Elementary and Middle School Social Studies

Fifth Edition

Elementary and Middle School Social Studies

An Interdisciplinary, Multicultural Approach

Fifth Edition

Pamela J. Farris
Northern Illinois University

WAVELAND

PRESS, INC.

Long Grove, Illinois

For information about this book, contact:
Waveland Press, Inc.
4180 IL Route 83, Suite 101
Long Grove, IL 60047-9580
(847) 634-0081
info@waveland.com
www.waveland.com

10-digit ISBN 1-57766-506-6
13-digit ISBN 978-1-57766-506-9

Printed in the United States of America

7   6   5

To my son, Kurtis, who shares a love of social studies

About the Author

Pamela J. Farris is a Distinguished Teaching Professor and former Coordinator of School–University Partnerships at Northern Illinois University. A former elementary teacher, she works closely with teachers in the schools in integrating social studies throughout the curriculum. Pam has presented throughout the United States and Canada as well as in Europe and Australia. A prolific writer, Pam has published over 175 articles and three other textbooks—*Teaching, Bearing the Torch; Language Arts: Process, Product, and Assessment;* and *Teaching Reading: A Balanced Approach for Today's Classrooms.* An avid reader of biographies and historical fiction, Pam devotes her free time to traveling with her husband and son throughout the United States and the world visiting historic sites.

Contents

Suggestions for Social Studies Units of Study and Lesson Plans

Africa – Chapter 11
Ancient Egypt – Chapter 9
Antarctica – Chapter 11
Apples – Chapter 2
Art – Chapter 14
Asia – Chapter 1, 11
Australia – Chapter 11
Biographies – Chapter 7, 10
Branches of Government (Executive,
  Legislative, and Judicial) – Chapter 12
Change – Chapter 10
Character Education – Chapter 12
Chicago Fire – Chapter 6
China – Chapter 6
Christopher Columbus – Chapter 9
Civil War – Chapter 5, 6, 7, 9
Colonial America – Chapter 6
Community Helpers – Chapter 8
Constitution – Chapter 12
Corn – Chapter 1
Cowboys – Chapter 14
Environment – Chapter 11
Europe (Modern day) – Chapter 6, 11
Far Western States – Chapter 10
Feudalism – Chapter 6
Folk Medicine – Chapter 2
Freedom – Chapter 10
Getting Along with Others – Chapter 8
Gold Rush of 1849 – Chapter 10
Great Depression – Chapter 2, 13
Great Plains States – Chapter 10
Historical Connections – Chapter 5
Historical Connections –
  Local Community – Chapter 9
Holocaust – Chapter 9, 10, 14

Jazz Age, The – Chapter 9
Latitude and Longitude – Chapter 11
Lewis and Clark – Chapter 1
Maps – Chapter 11
Mexico and the Mexican Culture –
  Chapter 4
Middle Ages – Chapter 2, 9
Middle East – Chapter 4, 11
Midwestern States – Chapter 1
Money – Chapter 13
Multicultural Education – Chapter 4
Native Americans – Chapter 1, 5, 11
North America – Chapter 11
Northeastern States – Chapter 10
Northwestern States – Chapter 10
Orphan Train – Chapter 13, 14
Pioneers – Chapter 7
Plague, The – Chapter 9
Potato Famine – Chapter 9, 10
Protest Songs – Chapter 4
Quilts – Chapter 6
Revolutionary War – Chapter 10
Salem Witch Trials – Chapter 2
Self – Chapter 8
Slavery – Chapter 10
South America – Chapter 11
Southeastern States – Chapter 10
Southwestern States – Chapter 10
Texas Revolution – Chapter 6
Underground Railroad – Chapter 5
Weather – Chapter 11
Westward Expansion – Chapter 11
Women's History Month – Chapter 7
World, The – Chapter 11
World War II – Chapter 1

Preface

"Let us put our minds together and see what life we can make for our children." These words of wisdom were shared by Sitting Bull with members of the U.S. Congress in the late 1800s. As elementary and middle school teachers, we have the same goal for our students, to make a better life for them. As teachers, we try to present social studies in meaningful, relevant ways.

Social studies has six basic tenets:

- Children should be actively involved in their learning.
- Children should be given opportunities to make decisions and become decision makers.
- Children need to use their previously gained knowledge and experiences as a learning scaffold.
- Children need to develop a positive self-concept in which they feel secure, effective, competent, and capable.
- Children need to develop an appreciation for the aesthetics of a subject.
- Children need to be productive, contributing citizens.

The fifth edition of *Elementary and Middle School Social Studies: An Interdisciplinary, Multicultural Approach* was developed on the basis of these tenets.

Approach

Based on interdisciplinary instruction as its pedagogical focus, this text puts "theory into practice," which preservice and inservice teachers can both understand and appreciate. Throughout the book, National Council for the Social Studies (NCSS) Standards are addressed and applied to the course content. Oftentimes this entails combining social studies concepts and objectives with those of other content areas, that is, geography and science, economics and math, history and language arts. The arts help students develop an appreciation for their own heritage and others.

The chapters are written by experts from their respective social science as well as elementary and middle school fields. Within the chapters are social studies activities and NCSS Standards-Linked Lesson Plans that can be linked with other content areas for effective and efficient interdisciplinary instruction.

Organization

Immediately following the preface is a listing of NCSS's Curriculum Standards for the Social Studies—Expectations of Excellence. These Standards are the foundation of social studies education and the approach of this book. Chapter objectives are listed at the beginning of each chapter followed by the theoretical background in social studies and interdisciplinary instruction. National social studies standards are stressed throughout. NCSS-based lesson plans are at the end of each chapter. In addition, several examples of activities for developing social studies concepts (particularly in the areas of history, geography, and civics, with lower and upper elementary as well as middle school students) are included in this textbook along with multiple Web site and WebQuest addresses. Diversity and technology content are thoroughly infused throughout the text. A thorough, updated annotated listing of social studies tradebooks is presented at the end of each chapter.

Chapter Previews

The opening chapter of the book is "Social Studies and Integrated Instruction: A Look at Social Studies." This chapter provides an overview of the social studies: anthropology, economics, history, geography, political science (civics education), and sociology. It includes current national standards and recommendations on how social studies is best taught.

Chapter 2, "Social Studies and Integrated Instruction: A Look at Interdisciplinary Instruction," provides the reader with insights into the philosophy, rationale, and goals of interdisciplinary instruction. The latter part of the chapter describes how social studies can be integrated in the elementary and middle school classroom. The end of the chapter presents an example of an interdisciplinary thematic social studies unit.

Chapter 3, "Classroom Assessment in Social Studies," presents ways of including authentic assessment in terms of rubrics, checklists, and portfolios. In addition, objectives and benchmarks for social studies instruction are discussed.

Chapter 4, "Multicultural and Bilingual Education: Making the Connections in Social Studies," discusses the role of the classroom teacher in helping students accept other cultures and beliefs. The chapter provides a vast array of integrated social studies activities for English language learners (ELLs).

Teaching strategies for diverse learners are provided in chapter 5, "Social Studies for All Learners," which explains how an interdisciplinary approach to teaching social studies can be used successfully with all students. Included are instructional methods for those students who have been diagnosed as having attention deficit disorder (ADD), learning disabilities (LD), as well as gifted students.

Meeting the learning needs of students is further expanded in chapter 6, "Facilitating Learning through Strategic Instruction in Social Studies." This chapter addresses instructional approaches that aid and assist student learning.

Chapter 7, "Communicating in Social Studies: Reading, Writing, and Discussing," gives suggestions for expository and narrative reading and writing. Classroom discussion and interview techniques are also presented in this chapter along with ways to use documents in the classroom.

Beginning with the youngest students, chapter 8 looks at "Early Childhood Social Studies" and the widening awareness of the social studies environment. The chapter elaborates on how the child moves from viewing self to family to neighborhood to community to state to nation to world and finally to the universe itself.

New to this edition is chapter 9, "History: Connecting Children to the Past," which expands on this important social science. This chapter helps the reader become better grounded in how to teach history in grades K–8. Several interdisciplinary techniques are shared.

Chapter 10, "Another Time, Another Place: Bringing Social Studies to Life through Literature," offers a plethora of activities and children's literature. Weaving the social studies curriculum with a cloth of quality children's books on geographic and historical themes, it also includes ways of using thematic units of study. Ample suggestions of current children's literature offer up a variety of choices for areas of study in the social studies thus providing for individual interests.

Chapter 11, "Geography: Exploring the Whole World through Interdisciplinary Instruction," includes Geography for Life Standards and provides numerous examples of K–8 literature-based instruction of geography skills and strategies.

Active participation is essential in political science and civic education. Chapter 12, "Civic Education in a Democratic Society," discusses democratic ideals and the core values of a democratic society. Character education is also examined in this chapter with several references to appropriate children's literature selections.

"Economics Education: Ways and Means" is the title of chapter 13, which presents an overview of economic concepts. Four thematic units of study are described.

Any interdisciplinary, multicultural instructional approach must include the arts. Chapter 14, "Social Studies and the Arts: From Inner Journeys to Faraway Lands," is a merging of the third edition chapters on the arts and drama. This chapter shares ways that music and the visual arts can readily be incorporated as part of social studies instruction, in particular utilizing the multiple intelligences. It demonstrates how social studies develops children's attitudes, values, and perspectives and provides ways that teachers can use drama as "living history."

Features of This Edition

Elementary and Middle School Social Studies: An Interdisciplinary, Multicultural Approach, Fifth Edition, offers several practical features for the preservice and inservice teacher, including:

- An emphasis on the NCSS Standards throughout the text
- "In the Classroom" boxes, providing additional information that the teacher needs and also additional teaching ideas
- The most comprehensive listing of related children's literature, keyed to each chapter
- A glossary elaborating on various social studies terminology

- Developmentally appropriate NCSS Standards-Linked Lesson Plans at the end of each chapter
- Actual children's work demonstrating instructional outcomes
- Plentiful teacher resources at the end of each chapter
- Related technology tools, including WebQuest sources, at the end of each chapter
- Activities on meeting the needs of all learners
- Inclusion of multicultural activities

These features and more make this a book that serves as both an instructional tool and a teaching resource. Accompanying the text is an Instructor's Manual with suggested class activities, discussion questions, resources, Web sites, WebQuests, test items, and PowerPoints.

The fifth edition offers the classroom teacher a shared belief that social studies instruction is best taught through interdisciplinary instruction while addressing multicultural considerations. This has meant additions in references to diversity in terms of culture, beliefs, and values. Specific suggestions for English language learners and diverse learners have been included.

Acknowledgments

At this point I would like to thank the various authors, all of whom who were selected on the basis of their expertise:

Martha Brady, *Northern Arizona University*
Karen Carrier, *Northern Illinois University*
Jill E. Cole, *Wesley College*
Richard A. Fluck, *Northern Illinois University*
Carol J. Fuhler, *Iowa State University*
Mary Louise Ginejko, *Samuel Gompers Junior High, Joliet, IL*
Marjorie R. Hancock, *Kansas State University*
Mary Beth Henning, *Northern Illinois University*
Bonnie L. Kuhrt, *Carl Sandburg Middle School, Rolling Meadows, IL*
Susan L'Allier, *Northern Illinois University*
Steven L. Layne, *Judson College*
Lisa M. Mehlig, *Rockford Public School District*
Pamela A. Nelson, *Northern Illinois University*
Carla Cooper Shaw, *Northern Illinois University*
L. Ruth Stryuk, *Utah State University*
Billie Jo Thomas, *Northern Illinois University*
Maria P. Walther, *Gwendolyn Brooks Elementary School, Aurora, IL*
Donna Werderich, *Rockford College*
Terry Whealon, *Northern Illinois University*

On behalf of all the chapter authors, we would like to gratefully acknowledge the significant assistance and encouragement we received from preservice and inservice teachers. Many of the ideas presented in this book either came from their suggestions or were field tested in their classrooms. For this, we are indebted to them.

I am greatly appreciative of the assistance and encouragement offered by my editor, Jeni Ogilvie. In addition, I'd like to thank Neil Rowe, who enthusiastically supported this edition. I'd also like to thank Lenny Walther, who assisted in the graphs and cartography of this edition.

A number of teachers and college professors offered their suggestions for improvement of the fifth edition. Such comments have strengthened the textbook for preservice and inservice teachers. These outside reviewers included:

Paul Egeland, *Wheaton College*
Phyllis M. Garcia, *Arizona State University*
Michele Jolivette, *Chicago State University*
Denee J. Mattioli, *East Tennessee State University*
Sharon O'Neal, *Southwest Texas State University*
Crystal L. Olson, *California State University, Sacramento*
Leslie Ricklin, *Eastern Connecticut State University*
Sister Catherine Stewart, *Mount Mercy College*
Bonnie L. Williams, *Bloomsburg University*

Certainly it takes lots of effort and encouragement from the home front for a book to come to fruition. To my husband and son goes my deepest gratitude for their support.

NCSS CURRICULUM STANDARDS FOR THE SOCIAL STUDIES

Performance Expectations

I. Culture

Social studies programs should include experiences that provide for the study of *culture and cultural diversity,* so that the learner can:

Early Grades

a. explore and describe similarities and differences in the ways groups, societies, and cultures address similar human needs and concerns;

b. give examples of how experiences may be interpreted differently by people from diverse cultural perspectives and frames of reference;

c. describe ways in which language, stories, folktales, music, and artistic creations serve as expressions of culture and influence behavior of people living in a particular culture;

d. compare ways in which people from different cultures think about and deal with their physical environment and social conditions;

e. give examples and describe the importance of cultural unity and diversity within and across groups.

Middle Grades

a. compare similarities and differences in the ways groups, societies, and cultures meet human needs and concerns;

b. explain how information and experiences may be interpreted by people from diverse cultural perspectives and frames of reference;

c. explain and give examples of how language, literature, the arts, architecture, other artifacts, traditions, beliefs, values, and behaviors contribute to the development and transmission of culture;

d. explain why individuals and groups respond differently to their physical and social environments and/or changes to them on the basis of shared assumptions, values, and beliefs;

e. articulate the implications of cultural diversity, as well as cohesion, within and across groups.

II. Time, Continuity, and Change

Social studies programs should include experiences that provide for the study of *the ways human beings view themselves in and over time,* so that the learner can:

Early Grades

a. demonstrate an understanding that different people may describe the same event or situation in diverse ways, citing reasons for the differences in views;

b. demonstrate an ability to correctly use vocabulary associated with time such as past, present, future, and long ago; read and construct simple time lines; identify examples of change; and recognize examples of cause and effect relationships;

c. compare and contrast different stories or accounts about past events, people, places, or situations, identifying how they contribute to our understanding of the past;

d. identify and use various sources for reconstructing the past, such as documents, letters, diaries, maps, textbooks, photos, and others;

e. demonstrate an understanding that people in different times and places view the world differently;

f. use knowledge of facts and concepts drawn from history, along with elements of historical inquiry, to inform decision making about and action taking on public issues.

Middle Grades

a. demonstrate an understanding that different scholars may describe the same event or situation in different ways but must provide reasons or evidence for their views;

b. identify and use key concepts such as chronology, causality, change, conflict, and complexity to explain, analyze, and show connections among patterns of historical change and continuity;

c. identify and describe selected historical periods and patterns of change within and across cultures, such as the rise of civilizations, the development of transportation systems, the growth and breakdown of colonial systems, and others;

d. identify and use processes important to reconstructing and reinterpreting the past, such as using a variety of sources; providing, validating, and weighing evidence for claims; checking credibility of sources; and search for causality;

e. develop critical sensitivities such as empathy and skepticism regarding attitudes, values, and behaviors of people in different historical contexts;

f. use knowledge of facts and concepts drawn from history, along with methods of historical inquiry, to inform decision making about and action taking on public issues.

III. People, Places, and Environments

Social studies programs should include experiences that provide for the study of *people, places, and environments,* so that the learner can:

Early Grades

a. construct and use mental maps of locales, regions, and the world that demonstrate understanding of relative location, direction, size, and shape;

b. interpret, use, and distinguish various representations of the earth, such as maps, globes, and photographs;

c. use appropriate resources, data sources, and geographic tools such as atlases, databases, grid systems, charts, graphs, and maps to generate, manipulate, and interpret information;

d. estimate distance and calculate scale;

e. locate and distinguish among varying landforms and geographic features, such as mountains, plateaus, islands, and oceans;

f. describe and speculate about physical system changes, such as seasons, climate and weather, and the water cycle;

g. describe how people create places that reflect ideas, personality, culture, and wants and needs as they design homes, playgrounds, classrooms, and the like;

h. examine the interaction of human beings and their physical environment, the use of land, building of cities, and ecosystem changes in selected locales and regions;

i. explore ways that the earth's physical features have changed over time locally and beyond and how these changes may be connected to one another;

j. observe and speculate about social and economic effects of environmental changes and crises resulting from phenomena such as floods, storms, and drought;

k. consider existing uses and proposes and evaluate alternative uses of resources and land in home, school, community, the region, and beyond.

Middle Grades

a. elaborate mental maps of locales, regions, and the world that demonstrate understanding of relative location, direction, size, and shape;

b. create, interpret, use, and distinguish various representations of the earth, such as maps, globes, and photographs;

c. use appropriate resources, data sources, and geographic tools such as aerial photographs, satellite images, geographic information systems (GIS), map projections, and cartography to generate, manipulate, and interpret information such as atlases, databases, grid systems, charts, graphs, and maps;

d. estimate distance, calculate scale, and distinguish other geographic relationships such as population density and spatial distribution patterns;

e. locate and describe varying landforms and geographic features, such as mountains, plateaus, islands, rain forests, deserts, and oceans, and explain their relationships within the ecosystem;

f. describe physical system changes such as seasons, climate and weather, and the water cycle and identify geographic patterns associated with them;

g. describe how people create places that reflect cultural values and ideals as they build neighborhoods, parks, shopping centers, and the like;

h. examine, interpret, and analyze physical and cultural patterns and their interactions, such as land use, settlement patterns, cultural transmission of customs and ideas, and ecosystem changes;

i. describe ways that historical events have been influenced by, and have influenced, physical and human geographic factors in local, regional, national, and global settings;

j. observe and speculate about social and economic effects of environmental changes and crises resulting from phenomena such as floods, storms, and drought;

k. propose, compare, and evaluate alternative uses of land and resources in communities, regions, nations, and the world.

IV. Individual Development and Identity

Social studies programs should include experiences that provide for the study of *individual development and identity,* so that the learner can:

Early Grades

a. describe personal changes over time, such as those related to physical development and personal interests;

b. describe personal connections to place—especially place as associated with immediate surroundings;

c. describe the unique features of one's nuclear and extended families;

d. show how learning and physical development affect behavior;

e. identify and describe ways family, groups, and community influence the individual's daily life and personal choices;

f. explore factors that contribute to one's personal identity such as interests, capabilities, and perceptions;

g. analyze a particular event to identify reasons individuals might respond to it in different ways;

h. work independently and cooperatively to accomplish goals.

Middle Grades

a. relate personal changes to social, cultural, and historical contexts;

b. describe personal connections to place—as associated with community, nation, and the world;

c. describe the ways family, gender, ethnicity, nationality, and institutional affiliations contribute to personal identity;

d. relate such factors as physical endowment and capabilities, learning, motivation, personality, perception, and behavior to individual development;

e. identify and describe ways regional, ethnic, and national cultures influence individuals' daily lives;

f. identify and describe the influence of perception, attitudes, values, and beliefs on personal identity;

g. identify and interpret examples of stereotyping, conformity, and altruism;

h. work independently and cooperatively to accomplish goals.

V. Individuals, Groups, and Institutions

Social studies programs should include experiences that provide for the study of *interactions among individuals, groups, and institutions,* so that the learner can:

Early Grades

a. identify roles as learned behavior patterns in group situations such as student, family member, peer playgroup member, or club member;

b. give examples of and explain group and institutional influences, such as religious beliefs, laws, and peer pressure, on people, events, and elements of culture;

c. identify examples of institutions and describe the interactions of people within institutions;

d. identify and describe examples of tensions between and among individuals, groups, or institutions, and how belonging to more than one group can cause internal conflicts;

e. identify and describe examples of tension between an individual's beliefs and government policies and laws;

f. give examples of the role of institutions in furthering both continuity and change;

g. show how groups and institutions work to meet individual needs and promote the common good, and identify examples of where they fail to do so.

Middle Grades

a. demonstrate an understanding of concepts such as role, status, and social class in describing the interactions of individuals and social groups;

b. analyze group and institutional influences on people, events, and elements of culture;

c. describe the various forms institutions take and the interactions of people within institutions;

d. identify and analyze examples of tensions between expressions of individuality and group or institutional efforts to promote social conformity;

e. identify and describe examples of tensions between belief systems and government policies and laws;

f. describe the role of institutions in furthering both continuity and change;

g. apply knowledge of how groups and institutions work to meet individual needs and promote the common good.

VI. Power, Authority, and Governance

Social studies programs should include experiences that provide for the study of *how people create and change structures of power, authority, and governance,* so that the learner can:

Early Grades

a. examine the rights and responsibilities of the individual in relation to his or her social group, such as family, peer group, and school class;

b. explain the purpose of government;

c. give examples of how government does or does not provide for the needs and wants of people, establish order and security, and manage conflict;

d. recognize how groups and organizations encourage unity and deal with diversity to maintain order and security;

e. distinguish among local, state, and national governments and identify representative leaders at these levels, such as mayor, governor, and president;

f. identify and describe factors that contribute to cooperation and cause disputes within and among groups and nations;

g. explore the role of technology in communications, transportation, information-processing, weapons development, or other areas as it contributes to or helps resolve conflicts;

h. recognize and give examples of the tensions between the wants and needs of individuals and groups regarding concepts such as fairness, equity, and justice.

Middle Grades

a. examine persistent issues involving the rights, roles, and status of the individual in relation to the general welfare;

b. describe the purpose of government and how its powers are acquired, used, and justified;

c. analyze and explain ideas and governmental mechanisms to meet the needs and wants of citizens, regulate territory, manage conflict, and establish order and security;

d. describe the ways nations and organizations respond to forces of unity and diversity affecting order and security;

e. identify and describe the basic features of the political system in the United States, and identify representative leaders from various levels and branches of government;

f. explain conditions, actions, and motivations that contribute to conflict and cooperation within and among nations;

g. describe and analyze the role of technology in communications, transportation, information processing, weapons development, or other areas as it contributes to or helps resolve conflicts;

h. explain and apply concepts such as power, role, status, justice, and influence to the examination of persistent issues and social problems;

i. give examples and explain how governments attempt to achieve their stated ideals at home and abroad.

VII. Production, Distribution, and Consumption

Social studies programs should include experiences that provide for the study of *how people organize for the production, distribution, and consumption of goods and services,* so that the learner can:

Early Grades

a. give examples that show how scarcity and choice govern our economic decisions;

b. distinguish between needs and wants;

c. identify examples of private and public goods and services;

d. give examples of the various institutions that make up economic systems such as families, workers, banks, labor unions, government agencies, small businesses, and large corporations;

e. describe how we depend on workers with specialized jobs and the ways in which they contribute to the production and exchange of goods and services;

f. describe the influence of incentives, values, traditions, and habits on economic decisions;

g. explain and demonstrate the role of money in everyday life;

h. describe the relationship of price to supply and demand;

i. use economic concepts such as supply, demand, and price to help explain events in the community and nation;

j. apply knowledge of economic concepts in developing a response to a current local economic issue, such as how to reduce the flow of trash into a rapidly filling landfill.

Middle Grades

a. give and explain examples of ways that economic systems structure choices about how goods and services are to be produced and distributed;

b. describe the role that supply and demand, prices, incentives, and profits play in determining what is produced and distributed in a competitive market system;

c. explain the difference between private and public goods and services;

d. describe a range of examples of the various institutions that make up economic systems such as households, business firms, banks, government agencies, labor unions, and corporations;

e. describe the role of specialization and exchange in the economic process;

f. explain and illustrate how values and beliefs influence different economic decisions;

g. differentiate among various forms of exchange and money;

h. compare basic economic systems according to who determines what is produced, distributed, and consumed;

i. use economic concepts to help explain historical and current developments and issues in local, national, or global contexts;

j. use economic reasoning to compare different proposals for dealing with a contemporary social issue such as unemployment, acid rain, or high quality education.

VIII. Science, Technology, and Society

Social studies programs should include experiences that provide for the study of *relationships among science, technology, and society,* so that the learner can:

Early Grades

a. identify and describe examples in which science and technology have changed the lives of people, such as in homemaking, child care, work, transportation, and communication;

b. identify and describe examples in which science and technology have led to changes in the physical environment, such as the building of dams and levees, offshore oil drilling, medicine from rain forests, and loss of rain forests due to extraction of resources or alternative uses;

c. describe instances in which changes in values, beliefs, and attitudes have resulted from new scientific and technological knowledge, such as conservation of resources and awareness of chemicals harmful to life and the environment;

d. identify examples of laws and policies that govern scientific and technological applications, such as the Endangered Species Act and environmental protection policies;

e. suggest ways to monitor science and technology in order to protect the physical environment, individual rights, and the common good.

Middle Grades

a. examine and describe the influence of culture on scientific and technological choice and advancement, such as in transportation, medicine, and warfare;

b. show through specific examples how science and technology have changed people's perceptions of the social and natural world, such as in their relationship to the land, animal life, family life, and economic needs, wants, and security;

c. describe examples in which values, beliefs, and attitudes have been influenced by new scientific and technological knowledge, such as the invention of the printing press, conceptions of the universe, applications of atomic energy, and genetic discoveries;

d. explain the need for laws and policies to govern scientific and technological applications, such as the safety and well-being of workers and consumers and the regulation of utilities, radio, and television;

e. seek reasonable and ethical solutions to problems that arise when scientific advancements and social norms or values come into conflict.

IX. Global Connections

Social studies programs should include experiences that provide for the study of *global connections and interdependence,* so that the learner can:

Early Grades

a. explore ways that language, art, music, belief systems, and other cultural elements may facilitate global understanding or lead to misunderstanding;

b. give examples of conflict, cooperation, and interdependence among individuals, groups, and nations;

c. examine the effects of changing technologies on the global community;

d. explore causes, consequences, and possible solutions to persistent, contemporary, and emerging global issues, such as pollution and endangered species;

e. examine the relationships and tensions between personal wants and needs and various global concerns, such as use of imported oil, land use, and environmental protection;

f. investigate concerns, issues, standards, and conflicts related to universal human rights, such as the treatment of children, religious groups, and effects of war.

Middle Grades

a. describe instances in which language, art, music, belief systems, and other cultural elements can facilitate global understanding or cause misunderstanding;

b. analyze examples of conflict, cooperation, and interdependence among groups, societies, and nations;

c. describe and analyze the effects of changing technologies on the global community;

d. explore the causes, consequences, and possible solutions to persistent, contemporary, and emerging global issues, such as health, security, resource allocation, economic development, and environmental quality;

e. describe and explain the relationship and tensions between national sovereignty and global interests, in such matters as territory, natural resources, trade, use of technology, and welfare of people;

f. demonstrate understanding of concerns, standards, issues, and conflicts related to universal human rights;

g. identify and describe the roles of international and multinational organizations.

X. Civic Ideals and Practices

Social studies programs should include experiences that provide for the study of *the ideals, principles, and practices of citizenship in a democratic republic,* so that the learner can:

Early Grades

a. identify key ideals of the U.S. democratic republican form of government, such as individual human dignity, liberty, justice, equality, and the rule of law, and discuss their application in specific situations;

b. identify examples of rights and responsibilities of citizens;

c. locate, access, organize, and apply information about an issue of public concern from multiple points of view;

d. identify and practice selected forms of civic discussion and participation consistent with the ideals of citizens in a democratic republic;

e. explain actions citizens can take to influence public policy decisions;

f. recognize that a variety of formal and informal actors influence and shape public policy;

g. examine the influence of public opinion on personal decision making and government policy on public issues;

h. explain how public policies and citizen behaviors may or may not reflect the stated ideals of a democratic republican form of government;

i. describe how public policies are used to address issues of public concern;

j. recognize and interpret how the "common good" can be strengthened through various forms of citizen action.

Middle Grades

a. examine the origins and continuing influence of key ideals of the democratic republican form of government, such as individual human dignity, liberty, justice, equality, and the rule of law;

b. identify and interpret sources and examples of the rights and responsibilities of citizens;

c. locate, access, analyze, organize, and apply information about selected public issues—recognizing and explaining multiple points of view;

d. practice forms of civic discussion and participation consistent with the ideals of citizens in a democratic republic;

e. explain and analyze various forms of citizen action that influence public policy decisions;

f. identify and explain the roles of formal and informal political actors in influencing and shaping public policy and decision making;

g. analyze the influence of diverse forms of public opinion on the development of public policy and decision making;

h. analyze the effectiveness of selected public policies and citizen behaviors in realizing the stated ideals of a democratic republican form of government;

i. explain the relationship between policy statements and action plans used to address issues of public concern;

j. examine strategies designed to strengthen the "common good," which consider a range of options for citizen action.

Source: National Council for the Social Studies. 1994. *Expectations of Excellence: Curriculum Standards for Social Studies.* Washington, DC: National Council for the Social Studies. © National Council for the Social Studies. Reprinted by permission.

Social studies should be the study of how citizens in a society make decisions on issues that affect themselves and the lives of others as well as the environment in which we live.

—Pamela J. Farris

Chapter One

Social Studies and Integrated Instruction
A Look at Social Studies

Pamela J. Farris and Terry Whealon, Northern Illinois University

■ CHAPTER OUTLINE

Introduction

An Ever-Changing World

Social Studies Learners

Teaching Social Studies

The Social Sciences

Integrating the Social Sciences

Skills Needed to Become a Good Citizen Actor

Building Curriculum for Integrated Instruction and Social Studies Integration

The Decision-Making Process

Scope and Sequence of Study in Social Studies

Illustrative Examples of Integrated Social Studies Activities

Celebrating Lewis and Clark in an Interdisciplinary Unit

Chapter Summary

CHAPTER OBJECTIVES

Readers will

- be aware of the six social sciences that make up social studies (anthropology, economics, history, geography, political science/civics, and sociology);
- be aware of the skills of a citizen actor;
- discover how the social sciences can be integrated for instruction;
- be aware of the steps in teaching social studies as a decision-making process; and
- be aware of the national curriculum standards for social studies instruction.

Introduction

The fresh smells of a new school year permeate the air—newly waxed floors, freshly painted rooms, chalk on the chalkrail. Marty Hammond's first graders are already engaged in learning an economic lesson about corn. On the first day of school Marty, a teacher in rural Illinois, asked her students several questions about their interests, what they liked, and what they didn't like. When she asked what their favorite vegetable was, most of the children responded, "Sweet corn!" She wasn't surprised because sweet corn is a common favorite; it is locally grown and very plentiful during August and September. Marty decided that since her students liked to eat sweet corn, she would take the opportunity to use corn as a social studies lesson.

A trip to her school media center and the public library helped Marty locate picture books about corn and maize that she read to her students. They discussed the importance of corn as a food for humans and livestock (cattle, chickens, pigs, and sheep) and as a fuel alternative to oil for driving a car. Afterward, they drew pictures about corn: planting, tending, and harvesting as well as pumping ethanol into the family van. During the first week of school, the class went to a nearby grocery store and purchased sweet corn still in the husks. After husking the corn, they cooked the corn in a big pot on a portable electric burner, buttered it, and ate it for lunch. The next day, a farmer who grows sweet corn commercially visited the class and brought some cornstalks with him. He showed pictures of the methods he uses to till the soil, plant, and harvest the corn to the students and explained the measures he takes to prevent soil erosion. The farmer also talked about how the corn must be picked at just the right time so that the kernels don't get too hard for people to eat. He explained to the students that corn must be kept cool and eaten soon after it is picked or it will spoil. The following day the first graders toured a local factory that cans corn and peas. Later, the class will visit a farm that is harvesting corn for livestock feed and see farm animals contentedly munching away on this important grain. Come early May, Marty's class will plant corn in a small garden plot on the school playground.

Another teacher, John Salter, and his fourth-grade teaching partner, Sue Kissinger, devoted several weeks of their summer vacation to developing their social studies units for the year. In addition to covering the exploration and development of the United States and the study of their own state of Ohio, they plan to focus on four major cultural studies during the year: African Americans, Asians, Jewish people, and Native Americans. In order to reduce the cost of books and materials, they alternate units between their two classrooms. While they use the same units they each tweak them with the activities they assign their students. John and Sue arrange for a field trip at a nearby university to a Native American Pow Wow each fall.

The year commences with John sharing children's literature about Native Americans with his students. His students read and discuss Lynne Cherry's (1992) *A River Ran Wild,* a picture book about how the Nashua Indians respected nature and the environment. Through reading and talking about the book, students gain a better understanding of the anthropological and ecological history of the Nashua River Valley in what is now lower New Hampshire and upper Massachusetts. Another picture book available for the students to read is Rafe Martin's (1992) *The Rough-Face Girl,* which is the Algonquin Indian version of Cinderella. In addition, each student selects one of three historical novels about Native Americans: Jean Fritz's (1983) *The Double Life of Pocahontas,* Paul Goble's (1990) *Dream Wolf,* or Scott O'Dell's (1988) *Black Star, Bright Dawn.* Each student reads the chosen book and writes about his or her reaction in a literature response journal. Every day, the students give their journals to John, who reads the journals and writes comments and questions for the students to read and react to. In addition, students discuss the books with peers who are reading the same selection.

One of the activities students engage in is making their own buffalo robe stories. This project gets students to think about the importance of their own lives and interests. The students cut brown paper bags donated by a local grocery store into ten-inch strips, soak the strips in water for a few minutes before wadding them into balls to give them a leathery look, then stretch them out on a table to dry. The next day, each student uses crayons or felt-tipped markers to draw four major events, one from each of the last four years of his or her life. While the students work, a CD of Native American songs plays in the background. After all the stories are finished, the students sit on the floor, legs crossed, around an unlit campfire made of sticks found on the playground during recess. The students then share the stories behind each picture on their buffalo robes. This enables the students and John to get to know each other better.

In addition to the picture books and novel studies, John has selected Gary Paulsen's (1988) *Dogsong* to read aloud to his students, while Sue has chosen Ken Kesey's (1991) *The Sea Lion* to read aloud to her students. Both teachers have elected to use Virginia Sneve's (1989) *Dancing Tepees: Poems of American Indian Youth* to integrate poetry and dance into the unit.

While John's class starts with Native Americans, Sue's begins with Asian culture. Sue opens her unit by reading to her class a Korean folktale, *The Sun Girl and the Moon Boy* (Choi 1997), which is similar to Little Red Riding Hood. Her students will read Momoko Ishii's (1987) *The Tongue-Cut Sparrow* (translated by Katherine Paterson), a Japanese folktale about a kind old man and his greedy wife, as a class discussion book. They will also read *El Chino* (Say 1990), a true story of a Chinese boy who became a famous bullfighter, and *The Land I Lost: Adventures of a Boy in Vietnam* (Nhuong 1982), which depicts daily life in Vietnam prior to the Vietnam War. English language learners who are still developing their English reading skills and struggling native English students read *Water Buffalo Days: Growing Up in Vietnam* (Nhuong 1997), a true story of adventure and excitement of growing up in a rural Vietnamese village. Sue has chosen *How the Ox Star Fell from Heaven* (Hong 1991) to read aloud because it is one of her favorite stories. Members of the Asian community come to speak to her class about their countries' customs and traditions.

In Oklahoma, Patricia Johnson's fifth graders incorporate technology and literature with their study of World War II. During the unit of study, she begins each social studies session with a read-aloud of one to two pages from Stephen E. Ambrose's (2001) *The Good Fight: How World War II Was Won*. Using the social studies textbook as a reference, the students create a time line around the top of the white board. A world map is used to mark battles. Patricia branches out, requiring all students to read *Snow Treasure* (McSwigan 1942), which is based on a story of how courageous Norwegian children hid gold bars from the German army during the occupation of Norway. For most of her students, this is a quick read. As they read, they write their reactions to the book in journals, which they then share in a grand conversation at the beginning of social studies class. Upon the conclusion of *Snow Treasure* (about five days of reading homework), Patricia lets her students select another novel to read as part of literature circle groups. The choices include *Lily's Crossing* by Patricia Reilly Giff (1997), a story about a British girl and a Hungarian boy who live through the bombing of England; *Number the Stars,* the Newbery Medal book by Lois Lowry (1989) that depicts how a family hides a Jewish girl and smuggles her family out of Denmark to Sweden, a book her lower ability readers have latched onto because of its readability and suspense; *Under the Blood Red Sun* by Graham Salisbury (1995), a book for above-average readers about Tomi, a Japanese boy who witnesses Pearl Harbor and must help his family when his fisherman father is sent to an internment camp in Texas; *Hitler Youth: Growing Up in Hitler's Shadow* by Susan Campbell Bartoletti (2005), about what life was like for German preadolescents and teenagers during World War II; and *Stones in Water* by Donna Jo Napoli (1998), about a group of Italian boys who attend a movie in Italy during World War II only to be kidnapped by the Nazis and used for forced labor. Students get into small groups to discuss the books as well as to identify historical events and concepts.

Patricia is fortunate as her classroom is equipped with four computers wired for the Internet. As a reference, students can get an overview of World War II from the CD-ROM *History of the World 3.0* (Dorling Kindersley 2001). The literature groups also seek out information from Google.com on their respective geographical settings (i.e., Great Britain, Denmark, Italy, Sweden, and Hawaii). Students then go to the World Wide Web for sites. Patricia gives the students a list with which they must start. Since a couple of her students are interested in art and cartooning, she has them look up Theodor Geisel (aka Dr. Seuss), who worked as a political cartoonist prior to and during the early part of World War II. They discover that Seuss was the cartoonist who first put the unique touches on the Hitler mustache.

Web Sites for World War II
Allied Victory
http://www.geocities.com/Athens/Oracle/2691/welcome.htm
> This page provides links to a wide variety of Web sites relating to World War II broken down into topical areas. A time saver for students to use.

Holocaust Sites
http://www.ushmm.org/
> This is the location for the U.S. Holocaust Museum.
http://www.jewishgen.org/ForgottenCamps/
> A Web site with a virtual museum on the Holocaust with text and images.
http://www.annefrank.org
> This is the official site for the Anne Frank House in Amsterdam.

Japanese Internment Sites
http://www.geocities.com/Athens/8420/camps.html
> Students can discover the locations of various sites where Japanese were taken during World War II at this site.
http://www.he.net/-sparker/cranes.html
> This is the Cranes for Peace site, a good accompaniment to the book *Sadako and a Thousand Paper Cranes* (Coerr 1979). Sadako was a young girl who died of leukemia as a result of the atomic bombing of her city.

Patricia has each literature circle group make a class presentation at the end of the unit. Each student contributes to a written report and the group project. Group projects may be a drama, diorama, or collage depicting an important scene from the book, a character chart comparing the attributes of the primary characters, an illustration of the sequence of the story, a museum exhibit, or other creative endeavors that the students propose and Patricia approves in advance. As a culminating activity, the students do origami and make paper cranes.

Tim Lamphere, a middle school teacher, also likes to use an interdisciplinary approach with units. Like those teachers depicted previously, Tim believes that through reading historical novels and nonfiction children's literature, students develop empathy for and a better understanding of the people, places, and events they study. In addition, Tim has discovered that students maintain a higher degree of interest in social studies when he uses children's literature to teach it. This allows students to become more personally involved with social studies because they can discuss or write about their own reactions to different events or aspects of social studies. He tries to incorporate the arts and science whenever possible. This is an interdisciplinary approach to the elementary curriculum as the instruction is integrated with different content area concepts being presented. Interdisciplinary instruction necessitates that the teacher plan well, be organized, and rely on meaningful, relevant materials for instruction.

Tim Lamphere's seventh graders never quite know what to expect from their lessons, except that social studies is always interesting. During the spring semester, Tim brought in firewood and made a campfire (unlit, of course) in the center of the classroom. With the desks pushed back and students seated on the floor around him, Tim beat on a drum and chanted the following:

The Spring
Behold, my brothers (and sisters), the spring has come; the earth has received the embrace of the sun and we shall soon see the results of that love!

Every seed is awakened and so has all animal life. It is through this mysterious power that we too have our being and therefore yield to our neighbors, even our animal neighbors, the same right as ourselves, to inhabit this land.

—Sitting Bull, Tatanka Yotanka, Hunkpapa Sioux, Lakota
(Philip, 1997)

Next, Tim had his students take turns reading *Many Nations: An Alphabet of Native America* by Joseph Bruchac (1997b), which gives a brief description about one aspect of the culture of various American Indian tribes. This was followed by having the students listen to Chief Lelooska narrate Kwakiutl tales courtesy of the CD to the accompanying picture book, *Echoes of the Elders: The Stories and Paintings of Chief Lelooska* (Chief Lelooska 1997). Next Tim shared poetry and short stories from *The Serpent's Tongue* (Wood 1997) and *Lasting Echoes: An Oral History of Native American People* (Bruchac 1997a). To change the pace and still keep his students interested, Tim had the students sit in a circle and handed each student a large handkerchief to use as a blindfold. One student was selected to be the "eagle" to silently capture the prey (a set of keys placed in the center of the circle) and escape—in other words, to retrieve the prey without making a sound and then leave the circle. The barefooted "eagle" deftly grasped the keys and noiselessly escaped from the circle. The next student chosen to be the "eagle" wasn't so successful; the keys jingled as he picked them up and the blindfolded students quickly pointed him out. This Sioux game proved to be an excellent listening activity for the middle schoolers.

After putting the students in groups of three, Tim took his class to the library to research tribes. During their time in the computer lab, the students searched for Web sites to locate additional information. For a reading activity, the class read two books. The first was *Trouble's Daughter: The Story of Susanna Hutchinson, Indian Captive* (Kirkpatrick 1998), a novel based on a true story. In 1643, Susanna's family lived in the wilderness near Long Island Sound during a period when the Dutch settlers and the native tribes were at war. Lenape warriors, an Algonquin-speaking tribe that later became known as the Delaware Indians, attacked the farm, massacring Susanna's family and taking nine-year-old Susanna captive. The Lenape tribe adopts her. Susanna learns the tribe's ways but never forgets her family. A few years later, Susanna is traded back to Dutch family members as part of a treaty agreement. The second book was Patricia McKissick's (1997) *Run Away Home*, the story of an Apache boy named Sky who escapes from a train taking him to the reservation. Sarah, a black girl, and her mother nurse Sky back to health after he contracts swamp fever. When the White Supremacist Knights of the Southern Order try to force Sarah's family off their farm, Sky helps fight them off.

The class was assigned to read three chapters each night. The following day, the students engaged in a lively conversation about the portion of the book they had read. Tim noted the comments made by various students on a legal pad on his clipboard. Tim gave the students in his class who had reading difficulties audiotapes of the book that had been recorded earlier by a volunteer parent. Following the 20 minutes of discussion, the students worked in their groups on their reports and projects. Three weeks after the unit begun, the students shared their reports and projects with the class.

An Ever-Changing World

Technology has always changed the face of our world. The engineering expertise of the Romans resulted in superior roadways and water systems improving communication, commerce, and daily lives of citizens. The creation of a smooth plow by John Deere helped increase the grain production by farmers. The invention of the steam engine by James Watt enabled not only factories to be powered, but transportation to haul cargo in steam powered boats and with steam powered trains. Passengers board jet planes and are whisked across the Atlantic or Pacific Oceans in a matter of hours—not weeks as was the norm 100 years ago. Today, computer engineers in India can repair home computers throughout the world through an Internet connection.

Despite all the advancements of technology, natural elements still impact humanity. King Phillip II's mighty armada of Spanish ships sent to invade England in 1588 was an impressive display of 130 of the finest naval vessels in the world— far superior to the English fleet of smaller, but faster vessels. The foul weather and winds of the English Channel and lack of maneuverability of the larger ships helped to undermine the Spanish navy, resulting in a military defeat as well as a severe psychological blow for Spain, which never regained its presence as a world power despite its wealth. In 2005, Hurricane Katrina dealt major devastation to the Gulf Coast states of Alabama, Louisiana, and Mississippi when man-made levees failed to hold back the waters flooding most of the cities of Gulf Port and New Orleans, causing several billions of dollars of damages and hundreds of deaths. Earthquakes, hurricanes, tornadoes, and typhoons all strike with little or no warning, destroying homes and businesses in various reaches of the world and upsetting the daily life and livelihood of thousands of people each year.

The Oklahoma City bombing in 1995 and the attacks that occurred on September 11, 2001, have made us aware of how easily a small number of human beings can destroy buildings, taking large numbers of lives in one fell swoop. In Oklahoma, the bomber used fertilizer to make a massive bomb and rented a truck to transport it. He drove to the Oklahoma federal building where the bomb exploded, blowing half of the nine-story building into oblivion and killing 168 people, from babies and preschoolers in the day care center to elderly citizens in the building's Social Security Office. At the time, it was the worst terrorist attack on U.S. soil; the perpetrators were U.S. citizens who had even served in the U.S. Army. Six years later, Americans and the world at large were shocked to learn that over 3,000 innocent people from different cultures, religions, and nations were killed when fanatic terrorists used two commercial jetliners loaded with volatile jet fuel as missiles to crash into the World Trade Center and another to crash into the Pentagon. A fourth plane was diverted into a field. Feelings of anger, disbelief, and sadness swept across the globe. These and other events have changed our world and our way of life, affecting how we teach social studies. Social studies instruction has become a focal point for all schools as teachers attempt to create knowledgeable citizens who are accepting of others.

Noted historian Diane Ravitch (2002) believes that the events of recent years have provided us with seven important lessons as we prepare students to become informed citizens who will both preserve and protect democracy. These lessons are:

1. *It's okay to be patriotic.* Good citizens feel a sense of attachment to the United States and its democratic values of freedom, justice, and individual rights.

2. *Not all cultures share our regard for equality and human rights.* The standards in the United States are equality, freedom, and human rights. Across the globe there are cultures in which political opposition is met with imprisonment or even death, religious freedom is nonexistent, women are oppressed, and schools teach hatred of differences from those in political power. Our nation, too, has had difficulty with equality and equal rights. Slavery was an accepted practice in parts of colonial America and the early years of the United States itself. Nine U.S. presidents were slave owners, and only one, George Washington, freed his slaves prior to his death. For nearly a century and a half, slavery has been forbidden in the United States. However, tragically slavery and the slaughtering of minorities still exists in the world. In the United States, equal rights continues to be an issue for women and minorities. Women earn roughly three-fourths of

what men take home. Minorities often encounter barriers when seeking employment, as the debate continues over what to do about the large number of illegal aliens, particularly those from Mexico, entering the United States.

3. *We must now recognize the presence of evil in the world.* The terrorists attacks of 1995 and 2001 were nothing less than evil, but this is not the first time in civilization that evil has reared its ugly head. In 1095, Pope Urban II, at the Council of Clermont, exhorted Christendom to war to retake the Holy Lands from Muslims. Over all, nine Crusades were undertaken by Christian armies from Europe. Richard the Lionhearted ordered his men to behead the Muslims, leaving the heads on stakes as a warning to others. The pathetic Children's Crusade saw thousands of European children start out for the Holy Lands only to die of illness or hunger while others were sold as slaves. Certainly slavery in America symbolized brutality as white slave owners treated their slaves as property, beating and raping African Americans as they pleased because they "owned" them. Long after the Emancipation Proclamation, African Americans were treated as second class citizens and forced to ride in the back of buses and forbidden to eat in restaurants with white citizens. During the twentieth century, the Japanese invaded China and ruthlessly murdered and raped innocent Chinese citizens; Jews were persecuted and sent to concentration camps and death chambers by the Nazis under Hitler; Communists removed opponents of Stalin and his policies through purging, which sent thousands to Siberia and their death. When human rights are violated, the world cannot stand aside.

4. *Pluralism and divergence of opinion are valuable.* Students need to understand other cultures and value their contributions to our society. Differing opinions can be dealt with through the democratic process. In our classrooms, students need to learn how to discuss, debate, and respect differences of opinion on issues. Everyone has the right to express an opinion, even a dissenting one. This is guaranteed in the First Amendment as the right to freedom of speech.

5. *Knowledge of U.S. history is important.* Students need to be familiar with the history of the United States. It cannot be cursory; rather, it needs to be solid and grounded. What are the origins and meaning of the U.S. Constitution? What are the major events that have shaped the United States? What issues have influenced history? Critical analysis by our students will ensure that, as future citizens, they can deal with political and social issues in a knowledgeable and reasonable manner.

6. *Knowledge of world history and geography is important.* The United States is made up of peoples from throughout the world. Knowing and understanding other nations, cultures, and religions is needed. Oftentimes geography impacts economy, history, and political situations.

7. *We must teach students to appreciate and defend our democratic institutions.* The public wants students to understand the fundamental processes of our government, including our Constitution and its meaning, as well as our history. Students need to be prepared to accept the responsibilities of citizenship—for example, paying taxes, serving on jury duty, and voting in elections.

Today we still have unsettled feelings about 9/11 and the subsequent 2003 war with Iraq. It is difficult for both students and teachers to understand and cope. As Ravitch (2002) writes, "The U.S. public supports public education, both to provide equality of opportunity and to prepare our young people to protect and preserve our experiment in democratic living. As long as our schools act on that vision, we will count them among the institutions of democracy that are worthy of the public's respect and gratitude" (9).

Social Studies Learners

Our role as teachers is to help students become **good citizens** by making informed decisions. Citizenship requires that we teach our students to think. By developing inquiry-based, problem-solving, and reflective activities for our students, we challenge their thinking, stretching them to higher intellectual growth. Informed citizens stop and ponder political candidates' platforms, question political issues, and raise ethical questions.

Social studies learners range from gifted students who read George Washington's farewell address to struggling readers who have difficulty reading the words to "America, the Beautiful." For some, learning comes seemingly easy; for others it is painfully difficult. Considering how students learn best is important. Lev Vygotsky (1962) believed that children negotiate meaning between themselves and others because children use language to explore. This is how children develop cognitively. The difference between what a child can do alone and what the same child can do while working collaboratively with others is called the **zone of proximal development.** Every child can do things with assistance that they cannot do alone, and what they can do while working cooperatively with others on one occasion, they will eventually be able to do successfully all by themselves later. This is important for teachers to keep in mind as social studies instruction often entails collaborative efforts as well as independent work.

Students who are **English language learners (ELLs)** need special consideration. Bilingual students also may be referred to as English language learners or **English as a second language learners (ESLs),** depending upon the terminology used by the state education agency. Thus, these terms are often used interchangeably. Such students will necessarily have a different cultural foundation as a basis for evaluating and making judgments. Their historical perspective will be based on different viewpoints than students who have spent their entire lives in the United States. Teachers should actively seek out these different perspectives from their ELLs, inviting them to share their experiences and views with the rest of the class. This validates the ELLs' experiences while inviting them to become part of the classroom community. Likewise, they should understand and develop an appreciation for the values and culture of our country.

English language learners are likely to have a different experience and response to issues of power, authority, and governance. They may have dealt with immigration and visa issues that most native-born American students have not. Cultural norms, such as unquestioning obedience and acceptance, as demonstrated by

Teachers need to be respectful of students as they nurture learning. Giving positive feedback and encouragement creates a sharing and caring classroom environment.

Asian students, or debate and dissent, as demonstrated by older Hispanic male students, are inherently powerful. Teachers should be aware of these different perspectives and invite discussion and open expression of them, adding them to the richness of the experiences students share with each other in the classroom.

In *Teaching What Matters Most,* Richard W. Strong, Harvey F. Silver, and Matthew J. Perini (2001) assert:

> Education is not designed to create new members of the history or science department. Public education is designed to create citizens—people who can collaborate to nurture families, build communities, pursue careers, and understand current issues. . . . Citizens who have these fundamental understandings will be able to use their knowledge in the decisions they make as parents, professionals, neighbors, and active members of the community. When you step into the voting booth, what are your hopes for the person in the next booth? Do you hope that person knows the facts of the nullification process—or knows how to work individually and collaboratively to address our common problems? (37–38)

Our actions and words in the classroom can have a major impact upon our students. A middle school teacher was honored with a retirement party attended by many former students. One student handed the teacher a note the teacher had written to him when he was a seventh grader. The note said, "I've enjoyed having you as a student. I hope that you'll continue to pursue math as you seem to have a talent for it." The retired teacher could not recall writing the note, but seeing the young high school math teacher before him made him feel glad that he did.

Consider the following poem and think about your comments to students each day.

Sticks and Stones May Break My Bones
By Herb Warren

"Sticks and stones may break my bones
But words could never hurt me."
And this I knew was surely true
And truth could not desert me.

But now I know it is not so.
I've changed the latter part;
For sticks and stones may break the bones
But words can break the heart.

Sticks and stones may break the bones
But leave the spirit whole,
But simple words can break the heart
Or silence crush the soul.

Peter Johnson (2004) reminds us that our interactions with students are critical as each encounter results in meaning making by the student, either as a positive or as a negative. He suggests that we as teachers do a number of positive interactions.

• *Did anyone notice?* Have students share things they observed.

• *Did anyone try?* Encourage students to use newly gained concepts and vocabulary.

• *Remember the first week of school when we only knew a few names of states? Now you guys know half of them and the year's barely begun!* Celebrate the history of students' learning.

• *You know what you just did, Claude? You put yourself in her place. You may not have realized it but you said . . . which is what (the character's name) was thinking.* Such a comment as this draws attention not only to the student (Claude) but to the class of a productive cognitive strategy. It also gives Claude a chance to claim competence, a moment of positive self-esteem.

• *I want you to tell me how it [group discussion] went. . . . What went well? . . . What kinds of questions were raised?* This draws student attention to group discussion being a process that is critical for both managing and arranging constructive learning by all students.

• *How are you planning to go about this?* Being able to plan is essential. Planning means organizing and thinking ahead to give oneself some direction and guidance.

• *I bet you're proud of yourself.* When a child is invited by his teacher to attend to internal feelings of pride in oneself, internal motivation is attached to the activity. While teachers commonly say "I'm proud of you" after a student accomplishes something, such words suggest that the student is to learn solely to please the teacher when indeed we truly want children to learn for their own benefit and self-satisfaction.

- *How did you figure that out?* Asking this after students have successfully solved a problem or answered a question invites them to review the process or strategies they used. The student is apt to say something like, "First, I tried . . . Then I thought about . . . Finally I . . ." The student is put in the position of a storyteller revisiting the strategy used and ensures that the student will be more apt to use the strategy in future ventures.

- *Why?* "Why" questions are higher level thinking questions and the essence of inquiry. "Once young children latch onto 'why' questions, they come to see how useful they are for getting to the bottom of things and finding the limits of others" (37). For instance, once they discover that France was involved in an expensive war and needed money, then they better understand why the United States was able to make the Louisiana Purchase.

By incorporating the above questions into our everyday classroom language as teachers we promote self-esteem in our students and encourage them as learners.

Teaching Social Studies

When children enter school they bring with them a wealth of knowledge that they have gleaned through informal schooling. They have likes and dislikes, opinions, and beliefs. Research gained from previous, firsthand, and vicarious experiences that a student brings to each encounter with a given topic in a discipline of study, such as social studies, influences learning in terms of depth, interconnectedness to other topics, and access to additional knowledge of that topic of study (Leinhardt 1992).

Learning is largely social in nature. Children learn from others: parents, siblings, relatives, friends, and other significant individuals in their lives. Thus, social studies instruction naturally lends itself to an integrated curriculum based on the personal and social aspects of learning. **Social studies** is more than a collection of facts for children to memorize; it is an understanding of how people, places, and events came about and how people can relate and respond to each other's needs and desires. Social studies is also how we develop respect for different viewpoints and cultural beliefs. In short, social studies is the study of cultural, economic, geographic, and political aspects of past, current, and future societies. In 1994, the National Council for the Social Studies (NCSS) developed new **standards for teaching the social studies.** Through ten themes, social studies are taught in an integrated approach (see In the Classroom).

Social studies at the elementary and middle school levels is usually taught by means of an integrated approach that combines two or more of the social sciences for instructional purposes. This chapter focuses on social studies instruction and the introduction of the six social sciences.

☞ **IN THE CLASSROOM**

Ten Themes for Social Studies, K–12

The National Council for the Social Studies (1994) has adopted the following 10 themes of study for social studies instruction in kindergarten through grade 12. The themes are interrelated and draw from all the social sciences and related fields of scholarly study.

1. **Culture.** Human beings create, learn, and adapt culture. Human cultures are dynamic systems of beliefs, values, and traditions that exhibit both commonalities and differences. Understanding culture helps us understand ourselves and others.

2. **Time, Continuity, and Change.** Human beings seek to understand our historic roots and to locate ourselves in time. Such understanding involves knowing what things were like in the past and how things change and develop—allowing us to develop historical perspective and answer important questions about our current condition.

3. **People, Places, and Environments.** Technological advancement has ensured that students are aware of the world beyond their personal locations. As students study content related to this theme, they create their spatial views and geographic perspectives of the world; social, cultural, economic, and civic demands mean that students will need such knowledge, skill, and understanding to make informed and critical decisions about the relationships between humans and our environment.

4. **Individual Development and Identity.** Personal identity is shaped by one's culture, by groups, and by institutional influences. Examination of various forms of human behavior enhances understanding of the relationships between social norms and emerging personal identities, the social processes that influence identity formation, and the ethical principles underlying individual action.

5. **Individuals, Groups, and Institutions.** Institutions exert enormous influence over us. Institutions are organizational embodiments to further the core social values of those who comprise them. It is important for students to know how institutions are formed, what controls and influences them, how they control and influence individuals and culture, and how institutions can be maintained or changed.

6. **Power, Authority, and Governance.** Understanding of the historical development of structures of power, authority, and governance and their evolving functions in contemporary society is essential for the emergence of civic competence.

7. **Production, Distribution, and Consumption.** Decisions about exchange, trade, and economic policy and well-being are global in scope, and the role of government in policy making varies over time and from place to place. The systematic study of an interdependent world economy and the role of technology in economic decision making is essential.

8. **Science, Technology, and Society.** Technology is as old as the first crude tool invented by prehistoric humans, and modern life as we know it would be impossible without technology and the science that supports it. Today's technology forms the basis for some of our most difficult social choices.

9. **Global Connections.** The realities of global interdependence require understanding of the increasingly important and diverse global connections among world societies before there can be analysis leading to the development of possible solutions to persisting and emerging global issues.

10. **Civic Ideals and Practices.** All people have a stake in examining civic ideals and practices across time and in diverse societies, as well as a stake in determining how to close the gap between present practices and the ideals on which our democratic republic is based. An understanding of civic ideals and practices of citizenship is critical to full participation in society.

Source: National Council for the Social Studies. 1994. *Curriculum Standards for Social Studies: Expectations of Excellence.* Washington, DC: National Council for the Social Studies. © National Council for the Social Studies. Reprinted by permission.

The Social Sciences

To integrate the social sciences fully, it is important that the teacher understand each of the six **social sciences** (anthropology, economics, history, geography, political science/civics, and sociology) that constitute social studies at the elementary and middle school levels. Each of these is described in this section.

Anthropology

Anthropology is the field of study concerned with the discovery of what people were like from earliest existence. Considered as part of this study are the how, what, and why people change over the years. Typically, an anthropologist conducts an on-site study. That is, an anthropologist actually visits and investigates the locale where the people lived or continue to live. This kind of research enables the anthropologist to better understand and appreciate the people and their culture by living with them and recording their actions and comments.

The two primary branches of anthropology are physical and cultural. *Physical anthropology* is the study of the physical aspects of humankind. Archaeology deals with the gathering of information about human cultures by "excavation of sites of former human habitations—ancient dwellings, monuments, objects of art, tools, weapons, and other human works covered over by the soil of time" (Pelto and Muessig 1980, 2). *Cultural anthropology* is concerned with the different types of human behavior, past and present, found throughout the world (Allen and Stevens 1998).

Consider that the North American continent had a myriad of indigenous cultures that were highly civilized before Europeans began exploring this "New World." The cities and roads of the Aztec culture astounded European conquerors. Advanced forms of irrigation and cultivation of foods by the Aztec and Mayan and other Native American cultures were superior to that of European cultures. Some of these foods (corn, potatoes, and peanuts) went on to later provide over 60 percent of Europe's diet and were responsible for the greatest population growth since the neolithic age (Feagin and Feagin 2005).

Some basic premises of anthropology are as follows:

1. **Culture** is a total way of life, not just a superficial set of customs. It largely shapes how we feel, behave, and perceive as we adapt to our world.

2. Every cultural system is an interconnected series of ideas and patterns for behavior in which changes in one aspect generally lead to changes in other segments of the system.

3. Every human cultural system is logical and coherent in its own terms, given the basic assumption and knowledge available to the given community.

4. Study of almost any behavior and beliefs among nonmodern peoples, no matter how unusual, is of direct relevance to understanding our own culture. Humans everywhere shape their beliefs and behaviors in response to the same fundamental human problems.

5. Many traditional cultural practices and beliefs that once seemed quaint and outmoded have been found to have a pragmatic basis.

6. Individuals differ from one another in attitudes, information, skills, culturally values resources, and other attributes.

7. Although the people of the world may be roughly and arbitrarily categorized into major population groups based on a very limited number of physical characteristics, there are no "pure races" and there never have been (Pelto and Muessig 1980).

Culture is a significant factor in anthropology; thus anthropologists study a people's contributions in terms of language, music, art, literature, religion, law, and so on. Artifacts, such as cooking utensils and weapons, also provide insight into a people's culture. Anthropologists analyze the data, then compare and contrast the culture with other cultures either of the same time period or throughout the ages.

Economics

Economics is the field of study concerned with the production, distribution, exchange, and consumption of products. An economist analyzes these four concepts and suggests ways to improve the distribution or production of various products or the economy in general. These basic concepts can be readily taught to elementary and middle school students. First or second graders can analyze **production** as they compare the goods and services provided by businesses in their community. For example, they might tour the premises of a local manufacturing company or visit a service business such as a restaurant or pizza parlor and observe its operation, from taking an order to cooking the food and serving it.

In a unit on the **distribution** of products third and fourth graders can study how goods and services are made available to consumers through advertising, selling, and shipping. For instance, they might visit a local shoe store to learn how the manager selects and orders sneakers and how the sneakers are shipped. By looking through newspapers and magazines and watching television advertisements, the students can compare how sneakers are promoted.

The third topic of economics, **exchange,** involves the study of money. Although this topic is introduced in kindergarten, it is typically studied in depth in the first through fourth grades. A visit to a local bank after a class discussion about currency and how checks and credit cards are used for exchange is an appropriate activity for this topic.

Children need to understand that **consumption** is determined by the needs and wants of the buyer. In addition, older children need to become familiar with federal and state agencies that protect the buyer from fraud or other illegal acts.

History

History is the study of how people lived in the past. This may include how people lived in the local community, the United States, or the world. The National Center for History in the Schools (1994, 29–30) suggests the following eight topics for study based on the National Standards:

1. Family life now and in the recent past; family life in various places long ago.

2. History of students' local community and how communities in North America varied long ago.

3. The people, events, problems, and ideas that created the history of their state.
4. How democratic values came to be, and how they have been exemplified by people, events, and symbols.
5. The causes and nature of various movements of large groups of people into and within the United States, now and long ago.
6. Regional folklore and cultural contributions that helped to form our national heritage.
7. Selected attributes and historical developments of various societies in Africa, the Americas, Asia, and Europe.
8. Major discoveries in science and technology, their social and economic effects, and the scientists and inventors from the many groups and religions responsible for them.

According to the National Assessment of Educational Progress (NAEP) (U.S. Department of Education, 1994, 18), students in grades 4 to 8 are to study the following four major historical themes across eight chronological periods of time:

1. *Change and continuity in American democracy.* This includes the basic premises on which the Declaration of Independence is founded, the U.S. Constitution, the Bill of Rights, slavery, the reasons for major wars (i.e., Civil War, World War I, and World War II), and civil rights.
2. *The gathering and interactions of peoples, cultures, and ideas.* How contributions of many peoples and cultures from different countries, races, and religious customs and beliefs have resulted in the heritage and development of society in America.
3. *Economic and technological changes and their relation to society, ideas, and the environment.* This considers the major changes in America that transformed it from an agrarian society to an industrial leader to the bellwether nation in technological innovations and how those changes affected society, ideas, and the environment.
4. *The changing role of America in the world.* This theme considers how America was initially an isolated country that was primarily self-sufficient to how today it depends on resources and goods from other nations. The relationship of geography, interests, and ideals as they pertain to foreign policy are examined.

The preceding themes are to be studied in the context of eight periods of U.S. history:

Years	Period Addressed
Beginnings to 1607	Three Worlds and Their Meeting in the Americas
1607–1763	Colonization, Settlement, and Communities
1763–1815	The Revolution and the New Nation
1801–1861	Expansion and Reform
1850–1877	Crisis of the Union: Civil War and Reconstruction
1865–1920	The Development of Modern America
1914–1945	Modern America and the World Wars
1945–present day	Contemporary America

Teachers should encourage students to be aware of the *chronology of historical events* as well as to dig through historical facts and information to discover why

Social studies requires the use of a number of media—artifacts, maps, illustrations, photos (like this one of the Great Wall of China), and even computer-generated pictures and graphics—as we attempt to familiarize our students with other cultures and locations.

events took place. This is known as *historical inquiry.* Understanding why things happen helps students to develop critical thinking skills as they create hypotheses for the reasons behind social movements, wars, and so on. Often students must weigh the evidence on its own merits. For example, the potato famine in the mid-1800s in Ireland resulted in millions of deaths among the lower-class citizens and the immigration of masses of Irish to the United States and mainland Europe. Potatoes were the staple food of the lower classes, and when a blight caused the potatoes to rot, millions of Irish starved. Yet there was an ample amount of food in the country to meet the needs of all of its people. Why did Ireland's neighbor, Great Britain, fail to send aid to help the Irish? By reading and uncovering the facts, students gain insights on the plight of the Irish during the late 1840s and early 1850s. Many wealthy Irish were large landowners who were afraid to give food to their starving tenant farmers for fear that other landowners would disapprove or that the large number of lower classes would cause a rebellion. Since Ireland was predominately Catholic, British politicians virtually ignored the situation, as they were members of the Church of England and were Protestants. Only one ship with aid, which was organized by a British charity group,was ever sent from Great Britain to Ireland during the potato famine.

There are other aspects of historical inquiry that upper elementary and middle school students may investigate. For instance, students could compare major breakthroughs or inventions in medical science that have taken place as a result of wars (e.g., nurses in battlefields from the Civil War, plasma during World War II, triage from the Vietnam War), or they might consider the development of specific weaponry (e.g., aircraft carriers during World War II, targeted missiles during the Persian Gulf War, minefields in Kosovo).

The history of the United States is one of diversity as numerous ethnic groups have arrived on both coasts. Beginning with the Western Europeans arriving in the original 13 colonies and in what later became Florida and the southwestern United States, these adventurers met many cultures of Native Americans with whom there was intermingling and/or confrontations. Later colonists imported slaves from the cultures of western Africa. During the westward movement, settlers encountered different Native American groups in the plains. English-speaking Americans ventured into what later became Texas, New Mexico, Arizona, Colorado, and California, homeland to yet other Native American cultures as well as Spanish-speaking heirs of relatives who had land grants dating back to the 1600s (Diaz-Rico and Weed 2002). Finally, in the nineteenth and twentieth centuries, immigrant groups from throughout the world poured into the United States. Today, in the twenty-first century, new immigrants seek refuge in our nation, the land of "liberty and freedom for all."

Geography

Geography is the study of the earth, including its features and the distribution of its human inhabitants and other life. Children should become familiar with five geography themes: location, place, relationships within places, movement, and regions (Joint Committee on Geographic Education 1984). Children are first introduced to these topics in terms of their own homes and neighborhoods.

The first geography theme, that of **location,** describes where specific places or points are on a map or on the earth's surface. It also describes the relationship between places—for example, the number of miles between San Diego and Phoenix.

The second theme, that of **place,** describes the unique or distinct characteristics of a place. This includes both physical and human characteristics. For instance, the flat land and fertile soil of the prairies of Illinois and Iowa allow for the production of large corn and soybean crops. On the other hand, the cool summers and acidic soil of Maine provide the perfect combination for growing blueberries.

The third geography theme, **relationships within places,** describes how people react to their environment and the changes they may make. Examples include preserving the wood owl by not cutting down a forest of trees for lumber or not allowing a company to build a plant on a river that would pollute the water and kill the fish.

Movement is the fourth geography theme. In a highly mobile society such as ours, movement is a very important topic in that it characterizes how people travel from place to place, how they communicate with each other, and how they depend

Displaying their work encourages students to be active participants as they learn about other cultures and nations.

on products (such as oil from the Middle East and auto parts made in Mexico) and information from other areas.

The last geographic theme, that of **regions,** involves categorizing areas according to their features: climate, landform, land use, natural vegetation, culture, and so forth. For instance, the Midwest is the biggest beef-producing region in the United States, and the South is the largest producer of tobacco in the world.

A geographic activity for third graders might be to have them visit a state park and make a map of the park. They could indicate where the people stay (in the park lodge) and eat (in the park restaurant) as well as illustrate the hills and meadows. Major hiking trails could be depicted along with paved roads.

Political Science/Civics Education

Political science, also referred to as **civics,** is the study of how people govern themselves. It includes the analysis of governing institutions, processes, and laws. The structure of government and the responsibilities and duties of elected and appointed government officials are all part of political science. For example, the political systems of North American indigenous peoples ranged from religious theocracies in Mexico, which were sources for advanced astronomical and mathematical achievement unparalleled anywhere else during that period of history, to the democratic councils of the Algonquin, Iroquois, and other nations that were greatly admired by such colonial leaders as Benjamin Franklin and Thomas Jefferson (Hardt 1992).

In elementary schools, the examination of the political system is important so that children gain an understanding of how government works. By creating a democratic classroom that allows for open discussion of issues and voting on those issues, the teacher can begin to set the stage for the students to become active participants in the democratic process. Later, such involvement will lead to active and concerned citizenship.

Upper elementary and middle school students need to develop a coherent and consistent set of values, particularly those contained in the political documents (e.g., U.S. Constitution, Declaration of Independence, and the Bill of Rights) that frame the values, beliefs, and ethical principles to which this nation adheres. Some educators are opposed to any overt involvement of students with value-related issues. "Efforts to protect students from serious value-related issues are counterproductive, as this forces them to look elsewhere for answers to serious questions" (Allen and Stevens 1998, 32).

A good yearlong political science activity is to create a self-governing board of the class. Members of the class should be elected to the governing board. Whenever disciplinary or other problems arise, the board can hold a hearing on the case and make a judgment. This may be as simple as a decision to request pizza be served more frequently in the cafeteria or that measures be taken to recycle used paper in the classroom.

Sociology

Sociology is the study of humans and their interactions in groups. Groups may be as small as a nuclear family or as large as the AFL-CIO union or the Catholic Church. Sociologists look for common values and beliefs. Unlike the *field study* of anthropologists, sociologists tend to conduct *case studies* of either individuals or a group over a period of time. A case study usually consists of information pertaining to the daily routine of the individuals or the group.

The study of sociology may begin with the study of families, followed by the study of neighborhoods and communities, and on to the study of larger groups. Sociology also involves the study of people from different cultures. A classroom of students itself is a study of sociology. As Ridgeway and Shaver (2006) write, "Helping our students develop positive social interactions is a primary focus of our school. . . . To this end, an important part of our school curriculum is social skills training" (15).

One powerful metaphor is the "salad bowl" culture of the United States, of having individual cultures blended together, thereby retaining their flavor and texture. Another metaphor used to describe the United States is that of the "kaleidoscope," inasmuch as shifting patterns of culture, language, and race combine and reconfigure based on a set of common ideals—life, liberty, and the pursuit of happiness—in a democracy (Diaz-Rico and Weed 2002).

The Six Social Sciences

Activities integrating the social sciences are helpful in being more efficient instructionally. For example, after presenting each of the social sciences, show a video or DVD of a film. For middle schoolers, *Johnny Tremain* can be used for the

Revolutionary War; *Gettysburg* or *The Red Badge of Courage* for the Civil War; *The Alamo* for Texas' independence from Mexico; and *The Longest Day* or *Tora! Tora! Tora!* for World War II. Other children's films may be used regarding social settings such as *Because of Winn Dixie* (for third and fourth graders) and *Holes* (for fifth and sixth graders). Have students identify an example in the film of each of the six social sciences.

Integrating the Social Sciences

At the elementary and middle school level, the six social sciences can be integrated as a unit of study. The social sciences are listed in table 1.1 along with examples of questions social scientists from each of these six areas of study would ask about the Civil War. Particular consideration during **integrated instruction** should be devoted to historical, geographical, and political/civic events prior to, during, and after the Civil War.

The classroom teacher should incorporate all the social sciences in social studies instruction because all are important in a democratic society. "Schools are a microcosm of global society. Within a country like the United States that is so culturally and linguistically diverse, the need for intergroup knowledge, understanding, and respect is critical" (Bieger 1996, 308). In addition, it is crucial that the teacher create a classroom environment that will help students become good citizens.

Students need to realize that the social studies are often intertwined with other content areas, such as science. Consider the evolution of transportation and the technology to move goods and people. When explorer Louis Joliet and missionary priest Jacques Marquette were sent by the governor of New France (now Canada) to verify that the Mississippi River did indeed flow south, they made an observation that changed the course of history. Joliet and Marquette believed if the Illinois and Des Plaines rivers could be connected by a canal, it would make a continuous route between the Mississippi River and the Great Lakes. In a political move, Congress moved the border between Illinois and Wisconsin north in 1818 so that the canal wouldn't be bogged down in political differences between the two states. A young politician named Abraham Lincoln supported the idea because anyone with a boat and toll money would gain access to water routes that linked the Midwest to the East Coast from the canal's construction. Thus, what became known as the Illinois and Michigan (I&M) Canal opened in 1848 at a cost of $6.4 million—an expense that nearly bankrupted the state of Illinois. It would affect all the social sciences—anthropology, economics, geography, history, political science, and sociology. In the five years following its opening, Chicago's population increased by over 400 percent. Towns sprung up along the 97 miles of banks of the I&M Canal, each adding to the culture of the Midwest.

Similarly, it is important for students to become familiar with the world through global education. Increasingly, what happens in another part of the world has an impact on the United States. For instance, in 1998, the economic decline in Asia and Brazil caused the United States and European stock markets to falter. What do the founders of eBay, Google, and Intel have in common? All are immi-

Table 1.1 The social sciences that constitute elementary social studies

Social Science	Definition	Type of Questions Asked about the Civil War
Anthropology	The study of human beings in terms of race, culture, physical characteristics, and environmental and social relations	What type of medical care was provided to wounded soldiers? How did the ratio of whites to African Americans differ between the North and the South? How did the two armies use African Americans during the war?
Economics	The study of the production, distribution, exchange, and consumption of goods and services	What were the primary products of the North? Of the South? Why was it important to the South to sell goods to England? What kind of bartering occurred between the soldiers?
Geography	The study of land, sea, and air and the distribution of animal and plant life, including human beings and their industries	Compare the types of agriculture used on Southern plantations with those of the Western states of the Union. How did the type of land influence the crops that were raised by each? Why was it important for the North to control the Mississippi River?
History	The study and recording of important events that may include an explanation of their causes	What was the significance of John Brown's raid and his later hanging? Why did the Union Army under Sherman try to destroy everything they encountered on their way to Atlanta? Why did President Lincoln appoint U.S. Grant to command the Union Army?
Political Science/Civics	The study of governmental institutions and processes	What was the significance of having Richmond, Virginia, as the capital of the South rather than New Orleans or some other city? How was the government of the Confederate states similar in structure to that of the United States?
Sociology	The study of people and their institutions and processes	In both armies, men joined regiments named for the state in which they lived. Why was this important? Compare the lifestyle of a freed slave living in the North with that of a slave in the South. Compare the culture of the agrarian South with that of the industrialized North.

grants to the United States. Inviting new immigrant students to share their experiences based on their home country's view of the world adds a different perspective to the classroom learning experience that can benefit all students.

Students need to learn about other continents, nations, and cultures. Consider that many elementary students believe that Africa is a country like France or Mexico. It is difficult for some students to fathom that Africa has 53 countries, each of which is quite unique. From a geographical standpoint, the immense size of Africa is difficult to comprehend. The area of China, Europe, and the United States could all fit at the same time within the African continent (Johnston Smith and Brown 1998). Such understandings are essential for students to become responsible citizens.

Skills Needed to Become a Good Citizen Actor

One goal of social studies is to produce **citizen actors.** That is, students must learn "how citizens in a society make personal and public decisions on issues that affect their destiny" (Linn 1990, 49–50). Children need to learn how to make good decisions. Unfortunately, too often children are not given the opportunity to demonstrate or even practice decision making. Parents, other adults, or even peers often make decisions for children that the children themselves should make. That is not to say that children should be permitted to make adult decisions. For example, an eight-year-old should not be asked whether her mother or father should take job A or job B. However, children should be allowed to have some options; this is essential in creating a learning environment that offers relevant and meaningful study material. For instance, in an integrated instruction classroom in which students are studying the topic of pioneer life, the students may work in small groups on projects. The grouping may be based entirely on the students' own selection of which project they would like to work on. In addition, the students can be given the option of selecting which of five or six books about pioneer life they would like to read and discuss in another small group. Students may individually prepare oral or written reports or write poems, or they may work with others to create a drama about a specific aspect of pioneer life and present it to the class.

In the field of social studies, one of the most basic documents for guiding curriculum development was presented by the NCSS in 1989. In its position statement, the NCSS (1989) reiterates the point that one major goal of social studies is to produce citizen actors through civic participation:

> Social studies programs have a responsibility to prepare our people to identify, understand, and work to solve the problems that face our increasingly diverse nation and interdependent world. . . . [P]rograms that combine the acquisition of knowledge and skills with the application of democratic values to life through social participation present an ideal balance in social studies. (377)

The NCSS (1989, 378) states that "skills essential to citizen participation in civic affairs can be grouped in a problem-solving/decision-making sequence in the following categories":

Skills Related to Acquiring Information
Reading skills
Study skills
Reference and information search skills
Technical skills unique to the use of electronic devices

Skills Related to Organizing and Using Information
Thinking skills
Decision-making skills
Metacognitive skills

Skills Related to Interpersonal Relationships and Social Participation
Personal skills
Group interaction skills
Social and political participation skills

Teachers need to consider these skills when creating an integrated social studies curriculum for elementary and middle school students.

In 1994, the NCSS adopted Curriculum Standards for Social Studies. The NCSS Standards appear on pages xxvi–xxxiii, prior to chapter 1.

Building the Curriculum for Integrated Instruction and Social Studies Integration

The National Commission on the Social Studies (1990), in its highly publicized document *Charting a Course: Social Studies for the 21st Century,* identified a set of characteristics for the social studies curriculum that establishes exemplary guidelines for integration. Social studies provide the obvious connection between the humanities and the natural and physical sciences. To assist students to see the interrelationships among branches of "knowledge, integration of other subject matter with social studies should be encouraged whenever possible" (3).

Central to social studies instruction should be observing, role playing, reading, and writing. Students must use creative and critical thinking skills for problem solving, decision making, and resolving differences. Students must also develop and use strategies that help them to be independent learners and responsible citizens. They must learn to work together with their peers through cooperative and collaborative efforts.

The study of social studies should avail itself of a wide variety of learning materials; not only textbooks but also children's literature (picture books, historical fiction, nonfiction, poetry, contemporary fiction) can be incorporated into the curriculum. For instance, Tomasino (1993, 7) believes that "good cultural literature and relevant social studies activities reveal people's similarities as well as differences and develop cultural literacy in young students." In addition, children should be able to examine original materials or sources whenever possible. For example, artifacts, documents, and maps available from local libraries and historical museums add relevance and meaning to children's discovery of social studies. Working with U.S. Census Bureau statistics can provide children with insights into demographic data and help them understand the role of mathematics in the study of social studies. Examining the effects of industrialization on the environment brings science into social studies. Media in the form of films, videotapes, interactive video, overhead transparencies, paintings, sculptures, quilts, and so on offer enrichment for social studies topics at all grade levels.

Hennings (2000, 8) adds to the rationale for integrating social studies instruction in the following statement: "Communication is central to learning. . . . Today's teachers are unleashing the power of communications by introducing learning strategies that rely on **social interaction.** Oral modeling of reading and writing, collaborative reading and writing, dialogue, and peer journals are just a few of these strategies." Social interaction is essential if children are to become responsible and literate citizen actors. Thus, a literate person does not become literate (acquire literacy skills) or use literacy in isolation. In fact, all literate people must use their literacy in a **social context** in which they interact with others in groups. Concurrently, people do not learn to become good citizens actors unless they engage in purposeful activities in which they **interact** and **communicate** with others in group situations. When asked why people need to be able to read and communicate, most pragmatists would say so that people can solve the everyday problems they encounter as members of society. Good citizens encounter problems that require the use of literacy skills to make wise decisions in consort with others for the good of society. In the next section we develop a curricular context for integrating social studies in the curriculum.

A model for curriculum integration was developed by Banks, Banks, and Clegg (1998) that is based on the **decision-making process.** This process can be integrated into the curriculum at all levels and provides an ideal opportunity for integrated instruction activities in social studies. The following section breaks down the various parts of the process and gives examples of the kinds of integrated instruction activities that can occur during each step.

The Decision-Making Process

Before describing the decision-making process, it is important to note that issues should be at the heart of the social studies curriculum. Banks, Banks, and Clegg (1998, 179) support this notion this way:

> [M]aking decisions can be one of the most interesting and important components of the social studies curriculum. It adds vitality to the curriculum and helps make it significant to both students and the teachers. The study of social issues gives students an opportunity to get a better understanding of the dynamic and changing nature of our society, their responsibilities as citizens in a democracy, and the importance of concepts such as equality and human dignity in maintaining a democracy.

Shirley Engle (1985, 265) states the case even more strongly:

> The failure to deal in a rigorous and uncluttered way with current social problems is one of the most unconscionable defects of the social studies today. . . . The direct study of social problems has been proposed as a cornerstone of our

specialty by social studies reformers over and over again, beginning as early as the recommendations of the Committee on the Social Studies in 1916.

Defining the Process

Step 1: Deriving an Issue

Students read and discuss ideas presented in myriad sources. This provides them with sufficient background information to see the issue, the dilemma it poses to society, and its relevance to them as members of society.

In this step students might read basic documents such as the Constitution, bills, laws, and so forth. They might also read journal, magazine, and newspaper articles, as well as literature in the form of biographies, other nonfiction, and fiction. They then might be asked to interpret and discuss in group situations both the implications and interconnectiveness of what they have read.

Step 2: Expressing Tentative Choices Based on Tentative Values

Students engage in group interaction activities in which they communicate alternate choices and explain and test the values that are driving their choices as they relate to the issues. This might include collaborative writing and analytical and synthesis writing, among other integrated instruction activities.

Step 3: Gathering Information to Test Choices

Students acquire research techniques that enable them to interact with primary documents such as bills, laws, the Constitution, personal journals, primary and secondary sources, and so on. They develop skills of oral inquiry through interviewing authoritative people on their topic. Students engage in analytical and synthesis writing as they organize the data presented. They also interpret data presented and use maps and graphs to find answers to their questions. As members of a group, they use collaborative reading and writing as they write drafts of positions based on their research.

Step 4: Evaluating Data and Identifying Tested Choices

Students master communication skills through debates and persuasive speaking and writing as they move toward group and individual choices on the issue. They evaluate their choices and values expressed earlier in light of their newly acquired knowledge. They arrive at choices on which they will act.

Step 5: Acting on Choices in Society

Students act on the choices agreed on by the group. They engage in purposeful and meaningful communications, both written and oral, as they become civic actors in trying to resolve the issue. They evaluate the impact of their decisions as they interpret the ramifications of their civic participation and realize the importance of their roles as citizen actors. They might conduct surveys, write letters to politicians proposing legislation, make posters, deliver talks and speeches, canvass people, and write journals.

It should be apparent that the process just outlined lends itself beautifully to the acquisition of literacy skills and citizen actors skills in an integrated fashion. Next we turn to more concrete examples of activities at various elementary levels that follow the steps of the decision-making process.

Scope and Sequence of Study in Social Studies

Topics of study for social studies involve **scope and sequence** decisions as to what is to be taught, when, and to what degree of depth. Such curricular decisions are influenced by state and local standards and expectations. Below is a scope and sequence for social studies as suggested by the Task Force on Scope and Sequence (1984):

Kindergarten—Awareness of Self in a Social Setting
Providing socialization experiences that help children bridge their home life with the group life of school.

First Grade—The Individual in Primary Social Groups: Understanding School and Family Life
Continuing the socialization process begun in kindergarten, but extending to studies of families (variations in the ways families live, the need for rules and laws).

Second Grade—Meeting Basic Needs in Nearby Social Groups: The Neighborhood
Studying social functions such as education, production, consumption, communication, and transportation in a neighborhood setting.

Third Grade—Sharing Earth-Space with Others: The Community
Focusing on the community in a global setting, stressing social functions such as production, transportation, communication, distribution, and government.

Fourth Grade—Human Life in Varied Environments: The Region
Emphasizing the region, an area of the earth defined for a specific reason; the home state is studied as a political region where state regulations require it.

Fifth Grade—People of the Americas: The United States and Its Close Neighbors
Centering on the development of the United States as a nation in the Western Hemisphere, with particular emphasis on developing affective attachments to the principles on which the nation was founded; Canada and Mexico are also studied.

Sixth Grade—People and Cultures: The Eastern Hemisphere
Focusing on selected people and cultures of the Eastern Hemisphere.

Seventh Grade—A Changing World of Many Nations: A Global View
Providing an opportunity to broaden the concept of humanity within a global context; focus is on the world as the home of many different people who strive to deal with the forces that shape their lives.

Eighth Grade—Building a Strong and Free Nation: The United States
Studying the "epic of America," the development of the United States as a strong and free nation; emphasis is on social history and economic development, including culture and aesthetic dimensions of the American experience.

Within the above framework, the emphasis is on civics education, history, and geography. Typically, grade four has a focus on the historical, geographical, and political events of the state in which the students reside.

Social Studies Instruction and Technology

Social studies instruction increasingly utilizes technology. Classrooms typically have from one to six computers with Internet access. Planning wisely for computer use is an important instructional task. If there is only one computer the teacher may rotate groups of two to four students to use it over a period of time, such as two weeks, to complete a project. With four or six computers, the students may be scheduled individually or in pairs to complete social studies tasks. The key is to find time and make certain that it be utilized wisely. This means that the teacher prepares in advance by providing appropriate Web sites for the students. A written list by subject may be posted in the technology center of the classroom or provided to each of the students, or both. The teacher should go to each site before putting it on the list to make certain the site is active and appropriate for the grade level.

If the school has a projector that can be connected to the computer, the teacher may locate a Web site on the Internet and display it on a full-size projector screen for all the students to easily view. While modeling a procedure, it is important for the teacher to demonstrate while observing the students to determine if they have any questions.

WebQuests

WebQuests provide a structured way to help students navigate and evaluate sources on the World Wide Web. Since 1995, when Bernie Dodge and Tom March first developed WebQuests, these Internet-based activities have spread throughout public schools. A quick look at the examples of social studies WebQuests posted on Bernie Dodge's Web page (http://www.webquest.org) shows that there are more WebQuests developed for social studies than for any other content area. There are thousands of WebQuests that have been developed by teachers and other educators that relate to civics, economics, geography, and history. WebQuests may include one or two activities for kindergarteners or encompass highly sophisticated activities requiring higher-level thinking skills and going to links at other Internet Web sites for middle school students. An example of a social studies WebQuest with strong use of media is http://www.plimoth.org, which depicts the Pilgrims and their first year's struggles in America.

Using a WebQuest, students complete an authentic task using Web sites selected by the teacher. Usually working in small groups, students use Web sites and other resources to create some product that they can share with others (Brucklacher and Gimbert 1999). For example, students might create a newspaper, persuasive essay, or poster. The beauty of WebQuests is that they allow teachers to screen Web sites that will be used by their students so time is not wasted in surfing the Web. Six tasks are essential to WebQuests:

- introduction to the problem,
- the task,
- the process to complete the task,
- the resources,
- evaluation of the task, and
- conclusion.

WebQuests can be time consuming as links to various Web sites can lead students to vast amounts of information. Increasingly, teachers are developing more refined WebQuests with pinpointed objectives and accompanying tasks that require less time to complete. Using QuestGarden (http://www.webquest.org/questgarden/author/), teachers can build their own WebQuests on a selected topic. (WebQuest sites are also listed at the end of each chapter.)

Although students often begin WebQuests with the goal of completing the task as quickly as possible, with time they begin to more reflectively evaluate multiple sources (Harpster and Gimbert 2000; Milson 2002). WebQuests that integrate an inquiry approach to teaching history and incorporate cooperative learning opportunities seem to improve the self-efficacy of students with special needs (Milson 2002).

Illustrative Examples of Integrated Social Studies Activities

The National Commission on the Social Studies (1990) and *Expectations of Excellence: Curriculum Standards for Social Studies* (NCSS 1994) provide examples of integrating activities that can serve as a stimulating springboard to more in-depth units of instruction. At the kindergarten level, children explore their own immediate environment as well as environments far distant in time and space. Meaningful understandings can be achieved through the use of songs, stories (including children's own pictures), artifacts, overhead transparencies, mapmaking, model building, and slide or videotape presentations of a drama.

In the remaining grades of early childhood education, grades 1 through 3, children can readily understand the concepts of communities past and present and how laws and individual behavior have an impact on the nature of communities. Combining children's literature with social studies affords students the opportunity to explore these concepts by reading stories about and descriptions of different kinds of people living under different conditions—for example, hunters in tropical rain forests, farmers of European, Central American, or Middle Eastern villages, pioneers and immigrant settlers in the United States, Native Americans, or urban and rural dwellers. Reading related children's picture and informational books give students an opportunity to expand their awareness. At this level, literature should be selected to provide children with insights into the diversity of people and social divisions that make up the multicultural community we call Earth. At this level, children's understanding should not come solely from printed material; drawing, building, quilt making, singing, and acting out parts can also be used to expand their consciousness of the variety of human social experience.

In middle childhood education, grades 4 through 6, the content should focus on U.S. history, world history, and geography, both physical and cultural. In the reading program, teachers should draw from literature that provides stories about Native Americans, early European explorers and settlers, the nation's founders, populists, suffragists, inventors, activists, business and labor leaders, and other political, economic, and cultural figures to demonstrate the diversity and historical complexity of American society. In addition, children should study in-depth the basic documents that provide the foundation of our democratic society. This same approach can be used to engage children in learning about world history as well.

At the early adolescent level or middle school level, students should study local and national social, political, and economic relationships and patterns of behavior in-depth. When exploring local history, children might study old buildings and successive architectural styles to discover how people in the area made their living, displayed their idealism, and organized and lived within their private spaces. Conducting oral interviews with older neighborhood residents and different cultural groups, analyzing historical census data, studying old photographs, and consulting newspaper files can introduce students to active historical and geographic research.

The ability to look carefully and productively at the worlds we have created in our neighborhoods, towns, cities, and countryside is a major goal of effective social studies education *at all levels*. In fact, such noted authorities on social studies as Shirley Engle (1985) suggest that each school should devote part of its academic year to the exploration of an identified issue at all grade levels.

By now it should be clear that social studies can be integrated into the curriculum to achieve one of the primary goals of education, that of producing good citizens. Other chapters expand on the broad examples of how social studies fit into the integrated curriculum. The following section is a close-up look at an interdisciplinary unit of study at the fourth grade level.

Celebrating Lewis and Clark in an Interdisciplinary Unit

Interdisciplinary instruction in social studies makes for a lot of planning by the teacher who reads, develops, and gathers prior to and during the unit of study. The bicentennial celebration of Lewis and Clark's incredible journey was targeted as an interdisciplinary unit by Kim Thomas for her fourth graders. Choosing Laurence Pringle's (2002) *Dog of Discovery: A Newfoundland's Adventures with Lewis and Clark* as a **read-aloud** to pique their interest, Kim shared the story of Meriwether Lewis's faithful dog, Seaman, who accompanied the expedition on its two-year military assignment. After reading the picture book, Kim had her students engage in literature response, writing about their reactions to Seaman's numerous adventures during the journey. Several students wrote about Seaman's heroic actions while others wrote about the special relationship between Seaman and the men, particularly his owner, Captain Lewis. One student linked his previously gained knowledge, pointing out that a Native American tribe on the Pacific Coast ate roasted dog meat and that a large dog such as Seaman might have looked pleasing to them as a giant meal. Even Lewis and Clark's men ate dog meat and refused to eat grilled salmon, a fish with which they were not familiar.

On the second day of the unit, a second picture book was read by Kim to her class, *Sacagawea: 1788–1812*, by Rosemary Wallner (2003). This book depicts the young Indian woman who accompanied Lewis and Clark serving as an interpreter for the Corps of Discovery. Sacagawea (also spelled as Sacajawea) used her knowledge of plants to determine which were edible and which poisonous plants and berries were to be avoided—an important task inasmuch as early in the expedition one man died of peritonitis, an infection in the abdomen. Kim's students were surprised to learn that more paintings and commemorative sculptures feature Sacagawea than any other woman in American history.

On the wall was a large sheet of butcher block paper on which Kim had traced from an overhead transparency a black outline of the United States along with the major rivers. When the unit began, Kim and her students drew the outline of the Louisiana Territory in a bold red outline on the map. This gave her students a perspective of the huge vastness of the purchase and how it significantly changed the United States. As they progressed through the unit, the students worked in pairs to identify landmarks on the map that were significant to the Lewis and Clark expedition. A dateline was created along the top of the map indicating the location, significant event, and date or dates. A copy of Peter Lourie's (2002) *On the Trail of Lewis and Clark: A Journey up the Missouri River* (a photo depiction of the journey in which he and three friends retraced Lewis and Clark's journey up the Missouri River) was kept accessible to the class, which helped her students gain a perspective of the different land forms and twists and turns of the mighty Missouri River and the Columbia River encountered by the expedition team. Another book, Rhoda Blumberg's (1998) *What's the Deal? Jefferson, Napoleon, and the Louisiana Purchase*, was used as a reference for all groups. Every day Kim shared additional information with the class through her read-alouds of selected passages from Stephen Ambrose's (1996) *Undaunted Courage: Meriwether Lewis, Thomas Jefferson, and the Opening of the American West* and Rhoda Blumberg's (2003) *York's Adventures with Lewis and Clark: An African-American's Part in the Great Expedition*.

Students selected from six different research groups to study the expedition. Over a 10-day period, the groups conducted their research, developed a presentation, and shared their findings with the class. One group of gifted students read *The Lewis and Clark Trail: Then and Now* (Patent 2002), following the path of Meriwether Lewis and William Clark, and concentrated on charting the anthropological, geographical, historical, and sociological changes that have taken place between 1804 and today. A second group composed of gifted students read the historical novel *Sacajawea: The Story of Bird Woman and the Lewis and Clark Expedition* (Bruchac 2000) and shared the contributions made by the young woman who started the journey heavy with child, gave birth to her son, nicknamed "Pomp," and cared for her infant son during incredibly difficult conditions. They shared with classmates that Sacagawea's husband, an unreliable French trader named Toussaint Charbonneau, had been hired to lead the group; however, it was Sacagawea who was able to guide and serve as interpreter for the expedition. Lewis later remarked that Charbonneau was "a man with no particular merit." Written as if the adventures of the journey were retold to Sacagawea's son, Jean Baptiste Charbonneau, the historical novel is extremely thorough. This group of students was able to share native tales along with a portrayal of what it would be like to travel on such an expedition as a young woman with a family. A third group included four struggling readers, all boys. The group read *How We Crossed the West: The Adventures of Lewis and Clark* by Rosalyn Schanzer (2002), a National Geography book that depicts the journey in comic strip illustration form with the route taken mapped out in the end papers.

The book shares entries from Lewis and Clark's diaries of the trip. This group contributed heavily to the completion of the wall map. Another group also read *How We Crossed the West* and took a different tack in the unit by developing minireports on the animals (i.e., the prairie dog, pronghorn antelope, grizzly bear, and bighorn sheep) and plants and rocks (flora and fauna) that Lewis and Clark discovered and the information they sent back to Washington, DC. They used the Lewis and Clark Web site to show how Lewis learned to read the celestial bodies (stars) to determine their location. The group's research helped Kim link science with social studies in this interdisciplinary unit of study. Another group of very low ability readers, including two ELL students, reported on the picture book *Lewis and Clark, Explorers of the West* by Steven Kroll (1996). They illustrated four major parts of the expedition: leaving St. Louis, wintering with the Mandan Indian tribe, crossing the Rocky Mountains, and seeing the Pacific Ocean for the first time. The last group of students read *Lewis and Clark for Kids: Their Journey of Discovery with 21 Activities* (Herbert 2002). The students created dioramas of the different Native American tribes that Lewis and Clark encountered on the way and gave a **reader's theater** of a dialogue between the two leaders of the journey and members of the expedition team.

Portions of Ken Burns's (1997) film, *Lewis and Clark—The Journey of the Corps of Discovery*, were shared with the class. This included President Thomas Jefferson's naming Lewis and Clark to head the military expedition of the Louisiana Purchase and the designing of the boats by Lewis that were to head up the muddy Missouri to the wintering fort before continuing their trip during the spring. The students learned that Clark took his slave, York, with them on the journey. When the expedition was almost at its farthest point west, Lewis and Clark decided to let all of the individuals in the group decide if the party should stay put or attempt to return to St. Louis. Lewis and Clark let every member of their party vote, including Sacagawea and York (Devoto 1997). This was unheard of for the period in which they lived, for only white men had the right to vote. Truly, this was an important democratic event in our history (Ambrose 1996). Upon their return to the east, both York and Sacagawea could not vote or own property as was the law. Neither received a land grant as did all other members of the expedition. The class debated the treatment of the black man and Native American woman by the government.

Two Web sites were also used as resources. The first Web site, http://www.lewisandclark.org, is a superb site with 19 different parts offering a synopsis of the expedition. Maps, journal entries, and summary are accompanied by illustrations. New terms and concepts have links that provide additional information and explanations. For example, the word *cache* was unfamiliar to many of Kim's students. When they clicked it they were given a definition and illustration of how the members of the expedition designed the storage area for their food and supplies. Likewise, students did not know some of the tribes and clicked on Blackfeet, Shoshone, and Sioux Indians to discover traits and culture about each tribe. The second Web site was a Public Broadcasting System site, New Perspective on the West—(http://www.pbs.org/weta/thewest/people/s_z/sacagawea.htm). This Web site is devoted to the Shoshone woman who guided Lewis and Clark in their military expedition of the Louisiana Purchase and presented students with information about her invaluable aid on the journey. For instance, students learned that when one of the boats capsized, Sacagawea calmly rescued important pouches of journals and logs of the expedition from the icy cold river waters. Looking at the NCSS Standards, Kim's two-week unit touched on all 10 of the standards.

A good book for upper elementary and middle school students to read is *Off the Map: The Journals of Lewis and Clark* (Roop and Roop 1993), which traces the journey of Lewis and Clark. The book begins with the letter from President Thomas Jefferson authorizing the expedition and continues with excerpts from the men's journals. The editors include an overview of the significance of the expedition.

NCSS STANDARDS-LINKED LESSON PLAN

Lewis and Clark Expedition

Theme: Influence of Climate and Geology on Findings of Lewis and Clark Expedition
Source: Pamela Farris, Northern Illinois University
Grades: 4–8
Objectives:

• Students will investigate the relationship between climate and weather.

• Students will investigate the relationship between climate and geological changes.

• Students will collect weather data for eight points along the Lewis and Clark trail for six weeks.

• Students will examine the weather data to seek patterns present in each site.

NCSS Themes:
  I. Culture
 III. People, Places, and Environment
VIII. Science, Technology, and Society

Materials: paper, colored pencils

   Students will seek information from a variety of sources that include reference books, science textbook (weather and geology units), and Web sites.

Salter, C. R. 2002. April. "Lewis and Clark's Lost Missouri." *National Geographic,* 90–97.
Web site: National Geographic's Research Division, (http://www.nationalgeographic.com/ngm/0204)

Process:

• Students will read the article by Salter.

• They will discuss how climate influences where people live and how it influences human lives.

• Next they will examine how the Missouri River changed course over time.

• Students will collect weather data on eight different sites along the Lewis and Clark trail over a six-week period.

• Students will compare and contrast weather differences among the eight sites. They will write an explanation why certain areas were settled and have a large population and others have a small population.

Instructional Comments: Students will seek information from a variety of sources that include reference books, science textbook (weather and geology units), and Web sites. A guest speaker could be a university or local television meteorologist.

Learning Styles Addressed: Verbal/linguistic, visual/spatial, interpersonal, intrapersonal, mathematical/logical

Evaluation: The rubrics for this lesson should include standard rules for writing letters. The evaluation should acknowledge the extent to which a student researches his/her topic of study. It should allow for creativity. Also included should be the impact of a PowerPoint presentation or Hyperstudio presentation.

Modifications for Diverse Learners: Students may work in diverse cooperative groups. Adult assistance may be requested. *Variations:* Students may hold a weather, geology, and geography fair to share their knowledge.

Chapter Summary

Social studies is the study of the cultural, economic, geographic, and political aspects of past, current, and future societies. When social studies is incorporated into an integrated curriculum, children are allowed to make decisions about what they want to learn and how they will learn it. Through the use of children's literature, writing, and discussion, students discover concepts in anthropology, economics, geography, history, political science, and sociology. Because self-selection of reading materials in children's literature and activities allows for personalization of learning, children become more fully engaged and interested in social studies, learning more than they would with teacher-assigned textbook readings. Students also learn to become decision makers.

The decision-making process consists of five steps: (1) deriving an issue, (2) expressing tentative choices based on tentative values, (3) gathering information to test choices, (4) evaluating data and identifying tested choices, and (5) acting on choices in society. Through active participation, children learn to become decision makers and responsible citizen actors. They also learn to be independent learners and thinkers.

By examining the development of their immediate and surrounding worlds, children gain insight into each of the social sciences that make up social studies. In so doing, they better understand the interdependency of people both locally and in the global society.

Children's Literature Recommendations

Ambrose, S. 1996. *Undaunted Courage: Meriwether Lewis, Thomas Jefferson, and the Opening of the American West.* New York: Simon and Schuster. This book gives a detailed account of the political and historical aspects of Lewis and Clark's journey. Good reference for teachers and gifted readers. (Gr. 6–8)

————. 2001. *The Good Fight: How World War II Was Won.* New York: Atheneum. A picture book for the upper grades that provides a thumbnail accurate overview of the events leading up to and during World War II. (Gr. 5–8)

Bartoletti, S. C. 2005. *Hitler Youth: Growing up in Hitler's Shadow.* New York: Scholastic. Describes life as a young teenager in Germany during WW II. (Gr. 5–8)

Blumberg, R. 1998. *What's the Deal? Jefferson, Napoleon, and the Louisiana Purchase.* Washington, DC: National Geographic Society. The twists and turns of the massive acquisition of the Louisiana Purchase are described in this 160-page informational book. (Gr. 4–8)

———. 2003. *York's Adventures with Lewis and Clark: An African-American's Part in the Great Expedition.* New York: HarperCollins. The life of York, the slave who accompanied Lewis and Clark. (Gr. 6–8)

Bruchac, J. 1997a. *Lasting Echoes: An Oral History of Native American People.* San Diego: Silverwhistle/Harcourt Brace. More than a hundred Native Americans stories are shared in this book. Bruchac, himself a Native American, presents the stories of seven generations. (Gr. K–8)

———. 1997b. *Many Nations: An Alphabet of Native America.* Illus. R. F. Goetzl. Boston: Bridgewater Books. From Anishanabe artists making birch bark bowls to Zuni elders saying prayers for the day that is done, this book is essential for a Native American unit. Twenty-six tribes are depicted. (Gr. K–8)

———. 2000. *Sacajawea: The Story of Bird Woman and the Lewis and Clark Expedition.* New York: Scholastic. This historical novel portrays the journey through the eyes of Sacajawea and William Clark. (Gr. 5–8)

Cherry, L. 1992. *A River Ran Wild.* Orlando, FL: Harcourt Brace Jovanovich. In this true story of the Nashua River, the author describes the environmental damage caused by civilization. (Gr. 1–5)

Choi, Y. 1997. *The Sun Girl and the Moon Boy: A Korean Folktale.* New York: Knopf. This story is similar to Little Red Riding Hood. A girl and a boy use their wits and a bit of luck to escape from a hungry tiger and bring the first rays of sunlight and moonlight to the world. (Gr. K–4)

Coerr, E. 1979. *Sadako and a Thousand Paper Cranes.* Illus. R. Himler. New York: Yearling. The poignant story of Sadako is a simple one. After the atomic bomb attack on her city, she develops leukemia. She believes if she makes one thousand paper origami cranes, she will survive. (Gr. 3–5)

Devoto, B., ed. 1997. *The Journals of Lewis and Clark.* Boston: Houghton Mifflin. The actual journal entries of Meriwether Lewis and William Clark are contained in this volume. Superb source of historical documents for upper elementary and middle school students. (Gr. 4–8)

Fritz, J. 1983. *The Double Life of Pocahontas.* New York: Putnam. A historical fiction account of the Indian princess, Pocahontas. (Gr. 3–6)

Giff, P. R. 1997. *Lily's Crossing.* New York: Delacorte. Lily is used to spending the summer at the beach but World War II changes her life. She finds a new friend, Albert, who has escaped from Hungary only to lose most of his family. Together they survive the bombing of England by the Germans. (Gr. 4–8)

Goble, P. 1990. *Dream Wolf.* New York: Bradbury. A beautifully illustrated book about a Native American legend. (Gr. 1–3)

Herbert, J. 2002. *Lewis and Clark for Kids: Their Journey of Discovery with 21 Activities.* Chicago: Chicago Review Press. An overview of the Lewis and Clark journey. The activities focus on the Native American tribes they discovered along the way. (Gr. 4–8)

Hong, L. T. 1991. *How the Ox Star Fell from Heaven.* New York: Whitman. A novel about an Asian legend. (Gr. 4–5)

Ishii, M. 1987. *The Tongue-Cut Sparrow.* Trans. K. Paterson. Illus. S. Akabar. New York: Lodestar, Dutton. A Japanese version of the well-known folktale of the fisherman and his wife, who is never satisfied with the gifts she receives. (Gr. 2–4)

Kesey, K. 1991. *The Sea Lion.* Illus. N. Waldman. New York: Viking. One of a few books about the Pacific Northwest Indians, this book depicts the legend of the sea lion. (Gr. 3–5)

Kirkpatrick, K. 1998. *Trouble's Daughter: The Story of Susanna Hutchinson, Indian Captive.* New York: Delacorte. Based on the true story of the massacre of Susanna's family by Lenape warriors in 1643 and her being taken captive by members of the tribe. A good book for middle school students. (Gr. 4–6)

Kroll, S. 1996. *Lewis and Clark, Explorers of the West.* Illus. R. Williams. New York: Holiday House. Good intermediate grade level book for examining the expedition of the Louisiana Purchase. (Gr. 3–6)

Lelooska. 1997. *Echoes of the Elders.* New York: Dorling Kindersley. A collection of five Native American tales that are rich with fablelike morals and tribal symbolism. (Gr. 4–7)

Lourie, P. 2002. *On the Trail of Lewis and Clark: A Journey up the Missouri River.* Honesdale, PA: Boyds Mills Press. Lourie and his friends retraced Lewis and Clark's journey up the muddy Missouri River. The photographs serve to give us a better understanding of the perils the expedition encountered. (Gr. 3–8)

Lowry, L. 1989. *Number the Stars.* Boston: Houghton Mifflin. Ten-year-old Annemarie and her best friend Ellen live in Copenhagen during the German occupation. When Jews are "relocated," Annemarie's family takes Ellen in and pretends she is a family member. Annemarie's courage saves her friend's life. A Newbery Award winning book. (Gr. 4–6)

McKissick, P. C. 1997. *Run Away Home.* New York: Scholastic. During the 1880s, Apaches were taken by train from their home in Arizona to reservations in Florida. This historical novel tells of Sky, an Apache boy, who escapes from the train and is rescued by Sarah, a black girl. When Sarah's family is threatened by a white supremacist group, Sky helps fight them off and save the family farm. A thought-provoking book for upper elementary children and middle schoolers. (Gr. 5–8)

McSwigan, M. 1942. *Snow Treasure.* New York: Dutton. During the 1940 occupation of Norway by the German army, Norwegian children smuggled gold bars to a cave for hiding. The story keeps students riveted. (Gr. 4–8)

Martin, R. 1992. *The Rough-Face Girl.* Illus. D. Shannon. New York: Putnam. This is the Algonquin Indian version of the Cinderella tale. It is one of the most haunting and beautiful of the more than 1,500 versions of Cinderella. (Gr. K–3)

Napoli, D. J. 1998. *Stones in Water.* New York: Scholastic. During World War II three teenage boys in Italy set out to see a movie. They are taken by soldiers and forced to work in a camp for the Axis powers. (Gr. 6–8)

Nhuong, H. Q. 1982. *The Land I Lost: Adventures of a Boy in Vietnam.* New York: Harper & Row. Describes daily life in Vietnam prior to the war, including the duties of parents and children. (Gr. 6–8)

———. 1997. *Water Buffalo Days: Growing Up in Vietnam.* New York: HarperCollins. This chapter book makes a good read-aloud for primary students. An autobiography, Nhuong tells how he fought off tigers and wild pigs that threatened his Vietnamese village. (Gr. 5–8)

O'Dell, S. 1988. *Black Star, Bright Dawn.* Boston: Houghton Mifflin. A compelling Native American story told by master storyteller Scott O'Dell. (Gr. 5–8)

Patent, D. H. 2002. *The Lewis and Clark Trail: Then and Now.* Photo. W. Munoz. New York: Dutton. A comparison of the path Lewis and Clark took on their mission. The entire region is considered with the rivers and mountains, Indian tribes, and animals of 1804 being contrasted with today's homes, farms, ranches, and cities that dot the trail's landscape. (Gr. 4–8)

Paulsen, G. 1988. *Dogsong.* New York: Bradbury. The story of a Native American boy growing up. (Gr. 4–7)

Philip, N., ed. 1997. *In a Sacred Manner I Live: Native American Wisdom.* New York: Clarion. Ranging from quotes by Chief Powhatan in 1609 to Leonard Crow Dog, a modern-day Sioux medicine man, this is an excellent book on Native American wisdom. Includes quotes from Blackhawk, Black Elk, Chief Joseph, Geronimo, Sitting Bull, and Tecumseh. (Gr. 5–8)

Pringle, L. 2002. *Dog of Discovery: A Newfoundland's Adventures with Lewis and Clark.* Honesdale, PA: Boyds Mills Press. The story of Seaman, the giant Newfoundland dog of Meriwether Lewis, who accompanied the military expedition to evaluate the Louisiana Territory. (Gr. 2–5)

Roop, P., and C. Roop, eds. 1993. *Off the Map: The Journals of Lewis and Clark.* New York: Walker. The journey of William Clark and Meriwether Lewis is traced through their own journal entries as they explored the territory of the Louisiana Purchase. (Gr. 3–8)

Salisbury, G. 1995. *Under the Blood Red Sun.* New York: Dell. After Pearl Harbor is attacked, a boy must become the man of the family when his Japanese father is sent to an internment camp on the mainland. (Gr. 6–8)

Say, A. 1990. *El Chino.* Boston: Houghton Mifflin. The true story of a Chinese boy who grew up to be a bullfighter in Spain. (Gr. 5–8)

Schanzer, R. 2002. *How We Crossed the West: The Adventures of Lewis and Clark.* Washington, DC: National Geographic. A condensed, simplified picture-book version of Lewis and Clark's diaries give the essence of this incredible expedition. (Gr. 3–6)

Sneve, V. 1989. *Dancing Tepees: Poems of American Indian Youth.* New York: Holiday House. A collection of poetry written by Native American children. (Gr. 2–6)

Wallner, R. 2003. *Sacagawea: 1788–1812.* New York: Bridgestone. A picture book biography of the young Native American girl who served as a guide and interpreter for the Lewis and Clark expedition. (Gr. 1–5)

Wood, N., ed. 1997. *The Serpent's Tongue: Prose, Poetry, and Art of New Mexico Pueblos.* New York: Dutton. A comprehensive book with lots of examples of Pueblo artwork and poetry as well as stories. Excellent resource book for middle schoolers and teachers. (Gr. 2–8)

Additional Children's Books About World War II

Books about War

Fox, M. 1989/2002. *Feathers and Fools.* San Diego, CA: Harcourt Brace. (Gr. 2–8)

Popov, N. 1996. *Why?* New York: North-South. (Gr. 3–8)

Books about the American Experience

Bunting, E. 1998. *So Far from the Sea.* New York: Clarion. (Gr. 4–8)

McKissick, P., and F. McKissick. 1995. *Red-Tail Angels: The Tuskeegee Airmen of World War II.* New York: Walker. (Gr. 5–8)

Mochizuki, K. 1993. *Baseball Saved Us.* New York: Lee & Low. (Gr. 4–8)

Stevenson, J. 1992. *Don't You Know There's a War On?* New York: Greenwillow. (Gr. 4–8)

Books about the Holocaust

Adler, D. A. 1993. *A Picture Book of Anne Frank.* New York: Holiday House. (Gr. 2–5)

Borden, L. 2004. *The Greatest Skating Race: A Story from the Netherlands.* New York: Margaret K. McElderry Press. (Gr. 4–6)

Deedy, C. A. 2000. *The Yellow Star: The Legend of King Christian X of Denmark.* Atlanta, GA: Peachtree. (Gr. 4–8)

Lowry, L. 1984. *Number the Stars.* Boston: Houghton Mifflin. (Gr. 4–6)

Nerlove, M. 1996. *Flowers on the Wall.* New York Margaret K. McElderry Press. (Gr. 4–8)

Oppenheim, S. L. 1992. *The Lily Cupboard: A Story of the Holocaust.* New York: HarperCollins. (Gr. 4–8)

Polacco, P. 2000. *The Butterfly.* New York: Philomel. (Gr. 3–6)

Warren, A. 2001. *Surviving Hitler: A Boy in the Nazi Death Camps.* New York: HarperCollins. (Gr. 4–6)

Books about the Japanese Experience
Coerr, E. 1985. *Sadako and the Thousand Cranes.* New York: Puffin. (Gr. 4–8)
Mochizuki, K. 1997. *Passage to Freedom: The Sugihara Story.* New York: Lee & Low. (Gr. 4–8)
Tsuchiya, Y. 1988. *Faithful Elephants.* (Trans. T. Dykes). Boston: Houghton Mifflin. (Gr. 4–8)

Nonfiction Books
Ambrose, S. E. 2001. *The Good Fight: How World War II Was Won.* New York: Atheneum.
   (Gr. 4–8)
Colman, P. 1995. *Rosie the Riveter.* New York: Crown. (Gr. 4–8)
Giblin, J. C. 2002. *The Life and Death of Adolf Hitler.* New York: Clarion. (Gr. 4–8)
Volakova, H. ed. 1993. *I Never Saw Another Butterfly: Children's Drawings and Poems from
   Terezin Concentration Camp, 1942–1944.* New York: Schocken. (Gr. 4–8)

Teaching Resources

The following resources are available from the African Studies Center at Boston University. Contact: African Outreach Program, Boston University, 270 Bay State Road, Boston, MA 02215. Web site: http://www.bu.edu/AFR

Africa Inspirer. This is a CD-ROM by Tom Snyder Productions (1997) that is good for grades
   4 to 8.
How Big Is Africa? This 31″ × 24″ full-color poster map shows how Europe, the United States, and
   China would all fit in Africa. Also included are lesson plans, reproducible maps, and cutouts.

Related Technology Tools

National Council for the Social Studies (NCSS)
   www.ncss. org
   www.socialstudies.org
   NCSS engages and supports educators in strengthening and advocating social studies.
Social Studies School Service
   www.socialstudies.com
   Includes information and guidance on: ice breakers, introduction to social studies, lesson
   planning, creative lessons, idea books, activities, and media resources.
Citizenship Central
   www.citizenshipcentral.org
   A clearinghouse for effective citizenship education from the National Council for the
   Social Studies.
Center for Critical Thinking Classroom Materials
   www.criticalthinking.org/K12/k12class/trc.nclk
   Includes lesson plans and classroom ideas to help teachers develop critical thinking skills
   in their students.

General Social Studies WebQuest Sites
Social Studies Lesson Plans and WebQuests (Gr. K–8)
   http://www.lessonplancentral.com/lessons/Social_Studies/ Social Studies WebQuests
   (Gr. 6–8)
   http://www.webquest.sdsu.edu/matrix/6-8-Soc.htm
Social Studies WebQuests (Gr. K–8)
   http://techtrekers.com/webquests
U.S. Government Web sites for Kids & Students (Gr. K–2, 3–5, 6–8—Lists government
   agencies in alphabetical order)
   http://bensguide.gpo.gov/subject.html

Specific Topic WebQuest Sites
Laura Ingalls Wilder Scavenger Hunt (Westward Movement) (Gr. 4–6)
    http://www.macomb.k12.mi.us/wq/WebQ97/LAURALES.HTM
Pearl Harbor Lives (Gr. 4–6)
    http://www.ga.unc.edu/NCTA/NCTA/WebQuests2001/FlatRock2/Pearl/index.html
Native Americans (Gr. 2–3)
    http://www.angelfire.com/tx4/lessons/Native_Americans2.html

Software and Videos
Dorling Kindersley. 2001. History of the World 3.0. New York: DK Multimedia.
Burns, K. 1997. *Lewis and Clark—The Journey of the Corps of Discovery.* Washington, DC: Flo-
    rentine Films and WETA. Available on DVD. This film is an excellent re-creation of
    Lewis and Clark's 1803 journey to locate the Northwest Passage.
Planning Integrated Units: A Concept-Based Approach. 1997. 65 minutes. Available from the Asso-
    ciation for Supervision and Curriculum Development (ASCD) at www.ascd.org. *Planning
    Integrated Units* examines how to design integrated units that not only help students see
    connections among different subject areas, but also challenges students to think at higher
    levels and promote a deeper understanding of what they're studying.
Explorers of the World Video, Lewis and Clark. 2000. 23 minutes. Available from Teacher's Dis-
    covery, 1-800-543-4180.

References

Allen, M. G., and R. L. Stevens. 1998. *Middle Grades Social Studies: Teaching and Learning for
    Active and Responsible Citizenship.* Boston: Allyn & Bacon.
Banks, J. A., C. A. M. Banks, and A. A. Clegg. 1998. *Teaching Strategies for the Social Studies.*
    5th ed. New York: Longman.
Bieger, E. M. 1996. "Promoting Multicultural Education through a Literature-Based
    Approach." *The Reading Teacher* 49 (4): 308–12.
Brucklacher, B., and B. Gimbert. 1999. "Role Playing Software and WebQuests—What's Pos-
    sible with Cooperative Learning and Computers." *Computers in the Schools* 15 (2): 37–48.
Diaz-Rico, L. T., and K. Z. Weed. 2002. *The Crosscultural, Language, and Academic Develop-
    ment Handbook: A Complete K–12 Reference Guide.* 2nd ed. Boston: Allyn & Bacon.
Engle, S. H. 1985. "A Social Studies Imperative." *Social Education* 49: 264–65.
Feagin, J., and C. Feagin. 2005. *Racial and Ethnic Relations.* 7th ed. Englewood Cliffs, NJ:
    Prentice-Hall.
Hardt, U. 1992. Teaching Multicultural Understanding. *Oregon English Journal.* 14 (1): 3–5.
Harpster, T. L., and B. G. Gimbert. 2000. "Tour USA—A WebQuest Embedding Technol-
    ogy and Standards in a Social Studies Curriculum." *Pennsylvania Educational Leadership*
    19 (2): 22–28.
Hennings, D. G. 2000. *Communication, Language and Literacy Learning.* 7th ed. Boston:
    Houghton Mifflin.
Johnson, P. 2004. *Choice Words.* Portland, ME: Stenhouse.
Johnston Smith, D., and B. Brown. 1998. "How Big Is Africa?" *Social Education* 62 (5): 278–81.
Joint Committee on Geographic Education. 1984. *Guidelines for Geographic Education.* Wash-
    ington, DC: Association of American Geographers.
Leinhardt, G. 1992. "What Research on Learning Tells Us About Teaching." *Educational
    Leadership* 49 (7): 20–27.
Linn, J. B. 1990. "Whole Language in Social Studies." *Social Science Record* 27 (2): 49–55.
Milson, A. J. 2002. "The Internet and Inquiry Learning: Integrating Medium and Method
    in a Sixth Grade Social Studies Classroom." *Theory and Research in Social Education* 30
    (3): 330–52.

National Center for History in the Schools. 1994. *National Standards for History (K–4).* Los Angeles: National Center for History in the Schools.

National Commission on the Social Studies. 1990. *Charting a Course: Social Studies for the 21st Century.* Washington, DC: National Council for the Social Studies.

National Council for the Social Studies (NCSS). 1989. "In Search of a Scope and Sequence for Social Studies." *Social Education* 53 (6): 376–79.

———. 1994. *Expectations of Excellence: Curriculum Standards for Social Studies.* Washington, DC: Author.

Pelto, P., and R. Muessig. 1980. *The Study and Teaching of Anthropology.* Columbus, OH: Merrill.

Ravitch, D. 2002. "September 11: Seven Lessons for the Schools." *Educational Leadership* 60 (2): 6–9.

Ridgeway, C., and T. Shaver. 2006. "Utilizing Children's Literature to Enhance Positive Social Interactions." *Illinois Reading Council Journal* 34 (2): 15–23.

Salter, C. R. 2002 (April). "Lewis and Clark's Lost Missouri." *National Geographic,* 90–97.

Strong, R. W., H. F. Silver, and M. J. Perini. 2001. *Teaching What Matters Most.* Alexandria, VA: Association for Supervision and Curriculum Development.

Task Force on Scope and Sequence. 1984. "In Search of Scope and Sequence for Social Studies." *Social Education* 48 (4): 376–85.

Tomasino, K. 1993. "Literature and Social Studies: A Spicy Mix for Fifth Graders." *Social Studies and the Young Learner* 5: 7–10.

U.S. Department of Education. 1994. *U.S. History Framework for the 1994 National Assessment of Educational Progress (NAEP).* Washington, DC: Author.

Vygotsky, L. S. 1962. *Thought and Language.* Cambridge, MA: MIT Press.

> *Students do not merely passively receive or copy input from teachers, but instead actively mediate it by trying to make sense of it and to relate it to what they already know (or think they know) about the topic.*
>
> —Jere Brophy,
> "Probing the Subtleties of Subject-Matter Teaching"

Chapter Two

Social Studies and Integrated Instruction
A Look at Interdisciplinary Instruction

Pamela J. Farris, Northern Illinois University

CHAPTER OUTLINE

CHAPTER OBJECTIVES

Readers will

- recognize that critical thinking skills need to be taught as part of social studies and interdisciplinary instruction;
- understand the relationship of language arts and social studies in interdisciplinary instruction; and
- be able to develop ways to promote decision making with students.

Introduction

Social studies serves as an integration of the social sciences: anthropology, economics, geography, history, political science, and sociology. In addition, social studies promotes the development of critical and creative thinking as children learn to assume their role as responsible citizens in a democratic society. According to Brophy (1992, 8):

> In social studies, students are challenged to engage in **higher-order thinking** by interpreting, analyzing, or manipulating information in response to questions or problems that cannot be resolved through routine application of previously learned knowledge. Students focus on networks of connected content struc-

tured around powerful ideas rather than long lists of disconnected facts, and they consider the implications of what they are learning for social and civic decision making.

For this to occur, learning must be both meaningful and relevant to students. When the curriculum allows students to make connections with learning and their own lives by being relevant, they plunge into social studies activities with a fervor—a phenomenon Parker Palmer (1998/1999, 8) refers to as "evoking the spirit."

The other content areas such as language arts, math, and science share many of the same basic principles of social studies. These include such basic learning principles as: (1) respect for the learner and the teacher, (2) belief in the role of the teacher as a facilitator of learning, and (3) encouragement of learners to experiment and take risks. Moreover, like the arts, social studies is both personal and social. Social studies is driven from the inside by the need to communicate and shaped from the outside toward the norms of society.

With these shared principles, it is appropriate that interdisciplinary instruction play a major role in the social studies curriculum. This chapter outlines interdisciplinary instruction and its essential elements. Other chapters describe how the integrated instruction approach can be effectively incorporated in the social studies curriculum.

Interdisciplinary Instruction

In the late 1890s and early 1900s, John Dewey and his mentor, Francis Parker, founded the progressive education movement. Their work at the University of Chicago's laboratory school encouraged teachers to provide more opportunities for **hands-on learning.** Dewey promoted "learning by doing," the belief that children learn best when they are active participants in the learning process.

In the 1950s and 1960s, Hilda Taba pointed out the need for character education. Perhaps her most important contribution to social studies was the **spiral curriculum,** in which social studies concepts are introduced and later continuously elaborated upon throughout elementary and middle school. Jerome Bruner further stressed the idea of the spiral curriculum.

In the 1970s and 1980s, James Banks pointed out the need to create citizens who were decision makers. He also emphasized the need for multicultural education in social studies and throughout the elementary and middle school curriculum. By the twenty-first century, the idea of **interdisciplinary instruction**—the teaching of more than one content area at the same time—had become well entrenched as an instructional technique.

By 2000, the issue of diversity of students, in terms of ability, background, culture, and language became pertinent as teachers considered the social studies curriculum and instructional strategies. **Differentiated instruction** was implemented by many teachers as they modified the activities to better meet the learning needs, previous experiences, and abilities of their students. This led to the idea of **parallel curriculum**, which has set learning objectives with up to four different venues of accompanying activities depending upon student needs to accomplish the objectives.

Traditional versus Interdisciplinary Instruction: Philosophical and Psychological Underpinnings

The traditional instructional approach is the direct instruction, skills-based, behaviorist approach. The interdisciplinary instructional approach has its roots in the progressive education, constructivist approach. These approaches differ in terms of views of knowing, learning, and motivation. Behaviorists believe that knowledge is present outside oneself and that it can be broken down into tiny, discrete units. Constructivists believe that knowledge develops from within as the individual attempts to "construct" meaning out of experience, both firsthand and vicariously (McCarty 1991). Inquiry becomes an essential aspect of learning.

Behaviorists believe that learning takes place *only* within the context of appropriately reinforced responses to events (or stimuli). These may be simple responses (one specific unit of behavior) or complex responses (a series of behaviors) (Weil, Calhoun, and Joyce 2003). Modeling or demonstrating an activity for students is an example of behaviorism. For average and struggling students, as well as English language learners (ELLs), explicit modeling of how to do an activity is especially helpful (Farris, Fuhler, and Walther 2003). Both directions for the activity and expectations are clarified. On the other hand, constructivists believe that learning takes place in the flow of daily human experiences and is an ongoing process. Thus, all individuals are learners and all are teachers. Children learn from each other as well as from the teacher. Likewise, the teacher learns from students and other teachers.

Behaviorists believe motivation to learn is extrinsic, based on external rewards. Constructivists believe that motivation to learn is based on the individual's own natural curiosity and interests as well as one's tendency to set and achieve self-determined goals. Students are given more choices in the interdisciplinary instructional approach than with direct instruction. In addition, they are expected to serve as active participants in their learning—making decisions, setting goals, and engaging real and relevant learning activities—thereby becoming more responsible for their learning.

Essential Elements of Literacy Learning

Literacy learning requires that the language arts (listening, speaking, reading, writing, viewing, visually representing, and thinking) be integrated in instruction. This section describes the role of listening, speaking, reading, and writing as part of social studies and interdisciplinary instruction.

Listening

Listening involves giving attention to others. As such it requires self-discipline. The listener must carefully consider what the other person is saying and, while doing so, think of a response. Thus, the listener must anticipate what the speaker will say and call on previously gained knowledge to judge what the speaker is saying.

Being a good listener aids learning. When the teacher uses a visual along with auditory presentation, retention goes from 25% to up to 80%.

In integrated instruction classrooms, listening is important because students are taught to value each other's contributions. Since students learn from each other, being a good listener is paramount to being a good learner. Much knowledge and understanding are gained via listening, which is in turn used in speaking, reading, and writing.

Listening to the teacher's instructions and questions as well as other students' comments is a very challenging task for learning disabled and English language learners. This oral medium of information delivery puts a heavy burden on nonnative English speaking students who are still developing their English language and listening proficiency. Speech that is intended for native speakers of English is naturally fast paced, full of colloquialisms, and frequented with reductions of natural oral speech (e.g., gonna/going to, hafta/have to). Unlike written text, which can be reviewed if needed, authentic oral text passes quickly in real time, and there are often few, if any, opportunities to relisten to the information.

Teachers can help their learning disabled and ELL students comprehend more of the oral information and instructions in the social studies classroom by making some straightforward modifications to their speech: simplify syntax and vocabulary; speak in a normal tone and at a normal rate (as well as avoid obvious cultural references that ELLs might not have the background knowledge for); and avoid or explain idioms. More importantly, teachers must use multiple channels of information input. Being demonstrative when speaking (using gestures, facial expressions, or pointing to pictures or realia) or talking while modeling a process can help struggling students comprehend the oral speech they are presented with. Another technique to ensure that learning disabled and ELL students understand instructions is to ask the student to repeat them in his/her own words, or alternately, demonstrate pictorially that he/she understands what is expected. Peer buddies in cooperative groups can also help with comprehension of oral information.

☞ IN THE CLASSROOM

Cooperative/Collaborative Attentive Listening

This listening-speaking activity is appropriate for students in grades 2 through 8. Begin by dividing the students into groups of six, and proceed to give each group member one-sixth of a paper circle that is eight inches in diameter. Next, inform the students that they are to listen carefully to a folktale as it is read aloud because each group of students must decide as a group what the six main events of the folktale are. Once a group has identified the six events, have each group member illustrate one of the events on his or her sixth of the circle. (Note: The number of students per group along with a corresponding number of events may be changed, depending on class size or number of significant events in a particular folktale.)

When a group has completed its illustrations, each member describes his or her illustration of one event. Then the events are put in proper order and the story is completely retold. Each group's final product becomes a completed circle of six pie-shaped illustrations that tell the story in clockwise order, starting at the twelve o'clock position. When glued to bright-colored construction paper, the completed circles make an effective bulletin board display.

This activity can be extended into the writing arena by having each student write the first draft of a story and then illustrate each event in the story. By drawing the various scenes and placing them in a desired sequence, students can modify and refine a story before they begin the final writing.

This activity is well-suited for struggling readers and writers as well as those English language learners whose language proficiency is not yet sufficient for writing in English. With the support of their group, they can demonstrate their understanding of the story through their drawings. Instead of writing a draft of the story, ELLs can write one- or two-word labels for the various frames of the circle story. This activity serves as a prewriting experience for these students, giving them the opportunity to participate in the activity and practice their English listening and prewriting skills.

Following are some suggested folktales for cooperative/collaborative attentive listening:

Aylesworth, J. 2001. *The Tale of Tricky Fox*. Illus. B. McClintock. New York: Scholastic.

Farris, P. J. 1996. *Young Mouse and Elephant: An East African Folktale*. Illus. V. Gorbachev. Boston: Houghton Mifflin.

Kellogg, S. 1991. *Jack and the Beanstalk*. New York: Morrow.

Historical informational picture books lend themselves to this activity. The first four books listed below can be used to introduce the Revolutionary War to students. For instance, *18 Penny Goose* (Walker 1999) is based on a true story of how a young girl and her family flee their home just prior to the British army's overtaking the area. The girl left a note for the soldiers not to kill her beloved pet goose. Upon the family's return they discover the goose alive and well, with a packet of 18 pennies and a note saying the money was for the food the British soldiers had eaten. *Katie's Trunk* (Turner 1989/1997) describes the life of a Tory family—the author's—during the Revolutionary War. Based purely on folklore, *Sleds on Boston Common* (Borden 2000) portrays the harsh winter of 1775 and the desire of a young boy named Henry, who is anxious to try out his birthday sled. Henry boldly asks a British general, General Gage, to permit them to sled on the hills of Boston Common, where the British army is camped. Impressed by the courage of Henry, Gage grants permission.

Borden, L. 2000. *Sleds on Boston Common: A Story from the American Revolution*. Illus. R. A. Parker. New York: McElderry.

Edwards, P. D. 2001. *Boston Tea Party*. Illus. H. Cole. New York: Putnam.

Fleming, C. 1998. *The Hatmaker's Sign: A Story by Benjamin Franklin*. Illus. R. A. Parker. New York: Orchard.

Turner, A. 1989/1997. *Katie's Trunk*. Illus. R. Himler. New York: Simon & Schuster.
Walker, S. 1999. *18 Penny Goose*. New York: Harper Trophy.

Below is the story of *Young Mouse and Elephant: An East African Folktale* as drawn by a group of six third graders. The story begins as Young Mouse brags that he is the strongest animal. His grandfather tells him that Elephant is the strongest animal. Young Mouse goes off to seek out Elephant and the adventure, and the fun, begins.

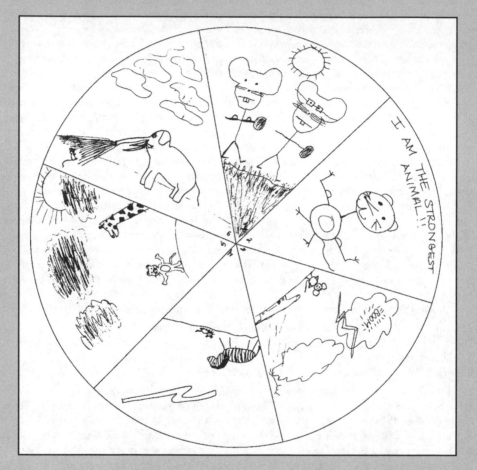

Folktales help children appreciate other cultures and also are good circle stories. After listening to their teacher read *Young Mouse and Elephant: An East African Folktale,* these third graders illustrated the primary events of the story and then retold it as a group.

Retelling stories from books improves comprehension of students. For English language learners and struggling readers, this activity can help language development through vocabulary expansion. It also aids the development of sequencing events, an important social studies skill.

Source: Farris, P. J. (2005). *Language Arts: Process, Product, and Assessment.* 4th ed. Long Grove, IL: Waveland Press.

Speaking

Although listening is a vital language art, it accompanies speaking in developing discussion and presentation skills. Children learn from interacting with each other. According to Eliot Wigginton (in Meek 1990, 35), "Learning is basically a social enterprise, and all the great educational philosophers have reiterated that point over and over again." A discussion based on a topic of mutual interest enables children to further their knowledge and to refine their understanding regarding that topic.

Developing discussion skills requires students to become good listeners and good speakers. They must also develop the ability to ask questions in order to probe the thoughts of others. Moreover, discussion skills require timing, patience, and the ability to interpret what has and has not been stated.

In addition to developing discussion skills, students need to develop the ability to speak before groups to share their knowledge and understandings. The more opportunities students have to speak before the class, the more at ease they become with the task. In social studies, this may begin as book talks about children's books with social studies themes. The student tells why the book was selected and briefly outlines the important aspects of the book. For instance, second or third graders might engage in reading biographies from David Adler's picture book series of famous Americans, such as *A Picture Book of Rosa Parks* (Adler 1993) and *A Picture Book of Eleanor Roosevelt* (Adler 1991), and present the information orally. Upper elementary and middle school students might begin the same way, sharing biographies they've read. Leonard Everett Fisher, Jean Fritz, Russell Freedman, and Diane Stanley are noted authors of biographies for children. Students should be encouraged to use appropriate props during their oral presentations. For example, one fourth grader, after reading *Now and Ben: The Modern Inventions of Benjamin Franklin* (Barretta 2006), wore wire rim glasses, a triangular paper hat, and carried a kite to present his overview of Benjamin Franklin's accomplishments as an inventor.

Other opportunities for speaking in front of the class include reports on specific historical or geographical topics. Students should be encouraged to use note cards or even create charts with markers to serve as low-tech teleprompters so that they will have easy access to the information they want to convey. This is especially helpful to low-ability students and English language learners. The use of visual displays of information, including time lines, pictures, and maps, reduces the language demand on these students, yet allows them to participate and share their knowledge with the class.

Reading

Reading used to be thought of as a sequence of skills that were taught in isolation. Today, reading is taught as strategies, with skills being taught as they arise and are needed.

To become a **strategic reader,** the students must become familiar with different ways to approach a topic or read textual material. For instance, if the topic is the independent countries that formerly made up the Soviet Union, the teacher may have students work together in groups to develop a schematic diagram of what they already know about these independent states (see figure 2.1). Thus, the students recall previously gained knowledge before reading about the independent states.

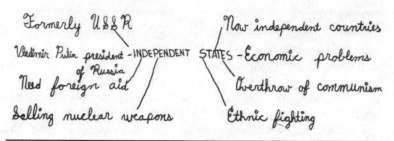

Formerly U.S.S.R

Vladimir Putin president -INDEPENDENT *of Russia*

Need foreign aid

Selling nuclear weapons

STATES

Now independent countries

-*Economic problems*

Overthrow of communism

Ethnic fighting

Figure 2.1 Schematic diagram of the independent states that were formerly republics of the U.S.S.R. by a group of sixth-grade students.

Newly gained information gleaned through their reading will be assimilated as they continue to read about and further discuss the topic.

Developing a schematic diagram of previous knowledge can also alert the teacher to gaps in background knowledge that some of his/her learning disabled and ELL students might have. Some ELL students will be relatively new to the United States and will not have the kind of cultural fund of knowledge that students who have lived continuously in the United States will have developed. With this information, the teacher can provide supplemental information or more support to those who need it.

Learning disabled and ELL students also benefit greatly by using explicit reading strategies. Encouraging students to use skimming and scanning techniques while reading (Peregoy and Boyle 2001) helps them manage what could be an overwhelming amount of reading. Providing advance organizers of the most important elements in the reading or providing guidance to students so that they can construct their own organizers as they read is very helpful to these learners.

Videos of certain books or historical events, when viewed prior to reading about them, can provide support for gathering meaning from the written text. In this way, students can develop some prior knowledge of what to expect in their reading. In other words, they are receiving the information on multiple channels of input.

Certain reading strategies in particular assist ELLs in attempting to construct meaning from text, no matter how basic their beginning English language proficiency is. For example, ELLs can make an initial pass through a reading passage to search for words that they might recognize so that they can get a general idea, clue, or sense of what the passage is about. They can think about what they know about that topic and then reread the passage with these cues in mind, inferring the meaning of unfamiliar words (Chamot and O'Malley 1994).

Writing

Writing instruction has changed dramatically within the past twenty years. Now reading and writing are both considered to be processes of meaning making. Writing is considered a recursive activity in that the students generate ideas and questions, gather information and organize their ideas, draft their compositions, and revise and edit the drafts before they share the final version of their writings (Farris 2005; Tompkins 2006).

The integrated instruction approach opened up writing instruction in that writing occurs across the curriculum. No longer are students limited to writing social studies reports; instead, new options are available, including writing in literature response journals and writing poetry, letters, plays, and so on.

English language learners and struggling writers do well with the process approach to writing because they can use the semantic maps, diagrams, pictures, and other graphic and pictorial representations of knowledge that they have been constructing in the class as entry points into writing. For those students who are at beginner or even early intermediate proficiency levels, drafts of writing can consist of bulleted information points or graphic organizers representing relationships between concepts or time lines. In this way, the student can participate in the writing process at a level that is manageable, given his/her current language resources. Adapting the writing requirements for ELLs and struggling writers in this way allows them to demonstrate their content knowledge.

Goal of Interdisciplinary Instruction

The goal of interdisciplinary instruction is to produce lifelong learners. This is done through respecting the learner, the teacher, and the content. The learning process is stressed as well as the final product. In addition, evaluation and assessment involve a variety of methods and techniques, not just paper-and-pencil tests.

Teaching the Way Students Learn

Advocates of integrated instruction focus on the learner, the concepts to be taught, and the environment. By interacting with books, materials, and other children, students expand their own knowledge and understanding. Enjoyable learning experiences are emphasized. Children are challenged, but not threatened. They are encouraged to take risks, knowing that they might fail, but in taking the risk they will gain from a failed experience as well. As a facilitator of learning, the teacher attempts to broaden students' interests in both breadth and depth. Refinement of interest is also supported.

Students develop a positive self-concept by being able to engage in activities of their own choosing and being decision makers. Freedom to choose results in students using their leisure time to pursue their interest in a topic.

One way to entice students is to provide choices of reading material as they engage in a unit of study. See the list of books about the Revolutionary War at the end of this chapter as an example.

Encouraging Decision Making

In making decisions of their own choosing, students are able to pinpoint and refine topics that interest them. In doing so, they are often allowed to work with other students who share a similar interest in a topic. Such collaboration and cooperative learning activities require group decision making as questions arise and decisions must be made, just as is true in any democratic society.

Teachers can establish a variety of social studies themes as part of the social studies curriculum. Students can help determine through the decision-making process

A quality, well-written historical or contemporary novel can spur students' interest in social studies.

how these themes are to be covered. What materials will be read? What activities are appropriate? What kinds of projects lend themselves to a topic? These and other questions can be addressed by the students either individually or as part of a group.

Creating Citizen Actors

Through democratic decision making, children learn to become **citizen actors;** that is, they learn the role of adult citizens by taking part in classroom civic activities. They learn to express their viewpoints without criticism, the first right of the Bill of Rights being freedom of speech. They learn the importance of casting an opinion or ballot on an issue, be it whether the school cafeteria should serve pizza once a week or who should be the class postmaster for the grading period.

Young and Vardell (1993) point out the value of using theater with nonfiction books such as Aliki's (1986) *Feelings* or Freedman's (1992) *An Indian Winter.* Reader's theater can help develop empathy in children and help them understand other points of view. For a reader's theater, students or the teacher develop a script using a portion of the book and students read it aloud so that the audience gains a sense of characterization, setting, and action as they paint an image in the listeners' minds.

If one explores the literature that is being developed on the purposes and goals of social studies and integrated instruction, one can find ample evidence for the logical incorporation of activities from the two to produce citizen actors. Why citizen actors?

As Linn (1990, 49–50) writes:

> Social studies should be the study of how citizens in a society make personal and public decisions on issues that affect their destiny. To keep us from becom-

☞ **IN THE CLASSROOM**

Reader's Theater

An effective vehicle for sharing a piece of historical fiction is through reader's theater. After reading the picture book or novel, students gather essential components of characters and the plot. Next they develop a sequence of events to organize the information. At that point, sentences and short phrases are selected and honed for the reader's theater. Below is a reader's theater for the Civil War historical novel, *Across Five Aprils* (Hunt 1969).

Reader's Theater
Across Five Aprils
by Irene Hunt
Directions: Reader 1—Reads standard print
Reader 2—Reads italicized print
Both Readers—Read bold print

Introduction (shared by Reader 1): *Across Five Aprils* depicts a farm family in southern Illinois that is split apart by different views of the Civil War.

April 1861
A young Boy's life just begun
Deep in Southern Illinois,
the small farming town of Hidalgo
A tight-knit family, the Creightons,
yet not untouched by tragedy
Twelve children borne by Matt and Ellen
Four no longer among the living,
Jethro, *called Jeth,* youngest in the clan,
preceded by Jenny, Tom, *Bill* and John
Sun-up to *sun-down, laboring,* toiling, striving
to coax an existence from the land
but piercing through the daily monotony
rumblings of civil unrest and dissension
secession, secession, secession
Differing beliefs and *opposing views*
cause a strain on a young country's unity
too soon, the inevitable,
"It's a war, Congress or no"
suddenly, a family divided
choosing to answer the call of patriotic obligation
Tom, Eb and John for the North
Bill, agonizing over his choice, *selecting the South*
A devastating war begins
Fueled by hatred and angry misconceptions
North against South
Slave against Free
Brother against brother
War no longer a distant rumor
but a sorrowful reality for all
Occasionally, letters trickle home,
rekindling a family's dying hope

A hope further extinguished with Tom's death at Pittsburg Landing
Many soon realize that
"being a soljer ain't that much"
Kept informed by newspapers
Union and Confederate names roll off tongues with ease
Sheridan, *Bragg, Jackson,* Grant, Sherman
Lee
Cancerous bitterness swells in the county
targeting the Creightons: the relatives of a Reb soldier
Ugly, yellow threats, a destroyed barn
each dealt with by young Jeth
An ailing and discouraged father
North against South
Slave against free
Brother against brother
The horrors of war produce deserters
Cousin Eb among the droves
A fugitive, a broken man
Looking to Jeth for mercy
Frightened by his choices
Jeth pens a letter seeking guidance
Guidance from a man known only through the news
Abraham Lincoln responds
Removing an ever present burden from Jeth's life
Amidst a cruel war,
Hope shines through
A marriage in Washington, DC.
Youthful Jenny and schoolmaster Shadrach Yale
Newfound hope grows greater
As the 13th amendment gives
Freedom to slaves in bondage
Yet lurking behind hope is *despair*
A murdered president, a broken land
Rage, mingled with grief and shock
Jeth five years older
Seeking answers that may never come
Yearning for hope to grow anew
Wishing for the day
One family can be reunited
North against South
Slave against free
Brother against brother
Across Five Aprils
places responsibility on Jeth's slight shoulders
The war rages on
one, *two,* three, *four years*
Fort Sumter, *Bull Run,* Fort Henry, *Fort Donelson*
Shiloh, Antietam, *Chancellorsville,* Fredericksburg.

ing a nation of observers instead of participants, students need to be shown early that the point of social studies is not to be found in terminology like ethnocentric, executive branch, and traditional values, but instead in one's own relationship and personal identification with these terms. One goal of social studies must be to assist youth in organizing concepts in line with their personal reality: connecting new concepts and ideas with known factors in their lives.

The role of the citizen actor is a crucial one for students. Without being cast as such, they are less apt to engage fully in the rights and privileges of being a citizen in a democratic society.

Interdisciplinary Instruction and the Social Studies

In the past, social studies instruction largely centered around the social studies textbook, with some hands-on projects added by the classroom teacher. Brophy (Bracey 1993, 654) referred to elementary social studies textbooks as being "remarkably uniform consisting of compendia of facts organized with the expanding communities curriculum structure." According to Routman (1991, 281):

> Typically, we have taught social studies by saying, "Take out your social studies book and open to page _____." Then there follows a whole-class, round-robin reading, with the teacher stopping occasionally to ask questions and lead the discussion. . . . Such exercises are boring and fail to engage many students.

For students to develop and sustain an interest in social studies, they must have a desire to learn more about it and be motivated to do so. At that point, they become **engaged learners.**

As Wells (1990, 15) so aptly states, "Unlike many other skillful performances, literate behavior cannot be learned simply by observation and practice." The same is true of being a citizen actor. To paraphrase Wells, democratic behavior cannot be learned simply by observation and practice. Students need to engage in democratic processes in the classroom—collaborative projects, discussions, cooperative learning, problem resolution, and so on—if they are to become effective and responsible citizens as adults.

From brain research, we've learned that learning is both personal and social with a major emotional component in each aspect. As social studies teachers we recognize we must engage our students both personally and socially in the learning experience. "To be fully literate is to have the disposition to engage appropriately with the texts of different types in order to empower action, feeling, and thinking in the context of purposeful social activity" (Wells 1990, 14).

The subject matter boundary of social studies needs to be broken down and integrated instruction principles erected. "At the very least, school tasks can be integrated through common reading and writing processes that cross subject matter. Interdisciplinary themes that provide opportunities to grapple with interpretations, understand others' perspectives, and solve problems require the content of social studies, science, and mathematics, not just of literature" (Hiebert and Fisher 1990, 63). Teaching social studies in an interdisciplinary curriculum serves to strengthen the tenets of the social sciences as well as the other content areas. As children listen, discuss, read, and write about social studies content, they develop a deeper understanding and appreciation of social studies and its respective social sciences. Political science and civics become more than voting in an election—they are how our government works. Supply and demand are understood through discussions and activities that demonstrate the need and demand for a product as well as the economic impact on a community. For instance, the protection of the spotted owl as an endangered species prohibited lumbering to occur in a major forest area in the western part of the United States. This action resulted in hundreds of lumberjacks and sawmill workers being forced out of work and the price of lumber greatly increased due to lack of supply.

Technology's Role in Interdisciplinary Instruction

Technology can be used effectively as part of interdisciplinary instruction. Students may use the computer to e-mail an expert on a social studies topic and ask a few pertinent questions. Thus, students gain information without having the expert visit the classroom in person as a guest speaker. Web sites and WebQuests enhance instruction as information shared during class discussions can be further elaborated upon.

The important thing to remember is to use technology efficiently. If the teacher wants to point out features of a Web site, then the Web site should be brought up on the computer *before* the students arrive in the classroom. If the server crashes, there need to be alternative activities that can readily be introduced and accomplished. Switching from one activity to a technology-based activity, like any transition from one lesson to another, must be done efficiently with little time wasted. The first time such a transition occurs, the teacher must make clear the parameters—this is down to business time and not chitchat, mess around time. Time on task is essential with so few precious minutes available for social studies instruction.

Building a Social Studies Curriculum

In building a social studies curriculum that utilizes interdisciplinary instructional principles, the first step is to identify which social studies concepts should be introduced to students. These should be important concepts that foster both critical and creative thinking and provide an intellectual challenge that students can achieve. The next step is to outline the type of learning experiences and skills to be taught. The types of student attitudes being developed must also be taken into consideration. Furthermore, it is imperative that the learning climate encourage both inquiry and choice (Routman 1991).

A variety of evaluation and assessment procedures need to be used to gather sufficient information to determine each student's growth and development in the social studies. Checklists, anecdotal records, attitudinal surveys, benchmarks met, lists of books read, journal entries, writing samples, rubrics, and videos of plays or projects are all appropriate measures for this type of curriculum. If there are state or local testing mandates, some provision must be made so that students become used to taking paper-and-pencil tests under a time limitation.

Interdisciplinary Literature Unit

Theme: Apples   Grade Level: K–2

Math concepts

- Predict the number of seeds in one apple.
- Sort apples according to size and color.
- Match word problems written on apples to answers on apples hanging on a bulletin board tree.
- Introduce fractions—1/2, 1/4, 3/4, 2/4, 4/4.
- Graph favorite apple foods.
- Measure ingredients when cooking.

Science concepts

- Learn parts of a tree.
- Analyze parts of a flower.
- Compare parts of different applies
- Describe seasons using pictures of trees.
- Look at apple seeds and the seeds of other fruits and vegetables with magnifying glasses.
- Compare the taste of different apples.
- Baked apples. (Observe raw apples. Predict changes. Describe changes in color, texture, and taste.)

Read other books

- *How Do Apples Grow?* (Maestro 2000).
- *Seasons of Arnold's Apple Tree* (Gibbons 1999).

Johnny Appleseed: A Tall Tale **(Kellogg 1996)**

Social studies

- Develop a time line of John Chapman's life.
- Develop a time line of tree to market apple life.
- Use map to find places Johnny Appleseed planted apple seeds.
- Make a map of an orchard.
- Play English games. (Snap Apple Night—twirl an apple on the end of a stick. Bob for Apples—if boy catches apple, it means his girlfriend loves him.)

Language arts

- Write a class big book on a field trip to an orchard.
- Discuss exaggeration vs. reality when reading about Johnny Appleseed.
- Keep a vocabulary book.
- Write poetry.
- Make a wheel book showing the steps to get apples from orchard to market.

Related arts

- Visit an apple orchard.
- Make apple prints with dried apples.
- Make applesauce.
- Illustrate the scene of an orchard.

(continued)

Interdisciplinary Literature Unit *(continued)*

Theme: The Great Depression   Grade Level: 5–8

Math concepts

- Study economics in reference to situations in the book.
- Study the stock market crash of 1929. Follow the current stock market.
- Compare wages and product prices from the depression era and now. Use newspaper advertisements.
- Study measurements, such as food rations.
- Create a bare minimum budget for your household.

Science concepts

- Research the causes of the Dust Bowl: Was it bad farming? Weather related?
- Learn about farming and cultivation.
- Learn about technological advancements and inventions since the Great Depression. What changes would occur in your life due to their absence? Would any aspect change for the better for you/society?

Read other books

- *The Grapes of Wrath* (Steinbeck 1939).
- *Bud, Not Buddy* (Curtis 1999).
- *Out of the Dust* (Hesse 1997).
- *Kids during the Great Depression* (Wroble 1999).

No Promises in the Wind (Hunt 1970/1999)

Social studies

- Develop time line of movement in book.
- Study the economics of the 1920s and 1930s.
- Map the movement of people during the Great Depression.
- Read through a collection of letters written to the first lady by needy children during the Great Depression along with Eleanor's responses (see http://newdeal.feri.org/eleanor/index.htm).
- Research bread lines, Hoovervilles, hobos, and soup kitchens.
- Compare today's housing to the 1930s bungalow. Discuss the variety of today's housing options, including single-family homes, apartments and condominiums, and the advantages of each for different lifestyles.

Language arts

- Write journal responses.
- Discuss conflicts in the story.
- Interview a person who lived during the Great Depression.
- Create stories for illustrations in *Kids during the Great Depression* (Wroble 1999).

Related arts

- Listen to music from the 1930s.
- Illustrate scenes from the book.
- Watch related videos such as *The Grapes of Wrath* and *O Brother, Where Art Thou?* Compare to the book.
- Examine photographs during the depression era.
- Prepare a meal that might be served during the depression era.

(continued)

Interdisciplinary Literature Unit *(continued)*

Theme: Salem Witch Trials   **Grade Level: 6–8**

Social action skills

• Develop a time line of the book according to the trials.

• Explore the handling of the death penalty in various states. What should a society do?

Reflective thinking

• Look at groups vs. individuals: the idea of connection vs. separation.

• Reflect on your own behaviors toward parents, peers, and community.

• Consider the judgments made during the trials. How would you have voted?

Problem solving

• Graph conflicts in the book. Look at the intensity or seriousness of the problem; compare Kit's perspective to your own.

• Evaluate the strategies of problem solving. How effective were the trials?

The Witch of Blackbird Pond **(Speare 1958)**

Critical ethics

• Look at the idea of "freedom from persecution."

• Study the ethics of law.

Cultural diversity

• Study the Puritan way of life in Connecticut in the 1600s.

• In relationship to the book, research gender behaviors of different societies and time periods.

Self concept

• Look at the roles of men and women. How have they changed and are today's roles acceptable?

• Compare Puritan traditions with our own.

Valuing

• Examine "traditions."

• Look at books such as *The Salem Witch Trials* (Yolen and Stemple 2004) or *Salem Witch Trials: How History Is Invented* (Wilson 1997). Note the issues/values expressed as the Puritan way of life. Correlate the view of the author to the social view of the day.

Applying Interdisciplinary Instructional Principles to Classroom Activities

An excellent way to use interdisciplinary instruction as part of the social studies in the elementary/middle school curriculum is through **thematic units** (Pappas, Kiefer, and Levstik 1998). A thematic unit may be based around a theme such as the Revolutionary War, coming-of-age ceremonies in different cultures around the world (Chinese, African, Native American, Muslim, Jewish, etc.), civil rights, economic systems, or any of the social studies standards and substandards. The teacher may provide a variety of books for the students to read in small groups or may select one or two books for the entire class to read. In their discussion groups, students formulate questions they want and expect to be answered in the next segment of their reading. After writing down their questions, they write down the answers as they read the material. When thematic units are used, the social studies textbook is used as reference material. (See the In the Classroom lesson plan on the next page followed by the interdisciplinary thematic unit on the Middle Ages.)

Routman (1991) offers informal guidelines for planning an integrated, interdisciplinary social studies unit. She suggests that the process and procedure be considered foremost in integrating a content area such as social studies with the language arts. Here are her specific recommendations (pp. 279–80):

1. Develop a semantic web as the class or group brainstorms the topic.

2. Have students select a subtopic by listing their first, second, and third choices of subtopics.

3. Divide the students into small groups of up to four students per subtopic.

4. Have the group develop questions to research for their subtopic of study.

5. Have each group meet with another group to confer over the questions each group generated for their respective subtopics.

6. Have each group establish a format for using resources to discover the answers to the questions they generated about their subtopic.

7. Have all the students take notes on their subtopics.

8. Let students use their notes to write rough drafts.

9. Have each group present the information they gathered to the entire class. (A variety of formats may be used: quiz shows, radio shows, festivals, plays, travelogues, etc.)

10. Have classmates evaluate presentations orally. At least two positive statements must be given by students before a suggestion for improvement can be given.

11. Evaluate group interactions and content learned. This is done by the teacher and through student self-evaluations. In addition, an essay test given by the teacher may be included at this point.

As part of this interdisciplinary unit, music from the Middle Ages was shared and discussed by the students. *Bartering* was introduced as an economic term as students were given a variety of different items to trade. Art projects included drawing illustrations of major scenes and characters. Students considered home remedies as part of science.

Routman's process/procedure approach allows for efficient classroom organization and structure. Little time is wasted as the students proceed through the eleven steps. All of the students contribute to one another's learning in the area of social studies. Thus, learning becomes a social activity.

☞ **IN THE CLASSROOM**

Interdisciplinary Social Studies Lesson Plan

The following lesson plan is based on national social studies standards as outlined in chapter 1 as well as the Illinois Learning Standards for Social Science (Illinois State Board of Education 1997). Other states have likewise created learning standards and substandards for social studies.

Theme: People and Places

National Social Studies Learning Standard: II. Time, Continuity, and Change: Social studies programs should include experiences that provide for the study of the ways human beings view themselves in and over time, so that the learner can demonstrate an understanding that different people may describe the same event or situation in diverse ways, citing reasons for the differences in views.

Illinois Learning Standard: State Goal 16. Understand events, trends, individuals, and movements shaping the history of Illinois, the United States, and other nations.

Substandard: Goal 16.A.1c. Describe how people in different times and places viewed the world in different ways.

Grade: Third

Lesson Plan Objective: Compare and contrast how two different groups of people perceived the geographic area in which they lived.

Time Span: Four days

Materials: Overhead transparencies and markers; overhead projector

Picture books:

Cherry, L. 1992. *A River Ran Wild*. Orlando, FL: Harcourt Brace.

Collard, S. B. 1999. *1,000 Years Ago on Planet Earth*. Illus. J. Hunt. Boston: Houghton Mifflin. (3 copies)

Heide, F. P., and J. H. Gilliland. 1999. *The House of Wisdom*. Illus. M. Grandpre. New York: DK Ink. (3 copies)

Jackson, E. B. 1998. *Turn of the Century*. Illus. J. Ellis. New York: Charlesbridge. (3 copies)

Kurtz, J. 2000. *River Friendly, River Wild*. Illus. N. Brennan. New York: Scholastic.

Procedures:

Day 1: Read to the class the picture book *A River Ran Wild* by Lynn Cherry. Have the class select three different time periods from the book. For each time period, have students in the class volunteer to offer views of the people who lived near the Nashua River. Make a semantic map on a transparency for each of the time periods. Display these on the overhead projector for discussion. Make a T chart listing how the different time periods were alike and how they differed in the ways they used the river.

Have the students get into small groups of three students. Each group selects one of the other four picture books mentioned in the earlier list. The students take turns reading their book aloud. After they read the book, they make a semantic map of two different groups of people and how they viewed the same event or situation. Next, have the students list comparisons and differences in a T chart. Finally, each student uses the information from the T chart to write a descriptive, expository piece comparing and contrasting the views and perceptions of the two groups of people.

Day 2: The students proof each other's work for accuracy and writing skills. The students then rewrite to produce their final drafts. They make an illustration to accompany their descriptive writing.

Day 3: The students are regrouped in groups of three so that each member of the group has read and written about a different book. The students each give a brief book talk and then read their descriptive paper and share their illustration.

Follow-Up Activity:

Have the students find newspaper or magazine articles. The students can compare how the same story (i.e., news, sports, weather) is reported by different journalists. Put the articles on construction paper and place on the bulletin board along with T charts of how the stories are similar and how they differ.

Assessment:

Scoring: 5 points—Student must include three similarities and three differences for the two groups of people.

4 points—Student must include total of five similarities/differences.

3 points—Student must include total of four similarities/differences.

2 points—Student must include total of three similarities/differences.

1 point—Student must include total of two similarities/differences.

The writing piece will be graded on a scale from 1 to 3, with 3 being well developed, 2 average, and 1 as needs work.

☞ IN THE CLASSROOM

Thematic Unit on the Middle Ages

Until recent years, few trade books about the Middle Ages have been available for children to read. The "age of chivalry" greatly interests children. This unit was designed for students in grades 5 through 8. The entire class reads Karen Cushman's *The Midwife's Apprentice* and engages in the integrated activities as outlined in figure 2.2. At the conclusion of these activities, each student then selects and reads a second novel about the Middle Ages and keeps a literature journal to record reactions and responses. Those who have selected the same book are paired to work together. They read and write in their response journals, then exchange journals to share their thoughts and reaction on the same material. They meet with their partner each day or every other day for ten minutes to discuss the book. The social studies textbook is used as needed for reference.

Children's Books

Aliki. 1983. *Medieval Feast.* New York: Thomas Crowell. Nobility of the manor house and their serfs prepare for a visit from the king and the queen, complete with their royal entourage. The illustrations demonstrate a variety of preparatory activities including hunting, fishing, and preparing food. (Gr. 2–7)

Barretta, G. 2006. *Now and Ben: The Modern Inventions of Benjamin Franklin.* New York: Holt. Thanks to Ben Franklin's cleverness, we now have illustrations and political cartoons in newspapers, bifocals to help people read as they grow older, and lightning rods to prevent buildings from catching fire upon being struck by lightning. This punchy read-aloud picture book shares Ben's inventions that did not quite catch on—a rocking chair that churned butter, etc. (Gr. 2–5)

Bellairs, J. 1989. *The Trolley to Yesterday.* New York: Dial. This time warp story takes Johnny and his friend, Fergie, back to 1453 and the Byzantine Empire. The two friends arrive in Constantinople just prior to the Turkish invasion. (Gr. 4–8)

Cushman, K. 1994. *Catherine, Called Birdy.* New York: Clarion. Birdy is fourteen and she faithfully keeps a diary of her experiences in England in 1290. The diary spans a one-year period during which Birdy's father attempts to marry her off for money or land. This book is a Newbery Honor Book. (Gr. 6–8)

Cushman, K. 1995. *The Midwife's Apprentice.* New York: Clarion. The setting is the Middle Ages where a young orphan must fend for herself until she becomes apprenticed to a midwife. Very accurate descriptions of details of the period. This book won the 1995 Newbery Award. (Gr. 4–8)

de Angeli, M. 1949. *The Door in the Wall.* New York: Doubleday. This award-winning book is the story of Robin, the son of a knight, who becomes ill and loses the use of his legs. A monk takes him in and teaches him woodcarving. Along the way, Robin also learns patience and strength. When the castle of Lindsay is threatened, Robin rescues the townspeople. (Gr. 5–8)

Hunt, J. 1989. *Illuminations.* New York: Bradbury. This alphabet book includes pictures of words that are from the Middle Ages. (Gr. 3–5)

Konigsburg, E. L. 1973. *A Proud Taste for Scarlet and Miniver.* Illustrated by the author, this historical fiction novel focuses on Eleanor of Aquitaine. Proud Eleanor is waiting for her young husband, King Henry II, to join her in heaven. Henry had died before she had, but has not yet been judged favorably by the angels. While she waits, Eleanor reflects on the various events of her life. Children will find this book to be both interesting and amusing. (Gr. 4-8)

Lasker, J. 1976. *Merry Ever After: The Story of Two Medieval Weddings.* New York: Viking. Two weddings, one of a couple from nobility and the other of a peasant couple, are described as the book looks at the betrothed couples as children and their marriages as teenagers. (Gr. 3–8)

Macaulay, D. 1973. *Cathedral: The Story of Its Construction.* Boston: Houghton Mifflin. This book is a classic picture book that goes into intricate detail, portraying the actual design and construction of a magnificent cathedral. (Gr. 3–8)

Macaulay, D. 1978. *Castle.* Boston: Houghton Mifflin. This book illustrates the various phases of the construction of a castle. (Gr. 3–8)

Osband, G., and R. Andrew, 1991. *Castles.* New York: Orchard. This pop-up picture book is filled with information that will intrigue students. Early designs of castles are depicted, including how they expanded over the years. Castle life is discussed along with the lives of knights. The book portrays and describes ten castles still in existence from a variety of European countries. (Gr. K–8)

Temple, F. 1994. *The Ramsay Scallop.* New York: Orchard. In a marriage designed to join their parents' estates, thirteen-year-old Elenor is betrothed to Thomas, who left on a crusade eight years earlier, in 1292. When they are reluctant to wed, Father Gregory sends Elenor and Thomas on a pilgrimage to Ramsey, Spain, where they receive a scallop shell. This book is targeted at the mature reader. (Gr. 7–8)

Winthrop, E. 1985. *The Castle in the Attic.* New York: Holiday House. William receives an old, realistic model of a castle as a gift from the housekeeper. She warns him that it is very special. This fantasy will appeal to students interested in magic and the wizards of the Middle Ages. (Gr. 4–7)

Winthrop, E. 1993. *The Battle for the Castle.* New York: Bantam. In this sequel to *The Castle in the Attic*, William is transported back to Sir Simon's castle in the Middle Ages using a magic token sent by his former housekeeper. With the help of his friend Jason, William must destroy the invading rats and save the kingdom. (Gr. 4–7)

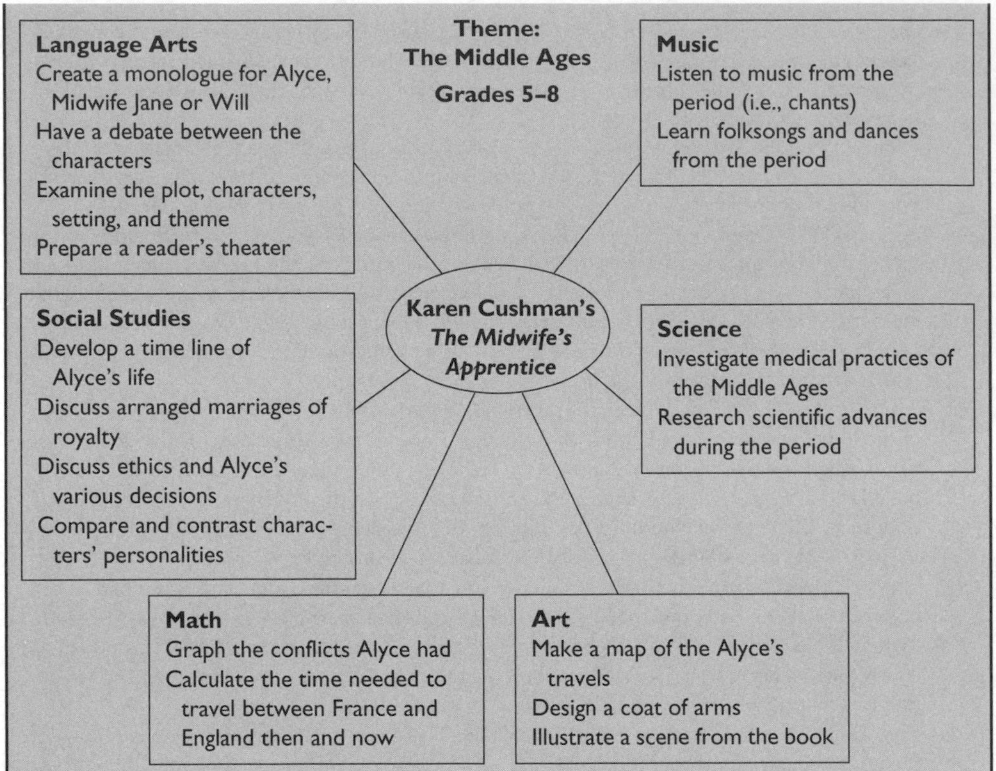

64

Language Arts
Create a monologue for Alyce,
 Midwife Jane or Will
Have a debate between the
 characters
Examine the plot, characters,
 setting, and theme
Prepare a reader's theater

Theme:
The Middle Ages
Grades 5–8

Music
Listen to music from the
 period (i.e., chants)
Learn folksongs and dances
 from the period

Karen Cushman's
The Midwife's
Apprentice

Social Studies
Develop a time line of
 Alyce's life
Discuss arranged marriages of
 royalty
Discuss ethics and Alyce's
 various decisions
Compare and contrast charac-
 ters' personalities

Science
Investigate medical practices of
 the Middle Ages
Research scientific advances
 during the period

Math
Graph the conflicts Alyce had
Calculate the time needed to
 travel between France and
 England then and now

Art
Make a map of the Alyce's
 travels
Design a coat of arms
Illustrate a scene from the book

Figure 2.2 Integrated unit. Theme: The middle ages, grades 5–8.

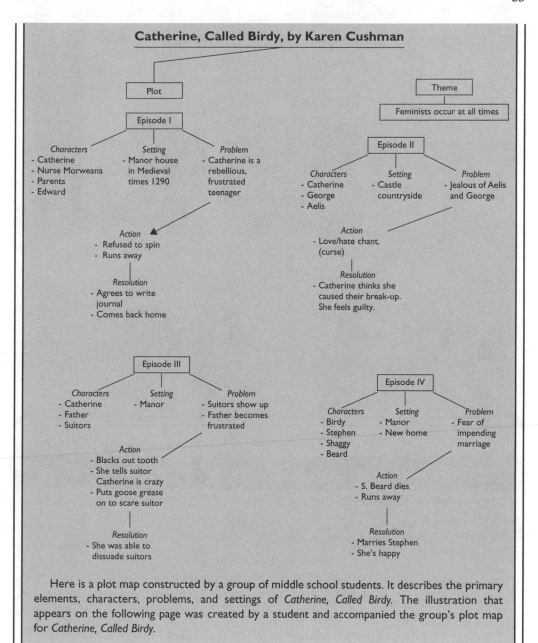

Catherine, Called Birdy, by Karen Cushman

Theme

Feminists occur at all times

Plot

Episode I

Characters
- Catherine
- Nurse Morweana
- Parents
- Edward

Setting
- Manor house in Medieval times 1290

Problem
- Catherine is a rebellious, frustrated teenager

Action
- Refused to spin
- Runs away

Resolution
- Agrees to write journal
- Comes back home

Episode II

Characters
- Catherine
- George
- Aelis

Setting
- Castle countryside

Problem
- Jealous of Aelis and George

Action
- Love/hate chant. (curse)

Resolution
- Catherine thinks she caused their break-up. She feels guilty.

Episode III

Characters
- Catherine
- Father
- Suitors

Setting
- Manor

Problem
- Suitors show up
- Father becomes frustrated

Action
- Blacks out tooth
- She tells suitor Catherine is crazy
- Puts goose grease on to scare suitor

Resolution
- She was able to dissuade suitors

Episode IV

Characters
- Birdy
- Stephen
- Shaggy
- Beard

Setting
- Manor
- New home

Problem
- Fear of impending marriage

Action
- S. Beard dies
- Runs away

Resolution
- Marries Stephen
- She's happy

Here is a plot map constructed by a group of middle school students. It describes the primary elements, characters, problems, and settings of *Catherine, Called Birdy*. The illustration that appears on the following page was created by a student and accompanied the group's plot map for *Catherine, Called Birdy*.

NCSS STANDARDS-LINKED LESSON PLAN

"Home Remedies" as Medicine

Theme: Folk Medicine
Source: Mary Louise Ginejko, Joliet Public School District 86
Grades: 3–8
Objectives:

• Students will research and summarize actual clinical remedies for fictitious illnesses.

• Students will understand how to write letters and replies similar to "Dear Abby" letters regarding requests for clinical remedies for fictitious illnesses.

• Students will understand how to prepare questions for a guest speaker or "ask an expert" using the Internet.

• Students will create and deliver a PowerPoint presentation or use Hyperstudio to compare culturally diverse remedies.

• Students will share information with another class using e-mail and the Internet.

NCSS Themes:
  I. Culture
VIII. Science, Technology, and Society

Materials: Heavy weight construction paper or white tagboard, bookbinding material, drawing utensils, glue, medical books, computer with Internet capabilities and PowerPoint or Hyperstudio.

Process:

• Students write three "Dear Abby" letters explaining an illness with which they are familiar.

• Students exchange letters.

• Students ask parents and other family members their advice to cure the illnesses.

• Students answer three "Dear Abby" letters using the information from family members.

• Students research the clinical cures to the illnesses.

• Students answer the same three "Dear Abby" letters using the information from medical books, medical professionals, or medical Internet sites. Students document sources.

• Students create a "Remedy Book," which includes three original letters, three folk remedies, and three clinical remedies. Students are encouraged to glue in actual plants or relevant items (e.g., possible cure for arthritis: copper bracelet or penny), or include the items in pictorial form, such as drawing, cutouts from magazines, graphics from the Internet, or an online encyclopedia.

• Students create a PowerPoint or Hyperstudio presentation to communicate the information they gathered.

• Using the Internet, students will contact another class to communicate information and request additional insight.

• Students visit a health food grocery store to inquire as to the purpose of natural healing items.

Instructional Comments: This is an activity that respectfully acknowledges diversity among students while gaining insight into cultures.

Learning Styles Addressed: Verbal/linguistic, visual/spatial, interpersonal, intrapersonal, mathematical/logical, emotional

Standards Addressed: Students will seek information from a variety of sources that include experts within their families and medical professionals.

Evaluation: The rubrics for this lesson should include standard rules for writing letters. It should acknowledge the extent of research conducted by the student. It should allow for creativity. Also included should be the impact of the PowerPoint or Hyperstudio presentation.

Modifications for Diverse Learners: Students may work in diverse cooperative groups. Adult assistance may be requested.

Variations: Students may hold a health fair to share their knowledge. The health fair may introduce health workers in the community.

Chapter Summary

Social studies instruction can be integrated into the elementary/middle school curriculum to meet common goals. As a result, the learner, the teacher, and the social studies content are respected. Students are encouraged to make choices and take risks in their learning. As citizen actors, they repeatedly engage in the democratic process in their classroom as they develop an interest in and greater understanding of social studies.

Children's Literature Recommendations

Adler, D. 1991. *A Picture Book of Eleanor Roosevelt*. New York: Holiday House. A biography of former First Lady and humanitarian Eleanor Roosevelt. (Gr. 1–3)

———. 1993. *A Picture Book of Rosa Parks*. New York: Holiday House. A biography of civil rights activist Rosa Parks. (Gr. 1–3)

Aliki. 1986. *Feelings*. New York: Morrow Junior Books. This picture book for primary-grade children explores different emotions.

Barretta, G. 2006. *Now and Ben: The Modern Inventions of Benjamin Franklin*. New York: Henry Holt. Franklin's timeless and not so successful inventions are shared in a humorous picture book. Great for sharing in a unit about the colonial or Revolutionary War period of U.S. history. (Gr. 2–5)

Curtis, C. 1999. *Bud, Not Buddy*. New York: Delacorte. During the Great Depression, Bud's mother becomes ill and passes away, leaving him to seek out a man he believes is his father, a jazz musician traveling throughout the Midwest. (Gr. 5–8)

Freedman, R. 1992. *An Indian Winter*. New York: Holiday House. Actual photos show the conditions Native Americans faced during the winter months.

Gibbons, G. 1999. *Seasons of Arnold's Apple Tree*. San Diego, CA: Harcourt. From the snow-covered buds to springtime blossoms being pollinated by bees, the summer forming of the fruit and subsequent harvesting of apples and making apple cider with a cider press, this book gives interesting details that will pique student interest. (Gr. 1–3)

Hesse, K. 1997. *Out of the Dust*. New York: Scholastic. Billie Jo shares her poignant story of life in the 1930s after the death of her mother. (Gr. 6–8)

Hunt, I. 1970/1999. *No Promises in the Wind*. Berkeley, CA: Berkeley Press. With food scarce during the Great Depression, two brothers and a friend hop a train seeking better times. (Gr. 6–8)

Kellogg, S. 1987/1996. *Johnny Appleseed*. New York: HarperCollins. A picture book biography of this noted American character. (Gr. 1–2)

Maestro, B. 2000. *How Do Apples Grow?* New York: Harper. All the seasons are presented so students get a perspective of what occurs in the apple orchard. (Gr. 1–3)

Speare, E. G. 1958/2002. *The Witch of Blackbird Pond*. New York: Laurel. Kit Tyler ventures from her Caribbean home to that of her Puritan aunt and uncle and befriends an old lady known in the community as a witch. (Gr. 5–8)

Steinbeck, J. 1939/2002. *Grapes of Wrath*. New York: Viking. The Pulitzer Prize-winning novel about a poor family of "Okies" who lose their farm due to the hard times of the Great Depression. Starving and desperate they seek work in the California fields all the while determined to keep their decency. (Gr. 7–8)

Wilson, L. L. 1997. *Salem Witch Trials: How History Is Invented*. Minneapolis: Lerner Publishing. Not restricted to the events of 1692, this well-documented and reasoned overview traces the primeval roots of humankind's belief in magic and the spirit world and carries it up to modern-day witch hunts. (Gr. 6–8)

Wroble, L. A. 1999. *Kids During the Great Depression*. Madison, WI: Powerkids Press. The social and economic hardships children encountered during the Great Depression are shared in this picture book. (Gr. 5–8)

Yolen, J., and H. E. Stemple. 2004. *The Salem Witch Trials: An Unsolved Mystery from History*. New York: Simon & Schuster. An overview of the Salem witch trials is presented with interesting facts shared. (Gr. 5–8)

Additional Children's Books about the Revolutionary War

Adler, D. A. 2001. *B. Franklin, Printer*. New York: Holiday House. (Gr. 1–4)

Barretta, G. 2006. *Now and Ben: The Modern Inventions of Benjamin Franklin*. New York: Henry Holt. (Gr. 2-5)

Borden, L. 2000. *Sleds on Boston Common: A Story from the American Revolution*. Illus. R. A. Parker. New York: McElderry Books. (Gr. 1–6)

Collier, J., and C. Collier. 1989. *My Brother, Sam, Is Dead*. New York: Scholastic. (Gr. 5–8).

Edwards, P. D. 2001. *Boston Tea Party*. Illus. H. Cole. New York: Putnam. (Gr. 1–4)

Forbes, E. 1987. *Johnny Tremain*. New York: Yearling. (Gr. 5–8)

Fritz, J. 1973. *And Then What Happened, Paul Revere?* New York: Coward, McCann & Geoghegan. (Gr. 2–6)

———. 1977. *Can't You Make Them Behave, King George?* New York Coward, McCann & Geoghegan. (Gr. 2–6)

Hopkins, L. B. 1994. *Hand in Hand: An American History Through Poetry*. New York: Simon & Schuster. (Gr. K–8)

Rinaldi, A. 1996. *Hang a Thousand Trees with Ribbons: The Story of Phillis Wheatley*. San Diego, CA: Harcourt Brace. (Gr. 4–8)

Turner, A. 1989. 1997. *Katie's Trunk*. New York: Aladdin. (Gr. 1–6)

Wanner, A. 2001. *Abigail Adams*. New York: Holiday House. (Gr. 2–4)

Related Technology Tools

Web Sites

A to Z Teacher Stuff Thematic Units Index
http://atozteacherstuff.com/themes/
Provides a collection of hundreds of resources organized into thematic units, such as family, around the world, and ancient Egypt.

ERIC Clearinghouse for Social Studies/Social Science Education
http://www.indiana.edu/~ssdc/multlinks.htm
A clearinghouse specializing in social studies and social science education. This site offers extensive resources for educators and educational research.

Ten Nifty Ways Teachers Can Use E-mail
www.electronic-school.com/0398f5.html
Learn how e-mail can enhance the learning experience of your students.

WebQuest Page
http://webquest.sdsu.edu/
Home of WebQuest, this site offers suggestions on how to create WebQuests as well as up and running WebQuest sites to use for social studies instruction with students.

WebQuests

Castle Builder (Medieval Times) (Gr. 6–8)
http://www.spa3.k12.sc.us/WebQuests.html
Place this WebQuest site on your favorites list as it offers a plethora of social studies WebQuests for grades 1–8.

Software and Videos

Integrating the Curriculum 2 Tape Series. (1994). 61 minutes. Available from the Association for Supervision and Curriculum Development (ASCD) at www.ascd.org. This series includes two videotapes, a Facilitator's Guide, and a copy of ASCD's Interdisciplinary Curriculum: Planning and Implementation. The series focuses on curriculum integration in elementary, middle, and high schools.

The ENTIRE 20th Century in One Video Collection. (2000). Teacher's Discovery. 12 and one-half hours total. Available at 800-543-4180. Also available in individual volumes. Watch how the world has been shaped from the beginning of the 20th century to the millennium.

Ancient Civilizations Video Set. (2000). Teacher's Discovery. Available at 800-543-4180. Also available in individual volumes. Travel to the ancient world and learn about Cleopatra, Caesar, Pharaohs, Great Pyramids and the Roman Empire.

References

Bracey, G. W. 1993. "Elementary Curriculum Materials: Still a Way to Go." *Phi Delta Kappan* 74 (8): 654, 656.

Brophy, J. 1992. "Probing the Subtleties of Subject-Matter Teaching." *Educational Leadership* 49 (7): 4–8.

Chamot, A., and J. M. O'Malley. 1994. *The CALLA Handbook: Implementing the Cognitive Academic Language Learning Approach.* Reading, MA: Addison-Wesley.

Farris, P. J. 2005. *Language Arts: Process, Product, and Assessment.* 4th ed. Long Grove, IL: Waveland Press.

Farris, P. J., C. J. Fuhler, and M. P. Walther. 2003. *Teaching Reading: A Balanced Approach for Today's Classrooms.* Boston: McGraw-Hill.

Hiebert, E. H., and C. W. Fisher. 1990. "Whole Language: Three Themes for the Future." *Educational Leadership* 47 (6): 62–63.

Illinois State Board of Education. 1997. *Illinois Learning Standards for Social Science.* Springfield: Author.

Linn, J. B. 1990. "Whole Language in Social Studies." *Social Science Record* 27 (2): 49–55.

McCarty, B. J. 1991. "Whole Language: From Philosophy to Practice." *The Clearing House* 65 (2): 73–76.

Meek, A. 1990. "On 25 Years of Foxfire: A Conversation with Eliot Wigginton." *Educational Leadership* 47 (6): 30–36.

Palmer, P. 1998/1999. "Evoking the Spirit in Public Education." *Educational Leadership* 56: (4) 6–11.

Pappas, C. C., B. Z. Kiefer, and L. S. Levstik. 1998. *An Integrated Language Perspective in the Elementary Schools: Theory into Action.* 3rd ed. New York: Addison-Wesley.

Peregoy, S. F., and O. F. Boyle. 2001. *Reading, Writing, and Learning in ESL.* 3rd ed. New York: Longman.

Routman, R. 1991. *Invitations: Changing as Teachers and Learners K–12.* Portsmouth, NH: Heinemann.

Tompkins, G. E. 2006. *Language Arts: Content and Teaching Strategies.* 6th ed. New York: Macmillan.

Weil, M., E. Calhoun, and B. Joyce. 2003. *Models of Teaching.* 7th ed. Englewood Cliffs, NJ: Prentice-Hall.

Wells, G. 1990. "Creating the Conditions to Encourage Literate Thinking." *Educational Leadership* 47 (6): 13–17.

Young, T. A., and S. Vardell. 1993. "Weaving Reader's Theatre and Nonfiction into the Curriculum." *The Reading Teacher* 46 (5): 396–406.

Teacher Materials

Benscoter, D., and G. Harris. 2002. *Social Studies Activities Kids Can't Resist.* Teacher Resources. (Gr. 3–6)

King, D. 1998. *Colonial Days: Discover the Past with Fun Projects, Games, Activities, and Recipes.* Illus. B. Moore. New York: John Wiley.

Kretzer, M., M. Slobin, and M. Williams. 1999. *Making Social Studies Come Alive.* New York: Scholastic. (Gr. 4–8)

Van Tine, E., S. Lee, and C. Cooper. 1999. *Super Social Studie*s. New York: Scholastic. (Gr. 4–8).

> *When educators talk of assessment, they generally think in terms of documented assessment systems. A completely different level of assessment takes place in the individual student, who is constantly assessing her own work, deciding what is right and wrong, what fits and what does not, what is a "good enough" job. This self-appraisal is the ultimate locus of all standards.*
>
> —Ron Berger, Social Studies Teacher, Massachusetts

Chapter Three

Classroom Assessment in Social Studies

L. Ruth Struyk, Utah State University
Lisa M. Mehlig, Rockford Public School District, Rockford, IL

■ CHAPTER OUTLINE

CHAPTER OBJECTIVES

Readers will

- understand the difference between assessment and evaluation in social studies;
- be able to explain different assessment methods;
- be able to construct a variety of different assessment tools for social studies;
- understand the Multiple Intelligences as they apply to social studies instruction; and
- be able to apply differentiated instruction and assessment for striving learners and ELLs.

Introduction

Teaching social studies as an interdisciplinary approach has resulted in increased instructional time at the elementary level as teachers integrate social studies into art, language arts, math, music, physical education, and science. Rather than "running out of time" to fit social studies in during the school day, many teachers have viewed social studies as a content area in which the other content areas can be extended and taught.

Over the past several years, social studies has become a more visible school subject, and the conception of learning social studies has evolved from doing and knowing to experiencing and making meaning. The tacit and piecemeal curriculum that has long characterized the social studies classroom seems to be gradually giving way to a more coherent and integrated set of objectives, benchmarks, and performance indicators. This approach is goal oriented with an emphasis on learner outcomes: the knowledge, skills, attitudes, values, and dispositions to action that teachers wish to develop in students. (Alleman and Brophy 1999b, 334)

The National Council for the Social Studies (NCSS 1994, 3–5) Advisory Committee on Testing and Evaluation recommends the following guidelines for assessment in social studies:

- Evaluation instruments should: focus on the curriculum goals and objectives; be used to improve curriculum and instruction; measure both content and process; be chosen for instructional, diagnostic, and prescriptive purposes; and reflect a high degree of fairness to all people and groups.

- Evaluation of student achievement should: be used solely to improve teaching and learning; involve a variety of instruments and approaches to measure knowledge, skills, and attitudes; be congruent with the objectives and the classroom experiences of the students examined; and be sequential and cumulative.

- State and local agencies should: secure appropriate funding to implement and support evaluation programs; support the education of teachers in selecting, developing, and using assessment instruments; involve teachers and other social studies professionals in formulating objectives, planning instruction and evaluation, and designing and selecting evaluation instruments; and measure long-term effects of social studies instruction.

Consider questioning as the spokes of a wagon wheel. **Convergent questions,** that is, questions with only one right answer, are like the spokes going in toward the hub of the wheel. Some teachers refer to convergent questions as "thin" questions as appropriate answers are narrowed down to a single response. **Divergent questions,** that is, questions with many possible correct responses, are like the spokes pointing outward with many possibilities. These questions are often referred to as "fat" questions as they offer inquiry that students need to mull over and discuss with more than one answer being correct.

Assessment and evaluation in social studies must be more than true-false or multiple-choice questions that measure low-level thinking skills. C. Frederick Risinger (2002), a former president of the NCSS, points out that the present push toward fact-based, multiple-choice tests that currently dominate the standards and testing movement of today may one day yield to authentic assessment. However, the goal, according to Risinger, is to prepare our students for "their role as informed, participatory citizens in a rapidly changing world" (233). This chapter examines how assessment can measure higher-level thinking skills through the use of testing and authentic, alternative measures.

Classroom Assessment in Social Studies

Classroom assessment involves more than creating, administering, and scoring paper-and-pencil tests. Assessment is the collection and interpretation of data to determine future instruction. Karen Wixson (2006) notes that assessment needs to occur on an ongoing basis as particular skills and content are being learned by the student; assessment focuses closely on that student's current level of functioning. She notes that assessment can be viewed as measurement (such as results for a multiple-choice or true-false exam), as procedure (such as when a student is observed going through a process), or as inquiry (such as when the student formulates questions and possible solutions to a problem, eliminating some solutions based on newly gained knowledge).

For many years, no one thought about how students learned or how learning styles affected students' ability to be successful on assessment activities. However, current literature and school reform reflect a growing belief that students do, indeed, learn differently (e.g., visually, auditorily, kinesthetically, spatially). Similarly, in recent years, to reflect the changes in understanding learning styles, teachers have designed classroom assessments that have moved from traditional paper-and-pencil quizzes and tests to a variety of assessment methods. In an attempt to combine classical assessment design factors with emerging assessment trends, teachers are utilizing a variety of assessment methods in conjunction with instructional activities to facilitate their ability to determine how well students understand and act on instructional objectives. By using a variety of assessment methods teachers can provide opportunities beyond the traditional paper-and-pencil tests, which often do not adequately demonstrate the level of understanding that English language learners (ELLs) and special needs learners have of the instructional objectives. Performance assessments can provide opportunities for such students to demonstrate their knowledge beyond their current language abilities. It is important to remember that no matter what type of assessment tools teachers use, those assessments must provide information about the instructional objectives.

As teachers we wrestle with how assessments should be used with regard to many factors. This perpetual evaluative tug of war persists in our classrooms as well as in the school district, our state, and across our country. Consider the following list developed by Robert J. Monson and Michele P. Monson (1997):

- teaching and learning versus evaluation, measurement, and accountability
- isolated disciplines versus integrated knowledge
- content knowledge versus processes and habits of the mind
- authenticity versus simulation
- student selection versus teacher selection
- interactive context versus object content
- on-demand word samples versus expanded process constructs
- comparability versus flexibility
- process versus product
- quantitative versus qualitative scoring

These all must be weighed as we go about our responsibility to properly assess our students' growth in social studies.

The first and foremost purpose of assessment should be to inform educators, students, and parents about the level of understanding and ability of the students in relation to the instructional objectives. Without clear and precise information relating to the objectives, the evaluations that teachers make are not going to generate informed instructional decisions. The stronger the information obtained from the assessment tool, the stronger the evaluation, whether the evaluation influences lesson planning or is used as a final indicator of students' understanding of the material (i.e., grades).

Assessment versus Evaluation

Because of the interactive nature of assessment and evaluation, it is often easy to confuse the two concepts. **Assessment** refers to the collection, storage, and retrieval of data (Cangelosi 1990; Popham 2006; Weber 1999). Assessments are merely tools for collecting the data or information about the students' levels of understanding of the instructional objectives. Data may be retained in a grade book, on individual tests stacked on the teacher's desk, or in an electronic grade book using a software program. In the classroom, some of the assessment tools used to collect information regarding students' performance include projects, portfolios, quizzes, homework, presentations, and traditional teacher-made tests. **Evaluations** involve teacher judgments that are made based on the information obtained from the assessment. When instructional objectives and assessments are aligned, then the more information obtained about the objectives through various assessments results in a greater potential to make accurate decisions regarding students' performance.

Although there are many methods of assessing students' performance, all of these methods fall into two basic categories, formal and informal. **Formal assessments** are very structured assessments that are planned in advance, administered under controlled situations, and have detailed scoring schemes. Formal assessment includes traditional teacher-made tests, oral presentations, and group projects. Standardized tests are the most formal tests schools use because the administration of the test, the scoring, and the interpretation of an individual student's score is compared with a grounded, well-defined framework or against predetermined levels of achievement. **Informal assessments** are unplanned, unstructured, and spontaneous. Informal assessments are the questions teachers ask to find out what the students know during class activities, discussions, and other activities. Informal assessments are also those nonverbal cues that teachers use to determine students' level of attentiveness or confusion (i.e., blank stares, daydreaming). More than 80 percent of teachers' daily activities are spent conducting informal assessment activities (Wiggins 1989).

Formative and Summative Evaluations

Similarly, evaluations can be broken into two categories, formative and summative (Cangelosi 1990; Popham 2006; Weber 1999). **Formative evaluations** are decisions made by teachers that influence their immediate teaching. Asking a series of questions over material and then deciding the students are ready to move on to new material is an example of a formative evaluation. **Summative evaluations** are those that indicate either an end point in a unit or level of student performance.

The teacher determining a grade for a particular grading period after adding all of the assessment scores is an example of a summative evaluation because it represents the final level of the students' performance. As with informal assessments, formative evaluations occur many times during a lesson, while summative evaluations are used to communicate individual performance on students' work throughout the year.

To make sound evaluation decisions (both formative and summative), quality assessments (whether formal or informal) that consider 10 key factors must be developed. According to Herman, Aschbacher, and Winters (1992, 13), those key factors are:

1. Assessments must measure the instructional goals and objectives.
2. Assessments must involve the examination of the processes as well as the products of learning.
3. Performance-based activities do not constitute assessments per se.
4. Cognitive learning theory and its constructivist approach to knowledge acquisition support the need to integrate assessment methodologies with instructional outcomes and curriculum content.
5. An integrated and active view of student learning requires the assessment of holistic and complex performances.
6. Assessment design is dependent on assessment purpose; grading and monitoring student progress are distinct from diagnosis and improvement.
7. The key to effective assessment is the match between the task and the intended student outcome.
8. The criteria used to evaluate student performance are critical; in the absence of criteria, assessment remains an isolated and episodic activity.
9. Quality assessment provides substantive data for making informed decisions about student learning.
10. Assessment systems that provide the most comprehensive feedback on student growth include multiple measures taken over time.

In relation to the preceding 10 key factors, assessment information should further relate to the instructional objectives not only by content but also by behavioral construct. Several models of taxonomies are currently in use (e.g., Bloom et al. 1969; Cangelosi 1990). No matter which taxonomy is used, the intent is to have a match between the behavior by which students learned the instructional objective (cognitive, psychomotor, and affective) and the assessment activities. **Bloom's taxonomy**, the taxonomy with which teachers are most familiar, subdivides cognitive behaviors into six levels (see figure 3.1). The following six levels of taxonomy are adapted from Bloom et al. (1969):

1. *Knowledge.* Knowledge is defined as the remembering of previously learned material. An example of a knowledge-level item would be: "Who was the second president of the United States?" +1 for John Adams.
2. *Comprehension.* Comprehension is defined as the ability to grasp the meaning of material. An example of a comprehension-level item would be: "In your own

words, paraphrase the second Bill of Rights." +1 for the right of each individual to own firearms.

3. *Application.* Application refers to the ability to use learned material in new and concrete situations. An example of an application-level item would be: "You and your friend are in the mall after school. As you walk out of one of the stores, the mall security guard stops you and accuses you of shoplifting. He places you in the mall security office and wants to search your bags. What should you do? Please explain why you choose to answer as you did." +1 for calling a parent or other adult. +1 for indicating that under the law you have the right to make a phone call.

4. *Analysis.* Analysis refers to the ability to break down material into its component parts so that its organizational structure may be understood. An example of an analysis-level question would be: "Analyze the effects of mass production on economical situations." One answer is that an economic situation will be enhanced by the increasing availability of cheaply produced goods while still maintaining quality. Goods are now available to more individuals at a price they can afford, thus increasing the standard of living.

5. *Synthesis.* Synthesis refers to the ability to put parts together to form a new whole. The following is an example of a synthesis-level item. "You are traveling along the Oregon Trail in late summer. You are at the base of the Rocky Mountains and are deciding whether to continue along the trail and be on the other side by winter or stay where you are for the winter. Defend your decision. Be sure to include dangers, if any, for continuing, cost of supplies for crossing or staying, and what you will do for housing if you stay."

6. *Evaluation.* Evaluation is concerned with the ability to judge the value of a poem, research project, or statement for a given purpose. An example of an evaluation-level item would be: "Using the following assessment criteria, evaluate four of your peers' research papers and provide comments to them so that they may include those revisions when they prepare the next draft."

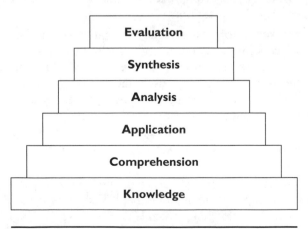

Figure 3.1 Bloom's taxonomy of educational objectives: Cognitive domain.

However, for most teaching activities, a breakdown of the cognitive taxonomy into two major divisions and five categories is appropriate. The two major divisions would be knowledge and intellectual levels. Knowledge-level assessment activities are those that measure simple memory, such as matching a state to its capital, remembering facts about the beginning of the Revolutionary War, and knowing the steps for amending the Constitution. Intellectual-level activities measure higher-level thinking skills, such as how well students comprehend a particular passage; how well they can identify examples of concepts; whether or not they can determine why a relationship exists; when it is appropriate to use a particular rule, theory, or law; and problem solving that involves a combination of synthesis, evaluation, and analysis. By matching what the student knows about the content of the objective (e.g., history of the Great Salt Lake from 1885 to 2000) and the construct of the objective (e.g., memorization), the assessment will be congruent with the instructional objective.

Gardner's Multiple Intelligences

Howard Gardner's (2006) theory of **Multiple Intelligences (MI)** suggests that there are different ways in which people learn and recognizes that individuals possess unique intellectual abilities. These distinct intellectual abilities include: **linguistic, musical, logical-mathematical, spatial, body and kinesthetic, intrapersonal, interpersonal, naturalistic,** and **spiritualistic.** Gardner has redefined human intelligence, suggesting that individuals may have several intelligences to varying degrees. The nine intelligences included in Gardner's theory are described below.

1. *Linguistic Intelligence.* Linguistic intelligence is the capacity to effectively use language, either orally or in writing. Students with this intelligence understand the structure, rules, and meanings of language.

2. *Musical Intelligence.* Musical intelligence is the capacity to perceive and manipulate the different musical forms. Students with this intelligence have sensitivity to rhythm, pitch, and timbre.

3. *Logical-Mathematical Intelligence.* Logical-mathematical intelligence is the capacity to effectively use numbers and objects, and involves deductive thinking and reasoning skills. Students with this intelligence have the ability to recognize abstract patterns and relationships.

4. *Spatial Intelligence.* Spatial intelligence is the capacity to perceive the physical world accurately and to perform transformations on these perceptions. Students with this intelligence have the ability to visualize and graphically represent spatial elements such as colors, lines, shapes, forms, and space.

5. *Body and Kinesthetic Intelligence.* Body and kinesthetic intelligence is the capacity to use the body in expressive and constructive ways. Students with this intelligence have physical abilities such as coordination, balance, dexterity, muscle strength, and speed.

6. *Intrapersonal Intelligence.* Intrapersonal intelligence is the capacity to understand one's own range of emotions and behaviors in order to act accordingly. Students with this intelligence are able to accurately self-evaluate themselves, recognizing both their strengths and weaknesses.

7. *Interpersonal Intelligence.* Interpersonal intelligence is the capacity to understand and assess the moods, behaviors, motivations, and intentions of others. Students with this intelligence are able to recognize and effectively respond to the body language of people.

8. ***Naturalistic Intelligence.*** Naturalistic intelligence is the capacity to recognize and classify living things and elements of the natural world. Students with this intelligence develop the ability to recognize and classify plants, minerals, rocks, and animals, as well as cultural artifacts.

9. ***Spiritualistic Intelligence.*** Spiritualistic intelligence is the capacity to make distinctions between appropriate and inappropriate behavior. Students with this intelligence are able to understand the differences between what is right and wrong.

Although Gardner has identified nine intelligences, he still is researching other human abilities to determine if other intelligences exist.

Learning styles are frequently addressed in social studies instruction. Table 3.1 gives multiple intelligence activities that may be assessed through checklists, teacher observation, or rubrics as well as other assessment measures.

In many instances, the assessment activities can be incorporated into the learning activity. This can be accomplished by using checklists or rubrics for oral presentations (see figure 3.2 on p. 88) or by having students use peer evaluations for group work. An example might be a group of students giving a presentation regarding what supplies must be included in a covered wagon, based on the number of travelers, the type of animal pulling the wagon, and the terrain. A group that presents what would be needed for a family of five when crossing the plains would present content different from that of a group giving a presentation on the same family preparing to follow the Oregon Trail across the Rockies. During the presentation a teacher can assess the content by following the criteria of the rubric for the oral presentation and the analytical scoring for the content. For the same learning activity, group members could follow their presentation by evaluating each member's contribution to the development and delivery of the project. The different ways that learning activities can be assessed by rubrics or combining rubrics with analytical scoring will be discussed later in the chapter.

It is extremely important that no matter what assessment tool is used, or the type of activity, the assessment results should be made available to the student in a timely manner. The longer an assessment activity is not returned to students, the less important and relevant it becomes. Traditionally, assessments are used to assign grades, yet the purpose of the assessment is to provide feedback to the teacher for instructional purposes. In other words, assessment enables the teacher to know what to teach next or what to reteach. If the assessment results are returned two weeks later, the assessment is for summative evaluation purposes only (i.e., assigning a grade). If assessment results are returned immediately and assessment components are reviewed with students, then the assessment activity truly becomes a learning activity. By incorporating learning activities with assessment activities, it is possible to create positive learning environments in relation to assessment as well as learning activities. By creating a nonthreatening learning environment that includes assessment, it may be possible that such activities may also help reduce the stigma of tests and assessment activities as threatening or punitive.

Undeniably, a primary function of assessments in the classroom is to provide educators with data on which they can determine and report levels of achievement, ability, and competency. Therefore, to make accurate and appropriate decisions based on assessment information teachers must use a variety of instruments that are closely aligned to instructional objectives. Instructional objectives identify the focus of the instruction, whereby teachers notify students of skills that must be acquired during the course of instruction and then demonstrated at times of assessment. In addition to the importance of matching delivery and assessment methods

Table 3.1   Multiple Intelligences

Sample Activities for Each Multiple Intelligence

Logical/Mathematical	**Verbal/Linguistic**	**Spatial/Visual**
• Abstract Symbols/Formulas	• Creative Writing	• Active Imagination
• Calculation	• Formal Speaking	• Color/Texture Schemes
• Deciphering Codes	• Humor/Jokes/Rhymes	• Drawing
• Relationships (> < =)	• Impromptu Speeches	• Guided Imagery/Visualizing
• Graphic/Cognitive Organizers	• Journal/Diary Keeping	• Mind Mapping
• Logic/Pattern Games	• Learning Logs	• Montage/Collage
• Number Sequences/Patterns	• Poetry	• Painting
• Outlining	• Reading	• Patterns/Designs
• Problem Solving	• Storytelling/Story Creation	• Pretending/Fantasy
	• Oral Debates	• Sculpting
	• Vocabulary	
Musical/Rhythmic	**Interpersonal**	**Naturalist**
• Environmental Sounds	• Collaborative Skills Teaching	• Archetypal Pattern
• Instrumental Sounds	• Cooperative Learning	Recognition
• Music Composition/Creation	Strategies	• Caring for Plants/Animals
• Music Performance	• Empathy Practices	• Conservation Practices
• Percussion Vibrations	• Giving Feedback	• Environment Feedback
• Rapping	• Group Projects	• Hands-on Labs
• Rhythmic Patterns	• Intuiting Others' Feelings	• Nature Encounters/Field Trips
• Singing/Humming	• Jigsaw Puzzles	• Nature Observation
• Tonal Patterns	• Person-to-Person	• Natural World Simulations
• Vocal Sounds/Tones	Communication	• Species Classification (organic/
	• Receiving Feedback	inorganic)
	• Sensing Others' Motives	• Sensory Stimulation Exercises
Bodily/Kinesthetic	**Intrapersonal**	**Spiritualistic**
• Body Language/Physical	• Emotional Processing	• Discuss Right/Wrong Behavior
Gestures	• Focusing/Concentration Skills	• Role Playing
• Body Sculpture/Tableaus	• Higher-Order Reasoning	• Write Reactions to Event in
• Dramatic Enactment	• Independent Studies/Projects	Story/Real Life
• Folk/Creative Dance	• Know Thyself Procedures	
• Gymnastic Routines	• Metacognition Techniques	
• Human Graph	• Mindfulness Practices	
• Inventing	• Silent Reflection Methods	
• Physical Exercise	• Thinking Strategies	
• Role Playing/Mime Arts		
• Sports Games		

☞ **IN THE CLASSROOM**

Implementing the Multiple Intelligences

According to Gardner (2006), his theory was originally developed as an explanation of how the mind works. As such, the Multiple Intelligences has implications for how teachers plan their instruction for their students. Gardener proposes that teachers focus on the particular intelligences of each student in terms of several relatively independent but interactive cognitive capacities. In short, these intelligences are more like LEGO building blocks. By using a number of blocks that have different shapes and that interconnect we can create a variety of patterns and structures rather than being limited to only one result. For example, if a student has strong spatial and logical-mathematical intelligences, the teacher should plan activities that encourage the student to develop these abilities. This requires that teachers be keenly aware of their students' abilities in order to plan effective learning experiences. Teachers can incorporate the Multiple Intelligences using lesson designs that involve individual and group projects, hands-on activities, apprenticeships, and interdisciplinary curricula.

Here are suggested multiple intelligence activities to accompany a unit on Native Americans:

Linguistic
• After reading different Native American legends, write your own legend.
• Research a tribe and make a pamphlet highlighting different aspects of the tribe.

Musical
• Listen to music representing different tribes.
• Play different Native American musical instruments.

Logical-Mathematical
• Develop a classroom trading system.
• Study the patterns of temples and totem poles.

Spatial
• Make a map showing the migration routes of various tribes in North and Central America.
• Identify different tribes on a map using push pins and compare different tribes using a Venn diagram.

Body and Kinesthetic
• Perform a Native American dance.
• Construct traditional Native American artifacts such as pottery, jewelry, or shelters.

Intrapersonal
• Pretend you are a member of a tribe and write a story about what it is like to live in that tribe.
• Explain the qualities you would want to find in a tribal council leader.

Interpersonal
• Role play a tribal council meeting.
• Participate in a service project to help protect the natural environment.

Naturalistic
• Write a Native American poem about nature.
• Compare and contrast everyday items such as utensils to items representing the lifestyles of Native Americans.

Existential
• Discuss your opinions on the historical treatment of Native Americans.
• Choose an animal that represents your own nature and feelings.

These suggested activities represent only a few adaptations of Gardner's theory of Multiple Intelligences. There are many models and formats for teachers to follow. More important is that teachers understand that there is more than one way to teach any concept or skill.

Monitoring student achievement also directs instructional practices by the teacher.

to instructional objectives in terms of content and construct, however, teachers must also be sure to gather sufficient data to make their decisions. Therefore, to increase the accuracy of decisions teachers should assess each objective with more than one tool. Furthermore, teachers should assess each object with variant tools to ensure that they are measuring the students' skill ability rather than the students' ability to complete the assessment task itself. Finally, teachers can increase the accuracy of their decisions not only through multiple measures of a given unit, but also through multiple measures over time.

Assessing Higher-Level Thinking Skills

As we develop our instructional units of study based on school and district goals and national, state, and local standards, we need to plan learning activities that develop higher-level thinking skills in the areas of knowledge acquisition, inquiry, problem solving, communication, and reflection. Strong, Silver, and Perini (2001, 38–39) offer these suggestions for increasing the development of students' thinking skills:

Knowledge Acquisition

- Organize instruction around a few core ideas.
- Model the use of organizational tools like graphic organizers and concept maps.
- Give students a wide variety of learning experiences and media with which to increase their potential for acquiring knowledge.

Assessment: To what extent does the curriculum engage students in acquiring and organizing information around concepts central to the topic?

Inquiry

- Teach students how to pose questions and substantiate claims.
- Build research and evidence-gathering opportunities into instruction.

Assessment: To what extent are students encouraged to pose questions, form and test hypotheses, and use evidence and proof to substantiate their findings?

Problem Solving

- Ask students to design easier and harder versions of the problems you give them.
- Set up a high-performance classroom in which students discuss problems they confront and solutions they find.
- Help students see the difference between first thoughts and second thoughts.

Assessment: To what extent do students concern themselves with pressing or problematic issues and use creative thinking to generate solutions?

Communication

- Show students how to use journals and logs for representing ideas and discoveries.
- Teach note taking and other means of representing thoughts.
- Allow students to compare ideas in pairs and small groups, as well as in class discussions.

Assessment: To what extent are students given the opportunity to speak, write, and elaborate on what they have learned?

Reflection

- Build units around criteria for growth.
- Write criteria in student-friendly language.
- Ask students to examine work at different stages of growth.

Assessment: To what extent do students think about their own learning in order to find gaps and improve as learners and thinkers?

Such activities stretch our students, challenging them to be reflective thinkers in an ever-changing world.

Benchmarks

Increasingly states are setting learning benchmarks for social studies instruction. In other words, students are expected to understand specific social studies concepts by certain grade levels. An example of a benchmark is the following: *By the end of fourth grade the student is able to state and describe the three branches of government.* Teachers need to make certain their social studies curriculum objectives and goals include their respective state's benchmarks.

Methods of Assessment

Students can be assessed in a variety of ways. Different techniques are used for informal assessments (i.e., those that are less structured, spontaneous) than are used for formal assessments (i.e., those that are structured, planned) (Cangelosi 1990; Miller 1995; Popham 2006; Weber 1999). Teachers can collect information in several different ways using informal assessments techniques.

For teachers, the most common method of informal assessment is that of questioning the students during class discussions and group activities. By asking questions that address the learning activities, teachers can get a general understanding of how well the students understand the material. It is important to remember that the teacher must be sure that all students are actively responding to the questions. In this way, the teacher receives a realistic picture of the level of understanding of the entire class rather than just a few students. An accurate measure can be accomplished by asking students by name to respond directly to questions. It is important, however, to remember that if a student does not know the answer the student should not be made to feel ignorant or less able. When the class as a whole doesn't know the answer to a series of questions, the teacher must clearly recognize the need to reteach or review the given information. In many instances, the teacher may need to prompt the students to facilitate their ability to formulate, articulate, or clarify responses. It is also appropriate to encourage students to pass the question on to a classmate as long as the student is not always allowed to demonstrate avoidance behavior.

During group activities, the teacher may not be able to pose questions to the class as a whole to get a measure of the students' understanding. Instead, the teacher may walk around the room and gather information about students' understanding by listening to the groups and documenting common understandings and misunderstandings. In addition, to get feedback about group understanding, or to assist the group in moving forward or considering different methods of approaching the activity, the teacher could ask questions of the individual groups and group members. By asking questions of the individual groups and the class as a whole, the teacher keeps the students focused on the instructional objectives and, therefore, the purpose of the activity. It is important for teachers to continually monitor the students' progress in the activity so that when the activity is finished the teacher can determine whether the students need to spend more time refining their knowledge or whether the teacher can begin to present new material.

Assessment Tools

If the purpose of assessment were to provide the teacher with information about students' understanding of the classroom activities, with no accountability to the students, their parents, other teachers, and so forth, formal assessments would not be necessary. However, this is not the case. Teachers must have detailed information that indicates how well students are achieving the instructional objectives in order to inform parents, students, school personnel, and the community of the students' achievement, ability, and competency. To better accomplish this, teachers must give formal assessment activities. In addition to providing the accountability needed within the educational community, formal assessment activities help determine how well each student understands the instructional objectives. Such information is extremely important if the goal of teaching is for the teacher to help the student

Honeybee conferencing is when the teacher floats around the room, stopping to answer questions that arise while the class is engaged in completing an assignment. This kind of conferencing aids anecdotal assessment as the teacher works with students on a one-to-one basis.

achieve the learning objectives. Without the formal assessment activities, teachers' perceptions of what a student understands may be misleading. If during informal assessment activities the teacher only asks the student questions that the student strictly can or cannot answer, then the teacher's perception of the student's ability to achieve the instructional objectives will follow accordingly. Formal assessments (i.e., those that are structured, planned, or have detailed scoring schemes) are a means by which teachers can gather further data to determine an overall picture of how well students have achieved the learning objectives. Formal assessments include paper-and-pencil tests, performance assessments, formal observations, and portfolios.

All assessments, whether formal or informal, are designed with instructional objectives in mind. An instructional objective takes into account the cognitive (i.e., thinking), psychomotor (i.e., physical), and affective (i.e., valuing) behavior that the teacher expects students to use when learning. Objectives should be listed in student outcome form (e.g., the student will be able to define the vocabulary words for the lesson). In addition, the objective should always be written so that the student's achievement of the objective is observable (e.g., define, remember, recall, analyze, paraphrase). The following is an example of an objective taken from the *Illinois Learning Standards for Social Science* (Illinois State Board of Education, 1997): "Students will identify concepts of responsible citizenship including respect for the law, patriotism, civility and working with others" (44).

Paper-and-Pencil Tests

Traditionally, instructional objectives have been assessed using paper-and-pencil tests. These tests rely on multiple-choice, true-false, matching, fill-in-the-blank, short answer, and essay questions. While every teacher is familiar with these tests, these tests do not necessarily provide information regarding the instructional objectives.

> The right kinds of tests, correctly applied, can help every teacher become a better teacher. But unless you know the nuts and bolts of effective test design and application, you may be collecting the wrong data; misinterpreting data; and drawing off-base conclusions about what students know and can do, what to teach next, and how effective your instruction has been. (Popham 2003, 6)

As indicated by Herman, Aschbacher, and Winters (1992), the number one factor when designing the assessment activity is that the assessment items measure the instructional goals and objectives. If the assessment items do not match the content and the behavioral construct of the objective, then the assessment is of little value (Cangelosi 1990). When writing items, teachers should ask, "When answering this assessment item, do students have to think about the content and use the construct of the instructional objective in order to be successful?"

Technology and Assessment

Assessment can be aided through technology as there are software programs designed to aid the classroom teacher in recording student grades. These programs automatically average the scores to yield percentages and letter grades.

Teachers need to be aware that lots of inexpensive and even free software exists. By typing in "computers/software/educational/teachers" at a search engine, a number of hits arise. Many of these will have lists of numerous assessment software programs that are available. Other good sources include www.ncss.org, the official Web site of the National Council of Social Studies and www.readwritethink.org, formerly the Marco Polo Web site. Another Web site not to be missed is www.ala.org, then go to "Great Books," which lists thematic units for grades K–12.

Besides the grade book capabilities, technology can be used in other ways. For instance, to meet the reading needs of students, go to either www.readinga-z.com or www.leveledbooks.com to locate social studies titles that match well with a child's reading level. Children's literature titles are suggested throughout this book. The annotated bibliography at the end of the chapters aids the selection process.

Alternative Assessment

According to Alleman and Brophy (1999a), the purpose of the learning situation determines the different forms and times for assessment. In addition, the purpose also determines how the assessment will be used to carry out social studies goals for the 10 thematic strands listed in the NCSS Standards. Alleman and Brophy (1999a) suggest developing **alternative assessment** tools to quizzes and teacher-made tests. They have created six guiding principles for such alternative assessment tools:

- Assessment is considered an integral part of the curriculum and instruction process;
- Assessment is viewed as a thread that is woven into the curriculum, beginning before instruction and occurring at junctures throughout in an effort to monitor, assess, revise, and expand what is being taught and learned;
- A comprehensive assessment plan should be goal oriented, appropriate in level of difficulty, feasible, and cost effective;
- Assessment should benefit the learner (promote self-reflection and self-regulation) and inform teaching practices; and
- Assessment results should be documented to "track" resources and develop learning profiles.

Assessment needs to be considered as an integral part of the curriculum and not as an additional task or afterthought.

Rubrics

Assessment activities other than the traditional paper-and-pencil test can be measured and evaluated using assessment instruments such as rubrics or checklists. **Rubrics** attempt to combine information that is assessed holistically (i.e., the assessment activity has a range of points but the points cannot be broken down specifically) and information that is assessed analytically (i.e., the assessment activity has a range of points and the points are clearly identified so that the student knows exactly where points were lost). Furthermore, rubrics, like traditional paper-and-pencil tests, may not assess one instructional objective but may focus on several. The rubric in figure 3.2 was created to provide information to students doing oral presentations. It assesses not only the student's oral presentation skills but also his/her understanding of the content. This type of rubric can be used to assess students in two content areas, language arts and social studies. To avoid unbalanced assessments, such as a strong presenter outscoring a weaker presenter with strong social studies skills, teachers must have an understanding of their instructional objectives

Name: _____ Date: _____

Content	4	3	2	1	0
Oral Presentation	Excellent voice and diction	Good voice and diction	Trouble hearing voice and understanding some words	Rarely could hear or understand words	No attempt
Historical Content	No errors	Only minor errors	Several major errors	Many errors	No attempt
Organization of Historical Content	No organizational errors	Only minor errors	Several major errors	Many errors	No attempt

Figure 3.2   An example of a scoring rubric for an oral presentation in social studies.

and what behaviors demonstrate a student's proficiency of those objectives. Figure 3.2 incorporates elements of oral presentation on a 0 to 4 scale.

Additionally, teachers of ELLs must make decisions on how much weight will be given to content and how much to language. These decisions need to be made on the basis of the ability levels of the individual students. For example, teachers should consider an adjustment in the oral presentation section of the rubric in figure 3.2 for a beginning ELL who has difficulty with pronunciation, yet clearly demonstrates a good level of mastery of the content. Likewise, there should be some adjustment in the scoring of an ELL's sentence structure and mechanics in the rubric on evaluating writing of reports in figure 3.3. Perhaps, in classrooms with large numbers of ELLs, teachers might want to design a different rubric specifically for ELLs. While teachers need to have high academic expectations of all their students, they also need to recognize that ELLs are still very much in the learning and development phase of their English language skills, especially their writing skills. Penalizing a beginning or intermediate language learner for developmental grammatical errors may take away any motivation on the part of the student to engage in the learning activities.

When creating a scoring rubric, it is important that teachers remember two important factors: First, the rubric should be easy to use and the number of scoring criteria should be kept manageable. Second, the number of possible points a student can score should be the same for each criterion. The more complex the rubric, the harder it is for teachers to score and to score consistently. The type of assessment activity also needs to be considered. The teacher can reread a written report and therefore provide an unrushed, thoughtful assessment. Oral presentations, on the other hand, require an instant response; teachers do not have the luxury of spending time thinking about what the student is saying and how well he or she is satisfying each of the criterion. If it is possible, teachers should videotape an oral presentation and then review it later to double-check scoring. However, limiting the number of scoring criteria for an oral activity as opposed to a written one makes immediate scoring more manageable.

The second critical factor in designing rubrics (as well as rating scales) is to consider the range of numeric or descriptive values that can be placed on a particular component of the activity. Teachers want to be sure to provide a range of points or descriptors that give the students and other members of the educational community appropriate levels of feedback. Teachers want to avoid designing rubrics that provide only holistic measures or provide meaningless and vague feedback. For example, the rubric in figure 3.3 (on the following page) does not allow the teacher or other evaluator to choose an insignificant, middle-of-the-road rating that would fail to provide the teacher and student with meaningful information about the student's achievement of the objective.

Initiating a rubric for an assignment can seem to be an overwhelming task. Students as young as first grade can help provide expectations for the learning assignment. As such they will feel they have ownership as part of the assessment process. If time is of the essence, two terrific Web sites offer rubric designs. These Web sites will develop your rubric for you if you put in your objectives for the lesson plan. These Web sites are http://www.rubistar.com and http://www.teachnology.com.

Figure 3.4 demonstrates a relatively simple, easy to apply rubric for a social studies task. Most assignments will fit into this rubric with only slight modifications to the rubric itself.

Evaluating Writing: Reports

	References (5)	Organization (5)	Presentation (5)	Sentence Structure (5)	Mechanics (5)

4	4+ references
	magazines
	encyclopedia
	books
	Internet
	video
	newspaper
	interview
		Strong content
		Strong beginning,
		  middle, and end
		Flow
		All ideas
		  sequenced
		All ideas logical
		Neat
			Fresh, original
			Focuses on topic
			Many supporting
			  details
			4+ visual aids
				Clearly written
				Complete sentences
				Compound/complex
				  sentences
				Variety of sentence
				  length
				Good content
				  vocabulary
					Few or no
					  errors:
					Capitalization
					Ending
					  punctuation
					Commas
					Paragraphs
					  indented
					Spelling

3	3+ references
	magazines
	encyclopedia
	books
	Internet
	video
	newspaper
	interview
		Most ideas
		  connected
		Good beginning,
		  middle, and end
		Most ideas
		  sequenced
		Most ideas logical
			Some original
			  ideas
			General focus on
			  topic
			Some support-
			  ing details
			  included
			3+ visual aids
				Most sentences
				  clearly written
				Most sentences
				  complete
				Simple sentences
				Some variety of length
				Some content
				  vocabulary
					Some errors:
					Capitalization
					Ending
					  punctuation
					Commas
					Paragraphs
					  indented
					Spelling

2	2+ references
	magazines
	encyclopedia
	books
	Internet
	video
	newspaper
	interview
		Some ideas
		  connected
		Attempts
		  beginning,
		  middle, and end
		Not always
		  sequenced
		Not always logical
			Few original
			  ideas
			Moves away
			  from focus
			Few supporting
			  details
			2+ visual aids
				Some unclear sen-
				  tences
				Some run-on, frag-
				  mented sentences
				Little variety of length
				Little content
				  vocabulary
					Many errors:
					Capitalization
					Ending
					  punctuation
					Commas
					Paragraphs
					  indented
					Spelling

1	1+ references
	magazines
	encyclopedia
	books
	Internet
	video
	newspaper
	interview
		Few ideas
		  connected
		Lacks beginning,
		  middle, and end
		Little sequence
		Little logic
			Incomplete ideas
			Unfocused
			Lacks details
			1+ visual aids
				Sentences not clear
				Frequent fragmented
				  sentences
				No variety
				No content
				  vocabulary
					Serious
					  errors:
					Capitalization
					Ending
					  punctuation
					Commas
					Paragraphs
					  indented
					Spelling

0	No attempt	No attempt	No attempt	No attempt	No attempt

Source: McWilliams, S., Vance, H., & Newsome, P. (1998). Tifton, GA: Omega Elementary School, Tift County School System. Used by permission.

Figure 3.3 An example of a scoring rubric for a written social studies report.

	No Attempt to Meet Basic Requirements and Standards	Attempted to Meet Basic Requirements and Standards	Met Basic Requirements and Standards	Met High Level Requirements and Standards	Clearly Exceeded Requirements and Standards
Ideas and Content	Product lacks connection to the topic	Product attempts to provide a recall of events related to the topic	Product provides a recall of events related to the topic and/or the effects of topic on our society	Product provides an understanding of the topic and/or the effects of topic on our society	Product provides a clear and thorough analysis or evaluation of topic and/or the effects of topic on our society
Voice	No personality or character (no voice)	Student's own voice may be present but lacks any clarity or may simply reflect routine, predictable communication	Student's own voice is somewhat present and clear (goes beyond the routine and predictable)	Student's own voice or the voice of a historical figure is definitely present and clear but may need to be louder and more poignant	Student's own voice or the voice of a historical figure is loud and clear and as poignant as Peggy Steele Clay's was in *Touchstone*
Quality	Final product is not ready to be shared	Final product can be shared within the classroom	Final product is of the quality to display in the hallway	Final product is of the quality to put on display in prominent area of the school	Final product could be published in a magazine or displayed in a museum
Creativity (overall)	Work does not reflect creativity	Work demonstrates limited creativity	Work demonstrates creativity	Work demonstrates a unique quality and is creative	Work is highly artistic or eloquent
Creativity (detail)	No detail is apparent	Detail is apparent	Detail is clear	Detail is focused on cultural elements and readily apparent	Detail is highly focused and highlighted in a unique manner
Work Effort	Evidence of only a limited amount of work or beginning draft of work	Evidence of a fairly complete rough draft	Evidence of a complete effort	Evidence of a complete, thorough, and careful effort	Evidence of a "professional" effort
Time Contributed	Shows a two-day effort	Shows a three- to four-day effort	Shows at least a five- to six-day effort	Shows over a week's effort	Shows two weeks of work

Figure 3.4 This rubric is appropriate for a social studies research project.

Teachers who use rubrics should be sure to provide students with a copy of the rubric when the activity is introduced. Such a practice enables students to evaluate their own work before it is evaluated by either another student or the teacher. This helps students to engage in self-teaching, self-reflection, and self-evaluation (Batzle 1992; Farr and Tone 1994; Miller 1995).

Portfolio Assessment

Portfolio assessment is one of many methods of collecting information about what the students know in relation to the instructional objectives. It is a way for teachers, students, and parents to see an overall picture of each student's growth. Perhaps more significantly, portfolio assessment enables students to see their progress in relation to themselves, not in relation to how they perform against their classmates.

Determining the content of a portfolio is a process that can include both the student and the teacher. It is important at this point to note that a portfolio is not just a random collection of student work or a file for all homework papers. The content is defined by the intent of the portfolio. If the portfolio is to be used to show a student's growth, then the collection should show early works of the student, including work that was not always the student's best work. If the portfolio is an assessment portfolio, then it should include only the student's best work since the student will be evaluated on that work.

The last part of any portfolio assessment is evaluation. How will the student's work be evaluated? This is where a clear statement of the purpose or the intent of the portfolio is important. Without clear evaluation processes, the evaluation of the portfolios will probably not be consistent. Portfolios can be assessed using checklists, a student-teacher conference, peer evaluation, and rubrics. Batzle (1992) suggests the following steps for involving students and parents in the evaluation process. First, the student chooses a sample and reviews it with a peer. Next, the student shares the sample with the class. Afterward, he/she then reflects and writes about why he/she chose the sample and explains its value. The student takes the sample home for his/her parents' comments and reflections. Finally, the student puts the work in the portfolio so that the teacher can write a formal evaluation. Figure 3.5 indicates how a summary sheet can include comments from the student, parents, and teacher about the student's work and progress in the portfolio. This is especially important for ELLs and students with different levels of ability. Portfolios can provide important motivation for them because it demonstrates their progress in both content and language.

Portfolio assessment has several advantages. One is that the students can see their improvement over time. In this respect, portfolios are also a great motivational resource for students. Throughout the educational process, students are always being compared with their peers. With portfolio assessments, students can look at how much they have grown in relation to themselves. This can be done by keeping progressive works in the portfolio, a growth chart, or any other type of communication works for showing the learning that has taken place. As the student and teacher work together to create the goals of the portfolio, the student also becomes increasingly involved in the learning process.

One of the primary limitations of portfolios is the space required for collection and storage. The responsibility of maintaining portfolios is also problematic, espe-

NAME: _____

SUMMARY SHEET FOR PORTFOLIO

Why I believe this piece should be included _____
_____
_____
_____
_____

This piece shows my progress _____
_____
_____
_____
_____

Parents' Comments:
My/our child's work shows _____
_____
_____
_____
_____

Teacher's Comments:
I think this student's work shows _____
_____
_____
_____
_____

Figure 3.5 An example of a student's, parent's, and teacher's summary sheet for including student work in student's portfolio.

cially if portfolios are moved through the school system along with the students. If the portfolios are assessment portfolios they can become very bulky over time, making storage for an entire school problematic. However, portfolios copied to disks or CD-ROMs require minimal storage space.

Projects

Projects are popular social studies activities designed to be engaging and open-ended. As such, they pose a challenge for evaluating the work. Projects tend to be done over a period of time and can be fairly complex in nature. A third-grade class may build a model community with each student contributing a building (hospital, school, grocery store, shoe store, gas station, auto dealership, etc.). Older students may be encouraged to select a country and present a small-group project that reflects the culture, economy, geography, and history of that nation.

Having students take notes is one important element. For elementary students, a loose leaf notebook works better than note cards, which are easily—and too often readily—lost. Spiral notebooks may contain other social studies material such as the student's social studies textbook reading log or vocabulary work. A loose leaf notebook or folder helps the student focus on the task at hand. Some teachers substitute a covered cereal box for the student to use as a file box to hold all the notes and rough drafts for the project. They offer a reasonable filing system requiring limited space to store (put on a shelf and retrieved each day until the project is completed).

For example, a sixth-grade class did individual projects on the Roman Empire. Some of the topics selected for the projects included Roman influences in Great Britain, Roman architecture, Julius Caesar, Cleopatra, Roman generals, life as a Roman citizen, and the Punic Wars. Over a six-week period, students developed and wrote a report on their topic along with a project to be presented to their parents. The time line was as follows:

Week One: Choose a topic; check resources (library and Web sites); gather written material on topic.
Week Two: Begin project notebook; outline/display.
Week Three: Complete research; write the first draft of report; start building display.
Week Four: Continue to collect items for display.
Week Five: Write a second draft of report; design graphs or charts for display; use PowerPoint to label display.
Week Six: Write and word process final report; set up display at home and do self-evaluation of project; make final adjustments/revisions; transport display and report to school for display.

An oral history project works well with middle school students. Grant Wiggins (1989, 42–43) suggests the following project:

> You must complete an oral history project based on interviews and written sources and present your findings orally in class. The choice of subject matter will be up to you. Some of the examples of possible topics include: your family, running a small business, substance abuse, a labor union, teenage parents, or recent immigrants. You are to create three workable hypotheses based on your preliminary investigations and come up with four questions you will use to test each hypothesis.
>
> To meet the criteria, [you] must:
> - investigate three hypotheses;
> - describe at least one change over time;
> - demonstrate that you have done your homework research;
> - interview four appropriate people as resources;
> - prepare at least four questions related to each hypothesis;
> - ask questions that are not leading or biased;
> - ask follow-up questions when appropriate;

- note important differences between fact and answers you receive;
- use evidence to support your choice of the best hypothesis; and
- organize your writing and your class presentation.

Projects, as with presentations, can be scored using a rubric or a checklist. The most important factors are clearly indicating to the students what they are to do, and then having a scoring scheme that clearly indicates those students who have met the project's criteria. For small groups, the rubric must consider both individual contributions and any group tasks that are accomplished. Figure 3.6 shows an example of a rubric that can be used for the Roman Empire project. The photo on page 348 shows one of the final projects.

Rubric for Roman Empire Project

Name of Student: _____ Room: _____

Title of Report: _____

WRITTEN REPORT   (10 PTS.) _____

DISPLAY   (10 PTS.) _____

CREATIVITY OF PROJECT   (10 PTS.) _____

THOROUGHNESS OF PROJECT   (10 PTS.) _____

                                         TOTAL POINTS: _____

Figure 3.6 An example of a rubric for a project.

Self-Assessment

Self-assessment calls for students to be objective about their own work. But if students are to engage in self-assessment, the criteria and other factors must be expressed using terms that students can both understand and use with confidence to accurately describe their efforts and accomplishments. They also need to procure an understanding that the assessment process and evaluation criteria help them develop their capacity as self-monitoring learners (Wixson 2006).

Diane Hart (1999), a firm believer of involving students in the evaluation process, suggests using self-evaluation for all long-term and group projects. For instance, Hart suggests having each group member complete a self-evaluation form at the end of a project, rating themselves from 1 (low effort) to 6 (highest effort). The form should have a place for the student's name and date as well as the title of the project. An opening statement regarding the amount of work the project required as well as an example of the need for each member to contribute substantially should be included. Examples of such statements include:

- I understood the project assignment and was able to help my group understand our task.

- I worked cooperatively with others. I took responsibility for some part of the project.
- I worked to the best of my ability and didn't waste time.
- I was willing to share my ideas with my group.

On the back of the form, the student would write a brief description of the role the student played in the project by answering the following questions:

- What did you do?
- How long did you spend doing it?
- How hard did you work?
- How did you interact with others in your group?
- Where did you get your ideas?
- What research did you do? What specific resources (list books, papers, primary and secondary sources, person interviewed, etc.) did you use?

Such a form would be appropriate for use starting at the fourth grade level. As an assessment tool it forces students to be reflective as a participating member of their respective groups.

Upper elementary and middle school students are often given one long-term project each year that requires an exceptional amount of time and effort to produce. Sometimes these projects are shared as part of an academic fair or open house. Usually the students are required to write a research paper along with developing a poster board display. Accompanying such an activity should be a self-assessment that includes questions that push the students to consider what they did, how they did it, and if they would do it differently if they had the opportunity to start all over again on the project. Here are some questions that push, probe, and stretch students:

- What goals did you set for yourself in conducting this project?
- How well did you meet your goals?
- What would you do differently if you had the opportunity to do this project over again?
- What did you find out about your problem-solving skills and strategies as you did this project?
- What new questions did your research for the project raise?
- What was the easiest part of conducting this project?
- What was the most challenging part of conducting this project?
- What was the most difficult aspect of presenting your project to the class?
- What one piece of advice would you give someone else who wants to do a similar project in the future?

Answering such questions encourages metacognition, that is, thinking about how we ourselves think and learn. It is probably best to model such questions with a student from the previous year, or perhaps a student from another class who has already completed and presented such a project. Have the student bring in his/her project and research paper and give a brief overview of the work to the class. Afterward, the instructor can then ask the above questions in a casual, conversational setting, giving the student time to ponder before responding. Further questions may develop based on the student's responses.

Manipulatives

Manipulatives are objects that students can use to demonstrate their knowledge of a project. Manipulatives can make excellent alternative assessment tools provided that content is stressed and the included materials provide a good match with the social studies learning goals. For example, primary grade students may be asked to draw the most important thing they learned from the project. Learning stations with manipulatives such as maps, globes, artifacts, and photographs can be used. When such learning stations are used with primary students, upper-level students can be used as peer assistants to record the younger students' responses (Alleman and Brophy 1997).

Using manipulatives as assessment tools with struggling students and English language learners allows them to demonstrate their knowledge beyond the limits of their current language resources and gives the teacher a clear picture of their grasp of the instructional objectives.

Differentiated Instruction Assessment and Grading for Striving and ELL Students

How does the teacher determine the grade of a struggling student? What standards are used? What criteria? Student ability varies widely within a classroom, from the gifted learner to the striving reader to the special education student with an IEP to the English language learner. How can a teacher fairly give each of these students a letter grade for a learning activity or the nine week summative letter grade that is reported on the report card? Rick Wormel (2006) believes that teachers in the elementary building or on a middle school team need to discuss and set up criteria for the performance expectations of all students. If a set of standards must be met by all students, that needs to be made clear to the students and adhered to by the teachers. With a diverse student population, differentiated instruction requires differentiated assessments and evaluation procedures.

Wormel believes that when grading differentiated instructional tasks, the report card or rubric needs to clearly state how the assignment differed from the one that most students in the class undertook. Checks and balances must be clearly set out so that the gifted student who earned an "A" for an outstanding project will not feel that a student who put forth much less effort but was likewise awarded an "A" was given the same grade. This is a difficult tightrope for teachers to walk as administrators and parents also weigh in on the issue. A comment section on each report card helps, but unfortunately such comments are usually limited to middle school report cards.

☞ IN THE CLASSROOM

Differentiated Assignments

Differentiated assignments can take many forms. Having students illustrate scenes from a historical novel and write an accompanying descriptive sentence about each to create a "movie" summary is an effective way to develop summarization skills. For this lesson, students read a novel and select six scenes. Using a black, medium marker, each student draws each of his or her selected scenes inside a movie "frame," like the one below. Next, each student writes a very descriptive sentence for the scene on the line above the frame. At this point, the teacher approves the illustrations and the sentences. Next, the teacher uses the photocopy machine to make a transparency of the scenes, which she gives back to the student. Using colored markers, the student finishes illustrating the scenes before cutting them apart and taping them together to form a strip of six "movie frames" (going left to right) of the critical scenes from the book. The student shares the movie with the class using the overhead projector. Following is a sample of instructions for the students and one of the six movie frames with a line above it for the descriptive sentence.

Making Movies

Book title or passage _____

Make a "movie" in your mind as you read! Think about six important parts of the book. In each movie "frame," sketch the scene that shows that important part. Remember details that you see, feel, taste, and hear. Write a descriptive sentence for each scene on the line above the frame. Use your sketches to help you write a summary of the story.

Chapter Summary

In summary, assessing students is a complicated and complex process. If assessment were easy, teachers would never question the results of their tests, the results of standardized tests, or their evaluation of portfolios. To create assessments that more accurately measure instruction, teachers need to plan learning and assessment activities based on predetermined instructional objectives. If the teachers create a strong link between the two, then the assessment will provide a solid basis for evaluating and reporting the student's performance. It is important to remember that assessment of student learning should include a variety of assessment activities, not just traditional paper-and-pencil tests.

When the teacher uses a variety of assessment tools to assess the student, the teacher will have a more complete picture of the student's level of understanding of instructional objectives. As information from assessment activities is collected during the grading periods, teachers have many pieces of information to use to communicate achievement to parents. More information is added throughout the year by the use of various assessment activities; by the end of the school year, teachers have a clear, more thorough understanding of the student's level of achievement. Because a multitude of assessment activities provide many pieces of information from which the teacher can make decisions, the final summative evaluation for the student will be far more accurate.

Related Technology Tools

WebQuest
Taxonomy of WebQuest Tasks (to evaluate WebQuests for Gr. K–8)
   http://webquest.sdsu.edu/taskonomy.html

Technology Resources
Assessment
   http://www.sarasota.k12.fl.us/g2K/64.htm
   This site provides a thorough overview of various types of assessment as well as a self-assessment for teachers.
Learning
   www.learning.org
   This Web site has a number of video clips that can be accessed on the Internet. Teachers demonstrate how they assess students using a number of different assessment techniques.
EdWeb
   http://www.edwebproject.org/edref.mi.intro.html
   Visit this site for an introduction to Multiple Intelligences as proposed by Howard Gardner. The site provides an introduction to Gardner's thinking, about Gardner himself, and discusses implications for classroom teaching.

Software and Videos
"Teacher's Toolbox 4.0 CD-ROM." Ablesoft. Available from www.amazon.com. The latest version of this comprehensive classroom administration system provides a lesson planner and report card generator, in addition to grading, scheduling, seating-chart design, attendance monitoring, test creation, and student reporting.

References

Alleman, J., and J. Brophy. 1997. "Elementary Social Studies Instruments, Activities, and Standards." In *Handbook of Classroom Assessment,* ed. G. Phye, pp. 321–57. San Diego, CA: Academic Press.

———. 1999a. "Current Trends and Practices in Social Studies Assessment for the Early Grades." *Social Studies and the Young Learner* 11 (4): 15–17.

———. 1999b. "The Changing Nature and Purpose of Assessment in the Social Studies Classroom." *Social Education* 65 (6): 334–37.

Batzle, J. 1992. *Portfolio Assessment and Evaluation: Developing and Using Portfolios in the Classroom.* Cypress, CA: Creative Teaching Press.

Bloom, B. S., M. D. Englehart, E. J. Furst, W. H. Hill, and D. R. Krathwohl. 1969. *Taxonomy of Educational Objectives: Handbook I, Cognitive Domain.* New York: David McKay.

Cangelosi, J. S. 1990. *Designing Tests for Evaluating Student Achievement.* New York: Longman.

Farr, R., and B. Tone. 1994. *Portfolio and Performance Assessment: Helping Students Evaluate their Progress as Readers and Writers.* Fort Worth, TX: Harcourt Brace.

Gardner, H. 2006. *Multiple Intelligences: New Horizons.* New York: Basic Books.

Hart, D. 1999. "Opening Assessment to Our Students." *Social Education* 63 (6): 343–45.

Herman, J. L., P. R. Aschbacher, and L. Winters. 1992. *A Practical Guide to Alternative Assessment.* Arlington, VA: Association for Supervision and Curriculum Development.

Illinois State Board of Education. 1997. *Illinois Learning Standards for Social Science.* Springfield: Author.

Miller, W. H. 1995. *Alternative Assessment Techniques for Reading and Writing.* West Nyack, NY: Center for Applied Research in Education.

Monson, R. J., and M. P. Monson. 1997 (September). "Professional Development for Implementing Standards: Experimentation, Dilemma Management, and Dialogue." *Bulletin*: 67–73.

National Council for the Social Studies. 1994. *Expectations of Excellence: Curriculum Standards for Social Studies.* Washington, DC: Author.

Popham, W. J. 2003. *Test Better, Teach Better: The Instructional Role of Assessment.* Alexandria, VA: Association for Curriculum and Development.

———. 2006. *Classroom Assessment: What Teachers Need to Know.* 4th ed. Boston: Allyn & Bacon.

Risinger, C. F. 2002. "Two Different Worlds: The Dilemma Facing Social Studies Teachers." *Social Education* 66 (4): 231–33.

Strong, R. W., H. F. Silver, and M. J. Perini. 2001. *Teaching What Matters Most.* Alexandria, VA: Association for Supervision and Curriculum Development.

Weber, E. 1999. *Student Assessment that Works: A Practical Approach.* Boston: Allyn & Bacon.

Wiggins, G. 1989. "Teaching to the Authentic Test." *Educational Leadership* 70: 40–44.

Wixson, K. 2006 (June 19). "Classroom Assessment: Where We Are and Where We Need to Go." Northern Illinois Reading Council's 27th Annual Summer Reading Conference, Sugar Grove, IL.

Wormel, R. 2006. *Fair Isn't Always Equal: Assessing and Grading in the Differentiated Classroom.* Portland, ME: Stenhouse.

Chapter Four

Multicultural and Bilingual Education
Making the Connections in Social Studies

Carla Cooper Shaw, Northern Illinois University;
Mary Louise Ginejko, Teacher, Curriculum and Technology Specialist, Joliet, IL;
Karen Carrier, Northern Illinois University;
Susan L'Allier, Northern Illinois University

CHAPTER OUTLINE

CHAPTER OBJECTIVES

Readers will

- acquire techniques for teaching about diversity;

- appreciate and understand the need to help students develop positive attitudes toward different cultural, racial, and ethnic groups;

- understand how to extend acceptance of others from the classroom to the multicultural community beyond;

- develop a greater awareness of the different cultures as well as their own;

- understand the need to learn the traditions and mores of the different cultural groups represented in their own school and community;

- understand that diversity occurs even with peoples from seemingly the same geographic area;
- understand the need to develop personal relationships in the classroom, both student to student and teacher to student;
- understand the changing demographics in the nation and the need to respond by adapting one's teaching; and
- acquire techniques for making content more accessible for English language learners.

Introduction

"Daddy, why did the Indians attack the settlers?"
"Because they were a wild and savage people."
"Who—the Indians or the settlers?"
"The Indians, of course. The settlers were just like you and me."

Children are not born **prejudiced,** but by the time they enter kindergarten they may possess misconceptions and negative attitudes about cultural groups different from their own (Banks and Banks 2004; Byrnes 1988). Among the causes of prejudice in children are two natural tendencies: to evaluate and categorize people and to adopt the attitude of respected adults and other children. The relationship between personal identity and the need for group membership also plays a role in the formation of prejudice. In their quest for belonging, children may express group loyalty by denigrating people belonging to cultures unlike their own (Byrnes 1988). Elementary and middle school teachers must "help children express, share, and take pride in their family cultures, and so to teach about the contributions of all the people who have helped build the United States. . . . [In addition, the teacher needs to create] a response to the increasing hostility in the United States toward immigrant groups" or people with lifestyles unlike their own culture (Singer and Harbour-Ridley 1998, 415). Teachers in particular need to be especially thoughtful in their word choice. The words that teachers use are critical as they set the tone for language in the classroom.

Regardless of the causes of prejudice, its pernicious effects are legendary. World history and current events, as they affect whole nations and races of people, are replete with the harmful results of prejudice. On an individual level, prejudice limits the opportunities of both those who are prejudiced and their victims, who often internalize society's negative stereotypes, leading to weakened self-esteem and ability to achieve. In a prejudiced society, the potential for various cultural groups to live together peacefully and to work together productively is greatly diminished.

This last effect assumes special significance in light of the large-scale demographic changes under way in the United States. The Hispanic population in the United States has surpassed that of African Americans and is rapidly exceeding it as a minority group. If current trends continue, and there is no indication that they will change, it is projected that by the year 2020, almost one out of two schoolchildren will be nonwhite. In addition to the large influx of Hispanics, there are large groups of Polish, Russian, and Indian people living in the United States. Many immigrants are living in the U.S. illegally. Concern is raised over what to do about the increasing numbers of illegal aliens who do not have insurance or pay taxes but still use social services such as health clinics and schools. Many institutions are having difficulty meeting high demands with limited resources.

"High quality preschool programs, computers in the home, and policies that allow for a more 'equitable distribution' of pupils from different racial and economic backgrounds across public schools can help reduce the learning deficits many children bring to kindergarten" (Jacobson 2002, 10). A recent study of 16,000 kindergartners was reported by Valerie E. Lee and David T. Burkam (2002) in *Inequality at the Starting Gate: Social Background Differences in Achievement as Children Begin School.* They found that kindergartners in the lowest fifth of socioeconomic status came from families who owned just 38 books as compared with 108 for kindergartners whose families are in the top fifth. Twenty percent of the poorest kindergartners have a computer in their homes as compared with 85 percent of kindergartners from the top-income level. Many low-income families use television more often than middle- and upper-class families to occupy their children's time. While children from the highest socioeconomic status watch television 11 hours a week, those from the lowest socioeconomic level view it 18 hours per week. Because many low-income parents must work two jobs to provide for their families, interaction between parents and their children may suffer. Educational and professional attainment is also a factor. Parents with professional jobs speak about 2,100 words an hour to their toddlers; those in poverty only about 600 words (Merrow 2002).

Diversity is rapidly becoming a fact of everyday life. As Carmen A. Rolón (2002/2003) writes:

> Racism is so pervasive in our society that it permeates our ideological orientations and our relations to people from racially and culturally diverse backgrounds. Even white teachers who are aware of racism should reflect on ways in which their own upbringing and education prevented them from learning about and appreciating the experiences and contributions of other groups to society. With the number of Latinos and other students of color increasing in our schools, it is time to embark on this most urgent endeavor. (43)

If diversity is to be a cause for celebration rather than a cause of contention, the prevention and reduction of prejudice are imperative.

Multicultural education and **bilingual education** are more than just learning about other cultures and languages. One of the major goals is to help all students— regardless of their cultural affiliations—develop more positive attitudes toward different cultural, racial, and ethnic groups (Banks and Banks 1997). A primary reason for developing positive attitudes toward people from different groups is that "being an active participant in American society requires individuals to assume many different roles and often requires the ability to interact with people from diverse backgrounds" (Sunal and Haas 1997, 378). Our task is no simple matter because, as Sleeter and Grant (1988, 208) put it, "People tend to live in small, rather insulated worlds with others who share their advantages or disadvantages."

For children, this insulation is heightened. Teachers need to consider multiculturalism as they plan for instruction (Weil, Calhoun, and Joyce 2003).

It would seem that learning about different ethnic groups, perhaps by researching and preparing reports on the contributions of diverse cultural groups, would lead to positive attitudes. But such is not necessarily the case, for knowledge or cognition alone does not lead to enlightenment. Prejudice is a complex phenomenon consisting of at least three related components—the cognitive, the affective, and the behavioral—and so it demands a multidimensional attack (Pate 1988).

Children who are low in prejudice show "more sensitivity and openness to other points of view" (Byrnes 1988, 269) and are able to think critically. Among the attitudes necessary for the growth of critical thinking are open-mindedness, flexibility, and respect for other viewpoints (Walsh 1988). Research suggests that activities and materials with a strong affective component that invite children to enter vicariously into the lives of people of different ethnic groups are effective in the development of this flexibility of perspective (Byrnes 1988). Once students begin to feel empathy, they are well on their way toward respecting diverse points of view and thus becoming less prejudiced.

Multicultural Unit of Study

The overarching goal of this chapter is to outline an instructional unit that represents the meshing of an important affective goal of multicultural and bilingual education with social studies content. The goal is the development of the ability to understand perspectives different from one's own and the content is knowledge about diverse cultural groups. The unit begins in Phase One with student participation in a variety of ethnic experiences. It proceeds to help students focus on a particular cultural group in Phase Two, and to develop an understanding of point of view and empathy in Phase Three. In Phase Four, students create characters from different cultural groups, writing from their characters' points of view, and share their products. The unit culminates in Phase Five, as students further immerse themselves by becoming their character's ally when they experience unjust treatment. An optional extension provides students with an opportunity to envision an entire multicultural community.

The unit uses children's books that invite vicarious experience with characters from a variety of cultural groups. These books, when taken together, represent a multicultural perspective. Research suggests that reading quality multiethnic literature can lead to increased awareness and decreased negative stereotyping of people from other cultures (Walker-Dalhouse 1993). At the end of the chapter is a bibliography of pertinent children's literature categorized by cultural group.

The unit's first three phases serve as rehearsal for subsequent stages of the writing process—revision, editing, and sharing—contained in the final phase. As the unit progresses, it also guides students through important aspects of the creative process: sensory stimulation, focusing, and incubation (see In the Classroom on the next page).

☞ **IN THE CLASSROOM**

Thematic Unit

Unit: Prejudice Reduction through Perspective Taking
Grade Levels: 5, 6, 7

Social Studies

• Research various cultures. Use new knowledge in the writing of language experience, point-of-view stories.

• Debate current issues. Encourage learners to assume different points of view from their own.

• Learn about the history of a variety of cultural groups—including those of students—in the United States.

• Engage in simulations such as "Bafa Bafa" and "Brown Eyes, Blue Eyes."

Math

• Write word problems using demographic data (see, e.g., Shaw 1993). Discuss implications of the data from the points of view of the cultural groups involved.

Science

• Explore the ways in which people are physiologically similar.

Art

• Learn about the use of perspective in drawing. Discuss the similarity between perspective in art and the ways in which our perspectives influence the ways we view people and events.

Physical Education/Health

• Learn and play games and dances popular in various cultural groups.

• Explore other cultures' views on wellness—for example, the holistic approach taken by many American Indians. Discuss how our views of health care could benefit from consideration of alternate views.

All Subjects

• Engage in activities that *require* the cooperation of all members of the group.

Phase One: Bombardment of Experiences

In Phase One, students participate in a variety of ethnic experiences, evidenced in both print and nonprint. The emphasis here is on exposure to diversity, on immersion without discrimination in the lives of people from a wide variety of cultural backgrounds. The teacher begins the unit by reading aloud a number of books that focus on the lives of children from various American cultures. The bombardment of experiences continues with whatever resources are available: guest speakers from the community; field trips to ethnic neighborhoods, restaurants, and museums with relevant exhibits; events for children during Black History Month (February) and Hispanic History Month (October); recordings of ethnic music, such as salsa, African American spirituals, rap, jazz, and reggae; and videotapes, DVDs, and films.

Teachers should also look to their own students, school, and local community and utilize the wealth of diversity of the people right at home. Many students and their parents, grandparents, and other relatives are happy to share their cultural history with interested students and teachers. Teachers and students alike also can invite school staff members, for example, cafeteria workers, bus drivers, custodians, bilingual aides, and tutors to give students a different perspective on their lives and cultures. High school and college students and white-collar professionals can have interesting stories to share. All of these resources can provide the material for life-expanding experiences and critical thinking opportunities for students of any age. Diversity includes not only those who have different cultural backgrounds, but also those who have experienced life from different points of view. For example, a person who has lived life with a disability can provide a different view of life on which students can reflect.

It is important in this phase for both print and nonprint experiences to be as primary and authentic as possible. That is, speakers should relate their own personal experiences in the spirit of storytelling rather than provide histories of their cultural groups. In selecting stories to read aloud, the teacher should try to choose those that reflect accurate patterns of language use, such as folktales and stories with realistic dialogue. In reading aloud, the teacher should remain true to those patterns and inflections to the best of his or her dramatic ability. Films and videos should be stories of lifelike, sympathetic characters rather than documentaries. When visiting ethnic neighborhoods, children should be encouraged to interact with residents and shopkeepers instead of communicating through the teacher or an interpreter.

The keys to continuity throughout this initial bombardment of experiences are quiet times, occurring at regular intervals, in which the teacher reads stories selected with an eye toward reinforcing and clarifying experiences students have recently had or whetting their appetites for experiences yet to come. Younger students may benefit from the shared book experience as created by Holdaway (1979). Through a series of seven steps, the entire class becomes involved in reading a single book. Typically, a "big book" is shared because the illustrations and print are large enough for children to see as they sit on the floor, gathered together around the teacher. The seven steps outlined by Holdaway are these:

1. The teacher selects a book and briefly introduces it to the students.
2. The teacher asks the students to make predictions about what they think will happen in the story.
3. The teacher reads aloud to the class, pointing to the words as they are read.
4. At preselected points, the teacher asks students to modify their predictions and to make new ones.
5. The book is reread, with the students joining in the oral reading with the teacher.
6. Students, singly or in pairs, volunteer to read the book or portions of it to the class.
7. The book is read either by the teacher or students to the class every day of the week.

Later, both students and teacher engage in sustained silent reading.

Primary-level students can engage in choral speaking or the reading of simple poetry. They can select a scene from a picture or a chapter from a book and act it out. They can make overhead transparencies to illustrate a story they have written about a specific culture and share them with the class. Upper elementary and middle school students can read the book themselves and engage in small group discussions.

Within the body of materials set aside for this phase of the unit, students should be encouraged to read whatever appeals to their interests of the moment. Time might be provided for students to respond actively and creatively to their reading. Students should be encouraged to think critically about the characters and situations of the stories they read. Questions can prompt reflection and discussion on ways in which the characters are different and similar to the students, ways in which the situation is familiar and unfamiliar, and so forth. Drawing students' attention to and inviting their reflection on the diversity of our world give students opportunities to express their opinions and, also, to ask questions about things that puzzle them, such as negative reactions to some people and some customs that they may have witnessed or engaged in themselves. Hoyt (1992) suggests that students add expression to their reading by dramatizing and illustrating stories and interpreting them through reader's theater. Students might also translate poetry into song and dance or write rap lyrics and perform them.

Phase Two: Focusing through Guided and Individualized Reading

After their immersion in a potpourri of diversity, students will probably be interested in particular cultural groups. Once students have deemed which group they would like to focus on for further study, the teacher divides the students into learning teams according to their stated preferences and assigns one or two books to each team. Each student reads silently and individually and engages in periodic conferences with the teacher or aide for the purpose of monitoring comprehension.

When a team finishes a book, the teacher conducts reading conferences with that team. Discussions are shaped by a sequence of questions designed to move students from the inside out—or getting inside the character's skin to achieve empathy. In Stage One, *viewing the character from the outside*, the teacher asks students to describe the character in terms of such characteristics as physical attributes, home life, family, school, food, feelings, beliefs, and religion. In Stage Two, *comparing oneself to the character,* the teacher prompts students to select the most important aspects of the character's life. To facilitate comparison, the teacher lists these aspects on a chart and instructs students to do the same. Students individually complete their charts, and the ensuing discussion focuses on comparing themselves with the character.

Still using the charts, in Stage Three, *identifying with the character*, students discuss the ways in which their lives are similar to the character's life. Finally, in Stage Four, *developing empathy,* the teacher asks students to predict their own and the character's responses to hypothetical situations. Introspection of one's own character traits, including faults, is something intermediate and middle school students often contemplate. Consider the problems Phil has in *The Jacket* (Clements 2002) when he searches the hallways to give his younger brother his lunch money. Spotting his brother's jacket, he quickens his step only to notice that the kid wearing it is not his brother but an African American boy named Daniel whom Phil has never seen before. A confrontation results with the principal interceding. Daniel was given the jacket by his grandmother, Phil's mother's cleaning lady. Daniel tells Phil, "You tell yo' mamma that my gramma and me don't need anybody being *kind* to us!" (15). His jumping to conclusions leads Phil to think about how he prejudges people who belong, who he chooses as friends, and how he reacts to people who look different than himself and his friends. This quick read (only 89 pages) for middle elementary grade students makes for superb class discussion on how appearances can lead to judgments that may be unwarranted.

The following is a sequence of questions that might be used with *The Jacket*.

Phase Two, Stage One: Viewing the Character from the Outside

- In what sort of a home does Daniel live—a house or an apartment building? How do you know? What sort of a home does Phil live in?
- Some children live in families with a mother and a father and sisters and brothers. Some children live in a family with just a mother. Sometimes the people in a neighborhood are like a family. What kind of family does Phil have? How about Daniel?
- How old do you think Phil and his brother are? How old is Daniel? What makes you think that?
- What do you know about Phil? About Daniel?

Phase Two, Stage Two: Comparing Oneself to the Character

With the teacher's help, students develop charts such as the one shown in figure 4.1 with the first two columns completed while the third and fourth columns vary from individual to individual. The following questions might be used with a predominantly white class in a middle-class suburban school:

- What is it like to move to a new school? How does it feel? How do you think Daniel felt?
- How do you get to school? How far away is your school from your house?
- How do you feel about your possessions and money? Have you ever been given a toy or clothes that someone else used to have but no longer needs? How did you feel about that?
- How is the way Phil talks different from the way you talk? From the way Daniel talks?
- When Daniel talks about his grandmother, how do you think he feels? What makes you think this way?

Phase Two, Stage Three: Identifying with the Character

- Think about your grandparents and aunts and uncles and cousins. How is your family like Phil's? Like Daniel's?
- How is Phil's mother like your mother?
- What TV show do you think you and Phil would both like? Would it be the same for Daniel and Phil?
- Think of all the ways that you and Daniel are alike.

Aspect	Daniel	Phil	Me	Same/Different?
Family				
Home				
Mother				
Economic background				
Attitude toward possessions				
Free time alone				

Figure 4.1 Sample comparison chart.

Phase Two, Stage Four: Developing Empathy

- Suppose you spent a Saturday with Daniel. What would you see and hear and smell? What would you and Daniel do?
- How would you feel if you transferred to Daniel's and Phil's younger brother's school?
- How would Daniel feel if he joined our class?
- What would you and Daniel do if you had him over to your house?
- Suppose you had to go without lunch because you didn't have enough money. How would you feel? How would you feel during the afternoon at school? Would you do well in your schoolwork?

- Do your sisters or brothers or friends ever borrow things from you and forget to return them? What do you do when that happens? If you were Phil and your friend borrowed an Xbox game and didn't return it, what would you do?
- How do you feel about the principal and what he did?

Sequence Flexibility

The progression suggested by this questioning sequence leads students in a gradual manner from viewing the character from an external, observer point of view to developing empathy, or viewing the world from the character's perspective. However, if students appear to be ready to empathize after completing their books, this sequence need not be followed in a lockstep manner. Depending on students' states of readiness, stages of the sequence might be omitted; the boundaries between the stages should remain flexible.

Similarly, at the conclusion of this phase of the unit, students should have a strong intuitive grasp of the concept "point of view" and may be ready to move immediately into the fourth phase of the unit, that of creating a character through language experience. However, the teacher may wish to use some or all of the activities in the Third Phase to provide students with additional practice in empathizing.

Phase Three: Point of View

The purpose of the third phase of the unit is to facilitate a deeper understanding of point of view and to discuss the concept with students in an explicit manner. Like the sequence of questions in the previous phase, the sequence of activities here moves students in a gradual progression—this time from their own physical points of view regarding an object to viewing life from the perspectives of people different from themselves.

Activity 1. The teacher places a globe in the center of the room, positions students around it in various locations, and asks them to draw it. The teacher then guides the students in comparing their finished pictures with questions such as these:

- You have all drawn the same thing. Why are all the pictures different?
- Tiffany and Jonathan were in almost the same place, but their pictures are still different. Why?
- Is one point of view right and the others wrong? Why or why not?

Activity 2. The students have learned that everyone has his or her own point of view (or own way of seeing things) and that no two points of view are ever exactly the same. Now the teacher asks the students to think about the globe's point of view with such questions as the following:

- If the globe had eyes, how do you think our room would look to it? What is the globe's point of view of our room?
- Is the globe a male or female or neither? Why?
- How does the globe feel being looked upon by us? Do you think it feels popular? Or do you think it would like a little privacy?
- How does the globe feel when we spin it around?

Teachers need to maintain high expectations as well as to provide enrichment activities for students in all school settings—urban, suburban, and rural.

Activity 3. Students simulate the experience of being visually or hearing impaired by wearing blindfolds or earplugs. Once they are sighted and hearing again, the teacher encourages them to discuss their experiences.

Visually Impaired

- How did you get around? Which senses did you use?
- Did you depend on other people to help you get around? How did you feel about having to depend on other people?
- Since you couldn't see the faces of people talking to you, how could you tell what they were feeling?
- Describe our classroom from your point of view as a person who is blind.

Hearing Impaired

- How did you communicate? How did you know whether you were talking loudly enough? Which senses did you use to understand other people?
- How did it feel to see people playing and talking and having a good time and not being able to hear them?
- Since you couldn't hear people's voices when they were talking to you, how did you know what they were feeling?
- Describe our classroom from your point of view as a person who is hearing impaired.

Up until Activity 2, when the teacher provides the meaning of point of view, the class has been "sneaking up" on a definition. When the teacher is sure that students grasp the meaning of the concept, she or he should reinforce it at every opportunity by relating point of view back to the characters in the books read in the second phase of the unit.

Phase Four: Creating a Character

At this point, students have been steeped in a wide array of ethnic experiences, and they have delved deeply and vicariously into the lives of one or more characters belonging to the cultural group in which they are the most interested. Students also possess a firm cognitive and affective understanding of point of view. They are now ready to create characters and write their own stories.

The fourth phase of the unit begins with a questioning sequence designed to help students imagine characters of their own creation, visualize settings for these characters, and as professional fiction writers do, view the world from the characters' perspectives. After informing students of the purpose of the upcoming activity, the teacher asks students individually to imagine people from the cultural groups they have explored in-depth. The teacher leads them though the process with questions, separated by pauses for reflection, such as the following:

• Is your person male or female?

• Is he or she a child or an adult?

• Is your person fat or thin or in between?

• What are the colors of your person's skin, hair, and eyes?

• What language does he or she speak?

• How does your person's voice sound? Is it soft or harsh, high or low?

• What is his or her name?

• Where does your person live? Does he or she live in the country with trees and rivers? Or in the desert? Or in the ice and snow? Does he or she live in the city?

• In what sort of dwelling does your person live—a house, an apartment, a tent, a cabin, or something else?

• What makes your person happy and sad?

The teacher then asks students to add flesh and bones to their characters by compiling portfolios consisting of completed character data sheets, such as the one shown in figure 4.2, and drawings of the character, his or her family, home, and other important aspects of his or her life. To help students get started, the teacher may wish to model the process with a character he or she has created. It is crucial that students begin work on their own portfolios as soon as possible before images fade.

When the portfolios are complete, students convene in teams representing their characters' cultural groups and are instructed to introduce each of their characters in such a way that all team members can "see each one in their mind's eye" and imagine each as a living person. After each introduction, students should be encouraged to ask each other questions similar to the questions from Stage Four in Phase Two. For example:

Character Data Sheet

Name _____ Age _____

Birthday _____ Ethnic group _____

Height _____ Weight _____ Hair color _____ Eye color _____

Address _____

_____

Place of birth _____

Describe your family _____

_____

_____

_____

What do you do during the day? _____

_____

What do you do for fun? _____

_____

If you go to school, what is your favorite subject? _____

What do people like most about you? _____

_____

Figure 4.2 A character data sheet such as this one is designed to help students flesh out their story characters.

- How would your character feel in our classroom?
- What is your character's point of view on McDonald's? Would it seem like a strange place to him or her?
- If your character had a whole free day, what would he or she do?

In answering these and similar questions, students round out aspects and visualize details of their characters that had not previously occurred to them. Before concluding this stage of character development, the teacher informs students that soon they will write stories from their characters' points of view.

Students engage in language experience as they dictate their stories. When the written versions are ready, students enter the writing process, as outlined by Robbins (1990), at the revision stage and proceed on to editing, either individually or in cooperative groups. The teacher works on her or his own story when not working with students.

Finally, students share their stories with the rest of the class and compile them in final form into a book. Students decide how they would like to present their creative efforts to parents and other students and teachers—perhaps via a program in which they dramatize their stories or read them in fireside storytelling sessions.

Phase Five: Becoming an Ally

At this point, students should have gotten the sense that for some people things are not as they should be. It is not enough to simply help the students to intellectually and emotionally identify with people's different experiences. The teacher must also help students develop the ability to become an active part of the solution when they see unjust things happening around them. According to Pang (2001b), one of the major goals of multicultural education is that "each child will examine social oppression and social privilege in both her/his personal life and in social institutions, and actively work toward eliminating inequalities" (103). Even very young children want to speak out as allies for their friends or others who they believe are being treated unfairly. Stern-LaRosa and Hofheimer Bettman (2000) encourage us to help children develop strategies for intervening when they are offended by jokes or hurt by name-calling, whether it is directed toward them or toward others.

In this phase, the teacher asks the students to think about a time when they heard someone tell a joke that was a put-down or an ethnic slur. The teacher leads them through a process of discussion and reflection about jokes with the following questions from Stern-LaRosa and Hofheimer Bettman (2000):

• What messages were conveyed in the joke?
• Who would be offended by the joke?
• What harm would there be in repeating the joke to one of your friends?
• Would the joke be okay to tell if someone who was being targeted by the joke was present?

The teacher then asks students to suggest ways in which to let the joke-teller know that his or her comments are offensive, hurtful, and unacceptable. These should include "I" messages such as "I don't think you're being fair when you say . . ." rather than "You" messages that assign blame and might make the person defensive and less likely to listen to the message. A poster listing the responses is created by the students and posted in the classroom.

The teacher then asks the students to work in groups and create a scenario in which someone tells a hurtful joke about one of the characters that they have created in Phase Four. Students write and perform a short play in which they take the roles of their characters and act as allies in support of one of their group who has been the target of an ethnic joke or hurtful comment. Each of the students should take a turn in speaking out against an injustice and thereby becoming an ally. As Stern-LaRosa and Hofheimer Bettman (2000) point out, simply practicing saying "I don't think that's funny" or "That name hurts my friend's feelings" is a powerful first step.

Extension: The Multicultural Community

This unit began with a wide-angle, multicultural view as students were immersed in a plethora of ethnic experiences. Starting with Phase Two the focus narrowed, with students selecting particular cultural groups they wished to explore.

The focus narrowed further as students articulated their visions of single characters. As the unit progressed, its focus became still finer and more specific.

If student interest remains strong, the teacher may consider widening the focus again to help students develop a fresh multicultural perspective. Implementing this extension, in which students create multiethnic communities and write stories about them, will bring the unit full cycle.

As a whole group, students decide which characters might live in the same community, with the only stipulation being that a variety of cultural groups must be represented. Arranged in community groups, students engage in discussions with a purpose similar to that of the previous character-creation questioning sequence. They travel together on a collective imaginative journey, hitchhiking off each other's ideas, to visualize a community: its physical setting, its name, the characters' relationships to one another, and the ways they interact. Materials in the group portfolio might include such items as maps of the community and phone books.

Keeping in mind the physical and interactive communities they have created, students engage in group language experiences as they discuss possible story lines with their ideas being recorded by a group member. Each group dictates its story, perhaps in "chain" fashion. When the initial version of the story is complete, students begin revising and editing, both of which promise to be more involved and time-consuming than before because students are now working with the whole class. Questions conducive to reflection on living together in multicultural communities include the following:

- As you were thinking of your story, did it matter that your characters came from different cultural groups? Why or why not?
- Were some people more powerful and important than others? Why or why not?
- You probably did not write down any rules or laws your community had for living together. If you had, what would these rules and laws be?
- How did the people in your community deal with conflicts?
- Do you think people in your community live together the way people *should* live together? Is your community a good model for us to follow in the real world?
- Let's think about our own country as a great big community with many, many different cultural groups. How should we treat each other if we are going to live and go to school and work together peacefully?

This extension takes an inductive approach as students derive codes of conduct from the ways their individual characters interact in a multicultural setting. To place special emphasis from the beginning on the means by which people live together in diverse communities, the teacher may wish to take an opposite, deductive approach in which students first formulate rules and laws for peaceful coexistence and resolution of conflicts. Story lines then unfold in accordance with these predetermined codes of conduct. The ensuing discussion explores the extent to which their characters abided by the community's rules and whether these rules should be modified.

☞ IN THE CLASSROOM

Teaching about Culture

Culture can be defined as the values, beliefs, perspectives, and ways of interacting that distinguish one group of people from another. Another way of defining culture is its program for survival in and adaptation to particular environments. We can see an example of these definitions in groups of people who have experienced discrimination in their environments through their need to tightly cling to their cultures and sometimes to the language of their communities.

It is important for students to realize that we all have at least one culture—even if we are in the majority and are not aware of having a distinct culture. Culture often influences us at a subconscious level, and sometimes it is easier to see the cultural influences in other people than in ourselves.

It is also important for students to understand that there are many different kinds of culture: ethnic, gender, socioeconomic, religious, and geographic region, to name a few. Just because people come from one culture does not mean they cannot be part of another. For example, a person might grow up in the South but live as an adult in the Midwest, or a student might be African American but attend school with mostly European American classmates. Sometimes there may be more than one culture present in a person's home. For instance, a student's mother may be Christian and his or her father Jewish.

Finally, it is important for students to understand that no culture is superior to another: *every* culture makes significant contributions to society. In order to feel comfortable with people whose cultures are different from ours, we must first feel comfortable with our own cultural background. Next, we should learn about other cultures—and the easiest and most effective way to do that is to make friends with people who are different from ourselves.

Cultural Awareness

Cultural awareness means far more than the designated multicultural month of February celebrated in most American schools. It requires much more than speeches, reports, bulletin boards, displays, and school assemblies for one month of the year to acknowledge that everyone has a culture. Cultural awareness does not mean presenting the contributions of each culture in isolation. It does mean understanding the interactions of the contributions of various cultures. It means making cultural connections.

Cultural awareness means understanding that each of us has a culture that is part of our very being. Together, we all make up the tapestry called America. We each bring threads of cultural values, historical pride, experiences, and aspirations to this fabric. Understanding and respecting cultural differences and similarities perpetuate an environment conducive to an appreciation of life.

In the nineteenth and twentieth centuries, our society viewed the perfect solution to cultural differences as a melting pot. This ideological assumption fostered the idea of a nation where people of diverse backgrounds would blend into one. Ethnic groups would assimilate to form one culture identity. It expected each person to begin the process of acculturation, to trade in his or her own unique language and customs, in essence, his or her own consciousness, for the new culture. It resulted in no individual culture appreciation, no existence of ethnicity. If all the cultures in the United States could be melted together, they would only produce a tasteless homogenized pretense of humanity.

After society recognized the folly of the melting pot idea, the metaphor of a stew or salad began to capture society's view of its cultural self. However, this allowed individuals to dictate which cultural qualities should or should not be chosen as part of an American stew or salad. Such elitism promotes the destruction of cultural pride and esteem, encouraging discrimination and prejudice. It does not

---

☞ IN THE CLASSROOM

Multiethnicity

As the minorities become the majority in most U.S. schools, teachers recognize the need to develop appropriate curricula that will foster our country's democratic philosophy. It becomes necessary for teaching strategies and the classroom environment to change in order to meet the needs of the new majority. Pang (2001b) emphasizes the need for the teacher's understanding of self and other cultures before attempting to create a multicultural classroom environment.

Although current thought is caught between the clash of two paradigms, assimilationism and ethnic pluralism, the focus will be on the latter. A sensitivity to all students predisposes their academic success. All children should learn and take pride in their own ethnicity; they should learn and respect the ethnicity of others. In this chapter, two ethnic groups are explored: Asian and Pacific Americans (APAs) and Mexican Americans. An appreciation of diversity and unity must be developed through the encouragement of multiple perspectives. James Banks (Banks and Banks 1997) reminds us that the "west" in our "U.S. western movement" is, for Mexicans, the "north," for the Chinese, the "east," and for the Sioux, the center of the universe. An important part of this development is a willingness to make decisions through compromise. Students must learn to accept alternate perspectives regarding the same phenomenon. Cook and Gonzales (1994) offer the multiethnic classroom as the place for this to happen.

To reduce prejudice and foster tolerance, we must teach people history, not as facts and dates but as popular movements. Time lines and events must translate to the history of common people. Each historic figure should not be portrayed as a hero, but as a human being with both good and bad characteristics. George Washington and Thomas Jefferson were great men; however, they also owned slaves. Teach the whole story. Don't rewrite history to present a balanced picture. Focus on the major ideas of history and all the ethnic groups that are part of history. Don't focus on any one single cultural group for Cultural Awareness Month. And note that not just one culture can be singled out for prejudice. For instance, in the late 1800s, Irish immigrants arriving in New York were told there were no jobs for them, just as the Chinese were rudely being greeted with the same message in San Francisco Bay.

Labor and immigration are focal points of *Bread and Roses, Too*, a historical novel by Katherine Paterson (2006) of the mill worker strikes in Lawrence, Massachusetts. Rosa, a 12-year-old Italian immigrant, desires to obtain an education and feels humiliated when her mother and older sister join the laborers in walking out of the mills. When the tension increases, the children are sent to live temporarily with families in other towns. Rosa ends up living with a stonecutter in Barre, Vermont, as do other children. Before she gets to Barre, she meets Jake, an orphan, who convinces her to claim he is her brother since he has nowhere else to go. Ethnic rivalries and prejudices play an important role in this historical novel.

recognize the need for pluralism in society or the individual's need of encultura-tion, the process of absorbing one's own culture. The variations in culture patterns are the strength of a multigroup society with an emphasis on diversity. Today, the idea of the melting pot has given way to the idea that our society is a kaleidoscope, an ever-changing pattern of different cultures combined under the American cul-tural values of freedom, justice, and liberty for all. It is not necessary for a person to give up his or her first language/culture to learn a second. Biliteracy development is not only possible, but also should be encouraged. When schools help students become bicultural and biliterate, they are creating citizens capable of maintaining freedom and democracy for the United States.

The image of a national fabric or tapestry precludes a respect and acceptance of all humankind's diversities. It makes all of us a part of this nation and allows for the appreciation and interaction of cultures. There is the view that no social intimida-tion threatens the loss of any individual culture. While allowing for cultural assimi-lation, it does not rob the individual of his or her culture. This view is by no means universally accepted. Janzen (1994) offers an explanation of the ethnic pluralism/ assimilation (melting pot) debate, a debate that will be played out in schools.

The Complex Diversity within the Asian and Pacific American Communities

Based on 2000 census data, the fastest growing minority group in the United States was the Asian and Pacific Americans (APAs). By the year 2040, it is pro-jected that the APA population will increase from the current 7.3 million to more than 34 million. But confusion blankets the term APA. Ethnic ties include Chinese, Japanese, Filipino, Korean, Hmong, Vietnamese, Cambodian, Laotian, Thais, Malaysians, East Indians, and Pakistanis. Each of these groups of people maintains a separate thread of identity and history.

The first Asian immigrants were attracted to the California gold rush in 1848. They arrived from the district of Toishan, in the south China province of Kwang-tung. Ninety-five percent of this population was male. Large numbers of females did not arrive until after 1945. The first Japanese immigrants arrived in Hawaii in 1868. Their history in this country includes their 1942 removal from the West Coast and internment in relocation camps in various states. They differed greatly from the first Chinese immigrants in that they had the advantage of maintaining their family structure as they immigrated to the United States.

The third major Asian group to arrive in America were Filipino. Their num-bers grew in Hawaii and they eventually migrated to California. Like their prede-cessors, they too met with anti-Asian attitudes. They were followed by Koreans in the early 1900s.

The end of the war in Vietnam in 1975 resulted in a large number of educated Vietnamese entering the United States. This was followed in 1979 by a second large wave of mainly less-educated "boat people." Both groups have met with mixed reac-tions and success. Many of these refugees spent time in camps waiting to enter the United States. The Cambodians were next to follow. The formally educated Cambodians spoke their own language and French (the language of the educated and the government). They suffered many atrocities before arriving in the United States.

One of the authors of this chapter, Mary Louise Ginejko, spent several years teaching in an elementary school during that period. The school found it difficult to locate anyone who could translate for the many Asian immigrants. In Laos, Cambodia, and Vietnam at least 20 languages are spoken. Neither the Asian children nor their parents and members of their immediate family could speak English. Before arriving in this country, however, some children learned "military French" from the camps. This also proved to be a problem to those who understood French.

The immigrants' first Halloween in the United States was traumatic. They believed strongly in the spirit world and were shocked, frightened, and confused by children wearing masks and roaming the neighborhood in the dark. Mary Louise learned this from the Hmong when they started making masks in class. The families had no familiar support groups or other family waiting here in this country to help explain American customs.

Many of the APAs (children as well as adults) had never been in a school. Many were farmers and this was their first contact with formal education in any form. Teachers discovered a need to help parents adjust to our country. Mary Louise remembers trying to explain a water bill to a family who spoke no English and had no concept of "bill." Educators were fortunate to have church groups sponsor families; they played a big part in education as well.

As teachers, they learned early that not all Asian groups were friendly with each other. It was not uncommon to see two children begin fighting for no apparent reason until the teacher realized one was Vietnamese and the other Cambodian. It was a learning experience for children and teachers alike.

The APA children were eager to communicate. Teachers and children volunteered for English classes held before school began each morning. As more APA immigrants came into the school, they had the support of the first group.

Understanding Mexican Culture

The history of Mexico is both complex and fascinating. When Cortes landed on the continent, he brought horses and improved weaponry, including cannons and guns, along with the culture of Spain and Roman Catholicism. Cortes discovered that the Aztecs ruled by demanding tribute in the form of goods and people to sacrifice. Montezuma II, leader of the Aztecs, decided to persuade Cortes to leave rather than immediately blocking the Spanish invasion. Cortes led his army of conquistadors along with indigenous Indian tribes who had suffered under Aztec control against the Aztecs, killing their leader for his indecision. When smallpox broke out among the Indian people, the Spanish, who had more resistance against European diseases, were able to take the Aztec capital, now known as Mexico City. Spain sought to gain wealth as a nation while the Catholic clergy sought to convert the Indians to Roman Catholicism. Only Spaniards born in Spain were named to major governmental positions to ensure that Spain would maintain its control over colonial Mexico (Berger and Bratzel 2006).

Between 1960 and 1970, 200,000 Mexicans immigrated to the United States. This number grew to 2.1 million between 1980 and 1990. Today, between nine and ten million Mexicans live in the United States and approximately 40 to 50 percent of them are undocumented. In 2004, the amount of money transferred by Mexican workers living in other countries back to their families in Mexico was $16.6 billion. This is roughly the same amount as foreign investment in Mexico for the same year, $16.2 billion (Curzio 2006).

By 2000, the fastest growing minority group in the United States was Hispanic, due largely to the sizeable numbers of illegal immigrants crossing the border between Mexico and the United States. In the state of Arizona alone, it is estimated that over 50,000 illegal aliens attempt to cross the border each month. Understanding Mexican culture is important for us as teachers as well as our students. Crafts are evident in Mexican family life. The midday meal may be spread out on a handwoven tablecloth. Colorful stone containers decorate the kitchen. Celebrations of baptism, *quinceñiera* (a celebration for girls turning fifteen in which they are presented to the community at large; also called *quince anos*), and marriage may find clothing for females decorated with *mola* (brightly colored appliqué panels). Quince anos/quinceñiera rates even higher than marriage in importance in Mexican culture. As such, families spare no expense to produce a lavish gathering for their 15-year-old daughters. Weddings, on the other hand, are paid for by godparents and aunts and uncles.

Traditional crafts reveal a people's beliefs, history, and values and should be shared with students. Mexican handicrafts that are most widely recognized are Aztec stone carvings, Huichol (pronounced Wee-choi) Indian yarn painting, and Kuna Indian molas (traditional appliqué panels on clothing, particularly blouses). The Aztec Empire was a combination of several societies. The Aztecs, who had a calendar year 18 months in length, believed that the world would end every 52 years. In AD 1479, during the reign of the sixth Aztec monarch, a huge stone was carved and dedicated to the sun. Dianne Turner (2002) suggests having students make their own Aztec sun stones by doing the following steps:

Materials: 2 to 4 ounces of Crayola white Model Magic, acrylic paints (bright colors, including gold), paint brushes, and a clear-coat spray.

- Roll the Model Magic into a ball (it is a clean medium and will not stain desks).
- Flatten the ball on the desk.
- Using the top of a paper or plastic cup as a template and a plastic knife, cut out a circular shape.
- Make a radial template from a manila folder and cut the sun rays out of the Model Magic.
- Position the radial rays around the sun.
- Use more Model Magic to make facial features on the sun (nose, eyes, and lips).
- Paint the sun with acrylic or tempera paints; use gold paint around the rays as is traditional in Mexico.
- Let dry for three hours and spray with clear coat to protect.
- Mount on individual pieces of construction paper and paste on black poster board to display.

Turner also suggests an Aztec calendar Web site to accompany this project: http:// www.ai.mit.edu/people/monalvo/Hotlist/aztec.html.

Mola appliqué panels are brightly colored and are made by Kuna Indian women in Panama. Because the panels are labor intensive, it may take 100 hours to create a blouse. Students in grades three through six can make their own molas using four sheets of construction paper (one black sheet for the background and three different colored sheets to use for the design), scissors, paper clips, and glue. Students create their own designs with the colored construction paper and glue them to the black construction paper. Designs should include a border. The final molas can be displayed on a bulletin board.

Huichol Indians, who live in central Mexico, use yarn painting to communicate with the spirit world as a form of prayer. The men of the Huichol Indian tribe use beeswax warmed in the sun and spread on thin boards. Strands of colored yarn are pressed into the beeswax to form a yarn picture. Nature provides most of the designs—animals and plants. Colors are symbolic. Red is the east, grandfather, fire, and is deemed masculine. Blue is the south, the Pacific Ocean, water, rain, and feminine. White is the Cloud Spirits. Green represents earth, heaven, healing, and the heart. Students in grades 2 through 8 can use crayons to make their design on paper first then use cardboard, white glue, and yarn to make their final yarn paintings (Turner 2002). A Web site on yarn painting is "Yarn Painting: Images of a Vanishing Culture" and can be found at http://www.Mexconnect.com/mex_ huichol/ abt_huit.htm. See the Children's Literature Recommendations list at the end of the chapter for a list of children's books with a Hispanic focus.

Personal Observation of the Mexican American Community

The Mexican American enters the U.S. educational system with a rich literary, political, economic, and historical background. Acuña (1988), Kanellos (1990), and Keefe and Padilla (1987) provide an extensive account of the Mexican American experience in the United States. For our purposes, we will briefly examine the cultural values of Mexican Americans and how they influence teaching styles.

While recognizing the diversity within the Mexican American culture, one can make the following observations about the traditional Mexican American value system. This culture promotes a strong emotion of identity with its loyalty to family, community, and ethnic group. Achievement for children means achievement of the family, not necessarily individual achievement as is encouraged in many Anglo-American children. It is important to the education of Mexican American students to include parent involvement as part of the educational process. Parents provide a positive support system. Every possible attempt should be made to keep parents informed of their child's progress. Sending work home or accepting items from the home for display strengthens the necessary home-school relationship.

Competition in school can be confusing when one's culture dictates cooperation for mutual rewards. Mexican American students function better in cooperative learning situations. Motivation is found in the group activity rather than in the personal gain of achievement or grade.

Another strong value to be considered is sensitivity to the needs and feelings of other people. Relationships become personalized and interpersonal. Teachers should encourage children to help each other. Mexican American children are attuned to verbal and nonverbal calls for help. They are also the recipients of such help in their culture. This may in part explain their reluctance to ask the teacher a question; their request for help may be nonverbal.

The Mexican American humanistic orientation extends beyond the immediate family into the community. Extended families include: *primos* (cousins), those with the same last name but no blood relation; *tocayos* (namesakes), those with the same first name; *concuños* (brothers-in-law), two or more men married into the same family; *cuñadas* (sisters-in-law); and very important *padrinos* (godparents), *ahijados* (god-children), and *compadres,* natural parents of godparents. Children acquire two godparents at baptism, one godparent when they receive the Sacrament of the Eucharist, and one godparent when they make their confirmation in the Catholic Church. Female children may also choose to have a quinceñiera when they become 15 years old. It is possible at this ceremony for a girl to receive an additional 10 to 15 godparents. *Damas* (bridesmaids) and *chamberlans* (grooms) also become participants. In this ceremony, as throughout their life, the *abuelos* (blood grandparents) play a major role.

Mexican American children learn security through interpersonal relationships rather than institutional assistance. In school, students also expect a close and personalized relationship with the teacher. They view their teacher as a mother or father in a classroom environment. They expect to see personal family pictures or even visits from the teacher's family members. Mexican American students function better in a humanized curriculum. Traditionally, a more personalized curriculum offers more meaning. Their culture is child centered rather than task centered.

In such an extended family, the status and role of the individual is precisely defined. These roles are usually dictated by sex and age. Older children have more responsibilities than younger children. This should be a consideration when assigning homework. Mexican American parents may find it difficult to understand why teachers feel that schoolwork is more important than home responsibilities. Parents may feel that staying home for a family commitment is as important as going to school for the day. Sexual roles are clearly defined. Females are responsible for the condition of the home, preparation of food, health care, child rearing, and religious obligations. Males have a higher status. They are the wage earners. Teachers should be aware of this when assigning duties.

A powerful factor in the lives of Mexican Americans is their identification with Mexican Catholic ideology. This forceful power reinforces their value system. Lack of respect for parents or customs is sinful. Any interpretation of failure to meet family responsibilities is a serious infraction. Guilt becomes a serious consequence. A cycle of failure begins. This is evident in the psychological and physical school dropout rate. Teachers must intervene by making students aware of the educational continuum and long-range goals rather than let them become discouraged by immediate setbacks.

Second-language learners need to be given lots of opportunities to work with first-language learners in order to acquire English and become confident in using it.

English Language Learners in the Social Studies Classroom

While there is an increasing awareness of the diversity of students, there is also great controversy over the placement of English language learners. Rosalie Pedalino Porter (1990) has questioned whether placement decisions are based on the children's needs or on the needs of politicians and bureaucrats. She condemns Transitional Bilingual Education (TBE), which provides native-language instruction in content area subjects while students are also learning English as a second language. She purports that this is an unjust form of segregation, thereby sending a message that these students are remedial or less than acceptable in general education classes. The editors of *When They Don't All Speak English,* Pat Rigg and Virginia G. Allen, (1989, ix) agree: "[S]econd-language students need to be with first-language students. If they are isolated from active-English-speaking students, they cannot learn English from them, nor can they share any of the riches they have to offer." According to Lim and Watson (1993, 393).

> Combining authentic and natural language experiences with content-rich classroom practices leads to optimal language learning and optimal subject matter learning. When the instructional focus moves away from language as an object

and away from content as facts to a content-rich, usable language, second-language learners will gain confidence in themselves, and their knowledge of both language and content will flourish. Effective language learning, either native or second language, depends not on the direct teaching of identified skills, but rather on a sound philosophy of learning and teaching, underlying a meaning-filled curriculum.

Some educators disagree with this argument.

One of the boldest conclusions Porter (1990) offers is a rejection of the concept that first language and cognitive abilities should be learned in the native language so that these skills can be more easily transferred into the second language. This concept is based on the research that has consistently shown that it takes from five to seven years for ELLs to fully develop the cognitive academic language needed to compete with their general education peers (Cummins 1981, 1994; Thomas and Collier 1997). Conversational language ability (which Cummins calls Basic Interpersonal Conversation Skills or BICS) is usually mastered relatively quickly by ELLs, typically in one to two years. Teachers, administrators, and even parents often make the mistake of thinking that ELLs who speak fluently about social matters and simple, concrete concepts have reached mastery level or native-like proficiency in English. But ELLs also need to develop the higher and more complex level of Cognitive Academic Language Proficiency (CALP) (Cummins 1994) in order to comprehend the context-reduced, abstract concepts of content matter classes. Providing content matter instruction to students in their native language allows them to make progress toward grade-level content norms while they are still developing their cognitive academic English language proficiency. Although this is worthy of detailed examination, the focus of this chapter is on the challenges of the general education classroom teacher.

This part of the chapter addresses the concerns of the general education teacher who is becoming increasingly aware of the large number of students in the classroom who speak English only as a second language. It is becoming increasingly rare to find classrooms without a student whose native language is other than English. Nearly 40 million people in the United States communicate in 329 different languages. Spanish is the most commonly spoken language after English. Over half of first language Spanish speakers communicate at home in Spanish.

Many children are Mexican American students. They are part of a group referred to as people of color. Membership in this group is exclusively reserved for nonwhite minority individuals. James A. Banks (Banks and Banks 1997, xviii) defines *people of color* as follows:

> In most instances, the phrase *people of color* rather than *ethnic minority* is used to refer to groups such as Mexican Americans, African Americans, Puerto Ricans, and Native Americans. *People of color* is used to reflect new demographic realities: These groups are majorities rather than minorities in a growing number of schools and school districts.

Of the three major Hispanic groups, Mexican Americans are increasing in the U.S. population at a much faster rate than Puerto Ricans and Cubans. When considering statistics, one should keep in mind that the population figures given by the

U.S. Census Bureau are invalid in terms of the Mexican American population in the United States because a substantial number of undocumented Mexican aliens enter the United States in search of work every year. Moreover, the birthrate in Hispanic communities tends to be higher than in white communities.

Because of this unknown number of undocumented aliens and the large number of legal immigrants coming from Mexico to the United States, teachers have more Hispanic students to teach each year. Few general education teachers have had any specialized training in working with English language learners. Even so, teachers sometimes have predisposed expectations about the student and themselves that are not based on fact. Because xenophobia (fear of foreigners) is, unfortunately, still an intricate part of American society, teachers must strive to be sensitive to the needs of all children. General education teachers can gain confidence in themselves and their professional abilities by becoming more knowledgeable about Mexican American culture and the cultures of all their students, as well as by examining teaching strategies that promote rather than impede learning for all English language learners in both first-language and second-language classrooms. The next section offers insights into respecting and understanding culture to assist educators in carrying out their responsibility to support all their students in reconceptualizing American society.

Cultural Sensitivity through Interdisciplinary Teaching Strategies

Being sensitive to the educational needs of children means listening to all cultural voices and promoting the skills necessary to become a successful member of society (Parker and Jarolimek 1997). Integrated instruction provides a reason to learn both a new language and academic content at the same time, which helps students to become active learners. English language learners experience specific academic difficulties that teachers should consider. Factors that influence the success of an English language learner are past life experience, personal/family educational experiences, self-image, learning styles, multiple intelligence, classroom organization and management, perceived teacher/student roles, body language, proxemics, gestures, facial expressions, and the amount of cognitive academic language proficiency that the student has developed. Approaches to language and content acquisition require sensitivity to sociocultural interrelations. Teaching strategies can make a significant difference in second language and academic achievement (Feinberg and Morencia 1998). This section suggests ways in which teachers can use integrated instruction strategies to promote the language and academic development of these students. First, let's look at the situation ELLs may find themselves in.

Initially, English language learners are placed in a bilingual education classroom or an ESL classroom. In a bilingual education classroom, the students receive instruction in English as a second language as well as content area instruction in their native language. This use of two languages is deemed necessary because of the need to keep students on track with their academic content learning as their English language skills gradually improve. Learning in their first language is the most efficient and effective way in which to meet that need. The ESL program differs. Students attend ESL classes for part of the day and are mainstreamed into general education classes for the remaining portion of the day. Exit from either program is accomplished by passing a language proficiency test.

☞ IN THE CLASSROOM

Thematic Unit Activities: Immigration (Grade 6)

Making your English language learners a welcome and integral part of your classroom community is a key ingredient in the recipe for success for these students. Listed below are activities in which your students' wealth of diverse knowledge is brought to the forefront, celebrated, and validated. Through these activities, the entire class expands their multicultural knowledge base.

1. Draw your family tree: use pictures, write down any anecdotes you know about any family members, write about which member had the greatest influence on you.

2. When and how did your family arrive? How did historical events affect your family (Gold Rush, Irish potato famine, Industrial Revolution, Great Depression, World War II, the Korean War, Vietnam War)? What language did they speak? Create a profile of the year your family arrived in this country.

3. Describe your favorite family holiday. Does your family eat certain traditional foods? Does your family have any sentimental treasures? Have you ever been to a family reunion? How would you plan one? Interview family members.

4. Make a welcome booklet for students arriving from different cultures. Share information they will need at school and in the neighborhood. Don't forget to include idioms (e.g., "Don't dis me, man"), phone numbers (e.g., doctors), stores (e.g., grocery store), and so on. Plan a one-day tour around your town: list Places/times.

5. Make an ancestor doll; identify the doll by name, country, and interesting information.

6. Create a Venn diagram: Slavery/Indentured Servitude. Write three paragraphs: (1) Same, (2) Different, (3) Best.

7. Make a chart: Bread Basket listing country/name of bread/description (e.g., Mexico/tortilla); Fairy Tale listing title/country/hero/villain/magic/lesson (e.g., Sleeping Beauty); Folk Art listing country/name/materials/directions (e.g., Polish/wycinaki); Science, Spices listing country/spice/plant/use (can be accompanied by a display of spices in small jars with holes in the lids for sampling); Math, Population listing who/when/how many/why; Art, Population (e.g., pictorial time line showing waves of immigration).

8. Put on an International Festival: organize each classroom into cooperative groups with each group representing a different country. Students make themselves passports (including a self-portrait) that can be stamped at each country visited. Culmination includes a dinner and entertainment representing a variety of countries. Remember to invite parents and guest speakers. Participants may receive an international cookbook compiled by the students.

9. Assemble a bulletin board: Flag display (e.g., world flag quilt); Hall of Fame (e.g., famous immigrants); Word display (e.g., words borrowed from other countries); Welcome (e.g., foreign words).

10. Take a field trip to an ethnic restaurant.

☞ IN THE CLASSROOM

Using Literature and Technology to Teach about the Middle East

John W. Logan, PhD, Assistant Superintendent, Northbrook School District 27, Northbrook, IL

My life changed dramatically when I moved from Chicago to Saudi Arabia to accept a one-year sabbatical assignment as a curriculum director in an international school district. In this new role, I visited many classrooms and school libraries. After just a few visits to classrooms, I realized quickly that children from the international community share a keen, natural interest in learning about their transplanted home and its rich cultural heritage. To promote a better understanding of the Middle East, teachers use extensive literature collections and technology (especially video-tapes and CD-ROMs) to teach about all areas, including the fine arts, politics, language, geography, science, cooking, religion, architecture, and history. This article presents information about narrative and expository literature useful in teaching students about the Middle East. Also, it provides several videotape, DVD, and CD-ROM resources to support the suggested reading literature. Finally, the article provides classroom literacy activities to help teachers introduce students to the wonderful and mysterious world of the Middle East.

Exploring Middle Eastern Literature

In *The Day of Ahmed's Secret* by Florence Parry Heide and Judith Heide Gilliland (1990), readers share in a day of the life of a young Middle Eastern boy. The colorful illustrations reflect a realistic view of the sights and sounds of a Middle East town. The story is told from the main character's point of view and is especially appropriate for young readers.

A timeless, heartfelt book for children of all ages and written more than fifty years ago is Sue Alexander's *Nadia the Willful* (1983). The story is about a Bedouin family (Arab desert people) whose favorite son disappears forever and how his sister, Nadia, keeps his memory alive despite her father's proclamation that no one speak about the brother ever again.

Ali Baba and the Forty Thieves (Early 1989) retells the most popular story from the classic tales in *The Thousand and One Nights*. This retelling features the exquisite and highly detailed illustrations of Australian artist Margaret Early. The illustrations are designed to represent authentic Persian miniatures of the tenth century. In addition to reading the classic tale of Ali Baba and his encounter with robbers, teachers can use the illustrations to teach children about various components of art.

A most fascinating translation of a 3,000-year-old Egyptian fairy tale, written directly from an original papyrus manuscript (British Museum, London), is entitled *The Prince Who Knew His Fate* (Manniche 1981). In this book, Lise Manniche creates illustrations about one of the world's oldest known fairy tales. She copies Egyptian artwork done during the time the story was written on the original, ancient scroll. At the end of the book, she includes a narrative about how she came to write the book and provides her own perspective as an author about the historical value of ancient writing.

With U.S. soldiers currently stationed in Afghanistan and Iraq, students should learn about these countries. The following three books for fifth through eighth graders are appropriate. The first, *The Story of My Life: An Afghan Girl on the Other Side of the Sky* (Ahmedi and Ansary 2005), is the autobiography of a young Afghan girl portraying the struggles she faced with the Taliban. Another book is *Shabanu* (Staples 1989), which portrays arranged marriages that are part of Middle Eastern culture. The last book, *Under the Persimmon Tree* (Staples 2005), is a young adult novel with yet another female protagonist. Najmah's father and brother are taken away by members of the Taliban and a bombing raid kills her mother and baby brother, forcing the young girl to fend for herself. Believing that her very survival depends on crossing the border to a refugee camp in Pakistan, Najmah eventually meets an American woman, a teacher of refugee children, whose husband gives medical aid to the refugees.

Informational Books, Videotapes, and CD-ROMs That Teach about the Middle East

Beginning readers will enjoy learning how to count in Arabic (from 1 to 10) in Jim Haskins's *Count Your Way Through the Arab World* (1991). In this book, Arabic numbers are written phonetically to help the reader pronounce them. The numbers are written in both English and Arabic languages. Also, the book provides a brief overview of the Arab world and Islamic beliefs using language young children can understand. The book is an excellent resource for teachers who want to teach young children how to count in another language.

Informational book series generally contain descriptive chapters and colorful photography about specific countries in the Middle East. Series books explore a country's special geography, people, history, government, industry, culture, and other topics. Intermediate and middle grade level students will find the following series selections of interest. In *Enchantment of the World: Iran*, Mary V. Fox (1991) provides accounts of where and how Iranians live; the rich cultural heritage of Iran; and a photographic tour of Iran. *Iraq . . . in Pictures* (Lerner Publications 1992) is another example of a well-documented, yet highly readable chapter book from an informational books series that uses a variety of photographs to support the book's thorough content.

Ali, Child of the Desert (London 1997) is a picture book which portrays the modern life of an Arabian child. The story goes through a day for young Ali.

Young adult readers will find *The Gulf War Reader,* edited by Micah L. Sifry and Christopher Cerf (1991), a rich resource to learn the historical background and causes of Desert Storm. Several contributors are world leaders such as former Presidents George Bush and Jimmy Carter. Even Saddam Hussein provides a perspective of the war.

Desert Storm: The War in the Persian Gulf (Time-Warner New Media 1991), is a compelling interactive CD-ROM that chronicles the events of Desert Storm. This CD-ROM was assembled by the editorial staff of *Time* and provides a compilation of reports, eyewitness accounts, photographs, audio recordings, and research about Desert Storm.

The British-made videotape series *ARABIA: Sand, Sea, and Sky* (FF & McKinnon 1990) provides three perspectives of the unique natural history of the Arabian Peninsula. The first videotape in the series, *The Mountain Barrier,* explores Arabia's wildlife in the high Sarawat mountains of western Arabia. In this video, exotic birds, snakes, lizards, and the barren landscape are featured, including a look at the volcanic moonscape land and rugged mountains. In *Red Sea Rift,* the second videotape of the series, thousands of miles of the Red Sea off the coast of Arabia are visited, all teeming with spectacular sea life. This videotape also explains the feeding behaviors and lifecycles of various sea life. Characteristics of marine behavior of each zone are examined. The third videotape in the series is entitled *Eye of the Camel.* Filmed as a journey with a Bedouin family on their winter migration through the country's Empty Quarter, viewers also learn of the many survival strategies used by desert wildlife including camels, gazelle, oryz, plants, and insects. A visit to al-Hasa Oasis bridges modern life with the heritage of ancient traditions.

Classroom Literacy Activities That Promote Middle East Awareness

The following are literacy-based classroom activities that teachers can use to help children understand and learn about the Middle East.

• Read aloud and discuss Arabic folktales with your students from Iner Bushnaq's (1986) *Arab Folktales*. Compare the literary elements of Arabic folktales with those found in folktales from other countries.

• Introduce children to Arabic food by reading to determine a recipe to prepare in class from Christine Osborne's *Middle Eastern Food and Drink* (1988).

• Arrange for your class to visit a mosque and request a guided tour with a question and answer time built in. Encourage children to write about the experience and share their writing with others.

• Write a letter to a Middle Eastern embassy in Washington, DC, or to a consulate near your part of the country. Develop questions to ask the ambassador or consulate general about that country. Request a reply.

• Use *Butterflies of Saudi Arabia and Its Neighbors* by Torben B. Larsen (1984) to examine similarities and differences between Middle East butterflies with those of other continents.

• Form cooperative groups to research and report a topic about a Middle Eastern country. Examples for report writing can include dress, food, music, art, geography, climate, history, religion, architecture, and literature.

• Invite a speaker or author to your classroom who can discuss a topic relevant to Middle East studies. Create a panel of children to discuss what was presented and have the speaker interact with the panel and the whole class.

• If you live near a university, invite a professor of Arabic or Middle East studies to visit your class and talk with your students. Prepare and send a list of student-generated questions to the visitor prior to the class visit. Ask the professor to provide a bibliography for you and your students so you can learn more about the Middle East.

• Middle Eastern countries, except for Israel, are largely Muslim. There are over 1 billion people throughout the world who are Muslim. Explain how this religion is like other religions and also how it differs.

The collective use of literature and technology can help teachers create more realistic experiences for their students to teach them about the Middle East. Reading literature provides a rich blend of informational and narrative genres to explore about all aspects of life in the Middle East, while the use of technology helps teachers make real connections between and among diverse cultures. Literature and technology can be used to cultivate awareness and understanding while helping children learn that in most ways, peoples of the world are more alike than they are different.

References

Ahmedi, F. with T. Ansary. 2005. *The Story of My Life: An Afghan Girl on the Other Side of the Sky.* New York: Simon and Schuster.

Alexander, S. 1983. *Nadia the Willful.* New York: Random House.

Bushnaq, I. 1986. *Arab Folktales.* New York: Pantheon.

Early, M. 1989. *Ali Baba and the Forty Thieves.* Sydney: Abrams Books.

FF & McKinnon. 1990. *ARABIA: Sand, Sea, and Sky.* Videotape series. London: Author.

Fox, M. V. 1991. *Enchantment of the World: Iran.* Chicago: Children's Press.

Haskins, J. 1991. *Count Your Way Through the Arab World.* Minneapolis: Carolrhoda.

Heide, F. P., and J. H. Gilliland. 1990. *The Day of Ahmed's Secret.* New York: Lothrop, Lee, & Shepard.

Larsen, T. B. 1984. *Butterflies of Saudi Arabia and Its Neighbors.* New York: Stacey.

Lerner Publications. 1992. *Iraq . . . in Pictures.* Fort Worth, TX: Author.

London, J. 1997. *Ali, Child of the Desert.* Illus. T. Lewin. New York: Lothrop, Lee, & Shepard.

Mann, E. 1996. *The Great Pyramid.* New York: Mikaya Press.

Manniche, L. 1981. *The Prince Who Knew His Fate.* New York: Philomel.

Osborne, C. 1988. *Middle Eastern Food and Drink.* Los Angeles: Wayland.

Sifry, M. L., and C. Cerf. 1991. *The Gulf War Reader.* New York: Random House.

Staples, S. F. 1989. *Shabanu.* New York: Knopft.

———. 2005. *Under the Persimmon Tree.* New York: Farrar, Straus, and Giroux.

Time-Warner New Media. 1991. *Desert Storm: The War in the Persian Gulf.* CD-ROM. New York: Author.

Students need to learn about other cultures and their traditions and beliefs.

Placing English language learners in general education classrooms emphasizes the fact that there is a difference between the skills needed to communicate in English and the skills necessary to comprehend content materials. It may take five to seven years for students with limited English-speaking abilities to acquire the command of English they need to perform successfully in academic areas (Cummins 1981; Thomas and Collier 1997). Barriers to their effective communication, comprehension, and understanding exists, especially in tasks that involve reading and writing. Sometimes such barriers are disguised by students' relatively quick acquisition of conversational language and mastery of decoding skills in reading. Thus, those students who appear to have command of English may in actuality be struggling to communicate and discover meaning when they are faced with academic settings and tasks that are decontextualized and cognitively demanding (Sutton 1989).

This problem can be compounded by the age of the student. Academic content is much more difficult at the middle or high school level, where students may become frustrated by the difficulty of learning in another language and, as a consequence, be more inclined to drop out of the school system completely. If they have been isolated from content subjects because of time spent learning English, there will be gaps of knowledge in their schema. Teachers must consider this fact when establishing a foundation of prior knowledge before assigning an activity.

Vocabulary development also becomes an essential part of an English language learner's learning development. Strategies to elicit meaning from words must be taught. Vocabulary development is essential in language learning, language processing, communication, reading comprehension, and understanding concepts that are content specific. Teachers should be aware that vocabulary is learned most successfully through personal experiences and interaction with the environment. Taking the time to prepare students for a successful learning experience by introducing the vocabulary and language structures commonly used in social studies will lessen the anxiety that English language learners often develop upon encountering unfamiliar text. Chamot and O'Malley (1994) provide excellent guidelines and examples that teachers can use to help students access content material, as well as advance their English language skills at the same time. Using this knowledge, teachers can provide an environment rich in language experiences. They can emphasize a hands-on environment where a love for learning is nurtured through concrete experiences. Word webs and word walls help clarify concepts.

Journal writing provides a vehicle for a true communicative situation while allowing the teacher to become more aware of a student's development. A journal kept by a bilingual student explaining strategies used to elicit meaning from content material can provide the teacher with valuable insights into the student and the learning process. Such insights can then be used as a basis for future instruction to aid other students. An excellent example of this is provided by the RESPONSE method as conceived by Jacobson (1989) and further tested by Farris, Fuhler, and Ginejko (1991).

Journals allow the teacher to learn what students already know (prior knowledge), how well they understand the concepts that have been discussed, and what misconceptions they may hold. Through journals, the teacher can acknowledge the value given by students to certain teaching approaches and if the students believe the approaches have affected their learning, how aware students are of themselves as learners, and whether they perceive any problems with the material. Journals provide a personal glimpse of each student's feelings and emotions and are a window to each student's progress.

Even students whose English language resources are not yet sufficiently developed for them to write lengthy entries in journals can participate in this important activity. Students should be encouraged to draw pictures to represent their knowledge and understanding or questions, and/or to use one or two word phrases if writing full sentences is not yet within their reach. Teachers should be accepting of this mode of communication in student journals, always encouraging students to add more as their English language ability grows.

Because learning is a social process, cooperative learning is a viable strategy to foster the development of pragmatic skills. The learner interacts with people of diverse backgrounds, and a sharing of ideas and self results in better understanding. English language learners benefit tremendously when they participate in cooperative learning groups. The self-consciousness that they may experience when responding to the teacher in a whole class situation often disappears when working with their peers. They also have many more opportunities for interaction in cooperative groups, which provide a safe environment for trying out their developing English ability. Reading, writing, listening, and speaking in English can all occur naturally in well-designed and properly motivated cooperative learning groups.

Interdisciplinary instruction means interaction with the printed word, with people, and with learning. It allows the development of skills necessary to lead a fulfilling life. It includes an exposure to language through model reading, book sharing, LEA (Language Experience Approach), independent reading time, storytelling, student-authored books, literacy portfolios, brainstorming, choral reading, partner fluency reading, using visuals and manipulatives, and all the culturally sensitive strategies listed thus far in this chapter and highlighted throughout the book.

It also includes the addition of technology as a classroom tool to promote language, academic, and cognitive development for meaningful communication. Computers with microphones, CD-ROMs, digital cameras, scanners, projectors, printers, and tape recorders become part of the natural approach to acquiring English. Multimedia software and the Internet offer effective learning opportunities to acquire content in multiple ways and through multiple input channels. Technology also provides opportunities for students whose English language is still developing to communicate their understanding of important social studies material without such a heavy language burden. One example is the use of presentation software to make slides with meaningful phrases rather than complex sentences. Another example is the use of software that allows students to easily make concept or mind maps that demonstrate hierarchy and relationships among important ideas. As in all classes, technology and the experiences it provides can motivate students while engaging them in meaningful learning activities.

Facilitating Access to Social Studies for English Language Learners

This section provides a brief introduction to strategies and techniques that teachers can use to make the content matter of social studies more comprehensible and the classroom activities more accessible for English language learners. It also suggests how students can participate in the classroom and display their understanding of the social studies content by using less language-dependent ways of responding.

According to Chamot and O'Malley (1994), social studies can represent significant challenges for ELLs due to the academic language and prior knowledge that is required to fully comprehend its content. The teacher needs to present information in multiple ways that make use of visual, oral, written, and kinesthetic channels. Some examples of ways in which content information can be made more accessible for English language learners are suggested by Echevarria, Vogt, and Short (2000). They include:

- *Hands-on manipulatives* (such as maps, globes)
- *Realia* (real-life objects, such as historical artifacts, photographs)
- *Pictures* (photographs, illustrations, and drawings from texts, magazines, newspapers)
- *Visuals* (overhead transparencies, models, graphs, charts, props, puppets, maps, clip art, the Internet)
- *Multimedia* (tape recordings, videos, CD-ROMs, scanners, digital cameras, video cameras)
- *Demonstrations* (play musical instruments from different time periods, dye clothes with natural herbs, prepare food using period utensils)
- *Related literature* (stories or texts in simpler language or the student's native language)
- *Adapted text* (summarizing the most important sentences that relate the main ideas or sequence of events)

- *Graphic organizers* (visual maps of time lines of events, relationships of characters or events using text, lines, clip art)
- *Videos* (visually rich depictions of events that can be easily understood without text)

Other students in the classroom, both native English speaking and proficient bilingual peers, can participate in helping make content more accessible to their fellow students in cooperative learning groups and also as peer buddies. English language learners are often more at ease out of the spotlight of the whole class environment and will begin to use their developing language skills with their fellow students.

The teacher should also provide multiple ways in which students can demonstrate their understanding of the content while their English language proficiency is still developing. These can include the use of:

- *Graphic organizers* (hand drawn or done with the use of software such as Inspiration and Kidspiration to demonstrate his/her knowledge of sequences of events, relationships between individuals, cause and effect, etc.)
- *Drawings as prewriting* (beginning and struggling intermediate English language learners can draw or use software to depict their understanding of events, etc.)
- *Simple words, labels, phrases* (teachers can encourage students to participate in activities by allowing them to respond orally or in writing with one word answers, labels, and short phrases)
- *Process demonstrations* (instead of writing a summary or report, students demonstrate a process or procedure to show their understanding)
- *Manipulatives* (students use manipulatives to show action, events, etc.)
- *Presentation software* (students use PowerPoint and other presentation software with clip art and bulleted lists in place of written reports or as support for oral reports)

Further information on using these and other effective strategies can be found in *Fifty Strategies for Teaching English Language Learners* (Herrell 2000) and *The More-Than-Just-Surviving Handbook: ESL for Every Classroom Teacher* (Law and Eckes 2000). Numerous Internet resources can be found in *Multicultural Education and the Internet: Intersections and Integrations* (Gorski 2001).

Technology in a Multicultural Society

Technology use in the classroom is important. Impoverished students are four times less likely to have a computer with Internet access in their homes than are students from affluent families. Technology access in schools can help level the learning field for all students provided computer access is utilized wisely. Web sites are a great way to share our multicultural world with students. Setting up keypals for students with teachers in schools in another state or country enables students to develop a better understanding of different cultures and locations.

Now that computers can carry telephone conversations, it is possible for classroom hookups to link experts in the field. The class could generate a set of five or six questions to ask an expert on black history or Egyptian culture and have the teacher make arrangements for a teleconference phone call for the class. The person could then provide expertise during a 15-minute phone call in which the entire class may participate. Children's authors or university faculty often are willing to participate in such a role.

NCSS Standards-Linked Lesson Plan

"Traveling with Oliver K. Woodman"

Theme: Culture and Geography

Source: Pamela J. Farris, Northern Illinois University

Grades: 2–3

Objectives:

• Children will learn about different cultures as they listen to the story.

• Children will study other cultures and then write about Oliver's visiting another culture.

• Children will learn about different parts of the United States.

NCSS Themes:

   I. Culture

  II. People, Places, Environments

  V. Individuals, Groups, Institutions

Materials: Pattison, D. 2003. *The Journey of Oliver K. Woodman.* Illus. J. Cepeda. San Diego: Harcourt Children's Books. (Gr. 2–3)

    Tameka, an African American girl, writes a letter inviting her Uncle Ray, who lives in South Carolina, to visit her in California. Uncle Ray is unable to make the trip so he builds a life-size wooden man and sends it in his place. Along the way, Oliver meets many people of different cultures.

Process:

• The teacher displays a large U.S. map on the bulletin board and introduces the book, *The Journey of Oliver K. Woodman,* which is then read as a read-aloud.

• The students and the teacher place a pin in each location that Oliver visits.

• The students are assigned to talk with their parents about their own culture as well as different cultures that Oliver could visit throughout the world. Afterward, they can imagine what wooden Oliver would he made into if he would be a part of that culture. For instance, if Oliver visited Trinidad, he might become a wooden percussion instrument to accompany a steel drum band. In China, he might become chopsticks. In Kenya, he'd be made into a walking stick. In Thailand, he'd be carved into a jewelry box. In the Netherlands, he'd be shaped into wooden shoes. In Germany's Black Forest, Oliver might meet up with a clockmaker and become a cuckoo clock. In Sweden, a carpenter might turn him into clapboards to make a house. A sheepherder in New Zealand could turn Oliver into a crook to aid in herding sheep. In Brazil, Oliver might become a boat that floats down the Amazon River.

• The next day the students write about where they think Oliver should visit and what different cultures he would meet as well as what he would discover about the culture. After editing and illustrating, the pieces are collected and made into a class book.

Instructional Comments: This is an activity that acknowledges diversity and encourages students to discover other cultures.

Learning Styles Addressed: Verbal/linguistic, visual/spatial, intrapersonal, interpersonal, spiritual.

Evaluation: Students will be evaluated informally to see if there is acceptance of other cultures.

Modifications for Diverse Learners: Students may work in pairs. They may receive suggestions of book titles about different places and cultures in the world from the school librarian or classroom aide, as well as suggestions as to what culture "Oliver" will discover.

Variations: Consider the cultures represented in the community in which the school is located.

NCSS STANDARDS-LINKED LESSON PLAN

Protest Songs

Theme: "Songs for Life" from Thai Student Protesters during the 1970s
Source: Karen Carrier, Northern Illinois University
Grades: Middle grades
Objectives:

- To understand how music is used to express people's discontent with government.

- To analyze protest songs for elements that express the nature of the discontent and the action desired.

- To evaluate the effectiveness of the song in raising people's awareness of the problem.

- To relate to current issues and create a protest song raising awareness and support.

NCSS Themes:
  I. Culture
  II. Time, Continuity, and Change
 IX. Global Connections
  X. Civic Ideals and Practices

Materials:

1. Internet connection and computer with RealPlayer or other software for listening to music clips of the song "Man and Buffalo" by Caravan.

2. Copies of *Songs for Life,* a brief history of the origin of the political song movement in Thailand in the 1970s. This can be printed from the Web site of the Center for Southeast Asian Studies at Northern Illinois University: http://www.seasite.niu.edu/Thai/music/song4life/.

3. Copies of the English lyrics to "Man and Buffalo" by Caravan. These lyrics can be printed from http://www.seasite.niu.edu/Thai/music/song4life/kongapkwai.htm.

4. Paper, pencils, and colored markers for creating a graphic organizer, signs, and banners.

Process:

- Form students into cooperative learning groups and choose or assign roles as Reader, Recorder, and Encourager (keeps track of time and ensures that all students contribute to the task).

- Ask students to think about what they know of protest songs from different time periods in U.S. history.

- Prompts: Have they have heard songs like "The Times They Are A-Changin" by Bob Dylan or "People Got to Be Free" by The Rascals? What do they think the words mean?

- Ask students to think about the reasons why people write these songs.

- Prompts: Is it for money, fame, to help others, right a wrong, spread information, gather support?

- Tell students that during the 1970s in Thailand, a group of students protested the military dictatorship's unjust treatment of the farmers. Some of the students formed a musical group called Caravan and wrote and sang songs about the plight of the farmers and also about their disagreement with government policies. Review and briefly highlight some of the key points from the Internet article *Songs for Life.*

- Pass out one copy of *Songs for Life* to the designated reader in the groups. Have the groups locate the important elements of how and why the students wrote and used a protest song to help the farmers.

138

- Have each group create a graphic organizer (their choice of design) to illustrate these elements and their relationships to each other. Encourage students to use different colored markers for each different element and the related concepts under it. Also encourage them to draw pictures or symbols (or use clip art from Inspiration or Kidspiration software if they are working on a computer) to highlight the elements.

- Have students listen to "Man and Buffalo" and read the English lyrics. (The English lyrics are displayed on the Web site page while the song is playing, but you may want the students to have a copy of the lyrics for later analysis.)

- Have the groups analyze the music and the lyrics for melody, rhythm, volume, words, or phrases that:
  —express the plight of the farmers.
  —state what the student protesters think the farmers should do.

- Tell the groups to add this information to their graphic organizer in an appropriate relationship to the other information they have gathered and organized.

- After completing their graphic organizers, students discuss issues of importance that they would like to make known to authorities and what changes they want to be made. They should use their graphic organizers to remind them of the ways in which the Thai students gathered the support of the farmers, what remedy they wanted, and consider whether it would be useful in these times.

- Each group then writes its own protest song that informs and encourages support from other students, family, and community members on an issue of importance the group has identified. They can:
  —write it to the tune of their favorite song or can create their own music for it and perform it for the class.
  —make signs and banners promoting their cause.
  —create actions or moves to the music to highlight their message.

Instructional Comments: The groups have a great deal of freedom to design and illustrate their graphic organizers. However, their organizer should contain the main elements listed below, with their subsidiary points in some visually obvious relationship to the main element. Some students may choose to split a main element into two elements. This should be acceptable as long as the subsidiary points are arranged in proper relationships to the main element. The main elements are:

- the government structure (the three most powerful men and their jobs)

- the energy crisis (what the government did as a result, and the effect on the farmers and poor people)

- "buy Thai" (the boycott against Japanese goods)

- students and their songs (students helping farmers, how songs helped shy students communicate, how farmers responded, how new songs came about and their topics)

- the singing group Caravan (how it was formed, their message to their people and how it changed, what they did after the coup)

Learning Styles Addressed: Verbal/linguistic, musical/rhythmic, bodily/kinesthetic, interpersonal, intrapersonal.

Evaluation: Each group's protest song should have the following elements:
- a central theme or issue.

- a clear message to the group from which they are seeking support.

- a recommended remedy.

- words or phrases of encouragement that could serve as a slogan.

- action, movement, or enthusiasm for the message on the part of the performers.

Modifications for Diverse Learners: Cooperative learning groups present excellent opportunities for diverse students to participate in these learning activities. The group members can serve as peer buddies for an English language learner. Liberal use of drawings or clip art in the construction of the graphic organizer can help make the material more comprehensible to the ELL, who can also participate in adding information to the organizer. A student who is proficient in the ELL's native language might be assigned to the same group to assist the student in understanding and adding new English vocabulary to his/her repertoire. Physically challenged students can also participate with the help of peer buddies in the group. Group members might add elements or draw illustrations for a student who does not have the manual dexterity to do it alone. A hearing-impaired student can read the lyrics while the song is being played, can also participate in the creation of physical movement to express the song's emotions, and so forth.

Extensions:
• Students compare and contrast the Thai students' protest songs to student protest songs written during the Vietnam War or other conflicts (the civil rights marches, union organizing, etc.). For a list of Vietnam era songwriters, go to http://www.battlenotes.com/The_Songwriters.html.

• Students complete a WebQuest on Change Models in which students identify and analyze how change occurs in society. Go to http://webquest.sdsu.edu/designpatterns/all.htm for the design template on Change Models.

Variations:
• Students investigate other forms of political resistance, such as leaflet writing, banners, and graffiti. For some examples, go to this educational reference site covering all aspects of the Vietnam War: http://members.aol.com/TeacherNet/Vietnam.html#AntiMusic.

• Students compare "Buy Thai," the Thai boycott against Japanese goods, to the "Made In America" campaign to buy only U.S.-made goods.

Chapter Summary

The goal of the unit described in this chapter is to facilitate the development of the ability to view life from cultural perspectives different from one's own and to take steps to become an ally for those who experience unjust treatment. After immersing students in a variety of ethnic experiences in Phase One, the unit's scope is progressively refined. In Phase Two, students focus on particular cultural groups for further exploration; in Phase Three, they develop an understanding of point of view; in Phase Four, students become creative writers as they write from the points of view of characters of their own creation; and finally, in Phase Five, they develop steps that they can take to become allies with others against prejudice and discrimination. At the beginning of the unit, students view ethnic groups through their own cultural lenses. By the unit's conclusion, students add new cultural lenses to their repertoire of perspectives and a more personal and informed understanding of where prejudice and discrimination can harm others. In short, they achieve a flexibility of perspective and the tools with which to oppose injustice.

Implementation of the unit's extension leads to the development of a fresh multicultural perspective in two ways. Students create a diverse community, and in the process, they engage in the same kinds of cooperative interactions as their characters. Further, if students in the learning groups are from different cultural groups, prejudice will probably diminish in the process of working together toward a common goal (Slavin 1989/1990).

In addition to aiding both the reduction of prejudice and the growth of critical thinking in all subject areas, the skill of perspective taking, together with the knowledge gained about diverse cultural groups, provides students with an intuitive grasp of a number of issues related to living in a multicultural society. This deep understanding, which is at once cognitive and affective, can serve as a foundation for dealing with these issues in more complex ways later in life.

Integrated instruction can reflect the effective inclusion of culture in educational instruction. It is a bridge that connects the students and their individual cultures to an understanding of a cross-cultural society. Our national identity is dependent on successful learning by a culturally diverse population. Good teachers facilitate learning by providing opportunities for active learning by both monolingual and bilingual children. Teachers who appreciate the unique abilities of each student also recognize the importance of culture in self-development. Using strategies and techniques that provide access to the social studies curriculum for English language learners promotes an inclusive and democratic classroom environment in which all students can grow and prosper.

Children's Literature Recommendations

Criteria for Selecting Multicultural Literature

Selecting multicultural literature for children is not an easy task for teachers. For some ethnic groups, such as African Americans, there is a multitude of children's literature available from which to choose. However, for other cultures, such as Latvian, there are few titles available. The areas of Asian American and Latino children's literature can be confusing to teachers because these are conglomerates of many cultural groups. For instance, Asian American children's literature includes not only Chinese and Japanese children's books but also Cambodian, Indonesian, Korean, Laotian, Malaysian, Thai, and Vietnamese, among others. Likewise, Hispanic includes Cuban, Dominican, Mexican, Nicaraguan, and Puerto Rican cultures, as well as those from the South American countries—all very different cultural groups.

Cullinan and Galda (1999, 351) suggest that teachers look for books representing culturally diverse groups that

1. avoid stereotypes,

2. portray the cultural groups and their values in an authentic way,

3. use language that reflects standards set by local usage,

4. validate children's experience,

5. broaden our vision, and

6. invite reflection.

Through discussing and sharing multicultural literature with other teachers, teachers can become more familiar with appropriate titles to relate to students.

There should be enough books available to give students different perspectives on issues and historical events, such as the Native American view on the European settlement of North America, both on the eastern seaboard and in the Southwest. In addition, books should be available that correct distortions of information (Bishop 1992), such as the fact that many Native Americans died not at the hands of pioneers and soldiers, but from illnesses such as smallpox, a disease brought to North America by Europeans.

The following is a list of African American, Asian American, Hispanic, and Native American multicultural books by cultural group.

African American
Bradby, M. 1995. *More Than Anything Else.* New York: Orchard. (Gr. 1–4)
Bryan, A. 1991/2003. *All Night, All Day: A Child's First Book of African-American Spirituals.* New York: Aladdin. (Gr. 3–8)
Collier, J., and C. Collier. 1981/1987. *Jump Ship to Freedom.* New York: Bantam Doubleday Dell Books. (Gr. 5–8)
Cooper, F. 1994. *Coming Home: From the life of Langston Hughes.* New York: Philomel. (Gr. 3–8)
Cox, C. 1993/1996. *The Forgotten Heroes: The Story of the Buffalo Soldiers.* New York: Scholastic. (Gr. 5–8)
Cox, J. 2003. *My Family Plays Music.* New York: Holiday. (Gr. K–2)
English, K. 2004. *Speak to Me (and I Will Listen Between the Lines).* New York: Farrar. (Gr. 3–6)
Golenbeck, P. 1990/1992. *Teammates.* Illus. P. Bacon. New York: Voyager. (Gr. 3–8)
Grimes, N. 1998/2000. *Jazmin's Notebook.* New York: Puffin. (Gr. 5–8)
Hamilton, V. 1992/1997. *Drylongso.* Illus. J. Pinkney. San Diego: Harcourt Brace. (Gr. 3–6)
———. 1993/2000. *The People Could Fly: American Black Folktales.* Illus. L. Dillon and D. Dillon. New York: Knopf. (Gr. 3–8)
Hansen, J. 1986. *Which Way Freedom?* New York: Walker. (Gr. 5–8)
Hester, D. L. 2005. *Grandma Lena's Big Ol' Turnip.* Morton Grove, IL: Albert Whitman. (Gr. K–2)
Hoffman, M. 1991. *Amazing Grace.* Illus. C. Birch. New York: Dial. (Gr. K–3)
Hopkinson, D. 1993/1995. *Sweet Clara and the Freedom Quilt.* Illus. J. Ransome. New York: Knopf. (Gr. 2–5)
Hoyt-Goldsmith, D. 1993/1994. *Celebrating Kwanzaa.* Illus. L. Midgale. New York: Holiday. (Gr. K–8)
Igus, T. 1998. *I See the Rhythm.* New York: Children's Book Press. (Gr. 5–8)
Kimmel, E. A. 1994/1995. *Anansi and the Talking Melon.* Illus. J. Stevens. New York: Holiday. (Gr. K–3)
Knutson, B. 1990. *How the Guinea Fowl Got Her Spots: A Swahili Tale of Friendship.* New York: Carolrhoda. (Gr. K–2)
Lawrence, J. 1993/1995. *The Great Migration: An American Story.* New York: HarperTrophy. (Gr. 3–6)
Miller, W. 1999. *Richard Wright and the Library Card.* New York: Lee & Low Books. (Gr. 2–5)
Myers, W. D. 1988. *Scorpions.* New York: Harper & Row. (Gr. 5–8)
———. 1991. *Now is Your Time!: The African American Struggle for Freedom.* New York: HarperCollins. (Gr. 4–8)
Nelson, M. 2001. *Carver: A Life in Poems.* New York: Front Street. (Gr. 3–5)
Pinkney, A. D. 1993/1995. *Seven Candles for Kwanzaa.* Illus. B. Pinkney. New York: Dial (Gr. K–up)
———. 2000. *Let it Shine: Stories of Black Women Freedom Fighters.* San Diego, CA: Gullivar/Harcourt Brace. (Gr. 3–5)
Ringgold, F. 1991. *Tar Beach.* New York: Crown. (Gr. 1–3)
———. 1992/1995. *Aunt Harriet's Underground Railroad in the Sky.* New York: Crown. (Gr. 1–4)
Thomas, J. C. 2002. *Crowning Glory.* New York: HarperCollins/Joanna Cotler Books. (Gr. K–4)

Asian American

Carlson, L. 1995. *American Eyes: New Asian-American Short Stories for Young Adults.* New York: Fawcett. (Gr. 6–9)

Cheng, A. 2005. *Shanghai Messenger.* New York: Lee & Low. (Gr. 3–6)

Choi, N. S. 1991. *Year of Impossible Goodbyes.* Boston: Houghton Mifflin. (Gr. 4–8)

Coerr, E. 1993. *Sadako.* Illus. E. Young. New York: Putnam. (Gr. 3–8)

Compestine, Y. C. 2001. *The Runaway Rice Cake.* New York: Simon and Schuster. (Gr. K–3)

Haugaard, E. C. 1995/2005. *The Revenge of the Forty-Seven Samurai.* Boston: Houghton Mifflin. (Gr. 6–8)

Jiang, J. L. 1998. *The Red Scarf.* New York: HarperTrophy. (Gr. 6–8)

Lee, M. 2006. *Landed.* New York: Farrar/Frances Foster. (Gr. 3–5)

Lin, G. 2005. *The Year of the Dog.* New York: Little, Brown. (Gr. 3–5)

Lord, B. B. 1984/1986. *In the Year of the Boar and Jackie Robinson.* New York: Harper & Row. (Gr. 4–6)

Mak, K. 2001. *My Chinatown: One Year in Poems.* New York: HarperCollins. (Gr. 1–4)

Nhuong, H. Q. 1982/1986. *The Land I Lost: Adventures of a Boy in Vietnam.* New York: HarperTrophy. (Gr. 4–8)

Pak, S. 2003. *Sumi's First Day of School.* New York: Viking. (Gr. K–2)

Park, L. S. 2001/2003. *A Single Shard.* Boston: Houghton Mifflin. (Gr. 6–8)

Recorvits, H. 2003. *My Name Is Yoon.* New York: Farrar/Frances Foster. (Gr. K–2)

Salisbury, G. 1994/1995. *Under the Blood-Red Sun.* New York: Yearling. (Gr. 6–8)

Say, A. 1990/1996. *El Chino.* Boston: Houghton Mifflin. (Gr. 4–8)

———. 1993. *Grandfather's Journey.* Boston: Houghton Mifflin. (Gr. K–3)

———. 2005. *Kamishibai Man.* Boston: Houghton. (Gr. 1–5)

Shea, P. D. 2003. *Tangled Threads: A Hmong Girl's Story.* New York: Clarion. (Gr. 5–9)

Simonds, N., L. Schwartz, and the Children's Museum, Boston. 2002. *Moonbeams, Dumplings, and Dragon Boats: A Treasury of Chinese Holiday Tales, Activities, and Recipes.* Boston: Harcourt/Gulliver. (Gr. 4–6)

Uchida, Y. 1993/1996. *The Bracelet.* Illus. J. Yardley. New York: Philomel. (Gr. K–2)

Uegaki, C. 2003. *Suki's Kimono.* Toronto, Ontario: Kids Can Press. (Gr. K–2)

Yacowitz, C. 2006. *The Jade Stone.* Illus. J. H. Chen. New York: Pelican. (Gr. 1–3)

Yee, P. 1999. *Tales from Gold Mountain: Stories of the Chinese in the New World.* Illus. N. Ng. Toronto, Ontario: Groundwood Books/Douglas and McIntyre. (Gr. 4–8)

———. 2003. *Roses Sing on New Snow.* Illus. H. Chan. Toronto, Ontario: Groundwood Books/Douglas and McIntyre. (Gr. 3–6)

Yep, L. 1993/1995. *Dragon's Gate.* New York: HarperCollins. (Gr. 5–8)

Hispanic

Aardema, V. 1991/1998. *Borreguita and the Coyote: A Tale from Ayutia, Mexico.* New York: Dragonfly. (Gr. K–3)

Ada, A. F. 1995/1997. *Half Chicken.* New York: Dragonfly. (Gr. 2–3)

———. 1998. *Under the Royal Palms: A Childhood in Cuba.* New York: Atheneum. (Gr. 6–8)

———. 2002. *I Love Saturdays y domingos.* New York: Simon & Schuster/Atheneum. (Gr. K–3)

Albert, R. 1994/1996. *Alejandro's Gift.* San Francisco: Chronicle. (Gr. 1–3)

Anaya, R. 1999. *My Land Sings: Stories from the Rio Grande.* New York: HarperTrophy. (Gr. 5–8)

Ancona, G. 1994. *The Piñata Maker/El Piñatero.* San Diego, CA: Harcourt. (Gr. K–8)

———. 1995. *Fiesta USA.* New York: Lodestar. (Gr. K–2)

———. 1998. *Barrio: Jose's Neighborhood.* San Diego, CA: Harcourt. (Gr. 2–3)

Andrews-Goebel, N. 2002. *The Pot That Juan Built.* Illus. D. Diaz. New York: Lee & Low. (Gr. K–3)

Anzaldua, G. 1996/2001. *Prietita and the Ghost Woman/Prietita y la llorona.* San Francisco: Children's Book Press. (Gr. 2–4)

Argueta, J. 2001. A *Movie in My Pillow: Poems/Una pelicula en mi almohada: Poemas.* San Francisco: Children's Book Press. (Gr. 3–6)

Bernier-Grand, C. T. 2002. *Shake It, Morena! And Other Folklore from Puerto Rico.* Brookfield, CT: Millbrook Press. (Gr. 3–5)

Bunting, E. 1996/1998. *Going Home.* Illus. D. Diaz. New York: HarperCollins. (Gr. 1–8)

Canales, V. 2005. *The Tequila Worm.* New York: Wendy Lamb Books. (Gr. 5–9)

Castaneda, O. S. 1993/1995. *Abuela's Weave.* New York: Lee & Low. (Gr. K–3)

Charles, F., and R. Arenson. 1996. *A Caribbean Counting Book.* Boston: Houghton Mifflin. (Gr. K–1)

Cisñeros, S. 1997. *Hairs/Pelitos.* New York: Dragonfly. (Gr. K–3)

Clark, A. N. 1980. *Secret of the Andes.* New York: Puffin. (Gr. 4–8)

Corpi, L. 1997/2002. *Where Fireflies Dance.* San Francisco: Children's Book Press. (Gr. 1–3)

de Paola, T. 1980. *The Lady of Guadalupe.* New York: Holiday. (Gr. 3–6)

———. 1994/1997. *The Legend of the Poinsettia.* New York: Putnam. (Gr. 1–4)

———. 2002/2004. *Adelita: A Mexican Cinderella Story.* New York: Putnam. (Gr. K–3)

Dorros, A. 1991/1997. *Abuela.* New York: Dutton. (Gr. 4–8)

———. 1993/1997. *The Radio Man.* New York: HarperTrophy. (Gr. 2–3)

Encinas, C. 2001. *The New Engine: La Maquina Nueva.* Walnut, CA: Kiva. (Gr. 2–4)

Gerson, M. 2001. *Femenina: Celebrating Women in Mexican Folktale.* Cambridge, MA: Barefoot Books. (Gr. 4–8)

Gonzalez, L. M. 1997/2001. *Señor Cat's Romance and Other Favorite Stories from Latin America.* New York: Scholastic. (Gr. 1–3)

———. 1999. *The Bossy Gallito (Rooster): A Traditional Cuban Folktale* (Dual language edition). New York: Scholastic. (Gr. K–3)

Hernandez, A. 1999/2001. *Erandi's Braids.* New York: Putnam. (Gr. K–3)

Isadora, R. 1998/2002. *Caribbean Dream.* New York: Putnam. (Gr. 1–3)

Johnston, T. 1994/1998. *The Tale of Rabbit and Coyote.* New York: Putnam. (Gr. K–3)

Krull, K. 2003. *Harvesting Hope: The Story of Cesar Chavez.* San Diego, CA: Harcourt Children's Books. (Gr. 3–6)

Levy, J. 1995. *The Spirit of Tio Fernando.* Morton Grove, IL: Albert Whitman. (Gr. 2–4)

Lomas-Garza, C. 1996/2000. *In My Family* (Dual language edition). San Francisco: Children's Book Press. (Gr. 1–3)

———. 1999/2003. *Magic Windows* (Dual language edition). San Francisco: Children's Book Press. (Gr. 1–3)

Medina, J. 2004. *My Name Is Jorge: On Both Sides of the River.* Honesdale, PA: Boyds Mills Press. (Gr. 3–6)

Mohr, N. 1993. *All for the Better: Story of El Barrio.* Dallas: Steck-Vaughn. (Gr. 2–5)

Mora, P. 1995. *The Desert is My Mother/El Desierto Es Mi Madre* (Dual language edition). Illus. D. Leshon. Houston: Pinata. (Gr. 3–6)

———. 1997. *Tomas and the Library Lady.* New York: Knopf. (Gr. K–3)

———. 2002. *A Library for Juana: The World of Sor Juana Ines.* New York: Knopf. (Gr. 2–4)

Muñoz, P. R. 2000. *Esperanza Rising.* New York: Scholastic. (Gr. 6–8)

O'Dell, S. 1981/2006. *Carlota.* New York: Laurel-Leaf. (Gr. 5–8)

Palacios, A. 1992. *¡Viva Mexico!: The Story of Benito Juarez and Cinco de Mayo.* Dallas: Steck-Vaughan. (Gr. 2–5)

Paulson, G. 1995/1998. *The Tortilla Factory.* San Diego, CA: Harcourt. (Gr. 4–7)

Perez, A. 2000. *My Very Own Room/Mi Propio Cuartito* (Dual language edition). San Francisco: Children's Book Press. (Gr. 2–4)

Perez, E. 2004. *From the Winds of Manguito: Cuban Folktales in English and Spanish/Desde lo vientos de Manguito: Cuentos folkloricos de Cuba, en ingles y espanol.* Westport, CT: Greenwood/Libraries Unlimited. (Gr. 4–9)

Philip, N. 2003. *Horse Hooves and Chicken Feet: Mexican Folktales.* New York: Clarion. (Gr. 4–8)

Roe, E. 1994. *Con Mi Hermano—With my brother* (Dual language edition). New York: Aladdin. (Gr. 5–8)

Sandin, J. 2003. *Coyote School News.* New York: Holt. (Gr. 2–4)

Shute, L. 1995. *Rabbit Wishes.* New York: HarperCollins. (Gr. 2–4)

Soto, G. 1990/2000. *Baseball in April and Other Stories.* San Diego, CA: Harcourt. (Gr. 3–6)

———. 1992/2005. *Neighborhood Odes.* Illus. D. Diaz. San Diego, CA: Harcourt. (Gr. 5–8)

———. 1993/1996. *Too Many Tamales.* Illus. E. Martinez. New York: Putnam. (Gr. K–3)

———. 1995. *Canto Familiar.* San Diego, CA: Harcourt Brace. (Gr. 1–3)

Tamar, E. 1996/1997. *American City Ballet.* New York: HarperTrophy. (Gr. 5–8)

Villaseñor, V. 2003. *Walking Stars: Stories of Magic and Power.* Houston: Piñata. (Gr. 3–6)

Winter, J. 1996. *Josefina.* San Diego, CA: Harcourt Brace. (Gr. 2–4)

Winter, J., and J. Winter. 1994/2007. *Diego* (Dual language edition). New York: Knopf. (Gr. 5–8)

Native American

Anaya, R. 1999. *My Land Sings: Stories from the Rio Grande.* New York: HarperTrophy. (Gr. 5–8)

Baylor, B. 1997. *The Other Way to Listen.* New York: Aladdin. (Gr. K–8)

Bierhorst, J. 1992. *A Cry from the Earth: Music of the North American Indians.* Santa Fe, NM: Ancient City Press. (Gr. K–8)

Bruchac, J. 1998/2002. *The Arrow Over the Door.* Illus. J. Watling. New York: Dial. (Gr. 1–4)

Bruchac, J., and J. London. 1992/1997. *Thirteen Moons on Turtle's Back.* Illus. T. Locker. New York: Philomel. (Gr. 1–4)

Bushyhead, R. H., and K. T. Bannon. 2002. *Yonder Mountain: A Cherokee Legend.* New York: Marshall Cavendish. (Gr. 1–4)

Cohen, C. L. 1988. *The Mud Pony: A Traditional Skidi Pawnee Tale.* Illus. S. Begay. New York: Scholastic. (Gr. 3–7)

Curry, J. L. 2003. *Hold Up the Sky: And Other Native American Tales from Texas and the Southern Plains.* New York: Simon & Schuster/ Margaret K. McElderry. (Gr. 3–7)

Dennis, Y. W., and A. Hirschfelder. 2003. *Children of Native America Today.* Watertown, MA: Charlesbridge. (Gr. 3–8)

Dorris, M. 1992. *Morning Girl.* New York: Hyperion. (Gr. 3–5)

Ekoomiak, N. 1990/1992. *Arctic Memories.* New York: Holt, Rinehart & Winston. (Gr. 4–6)

Freedman, R. 1988/1995. *Buffalo Hunt.* New York: Holiday. (Gr. 3–8)

———. 1992/1995. *Indian Winter.* Photo. K. Bodmer. New York: Holiday. (Gr. 5–8)

Fritz, J. 1983/2002. *The Double Life of Pocahontas.* New York: Putnam. (Gr. 3–7)

George, J. C. 1983/1987. *The Talking Earth.* New York: HarperTrophy. (Gr. 4–8)

Goble, P. 1988/1991. *Iktomi and the Boulder: A Plains Indian Story.* New York: Orchard. (Gr. K–4)

———. 1990/1997. *Dream Wolf.* New York: Aladdin. (Gr. 1–3)

Gregory, K. 2002. *The Legend of Jimmy Spoon.* Orlando, FL: Harcourt. (Gr. 4–8)

Grossman, V. 1991/1995. *Ten Little Rabbits.* Illus. S. Long. San Francisco: Chronicle. (Gr. K–2)

Hoyt-Goldsmith, D. 1991/1994. *Pueblo Storyteller.* Photo. L. Migdale. New York: Holiday. (Gr. 1–4)

Lind, M. 2003. *Bluebonnet Girl.* Illus. K. Kiesler. New York: Holt. (Gr. K–2)

Martin, R. 1992/1998. *The Rough-Face Girl.* Illus. D. Shannon. New York: Putnam. (Gr. K–4)

Moore, R. 1990. *Maggie Among the Seneca.* New York: HarperCollins. (Gr. 5–6)

O'Dell, S. 1988/1989. *Black Star, Bright Dawn*. Boston: Houghton Mifflin. (Gr. 5–8)

Paulsen. G. 1988/2000. *Dogsong*. New York: Atheneum. (Gr. 5–8)

Rodanos, K. 1992/1995. *Dragonfly's Tale*. New York: Clarion. (Gr. 5–8)

Roessell, M. 1993. *Kinnalda: A Navaho Girl Grows Up*. Minneapolis, MN: Lerner. (Gr. 3–6)

Smith, C. L. 2000. *Jingle Dancer*. New York: HarperCollins. (Gr. K–3)

———. 2002. *Indian Shoes*. New York: HarperCollins. (Gr. 3–5)

Sneve, V. 1989. *Dancing Teepees: Poems of American Indian Youth*. New York: Holiday. (Gr. 4–8)

Swann, B. 1998. *Touching the Distance: Native American Riddle Poems*. San Diego: Brown Deer/Harcourt Brace. (Gr. 4–6)

Wisniewski, D. 1991/1995. *Rain Player*. New York: Clarion. (Gr. K–3)

Yolen, J. 1992/1996. *Encounter*. Illus. D. Shannon. San Diego, CA: Harcourt. (Gr. 3–8)

Other Multicultural Works

Adolf, A. (2002). *black is brown is tan*. New York: HarperCollins. (Gr. K–3)

Ajmera, M., and J. D. Ivanko. (2004). *To Be an Artist*. Watertown, MA: Charlesbridge. (Gr. K–4).

Crew, G. 2000. *The Kraken*. Melbourne, Australia: Lothian Books. (Gr. 3–6)

Heide, F. P., and J. H. Gilliland. 1990/1995. *The Day of Ahmed's Secret*. Illus. T. Lewin. New York: HarperTrophy. (Gr. K–3)

———. 1992. *Sami and the Time of the Troubles*. New York: Clarion. (Gr. 2–5)

Johnson-Davies, D. 2005. *Goha the Wise Fool*. New York: Philomel. (Gr. 1–6)

Lankford, M. D. 1992/1996. *Hopscotch Around the World*. Illus. K. Milone. New York: HarperTrophy. (Gr. 1–2)

McDonald, A. 2002. *Please, Malese! A Trickster Tale from Haiti*. New York: Farrar/Melanie Kroupa. (Gr. 2–4)

Nye, N. S. 1997. *Sitti's Secrets*. New York: Aladdin. (Gr. 2–5)

———. 2002. *19 Varieties of Gazelle: Poems of the Middle East*. New York: Greenwillow. (Gr. 6–9)

Rosenburg, M. 1994/1998. *Hiding to Survive: Stories of Jewish Children Rescued from the Holocaust*. New York: Clarion. (Gr. 6–8)

SanSouci, R. D. 2000. *Cut from the Same Cloth: American Women of Myth, Legend, and Tall Tale*. New York: Putnam. (Gr. 3–6)

Steig, W. 2005. *When Everybody Wore a Hat*. New York: HarperTrophy. (Gr. K–3)

Wing, N. 1996. *Jalapeno Bagels*. New York: Atheneum. (Gr. K–3)

Winter, J. 2005. *The Librarian of Basra: A True Story from Iraq*. Boston: Harcourt. (Gr. 3–8)

Children's Literature Resources

Clements, A. 2002. *The Jacket*. Illus. M. Henderson. New York: Simon & Schuster. When Phil sees a boy wearing his brother's jacket, he assumes the boy stole it. After all, he's never seen the boy in school or in the neighborhood before and the kid is black. An excellent book on prejudice. (Gr. 4–7)

Paterson, K. 2006. *Bread and Roses, Too*. New York: Clarion. When her militant Italian immigrant mother and sister join the mill workers' labor strike, twelve-year-old Rosa finds herself on a train to Barre, Vermont, along with other children as they are protected from the violence accompanying the strike. She meets thirteen-year-old Jake, an orphan who persuades her to say he is her older brother. They are put up with a stonecutter's family, where the father helps them sort out their differences. (Gr. 5-8)

Teaching Resources

Barrett, K., L. Bergman, and G. Dornfest. 1996/2000. *Investigating Artifacts: Making Masks, Creating Myths, Exploring Middens—Teacher's Guide*. Berkeley: University of California.

Bigelow, B., and B. Peterson. 1998. *Rethinking Columbus: The Next 500 Years.* Minneapolis, MN: Rethinking Schools.

Gorski, P. C. 2001/2004. *Multicultural Education and the Internet: Intersections and Integrations.* Boston: McGraw-Hill.

Joyce, W. W., and J. F. Bratzel. 2006. *Teaching About Canada and Mexico.* Silver Spring, MD: National Council for the Social Studies.

Lee, E., D. Menkart, and M. Okazawa-Rey. 1998. *Beyond Heroes and Holidays: A Practical Guide to K–12 Anti-Racist, Multicultural Education and Staff Development.* Berkeley, CA: NECA.

Videos

The World Through Kids' Eyes. 1997. 67 minutes. Maryknoll World Productions. Available from www.americas.org. Six short segments of children at risk from six different countries (Philippines, Peru, Brazil, United States, India, and South Africa).

Web Sites

http://www.tenet.edu/halls/multiculturalism.html
Hall of Multiculturalism, Texas Education Network
http://www.indigenouspeople.net/ipl_final.html
Indigenous People's Literature

Related Technology Tools

Web Sites

http://www.ncela.gwu.edu/
The National Clearinghouse for English Language Acquisition & Language Instruction Educational Programs (formerly National Clearinghouse for Bilingual Education)
http://www.cal.org/
Center for Applied Linguistics
http://www.nameorg.org
The National Association for Multicultural Education
http://www.ed.gov/about/offices/list/oela/index.html?src=mr
The Office of English Language Acquisition, Language Enhancement, and Academic Achievement for Limited English Proficient Students (OELA)
http://www.tesol.org/s_tesol/index.asp
Teachers of English to Speakers of Other Languages
http://nces.ed.gov/
The National Center for Education Statistics (NCES)
http://www.ets.org/research/
Educational Testing Service
http://www.elfs.com
English Learning Funsite
http://www.kids-space.org/
International Kids Space
http://www.estrellita.com/bil.html
Bilingual Education Resources on the Net
http://curry.edschool.Virginia.EDU/go/multicultural
Multicultural Pavilion at the University of Virginia

WebQuests

Cinco de Mayo (Gr. 2–3)
http://www.zianet.com/cjcox/edutech4learning/cinco.html

Day of the Dead—A Mexican Holiday (Gr. 3–6)
   http://its.guilford.k12.nc.us/webquests/dayofdead/dodead.htm

Technology Resources

The Odyssey
   http://www.worldtrek.org/odyssey/index.html
   Teachers and students can follow six explorers who are traveling to Mexico, Latin America, Africa, the Middle East, India, and China.

Multicultural Pavilion
   http://curry.edschoolVirginia.EDU/go/multicultural/home.html
   Teachers can gain multicultural teaching practices, activities, and tools.

Software and Videos

Roll of Thunder, Hear My Cry. 1978. 95 minutes. Teacher's Video Company. Available from www.teachersvideo.com. Morgan Freeman stars in this poignant drama that follows a black family's struggle to maintain dignity in the Depression-era South. They fight to keep their land, and their strong family values pull them through. Students love this portrayal of Mildred Taylor's famous novel.

The Story of Immigration. 1994. 45 minutes. Teacher's Video Company. Available from www.teachersvideo.com. Kids learn that our nation was built by millions of people who left the shores of foreign nations to pursue a dream in America. Revisit Ellis Island, where immigrants first arrived, and witness how families struggled to find their place in the new land. Historic footage and fascinating anecdotes provide a remarkable view of our ancestors' brave journeys to the United States.

Travel to Africa with NBC's Today Morning Show. 1993. 56 minutes. NBC. Available at Teacher's Discovery, 800-543-4180. Journey through Africa and learn about its geography, history, and culture.

Microsoft Encarta Africana Third Edition. Microsoft. Available from www.amazon.com. "Encarta Africana" is an absorbing interactive exploration of the history of African culture.

References

Acuña, R. 1988. *Occupied America: A History of Chicanos.* New York: Harper & Row.

Banks, J. A., and C. A. Banks. 1997. *Teaching Strategies for Ethnic Studies.* 6th ed. Boston: Allyn & Bacon.

———. 2004. *Multicultural Education: Issues and Perspectives.* 5th ed. Boston: Allyn & Bacon.

Berger, D. M., and J. F. Bratzel. 2006. "From Conquest to Modernity: Mexico 1519–1946." In *Teaching About Canada and Mexico,* ed. W. W. Joyce and J. F. Bratzel. Silver Spring, MD: National Council for the Social Studies.

Bishop, R. S. 1992. "Multicultural Literature for Children: Making Informed Choices." In *Teaching Multicultural Literacy,* ed. V. Harris, pp. 37–54. Norwood, MA: Christopher Gordon.

Byrnes, D. A. 1988. "Children and Prejudice." *Social Education* 52: 267–71.

Chamot, A. U., and J. M. O'Malley. 1994. *The CALLA Handbook: Implementing the Cognitive Academic Language Learning Approach.* Reading, MA: Addison-Wesley.

Cook, L., and P. C. Gonzales. 1994. "Helping ESL Students in English-Only Classes." *Reading Today* 12 (2): 25.

Cullinan, B., and L. Galda. 1999. *Literature and the Child.* 3rd ed. San Diego, CA: Harcourt Brace.

Cummins, J. 1981. *Bilingualism and Minority Language Children.* Toronto: Ontario Institute for Studies in Education.

———. 1994. *Bilingual and Special Education: Issues in Assessment and Pedagogy.* Clevedon, England: PRO-ED.

Curzio, L. 2006. "Mexico: Contemporary Achievements and Challenges." In *Teaching About Canada and Mexico*, ed. W. W. Joyce and J. F. Bratzel. Silver Spring, MD: National Council for the Social Studies.

Echevarria, J., M. Vogt, and D. J. Short. 2000. *Making Content Comprehensible for English Language Learners: The SIOP Model*. Boston: Allyn & Bacon.

Farris, P. J., C. Fuhler, and M. L. Ginejko. 1991. "Reading, Writing, Discussing: An Interactive Approach to Content Areas." *Reading Horizons* 31 (4): 261–71.

Feinberg, R. C., and C. C. Morencia. 1998. "Bilingual Education, an Overview." *Social Education* 62 (7): 427–31.

Gorski, P. C. 2001. *Multicultural Education and the Internet: Intersections and Integrations*. Boston: McGraw-Hill.

Herrell, A. L. 2000. *Fifty Strategies for Teaching English Language Learners*. Upper Saddle River, NJ: Merrill.

Holdaway, D. 1979. *The Foundations of Literacy*. Urbana, IL: National Council of Teachers of English.

Hoyt, L. 1992. "Many Ways of Knowing: Using Drama, Oral Interactions, and the Visual Arts to Enhance Reading Comprehension." *The Reading Teacher* 45 (6): 580–84.

Jacobson, J. M. 1989. "RESPONSE: An Interactive Study Technique." *Reading Horizons* 29 (2): 86–92.

Jacobson, L. 2002 (October 2). "Kindergarten Study Links Learning Deficits to Poverty." *Education Week* 22 (4): 10.

Janzen, R. 1994. "Melting Pot or Mosaic?" *Educational Leadership* 51 (8): 9–11.

Kanellos, N. 1990. *A History of Hispanic Theatre in the United States: Origins to 1940*. Austin: University of Texas Press.

Keefe, S. E., and A. M. Padilla. 1987. *Chicano Ethnicity*. Albuquerque: University of New Mexico Press.

Law, B., and M. Eckes. 2000. *The More-Than-Just-Surviving Handbook: ESL for Every Classroom Teacher*. 2nd ed. Winnipeg, Canada: Portage & Main/Peguis.

Lee, V. E., and D. T. Burkam. 2002. *Inequality at the Starting Gate: Social Background Differences in Achievement as Children Begin School*. Washington, DC: Economic Policy Institute.

Lim, H. L., and D. J. Watson. 1993. "Whole Language Content Classes for Second-Language Learners." *The Reading Teacher* 46 (4): 384–93.

Merrow, J. 2002 (September 25). "The 'Failure' of Head Start." *Education Week* 22 (4): 52.

National Council for the Social Studies. 1992. "The Columbia Quincentenary Position Statement." *Social Studies and the Young Learner* 4.

Pang, V. O. 2001a. "Why Do We Need This Class? Multicultural Education for Teachers." *Phi Delta Kappan* 76 (4): 289–92.

———. 2001b. *Multicultural Education: A Caring-Centered, Reflective Approach*. Boston: McGraw-Hill.

Parker, W. C., and J. Jarolimek. 1997. *A Sampler of Curriculum Standards for Social Studies: Expectations of Excellence*. Englewood Cliffs, NJ: Merrill/Prentice-Hall.

Pate, G. S. 1988. "Research on Reducing Prejudice." *Social Education* 52: 287–89.

Porter, R. P. 1990. *Forked Tongue: The Politics of Bilingual Education*. New York: Basic Books.

Rigg, P., and V. G. Allen, eds. 1989. *When They Don't All Speak English*. Urbana, IL: National Council of Teachers of English.

Robbins, P. A. 1990. "Implementing Whole Language: Bridging Children and Books," *Educational Leadership* 47 (6): 50–54.

Rolón, C. A. 2002/2003. "Educating Latino Students." *Educational Leadership* 60 (4): 40–43.

Shaw, C. C. 1993. "Taking Multicultural Math Seriously." *Social Studies and the Young Learner* 6 (1): 31–2.

Singer, J. Y., and T. Harbour-Ridley. 1998. "Young Children Learn about Immigrants to the United States." *Social Education* 62: 415–16.

Slavin, R. E. 1989/1990. "Research on Cooperative Learning: Consensus and Controversy." *Educational Leadership* 47 (4): 52–54.

Sleeter, C. E., and C. A. Grant. 1988. *Making Choices for Multicultural Education: Five Approaches to Race, Class, and Gender.* Columbus, OH: Merrill.

Stern-LaRosa, C., and E. Hofheimer Bettman. 2000. *Hate Hurts: How Children Learn and Unlearn Prejudice.* New York: Scholastic.

Sunal, C. S., and M. E. Haas. 1997. *Social Studies and the Elementary/Middle School Student.* Orlando, FL: Harcourt Brace Jovanovich.

Sutton, C. 1989. "Helping the Non-Native English Speaker with Reading." *The Reading Teacher* 49 (9): 684–86.

Thomas, W. P., and V. Collier. 1997. *School Effectiveness for Language Minority Students.* NCBE Resource Collection Series, No. 9. Retrieved at http://www.ncela.gwu.edu/ncbepubs/resource/effectiveness/index.htm.

Turner, D. 2002. "Understanding Mexican Culture through Crafts: Three Activities." *Social Studies and the Young Learner* 15 (2): 6–8.

U.S. Census Bureau. 2000. *2000 Census Report.* Washington, DC: Author.

Walker-Dalhouse, D. 1993. "Using African-American Literature to Increase Ethnic Understanding." *The Reading Teacher* 45 (5): 416–22.

Walsh, D. 1988. "Critical Thinking to Reduce Prejudice." *Social Education* 52 (4): 280–82.

Weil, M., E. Calhoun, and B. Joyce. 2003. *Models of Teaching.* 6th ed. Englewood Cliffs, NJ: Prentice-Hall.

> *Child, teacher, and parent should celebrate each new learning by focusing on what is known rather than what is lacking.*
> —Dorothy S. Strickland, "Emergent Literacy: How Young Children Learn to Read and Write"

Chapter Five

Social Studies for All Learners

Carol J. Fuhler, Iowa State University

CHAPTER OBJECTIVES

Readers will

- apply a variety of interdisciplinary strategies to enhance the learning of social studies content for all students;

- examine and explain the similarities and differences of students in the learning community labeled as gifted, learning disabled, or educationally challenged;

- summarize why social studies content can be thought provoking and engaging to all learners; and

- design quality, appealing learning opportunities for students at various stages of the learning spectrum.

Introduction

The world within today's classroom is a reflection of the world outside its doors. Each year teachers will be confronted with greater ethnic diversity among students, an ever-present range of socioeconomic backgrounds, and a widening range of intellectual abilities. Children labeled as gifted, learning disabled, attention deficit disorder (ADD), or other educationally challenged learners will be thrown into the mix of eager faces looking toward the teacher. One reason for these changes is the current inclusion movement. Although there is far from a consensus on the subject, advocates for inclusion strongly believe that students with learning disabilities increasingly benefit, both academically and socially, from placement in the regular classroom (Dugger 1994; O'Neil 1994/1995). In numerous schools, these often segregated learners will return to the regular classroom from either the

151

self-contained or the resource classrooms where many currently receive all or part of their education. Proponents have put forth the convincing rationale that the regular classroom can bolster academic performance because students would be held to higher expectations, exposed to more challenging content, and motivated by classroom peers; their social growth can also be strengthened (Dugger 1994; Willis 1994). When teachers teach to student strengths, students also see themselves as learning positively while their peers see strengths in every student. Teaching to student strengths helps students overcome their weaknesses (Tomlinson and Jarvis 2006). Although some educators and members of the media argue against inclusion, these changes are already occurring in classrooms across America.

A possible secret to success lies in **differentiated instruction.** When teachers do so, they teach learners based upon their individual abilities, selecting from a variety of methods and materials. As a result, they are better able to match the present skills

---

☞ IN THE CLASSROOM

Successful Teaching Premises for All Learners

1. Each learner is unique. Therefore, all learning experiences must take into account the abilities, interests, and learning styles of the individual.

2. Learning is more effective when students enjoy what they're doing. Therefore, learning experiences should be designed and assessed with as much concern for enjoyment as for other goals.

3. Learning is more meaningful and enjoyable when content (e.g., knowledge) and process (e.g., thinking skills) have a real problem as their context. Therefore, students should have some choice in problem selection and teachers should consider the relevance of the problem for individual students as well as authentic strategies for addressing the problem (Taylor and Larson, 2000).

4. Enrichment learning and teaching focus on enhancing knowledge and acquiring thinking skills. Therefore, applications of knowledge and skills must supplement formal instruction (Levstik and Barton 1997; Renzulli 1994/1995, 77).

5. Teach to the strengths of each learner. Remediate other areas, developing compensatory skills in the process (Tomlinson and Jarvis 2006).

6. Use direct instruction to ensure understanding.

7. Allow enough time for students to read and to write as students integrate skills across the curriculum.

8. Give directions in different ways—oral, written, visual, and/or auditory—cueing the learners as is necessary.

9. Model new learning strategies, actively demonstrating how they work rather than just giving an assignment.

10. Provide peer buddies to be learning partners or tutors when necessary.

11. Evaluate each learner on his or her individual performances, looking at alternative assessment options that reinforce success.

12. Stay positive. Be patient. Every child is a learner and can grow within a supportive and thoughtfully managed classroom (Farris, Fuhler, and Walther 2004).

of a particular learner (Franklin 2002). One way to find out where students are in their social studies learning is to apply a self-assessment procedure (Brimijoin, Marquissee, and Tomlinson 2003). Using a car windshield metaphor, the teacher asks, "How many of you are as clear as glass about the reasons for the American Revolution? How many of you have bugs on your windshield? How many have windshields covered with mud?" On the basis of their spontaneous self-assessment of "glass, bugs, and mud," along with the teacher's own observations of comments during class discussion and group interactions, students are then assigned to one of three different follow-up activities depending on each student's own learning needs. This differentiated instruction approach helps to meet the needs of all students in the classroom.

Depending on the school district, inclusion may extend to those students identified as **gifted.** This change is impelled by a spreading philosophy that encourages mixed-ability grouping and is facilitated by decreasing funding for separate programs for these bright learners (Renzulli and Reis 1993; Willis 1995). Such a move raises the ire of some educators and is strongly supported by others. On one hand, concerned educators worry that "detracking" (Sapon-Shevin 1994/1995, 64) will dilute the quality of education, will force students to learn the pallid fare of a dumbed-down curriculum, and will deny the existence of individual differences. On the other hand, advocates claim these bright young students should learn in a classroom reflective of the community they will eventually work in. Thus, gifted students may be an integral part of the classroom, no longer served by pull-out programs or by completely separate programs. The burden of meeting all these learners' needs ought not to rest entirely on the classroom teacher. Joseph Renzulli, a noted authority in the field of gifted education, suggests that in addition to classroom instruction extremely bright children might benefit from mentor programs, special study groups, and classes outside their grade level (Renzulli and Reis 1993; Silverman 1993; Willis 1995).

Reaching and teaching students along an extensive continuum of skills and abilities within the realm of social studies is the focus of this chapter. Based on the firm belief that all students can learn, suggestions are offered here that will perhaps "raise the floor and raise the ceiling" (Wheelock 1992, 6) of learning for students described as slow learners or learning disabled, students struggling with attention deficit difficulties, or exceptionally bright students. Despite their labels, all children deserve the opportunity to be tuned in and turned on to social studies. One of the best predictors of students' effort and engagement is the relationships they have with teachers (Scherer 2006). Social studies provides teachers with the opportunity to listen to students' perspectives and be supportive of their feelings and interests. The challenge facing the teacher is just how to accomplish such an exciting but seemingly overwhelming task. The first step is to understand a little about some of the different students within the class.

A Look at Gifted Learners

According to Renzulli (1994/1995), there is no single criterion that determines who is gifted and who is not. Instead, giftedness consists of behaviors that indicate interaction among three clusters of human traits:

1. Above average (not necessarily superior) general and/or specific abilities, which means performance—or the potential for performance—representative of the top 15 or 20 percent of any given area of human behavior.

2. High levels of task commitment, which is the perseverance, hard work, and self-confident energy applied to a particular problem or performance area.

3. High levels of creativity, including fluency, flexibility, originality of thought, openness to experiences, curiosity, and sensitivity to detail (Siegel 1990).

These are simple guidelines, however. Some children may display these characteristics while others don't fit into any gifted mold. Brian, a primary-age gifted child, explains the term as meaning, "You have lots and lots of ideas in your head that are bumping into each other all trying to get out" (Siegel 1990, 8). At present, we have no definitive description of what gifted children are like. New ideas of what the term means are constantly being developed; in the meantime, these learners will distinguish themselves in the social studies classroom in one way or another.

Suggested Classroom Strategies

The suggestions for teaching the brightest children in a classroom are exciting because they are strategies that can be adapted to challenge every learner. For example, in an effort to teach all the children in the classroom, strategies such as **flexible grouping** or **differentiated assignments** can be implemented. In differentiated assignments, all students explore the same topic but the level of questioning or the expected product varies depending on ability levels. Ability-based reading and discussion groups could be formed for some projects. Learning centers could be filled with a wide range of materials for reading and research. Individual student contracts could be tied to specific research projects based on personal interest. Finally, mentorships with adults outside the classroom or the school could be carefully worked into the social studies curriculum (Silverman 1993; Willis 1995).

Another effective suggestion for bright students is **curriculum compacting** (Reis and Renzulli 1992). In this process, the teacher tests students on upcoming units to ascertain what they already know. While a specific unit is being taught to the rest of the class, students who have mastered the content can pursue enrichment activities. That is, the teacher defines goals and outcomes of a unit and determines which students have already mastered the learning outcomes and which students can master outcomes in less time than their classmates. Then, in place of mastered material, more challenging and productive activities are provided, including content acceleration, peer teaching, and involvement in outside-the-class activities. Another important step for the teacher is to analyze the textbook, deciding which material is necessary for review, what else is necessary to cover quickly, and what should be covered in an in-depth manner (Renzulli 1994/1995).

An additional strategy is to allow students of varying abilities to work together on topics in which they are mutually interested as a kind of flexible grouping strategy. The major criteria for group effectiveness are commonality of purpose, mutual respect among students, harmony, specific interests, complementary skills, or even friendships. Group work based occasionally on friendships can help promote self-concepts and self-efficacy in students with high abilities as well as in students who struggle with academic demands. This type of grouping enables each child to stretch as a project is completed. To help children grow as learners, teachers need to tap outside sources when developing thematic units. Gifted children might develop a mentorship with an authority outside the classroom, but all children should be exposed to quality speakers, interesting field trips, or other projects that connect the outside world with the classroom world in real ways.

In a social studies classroom that reflects a wide range of abilities, another critical step for the teacher is to change focus. Rather than focus on skill development and the memorization of facts, teachers should refocus on **interdisciplinary teaching** and theme-based units, student portfolios, and cross-grade grouping whenever possible while continually keeping the individual child in mind. (Renzulli 1994/1995; Siegel 1990). The new focus of all students' work should be an inquiry-based curriculum that develops higher-level thinking skills (Silverman 1993; Wheelock 1992). In the process, students pursue topics as firsthand investigators rather than as traditional passive learners. For example, the Internet offers a world of fascinating Web sites to extend learning opportunities for the gifted student. Start off with several carefully previewed sites relating to the social studies content under study. Then, tie information gleaned on the Internet to varied classroom resources in the form of a multigenre writing project as suggested later in this chapter (In the Classroom: Dissolving the Classroom Walls through Technology with a Closer Look at the Underground Railroad). In this case, students present final projects integrating different genres of writing to represent a captivating slice of history. Perhaps a combination of fictional journal entries, shopping lists, telegrams, new articles, letters, or posters might be some of the options chosen. This type of writing is sure to stretch thinking and creativity. Involved in the process, students grow as researchers, thinkers, and writers who understand the possibilities of different types of text (Grierson, Anson, and Baird 2002).

A further strength of interdisciplinary teaching is that it broadens the arena for learning for all players, opens large blocks of time for in-depth study of a topic, and allows for more opportunities for student choice, a boon to every learner. Using this approach, students are actively "doing history" rather than being stuck in the traditional roll of chapter by chapter review of the year's social studies curriculum (Levstik and Barton 1997; Moore, Moore, Cunningham, and Cunningham 2003). If you are worried that some learners might falter using the preceding strategies, consider this advice. Teaching to the top helps meet the needs of the brightest in the class while the teacher strives to bring the others along; this tactic is much more efficient than teaching to the middle (Willis 1995).

A Look at Students with Learning Disabilities

A teacher entering an elementary school or junior high social studies classroom probably cannot at first glance single out a mainstreamed student with a **learning disability.** For the most part, these unique learners do not display an observable collection of symptoms. Because no two students labeled as learning disabled are alike, a straightforward, accurate definition remains elusive. More than 50 attempts to pigeonhole this group of learners are currently on the books. It is no wonder that numerous children have been misidentified, swelling the ranks of this catchall category to include a large number of underachievers and slow learners as well ("Learning Disabilities" 1990). Briefly, these children have a disorder in the basic psychological processes involved in understanding or using spoken or written language such that it hampers that student's ability to think, speak, read, or make mathematical calculations. If a severe discrepancy between ability and achievement is found based on the use of a discrepancy formula, the student is considered to be learning disabled.

In creating an appealing educational setting for these learners, teachers must consider the issue of motivation. After years of failure in and out of self-contained classrooms, many students with learning disabilities are reluctant to risk any more. Their battered, fragile egos are buried under a thick, protective covering of feigned indifference and negative or cocky attitudes. Their discouragement can be traced by backtracking along a lengthy trail of incomplete assignments. At a time when conformity and peer approval are a top priority, these students spend much time and energy proving they are not different from their agemates. This potent social-emotional overlap to basic cognitive deficits presents teachers and learners with a formidable challenge.

Here, too, working across the curriculum, making a serious effort to connect thinking content areas, is a sound educational strategy for learners identified as **learning disabled (LD)** or **Attention Deficit Disorder/Attention Deficit Hyperactivity Disorder ADD/ADHD** with an individualized education plan, or to slow learners who have slipped through the cracks of the identification system. For instruction to be most beneficial, teachers must consider a learner's identified strengths and weaknesses. Isn't this just highlighting the fact that learning is an intensely personal endeavor? At first glance, integrating instruction while still individualizing or differentiating instruction to meet student's needs might seem incompatible, but that is not the case. They mesh with a complementary, syncopated beat. When the class as a whole moves forward with a basic rhythm of its own, the educational accent shifts to a different beat, acknowledging specific individual needs that can be met with direct instruction. To maintain a toe-tapping tempo, then, teachers directly teach individual students what they need, when they need it, within the context of their own reading and writing (Routman 1991; Taylor and Larson 2000). These teachers maintain a catchy educational rhythm because they have learned to take advantage of individual and collective teachable moments.

To get a better picture of a student with learning difficulties, let's look at the area of reading. Middle school and junior high students with learning difficulties are commonly reading three to four years below grade level, plateauing at the fifth or sixth grade level late in high school (Whyte 1983). Compare this to their gifted counterparts, who may be reading two years or more above grade level. In addition, learning disabled students may have short attention spans or auditory memory problems that hamper the development of proficient listening abilities. Some of these learners have difficulty forming thoughts well enough to speak smoothly in front of class, while others are lacking useful study strategies. The often segregated skills of reading, writing, listening, and speaking, inherent in the successful naviga-

Additional time should be provided for special needs students to complete their assignments.

tion of the social studies curriculum, need to be addressed in a different way to meet this population's needs. An integrated teaching approach taught by enthusiastic, well-versed educators offers hope to students with learning difficulties.

Specific Teaching Strategies

One general tactic that will benefit students who are slow learners, or others with learning disabilities, is to carefully scaffold instruction (Moore et al. 2003). Simply put, scaffolding means that the teacher makes certain each learner has enough support to complete a learning task successfully (Larkin 2001). Thus, a teacher provides one-on-one guidance through a new activity until he or she senses that the learner is gaining competence and confidence. Assistance is gradually removed as the learner masters the skill or task. For example, before beginning a project as part of a unit on the study of Native Americans, the teacher would chat with the student, zeroing in on a topic of personal interest. Next, teacher and student would establish a goal related to the project. Instruction and guidance would be tailored to the student's needs and abilities.

Support and feedback would continue as the student worked toward the established goal. Once the project was completed, both the teacher and student would conference, discussing the progress made. It is hoped that the skills acquired throughout the project will generalize to the next learning task where the learner would be supported less as he or she becomes more independent.

The adage "practice makes perfect" ought to be elevated to an interdisciplinary educational golden rule. Its application can improve all students' skills and should be kept in mind as learners read, write, think, and integrate knowledge across the curriculum. Teachers addressing the needs of students who have learning disabilities, or who are considered slow or struggling learners, or who display symptoms of ADD/ADHD, should remember the following premises:

1. Allocate time for practice in reading and writing across the curriculum. Continue to teach critical skills and thinking strategies within the context of the students' reading and writing (Graham and Harris 1988; Routman 1991).

2. Whenever new concepts or learning strategies are taught, model, model, model.

3. Expose students to a broad range of reading and writing tasks. Replace contrived writing assignments with more natural writing activities (Farris et al. 2004; Negron and Ricklin 1996).

4. Create a supportive learning climate. Students will need to reestablish confidence so that they can risk without ridicule.

5. Integrate a writers' workshop format into social studies, breaking writing projects into less overwhelming stages.

6. Individual conferences can be used for a quick assessment of progress. They may be as short as 45 seconds or as long as necessary. It is the concerned, personal touch that counts.

7. Small group work promotes constructive peer interaction. Combined efforts with everyone doing his or her share yield rewarding results.

8. Hold miniworkshops—skills still need to be taught directly and reinforced frequently to promote academic success. Take a few minutes to highlight a skill that a number of students need to review before starting a new project.

   a. Present new information both orally and in writing, modeling procedures on the chalkboard or an overhead transparency.

   b. Repeat important information several times to ensure learning. Begin each day's reading or lecture with a review of previous materials to aid connections with social studies content. Teach the use of mnemonic devices to help organize key information (Taylor and Larson 2000).

   c. Continue to teach skills—such as previewing, questioning, and making predictions—within the context of literature books and the social studies text. Urge students to use what they know about language to continually construct meaning from text.

9. Allow for personal choices. Students have a greater vested interest in reading a book or poem or pursuing a project that they have personally selected than one that is assigned by the teacher. That critical element of choice facilitates the development of independence, which is so important for the academic and social growth of students with learning difficulties.

10. Implement Gardner's theory of Multiple Intelligences by supporting students who want to present projects in creative ways rather than in the frequently requested written format. Students might opt to write and perform a rap or bal-

lad (musical intelligence). Others might create a diorama, wall mural, or **jack-daw** (kinesthetic and visual/spatial intelligence). Another group could develop a skit or a tableau of a pertinent moment in history (intrapersonal and interpersonal intelligences) offering learners a memorable opportunity to highlight what they have learned (Taylor and Larson 2000).

A Look at Students with Other Educational Challenges

In the diverse mix that makes up an inclusive classroom it is highly likely that other educationally challenged students will be represented. It is probable that a child with **visual impairments,** a hearing loss, an attention deficit disorder, or the designation of slow learner will be a part of the classroom community. While support staff in the school system can provide guidance for optimal learning for these learners, the following suggestions will also be of use. Because the goal is to facilitate connections with social studies and with learning across the curriculum for each student, there are some basic adaptations to instruction and the learning environment that will help them to be their best.

The Visually Impaired Learner

If a student's sight is impeded by a visual impairment, there are a number of practical options to facilitate learning. Teacher support will include something as simple as placing the student near the board in a well-lighted area, but away from possible glare. Using assistive technology like felt-tipped pens to write assignments for the learner or for the student's use, providing enlarged texts, or adding a magnifying glass to the student's supplies will aid the student in reading assignments. If needed, request a Braille writer and stylus for the student. Another idea is to encourage the student to reach for a cassette recorder if books on tape are available. Sometimes classmates can pitch in and take notes for their peer as well. Consider allowing this student to turn in audiotapes of some assignments rather than having to write them out. Finally, Williams (2002) suggests that teachers look for computer software that can read text aloud or even offer spelling assistance like Write:OutLoud or Co:Writer. Programs like these would also benefit children with learning disabilities or the child with attention deficit difficulties. See figure 5.1 for further assistive technology suggestions. Remember, too, that district personnel are available to offer their expertise.

The Hearing Impaired Learner

The child with a hearing impairment will achieve success with some thoughtful adaptations such as using an overhead projector during direct teaching so that he or she can read key information being presented as well as providing an outline of notes when social studies materials are presented to the rest of the class. If the learner is assigned materials to read in a textbook or other trade books, create a study guide ahead of time to direct the reading process. Visual organizers like a popular Venn diagram, time lines, story maps, or sequencing charts will aid in visually organizing information for these learners (Taylor and Larson 2000; Moore et al. 2003). Teach students to use software like Kidspiration (best suited for kindergarten through grade five) or Inspiration (appropriate for grade six and higher) to facilitate visually organizing information. Students can form webs or diagrams using symbols and pictures along with simple text to help them brainstorm ideas for projects or to organize previously gathered information. This visual format serves to illuminate how facts and ideas might fit together, making the transition to an ensuing project that much easier.

In addition, whenever possible, select captioned films or videotapes to make content knowledge more accessible. As with their classmates, hearing impaired students will enjoy hands-on opportunities to learn. Integrate the computer by posting assignments on a Web page for him or her to download or offer Internet explorations to enrich the lesson and challenge the student. Without a doubt, the computer is a tool that can be adapted to meet the needs of every learner in the classroom, including one identified as having an attention deficit disorder.

The Learner with an Attention Deficit Disorder

Attention deficit disorder (ADD) students frequently distinguish themselves by their high levels of activity and relatively short attention spans. They are characterized as having developmentally inappropriate levels of inattention, impulsivity, and hyperactivity (Carbone 2001). Helping them to stay focused on the task at hand can be done in a variety of ways. First, seat the child in the front row away from distractions like windows, the door to the hallway, or the pencil sharpener. Second, add movement to the classroom routine in the form of drama, role playing, or other creative curricular responses like coming up to the front of the class to write answers on an overhead transparency. Another opportunity to vary the daily routine would involve giving students different classroom management jobs with clearly set expectations (Taylor and Larson 2000). For instance, being the door monitor or taking attendance to the office allows for a little movement while building a sense of responsibility in the student. Then, maintain eye contact with this learner when giving verbal directions, keeping those directions clear and concise. Here, too, scaffolding instruction will help the child stay focused or be better able to follow through on an assignment. Another suggestion is to partner them with classmates who can serve as good role models. Finally, if tasks are interesting and varied, it is more likely that these students will do their best to be attentive (Carbone 2001; Farris et al. 2004). One way to incorporate interest and variety into social studies is through wonderful children's literature.

Assistive Technology for Students

Each special needs student's current level of educational performance needs to be discussed by the classroom teacher, special education teacher, school psychologist, parents or guardians, and other pertinent personnel in order to create an **individualized education plan (IEP)**, which specifies specific learning goals for the student for the academic year. These goals must be measurable in some way, such as recognizing 25 of the 50 states by shape. **Assistive technology** may be needed by some students with disabilities. Any item, piece of equipment, or product, either made commercially, modified, customized, or made by the teacher, that is used to

1 1 1

What is Assistive Technology (AT)?

• It refers to items, pieces of equipment, or products used to increase, maintain, or improve the capabilities of individuals with disabilities.

• These items are often categorized according to their level of complexity.

Examples of low- and high-technology solutions for reading and writing:

Activity	Low-Technology Solutions	High-Technology Solutions
Reading		
• Holding book	• Nonslip mat • Book holder	• Electronic version of book on the computer
• Turning pages	• Rubber finger • Universal cuff with pencil and eraser	• Electric page turner
• Reading words • Writing	• Reading glasses • Magnifying glass • Enlarged print • Slant board • Cardboard "jig" to isolate words (a "jig" is a cutout rectangle used to read word by word) • Ruler to read line by line	• Enlarged computer monitor • Books on tape • Software that "reads out loud" • Reading pen • Language master with books
Writing		
• Holding a pencil	• Built-up pencil • Larger writing instruments • Weighted pen or pencil • Head or mouthstick to hold the instrument	• Orthotics • Prosthetics • Word processor • Laptop computer • Handheld computer
• Keyboarding	• Keyboard mitt with isolated finger • Keyboard overlap • Head or mouthstick • "T-bar"	• Voice-recognition software • Scanning software • Alternative keyboards (expanded or miniature) • Spell check • Cassette recorder • Augmentative communication devices
• Using paper	• Templates • Color-coded or textured-line paper • Tape paper to the desk • Clipboard	• Augmentative communication devices • World processor • Beam assignments to the teacher's handheld or to the classroom printer

Source: Adapted from *Assistive Technology for Individuals with Learning Disabilities, Project ACCEPT* by Toni Van Larrhoven, Dennis Munk, Julie Bosma, and Joanne Rouse. Used by permission.

Figure 5.1 Assistive technology.

increase, maintain, or improve the functional capabilities of a child with a disability is considered an assistive technology device. These devices may be low tech (i.e., word cards containing geography terms such as latitude and longitude, Tropic of Cancer, Tropic of Capricorn, and equator), mid tech (i.e., word processing with spell-checker), or high tech (i.e., voice recognition software that shows the word on the screen ["equator"] when the child says it) (see figure 5.1).

An "Assistive Technology Consideration Quick Wheel" can be obtained for $8.95 plus shipping from the Council for Exceptional Children (1110 N. Glebe Road, Suite 300, Arlington, VA 22201-5704) at www.cec.sped.org at the CEC store (type in "Assistive Technology" at "Books" "Content Area"). The Quick Wheel provides numerous suggestions for low- , mid- , and high-tech assistive technology for communication, reading, learning/studying, math, writing, motor aspects of writing, and computer access. It covers students' needs in terms of hearing, vision, motor skills, and mobility.

Other Web sites for suggestions regarding assistive technology include the Family Center on Technology and Disability (www.fctd.info), which has extensive reviews of assistive technology devices and suggestions. Learning disabilities and technology are addressed at the LDOnline site (www.ldonline.org/indepth/technology). The Wisconsin Assistive Technology Initiative has assessment forms, updates, lending library, information, best practice tips, and more at its site (www.wati.com).

A Case for Children's Literature

In an effort to stretch across the curriculum and integrate subject matter, teachers should infuse their courses with children's literature rather than unappealing textbook fare. A multitude of fiction and nonfiction offerings are available to stimulate a student's personal involvement with history (Temple, Martinez, Yokota, and Naylor 2002). A judicious match between literature book and learner, whatever his or her abilities, can fill in the gaps left by a social studies textbook's factual approach, providing an opportunity to study a "frozen" slice of history at whatever pace or depth is desired (Cline and Taylor 1987). Within the pages of a narrative children's book are new worlds, thought-provoking experiences, and interesting people to widen a student's horizons and deepen understanding as he or she steps across the years (McGowan, Erickson, and Neufeld 1996). In addition, nonfiction children's literature provides an "interesting, lively way to share up-to-date information" (Young and Vardell 1993, 405). Harvey (2002) urges teachers to surround students with compelling nonfiction in various forms including picture books, segments of longer books, newspapers, and magazines. In order to broaden student exposure to this often-ignored genre, teachers should read it aloud regularly. They should use it for instruction, model how to use it to gather information, or as a model for personal writing. Because some nonfiction offerings are quite short, they are less intimidating to struggling readers, while others can challenge the most adept. Fine selections of children's literature will push back the walls erected by the traditional remedial curriculum with impediments to learning so familiar to the student and make room in every learner's mind for fascinating historical worlds yet unexperienced.

In considering other types of nonfiction, one quickly thinks of reference materials. Books that fall into this category need to be brief and to the point for struggling readers, yet presented in an enticing manner. One such book is *Civil War A to Z: A Young Readers' Guide to Over 100 People, Places, and Points of Interest* (Bolotin 2002), a thin encyclopedia of facts about the War between the States. Complete with pictures and simple maps, the book covers abolitionists through the Zouaves regiments, who were largely units of French soldiers fighting for the French in North Africa and for both sides during the Civil War. The book provides a balanced account of the period, including the roles blacks and women played. Written in short text, the book provides information in an interesting fashion that is relevant to today's students. For instance, in presenting the data about the vast numbers of soldiers who died, a small side margin note says:

How Do You Picture 600,000 Battle Dead?
Can you imagine just how many 600,000 people really are? The Union and Confederate dead would fill 2,000 theaters, 13 Major League baseball stadiums, six Super Bowl stadiums, or more than 1,000 elementary schools.

In short measure, students can readily grasp the magnitude of the fatalities both sides suffered via these relatively simple comparisons. Another book is *From Slave Ship to Freedom Road* (Lester 1999), a picture book with vivid descriptions of slavery such as how the captured men were stacked in the slave ships and those who died were tossed overboard to be eaten by sharks.

Such enticing tools of the trade can also extend a teacher's capacity to reach every student in the class. Students' varying reading levels can be accommodated along with their individual interests when a large number of historically related children's literature books and magazines are available to complement the current textbook unit. The more adept reader can travel back in time to the siege of Petersburg during the Civil War, suffering the realities of the war with William, a plantation owner's son in *Across the Lines* (Reeder 1996). This book affords the reader a different perspective as well as Simon, a slave, recounts the siege from amidst Union lines. The less able reader can gather information from *Cecil's Story* (Lyon 1991), as a young boy awaits his father's return from the war realizing how it may tragically change his life. *The Last Brother* (Noble 2006) is based on a true story of how the two eldest brothers had already been killed in battle when the third brother joined the Union Army. The youngest brother tagged along, only for both of them to encounter the battle of Gettysburg. Titles such as these enable the teacher to start where the learner is, progress from there, and create a richer, more diverse educational environment for the entire class.

To overcome flagging motivation often attributed to students with learning disabilities, to challenge the gifted readers, and to hook the child with ADD/ADHD, lively children's literature books are the answer (Hansen and Schmidt 1989; Harvey 2002; McGowan et al., 1996; Tunnell and Ammon 1993). Making an assortment of literature available in both reading and social studies increases the possibility that reluctant learners and inquisitive students alike will become captivated by ideas and events in history. Ducking flying bullets with Tillie in *Thunder at Gettysburg* (Gauch 1990), reacting in horror after shooting a man as Charley does in *Char-*

Dividing large tasks so they are of short duration and accomplished in smaller chunks helps students with closure, making them feel a sense of accomplishment as opposed to being overwhelmed.

ley Skedaddle (Beatty 1987), or cringing under the crack of the whip as it impacts bare skin in *True North* (Lasky 1996) makes history live within the mind of the reader. The magic of reader response is at work here. Readers and listeners are busy people. They reflect on what they hear, interpret it in their own unique way, make connections to an accumulation of previous knowledge, and often predict what might happen next. This process is the basis of the popular premise that a response to a book is a transaction between reader and writer, a personal exploration of meaning (Rosenblatt 1983, 1991).

For striving readers, graphic novels offer an enticing change of pace. While they certainly cannot be viewed as quality literature, with their comic book format they do offer a medium that appeals to many struggling readers, especially boys. Capstone Press (1-800-747-4992 www.capstonepress.com) has a series of graphic novels appropriate for upper elementary and middle schoolers who are low-ability readers. These include biographies on such noted individuals as Benjamin Franklin, Patrick Henry, Nathan Hale, and Helen Keller as well historical-events books about topics such as the Revolutionary War, John Brown's raid, the Civil War, and World War II. Such books can be used to supplement more polished children's and young adult literature while still enabling the students to grasp the social studies concepts put forth.

The teacher should capitalize on this premise by encouraging memorable connections between reader, writer, book, and history. The teacher can facilitate these personal transactions by presenting students with choices from numerous reading materials beyond the textbook. In addition to fiction and nonfiction books, poetry, song lyrics, recipes, maps, and old letters can be included. Their use can heighten enthusiasm, increase time spent in contact with social studies content, and invite a variety of written responses. It is highly probable that these efforts will have a positive impact on learning within the classroom (Cox and Many 1992; Tunnell and Ammon 1993). Levstik (1989, 183) reminds us of the value of historical fiction:

> It can lead to a richer, fuller, and more empathetic understanding of history. Through historical fiction children learn that people in all times have faced change and crisis, that people in all times have basic needs in common, and that these needs remain in our time. Children can discover some of the myriad ways in which humans depend on each other, and of the consequences of success and failure in relationships, both personal and historical.

To pique students' interest in a new area of study, the teacher can read an appropriate children's literature book aloud. Reading aloud daily, even briefly, should be a comfortable niche in the social studies regimen. There is nothing like a book that is read aloud well to entice listeners and to tantalize children's imaginations (Fuhler 1990; Gambrel 1998; Temple et al. 2002). Listening to a book provides an opportunity for readers with disabilities to "taste the delicacy of well-written books regardless of the reading level" (Fountas and Hannigan 1989). As listeners, students are exposed to rich vocabulary and complex sentence structure that would frustrate them if they tackled it on their own.

Students can read coordinated titles independently during reading class or as extra reading in social studies. The teacher then encourages readers to share their reactions and connections to the read-aloud sessions or to text lectures during both large- and small-group discussions. It is not too much to hope that students will carry their reading right out of the classroom when they walk side by side with a main character, caught up in the tale unraveling within the covers of their books.

As they read informational books, students can take notes. This may involve writing down questions developed from their reading, writing down new information, or drawing a pictorial representation of the text or illustrations in the book. By letting students use a wide range of ways to think and record information, students learn to determine importance and interpret information and its value (Buhrow and Garcia 2006). Students can learn of historical firsts that took place during the Civil War: aerial reconnaissance (with hot air balloons), ambulance corps, battle photography, hospital ships, income tax, machine gun, ready-made factory clothing, repeating rifles, ironclad ships, and smoke screen. There were many more firsts in the kinds of weaponry used: bayonet, field and garrison cannon, Gatling gun, grenades, land mines, naval swivel cannon, revolving rifle, and smoothbore guns. Those with musical interests may lean toward discovering what songs were popular in the 1860s, such as "Aura Lee," "Beautiful Dreamer," "Dixie," "Shenandoah," and "When Johnny Comes Marching Home." Other information students will find interesting is that northern white soldiers were paid $13 a month with no clothing allowance withheld while black soldiers were paid $10 a month with $3 deducted for clothing (Partin 2003).

Caught in their quest for knowledge, every learner is empowered with the responsibility for his or her own reading, writing, speaking, listening, and thinking in the process of getting an education. Working in small groups or paired with a partner, each child has more opportunities to be a successful learner despite the complexities of being categorized—either as gifted or with academic underachievement, inefficient learning strategies, cognitive processing deficits, personality problems, or inhibiting emotional reactions to their deficiencies. Thus, working across the curriculum, impelled by captivating literature, is a giant step in the right direction as students acquire skills in how to become independent learners across the curriculum.

Travels Back through Time

Teachers can invigorate the social studies curriculum by mixing and matching the activities suggested in this section to inspire and ignite learners of varying abilities. The thematic units on the Civil War and Native Americans that are presented here encourage interdisciplinary learning. With an eye to district curriculum guidelines and the Standards for Social Studies, teachers can adjust or adapt the following ideas.

The Civil War

Introduce the Civil War with an appropriate read-aloud like *Pink and Say* (Polacco 1994) or *Bull Run* (Fleischman 1995), two fascinating books that will quickly capture the students' interest. Invite students to choose companion books from those listed at the end of this chapter or others that are readily available at the public library or school learning center. Choice should be based on personal interests and appropriate reading levels. In addition, you may want to refer students to the following issues of *Cobblestone* magazine: April 1981 (on highlights of the Civil War), January 1985 (on the making of a newspaper), May 1987 (on Reconstruction), July 1988 (on Gettysburg), January 1989 (on children who influenced history), February 1989 (on Frederick Douglass), February 1993 (on the antislavery movement), April 1997 (on Stonewall Jackson), October 1997 (on the battle of Antietam), December 1998 (on the battle of Vicksburg) and December 1999 (on a child's view of the Civil War). Or purchase the Civil War theme packs from Carus Publishing (www.cobblestonepub.com/themepack/). Civil War Highlights, Reconstruction, Robert E. Lee, Abraham Lincoln, Gettysburg, and the Antislavery Movement are contained in Pack I; Battle of Manassas, Clara Barton, Sengbe and the *Amistad*, Stonewall Jackson, Ulysses S. Grant, and the Battle of Vicksburg are in Pack II. The articles are written at a fifth grade level. These issues are relatively easy reading and might spark some intriguing group projects.

1. As the read-aloud unfolds, ask the students how events in the book mesh with information in the social studies textbook, the book they are reading, or research being conducted for group projects. Have students discuss and then list in their personal journals similarities and differences that they discover (Negron and Ricklin 1996). Encourage learners to continue observations on their own. Check progress periodically.

2. Provide students with spiral-bound notebooks or have students make their own and entitle them Nonfiction Notebooks or Wonder Books (Harvey 2002). Stu-

dents will use these to record their thinking and reactions to the nonfiction reading and writing they are doing. As they investigate topics in the text or on the Internet, these books become places to record things they wonder about. Teacher modeling will inspire students to add questions and wonderings, project ideas, responses to nonfiction writing, notes on topic of interest, drawings, and sketches, or even drafts of poems. The list can be extended as these notebooks help students reflect and make learning a personal experience.

3. Have students keep track of colorful vocabulary words from the read-aloud along with words from literature books they are reading in social studies or reading class. Students can record in their journals words and meanings as well as sentences in which each word is used correctly. Share words with the class on a weekly basis, adding the words, along with a pertinent illustration, to a class dictionary. Dedicate the finished dictionary to future classes.

4. Choose a political figure from the period. Divide students into pairs to do research on the person, on his or her views of the war, and on the dress of the times. Students can present a vignette or play, capturing a day of debates in Congress over issues underlying the war. Students can also take the roles of citizens of the time, displaying thoughts and emotions through conversation in a general store or a chance meeting on the street. Students can play two individuals representing opposing views who meet on a train. This information can also be presented in a town forum. In the process, students will feel like a part of history.

5. Have students compare and contrast the kinds of information they can learn about the Civil War from literature books versus nonfiction selections, a textbook, and the Internet. Make a large chart with a catchy title for the classroom wall, listing information acquired from various literature books. Add to it as new information emerges. Ask students to examine their books for prologues, epilogues, or author's notes to glean historical facts on which their books might be based. Invite the readers to discover if the information is accurate.

6. Involve the class in a discussion of the key issues involved in the Civil War. Groups are formed as students select which side of an issue they support. After students research the issue thoroughly, they present their findings to the class in the form of a presentation with visual aids, a play, interviews with prominent thinkers of the time, or other student suggestions. This is one way to demonstrate how students are able to produce rather than reproduce knowledge as they build on what they knew initially, reflect on what they have learned, and then share the results (Levstik and Barton 1997).

7. As students complete self-selected literature titles, divide the class into groups based on the setting of their stories, the time period covered, or issues such as slavery or the running of the Underground Railroad. Assign a recorder to each group. Ask students to share information that is similar or different in their individual books as you monitor group work. Encourage students to discuss their personal reactions, the feelings of their characters, or the resolution of war-related conflicts within each story. Have each group write a summary of its findings to be shared with the class. Invite the groups to compare and contrast their findings to information from the textbook, class lectures, or both.

8. Work across the curriculum to create an edition of a Civil War newspaper. Provide actual models for the students to study. Perhaps students would like to compare separate issues reflecting the views of the North and of the South. Students can study and write editorials, want ads, ads for runaway slaves, or notices for upcoming slave auctions. They may write reports of the naval battles between the ironclads or of major battles in the field. After studying styles of clothing or menus of the times, they should intersperse that information along with daily news and war correspondence. A review of the use of sketches and photography to capture battle scenes might prompt artistic renditions along with articles by correspondents from different parts of the United States. Publish the final editions by displaying them in the learning center.

9. Have a Civil War reenactor come to class in uniform and discuss a segment of the Civil War. Women often followed the troops. A female participant in a reenactment group could shed light on the reality of life on the battlefield and at home. Students can integrate this information with what they have learned from other resources.

10. If possible, visit a museum that has displays covering the Civil War. Students could research answers to questions they are personally interested in as they study the museum artifacts. Notes taken during the trip can become references for individual research or group projects.

11. Students can be assessed on their research and group work based on conditions set up in individual contracts at the beginning of the thematic unit. Select three or four students a day to meet with briefly, noting progress via anecdotal comments. In that way all students in the class can be monitored during the course of a week. A final conference with each student at the end of the unit that includes the student's written self-evaluation will indicate his or her progress and grasp of knowledge.

Native Americans

The study of Native Americans traditionally falls into the elementary social studies curriculum. The following readings and activities are appropriate for younger students but have strong appeal for older students as well. It is imperative that students of all ages develop a better understanding of different cultures. One place to begin is right here in America. By meeting Native Americans in another time or in another way, students may begin to better appreciate the rich heritage that Native Americans have bequeathed to all Americans. In addition, the knowledge gained at this level provides a firm base on which to later study the contemporary life of Native Americans.

Although the study of Native Americans can take many directions, a good place to start is with their myths and legends. Beautifully illustrated, wonderfully written picture books are available that will appeal to readers of all ages and abilities. You may want to choose a sampling of tales from tribes spanning the country or decide to concentrate on one section of the country, highlighting the Plains tribes, for example. As each tribe is discussed, locate it on a map of the United States.

Begin the thematic unit with a K-W-H-L chart to be posted on a bulletin board or chalkboard throughout the unit. Activate prior knowledge by asking children what they already *know* about Native Americans. This is a critical step for every learner and is rooted in cognitive learning theory, more specifically in schema theory. This theory explains how people attach new information to previously existing

☞ **IN THE CLASSROOM**

Dissolving the Classroom Walls through Technology with a Closer Look at the Underground Railroad

One topic that intrigues many students is the Underground Railroad. To further study this road to freedom for slaves, invite students to learn about the Underground Railroad in a number of ways. Introduce the following Web sites to the students as one option to learn about the people and places involved in moving fleeing slaves to freedom.

Underground Railroad
http://www.nationalgeographic.com/features/99/railroad/
Students follow in the footsteps of Harriet Tubman as they learn about the inner workings of the Underground Railroad from a slave's perspective on this superb site.

Miles to Go Before I Sleep
http://www.exchange.co-nect.net/Teleprojects/project/Railroad
It is 1850 and you are part of a small group of runaways who start from Ripley, Ohio, and must navigate your way to Canada via the Underground Railroad. This is an excellent teleproject with a free teacher's guide and student materials. You must register for the project.

The History Channel
http://www.historychannel.com/exhibits/undergroundrr/
Students in upper grades will find this an outstanding site for research.

Before they begin work, provide students with an appropriate graphic organizer to aid them as they gather and organize information about the Underground Railroad. Another option is to let students create their own organizers using Kidspiration or Inspiration software.

• Read a selection of picture books, analyzing them for facts on the Underground Railroad. Good examples are *Sweet Clara and the Freedom Quilt* (Hopkinson 1993), *The Underground Railroad* (Bial 1999), *Barefoot: Escape on the Underground Railroad* (Edwards 1999), or *Follow the Drinking Gourd* (Winter 1992). Students can then convey directions for a safe route on the Underground Railroad by making their own quilt or compose their own version of Peg Leg Joe's song. Make the directions apply to the school vicinity so other students can try to follow them.

• Read other selections about escapes, such as *Escape from Slavery: Five Journeys to Freedom* (Rappaport 1999), *If You Traveled on the Underground Railroad* (Levine 1993), *Letters from a Slave Girl* (Lyons 2002), or *Running for Our Lives* (Turner 2004). Students can reenact one of the journeys.

• Write or illustrate a book about a real or a fictitious character involved with the Underground Railroad.

• Students may prefer to showcase their learning through multigenre writing (Grierson et al. 2002). The final project showcases a student's learning by blending different types of writing and genres. For instance, a student may study an original bill of sale for a slave and create one as part of his project. He might write a newspaper article discussing the escape of several slaves, prepare a wanted poster describing the slaves, and create diary entries from the owner of a safe house on the route the slave took to freedom. Written from different perspectives and using varying genres, the final project is bound to be engaging to read and to create.

information, or schemata, which are described as collections of related ideas. Learning occurs, then, as new ideas are integrated into a learner's current knowledge. Translating this information into classroom teaching practices suggests that in order for all students to learn most advantageously, it is imperative that new knowledge be built on what students already know. Therefore, being aware of just how much existing knowledge a student has before beginning a new unit of study is the first step in ensuring that every student, regardless of ability, has the best opportunity to learn (Duis 1996; Levstik and Barton 1997). Schema theory makes the Know segment of the K-W-H-L chart particularly important. Furthermore, judicious use of this chart or similar graphic organizers can facilitate thinking skills and offer time for reflecting on what has been learned, both of which are valuable skills needed long after students leave the classroom (Farris et al. 2004).

Then move to the column on what they might *want* to know and fill that in. The column headed by an H asks the students *how* they might find the information in which they are interested. Finally, at the conclusion of the unit, ask the students to explain what they have *learned,* the final column on the chart. The responses that fill this column are one way to assess growth in understanding of the group as a whole.

1. Explain the value of storytelling and its critical role in many cultures since the earliest times in human society. A good example of the importance of storytelling is *Spider Spins a Story* (Max 1997). Although the discussion may be quite familiar to elementary students, tell them that stories were the way Native American heritage was passed on to other generations. Help listeners consider the value of the spoken word in a different light. To the Native Americans, the spoken word was sacred because they used it to pass stories, songs, and chants on to the younger generation. Respectful children who revered their elders retained these messages, regarding them as invaluable. As those children transmitted the words of their elders to their children, a body of knowledge gradually formed, one that future generations would be able to study and to enjoy.

2. Read a selection of chants or poems to the students and discuss their underlying meaning to the Native Americans. Invite students to browse through a collection of wonderful poetry books. Have them select a favorite and read it aloud to the class in a poetry session. Students might use *Spirit Walker* (Wood 1993), *Earth Always Endures: Native American Poems* (Philip 1996), *Dancing Tepees: Poems of American Indian Youth* (Sneve 1989), or *Navajo: Visions and Voices* (Begay 1995).

3. A natural art activity is to create pictures or papier-mâché masks to be displayed in the room or learning center. Children can write a brief explanation of what their mask represents because it is an original work of art.

4. After more exposure to the Native American culture, students may want to write their own chants or poetry as they reflect on their own cultures. Older students might illustrate their writing with appropriate Native American artwork used as a border.

5. Demonstrate the power of the oral tradition by telling a Native American legend that is a personal favorite. Encourage students to discuss why the story might have been passed along over the years. Follow up by reading a selection such as the amusing *Iktomi and the Boulder* (Goble 1988), the beautifully illus-

trated *Beardance* (Hobbs 1997), the pleasing *Sunpainters: Eclipse of the Navajo Sun* (Whitethorne 2002), or a selection from *Earthmaker's Tales* (Mayo 1989). These easily read books will be picked up and reread by young readers as soon as you put them down. Bring storytelling into contemporary times by reading and discussing *Pueblo Storyteller* (Hoyt-Goldsmith 1991). If possible, invite a Native American speaker into class to tell several favorite stories.

6. Older students can research their family background for a story to share with the class. Invite parents or younger students to come to class for a Family Story Sharing Day. While the parent tells the story, the child might hold up an illustration he or she created. The oral tradition is a strong influence in many cultures and is a fine lesson for children to learn.

7. Provide a large selection of books of myths and legends for the students to read independently. Give brief book talks on several titles to entice readers to sample the fare. *Where the Buffaloes Begin* (Baker 1981), *The Star Maiden* (Esbensen 1991), *Snail Girl Brings Water* (Keams 1998), or *How Chipmunk Got His Stripes* (Bruchac and Bruchac 2001) are a few suggestions. *Spider Spins a Story* (Max 1997) is an appealing collection of trickster tales that will delight readers and listeners from first through sixth grades. Consult the school librarian or visit the public library in search of other appropriate titles. The students should keep a record of the books they read, write a sentence or two in reaction to the book, and rate it on a class rating scale. Use this information to assess progress, interest level, and comprehension.

8. Discuss the structure of myths and legends, noting the simple plot that usually relates just one incident. Explain that if several events occur in a story, they are usually "chained together" in sequential order rather than having one event building on another to create a more complex plot. For example, read *Iktomi and the Buzzard* (Goble 1996) through from beginning to end. Then reread the story, having students pick out each incident. Work as a class to start an original Native American tale. After the first few incidents are recorded, let the students break into small groups to finish the story. Read the polished, illustrated versions in class or share them with another class.

9. Investigate the lives of Native American children and their families today. Hobbs's (1989) *Bearstone* is a fictional account of Cloyd Atcitty's struggle to find a place for himself, making it thought-provoking reading for older elementary students. *Lakota Hoop Dancer* (Left Hand Bull and Haldane 1999) will demonstrate how important it is for many Native American tribes to keep their traditions and their culture alive.

10. Visit a local museum to study a display depicting the daily lives of Native Americans in the past. Have an informed adult explain the display. Ask students to write about what they learned or what they want to know more about after returning to the classroom.

11. Invite Native Americans to share their music and their dances with the class. The symbolism behind the dances and the costumes can be explained in simple terms to the listeners.

12. As a culminating activity, children can act out their favorite myth or legend, or the one they created in class. Parents can help with simple costumes, and background music can be provided by a tape of authentic Native American music. Parents, another class, or both can be the delighted audience (Negron and Ricklin 1996).

Technology: Handhelds in the Social Studies Classroom

Technology is increasingly making itself an integral part of the educational realm. At the forefront of new options are **handhelds,** also referred to as handheld computers or personal digital assistants (PDAs). These minute computers fit into one's palm with ease and readily tuck into a backpack or purse (Brown 2001). If they are integrated into the curriculum wisely, they have the potential to facilitate learning in a myriad of ways for nearly all learners. By using these easily transported devices, learning can take place almost anywhere at any time, expanding it beyond the classroom and typical school hours. With the appropriate downloaded programs students might:

• Take and store digital pictures related to a project

• Draw a picture

• Make a concept map that summarizes chapter content

• Record observations on a field trip

• Graph pertinent data

• Make a time line of historical events

• Take notes in class or type a draft using an accompanying keyboard

Most handhelds come with a cradle attachment that enables information to be transferred from the handheld to a desktop computer. The invitation to use them to differentiate instruction to meet the needs of all learners in the social studies classroom is tantalizing. Visit the following sites to learn more about this up and coming technological innovations.

K–12 Handhelds: Handheld Solutions for Educators
http://www.k12handhelds.com/
Packed with information, this site offers free programs to download, a list of 101 ways to use Palms in the classroom, a discussion board, and more.

Learning in the Palm of Your Hand
http://www.handheld.hice-dev.org/
Educators who are using handhelds have created this site. Read their success stories, browse through the archives, and learn about free downloads.

Planet 5th: Mr. Vincent's Fifth Grade
http://www.mpsomaha.org/willow/p5/handhelds
Learn how enthusiastic fifth grade students use some of the programs available for handhelds and pick up additional ideas from their teacher as he shares some of his classroom experiences.

NCSS STANDARDS-LINKED LESSON PLAN

Theme: Historical Connections

Source: Carol J. Fuhler, Iowa State University

Objectives:

• Students will explore different periods of history in small groups using children's literature, non-fiction resources, and the Internet.

• Students will learn how to use a time line to portray a series of historical events.

• Students will present a researched segment of history through art and drama.

NCSS Themes:

   I. Culture

   II. Time, Continuity, and Change

   III. People, Places, and Environments

Materials: Butcher paper and art supplies, simple costumes, additional fiction and nonfiction resources, paper, pens/pencils for data collection, one of the following book titles:

     Primary-middle level elementary: Miccucci, Charles. 1994. *The Life and Times of the Apple.* New York: Orchard Books.

     Middle school: Kurlansky, Mark. 2001. *The Cod's Tale.* Illus. S. D. Schindler. New York: G. P. Putnam's Sons.

Process: Following the introductory read-aloud, the research and resulting art and drama project will be completed in small groups. After reading aloud *The Life and Times of the Apple* or *The Cod's Tale,* the teacher will:

• discuss and review the main points, examining how they affected society over time.

• teach key vocabulary at the primary level like past, present, future, and long ago.

• teach concepts such as chronology, causality, change, conflict, and complexity at the middle school level to explain and analyze changes over time.

• divide the class into cooperative learning groups based upon topic interest as related to the books above.

• begin research on a topic, person, or period of history from the selected book using materials and Web sites gathered ahead of time.

• teach how to organize data being gathered using a web, graphic organizer, software like Inspiration or Kidspiration, or a graphic option on a handheld.

• demonstrate how each group will present the information.

• monitor the design and creation of each section of the mural. Each group's segment will serve as a piece of the time line, thus organizing the presentations in chronological order. It will also become the backdrop for their historical dramatic portrayal.

• suggest that the drama might take the form of a pantomime with a speaker relating key historical points during the actions. It might also become a tableau of actors with the speaker again highlighting the events being depicted.

• invite an appropriate audience to view the completed work.

Instructional Comments: This is an activity that could take two to three weeks depending on the time a teacher would like to allocate to it. It will facilitate learning to work in groups at both grade levels. In the process it will enable students with varying educational needs to be supported in their learning by their peers. The final project will make an appealing presentation to other classes in the school and to parents at an evening school event.

Learning Styles Addressed: Verbal/linguistic, visual/spatial, interpersonal, intrapersonal, logical/mathematical.

Standards Addressed: Time, Continuity, and Change

Early Grades

a. Demonstrate an ability to use correctly vocabulary associated with time, such as past, present, future, and long ago by reading and constructing simple time lines; identify examples of change; recognize examples of cause-and-effect relationships.

Middle Grades

b. Identify and use key concepts such as chronology, causality, change, conflict, and complexity to explain, analyze, and show connections among patterns of historical change and continuity.

c. Identify and describe selected historical periods and patterns of change within and across cultures, such as the rise of civilizations, the development of transportation systems, the growth and breakdown of colonial systems, and others.

Evaluation: The research, time-line mural, and presentation should be evaluated based upon the following questions that may form the basis of a rubric:

• Did students research their selected topic using appropriate resources?

• Was information organized into a web or other graphic organizer before the written work was completed?

• Was the written portion of the presentation adequately edited and polished for presentation?

• Did the group interact collaboratively and share equally in the learning?

• Was the related section of the time line mural backdrop created by all members of the group?

• Were the drama, pantomime, and speaking role practiced and polished?

• Was each student required to complete a thoughtful and honest self-evaluation?

Modifications for Diverse Learners: Prepare audiotapes of each book so that learners can "reread" the text as necessary. Supply magnifying glasses to students who have visual handicaps so that they can see and appreciate the details in these books. Scaffold instruction using one-on-one conversations, prompts, and graphic organizers. Using small groups and/or a teacher's aide will also provide additional reading, writing, and speaking support to diverse learners.

Extensions: A variety of activities can evolve from this project.

• Provide fiction and nonfiction titles related to the read-aloud books so that students can extend their knowledge. For example, primary readers might select fictional titles like *How to Make an Apple Pie and See the World* (Priceman 1994), *The Apple King* (Bosca 2001), or *Johnny Appleseed* (Kellogg 1988). An appealing nonfiction choice is *Apples Here!* (Hubbell 2002). Middle grade readers might choose from a wealth of nonfiction titles like *Around the World in a Hundred Years* (Fritz 1994), *Ocean* (MacQuitty 2000), or *Food Watch* (Bramwell 2001). Finally, *Giving Thanks: The 1621 Harvest Feast* (Waters 2001) is a fictional reenactment of the harvest celebration involving the Pilgrims and the Wampanoag people.

• Interview owners of a local orchard and summarize the information in a newspaper article format addressing the questions who, what, where, when, and why.

• Interview owners of a local grocery store, a truck driver, or a representative from the railroad to learn about transporting goods cross-country. Present the information to the class in a PowerPoint presentation, chart, or news article as mentioned above.

• Write and illustrate an A B C book as a variation on the read-aloud title, incorporating information gleaned from research.

Variations: Pick another product that can travel through time and connect different periods of history. Instead of presenting information via a time line mural and drama, students might try the multigenre approach discussed in the chapter.

Bibliography

Bosca, F. 2001. *The Apple King.* Illus. G. Ferri. New York: North-South.

Bramwell, M. 2001. *Food Watch.* New York: DK Publishing.

Fritz, J. 1994. *Around the World in a Hundred Years: From Henrythe Navigator to Magellan.* Illus. A. B. Vent. New York: G. P. Putnam's Sons.

Hubbell, W. 2002. *Apples Here!* New York: Albert Whitman.

Kellogg, S. 1988. *Johnny Appleseed.* New York: Morrow.

MacQuitty, M. 2000. *Ocean.* Photo. F. Greenaway. New York: Dorling Kindersley.

Priceman, M. 1994. *How to Make an Apple Pie and See the World.* New York: Alfred A. Knopf.

Waters, K. 2001. *Giving Thanks: The 1621 Harvest Feast.* Illus. and photo. R. Kendall. New York: Scholastic.

Chapter Summary

Social studies becomes more relevant when teachers nurture all dimensions of intelligence rather than define and measure fixed ability, as so often happens in a labeling process. Such nurturing is facilitated when students are given a choice of materials they can readily read, write about, and discuss. Pertinent integrated instructional activities can assist the classroom teacher in facilitating social studies instruction by treating students as citizens of a learning community rather than as products of an assembly line.

The wide range of narrative and nonfiction children's books currently available makes it easier to develop interdisciplinary thematic units for social studies. This chapter provided examples of children's literature and activities for the Civil War and an introduction to Native Americans. In actuality, most topics in social studies can be taught through thematic units because of the vast variety and number of children's literature books and the activities that teachers and students can develop to accompany them. Wrapped up in history, literature, and choice, all learners can discover that "persistent effort is the precursor to success in life and is the basis for lifelong learning" as future productive citizens in our democracy (Wheelock 1992, 8).

Children's Literature Recommendations

The Civil War

Ackerman, K. 1990. *The Tin Heart.* Illus. M. Hays. New York: Atheneum. Mahaley and Flora are best friends who live on different sides of the Ohio River. Traveling back and forth on her father's ferryboat, Mahaley is able to visit Flora frequently. Each wearing one-half of a tin heart, they pledge their friendship forever. As the Civil War erupts, more than the river threatens that pledge. (Gr. 3–5)

Beatty, P. 1984. *Turn Homeward, Hannalee.* New York: Morrow. Twelve-year-old Hannalee and her brother Jem are branded as traitors for making cloth and rope for the Confederacy. When they are sent north to work, Hannalee must serve a harsh employer while

Jem is sent to a farm. Disguised as a boy, Hannalee runs away, finds Jem, and they return to devastated Roswell, Georgia. (Gr. 4–8)

———. 1987. *Charley Skedaddle.* New York: Morrow. A tough New York street kid and member of the Bowery Boys, Charley finds himself a drummer boy in the Union Army. Underneath the tough exterior is a young man who is lonely on the troop ship, horrified in battle, repulsed when he shoots a Rebel, and filled with guilt when he "skedaddles" from battle. An old mountain woman teaches him to believe in himself again. (Gr. 4–8)

Bial, R. 1999. *The Underground Railroad.* Boston: Houghton Mifflin. Ray Bial has retraced a portion of the Underground Railroad via his sensitive color photos and insightful word crafting. (Gr. 4–7)

Bolotin, N. 2002. *Civil War A to Z: A Young Readers' Guide to Over 100 People, Places, and Points of Interest.* New York: Dutton. Personality sketches and career briefs as well as explanations of battles and their significance are presented in this handy reference to the Civil War. (Gr. 3–6)

Brill, M. T. 2000. *The Diary of a Drummer Boy.* Illus. M. Garland. Brookfield, CT: Millbrook Press. When 12-year-old Orion Howe joined the Union Army he never thought he would miss his younger sister or the daily routine at home. The grim days of battle changed his perspective but he emerged from the war a real hero. He was awarded the Congressional Medal of Honor. (Gr. 3–6)

Bunting, E. 1996. *The Blue and the Gray.* Illus. N. Bittinger. New York: Scholastic. A young African American boy and his friend watch the construction of a house that will make them neighbors. Images of a Civil War battle vividly connect the past and the present as the boys reflect on the roots of their friendship. (Gr. 3–5)

Crane, S. 1981. *The Red Badge of Courage.* New York: Tor Books. Young Henry Fleming is skeptical as he and his fellow U.S. Army men prepare to fight Confederate soldiers during the Civil War. Henry thinks of soldiers as heroes one moment and as cowards the next. As a result of his own cowardice, he must face his own worth both as a U.S. soldier and as a human being. (Gr. 6–8)

Diouf, S. A. 2001. *Growing Up in Slavery.* Brookside, CT: Millbrook Press. A valuable classroom resource that illustrates the strength and the suffering endured by children who were raised in slavery. The photographs and prints add further insight. (Gr. 2–8)

Edwards, P. 1999. *Barefoot: Escape on the Underground Railroad.* Illus. H. Cole. New York: Harper Trophy. Dark shadows follow a young boy as he runs away from his slave owner as the heavy boots rush after him. A superb book about slavery. (Gr. 3–5)

Fleischman, P. 1995. *Bull Run.* Illus. D. Frampton. New York: HarperCollins. The first engagement of the Civil War is described through the vignettes of 16 memorable characters. Each distinctive voice contributes to a picture of the life-shattering tragedy for anyone involved in this war. (Gr. 4–8)

Freedman, R. 1987. *Lincoln: A Photobiography.* New York: Clarion. The author shapes a vivid portrait of the sixteenth president from historical photographs, magazine prints, and other pertinent documents. The facts of Lincoln's life, from the growing-up years to the turmoil of his presidency, are presented in informative, straightforward text. (Gr. 4–12)

Fritz, J. 1987. *Brady.* Illus. L. Ward. New York: Coward, McCann. Brady cannot keep a secret, a fact that worries his parents when he discovers their activities with the Underground Railroad. Brady's resourcefulness in time of need saves the life of a runaway slave and proves he can do a man's work. (Gr. 5–8)

———. 1993. *Just a Few Words, Mr. Lincoln: The Story of the Gettysburg Address.* Illus. C. Robinson. New York: Putnam. This relates the story of the Gettysburg Address at an easy reading level. (Gr. 4–8)

Gauch, P. L. 1990. *Thunder at Gettysburg.* New York: Coward, McCann. Young Tillie is excited as she watches the beginning of the battle from an upper window of her home.

Before the battle is over, she has experienced the pain and horror of war as she ducks flying shells and tries to comfort the wounded. Very easy to read book. (Gr. 3–5)

Hamilton, V. 1984. *The House of Dies Drear.* Illus. E. Keith. New York: Macmillan. Add together one huge Civil War era house with secret tunnels, a cranky caretaker, buried treasure, and the possibilities of a ghost and you have the makings of fascinating reading. Thirteen-year-old Thomas leads readers through the pages and through history as they learn together about the Underground Railroad and the mysteries of Dies Drear. (Gr. 3–6)

Hopkinson, D. 1993. *Sweet Clara and the Freedom Quilt.* Illus. J. Ransome. New York: Random House. Sweet Clara applies her needlework skills to the scraps she collects in an effort to make a quilt showing the way to freedom. (Gr. 2–6)

Hunt, I. 1964/1987. *Across Five Aprils.* Chicago: Follett. The hardship, suffering, and courage of a young farm boy living near Newton, Illinois, are related as nine-year-old Jethro Creighton gradually takes full responsibility for the farmwork as a result of tragic home situations caused by brothers and cousins who fight on opposite sides in the war. (Gr. 6–8)

Johnston, T. 1996. *The Wagon.* Illus. J. E. Ransome. New York: Tambourine. Born into slavery and supported by his caring family, a 12-year-old boy relates the anger he feels as a slave and the sorrow he carries when he gains his freedom and Lincoln loses his life. (Gr. 3–5)

Lasky, K. 1996. *True North.* New York: Blue Sky Press. This story unfolds through alternating voices. Fourteen-year-old Lucy lives a life of comfort in Boston while Afrika, a young slave girl, works her way alone along the Underground Railroad. The girls become bound together when Lucy follows her abolitionist grandfather's beliefs and helps Afrika complete her journey. (Gr. 5–8)

Lester, J. 1968. *To Be a Slave.* Illus. T. Feelings. New York: Dial. In this Newbery Honor book, the author combines the actual testimony of former slaves with his own commentary in an effort to bring the reality of the institution of slavery to the reader. (Gr. 6–8)

———. 1999. *From Slave Ship to Freedom Road.* Illus. R. Brown. New York: Puffin. A picture book with the factual detail of slavery and how freedom was eventually gained. (Gr. 4–8).

Levine, E. 1988. *If You Traveled on the Underground Railroad.* Illus. R. Williams. New York: Scholastic. A well-concealed railroad helped thousands of slaves escape from owners in the South to freedom in the North. How it worked, what the dangers were, and who helped along the way are explained in this fascinating, easy to understand book. (Gr. 2–6)

———. 1993. *If You Traveled on the Underground Railroad.* New York: Scholastic. Part of the "If You Traveled . . ." series, this picture book depicts the hardships and danger that the slaves and their protectors faced. (Gr. 4–8)

Lewin, T. 2001. *Red Legs: A Drummer Boy of the Civil War.* New York: HarperCollins. A modern day reenactment brings the past to life as young Stephen assumes the role of a Union drummer boy. The reality of war is vividly portrayed as it becomes apparent that Stephen dies in battle. (Gr. 2–6)

Lincoln, A. 1995. *The Gettysburg Address.* Illus. M. McCurdy. Boston: Houghton Mifflin. Lincoln's powerful words penned in 1863 carry their strong impact to today's reader as well. (Gr. 3–6)

Lunn, J. 1983. *The Root Cellar.* New York: Scribner's. When her grandmother dies, shy Rose is sent to the northern shores of Lake Ontario to live with her Aunt Nan's lively family. The discovery of a vine-covered root cellar door draws her into a world of more than 100 years ago, where she is eventually pulled into the tragedies of the Civil War. (Gr. 5–8)

Lyon, G. E. 1991. *Cecil's Story.* Illus. P. Catalanotto. New York: Orchard. When his father goes off to war, a young boy takes on his father's chores while worrying and waiting for news about his safety. (Gr. 2–8)

Lyons, M. 2002. *Letters from a Slave Girl*. New York: Glencoe/McGraw-Hill. Based on the letters and diaries of Harriet Jacobs's own life, this biography is poignant. (Gr. 5–8)

McKissick, P., and F. McKissick. 1994. *Sojourner Truth: Ain't I a Woman?* New York: Scholastic. This is a particularly well-written biography detailing the life of a slave born in New York who changed her name from Isabella to Sojourner Truth. A tall woman and a powerful speaker, she was a preacher, abolitionist, and activist for the rights of blacks and women during her memorable lifetime. (Gr. 6–8)

Marston, H. I. 1995. *Isaac Johnson: From Slave to Stonecutter*. Illus. M. M. Brown. New York: Cobblehill. Based upon extensive research, this book details Isaac's life from the time he was sold into slavery as a seven-year-old to his escape to a better life in Canada. (Gr. 2–5)

Meltzer, M. 1989. *Voices from the Civil War*. New York: Crowell. The author depicts life during the Civil War through the words of people who were there, using such primary sources as letters, diaries, ballads, newspapers, interviews, speeches, and memoirs. The text is highlighted with engrossing photographs. (Gr. 6–8)

Murphy, J. 1990. *The Boys' War—Confederate and Union Soldiers Talk about the Civil War*. New York: Clarion. This book presents a riveting picture of the Civil War through the eyes of boys involved in it. More than 50 archival photographs are included. (Gr. 3–8)

———. 1992. *The Long Road to Gettysburg*. New York: Clarion. Firsthand impressions of two teenage soldiers, one a 17-year-old corporal in the Union Army and the other a 18-year-old Confederate lieutenant, of the battle of Gettysburg. (Gr. 5–8)

Noble, T. H. 2006. *The Last Brother: A Civil War Tale*. Chelsea, MI: Sleeping Bear Press. When his two older brothers die in the Civil War, the third brother joins the Union Army only to be followed by eleven-year-old Gabe, who tags along as a bugler. Based on a true story. (Gr. 3–5)

Paterson, K. 1998. *Jip, His Own Story*. New York: Puffin. Jip is an orphan who was raised on a poor farm in Vermont. He becomes caught up in issues between slave owners and the abolitionists. (Gr. 4–8)

Pinkney, A. D. 2001. *Abraham Lincoln: Letters from a Slave Girl*. Delray Beach, FL: Winslow Press. This carefully researched fictional text includes letters written between 12-year-old Lettie Tucker, a slave girl, and President Lincoln. It is illustrated with interesting primary source materials. (Gr. 3–6)

Polacco, P. 1994. *Pink and Say*. New York: Philomel. Two young Union boys from different backgrounds try to recover from wounds in Confederate territory. (Gr. 2–8)

Rappaport, D. 1999. *Escape from Slavery: Five Journeys to Freedom*. New York: Harper Trophy. Based on primary source material, Rappaport depicts actual escapes of five slaves including one who shipped himself as freight in a wooden box to Philadelphia. (Gr. 5–8)

———. 2002. *No More! Stories and Songs of Slave Resistance*. Illus. S. W. Evans. Cambridge, MA: Candlewick Press. While one can never truly walk in another's shoes, this book gives readers a glimpse into the lives of 11 African Americans as they battle the chains of slavery through resistance, escape, and through their religion and songs. (Gr. 3–8)

Reeder, C. 1996. *Across the Lines*. New York: Atheneum. Readers get an understanding of the siege of Petersburg through the eyes of the son of a plantation owner and a slave serving in the Union army. (Gr. 3–6)

———. 1997. *Shades of Gray*. New York: Macmillan. Twelve-year-old Will Page regards the Yankees as the enemy because all his family lost their lives as a result of the war. He works the land and hunts the fields in the Virginia Piedmont beside his Uncle Jed, who has offered him a home. Will eventually comes to accept the fact that good people have different, but still acceptable ideas, and that all people suffer from war. (Gr. 3–6)

Rinaldi, A. 2000. *Girl in Blue*. New York: Scholastic. Sixteen-year-old Sarah masquerades as Neddy Compton, a Union soldier, and later becomes a Pinkerton spy in this fast-paced piece of historical fiction. (Gr. 3–8)

Rosen, M. 1995. *A School for Pompey Walker.* Illus. A. B. L. Robinson. San Diego: Harcourt Brace. A former slave relates the ingenious ways in which he tried to raise money to build a school for all children. (Gr. 3–6)

Ruby, L. 1994. *Steal Away Home.* New York: Macmillan. Fascinating reading as history and mystery are woven into two integrated stories, one of the Underground Railroad and the other of a curious girl in Kansas in the 1990s. (Gr. 4–8)

Schomp, V. 2002. *Letters from the Homefront: The Civil War.* New York: Benchmark-Marshall Cavendish. This is an excellent resource to show the value and impact of original sources when examining history. Pertinent letters serve as a backdrop as events are traced from the beginning to the end of the Civil War. (Gr. 3–8)

Seymour, T. 1998. *We Played Marbles.* Illus. D. Andreasen. New York: Orchard. Two young boys play marbles, make mudpies, and run races in an area that was once the site of a great Civil War battle. Pawpa teaches the boys another use for relics left on the grounds of old Fort Craig. (Gr. K–4)

Sullivan, G. 2001. *The Civil War at Sea.* Brookside, CT: Millbrook/Twenty-first Century Books. Learners interested in battles waged at sea will find this to be an excellent volume of informative pictures and clearly written text. Sea battles are rarely highlighted in the study of the Civil War so this volume could be a starter for some fascinating research. (Gr. 4–8)

Turner, A. 1987. *Nettie's Trip South.* Illus. R. Himler. New York: Macmillan. The realities of slavery are portrayed in a sensitive manner as seen by a young girl of the North. Nettie writes her impressions of a trip in the pre-Civil War South to a friend. Her comments center on the institution of slavery as it includes the maid at the inn and those at a slave auction. (Gr. 2–5)

Turner, G. 2004. *Running for Our Lives.* Illus. S. Johnson. Chicago: Newman Educational Publishers. Luther and his family split up after their escape from their slave owner, vowing to meet in Canada. (Gr. 5–8).

Winter, J. 1992. *Follow the Drinking Gourd.* New York: Knopf. This book describes how songs were used to direct slaves to freedom via the Underground Railroad. (Gr. 2–8)

Wisler, G. C. 1995. *Mr. Lincoln's Drummer.* New York: Lodestar. Based on a true story, this historic novel tells of Willie Johnston, a skinny boy from Vermont who enlisted in the Union Army along with his father. Willie was awarded the Congressional Medal of Honor for his heroics by President Abraham Lincoln. (Gr. 4–8)

———. 2001. *When Johnny Went Marching: Young Americans Fight the Civil War.* New York: HarperCollins. Vivid and at times, heart wrenching, these short stories of young people who served during the Civil War can add depth to the study of the many facets of this war. (Gr. 6–8)

Native American Literature: Myths, Legends, Poetry, and Nonfiction

Baker, O. 1981. *Where the Buffaloes Begin.* Illus. S. Gammell. New York: Viking. A Caldecott picture book that describes Native American life on the plains. (Gr. K–3)

Begay, S. 1995. *Navajo: Visions and Voices Across the Mesa.* New York: Scholastic. A personal view of the contemporary life of the Navajo is presented through art and poetry. (Gr. 4–8)

Bierhorst, J. 1998. *The Deetkatoo: Native American Stories about Little People.* Illus. R. H. Coy. New York: Morrow. Fourteen different Native American cultures are represented in the 22 stories about little people. Includes notes, a cultural guide, and a bibliography. (Gr. 4–8)

Bruchac, J. 1996. *Between the Earth and Sky: Legends of Native American Sacred Places.* Illus. T. Locker. San Diego: Harcourt Brace. An elder teaches his nephew about the sacredness of living things. A number of sacred places are highlighted through Native American legends. (Gr. 4–8)

————. 2000. *Crazy Horse's Vision*. Illus. S. D. Nelson. New York: Lee & Low. This book relates the life of Crazy Horse, one of the best known Native American heroes. (Gr. 3–6)

————. 2002. *Navajo Long Walk*. Illus. S. Begay. Washington, DC: National Geographic Society. A recounting of the tragic forced march of thousands of Navajos from their homeland to a desolate reservation at Bosque Redondo. (Gr. 5–8)

Bruchac, J., and J. Bruchac. 2001. *How Chipmunk Got His Stripes*. Illus. J. Aruego and A. Dewey. New York: Dial. Here is a perfect pourquoi tale to read aloud. It will quickly involve young readers with its repetitive text. (Gr. 1–3)

Burks, B. 2000. *Walks Alone*. San Diego, CA: Harcourt Brace. A NCSS-CBC Notable Book in Social Studies, this historical fiction novel takes readers into the New Mexico Territory in the late 1800s to struggle to survive alongside 15-year-old Walks Alone. Persecuted by U.S. soldiers and Mexican scalp hunters, her Apache tribe members face constant danger. (Gr. 6–8)

Doner, K. 1999. *Buffalo Dreams*. Portland, OR: Westwinds Press. When she travels with her family to see a newly born white buffalo calf, Sara Bearpaw experiences some magic that will last a lifetime. A retelling of the White Buffalo Calf legend is included. (Gr. 3–6)

Erdrich, L. 1999. *The Birchbark House*. New York: Hyperion. Set during the westward movement, seven-year-old Omakayas takes readers through events in her daily life with her Ojibwa tribe on an island in Lake Superior. (Gr. 2–6)

Esbensen, B. J. 1991. *The Star Maiden*. Illus. H. K. Davie. Boston: Little, Brown. The retelling of a Native American legend. (Gr. 2–5)

Goble, P. 1988. *Iktomi and the Boulder*. New York: Orchard. The plains Indian trickster Iktomi encounters a boulder that causes him some problems when it refuses to return his blanket. (Gr. 1–3)

————. 1996. *Iktomi and the Buzzard: A Plains Indian Story*. New York: Orchard/Jackson. The trickster is at work again in a humorous tale. (Gr. 1–3)

————. 2001. *Storm Maker's Teepee*. New York: Atheneum. This is a retelling of the myth about how teepees were given to the Blackfoot people through Sacred Otter's dream. It also explains why the designs painted on teepees are believed to have special meaning and power. (Gr. 1–3)

Hobbs, W. 1989. *Bearstone*. New York: Atheneum. As he works for an elderly rancher during the summer, Cloyd searches for his identity in a world where he feels he doesn't belong. (Gr. 6–8)

————. 1997. *Beardance*. Illus. J. Kastner. New York: Camelot. In a tale that explains how the Ute Bear Dance began, a young boy seeks out an elderly bear who hasn't appeared with the coming of spring. (Gr. 6–8)

Hoyt-Goldsmith, D. 1991. *Pueblo Storyteller*. Photo. L. Midgale. New York: Holiday House. A book about a young girl who is the storyteller of her village. (Gr. 2–4)

Keams, G. 1998. *Snail Girl Brings Water*. Illus. R. Ziehler-Martin. Flagstaff, AZ: Rising Moon. The story of how the Navaho people got water. (Gr. K–3)

Left Hand Bull, J., and S. Haldane. 1999. *Lakota Hoop Dancer*. Photo. S. Haldane. New York: Dutton. A Lakota man performs the Hoop Dance in order to share his culture with audiences. (Gr. 2–6)

Martin, R. 1993. *The Boy Who Lived with the Seals*. Illus. D. Shannon. New York: Putnam. A Chinook tale about a boy who disappears while playing in the river only to return years later after living with the seals. Unable to adapt to his former life, he returns to the sea. (Gr. 1–4)

Max, J., ed. 1997. *Spider Spins a Story: Fourteen Legends from Native America*. Flagstaff, AZ: Rising Moon Press. In a book endorsed by tribal authorities, the power of myths and legends is revealed through spider, a character common to many Native American tales. (Gr. K–2)

Mayo, G. W. 1989. *Earthmaker's Tales: North American Indian Stories about Earth Happenings.* New York: Walker. Depicts how the earth was created and how it should be cared for by its people. (Gr. K–8)

Miles, M. 1985. *Annie and the Old One.* Illus. P. Parnell. New York: Orchard. A young girl befriends an elderly Native American woman. (Gr. 1–3)

Moroney, L. 1995. *Moontellers: Myths of the Moon from Around the World.* Illus. G. Shedd. Flagstaff, AZ: Northland. Readers can travel the world as they investigate 11 different cultures along with their legends tied to the moon and its cycles. Story sources and suggestions for further reading are included. (Gr. 3–8)

Normandin, C., ed. 1997. *Echoes of the Elders: The Stories and Paintings of Chief Lelooska.* New York: DK Publishing. A collection of five tales that were long a part of the oral tradition of the Northwest Coast Indians are recorded for the first time. They teach the importance of revering the natural world and all of its creatures. (Gr. 3–8)

O'Dell, S., and E. Hall. 1993. *Thunder Rolling in the Mountains.* New York: Yearling. This book tells of the desperate flight for freedom by the Nez Peace. It describes the wisdom and courage of their leader, Chief Joseph. (Gr. 4–6)

Philip, N. 1996. *Earth Always Endures: Native American Poems.* Illus. E. S. Curtis. New York: Viking. Photographs complement this collection of poetry illuminating a number of facets of the Native American cultures. (Gr. 4–7)

Sneve, V. D. H. 1989. *Dancing Tepees: Poems of American Indian Youth.* New York: Holiday House. Poetry written by Native American children. (Gr. K–8)

Turcotte, M. 1995. *Songs of Our Ancestors: Poems about Native Americans.* Illus. K. S. Presnell. Chicago: Children's Press. This collection of poems focuses on famous Native Americans and events in their history. (Gr. 2–8)

Whitethorne, B. 2002. *Sunpainters: Eclipse of the Navajo Sun.* Illus. B. Whitethorne. Flagstaff, AZ: Northland Publishers. A grandfather explains the solar eclipse to his grandson. (Gr. 3–8)

Wood, N. 1993. *Spirit Walker.* Illus. F. Howell. New York: Doubleday. Beautiful poetry that reflects the determination, courage, and powerful spiritual faith of her friends, the Taos Indians of New Mexico. (Gr. 2–6)

Yolen, J. 1996. *Encounter.* Illus. D. Shannon. San Diego: Harcourt Brace. A Taino boy tells of Christopher Columbus's landing on San Salvador in 1492. Later, Spanish colonization alters the lifestyle, language, and religion of his tribe. (Gr. 2–6)

Related Technology Tools

General Social Studies Sites

http://www.education-world.com/

If the only site available to a teacher were this one, classroom life would still be rich indeed. Choose from a wealth of information across the curriculum. Check the links to social studies and try some of the wonderful teaching ideas

http://www.nationalgeographic.com

With a reputation long established, you know this site just has to be good.

The Internet Public Library

http://www.ipl.org/

Here is an excellent spot to begin research on numerous topics across the field of social studies, especially because it promotes quality information resources. Students might work within the Youth section that is further divided into other areas. The Resources for Teachers and Parents section has a number of links to sites about literature and reading. Teens will find areas for research help and a useful writing guide.

http://execpc.com/~dboals/k-12.html

Part of the History/Social Web Site for Teachers. Look for separate links for K–6 grades with specific lesson plans for social studies, educational resources for parents, and information about professional development.

Sites Focusing on Special Learners

National Center for Learning Disabilities

http://www.ld.org/index.html

Spend time on this site to learn more about learning disabilities in children and adults. The site provides information, resources, and referral services. Visit the Tips for Teachers section for innovative ideas to support classroom instruction.

The National Information Center for Children and Youth with Disabilities

http://www.nichcy.org

Log on for information on a wide range of disabilities and disability-related issues. Read pertinent publications and connect with useful resources. Don't miss Zagawhat, an area packed to the brim with information and links just for students. The site is available in Spanish and English.

The National Research Center on the Talented and Gifted

http://www.gifted.uconn.edu/nrcgt.html

This is a cooperative directed by Dr. Joseph Renzulli. It involves researchers, educators, and policy makers who are dedicated to trying to understand the nature of being gifted in order to increase the success of all types of learners. Find online resources, educational links, and newsletters.

KidSource

http://www.kidsource.com/kidsource/pages/ed.gifted.html

This is a directory of valuable articles about gifted and talented students and provides additional information, including pertinent Web sites and online forums. The appealing student pages will be welcomed at home and in the classroom.

The Council for Exceptional Children

http://www.cec.sped.org

This site offers information about a range of learning challenges, provides ideas on classroom management, and gives viewers the opportunity to read articles from the Council's journal, *Teaching Exceptional Children*.

Civil War Sites

http://www2.lhric.org/pocantico/civilwar/cwar.htm

For a change a pace, join Mrs. Huber's class and learn about a variety of Civil War related topics together. It is refreshing to see examples of students' work while learning about the Civil War. It is also a good place to gather ideas for classroom projects.

Gettysburg National Military Park

http://www.nps.gov/gett/

Here is one way to make a location real by visiting the sites of a number of Civil War battles at the Gettysburg National Military Park.

The United States Civil War Information Center

http://www.cwc.lsu.edu/index.htm

From the Web page of the U.S. Civil War Center, one can travel for hours to many destinations. Check out the site and bookmark links for student use. With 8,000 links available, there are a myriad of topics to choose. For instance, one can read diaries or documents, visit historic places, or learn about the role of African Americans, Native Americans, and other minority groups during the Civil War era.

http://lcweb.loc.gov/exhibits/G.Address/ga.html

This site allows students a close-up of the two versions of the Gettysburg Address.

Native American Sites

http://www.hanksville.org/NAresources/
   Index of Native American Resources on the Internet.

http://www.nmai.si.edu/
   Smithsonian Institute National Museum of the American Indian.

http://www.cobblestonepub.com/themepack/
   Cobblestone, a superb social studies magazine for grades 4–8, has theme packs for many topics. There are three theme packs for Native Americans.

http://www.oyate.org/aboutus.html
   This popular Native American site is designed to promote the use of quality Native American literature in classrooms. It is focused on helping children develop an unbiased understanding of Native Americans as well.

Technology Resources

General Social Studies Sites

http://www.ncss.org
   National Council of Social Studies presents an award-winning Web site packed with information for the professional social studies educator that includes numerous resources, professional development programs, and a section devoted to student use.

The Council for Exceptional Children (CEC)
   http://www.cec.sped.org
   The Council for Exceptional Children gives teachers support for teaching students with special needs.

Special Education Resources on the Internet (SERI)
   http://www.hood.edu/seri/serihome.htm
   Search this site under categories including "Special Education Discussion Groups," "Learning Disabilities," and "Inclusion Resources."

Attention Deficit Disorder Association
   http://www.add.org
   ADDA focuses especially on the needs of ADHD adults and young adults with ADHD. This site is packed with articles, personal stories, interviews with ADHD professionals, book reviews, and links to other ADHD-related sites

Hard of Hearing and Deaf Students Resource Guide for Teachers
   http://www.bced.gov.bc.ca/specialed/hearimpair/toc.htm
   Often-asked questions, information and communication, and teaching strategies are included to help broaden your awareness and experience of the language and world of your student who is hard of hearing or deaf.

Learning Disabilities Association of America
   http://www.ldanailorg
   LDA provides information, support, education and resources through its network of nearly 300 state and local affiliates in 50 states and Puerto Rico.

Gifted Resources
   http://www.eskimo.com/~user/kids.html
   Contains links to all known online gifted resources, enrichment programs, talent searches, summer programs, gifted mailing lists and early acceptance programs.

Software and Videos

Inspiration and Kidspiration. CD-ROM. Available from Inspiration Software, Inc. (800-877-4292).

Co:Writer (Version 2.0). CD-ROM. Don Johnston, Wauconda, IL.

Write:OutLoud (Version 2.0). CD-ROM. Don Johnston, Wauconda, IL.

Speeches of Abraham Lincoln. 45 minutes. Teacher's Video Company. Available from www.teachersvideo.com.

Liberty's Kids. CD-ROM. The Learning Company. Available from www.amazon.com.
Students encounter soldiers, spies, Indians, Loyalists, statesmen, and townsfolk in a series of adventures that place them right in the middle of one of the most important eras of America's history, the American Revolution.

Oregon Trail. 6th ed. CD-ROM. The Learning Company.
For ages 6–10, students can travel through 2,000 miles of adventure while building decision-making and problem-solving skills.

References

Brimijoin, K., E. Marquissee, and C. A. Tomlinson. 2003. "Using Data to Differentiate Instruction." *Educational Leadership* 60 (5): 70–73.

Brown, M. D. 2001. "Handhelds in the Classroom." *Education World.*
Available http://www.education-world.com/a_tech/tech083.shtml

Buhrow, B., and A. U. Garcia. 2006. *Ladybugs, Tornadoes, and Swirling Galaxies.* Portland, ME: Stenhouse.

Carbone, E. 2001. "Arranging the Classroom with an Eye (and Ear) to Students with ADHD." *Teaching Exceptional Children* 34 (2): 72–81.

Cline, R. K. J., and B. L. Taylor. 1987. "Integrating Literature and 'Free Reading' Into the Social Studies Program." *Social Education* 42: 27–31.

Cox, C., and J. E. Many. 1992. "Toward Understanding of the Aesthetic Response to Literature." *Language Arts* 69 (1): 28–33.

Dugger, J. M. 1994. "Perceptions and Attitudes of Teachers toward Inclusion of Handicapped Students." *Illinois School Research and Development* 30 (2): 5–7.

Duis, M. 1996. "Using Schema Theory to Teach American History." *Social Education* 60 (3): 144–46.

Farris, P. J., C. J. Fuhler, and M. P. Walther. 2004. *Teaching Reading: A Balanced Approach for Today's Classrooms.* Boston: McGraw-Hill.

Fountas, I. C., and I. L. Hannigan. 1989. "Making Sense of Whole Language: The Pursuit of Informed Teaching." *Childhood Education* 65 (3): 133–37.

Franklin, J. 2002. "The Art of Differentiation: Moving from Theory to Practice." *Education Update* 44 (2): 1, 3, 8.

Fuhler, C. J. 1990. "Let's Move toward Literature-Based Reading Instruction." *The Reading Teacher* 43: 312–15.

Gambrel, L. B. 1998. "Creating Classroom Cultures That Foster Reading Motivation." In *Teaching Struggling Readers,* ed. L. Allington. Newark, DE: International Reading Association.

Graham, S., and K. Harris. 1988. "Instructional Recommendations for Teaching Writing to Exceptional Students." *Exceptional Children* 54 (6): 506–12.

Grierson, S. T., A. Anson, and J. Baird. 2002. "Exploring the Past through Multigenre Writing." *Language Arts* 80 (1): 51–59.

Hansen, M. B., and K. S. Schmidt. 1989. "Promoting Global Awareness through Trade Books." *Middle School Journal* 21 (1): 34–37.

Harvey, S. 2002. "Nonfiction Inquiry: Using Real Reading and Writing to Explore the World." *Language Arts* 80 (1): 12–22.

Larkin, M. J. 2001. "Providing Support for Student Independence through Scaffolded Instruction." *Teaching Exceptional Children* 34 (1): 30–34.

"Learning Disabilities: A Definitional Problem." 1990. *Education of the Handicapped* 16 (21): 5–6.

Levstik, L. 1989. "A Gift of Time: Children's Historical Fiction." In *Children's Literature in the Classroom: Weaving Charlotte's Web*, ed. J. Hickman and B. Cullinan. Portsmouth, NH: Heinemann.

Levstik, L. S., and K. C. Barton. 1997. *Doing History: Investigation with Children in Elementary and Middle Schools*. Mahwah, NJ: Lawrence Erlbaum.

McGowan, T. M., L. Erickson, and J. A. Neufeld. 1996. "With Reason and Rhetoric: Building the Case for the Literature-Social Studies Connection." *Social Education* 60 (4): 203–7.

Moore, D. W., S. A. Moore, P. M. Cunningham, and J. W. Cunningham. 2003. *Developing Readers and Writers in the Content Areas K–12*. 4th ed. Boston: Allyn &Bacon.

Negron, E., and L. P. Ricklin. 1996. "Meeting the Needs of Diverse Learners in the Social Studies Classroom through Collaborative Methods of Instruction." *Social Studies and the Young Learner* 9 (2): 27–29.

O'Neil, J. 1994/1995. "Can Inclusion Work? A Conversation with Jim Kauffman and Mara Sapon-Shevin." *Educational Leadership* 52 (4): 7–11.

Partin, R. L. 2003. *The Social Studies Teacher's Book of Lists*. San Francisco: Jossey.

Reis, S., and J. Renzulli. 1992. "Using Curriculum Compacting to Challenge the Above Average." *Educational Leadership* 50 (2): 51–7.

Renzulli, J. 1994/1995. "Teachers as Talent Scouts." *Educational Leadership* 52 (4): 75–81.

Renzulli, J., and S. Reis. 1993. "The Reform Movement and the Quiet Crisis in Gifted Education." *Oregon English Journal* 15: 9–17.

Rosenblatt, L. M. 1983. *Literature as Exploration*. New York: Modern Language Association of America.

———. 1991. "Literature—S.O.S.!" *Language Arts* 68: 444–48.

Routman, R. 1991. *Invitations: Changing as Teachers and Learners*. Portsmouth, NH: Heinemann.

Sapon-Shevin, M. 1994/1995. "Why Gifted Students Belong in Inclusive Schools." *Educational Leadership* 52 (4): 64–70.

Scherer, M. 2006. "Discovering Strengths." *Educational Leadership* 64 (1): 7.

Siegel, D. 1990. *Educating the Gifted is a Community Affair: An Educator Handbook*. Helena: Montana Association of Gifted and Talented Educators.

Silverman, L. K. 1993. "Instructional Strategies for the Gifted." *Oregon English Journal* 15: 18–20.

Strickland, D. S. 1990. "Emergent Literacy: How Young Children Learn to Read and Write." *Educational Leadership* 47: 18–23.

Taylor, H. E., and S. M. Larson. 2000. "Teaching Elementary Social Studies to Students with Mild Disabilities." *Elementary Education* 64 (4): 232–35.

Temple, C., M. Martinez, J. Yokota, and A. Naylor. 2002. *Children's Books in Children's Hands: An Introduction to Their Literature*. 2nd ed. Boston: Allyn & Bacon.

Tomlinson, C. A., and J. Jarvis. 2006. "Teaching Beyond the Book." *Educational Leadership* 64 (1): 16–21.

Tunnell, M. O., and R. Ammon, eds. 1993. *The Story of Ourselves: Teaching History through Children's Literature*. Portsmouth, NH: Heinemann.

Wheelock, A. 1992. "The Case for Untracking." *Educational Leadership* 50: 6–10.

Whyte, L. A. 1983. "The Learning Disabled Adolescent: A Review of the Research on Learning Disabled Adolescents and Its Implications for the Education of This Population." *Mental Retardation and Learning Disability Bulletin* 11: 134–41.

Williams, S. C. 2002. "How Speech-Feedback and Word-Prediction Software Can Help Students Write." *Teaching Exceptional Children* 34 (3): 72–78.

Willis, S. 1994 (October). "Making Schools More Inclusive." *Curriculum Update*: 1–8.

———. 1995. "Mainstreaming the Gifted." *Curriculum Update* 37 (2): 1, 4–5.

Young, T. A., and G. Vardell. 1993. "Weaving Readers' Theatre and Nonfiction into the Curriculum." *The Reading Teacher* 46: 396–405.

> *Above all, textbooks must try to lay bare the fundamental structures of history, geography, health, and science—and in a manner that permits children and youth to grasp the structure.*
>
> —Richard Anderson et al.,
> Becoming a Nation of Readers

Chapter Six

Facilitating Learning through Strategic Instruction in Social Studies

Pamela J. Farris, Northern Illinois University;
Bonnie L. Kuhrt, Carl Sandburg Middle School, Rolling Meadows, IL;
Donna E. Werderich, Rockford College

CHAPTER OUTLINE

CHAPTER OBJECTIVES

Readers will

- be able to apply brain research findings as part of strategic instruction in social studies;
- be able to apply strategies to activate learning;
- be able to model thinking strategies used in social studies;
- understand how to teach strategic sequencing in social studies;
- recognize the need for teaching history as perspective taking;
- be able to apply Internet reading strategies in social studies instruction;
- learn ways to expose students to multicultural perspectives; and
- apply concept muraling as a visual learning strategy.

Introduction

Children need to develop **learning strategies** that they can apply effectively in social studies as they read, write, and discuss. The student constructs meaning from within. The teacher does not merely facilitate the process but works cooperatively with the student in developing the meaning. Creation of the student's own meaning is also an essential element to the **constructivist** model identified by Gaskin et al. (1994), which describes how classroom discussion of text can help in the active construction of meaning. However, discussion of text encourages the student to construct personal meaning only when the initiating problem or question allows for a variety of student responses. Increasing the accessibility of the information locked in the **expository** material of textbooks becomes more important with the increased literacy demands of authentic assessment and the increased language diversity of the students.

The current shift from an overdependence on norm-referenced testing to the higher literacy demands associated with authentic assessment suggests that avoiding expository material is not a viable alternative. Students are held accountable for the knowledge locked within the informational text passages, including some that may not be accessible. When the teacher models comprehension strategies for students the resultant student interaction with textbooks can increase understanding (Hadaway and Young 1994). Resnick and Klopfer (1989, 206–7) suggest "Knowledge is acquired not from the information communicated and memorized but from the information that students elaborate, question, and use." Therefore, the question becomes: How can the reasoning activities necessary for knowledge acquisition be activated to give students control over their learning in social studies?

This chapter examines strategies for helping students gather, organize, relate, and retain knowledge in social studies. We look at strategies that activate learning and questioning techniques and describe the characteristics of graphic organizers. This chapter provides a basic framework for strategic instruction as well as integration of reading, writing, and reasoning in social studies.

Brain Research and Strategic Instruction in Social Studies

"Attention is the gateway to retention. If the information doesn't get in to begin with, forget trying to save it and access it later" according to Dr. Barry Gordon, professor of neurology and cognitive science at Johns Hopkins Medical Institutions (as quoted by Bailey 2006, 70). New research in neuroscience gives teachers insights into how social studies instruction can be more effective. Brain research suggests that teachers need to set the stage for learning in order to help students attend to relevant knowledge to be presented in upcoming instruction. When introducing the topic, make certain that all of the students are looking at you. Thus, the teacher should ask focusing questions about the topic and have the students recall previous information, often referred to as activating prior knowledge. The objective of a lesson should be made clear by the teacher for the students (Wolfe 1999).

Lastly, instructions need to be clear and concise. Detailed instructions should be presented in a handout and by using a transparency so that students can follow along and use the handout for a reference as they do the research or project.

One way to activate prior knowledge is to use an alphabet grid. Make 26 boxes about 12 inches square on the chalkboard or bulletin board and write a letter of the alphabet in each box. Then have students take turns writing something about the upcoming topics in a box until no one in the class has any more words to put in the boxes. For example, if our topic is China, a student might write "tea" in the box for the letter "T" while another student might write "Great Wall" in the "G" box and yet another writes "Asia" in the "A" box. Some boxes will have more than one word or phrase while others may be empty. After everyone in the class has had a chance to write a word, the class can discuss the words and their meanings. By having students with diverse backgrounds or limited abilities go among the first students, the teacher affords those students the opportunity to be successful. At the end of the unit, the activity is repeated until the students have exhausted all of their newly gained knowledge and information. The "A" box may have "Asia" and "acupuncture," for instance. This can now serve as an evaluation technique for the success of the unit. The alphabet box technique works with grades 2 through 8.

Brain research points out the need to use more than one modality for learning. In fact, the more modalities used, the better. In planning a unit of story, the teacher should keep in mind ways to incorporate students' use of their senses. Research indicates that when students use more than one sense, learning increases dramatically. For instance, combining listening and a visual activity may yield up to 80 percent recall and understanding of a topic. Obviously videos/DVDs and CDs are important supplementary materials. Overhead projectors should be used frequently by both the classroom teacher and students to demonstrate social studies concepts along with an oral explanation. PowerPoint demonstrations are also quite effective for presenting new content and concepts, provided that short summarizing phrases are used rather than extended and elaborated text.

Social studies offers tactile (artifacts, locating capitals of countries on a globe, relief maps), smell (field trips to demonstration of pioneer village—candle making, blacksmithing, etc.), and taste (class makes Johnny cakes or applesauce, dishes from various cultures) experiences. Various CDs offer students the chance to be taken to another culture, hear folk songs, or listen to a famous speech. Such stimulation of the learning modalities of seeing, hearing, touching, smelling, and tasting helps to aid the student in understanding and retaining new material.

If a task is either too difficult or too easy, students will have little motivation to continue to do it. Likewise, if students find that the level of stress is too high or too low, learning becomes less efficient (Hunter 1982). Basically, brain research points out that these are "fight or flight" survival tactics by the brain. In other words, teachers need to adopt instruction that reaches out to the emotions of the students. If the task seems to have little or no value to the students, they will drop it from their brains. If the emotional content (i.e., stress) is too extreme, thinking processes of the students become less efficient.

Teachers need to be able to break down skills into their subcomponents to explain them piece by piece to students (e.g., how to identify the focus of a passage in a social studies textbook, how to locate a specific longitude and latitude on a map, or how to define the Articles of Confederation). Memory is stored in the brain in different ways. When a student repeatedly practices something, such as saying the capital of a state, in order to remember it, the brain cells "fire" and eventually become wired together (hardwired); the brain automatically embeds the fact. Thus, if a student continually repeats information that is incorrect, such as the capital of Kentucky is Louisville (instead of Frankfort), the wrong information will be hardwired and recalled automatically by the student. As Madeline Hunter said, "Practice doesn't make perfect; it makes permanent" (quoted in Wolfe 1999, 63).

Behaviorism and Constructivism

The **behaviorist** view of learning focuses on rote memorization and the collecting of facts and information which are recalled by the learner for exams. Learning takes place in isolation. Most behaviorist instruction is **direct instruction** or **explicit instruction** in which the teacher demonstrates or stages and manages the learning event. The teacher, therefore, presents the lesson in a manner that is concrete.

The constructivist view of learning is that learning takes place as students relate what they have previously learned, or past experiences, to new situations, or new experiences. In other words, learning is an active process of "sense making" and transfer of learning is commonplace as learning does not occur in isolation from previously gained knowledge. Indeed, constructivists believe that students learn by adapting to the world in which they live. Past learning helps to build a base on which new learning occurs, a kind of scaffolding or strategic cognitive processing that in turn provides the seasoned reasoning and wisdom from which decisions are made and actions taken. **Inquiry** and **higher-order thinking** along with **problem solving** are featured as part of constructivism.

Teachers who follow the constructivist theory key in on such previously gained learning by **activating prior knowledge** to help students tie new information and concepts to old. In order to take advantage of students' earlier experiences, teachers need to create activities that are engaging to students so that they are motivated to learn and thereby willingly respond to the learning situation. **Guided learning experiences** are those instructional activities that pique students' curiosity, evoking questions as they explore social studies. Students' intellectual abilities are linked with their own innate, personal drive to discover the unknown (Caine, Caine, and McClintic 2002).

Here is an example of a need for prior learning to be activated as they learn about the fire that destroyed Chicago in 1871 from *The Great Fire* (Murphy 1995).

> Once the fire broke through the circle of engines, it pushed out fists of flame that ate up clapboard siding, shingled roofs, fences, trees, outhouses, and chicken coops. Raised wooden sidewalks caught fire and the wind drove the flames along at a brisk pace. The wind and updraft lifted flames hundreds of feet into the sky and created such a bright light that it reminded some people of daylight. (43)

Before grasping the magnitude of the Chicago fire that destroyed 17,500 buildings and left 100,000 people homeless, students need to understand basic social studies and science concepts and link them in their knowledge bases in order to give them the proper perspective of the period in terms of setting, both time and place. In the 1870s, houses and small neighborhood stores were spaced tightly together with wooden, raised sidewalks used as walkways for pedestrians. The primary building material of the period was wood, a material also used for kindling because it burns relatively quickly when dry. A slight breeze in dry weather can move flames and embers of a fire swiftly over great distances. Since stores, houses, apartment buildings, fences, outhouses, chicken coops, and raised wooden sidewalks were all constructed of dry timber and located within close proximity, the fire was fueled naturally as it spread across the city. Understanding the need to control the amount of air reaching a fire to keep it burning, called the draft, is yet another concept as the wind hampered firefighters in their attempt to gain control over the massive blaze. So profound was the damage to Chicago that few people thought the city could ever be rebuilt. Cities today are viewed as concrete jungles, not the plank and board towns of old, largely because Chicago was rebuilt with concrete and bricks—construction materials that resist burning. Indeed, the first skyscrapers were built in Chicago shortly after the great fire.

An example of creating a compelling classroom event to stimulate students' interest in a subject is that developed by Carol McClintic (Caine, Caine, and McClintic 2002), an eighth-grade teacher from California. Carol worked with two education consultants in developing a Civil War unit. Carol's class already had a strong sense of community with students working together and being able to hold discussions in which they could agree to disagree without being judgmental. After determining the topics to be covered—causes of the war, the nature of slavery, and the development of the union—Carol selected core facts, sequence of events, battles, and individuals who played significant roles in the war to share with her students.

Using a read-aloud format, Carol opened the unit by reading about Sarah Rosetta Wakeman, a woman who enlisted in the Union Army and served as a coal handler on a canal boat in order to help support her impoverished family. This was followed by an excerpt from the video *Gettysburg* (Turner Pictures and Maxwell 1993), that of Picket's Charge in which Confederate soldiers lined up and then marched into the face of Union cannon fire. Rather than playing the film's sound track, Carol played an audiotape of Charlotte Church's (1998) singing of "Pie Jesu." Church's clear voice contrasted with the violent scene of soldiers being cut down helplessly on the battlefield. Student emotions heightened as Carol added yet another piece of media, that of an overhead transparency describing how Sarah Rosetta Wakeman's female identity went undiscovered during the war and that she was one of over 400 women who served as Civil War soldiers. A second overhead, displaying statistics about the battle, was then turned on. One citation included the deaths of 51,000 soldiers during the three-day Battle of Gettysburg, more than all of the U.S. soldiers killed in the Vietnam War. Other facts were included. This ended the 10-minute media presentation that served to activate students' prior knowledge. The classroom was silent as students reflected on all they had seen, heard, and felt.

After a few moments, Carol asked if they had any questions. Hands shot up. "Why did they fight?" "Why did the soldiers walk straight into the gunfire?" "Were women really fighting, and why did no one know who they were?" (Caine, Caine, and McClintic 2002, 71). The questions were used as guides for the unit of study. Carol then divided students into interest groups and had them research various aspects of the Civil War, reporting their findings back to the class at large later. The class decided on time limits for researching their topics and developed a rubric for the assessment of the reports. Through the unit, all the core issues Carol had intended to present were touched on through the group sharing. Most of the core facts were also introduced through the group reports. There were times that she had to prod or even directly introduce some issues or facts herself. This ensured that the unit's goals and objectives were properly met. Students were given time to rehearse their oral reports, and Carol gave them pointers on proper diction, eye contact with the audience, and pausing between topics to let the audience have time to mull over an idea. Carol used memory games to encourage her students to memorize key facts.

Inquiry-Based Social Studies

Using the definition of student inquiry as "raising and pursuing genuine concerns" Nancy L. Roser and Susan Keehn (2002, 416) developed a three-phase plan for implementing an **inquiry-based** social studies unit that is constructivist in nature. They observed student involvement in discussion and noted instances of inquiry written in the student reader response journals. Designed for a five or six week social studies unit of study, each phase comprises two weeks of study for a two-hour period each day.

In Phase 1 (weeks 1–2), the teachers introduce the unit of study through read-alouds of a quality biography or historical fiction related to the unit of study. A biography is preferred inasmuch as it ushers students into the historic period through the perspective of an actual participant and provides for the literary examination of character. A well-written biography reveals human conflict, courage, ethical dilemmas, and sacrifice, which serve as important discussion points with students.

Phase 2 (weeks 3–4) begins with the teacher giving book talks about three different pieces of historical fiction set in the same period. After selecting one of the three texts to read, each student then joins peers in a book club or literature circle. Each student is given a task and each day shares the results of that task with the entire group (see Literature Circles in Chapter 7). All three books need to both unveil the historical period and entice open-ended inquiry. Children's responses have been found to be deeper and richer in a risk-free setting, such as small group book clubs, and when they are encouraged to say "I wonder if . . ." and "I wonder why . . ." (Raphael and McMahon 1994).

The final two weeks, Phase 3 (weeks 5–6), brings the entire class back together as one group to pose questions that arose during their reading or discussions in their respective book clubs. The questions are collected by the teacher for the class to answer through investigating informational books about the historical characters and period.

The focus of the six-week inquiry study at the fourth grade level was the Texas Revolution. The class read aloud Jean Fritz's (1986) *Make Way for Sam Houston.* A hero who also possesses a number of character weaknesses, Houston makes for interesting reflection and discussion. Houston was the only person to have ever been elected governor of two states, Tennessee and Texas. His leadership skills were superior but his personal life had much conflict and sorrow. After listening to a chapter read-aloud each day for seven days, the students then completed an introspection characterization form consisting of three questions: (1) What is Sam Houston like so far? (2) What makes you think so? and (3) What traits has Houston shown? Comments by students fall under one of eight different types of responses:

Informs   Provides new information not immediate in the text.
Connects Self to text.
Infers   Links ideas within text
Wonders   Raises questions (often unanswerable); speculates; hints at future inquiry attempts.
Predicts Poses hypotheses about upcoming events in the book.
Interprets Tries to make sense of or clarify text or dialogue.
Recalls   Recovers information from the text or dialogue.
Evaluates Judges quality, worth of text; accuracy of accounts; merits of actions.

The diverse student population in the study gave interesting views of the famous, multidimensional Texan. A farmer, a teacher, a slave owner, a drunk, a military leader, and governor of Texas are all "character and skill" traits present in the same person. Some students resented his multiple wives and large number of children. African American students had difficulty understanding Houston's view toward slavery—he owned slaves. Hispanic students were quick to point out the complexity of the Texan's desire to take land away from Mexico and create a new republic (Roser and Keehn 2002). Different cultural models are often constructed depending upon the cultural backgrounds present in the class. Students will present different cultural models and worldviews in their own words as they tell what they understand and how they judge it (Beach 1995).

Phase 2 involves students engagement in book clubs. Students actively participate in small group discussions about what they have read and notes they have jotted down. Prior to getting into small groups the teacher models with a couple of students how to make contributions to a discussion based on reading and notes, ideas, and inferences made. Historical fiction naturally invites children to share, seek, and clarify their knowledge of actual historical events, weighing that knowledge against accounts presented in fictionalized versions of history (Roser and Keehn 2002; George 2006).

During Phase 3, the final phase, students seek out answers to questions that arose during their reading of the historical fiction texts. During the entire class discussions, the teacher recorded questions that evolved. Later, using informational books, the students pursue answers to their questions. Roser and Keehn (2002) found that sustained talk during Phase 3 centered on making inferences, informing classmates about discoveries made in texts, and interpreting information found in the informational texts.

The Project Method

Project-based learning allows for student choice in the learning process. As such, the **project method** makes the

> inquiry more meaningful to students than does teacher-assigned work. Projects provide many opportunities to integrate the curriculum, and the very nature of the work is active. Students work together in different parts of the classroom, on different tasks related to the project. Because project-based learning is meaningful, integrated, and active, teachers find more opportunities to challenge students at their own levels of ability. As students become experienced in doing project work, they challenge themselves and each other to ask more questions, find more resources, and create more informative projects. (Diffily 2002, 17)

The collaborative nature of projects that engage students over a period of several days or weeks makes for a learning community. Upon selecting an area of interest, students work together in groups to research the topic from several different sources: books, articles, interviewing experts in the area, Web sites, and personal observation during fieldwork. The textbook serves as a resource.

Well-designed projects are predominately student-directed with the teacher serving as a facilitator. The projects are connected to the real world, informed by several sources, and are research-based. The projects reflect the knowledge and skills gained over a period of time. The final product is then shared with the rest of the class during a presentation. Any written report is given to the teacher for evaluation. Generally each member of the group researches and writes a portion of the final paper.

Guided reading is a well-used instructional strategy in which the classroom teacher initially shares a carefully selected text with the class or small group through a read-aloud, providing a reading model as well as exposing the students to quality literature. Such read-alouds and guided reading experiences stimulate thinking, expand students' attention span, build vocabulary, and create yet another linkage between reading and writing. In particular, nonfiction social studies books make for great read-alouds as they appeal to strong readers and striving readers alike. Such informational books add to students' topics of interest and can spur them on to read both in guided reading and in independent reading (Dreher 2003).

Left for Dead: A Young Man's Search for Justice by Peter Nelson (2002) is an actual accounting of the sinking of the USS *Indianapolis* by the Japanese in the Pacific Ocean near the end of World War II. The book chronicles how 880 of the ship's crew struggled for survival in the shark-infested waters for days. Only 317 men were rescued. The ship's commander, Captain McVay III, had been ordered to cease sailing in a zigzag pattern and return to a straight line, which ultimately resulted in the ship becoming an easy target. The book also details how Hunter Scott, an 11-year-old-boy, latched onto the topic and the court martial of the ship's captain as a project for his school history fair and subsequently helped to clear the captain's name after 50 years of repeated attempts by former crew members and their families had been unsuccessful. Carolyn, a seventh-grade teacher, opted to read aloud *Left for Dead* for 15–20 minutes a day and aligned the book with the cross-curricular themed unit on disaster that her school district had created (Meehan 2006).

Students in Carolyn's class engaged in accompanying projects. Some wrote papers on related topics such as sleep deprivation, hypothermia, and shark attacks. A number of students researched Hunter Scott and how he had "sought justice" for Captain McVay. Other students wrote and performed short skits that simulated a live broadcast of the sinking of the USS *Indianapolis* and interviewing of some survivors. One student discovered a survivor and interviewed him via e-mail. All the students worked on displays that pertained to the events surrounding the USS *Indianapolis*.

Carolyn was able to contact yet another survivor, Mike Kuryla, who came to her school and shared his recollections of the ship's sinking and ultimate court martial of Captain McVay with all the students in the junior high school. The real-life situation for then seaman Kuryla was harrowing and treacherous and his remarks clearly made an impact on the students. Likewise, the class had great admiration for Hunter Scott's continued efforts to clear the name of Captain McVay. Hunter was a "kid" just like the seventh graders and was able to make a significant difference as a single individual. By combining guided reading and read-alouds with the project method, Carolyn was able to involve her entire class, and ultimately the entire school, in presenting the importance of how a single person can make a difference.

Strategies to Activate Learning

Prior knowledge is the knowledge a student already possesses and brings to the learning experience. It differs for every student because each student has had different experiences, both first-hand and vicarious. The learner attempts to relate new information to the information already known in order to make sense of the world. It is said that the learner is drawing a **schema** (pl., **schemata**), or a cognitive blueprint or diagram in the brain. Consider a 1,000-piece picture puzzle. When the contents are emptied onto the table, there isn't any diagram or map to be viewed. It appears to be nothing more than a mess of tiny cardboard pieces, some of which are colored and others are even upside down. By sorting out the pieces by colors—browns, blues, reds, yellows, greens—and then by the various shades within each color, patterns begin to form. Next, the shape of each piece is considered, and the notches that interlock the pieces are closely scrutinized. Piece by piece the picture begins to form. Learning occurs by planning and building information much the same as a picture puzzle is built slowly with one part of the puzzle being filled in at a time. Unlike the person completing the puzzle, the learner doesn't have the opportunity to first view the entire picture—or schema—before venturing forth on the learning experience. This is why it is so important for teachers to model behavior before asking students to demonstrate it on their own.

Schema theory is one way of explaining how prior knowledge is stored in an individual's memory. The information a learner acquires about a topic is organized into a framework, or schema. As other topics are added, the framework grows, creating larger and larger schemata that are arranged in a hierarchy. Information is retrieved by the learner through understanding how newly encountered knowledge links to what has already been organized cognitively in the blueprints or diagrams in the brain. Interrelationships among schemata assist understanding. Psychologists emphasize that learning new information depends on relating the new knowledge to something the learner already knows (Richardson and Morgan 2000). Pressley (2000) presents the following example of the schemata for a ship christening. The schemata include the purpose—to bless the ship; where the ship is christened—dry dock; by whom—a celebrity or person who has a connection to the ship (i.e., Nancy Reagan christened the aircraft carrier, USS *Ronald Reagan* named in honor of her husband); when it occurs—just before the launching of a new ship; and the action of christening—breaking a bottle of champagne that is suspended from a rope by swinging it against the bow of the ship.

The development of the schemata involves the following phases: (1) activating prior knowledge by *searching* for appropriate information related to the topic, (2) monitoring comprehension by *applying* selected related information to interpret the topic, (3) evaluating the meaning and inconsistencies with regard to prior knowledge by *selecting* and *evaluating* information to be stored in memory or used to construct a new schema, and (4) *composing* by thinking (silently, orally, or by writing) based on information encountered through discussing, reading, viewing, and so forth. As students internalize the when and why for the application of these patterns, the conditions for transferring these structures to a new context emerge.

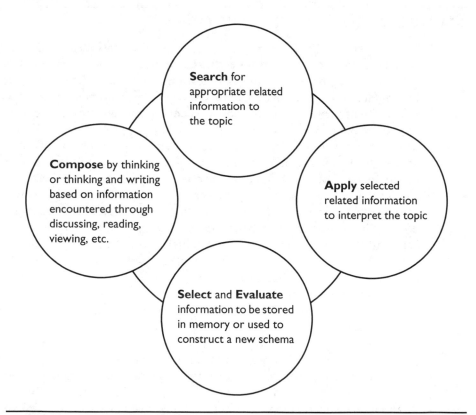

Figure 6.1   How information is processed according to schema theory.

Finally, the interplay between the process of prediction and verification that takes place during discussing or reading suggests strategies to activate prior knowledge and to analyze new material. Kindergartners understand that sharing materials makes for good citizenship in the classroom. This idea can be expanded by having them make art projects to share with individuals living in retirement homes as they learn that giving to others makes for a good feeling for those receiving as well as those giving the items.

Modeling Thinking

Teachers need to model thinking processes for students. How we relate new knowledge to our prior knowledge, how we understand concepts, how we develop questions, and so forth needs to be taught explicitly to students. This can be done by taking nonfiction text, reading it aloud to the students, and sharing our thoughts aloud as we proceed. Have the students clear their desks or, better yet, gather on the floor quietly with a pencil and notebook, eyes forward. Share the nonfiction piece on an overhead transparency or give each student a copy. As you read the text aloud, point out how the text itself reveals information—first the title of the piece; headings; photo or illustration captions; bold print; sidebars; graphs; and so forth. As you read the piece aloud, stop and ponder aloud as you demonstrate how to incorporate the information. Do the same when material is confusing or unclear. Reread it aloud. Ask questions that come to mind aloud. What is the author trying to say here? Reread it again aloud, this time more slowly. Using clear sticky notes with an arrow, mark the section that is confusing with a large question mark. After you have read the piece aloud, share what you think is the main idea with the class. Students then understand that reading factual, nonfiction material is more than gathering facts; it is really understanding the big idea (Harvey and Goudvis 2000).

Teachers need to model how to make a prediction, ask questions, clarify, make comments, and make connections. Here are suggestions from Kylene Beers (2003):

Make a Prediction
- I predict that . . .
- I think that . . .
- Since this happened _____, then I think the next thing to happen will be _____
- I wonder if . . .

Ask a question
- Why did . . .
- What's this part about . . .
- How is this _____ like this _____
- What would happen if _____
- Why . . .
- Who is . . .
- Do you think . . .
- I don't understand _____

Clarify Something

- Oh, I get it . . .
- Now I understand . . .
- I think it means . . .
- At first I thought _____ but now I think _____
- What this part is really saying . . .

Make a Comment

- This is good because . . .
- This is hard because . . .
- This is confusing because . . .
- I like the part where . . .
- I don't like the part where . . .
- I think that . . .

Make a Connection

- This reminds me of . . .
- This character _____ is like _____ because . . .
- This is similar to . . .
- This differs from _____ because
- This reminds me of . . .
- This part is like . . .
- I have never (name something from the book) . . .

With the class, view a video or DVD. Watch a short portion such as 5 or 10 minutes and then stop. At this point, discuss what you have learned so far. Divide an overhead transparency into two halves. On the left hand side, use phrases to jot this information down in rapid fashion. Explain to the students how the information relates to what you already know. Next, on the right half of the overhead transparency, write two or three questions that are still unanswered and that you expect the remainder of the video to resolve. Continue viewing the selection, stopping every 5 to 10 minutes and repeating the above steps. At the end of the video, compare the information gathered with the questions asked. Then have the students view the entire video a second time.

Do such demonstrating frequently and early in the school year, then once every other week midyear, and finally once a month by the last three months of the school year. The exception would be if the class is highly transient, receiving new students every couple of weeks, or if the class has a large number of struggling readers and/or ELLs, in which instances modeling this strategy every two weeks throughout the entire year would be appropriate.

On chart paper have students generate ways to read social studies text. This serves as a "reading guide" and should be posted where students may refer to it throughout the year. Some student may point out that bolded words are often new vocabulary, while another may say to key in on headings as they summarize the

Teachers need to model their thinking, including how they make predictions and self-question as well as how they seek out information from the text.

upcoming topic. Someone will likely announce that captions under pictures reveal information. Yet another student will remind the class that reading the headings first and then going back to read the entire text can serve as a road map to what the author is trying to share. Asking questions at the end of one section may sometimes predict what will unfold in the text in the next section. Such insights help students develop their thinking strategies for information texts. The "reading guide" chart should be added to throughout the school year as new strategies evolve or are discovered.

Good texts to use with this approach include: *My Weekly Reader* (current events information for primary students), *Appleseed* (monthly social studies magazine for primary students), *National Geographic Young Explorer* (published seven times a year for K–1 students), *Cobblestone* (monthly social studies magazine that focuses on history for intermediate grades), *Ranger Rick* (monthly magazine with both fiction and nonfiction for ages 7–10), *National Geographic World* (monthly magazine for intermediate through middle school grades), *National Geographic Explorer* (science and social studies content for elementary students), and *Faces* (monthly magazine on world cultures and geography for upper grades/middle school). Using the opening portion of a chapter in the social studies textbook is also appropriate. By first sharing a portion of an article on the overhead projector as you demonstrate a reading skill and then having the students apply the skill as they read the text themselves, the students will be more likely to utilize the skill in their own reading. It is important to have a copy of the text for all of the students to read in pairs or at their own desks.

K-W-L

One strategy to help students take an active role in reading social studies text is **K-W-L** (Ogle 1986, 1989), which stands for *k*now, *w*ant to know, and *l*earned. This strategy is a three-step approach to help students read and understand informational text such as social studies materials. The teacher and each student begin with a chart containing three columns: (1) Know, (2) Want to Know, and (3) Learned. By using K-W-L prior to the whole-class discussion, the student assesses what she or he already knows before group activity begins (Gaskin et al. 1994). Naive beliefs become apparent during the examination of the new information in the text. Figure 6.2 provides an example of a K-W-L chart constructed on the topic of France; the learning activities associated with this strategy are discussed in the section on strategic sequencing.

Using specific reasoning strategies to activate prior knowledge helps students comprehend the ideas contained in the text. Through this active engagement, readers are able to link new information with their personal knowledge of the subject. By learning to monitor and control such strategies students develop an understanding of how they learn. This metacognitive awareness allows them to control the learning process.

Young learners, such as first and second graders, need a modified version of K-W-L. Rather than asking them what they want to know, they should be told to share what they "wonder" about. For instance, "I wonder" what Abraham Lincoln was like as a boy; "I wonder" what he did before he became president; "I wonder" why he wanted to become president; "I wonder" what he did as president. This gives the students a framework from which they can work and to which they can also relate.

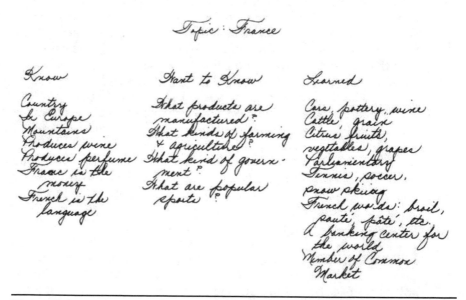

Figure 6.2 An example of K-W-L on the topic of France by a fourth-grade class.

Graphic Organizers

When used with social studies textbooks, graphic organizers or semantic maps, help activate student learning. **Graphic organizers** present information in a diagram in a simplistic manner. They are also very appropriate for use with nonfiction informational books. When students are reading material that contains a large amount of information, a visual display can help them remember what they have read.

The teacher can demonstrate the use of graphic organizers by reading aloud five or six pages from the social studies textbook or an informational children's literature book. Students working in pairs reread the passage the teacher read aloud and begin to map information. The students identify key information, which is then classified under a heading and related to the nucleus word or words that identify the primary topic. An example at the first-grade level is to purchase two hula hoops. For Presidents' Day, read about Presidents George Washington and Abraham Lincoln. On 5 by 8 cards, write facts about each. For instance: Army officer, general, fought Indians, from Virginia, from Illinois, owned slaves, freed slaves, a farmer, a surveyor, a lawyer, a storekeeper, and so forth. Next have the students place the facts in the circle for Washington, the circle for Lincoln, or where the two circles overlap for both presidents. This is a simple way to introduce students to a Venn diagram.

A simple graphic organizer for first and second graders is to draw a spider, a circle with eight legs extending from it. Inside the circle, put the topic. From each leg, write something that relates to the topic. Community could be the topic with fire department, city government, hospital, police department, post office, bank, stores, and school as the "legs." As students progress, they further refine the graphic organizer, for instance, making subheadings for each extended arm (for fire department the student might add firefighters, paramedics, fire chief, fire trucks, hook and ladder truck, water tanker truck, ambulance).

The graphic organizer shows the learner the relationship patterns developed in the text that have similarities to the structures inherent in the schemata. However, distinctive differences exist between the graphic organizer and reasoning. Although the graphic organizer can activate the reasoning strategies, the learning takes place during the interaction between the learner's prior knowledge, the demands of the graphic organizer, and the information contained in the textbook. Therefore, differences appear in the visual representations created from text material because of variations in the learner's prior knowledge as well as in the reasoning strategies applied.

Using a graphic organizer (see figure 6.3) aids comprehension of the social studies text by making the patterns clear. Designed as a means of organizing text material into relationship patterns, the graphic organizer centers attention on the key information contained in the text. Hadaway and Young (1994) advocate the development of literacy through content and the use of the graphic organizer to promote comprehension. More important, they suggest that the current trend toward more language diversity in the schools necessitates this instructional strategy. By building background knowledge and developing language simultaneously, the instructor can promote cooperative problem-solving activities, which is an effective pattern of instruction where language diversity is a consideration. However, Hadaway and Young stress that these activities benefit all children, because

Feudal Society Groups

Clergy	Nobles	Peasants
- teach religion	- govern	- farm land
- help poor and sick	- enforce laws	- provide services
- have more rights	- protect people	- work for clergy and nobles
	- have more rights	- largest group

Believed God wanted it that way →

- few tried to make improvements or change way of life

→ remained in groups they were born into

(a)

	Ties of Loyalty	Duties
Lord	- protected vassals from enemy attack - if he failed to do this, vassal owed no loyalty	- gave vassal a fief - gave symbol of trust - gave right to govern
Vassal	- less powerful noble - fief vassals for life - upon death, passed to son - did not lose respect for seeking protection - gave loyalty to lord - some supported the one likely to win	- helped lord in battle - supplied knights - owed 40 days of battle a year - paid lord when sons became knights and daughters married - paid ransom for lord's release - supplied food and entertainment - decided cases

(b)

Figure 6.3 Sample graphic organizers developed by students.

Residence

Type	Time period	Description
Manor	9-11th centuries	- wooden buildings high wooden fences - 1 room, high ceiling and straw floor - all activities - fire for cooking and heating
Castle	12th century	- stone fortress - lookout tower and arches - moat -- soft muddy bottom - drawbridge -- heavy door - portcullis -- heavy oak/iron gate - keep -- tall tower with all, many rooms and dungeon

(c)

Figure 6.3 (continued)

the relationship between the concepts and the main ideas is reinforced through the manipulation of text material. With the graphic organizer, students can better control and comprehend large amounts of information.

In examining the impact of the graphic organizer on meaningful learning, Armbruster (1985) identifies three stages leading to meaningful learning: (1) selection of information from the text, (2) organization into a coherent structure, and (3) integration of the new information. Armbruster applies this model to three basic structural patterns used in social studies texts: (1) description, (2) comparison/contrast, and (3) explanation. Figure 6.3 shows three examples of graphic organizers. These represent three different approaches to feudal societal groups generated by sixth-grade students.

Armbruster, Anderson, and Ostertag (1989) expanded the list of patterns by dividing the explanation pattern into (4) sequence, (5) cause-effect, and (6) problem solution. Regardless of the labels, these organizational patterns are used in most social studies text materials. Graphic organizers, as visual representations of these patterns, help the learner focus on the important information within the text and clarify the purpose in reading.

By setting the focus for learning, the graphic organizer gives the student control over the text and assistance in comprehension. The value of these visual models lies in directing the integration of reading, writing, and group work toward a specific learning outcome.

Questioning Strategies

Developing appropriate questions is not an easy task for students. Thus, it is important that teachers model such behavior. Sharing a read-aloud and then writing down questions on an overhead transparency that relate to what was read is one technique. Another is to use two overhead projectors, one displaying a passage from a piece of historical fiction, for example, and the other projecting questions that the class creates. Students may then be given a short story or piece of nonfiction text and, working with a partner, develop a list of five or six questions to be shared with the entire class.

Certainly the level of difficulty of questions varies from low-level, literal recall, knowledge questions to inferential questions to evaluative higher-level, critical-thinking questions. Some teachers refer to low-level questions as "thin" and to inferential and evaluative questions "thick." Nancy Carnahan, a third-grade teacher, labels the questions her students create by the level of difficulty as "25 cent" or "two dollar" questions. A question whose answer can readily be found in the text, a literal question, is a "25 cent" question; one that requires inferential thinking, taking information and interpreting it, is a "two dollar" question. The "two dollar" questions may not have a right or wrong answer but serve to stretch students to think about what they have read. Some teachers refer to such questions as "thin" and "fat" questions, as thin questions have little to "chew on" discussion-wise while "fat" questions serve up juicy options of possible solutions that can be discussed by a group of students. Evaluative questions require that the student take information from a variety of sources, weigh each, and make a final judgment.

Strategic Sequencing

The **sequencing of strategies,** like the phases of learning, involves (1) prereading to activate prior knowledge, (2) using graphic organizers to monitor comprehension, and (3) evaluating inconsistencies between new information and prior knowledge. These three steps, especially the first one, are central to comprehension of the text materials. The following sections apply sequencing strategies and the use of graphic organizers to a middle school geography lesson.

Phase One: Activating Prior Knowledge

Before students read social studies texts, learning theory suggests engaging them in activities that tap their prior knowledge of the topic, or schema. Because of the descriptive pattern used in social studies books—particularly when describing geography—the text provides an opportunity to classify specific characteristics of a geographic region. During this initial introduction to a region, students access their prior knowledge. This follows the same logic as the K-W-L strategy (Ogle 1986, 1989). During the prereading stage, students brainstorm about what they already know of the topic. The pooled information is recorded on the class chart under the "Know" column. As students contribute information, some conflicts and disputes will arise. These discrepancies are turned into questions and listed under the "Want to Know" column.

Drawing on the same thinking strategies as the K-W-L, Davidson (1982) presents another strategy: the whole class uses mapping strategies to assess the group's level of prior knowledge. For this geography unit, the students independently list random associations for Western Europe in their learning logs. The teacher uses an overhead transparency to record student responses about the topic. This activity gives students a model for the process of anticipating the information contained in the chapter.

By mapping the predicted material for the text, students determine what they know, predict what will be discussed, and assess what was learned. They are using the K-W-L thinking strategy in a new format. Students activate their prior knowledge by writing what they know into a learning log. Fulwiler (1978) defines this kind of writing as a means of connecting the personal and the academic functions of writing. This learning log strategy actively engages the student in learning by encouraging rehearsal of ideas and establishing the level of background knowledge prior to the whole-class discussion. Following a time span of three to five minutes, the teacher records the student associations of Western Europe on an overhead transparency (see figure 6.4). All student associations are recorded regardless of their accuracy. Associations are removed from the list only when they are disproved or are not validated in the textbook. No attempt at classification occurs during this stage. Information is recorded in the random order in which the students present it.

After listing the known information on the overhead projector, the teacher uses another transparency to model the classification of this information. For the topic of Western Europe, the teacher starts with "country," the obvious category of

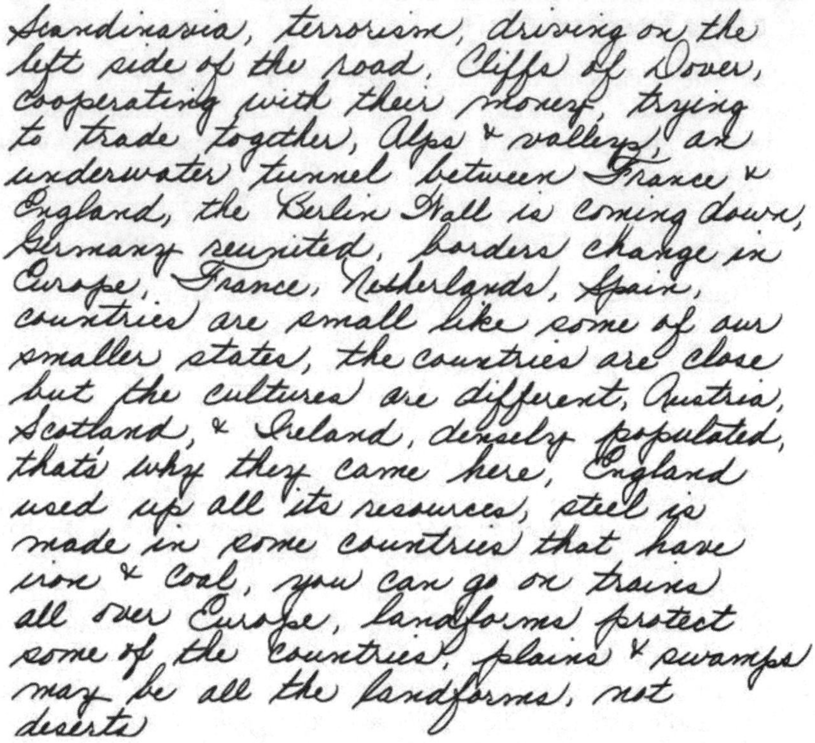

Scandinavia, terrorism, driving on the left side of the road, Cliffs of Dover, cooperating with their money, trying to trade together, Alps & valleys, an underwater tunnel between France & England, the Berlin Wall is coming down, Germany reunited, borders change in Europe, France, Netherlands, Spain, countries are small like some of our smaller states, the countries are close but the cultures are different, Austria, Scotland, & Ireland, densely populated, that's why they came here, England used up all its resources, steel is made in some countries that have iron & coal, you can go on trains all over Europe, landforms protect some of the countries, plains & swamps may be all the landforms, not deserts

Figure 6.4 Listing random Western Europe associations.

countries. By circling each country and listing it under the category on the transparency, the teacher demonstrates the classification process. Students continue the process by classifying the information in their learning logs and recording the reasoning for each classification. Finally, the teacher records the students' categories (e.g., land forms, natural resources, etc.) on the transparency (see figure 6.5) and identifies similar and overlapping categories. Depending on the group's familiarity with the text, categories based on geography concepts may emerge. Following this predictive activity, the students move to the next phase and preview the chapter.

Phase Two: Assessing and Monitoring Comprehension

By comparing the subtopics in the text with their classification categories, students evaluate their initial predictions and determine the need for additional topics. The teacher directs the evaluation process through questioning. Were any categories overlooked during the brainstorming activity, and is there a need to extend the categories? What possible relationships are seen in the subtopics, and how do they appear to be organized? The teacher gains insight into the group's knowledge of text cues by following student input on these topics.

Students examine the pictures, maps, graphs, and subheadings as they revise their original predictions. Graphic displays used in expository text reinforce the

WESTERN EUROPE					
Countries	Land Forms	Natural Resources	Economics	Transportation	Problems
France	Alps	coal	economic	drive on wrong	terrorism
Netherlands	valleys	farms	community	side of the road	Wall coming
Germany	Cliffs of Dover	iron ore	cooperate with	trains all over	down
Austria	swamps	steel	money	underwater tunnel	small like
Spain	plains		trade together	between France	states
Ireland	all types		European	and England	England used
Great Britain	no desert		Union		up resources
	can protect		"Eurodollar"		densely
	countries		Great Britain		populated
			has own		close but
			currency		different
			(pound)		cultures
					borders
					change

Figure 6.5   Classifying associations.

connections between concepts and help students discover patterns. Students can preview the graphic displays (i.e., headings, graphs, maps, bold prints) in the text and discuss what is illustrated. During the group discussion, the teacher guides and clarifies the information. Gillespie (1993, 352) suggests using questioning strategies similar to those used with prose: What is the main idea? What are the supporting details? What is the purpose of the graph? How are the details related?

Students may depend on the subheadings of the social studies chapter to suggest concepts presented in the text. Another helpful strategy, however, is to use the introduction and the first sentence of each paragraph to identify central concepts. After this research, students will add to their learning logs and the group will discuss the following question: What signals are found in the chapter introduction, and what organization can be predicted?

Using the text overview, the teacher begins to record the questions that the students believe will be answered in the text (see figure 6.6 on the following page). These questions establish the purpose for reading. Taking one subtopic at a time, the teacher records the questions on the overhead transparency as students predict what the material will cover. The students then read the text to find the information that answers the questions. This strategy combines the thought process of the K-W-L strategy and the explicit framework of the graphic organizer.

Phase Three: Evaluating Inconsistencies and Written Extensions

Finally, in a class discussion, students reflect on what they have learned. During this time, the students share what they have recorded under the column titled "Learned." The teacher moves students to the evaluation level during this final phase of instruction, beginning with an analysis of the classification of associations and the descriptive map of the text. Examination and discussion of the similarities and differences between the predicted structure and the actual text organization help students refine this knowledge and apply this learning to their preview of the next chapter.

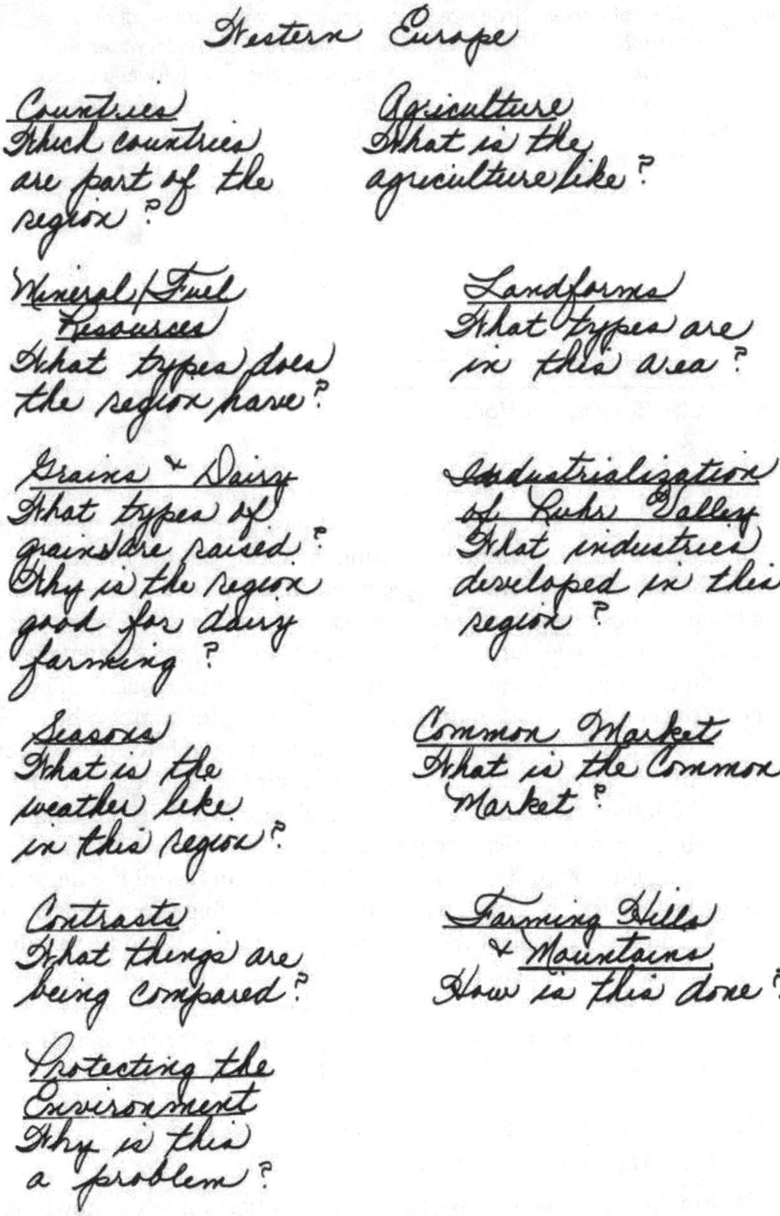

Western Europe

Countries
Which countries are part of the region?

Agriculture
What is the agriculture like?

Mineral / Fuel Resources
What types does the region have?

Landforms
What types are in this area?

Grains & Dairy
What types of grains are raised?
Why is the region good for dairy farming?

Industrialization of Ruhr Valley
What industries developed in this region?

Seasons
What is the weather like in this region?

Common Market
What is the Common Market?

Contrasts
What things are being compared?

Farming Hills & Mountains
How is this done?

Protecting the Environment
Why is this a problem?

Figure 6.6 Class-generated questions about a topic help direct students' reading. These are the "What" questions the class brainstormed regarding Western Europe.

By placing the classification of associations (see figure 6.5) on the overhead transparency and having students refer to the descriptive map that they have created while they were reading the text, the teacher ensures that students can evaluate the effectiveness of their predictions. The focus on this analysis should center on the students becoming more effective in making future predictions. Through awareness of concepts covered in the first chapter, expectations for future chapters are changed.

As the students examine the descriptive maps, they find that many of the countries originally classified as part of the region were correct. Their classification contained too few countries: one incorrect country in the original prediction will appear in another region. Because the students gave no consideration to the categories of agriculture and climate in their initial classifications, they learn that these categories need to be added to the predictions of future chapters. In this chapter, students find the concept of transportation appears under the category of industrialization. The problems cited in the chapter are more environmental and general than those in TV and radio newscasts, and in newspapers and magazines. Using this critique as a basis, the predictive process can be repeated for subsequent chapters.

Each time the students perform this predictive process, they further refine the organizational pattern for more effective predictions. Descriptive mapping strategies can extend into group discussion, research, and writing. Students can experience more rehearsal for the material, for example, by manipulating the information on the maps generated for the chapters on Northern and Western Europe and writing a paper comparing and contrasting the two regions.

The descriptive maps, generated from the expository text, provide a structure for the points of comparison so that students become sensitive to the structures required in expository writing. Signal words cue the reader to the structure of the written product as students make transitions from material on one descriptive map to material on another (see figure 6.7 and figure 6.8 on the following pages) to produce the final product as Shannon did in creating her final draft.

Clues for Teaching Further Thinking Skills

By examining the influence of the descriptive mapping activity on expository writing, one can see how the mapping process gives students control over focus and organization. Students use the descriptive maps to identify points of comparison in the text. This establishes the focus and organization of their paper. Once students establish their series of topics in the introductory paragraph, they can go on to isolate each point of comparison and examine it for similarities and differences in a Venn diagram (see figure 6.9 on p. 214).

The students make appropriate transitions between the information contained in each chapter to establish these comparisons. As a result, the information drawn from each chapter does not remain isolated facts but emerges as an interrelated information bank. This process of creating connections between the information encourages rehearsal of the information and facilities long-term retention of the material. The positive impact of this type of manipulation and integration of material is supported by the research of Langer and Applebee (1987) and the results of their three-year study funded by the National Institute for Learning. Moreover, the

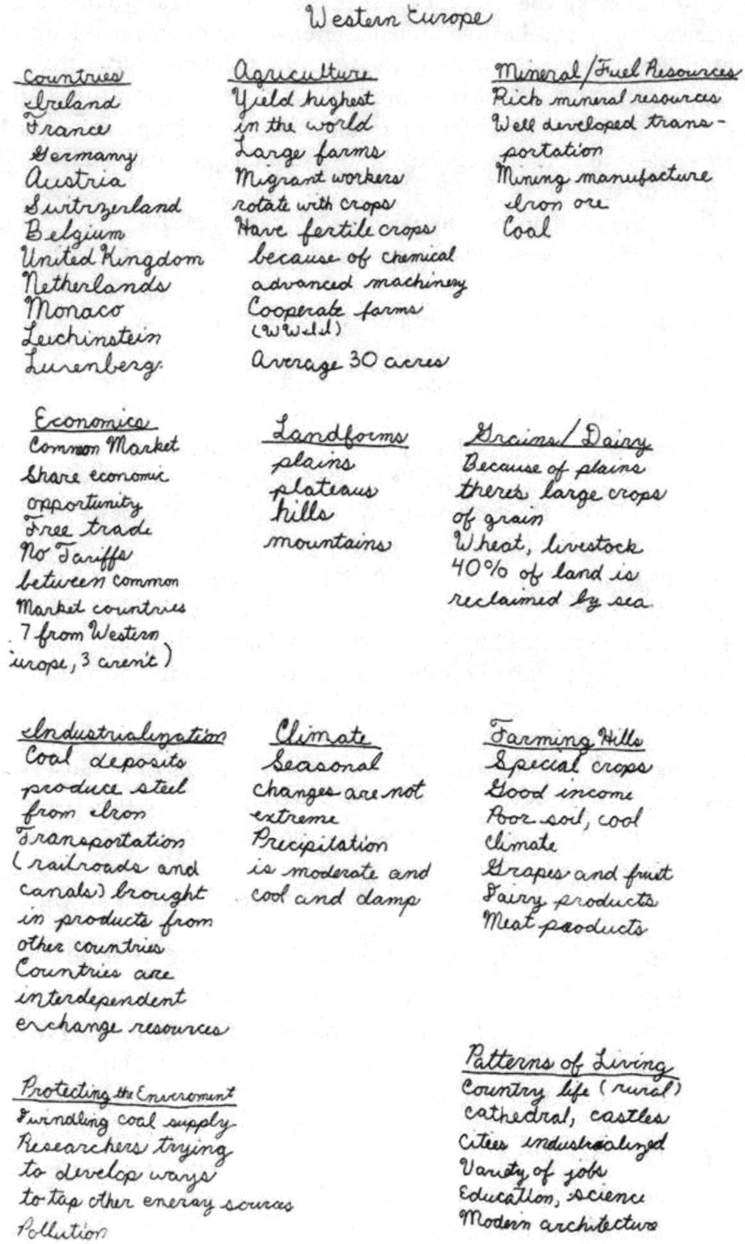

Western Europe

Countries
Ireland
France
Germany
Austria
Switzerland
Belgium
United Kingdom
Netherlands
Monaco
Leichinstein
Luxenberg

Agriculture
Yield highest
in the world
Large farms
Migrant workers
rotate with crops
Have fertile crops
because of chemical
advanced machinery
Cooperate farms
(WWild)
Average 30 acres

Mineral/Fuel Resources
Rich mineral resources
Well developed trans-
portation
Mining manufacture
Iron ore
Coal

Economics
Common Market
Share economic
opportunity
Free trade
No Tariffs
between common
Market countries
7 from Western
urope, 3 aren't)

Landforms
plains
plateaus
hills
mountains

Grains/Dairy
Because of plains
there's large crops
of grain
Wheat, livestock
40% of land is
reclaimed by sea

Industrialization
Coal deposits
produce steel
from Iron
Transportation
(railroads and
canals) brought
in products from
other countries
Countries are
interdependent
exchange resources

Climate
Seasonal
changes are not
extreme
Precipitation
is moderate and
cool and damp

Farming Hills
Special crops
Good income
Poor soil, cool
climate
Grapes and fruit
Dairy products
Meat products

Protecting the Environment
Dwindling coal supply
Researchers trying
to develop ways
to tap other energy sources
Pollution

Patterns of Living
Country life (rural)
cathedral, castles
cities industrialized
Variety of jobs
Education, science
Modern architecture

Figure 6.7 Student-generated descriptive map by Shannon.

Northern and Western Europe
by Shannon

Have you ever visited Europe?
Examination of Northern and Western
Europe shows that many similarites
and differences can be seen in many
areas. By refering to agriculture, resources,
climate, contries, and land, you can see just
how alike and different they really are.

When comparing Northern European
agriculture to Western European agriculture,
it becomes clear that there are many
similarties and differences.
Western Europe prows to be more of an
agriculture region, unlike Northern
Eurpe in many ways. Farming in Western
Europe is more basic since boulders and
rocks soil don't interfere with the
flurishing plains and basins. Western
Europe produces a large variety of grain,
wheat, and livestock, similar to its
neighbor, Northern Europe. Northern Europe
although it has swamps and marshes, and
rocky soil yields more than Western
Europe. Northern Europe produces large
quantities of daily, grains, and livestock.
Such examples are exported cheese,
butter, oats, wheat, rye, barley, and livestock
products like meat and hide. This conclusion
is drawn from the hard workers and the
various farming techniques. Northern
Europe and Western Europe are similar

Figure 6.8 An example of expository writing.

since they both use cooperative farms to help keep costs down. Unlike most Western farmers, in Northern Europe, farmers often share their equipment and profits. Western Europe benefits by having migrant workers rotate with their crops. Also, crops are more fertile because of chemical advanced machinery.

Resources play a great deal of importance in Northern and Western Europe. While Northern Europe is famous for its fish and forests, Western Europe has rich mineral resources. Both areas produce steel and iron or, although Western Europe also has coal deposits. In order to trasport the products, Western Europe has many railroads and canals which have their transportion well developed. In comparison, Western Europe produces more natural resources while Northern Europe stays less industrialized.

Through climate, simalarties and differences became clear in Western and Northern Europe. Northern Europe has a moderate climate, as well as Western Europe, until you reach areas north of the Artic Circle. This area includes long winters and short growing seasons. Western Europe doesn't appear to have extreme seasonal changes and precipitation is moderate. Over all, most of this area is cool and damp.

Figure 6.8   *(continued)*

Such countries within Western Europe are Ireland, France, West Germany, Austria, Switzerland, Belgium, United Kingdom, Netherlands, Monaco, Liechtenstein, and Luxenburg. Countries located in Northern Europe are Iceland, Norway, Sweden, Finland, and Denmark. These countries make up all the similarities and differences contained in this article.

A distinctive difference between northern and western Europe is the land type. In northern Europe glaciers remain, while marshes and swamps are present. This land permits limited farming because of its infertile soil with boulders and gravel. On the other hand, western Europe has large farms and fertile crops, the average being thirty acres. Landforms there include plains, plateaus, hills, and mountains.

As concluded from information gathered, many similarities and differences have arisen between the two countries. While western Europe proves more as an agriculture region, northern Europe is big in the fishing industry. Through examination of agriculture, resources, climate, countries, and land a better understanding can be reached about these two famous countries.

Figure 6.8 *(continued)*

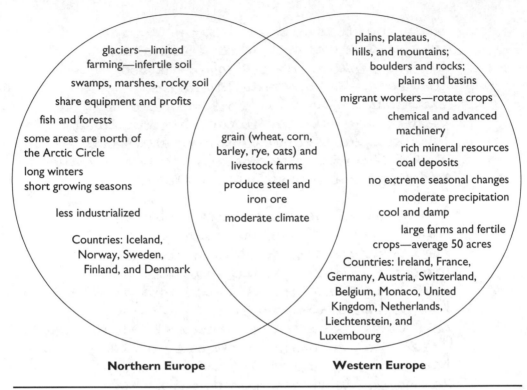

Figure 6.9 A Venn diagram is good to use to compare and contrast.

research of Armbruster, Anderson, and Ostertag (1989) concludes that instruction on the text structure has a positive impact on reading and writing expository text. This finding is based on their research on the problem-solution structure with the fifth-grade population. Since expository text is one of the most difficult text structures, the researchers suggest that the text structure instruction could be beneficial in learning content area material such as social studies and could have a positive impact on writing as well. As mentioned earlier, the Venn diagram helps students organize material (see figure 6.9).

Finally, through the use of their learning logs, students can think about how they evaluate the structure of the information presented in the chapters and how they process that information; in other words, students develop a metacognitive awareness.

Reading Strategies for New Technology Sources

"New technologies have not diminished our students' need to read. In fact, the arrival of computers and the Internet has increased the importance of reading" (Lewin 1999, 17). As teachers help students develop new reading strategies, it is good to use guided reading to assist students in using information gathered from the Internet. Students create an "e-sheet," which contains the topic or related topic to what is being studied (i.e., the Revolutionary War, a comparison of All Soul's Day and The Day of The Dead [*Dia de los Muertes*], the Punic Wars). Below are examples of specific Web sites, questions related to each one, and a question for extra credit (Lewin 1999). The e-sheet serves as a kind of semantic map for the net-surfing student.

Guided Reading: E-Sheet
Topic: The Punic Wars

Web Site #1: History of Western Civilization, Boise State University
http://www.history.idbsu.edu/westciv/punicwar

Questions:
1. Who wrote this Web site?
2. Which countries were involved in the Punic Wars?
3. Why did the Romans lose the first Punic War?
4. What role did Hannibal play in the Punic Wars?
5. Describe two war strategies that Hannibal used.

Extra Credit Question:
6. Who was Scipio? Which side did he fight on?

Web Site #2: The University of Virginia
www.cti.itc.Virginia.edu

Questions:
1. Who wrote this Web site?
2. Where is Carthage located?
3. Who was Hannibal?
4. How did Hannibal get his troops to Italy to battle the Romans?
5. Elephants were important in the Punic Wars. How were they used?

Extra Credit Question:
6. What was Fabius's strategy? Was he correct?

The use of e-sheets aids students to define the topic they are studying and gather the information needed in a reasonable amount of time.

Handhelds can be used by the teacher to jot down observations about students. Such comments can then be transferred to the hard drive of the classroom's computer for permanent storage. Middle school students can use handhelds to record data for research reports.

History as Perspective Taking

As students get older, they can better interpret and understand history if they take different **perspectives.** For instance, a third grader may take the perspective as a pioneer going west and then investigate the same topic from the viewpoint of a member of a tribe of Native Americans. A fifth grader may take the position of a sister of two Civil War soldiers, with one fighting for the Confederate Army and the other for the Army of the Potomac. Each of her brothers could present their sides of the issue of slavery.

In preparation for exploring multiple perspectives, Roberta Linder (2006) believes the teacher needs to critically examine the text to be presented to the students to determine the perspective present in the text as well as those that are absent. Should any additional materials be gathered to supplement the information about any absent perspectives? What activity or strategy would be most appropriate? Linder then front loads information by sharing some insights or information that the text is missing. For instance, the Japanese had control of Korea for 30 years prior to the U.S. getting involved in WWII, and the communists in Korea wanted the Japanese ousted from their country. Thus the communists and Americans helped push the Japanese back to Japan. Today the U.S. and North Korea take opposite sides.

Linder gives her middle school students a "Character Perspective Chart" to complete as they read their historical fiction novels. To get them started she shares a picture book as a read-aloud and completes a Character Perspective Chart on the overhead with the class. For her WWII unit, Linder shares *Faithful Elephants* (Tsuchiva 1988), an informational picture book based on actual facts of what the Tokyo zookeepers did to euthanize the wild animals at the end of the war to prevent them from running loose in the streets and harming people. When the elephants refused to eat the poisoned potatoes, they were starved to death.

Mac Duis, an eighth-grade teacher at Haverford Middle School in Haverford, Pennsylvania, capitalizes on his students' ability to conceptualize and think in abstract terms (Duis and Duis 1998). Students at this age are searching for their

☞ IN THE CLASSROOM

Character Perspective Chart

Who is your character? _____

Setting: Where and When does the story take place? _____

Conflict: What is your character's problem? _____

Goal: What does your character want? _____

Attempt: What does your character do to solve the problem or reach the goal? _____

Outcome: What happened as a result of the character's attempt? _____

Reaction: How does your character feel about the outcome? _____

Theme: What point did the author of the book want to make? _____

own identity, a process that requires them to draw on the present as well as the past. Seventh and eighth graders are able to take on perspectives of others and gain new insights about opinions that may be different from their own. Duis has his students engage in perspective taking in teaching about early American history through an activity he calls the Colonial Convention. This activity is set in the year 1750. Each student adopts the role of a character from the late colonial period and must present the views of that character at the Colonial Convention. Duis gives each student the hometown and the background of each character. At this point, the students give their characters' background.

Character Development Planner

Student:
Character's name:
Character's hometown:
Character's occupation:
Character's gender:
Character's age:
Character's religion:
Character's family members and their ages:
Character's family history:
Character's interests:
Character's unique characteristics:
Character's influential experiences:
Character's opinion about colonial trade:
Character's opinion about the "*Indian* problem":
Character's opinion about the role of religion:

Duis has the students research the period. In addition, the students read *The Light in the Forest* (Richter 1995), the classic story about a white boy raised by Native Americans when his parents are killed in a skirmish. The class takes a field trip to a working farm where they engage in such colonial tasks as carding wool, making crafts, and preparing Early American food dishes.

The students present their characters' views at the Colonial Convention. The other students may question or challenge a student's character if the views presented seem to change during the presentation. At the end of the Colonial Convention, the students write compositions comparing the views of the colonists from the three different regions: New England, the Middle Colonies, and the South.

The assessment of the students includes three criteria: (1) the thoroughness of the character development planner, (2) historical accuracy of character attributes, and (3) historical appropriateness of stands on issues. Each of these is graded on a three-point scale with the total score being worth nine points. Culminating events can be a class version of a colonial newspaper or a fair reflecting the period's food and crafts (Duis and Duis 1998).

This unit by Duis incorporates several social studies standards. These are listed as follows:

Integrated Instructional Unit: Theme: Colonial America

Standard I. Culture

a. Compare similarities and differences in the ways groups, societies, and cultures to meet human needs and concerns.

b. Explain why individuals and groups respond differently to their physical and social environments and/or changes to them on the basis of shared assumptions, values, and beliefs.

Standard II. Time, Continuity, and Change

c. Identify and describe selected historical periods and patterns of change within and across cultures.

d. Develop critical sensitivities such as empathy and skepticism regarding attitudes, values, and behaviors of people in different historical context.

Standard V. Individuals, Groups, and Institutions

b. Analyze group and institutional influences on people, events, and elements of culture.

Standard X. Civic Ideals and Practices

c. Locate, access, analyze, organize, and apply information about selected public issues—recognizing and explaining multiple points of view.

d. Practice forms of civic discussion and participation consistent with the ideals of citizens in a democratic republic.

By using these standards as guidelines for his integrated unit of study on Colonial America, Duis strengthens his students' understanding of the social studies.

Reading from a Resistant Perspective

Different layers of meaning can be "peeled" from reading a text when the reader is encouraged to approach the text from different identities based on age, race, ethnicity, class, gender, language, sexuality, and religion (Foss 2002). "Reading from a resistant perspective requires a conscious awareness of the influences upon text interpretation" (Behrman 2006, 493). For instance, while studying the state history of Wisconsin, a teacher organized the class into small groups, each taking on a family identity (e.g. English American, German American, Scandinavian American, and Native American). Each group expressed their views as Wisconsin evolved from being part of the Northwest Territory to being a separate territory and then later gaining statehood (McCall 2002).

Economics can be likewise studied with a resistant perspective. A study of capitalism and degree of wealth and the effects upon social classes can be studied by considering the murder of a middle schooler by a classmate solely to steal his iPod. Or capitalism versus communism using chocolate candy to interpret the effects of communism and resource allocation versus the free enterprise system.

Infusing Critical Multicultural Perspectives into Integrated Language Arts and Social Studies Instruction

Literature-based social studies instruction along with well-defined accompanying activities can provide for sophisticated, challenging, relevant, connected, in-depth, critical, and multicultural learning to take place asserts Nelly Ukpokodu (2002). She believes such instruction has seven essential ingredients:

1. *Good literature.* Books must be interesting and well-written if students' understanding of multicultural perspectives about the human experience are to be fostered. Seek out such books for all grade levels by going to the lists of Notable Trade Books for Youth at the NCSS Web site, www.socialstudies.org.

2. *Meaningful theme.* Select a broad instructional theme that the book represents—historical events, social concepts, current issues, and moral questions.

3. *Challenging academics.* The combination of language arts and social studies allows for students to learn social studies content as they practice the language arts (listening, speaking, reading, writing, viewing, and visually representing) and think critically. Students need the opportunity to discuss, write, dramatize, debate, read aloud, visually represent, view, and/or get involved in school or community service projects.

4. *Multiple perspectives.* Encourage students to consider the social perspectives and social relationships demonstrated by the characters of the book. What actions do they take? What cultural and social groups are portrayed?

5. *Social activism.* The book selected should be of top quality in terms of encouraging students to become socially active. Are there examples in the book of individuals or groups shouldering responsibility and taking action? Is a social problem presented and resolved?

6. *Critical multiculturalism.* Design accompanying activities that inform students about the core beliefs and traditions of another culture as well as promote critical thinking.

7. *Collaboration.* Work with other teachers in your school or district to gain input about the unit of study. In particular, seek out those who are culturally and socially different from yourself. They may be able to provide insights that cannot be found in your social studies textbook and the teacher's manual.

Children's literature is a superb vehicle for assisting students in learning about and understanding other peoples and their cultures and traditions. According to Ukpokodu (2002):

> When teachers do not help students examine critical issues embedded in trade books, they lead them to believe that society is perfect, all is well, and there is no need to get involved in civic life. . . . When we assist students in seeing how injustices come about, how they can be understood, and how we work to overcome them, then we prepare them to be effective citizens in a culturally diverse, democratic society. (23)

Concept Muraling

Visual literacy is increasingly gaining attention as a learning strategy. We remember visual images and patterns in our minds relatively easily. So, too, do our students. **Concept muraling** is an expository text strategy in which visual images are presented as a prereading activity to teach concepts and new ideas. A direct instruction approach, concept muraling enables students to preview the topic by seeing images and hearing the teacher describe important concepts prior to being asked to read the accompanying textual material. Learners—gifted, average ability, struggling readers, language delayed, learning disabled—all benefit from this strategy because it combines the brain's natural tendency to recall structured patterns with an oral overview. Based on schema theory, it has been found that even young children can see, hear, understand, and store well-structured images and verbal information in their long-term memory. Consider that every four-year-old in America can identify the golden arches of McDonald's whether it is a visual on a piece of paper or the sign in front of the restaurant itself. This process allows students to access this prior learning as they read and helps them to comprehend the textual material.

Concept muraling involves the teacher gleaning the primary goals and objectives from the social studies unit. Next, the teacher searches for pictures from the textbook, photos, postcards, Web site pictures, hand-drawn illustrations, computer clip art, or a combination of these. Between four and eight clearly defined, simple visuals are selected and presented in the same order in which they appear in the text to be read, such as the social studies chapter or a biography about a famous person. After reducing the size of the visuals using a photocopying machine, they are then taped or glued to a sheet of paper from the upper left-hand corner, flowing like a river down the page in a left to right, right to left, then left to right fashion until there are no more visuals. Figure 6.10 is an example of concept muraling for a unit on China. The visuals beginning with the upper left and in sequence a chain to bottom of the page are:

- Imperial Summer Palace, home of the Emperor's family, Tiananmen Square, and the Forbidden City are in Beijing; the 10 posts each represent one of the ten great Chinese dynasties.

- The Great Wall of China, over 1,500 miles in length, was built starting in the third century across the northern part of China to keep out invaders; it is wide enough that an army can march on it.

- Longtime products of China: finely painted china and tea.

- Confucius, moral and religious leader who lived 551–479 BC; three major teachings were respect for elders, statesmen were to take care of and respect citizens, and a sense of morality.

- Mao Zedong, Chairman of the Communist Party and former head of China.

- Pandas are found in China; two were gifts to American people when President Nixon went to China in 1970s.

- Modern Hong Kong, the former British colony that was turned over to China in 1997.

While this concept mural contains seven images for presenting to upper elementary or middle school students, the number for K–1 students should be four or five, for grades 2–3 students, five or six images.

Figure 6.10 Concept mural for China unit.

Steps in Concept Muraling:

1. Have the students clear their desks and look to the screen.

2. Share the theme of the unit of study, in this case, China.

3. Turn on the overhead projector and describe what each of the images represents, starting with the upper left-hand corner and moving in sequence from top to bottom as the pictures flow toward the bottom of the page. Give up to three facts that relate to each illustration.

4. When finished, go back to the first image and point to it. Ask the students what it is and what it represents. Do the same for the remaining illustrations.

5. Turn off the projector and point to where the first image was. Ask "what was here?" In sequence, ask what was in each of the positions. For each image, have the students explain who, what, where, and how.

6. Next, have each student either draw a picture of each image or list each image and the major points for each.

7. A variation is to have students work in pairs with each recording what they recall about each concept image in their social studies learning logs.

8. This can be used as an assessment measure.

Primary students as young as kindergartners who cannot write can recall the different scenes from memory and draw them. Intermediate students can either draw or number their paper from 1 to 15 and list the concepts presented. Upper elementary and middle school students can write a paragraph about each image presented, explaining what it means. This is a good follow-up activity to do the day after the concept muraling is initially presented.

Students can use this technique as a media approach in sharing their reports. They may use thin transparency markers to draw their images or clip art. Students who tend to become nervous while giving oral presentations are often more comfortable with this type of presentation because their peers are looking at the screen and not at them.

☞ IN THE CLASSROOM

Strategies for Synthesizing Information

When Lewis, Wray, and Rospigliosi (1994) work with expository material, they have several strategies to help students transform the information and make it their own.

• By drawing pictures of the steps in a procedure and labeling the process, students can restructure the information obtained from sequential text material.

• Students can synthesize text information into a graphic display that corresponds to the structure of the material. For example, a Venn diagram can be used to reinforce the information drawn from a compare and contrast selection.

• Students can take information from the text and use it to create a newspaper article.

☞ IN THE CLASSROOM

Strategic Instruction and Diverse Learners

Struggling readers and writers need additional assistance as do ELLs. In addition, each student brings a different perspective and background of experiences to the social studies lesson. To facilitate communication of social studies, Rolón (2002/2003) believes that "culturally appropriate pedagogy is about welcoming students' language, culture, and experiences to the classroom" (43). Teachers can offer support in the following ways:

• "Plan adequate time to activate students' prior knowledge and encourage students to share what they already know in journals, small groups, or paired brainstorming sessions. Identify which concepts and vocabulary words students are missing; supply definitions" (Rolón 2002/2003: 42), and, if possible, provide the translations in the students' native language.

• Visuals such as concept murals provide aid for struggling readers and writers as well as ELLs. Incorporate visuals such as pictures, drawings, graphs, video clips with the closed captions on, and maps, of course, as part of instruction.

• Graphic organizers, mentioned earlier in this chapter, and outlines are an asset for introducing new and reviewing old material with students.

• Model new skills for diverse learners so they will understand the process and the expectations.

• Use body language and facial expressions to convey new concepts. Be alert to the body language and facial expressions of students, as a blank look is indicative that the point being made is not getting across.

• Classroom routines should be set and predictable for students with transitions from one topic or subject to another being clear and distinct.

• At the end of the class, use summaries to bring closure and reinforce students' understanding.

NCSS STANDARDS-LINKED LESSON PLAN

Quilts as a Fabric of Culture

Theme: Quilts
Source: Ava McCall, University of Wisconsin-Oshkosh
Grades: Primary/Intermediate; Upper Elementary/Middle School
Objectives:

• Quilts as artistic creations, economic status, and historical documents are examined.

• Children will create a quilt expressing personal reaction to literature or textbook reading selection.

• Children will make a connection to quilters from other eras using a short creative writing exercise.

NCSS Themes:
   I. Culture
  II. Time, Continuity, and Change
VIII. Production, Distribution, and Consumption

Materials: Cotton material of various colors and sizes to be cut into quilt blocks. Needles, thread, thimbles, scissors, a quilting frame (made from 2 by 4 boards and two saw horses), cotton filling.

For Gr. K–2, give each child a like-color 12 square to decorate with markers. For grades 3 and up, the students should be given material to make a class quilt using the quilting frame.

Handmade quilts with different designs (i.e., wedding ring, flying geese).

Primary–Intermediate Level Elementary:

Bial, R. 1996. *Needle and Thread: A Book About Quilts.* Boston: Houghton Mifflin.

Ernst, L. C. 1983. *Sam Johnson and the Blue Ribbon Quilt.* New York: Mulberry Books.

Hopkinson, D. 1993. *Sweet Clara and the Freedom Quilt.* New York: Knopf.

Vaughan, M. 2001. *The Secret Freedom.* New York: Lee & Low.

Upper Level Elementary and Middle School:

Atkins, J. 1999. *A Name on the Quilt: A Story of Remembrance* (Illus. T. Hills) New York: Atheneum.

Benberry, C. 1992. *Always There: The African American Presence in American Quilts.* Louisville: The Kentucky Quilt Project.

Coerr, E. 1986. *The Josefina Quilt Story.* New York: HarperCollins.

Fry, G. M., J. L. Tobin, and R. G. Dobard. 1999. *Hidden in Plain View: A Secret Stag of Quilts and the Underground Railroad.* New York: Doubleday.

Lyons, M. E. 1993. *Stitching Stars: The Story Quilts of Harriet Powers.* New York: Scribner's.

Pulford, F. 1989. *Morning Star Quilts.* Los Altos, CA: Leone.

Ruskin, C. 1988. *The Quilt: Stories from the NAMES Project.* New York: Pocket Books.

Process: This project is done with primary students after the teacher shares a read-aloud with the class. After sharing the book, *Sam Johnson and the Blue Ribbon Quilt,* talk about why quilts were important to people on the prairie.

• Review or highlight the main points of the historical or societal event being explored.

• Provide students with the materials needed to make a quilt square. Instruct students on how to make a design as part of a math lesson using geometry and measurement.

• Softly play appropriate folksongs in the background (i.e., "Old Dan Tucker," "Wait for the Wagon," "Red River Valley," "Get Along Home Cindy").

• Have students use the materials provided to each create a quilt square.

• Each day, share a different book on quilting. Point out how many cultures made quilts (Native Americans, Mexicans, African Americans, Amish).

• Use the children's literature to share how quilts have many purposes: artistic, map (Underground Railroad), remembrance (AIDS quilt), and practical (bedding for warmth). Have students discuss how these purposes are similar and how they differ.

• After students have finished the quilt, ask them to write a letter, poem, or other type of creative communication to an individual with the historical time frame being explored through the text. This could be a character from history or historical fiction book they are presently reading.

Instructional Comments: This is a powerful activity that requires modeling of making a quilt square by the teacher. Since quilting is popular, invite a quilter to share her work and talk about the different designs of quilts. Time should be allocated for questioning.

Learning Styles Addressed: Verbal/linguistic, music/rhythm, visual/spatial, interpersonal, intrapersonal, mathematical/logical.

Standards Addressed: Students will use a variety of means to express their connections, thoughts, and reactions to literature and historical events.

Evaluation: The quilt block and writing should address the following questions:
• Does it create a feeling?
• Does the piece have a theme?
• Does it relate to the topic shared?
For writing,
• Did the student's word choice add to the piece?
• Was it organized?
If poetry, did it follow the proper format (i.e., cinquain, diamente)?

Modifications for Diverse Learners: Have an aide or another student assist the student with the sewing. Physically challenged students will need to have the materials set up for them.

Extensions: Numerous activities can evolve from this one.
• Have students read one of the picture books about quilts as maps to escape slavery and keep a journal of their thoughts as the characters flee along the Underground Railroad.
• Have students interview neighbors and relatives who make quilts.
• Take students to a local historical museum to see quilts.
• Have students engage in a quilting bee.
• Have the students complete a WebQuest, either one you create or one already developed.

Variations: Other possibilities would be to use the same activity with appropriate children's literature for such topics as the Great Depression, AIDS, and so forth.

Web Sites:
   A "Star" is Born
   http://www.starquilts.com/starborn.htm
   The morning star is significant in the Native American culture and is often symbolized in quilts. In the Lakota tribe, the morning star represents the direction from which the spirits of the dead travel to earth, provides a link between the living and the dead, and is a symbol for immortality. The morning star also represents a new beginning and a new dawning. The star pattern had been painted, quilled, or beaded onto animal skins used for clothing, shields, or teepees. Examples of morning star quilts are shared on this Web site.

   African American Historical Quilts
   http://www.quiltethnic.com/historical.html
   Slaves made inexpensive quilts for their families and more expensive, elaborate quilts for their owners. Examples of pieced, appliquéed, embroidered, whole cloth, broderie perse, and reverse appliqué historic quilts made by African Americans are on this Web site.

Chapter Summary

Students and teachers are held accountable for the student performance in social studies as well as in reading and expository writing. Awareness of the active nature of the learner in constructing the meaning of the text suggests direction in addressing this issue. Combining selections from children's literature with the social studies textbook and applying learning strategies may be the most efficient way to help students understand and relate concepts. Students can use strategic sequencing and graphic organizers to acquire the necessary awareness of text structure. Developing descriptive maps while reading the text helps students compare and contrast the information as well as link the concepts they are learning. This procedure of generating writing from graphic representations enhances students' expository writing by centering their attention on the focus and organization, which are primary traits on most writing assessment measures. Finally, as students use their learning logs in this procedure, they develop metacognitive awareness necessary to take control of their own learning. By using this learning method, students can facilitate their reading comprehension and improve the focus and organization of their writing.

Children's Literature Recommendation

Fritz, J. 1986. *Make Way for Sam Houston.* New York: G. P. Putnam's Sons. Part Cherokee, Sam Houston led an astounding life. Schoolteacher, Texan, military leader, slave owner, alcoholic, and governor of Texas, Houston's life is full of twists and turns. In the Battle of San Jacinto, Houston led his army to defeat General Santa Ana's army and ensured the independence of Texas. (Gr. 3–4)

Nelson, P. 2002. *Left for Dead: A young man's search for justice.* New York: Delacorte. The true story of Hunter Scott and how his school history project cleared the name of Captain McVay of the USS *Indianapolis,* a ship sunk during World War II. (Gr. 6–8)

Richter, C. 1995. *The Light in the Forest.* New York: Turtleback. When a white boy's parents are killed in a battle with Native Americans, he is taken back and raised by the tribe as a True Son. Attitudes toward Native Americans during the colonial period are presented. (Gr. 5–8)

Tsuchiva, Y. 1988. *Faithful Elephants.* Boston: Houghton Mifflin. As Japan braces for bombing by the Allies at the end of WWII, the Tokyo zookeepers give the word to the caretakers to euthanize the dangerous animals so no harm will come to people in the city. (Gr. 3–8)

Related Technology Tools

Web Sites
FirstGov for Kids
www.kids.gov
This is a U.S. government interagency site for children, developed and maintained by the Federal Citizen Information Center. It has links to best kids' sites from other organizations, all grouped by subject.

WebQuests
All Roads Lead to Rome (Gr. 5–8)
http://www.techtrekers.com/webquests/#Social%20Studies
Constructivist Unit on How the World Would Have Changed if Outcome of Wars Had Been Different (e.g., WWII won by Axis; Islam had conquered Europe during Middle Ages)
http://webquest.sdsu.edu/designpatterns/AH/webquest/htm

Technology Resources
Graphic Organizers
http://teachervision.com/lesson-plans/lesson
This collection of ready-to-use graphic organizers will help teachers and students to communicate more effectively. Includes graphic organizers for describing, comparing, contrasting, classifying, sequencing, causal, and decision making.

Software and Videos

Teacher's Puzzle Creator 5.0. Ablesoft. Available from www.amazon.com. Teachers can build crosswords and word searches for reinforcing vocabulary and spelling lessons, create quizzes and homework assignments for any subject, and design extra-credit worksheets.

Problem-Based Learning with Multimedia CD-ROM. 2001. Available from the Association for Supervision and Curriculum Development (ASCD) at www.ascd.org.

The Brain, the Mind, and the Classroom on Compact Disc. 1997. Available from the Association for Supervision and Curriculum Development (ASCD) at www.ascd.org.

Jeopardy. Available from www.schoolaids.com/technology.htm
Students and teachers can create their own versions of the TV shows *Jeopardy* and *Who Wants to Be a Millionaire* using social studies facts.

Kidspiration and Inspiration. Kidspiration is for grades K–5; Inspiration spans grades 1–12. Available from Inspiration Software, Inc., 7412 SW Beaverton Hillsdale Hwy, Suite 103 Portland, OR 97225-2167 Teachers and students can create graphic organizers.

References

Anderson, R. C., E. H. Hiebert, J. A. Scott, and I. A. G. Wilkinson. 1984. *Becoming a Nation of Readers: The Report of the Commission on Reading.* Washington, DC: National Institute of Education.

Armbruster, B. B. 1985. "Using Graphic Organizers in Social Studies." *Ginn Occasional Papers* 22.

Armbruster, B. B., T. H. Anderson, and J. J. Ostertag. 1989. "Teaching Text Structure to Improve Reading and Writing." *The Reading Teacher* 43: 130–37.

Bailey, J. 2006, July. "Trying to Remember." *Good Housekeeping:* 68, 70, 72.

Beach, R. 1995. "Constructing Cultural Models through Response to Literature." *English Journal* 84 (6): 87–94.

Beers, K. 2003. *When Kids Can't Read: What Teachers Can Do.* Portsmouth, NH: Heinemann.

Behrman, E. H. 2006. "Teaching about Language, Power, and Text: A Review of Classroom Practices that Support Critical Literacy." *Journal of Adolescent and Adult Literacy* 49 (6) 490–98.

Caine, G., R. N. Caine, and C. McClintic. 2002. "Guiding the Innate Constructivist." *Educational Leadership* 60 (1): 70–73.

Davidson, J. L. 1982. "The Group Mapping Activity for Instruction in Reading and Thinking." *Journal of Reading* 26 (1): 52–56.

Diffily, D. 2002. "Classroom Inquiry: Student-Centered Experiences." *Social Studies and the Young Learner* 15 (2): 17–19.

Dreher, M. J. 2003. "Motivating Struggling Readers by Tapping the Potential of Information Books." *Reading and Writing Quarterly,* 19: 25–38.

Duis, M. S., and S. S. Duis. 1998. "Teaching History as Perspective Taking: The Colonial Convention." *Middle Level Learning* (September 1998, no. 3): M9–M11.

Foss, A. 2002. "Peeling the Onion: Teaching Critical Literacy with Students of Privilege." *Language Arts* 79: 393–403.

Fulwiler, T. 1978. *Journal Writing Across the Curriculum* (Report No. CS 204 467). Denver, CO: Conference on College Composition and Communication. (ERIC Document Reproduction Services No. ED 161 073)

Gaskin, I., E. Satlow, D. Hyson, J. Ostertag, and L. Stix. 1994. "Classroom Talk about Text: Learning in Science Class." *Journal of Reading* 37 (7): 558–65.

George, M. 2006, June 22. "Book Club: A Framework for Organizing Literacy Instruction." A paper presented at the Northern Illinois Reading Council/Northern Illinois University Summer Reading Conference, Sugar Grove, IL.

Gillespie, C. 1993. "Reading Graphic Displays: What Teachers Should Know." *Journal of Reading* 36 (5): 350–54.

Hadaway, N., and T. Young. 1994. "Content Literacy and Language Learning: Instructional Decisions." *The Reading Teacher* 47 (6): 522–27.

Harvey, S., and A. Goudvis. 2000. *Strategies that Work: Teaching Comprehension to Enhance Understanding*. Portland, ME: Stenhouse.

Hunter, M. 1982. *Mastering Teaching*. El Segundo, CA: TIP.

Jones, B. F., A. S. Palincsar, D. S. Ogle, and E. G. Carr. 1987. *Strategic Teaching and Learning: Cognitive Instruction in the Content Areas*. Alexandria, VA: Association for Supervision and Curriculum Development.

Langer, J., and A. Applebee. 1987. *How Writing Shapes Thinking*. Urbana, IL: National Council of Teachers of English.

Lewin, L. 1999. "'Site Reading' the World Wide Web." *Educational Leadership* 56 (5): 16–20.

Lewis, M., D. Wray, and P. Rospigliosi. 1994. "And I Want It in Your Own Words." *The Reading Teacher* 47 (6): 528–36.

Linder, R. 2006, June 19. "Yours, Mine, and Theirs: Examining Multiple Perspectives with Young Adult Literature." Northern Illinois Reading Council's 27th Annual Summer Reading Conference, Sugar Grove, IL.

McCall, A. L. 2002. "That's Not Fair! Fourth Graders' Responses to Multicultural State History." *Social Studies* 93: 85–91.

Meehan, J. 2006. "Generating Excitement for Reading in the Middle Grades: Start with Non-Fiction Read Alouds!" *Illinois Reading Council Journal* 34 (4): 13–16.

Murphy, J. 1995. *The Great Fire*. New York: Scholastic.

Ogle, D. M. 1986. "K-W-L: A Teaching Model that Develops Active Reading of Expository Text." *The Reading Teacher* 39 (6): 564–70.

———. 1989. "The Know, Want to Know, Learn Strategy." In *Children's Comprehension of Text: Research into Practice*, ed. K. D. Muth, pp. 205–23. Newark, DE: International Reading Association.

Pressley, M. 2000. "What Should Reading Comprehension Instruction Be the Instruction Of?" In *Handbook of Reading Research (Volume III)*, ed. M. L. Kamill, P. B. Mosenthal, P. D. Pearson, and R. Barr, pp. 545–62. Mahwah, NJ: Erlbaum.

Raphael, T. E., and S. I. McMahon. 1994. "'Book Club': An Alternative Framework for Reading Instruction." *The Reading Teacher* 48 (2): 102–16.

Resnick, L. B., and L. E. Klopfer. 1989. "Toward Rethinking the Curriculum." In *Toward Rethinking the Curriculum*, ed. L. B. Resnick and L. E. Klopfer, pp. 29–34. Arlington, VA: Association for Supervision and Curriculum Development.

Richardson, J. S., and R. F. Morgan. 2000. *Reading to Learn in the Content Areas*. 4th ed. Belmont, CA: Wadsworth.

Rolón, C. A. 2002/2003. "Educating Latino Students." *Educational Leadership* 60 (4): 40–43.

Roser, N. L., and S. Keehn. 2002. "Fostering Thought, Talk, and Inquiry: Linking Literature and Social Studies." *The Reading Teacher* 55 (5): 416–26.

Ukpokodu, N. 2002. "Breaking through Preservice Teachers' Defensive Dispositions in a Multicultural Education Course." *Multicultural Education* 9 (3): 25–33.

Wolfe, P. 1999. "Revisiting Effective Teaching." *Educational Leadership* 56 (3): 61–64.

> We write and read in order to know each other's responses, to connect ourselves more fully with the human world, and to strengthen the habit of truth-telling in our midst.
> —Benjamin DeMott, "Why We Read and Write"

Chapter Seven

Communicating in Social Studies
Reading, Writing, and Discussing

Pamela J. Farris, Northern Illinois University

CHAPTER OUTLINE

Introduction

Family Involvement

Reading

Writing

Writing and Social Studies

Wonder Books

Multigenre Writing for Research

Structuring the Writing Research Project

Internet Searches

Aesthetic and Efferent Reading and Writing

Historical Documents: Diaries, Journals, Letters, and Newspapers

Using Technology to Keep Abreast of Current Events

Discussion

Writing, Reading, and Discussing as Learning Strategies

Field Trips

Chapter Summary

CHAPTER OBJECTIVES

Readers will

• understand ways to incorporate language arts and social studies;

• understand the steps of the writing process; and

• be able to generate language arts activities based on social studies and language arts learning goals.

Introduction

Social studies offers many opportunities for reading, writing, and discussing—skills that good citizens need to develop to their fullest. It is essential that the citizenry in a democratic society be well-educated, with each citizen able to gain information through reading and to communicate effectively through speaking and writing. As former U.S. Commissioner of Education Ernest L. Boyer (1990, 5) writes:

> While economic purposes are being vigorously pursued, civic priorities also must be affirmed. Indeed, unless we find better ways to educate ourselves as *cit-*

izens, Americans run the risk of drifting unwittingly into a new kind of dark age, a time when specialists control the decision-making process and citizens will be forced to make critical decisions not on the basis of what they know but on the basis of blind belief in so-called "experts."

The interdisciplinary philosophical tenet is based on sharing relevant material from the content area(s) with children. Decision making is promoted as children make choices about how and what they will learn. Children are also encouraged to interact with each other as they learn.

Reading, writing, and discussing allow children the individual freedom to learn as well as maintain a social responsibility to the class to share what has been learned. As Banks (1991/1992, 32) states:

> To create and maintain a civic community that works for the common good, education in a democratic society should help students acquire the knowledge, attitudes, and skills they will need to participate in civil action to make society more equal and just.

Students are encouraged to challenge and question both themselves and others; therefore, such a classroom is a democratic community.

A democracy is established on the belief that each citizen has worth and can offer something of value to the group. This necessitates that *trust* be gained and maintained if a democracy is to survive. In the classroom, the teacher must first establish the basic principles of democracy. In the areas of reading, writing, and discussing, this means that every child's ideas must be respected.

Support and encouragement must also pave the way if trust is to evolve in the classroom. This is not purely a unidirectional matter of teacher to student but also of student to teacher, for the teacher must be willing to submit ideas that the class may openly criticize. For example, when the teacher shares a piece of his or her own writing with a class for the first time, both the teacher and the students are somewhat anxious and uncomfortable. The teacher wants the students to like what he or she has written because writing is very personal. The students feel that the situation is precarious because they are unsure of whether they should make only positive comments. That is, will the teacher consider negative comments to be ill-suited for the occasion? By opening up through sharing his or her own writing with the class, the teacher is demonstrating democratic principles: We all have different talents, we all have feelings, we all have beliefs, and we all can profit by sharing our thoughts and ideals.

According to Kohn (1996, 499), "If we had to pick a logical setting in which to guide children toward caring about, empathizing with, and helping other people, it would be a place where they would regularly come into contact with their peers and where some sort of learning is already taking place." Laura Schiller (1996), a sixth-grade teacher at Birney Middle School in Southfield, Michigan, teaches a year-long thematic unit titled "Coming to America: Community from Diversity" to her students. Schiller finds that by having her students investigate their families' heritage and immigration to the United States, many social studies concepts are learned and a sense of community evolves in her classroom.

The San Ramon Valley Unified School District in San Ramon, California, fosters democratic principles by rooting its elementary curriculum in the development of social values (Schaps and Solomon 1990). This school system relies on children's literature and cooperative learning to encourage a caring climate where learning takes place. Quality literature that depicts how values "work" is the basis for reading instruction. For instance, books with themes of fairness and kindness help students develop empathy for others; books about other cultures and circumstances represent universal issues and concerns. Cooperative learning emphasizes collaboration, extensive interaction, division of labor, use of reason and explanation, and consideration of values related to the activity in which the group is engaged. Cooperative learning activities in the social studies often rely on a cycle of discussing, reading, and writing.

Family Involvement

The extent to which a student communicates in and relishes social studies depends in part on the family, which plays a central role in children's attitudes towards school and their attitudes toward learning (Henderson and Berla 1994). Parents and guardians establish the foundation by talking to their child about social issues and demonstrate, themselves, the importance of participating in democracy by voting at each election. Interactive homework assignments in which families share a slice of their own lives through family history help reach out to parents while supporting students. Such an approach creates a positive, interactive environment for parents, students, and teachers. Parents whose language is not English may be invited to share their thoughts in their native language. Homework assignments might include giving helpful advice to each other about life, creating "I Am ____" poems, or providing responses to the Nobel Prize for Peace acceptance speech by the Dalai Lama as part of a multicultural unit. A culminating event might be a social gathering at the end of each grading period (Barillas 2001).

Creating home-school journals is a great way to communicate with primary grade parents on a weekly basis. These may be inexpensive folders containing lined paper in which the teacher jots a couple of sentences down along with a couple of plastic paper covers in which the teacher can insert a weekly one-page classroom newspaper. Such journals provide a vehicle for sharing social studies and activities from other subjects as well as a written note system between the teacher and parents. All in all it is important to reach out to students and parents.

Reading

Research studies in reading indicate that when children can relate their daily life experiences as well as prior knowledge to the content of a textbook, they are better able to understand and assimilate new concepts and knowledge (Alvermann, Smith, and Readance 1985). Thus, the engaging narrative style of a children's book may result in a student's discovery and retention of social studies concepts (McGowan and Guzzetti 1991).

Reading enables children to gather information directly and to gain knowledge through vicarious experiences. By reading a social studies textbook or nonfiction book, students can acquire background information about a specific social studies concept or topic. Consider Joseph Slate's (2002) *The Great Big Wagon that Rang: How the Liberty Bell Was Saved*, which relates how a wagonload of hay hid the Liberty Bell from the Redcoats. By reading quality fiction, children can develop empathy for others as well as a better understanding of their own feelings and values. There are numerous award-winning books in this area that are shared in this text.

Children's Literature

Reading quality children's literature enhances a child's understanding of social studies. According to McGowan and Guzzetti (1991, 18):

> Literary works are packed with conceptual knowledge about the human condition and can supply meaningful content for skill-building experiences. . . . Perhaps more completely and certainly more intensely than with textbooks, a creative teacher can use trade books to engage students in the pursuit of such citizenship competencies as processing information, examining other points of view, separating fact from opinion, and solving problems.

The teacher must take care to provide good books. Numerous children's and young-adult authors have written books that create vivid and accurate historical settings. For instance, Joan Lowery Nixon's (1992, 1993, 1994) Ellis Island series depicts the lives of three immigrant girls in the early 1900s—Rebeka, a Russian Jew; Kristyn, an independent Swedish girl; and Rose, whose family was escaping famine in Ireland. A great number of quality children's and young adult books are available that are appropriate for teaching social studies. Each year the NCSS names "Notable Social Studies Trade Books for Young People." The titles are shared at the NCSS Web site (www.ncss.org). This annotated bibliographical list is printed in NCSS's *Social Education* along with subject categories such as biography, contemporary issues, environment, folktales, geography, history and culture, reference, social interactions, and world history and culture. In addition, each book is identified by the social studies themes depicted.

The increased use of children's literature in social studies instruction has provided more relevant textual material for students than the sole use of social studies textbooks. By incorporating both, the classroom teacher can capitalize on the best of both types of reading material.

Fiction

The rich proliferation of quality children's literature with a social studies base permits the classroom teacher to enrich and expand a topic by having children read beyond the social studies textbook. For instance, Patricia MacLachlan's *Sarah, Plain and Tall* (1985) outlines a widower's search for a mail order bride to "make a difference" for his young son and daughter. Because of its rich descriptions of the Maine coastline and the Nebraska prairie, the book provides an excellent opportunity for comparing and contrasting the two geographic settings and discussing the differences in the plant and animal life native to each of the two regions as a third or fourth grade social studies and science link.

Economics is the focus of *Lyddie,* a book by Katherine Paterson (1991), set in 1840. Lyddie is a young farm girl who ventures to Lowell, Massachusetts, in search of a better life. She finds work in the mills and discovers the anguish and frustrations of the dangerous mill work. The long hours, low pay, and inadequate living and working conditions are suitably portrayed by Paterson, providing today's upper elementary and middle school students with insights as to the sacrifices made by workers and, in this case, children during the Industrial Revolution.

Other books encourage students to reflect on their own lives. Cynthia Rylant's (1982) *When I Was Young in the Mountains* is a picture book that introduces children to the simple pleasures Rylant engaged in while growing up in the Appalachian Mountains. Rylant depicts the social and psychological aspects of life there. Ed Lane, a fifth-grade teacher, wrote his reflections about his experiences as a child in the fifth grade and shared them with his class. Next, Ed had his fifth graders write their own reflections of being in second grade. Since most of the students attended the same elementary school as second graders, they wrote not only about their own remembrances but also about the culture and history of the school itself. After writing about and editing their memories of second grade, the class went to the second-grade classroom, where each fifth-grade student was paired up with a second grader to share their experiences.

Concepts can be introduced by sharing a children's book with students. The picture book *How Many Days to America?* by Eve Bunting (1988) describes how a Caribbean family flees to the United States and freedom in a fishing boat. Through a dramatic and touching story, students learn the importance of freedom and the value people from other countries place on it. In *Mark Twain and the Queens of the Mississippi* (Harness 1998), students see the Mississippi River and its steamboats in the 1800s through Twain's own words.

Cultural and sociological differences can also be presented through children's literature. Folktales often provide insight into a different culture. A Russian folktale, *The Enormous Carrot* (Vagin 1998), tells how animals join together to pull a large carrot out of the ground; kindergartners and first graders will delight in this story while learning about the concept of being a community. Upper elementary and middle school students can also enjoy folktales. *The Crane Wife* (Bodkin 1998) is a retelling of a Japanese folktale of a poor fisherman who gains a beautiful and talented wife in a very moving, touching story. Folklore is the basis of David Wisniewski's (1991) *Rain Player,* a richly illustrated picture book based on Mayan folklore that has extensive information about Mayan history and culture in the author's note. An example of a collection of folktales appropriate for social studies instruction is Laurence Yep's (1991) *Tongues of Jade,* which contains seventeen Chinese folktales.

Historical fiction that accurately depicts cultural and sociological commonalities and differences are quite useful. In *Choosing Up Sides* (Ritter 1998), Luke, a left-handed preacher's boy in the 1920s, finds he lives in a right-handed world. His family considers left-handedness to be a sign of Satan and contrary to God. Luke is a talented pitcher who struggles not to disgrace his family. In keeping with the baseball theme, other books might include *Teammates* (Golenbock 1990), the story of Jackie Robinson's becoming the first African American major league baseball player, accompanied by the nonfiction picture book *A Negro League Scrapbook* (Weatherford 2005). Yet another poignant story on the ball field is *Baseball Saved Us* (Mochizuki 1993), which depicts baseball in a camp for displaced Japanese during WWII.

Nonfiction and Informational Books

Informational books must be a part of social studies instruction so that children can become familiar with "what really happened." Unfortunately, many school libraries have informational books that are either outdated or present a view from only one perspective. Newly published informational books relating to social studies tend to present a variety of perspectives. For instance, *Pueblo Storyteller* by Diane Hoyt-Goldsmith (1991) depicts the contemporary life of a Cochiti (Pueblo) Indian girl, while David Weitzman's (1982) *Windmills, Bridges, and Old Machines: Discovering Our Industrial Past* relates how specific machines were developed and how they work. Novelist Walter Dean Myers (1991) turned his pen to nonfiction in the book *Now Is Your Time! The African American Struggle for Freedom,* which traces the civil rights movement in America by following African American slaves, soldiers, political leaders, inventors, and artists. Jerry Stanley's (1992) *Children of the Dust Bowl* is a true story of families who were lured to California by a desire for a better life during the Great Depression.

Book Links is a professional journal that provides articles in each issue on ways to integrate literature in the curriculum. "Women and the Way West" by Loftis (1996) gives several suggested titles of children's books, including picture books and

During March as students engage in Women's History Month, having students do reports on women in the community or in their own family, who have made an impact on others' lives, can lead to increased knowledge and respect for females in general.

historical novels, that portray the harsh life of pioneer women. Another article by Scales (1995) outlines ways of studying the First Amendment in middle schools using literature as the primary vehicle. "Shining the Light, Meeting the Standards: Books about Lighthouses" (Buzzeo 2003) provides nonfiction and fiction titles about lighthouses based on the NCSS thematic strands. Described as "beacons along the coastlines," Buzzeo portrays different ways of incorporating a lighthouse theme in social studies instruction.

By acquainting children with literature that contains social studies themes and content, the teacher may find that student motivation is increased. In addition, for these students who find the textbook either too difficult or not very exciting, children's literature may unlock doors to historical events, light a path for geography, or explain in simple terms an economic or sociological concept.

Guiding students in their reading to locate appropriate information is an important role for teachers. As mentioned earlier, we need to share well-written nonfiction books that serve as models for writing, not merely the dry factual information presented in encyclopedias. Nancy Leifheit, a fifth-grade teacher, integrates a three-week unit on electricity and inventors as she combines science and social studies along with language arts and math. Nancy opens the unit with a read-aloud of *Airborne: A Photobiography of Wilbur and Orville Wright* (Collins 2003) to pique the interest of her students. Later her students are encouraged to read a biography about an inventor. The students are also required to write a research report about an invention as part of the three-week unit. Keep in mind that for this three-week period, the sole focus is this unit of study. Even math problems and spelling assignments come from the unit itself. Nancy is well-organized and prepared and she keeps her students informed. The unit's goals are posted and gone over with the entire class. Activities are modeled and rubrics for each of the activities are shared at the appropriate time.

A couple of weeks prior to starting the unit on electricity, Nancy heads to the library to garner these and other biographies that both interest her students and are within their range of reading abilities, roughly grades two through eight. While Benjamin Franklin, Robert Fulton, Marie Curie, Thomas Edison, and Henry Ford are familiar names to Nancy's students, her students are stretched to find other inventors who may not be so famous, including female inventors. After all, as Nancy says, necessity is said to be the "mother of invention." Although most of the boys stick to doing research on male inventors, many girls seek female inventors who become, at least for the moment, heroines and role models.

Doing research on inventors in the library and on the Internet can uncover some interesting findings, especially about female inventors. Throughout history, women have been innovative with ideas that have improved conditions for humankind. In 1715, Sybilla Masters came up with the first invention by an American woman. Upon observing Native American women using heavy pestles to grind corn by hand, Masters used a power-driven source by having the corn ground between two millstones powered by a waterfall. Even tools, thought to be part of the man's world, have been invented by women. Tabitha Mather, a Shaker woman, observed that hand saws were very inefficient in terms of the amount of labor and time needed to produce a single board. The two-man saws had a handle on both ends attached to a thin metal blade and were used to cut logs. The saw's design required one man to stand on top of the log while the other worked below the floor in the sawmill, fending off sawdust as he pushed the saw back up to the man up above. Both men had to work extremely hard to produce each board. Noting that her spinning wheel was an efficient device that constantly moved in a very able way, Tabitha designed a circular saw blade that could be "powered either" by a single man turning a wheel by hand or with water. The result radically transformed lumbering and carpentry. Later powered by gas engines or electric motors, the circular saw became one of the most popular power tools ever invented and the circular cutting blade design is still the most efficient sawing device.

Other women have made a major impact on how we live. One problem that top-notch engineers had failed to solve was poor visibility in streetcars during rain and snowstorms. Mary Anderson devised a lever on the inside of the streetcar that moved an arm outside that swept snow and rain off the glass—the invention of the windshield wiper—one of the greatest safety devices ever invented. Unfortunately, companies were not interested in her idea and her patent expired without her gaining any financial reward. In *Girls Think of Everything: Stories of Ingenious Inventions by Women,* Catherine Thimmesh (2000) presents an excellent overview of inventions by women suitable for sharing with upper elementary students. This book is a good prewriting read-aloud as well as a source to share with students. Included in the book is a chronological listing of inventions by women, including those discovered in 3000 BC. Here are some examples: Hsi-ling-shi's creation of a method to gather and weave silk, the 1793 improvement by Mrs. Samual Slater of cotton sewing thread, to the 1930 chocolate chip cookie created by Ruth Wakefield. A second book by Thimmesh (2002), *The Sky's the Limit: Stories of Discovery by Women and Girls,* describes the more recent inventions women have made that middle schoolers will enjoy. Reading aloud to the class a section on a single inventor is enough to entice students. Two other books about inventions are *So You Want to Be an Inventor?* (St. George 2002), which offers a clever introduction to 40 inventors, and *1,000 Inventions and Discoveries* (Bridgeman 2002), which begins three million years ago and ends with the self-cleaning oven. These true tales of adventure and discovery are certain to captivate both girls and boys who are interested in science and technology. Having students follow news reports of new discoveries in medicine, archaeology, and so forth and sharing the reports as part of current events each week encourages them to be curious and seek out solutions to problems they encounter.

Students are interested in money-making inventions, so economics is easily incorporated into such a unit of study. The first American woman who was a self-made millionaire was Madam C. J. Walker, the daughter of slaves. She invented and sold hair products for African American women. Starting out with a single product she had concocted, $1.50, and self-assurance, she went door-to-door giving free demonstrations.

Two Web sites that serve as good resources for elementary and middle school students in a study of the contributions of women are Distinguished Women of the Past and Present (www.distinguishedwomen.com) and the Gallery of Achievers (www.achievement.org/gallery.achieve.html), which also includes famous men who have had made a major impact on society during the twentieth century.

Providing ample quantities of nonfiction, informational books is important and may require a trip to the school library as well as the local public library to gather sufficient titles. Each year the school librarian will likely put out a request for new titles to purchase so keeping a list of titles, authors, and ISBN numbers of books on topics related to the social studies curriculum is important. Passing along such information each semester can lead to well-stocked library shelves. Stephanie Harvey (2002) suggests selecting nonfiction books based on three categories:

- Content—relate to the curriculum or topic of study;

- Text features—headings, subheadings, charts, graphs, and maps that support students as they seek out information as they read; and

- Writing quality—books selected should be written in a compelling, visual way that engages students and provides them with strong models for writing.

Reading nonfiction informational books is a major component of a prewriting activity. "Nonfiction breeds passionate curiosity; passion leads to engagement" (Harvey 2002, 15). It is such passion that creates learners who are curious about social studies and want to know more. Unlike novels and biographies, informational books do not require being read cover to cover. Scanning for the information being sought is perfectly okay. The structure of nonfiction books requires that we help our students become familiar with how best to utilize the features available. The best way to share such information is by modeling how we, ourselves, use each feature to locate information. By sharing a feature with our students every two or three days at the beginning of the school year and then reinforcing it the following day and in successive weeks, students likewise find the features to be of practical use for their reading needs. Below is a list of such features along with their purpose.

Feature	Purpose
Bold print	Makes the reader stop and pay attention as new information or vocabulary is being introduced
Caption	Brief description of the photograph or illustration
Table of contents	Division of the book into sections or chapters
Index	Tells location of specific topics
Heading	Tells what the text that follows is about
Subheading	Breaks the text into smaller parts
Distribution map	Shows where something occurs

In addition to the above features, nonfiction books have maps, graphs, and charts. Students need to be taught how to read each of these distinctive text features. Fortunately, these text features can often be taught using overhead transparencies or through PowerPoint presentations.

While fiction needs to be read cover to cover, nonfiction can be short in length. The caption under a picture holds much information. A letter may only be a page in length. A newspaper article may be equivalent to two or three typed pages. We glean significant amounts of information through reading short texts. Short nonfiction text is (Harvey and Goudvis 2000):

- *well-crafted* with vivid language and striking illustrations and photographs;

- *self-contained* and provides a complete set of thoughts, ideas, and information;

- *focused on issues* of critical importance to readers of varying ages;
- *easily read aloud*, giving a common experience to everyone in the room;
- *accessible* to all kinds of readers—the length is less likely to intimidate;
- *a realistic model* for writing; and
- *authentic* and prepares kids for real-world reading.

Such text makes for good "filler read-alouds." It is the stuff of current events but also the dropping in of information that can add to a unit of study. A report about the recovery of a Confederate submarine sunken in the depths of the Atlantic for over 100 years, its crew still at their assigned duty, can add to a unit on the Civil War. The sharing of an opening of a display of Fabergé eggs when engaged in a unit on Russia or the deep cultural traditions associated by the Japanese with samurai swords of old when studying Asian cultures will also be of great interest to the students.

Short text includes newspaper articles, letters, book reviews, and magazine articles. Fourth through sixth graders may prefer reading a short article in *Cobblestone* or *Calliope* instead of trying to ferret out information from a full-length informational book. Likewise, middle schoolers may find an article in the *National Geographic* much more palatable than encountering a full-length nonfiction book on the same topic. Struggling readers find such short text materials to be both reader friendly and face saving as all students can utilize these same sources as the need arises.

Below is a list of informational magazines for students in grades K–8:

Appleseed (www.cricketmag.com) is a social studies magazine for young children (Gr. K–2)

Click (www.cricketmag.com) has a different theme each issue (Gr. K–2)

Dig (www.digonsite.com) is a publication of the Archaeological Institute of America that has themed issues (Gr. 4–8)

Muse (www.cricketmag.com) is a nonfiction magazine that includes articles, interviews, and photo essays (Gr. 3–7)

KIDS Discover (www.discover.com) is a themed magazine on high interest topics (Gr. 2–6)

Cobblestone (www.cricketmag.com) focuses on American history and includes articles, primary documents, colorful visuals, maps, time lines, and activities (Gr. 4–8)

Calliope (www.cricketmag.com) is a themed magazine based on world history (Gr. 5–9)

Faces (www.cricketmag.com) is a themed magazine based on world cultures and geography (Gr. 6–8)

National Geographic Explorer (www.nationalgeographic.com) covers history, natural history, geography, and world cultures as well as science (Gr. 6–8)

National Geographic World (www.nationalgeographic.com) includes articles on world geography, science, and natural history (Gr. 3–5)

National Geographic Young Explorer (www.nationalgeographic.com) themed issues of 24 pages that combines science and social studies (Gr. K–1)

While most school libraries subscribe to some of the above magazines, it is worthwhile to try to have a subscription in your own classroom. Ask the PTA to give you a subscription or put on a list for parents to purchase a subscription as a holiday gift. Keep the issues as part of your own classroom library as they can readily be accessed in case of a breaking news story.

Writing

Children enjoy reading about what interests them most; the same is true for writing. Children write best when they write about what is most familiar and interesting to them (Graves 1983). Assigning children topics in which they have little interest makes it difficult for them to write about them because they not only lack motivation but may have no background in the topics. According to Gammill (2006):

> Writing is a tool for thinking. All knowledge is best absorbed and applied when students make it their own. Writing-to-learn allows students to make inferences, draw upon prior knowledge, and synthesize material, therefore taking their thought processes to an evaluative level (according to Bloom's Taxonomy). Educators are better able to access what students learn. . . . A student's ability to simply repeat the facts is not a true measure. . . . No other exercise in the classroom generates higher thinking skills than does writing. (760)

Writing also helps striving and struggling readers and writers. Writing helps students with learning disabilities as they discover they can do far more than write

A writing center, complete with dictionary, thesaurus, note pads, pencils, and computers with Internet connections and printers, is important for grades 3–8 if students are to develop informational reports in social studies.

and they come to terms with a image of themselves as thinkers (Marchisan and Alber 2001).

Different forms of writing, including informational (descriptive, explanatory, and persuasive), poetic, and narrative, should be used to meet different social studies goals. By using a variety of writing forms, students will maintain their interest in social studies and writing (Walley 1991). Writing gives students the opportunity to reflect on what they have just read or discussed (Abel, Hauwiller, and Vandeventer 1989).

Writing can also help students understand concepts and attain knowledge. For example, Langer and Applebee (1987) found that thinking is enhanced by writing. Kuhrt (1989) conducted a study with sixth graders regarding their acquisition of social studies concepts and found that writing in learning logs or journals about what they have read in a chapter in a social studies textbook enhanced the students' knowledge of concepts.

Writing Models

Our students need to see models of exquisite nonfiction writing in social studies. Rich, powerful writing must be shared on a frequent basis to demonstrate that informational writing does not have to be dull. Consider the following information about Abraham Lincoln:

> Abraham Lincoln (1809–65), the sixteenth president of the United States, was born in Hardin County (now Larue County), Kentucky. Born in a log cabin in the backwoods, Lincoln was almost entirely self-educated.

The above was copied word for word by a fourth grader from an encyclopedia. Now consider the dramatic, stirring lead from Russell Freedman's (1997) Newbery Award-winning *Lincoln: A Photobiography.*

> Abe Lincoln wasn't the sort of man who could lose himself in a crowd. After all, he stood six feet four inches tall, and to top it off, he wore a tall silk hat. His height was mostly in his long bony legs. When he sat in a chair, he seemed no taller than anyone else. It was only when he stood up that he towered above the other men.

The difference in prose is day and night. Such is the vibrancy of language and voice in well-written nonfiction. Clearly the reader comes away from Freedman's book with a vivid image of Lincoln. By placing the two samples of writing illustrated above on overhead transparencies and having the students comb through it, they will immediately begin to grasp the importance of wordsmithing in their own informational writing, carefully considering each and every word that they use to write an opening sentence or two that will pique the interest of readers.

Writing Traits

According to Ruth Culham (2003; 2005), writing can be broken down into seven traits: ideas (the message of the piece), organization, word choice, sentence fluency, voice, conventions (grammar, usage, and spelling), and presentation (handwriting and word processing). Using the paragraph from Freedman's (1997) *Lincoln: A Photobiography* we can point out a number of these traits to students:

Ideas	The author wants to give the reader the impression that Lincoln stood out in a crowd and was looked up to by people.
Organization	The paragraph has an opening topic sentence with each additional sentence adding more details.
Word Choice	The author is careful to use descriptive words: long *bony* legs, *towered* above the other men.
Sentence Fluency	The author varies the length of the sentences and their structure by including clauses.
Voice	The reader gets a sense that the author has researched the subject and is knowledgeable.
Conventions	Note that the author uses commas to set off clauses.

Each writing trait is used for every social studies writing genre: narrative, poetic, expository (informational), and persuasive.

Writing Process

The writing process consists of five stages typically referred to as prewriting, drafting, revising, editing, and publishing/sharing (Farris 2007; Graves 1983). Figure 7.1 presents a summary of these stages.

Stages of the Writing Process

Prewriting	The teacher needs to provide students with essential background experiences for writing. In addition, the assignment needs to be clearly delineated and explained. At this point the students may brainstorm to discover what they already know about the writing topic and what remains to be learned. Questions may be generated and lists made of possible sources of information. The information is then gathered and organized for the next stage.
Drafting	Drafting involves actually putting the pencil to paper. This stage focuses on content, not mechanics. In essence, it is getting the principal ideas down on paper.
Revising	In the revising stage, the writer rereads the draft and makes changes on the draft itself, such as writing in corrections for misspellings, crossing out words or phrases and writing in replacements, or making notations for moving paragraphs.
Editing	This stage is a polishing stage. Editing also occurs in the prewriting stage as the writer thinks about ideas, adopting some and discarding others. Likewise, editing takes place in the drafting stage as the writer makes decisions about word choice, sentence order, and so on. In the editing stage, the writer reads through the revised draft, correcting errors in both content and mechanics. The piece of writing is then recopied as a finished product.
Publishing/ Sharing	In this stage the finished product is shared with the class. This may be done by having each child read his or her final draft, by making a class book of all the students' pieces of writing, or by placing all of the final pieces on a bulletin board. The students should discuss each other's work so that they not only learn from each other but also appreciate each other.

Figure 7.1 Effective writing is a five-stage process.

Prewriting

In social studies, teachers may want to give the students a broad topic and allow them to write on a subtopic in which they are interested. In the **prewriting** stage, it is the teacher who establishes a purpose for the writing and gives students time to think about their individual topics. Each student brainstorms to gather her or his already collected ideas and thoughts about the topic. The student may brainstorm with another student to share information and to formulate questions for which they may both want to find answers.

Many teachers find *graphic organizing*, also called *semantic mapping*, to be a successful prewriting activity (Rico 1983). A concept, in the form of a word or phrase, serves as the nucleus. Words or phrases are then generated by the students and placed in a separate circle to be linked to the nucleus. Students then contribute related ideas and information that they already know about the concept or topic. These ideas are also written down, either on the chalkboard if it's a class discussion or in the student's notebook if it's an individual writing assignment. Figure 7.2

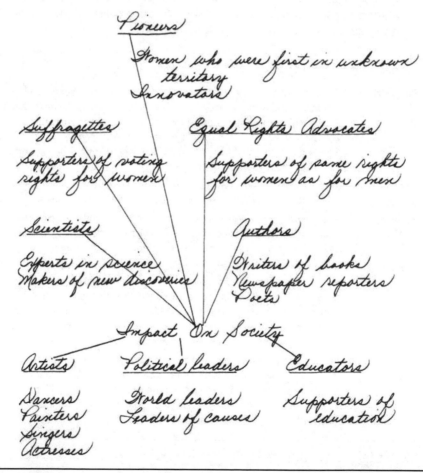

Figure 7.2 Identifications and definitions of clusters for Women's History Month.

shows an example of clustering done by a sixth-grade class in reference to National Women's History Month (March).

Graphic organizers can entail both brainstorming and discussion. For instance, the sixth-grade class brainstormed the primary theme of the cluster: women who have made an impact on society as part of Women's History Month. The result was the various subclusters. These were discussed and refined until the students agreed on those shown in figure 7.2. The class then identified specific women for each cluster and library time was devoted to the project. A variety of books were checked out, such as *With Courage and Cloth: Winning the Fight for a Woman's Right to Vote* (Bausum 2004), a book about the women's suffrage movement from 1906–1920. Both well-known and little-known names were included as part of the class's study: Agnes de Mille, an innovator in dance choreography, who

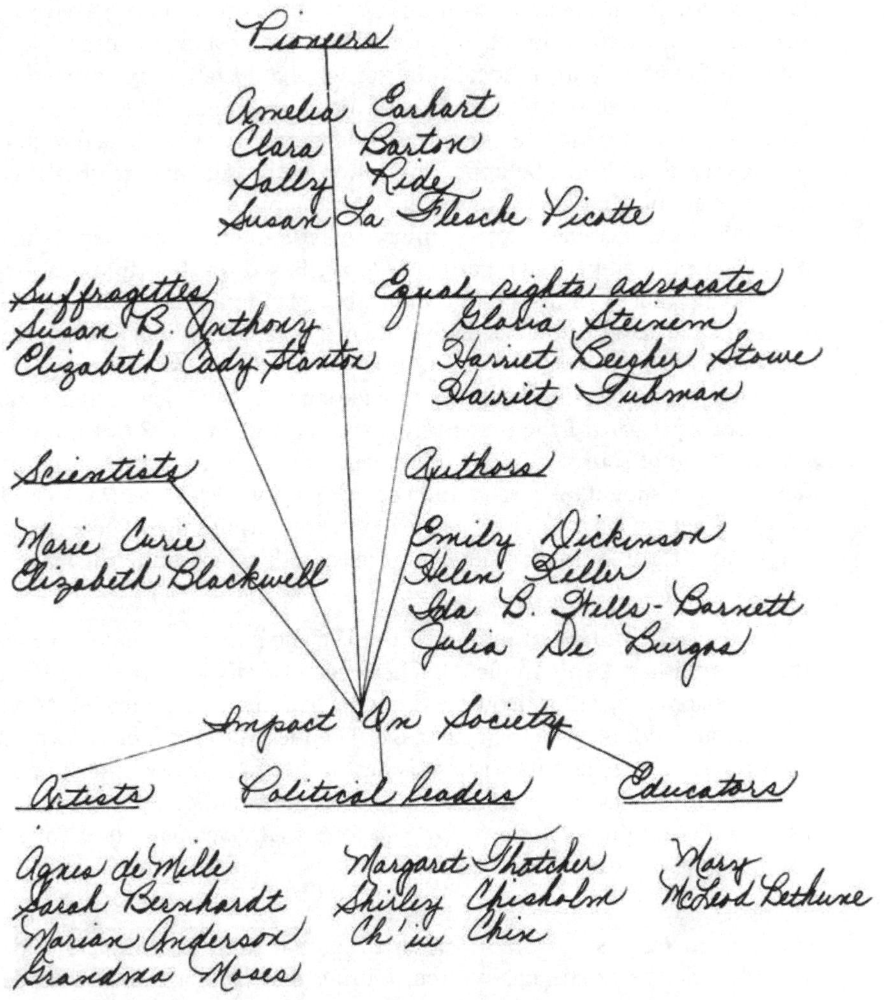

Figure 7.2 *(continued)*

was responsible for the dances in the musical *Oklahoma!*; Ida B. Wells-Barnett, the first black investigative reporter, who led the effort against the lynching of blacks by white mobs; Julia De Burgos, a Puerto Rican poet; Ch'iu Chin, a Chinese feminist and political leader who was beheaded for leading an uprising against the Ch'ing dynasty; and Susan La Flesche Picotte, the first Native American female physician. The teacher introduced the class to Fanny Mendelssohn, who was Felix Mendelssohn's sister. Many music historians believe that Fanny was the better composer of the two, but because she was a woman, her works were not given the attention received by her brother's musical compositions. The class discussed the reasons why this occurred and listened to music by both Fanny and Felix.

The prewriting stage may also involve *interviews*. The local community can provide a wealth of individuals who are knowledgeable about specific topics. For instance, Sarah Wheeler's fifth-grade class was studying the Civil War. Living in a fairly remote rural community in Illinois, the students did not have ready access to historians and well-endowed libraries. However, several townspeople were interested in the Civil War. A local minister who collected songs from the Civil War period was interviewed by members of the class. Miller (2000) suggests having an older student interview a younger student and then write a biography of the younger student. Both the upper and lower grade students are challenged to think critically about what goes into the final writing piece.

Individually, students may interview community members. First, students should identify and study a particular topic. Based on their findings they can then develop a protocol, or a set of questions they plan to ask. This may be done in pairs or in small groups of students. People such as an anthropologist or economist from a local college, the manager of a fast-food restaurant, a newspaper reporter, a circuit court judge, or a state legislator can provide students with new insights on their topic.

Reading is part of the prewriting stage, as students seek out information from various textual sources: books, newspapers, magazines, almanacs, and so forth. The students should take notes and write down sources. *Viewing* DVDs, videotapes, and Internet videos may also be part of the prewriting stage. These are just a few of the various forms of media that can be used in this data-gathering stage.

Drafting

The actual writing of the initial draft of the paper begins when most or all of the research has been completed. The focus of **drafting** a piece of writing is content, or the message that the writer is trying to convey to the reader. Mechanics and spelling are addressed in the next stage. The idea is to get ideas down on paper for later revision. As students write, it is best if they skip every other line so that they will have ample room for revising later. Teachers and students should refer to this as a "draft" and not "sloppy copy"—a term that gives parents the image that the teacher does not care about quality.

Revising

The **revising** stage occurs when the initial draft is complete and the writer rereads what he or she has written. During this stage, the writer reads the draft, crosses out words and phrases for permanent deletion or replaces them with other words and phrases, and circles misspelled words to be checked for accuracy later.

During the revising stage, the student tries to view the piece as a reader would. This involves asking questions: Does it have a lead that entices the reader to continue? Is the piece clear? Is it interesting to read? Is it well-organized? Are the facts accurate? Children often have difficulty realizing that not everyone has the same amount of knowledge about a topic as they possess. This in turn may cause difficulty for the reader. Therefore, it is important for the writer to consider the audience for whom the piece is written.

Editing

Editing is the stage in which the piece is polished before publishing/sharing takes place. Some teachers have the students exchange papers and edit each other's writing. Other teachers encourage effective editing by having students, particularly those for whom writing is difficult, read their work out loud to themselves.

After making all the necessary corrections, the students recopy their papers or make their changes on the computer. This ensures that the papers not only look nice to the reader's eye but also are easier to read. When students use computers for writing, spelling and grammar checkers are useful in their editing.

Publishing/Sharing

The last stage of the writing process is that of **publishing/sharing**. In this stage each student shares his or her writing with the class or members of the student's group. When the piece is presented, each student should find something positive to say about it. This helps build trust among classmates.

It is important to note that this stage allows students to learn from each other. Thus, students should be encouraged to ask questions of the writer after the presentation. This also enhances the writer's self-esteem and self-confidence. Having written a piece, the student has expanded his or her knowledge in that particular area.

Portfolios

It is a good idea to date all pieces of writing in the area of social studies and then have each student file his or her piece in a *portfolio* of writing samples. As Kaltsounis (1990) points out, writing in social studies is both a method of assessing students' work and a tool of learning. Titles of books the student has read should also be listed and put in the portfolio. These books will then serve as resources or motivation for the child's own writing. Chapter 3 has more on assessing portfolios.

Periodically, perhaps once every month or evaluation period, the teacher and the student should review the student's progress together by examining the contents of the portfolio. The student can critique the various pieces, thereby engaging in self-evaluation to determine his or her own strengths, weaknesses, likes, and dislikes. Portfolio assessment also enables the child and teacher to establish new goals.

Writing and Social Studies

Four types of writing are appropriate for social studies. These are narrative, poetic, expository (informational), and persuasive writing. **Narrative** writing can be described as story writing; that is, all the elements of a story, including character, plot, and setting, are present. There is a beginning, a middle, and an end. Children between five and eight years old tend to use this form of writing for social studies.

Poetic writing, which is often ignored in content areas such as social studies, should be included in social studies instruction. Some forms of poetry offer natural links to social studies, such as haiku poetry (three-lined poems with five, seven, and five syllables per line respectively), which often reflects nature. Another form is parallel poetry, or definition poems, which examines feelings or concepts. Examples of these two kinds of poetry are shown in figure 7.3, along with free verse.

The sharing of children's literature can serve as a stimulus for writing poetry. For example, the picture book *Nettie's Trip South* (Turner 1987) is a story that was inspired by the diary of the author's great-great-grandmother who, as a young child, took a trip in 1859 from her home in Albany, New York, to the southern states. On her journey, she viewed a slave auction firsthand. The book is a superb choice to share with students as part of a Civil War unit. Afterward, the students may, either individually or in small groups, compose poetry that reflects their own thoughts and feelings about what Nettie saw on her trip. One of the poems in figure 7.3, "Slave Auction," is by a fifth-grade student whose teacher had read *Nettie's Trip South* to her class.

Expository or informational writing includes writing factual works such as research reports. This type of writing may be done on an individual basis or as a collaborative effort. Biographies, including historical biographies, also fall into this type of writing.

Students must narrow their topic for informational writing and develop questions to be answered. Then they should use the library to research the information. After gathering facts, students organize the information, write their first draft, and then revise and edit the piece.

Tompkins (2004) suggests having the students write class collaboration reports as a form of expository writing. She divides her writing approach into six steps.

1. *Choose a broad topic.* For instance, the topic might be the Middle Ages.

2. *Design research questions.* Questions such as these would be appropriate: What kinds of work did people do in the Middle Ages? What kind of political system existed?

Haiku

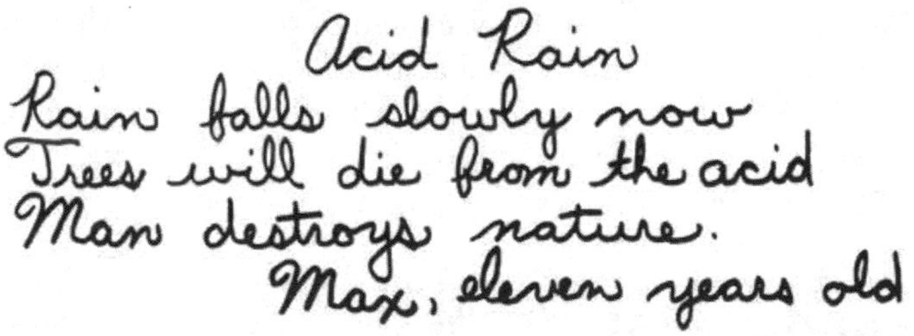

Acid Rain
Rain falls slowly now
Trees will die from the acid
Man destroys nature.
Max, eleven years old

Here is an example of haiku poetry, which focuses on nature. Max has incorporated a social issue, acid rain, with nature in his poem.

Figure 7.3 Three examples of poetic writing.

Parallel Poetry

Freedom

Freedom is powerful.
Freedom is being able to vote
for who you want.
Freedom is being able to walk
the streets.
Freedom is sharing the
responsibility for peace.
Freedom means being on
constant guard so no one
can take it away from you.
Group of ten-year-old students

Freedom was the focus of this parallel poem by a group of fourth graders.

Free Verse

Slave Auction

Here I stand on the auction block,
Waiting my turn to be sold.
I clasp my sister's hand tightly,
youth wanting together to
grow old.
Will this be the last time we'll see each
other?
A man pulls her away as she cries and leaves.
We've already lost our father, our mother.
Now we are left to face the world
Alone.

JAKE fifth grade

Jake wrote "Slave Auction" after his teacher read *Nettie's Trip South* aloud to the class.

Figure 7.3 *(continued)*

3. *Gather and organize information.* The students work in pairs to gather the information.

4. *Draft sections of the report.* Students use their notes to write their section reports. (It is helpful if the students skip every other line so they will have space for revising and editing later.)

5. *Compile the sections.* The students put together the sections, and the class as a group under the teacher's supervision writes the introduction, conclusion, and summary.

6. *Publish the report.* The final copy is published on a word processor if the students did not use a word processor for their section reports. Each student receives a copy of the final report.

The Web site ReadWriteThink.org offers useful interactive lesson plans and tools for teaching social studies with reading and writing. Figure 7.4 is an example of a rubric used to evaluate a type of expository writing.

Expository writing can also be used to introduce students to the use of references and a bibliography. A simple bibliography can be introduced as early as second grade by having the students write the name of the author and the title of the book on the last page of their reports. Later, a more elaborate bibliographical style can be introduced.

Persuasive writing includes **propaganda** statements designed to influence people's thinking. Students in grades 4 through 6 should be encouraged to write persuasive arguments as well as to learn the various devices of propaganda. Persuasive writing requires that the student present a case and take a stance, followed by giving three or four sound reasons for the stance. The student then concludes by restating the problem and proposes reasons and way(s) to resolve it. Typically, a community or school issue provides an excellent opportunity for introducing students to this form of writing as it applies to social studies. Figure 7.5 (on p. 252) is an example of a rubric to evaluate persuasive writing.

Bio-Cube

Bio-Cube is an interactive tool on the Internet that allows students to develop an outline of a person whose biography or autobiography they have just read. It can also be used by a student in writing his or her own biography. The prompts in the Bio-Cube ask the students to describe a person's significance, background, and personality. The Web site is located at http://www.readwritethink.org/materials/bio_cube/ and has other writing suggestions. Lessons that accompany this tool include: "Paul Revere: American Patriot" (Gr. 3–5), "Biography Project: Research and Class Presentation" (Gr. 6–8), and "My Life, Your Life: A Look at Your Parents' Past" (Gr. 6–8). These lessons require the use of graphic organizers, rubrics, and cooperative learning with a culminating presentation to the class.

Wonder Books

Many writers and researchers record their thoughts on a daily basis through journals or notebooks. Harvey (2002) suggests requiring our students to keep "Wonder Books," a nonfiction journal in which they can jot down their thoughts

Evaluating Writing: Biography

	Elements of Biography (5)	Ideas (5)	Organization (5)	Sentence Structure (5)	Mechanics (5)
4	All elements of biography developed: who, life span Early years (schooling, family) Contributions/ awards/honors Impressions	Fresh, original Focuses on topic Supporting details	Ideas connected Sequenced and logical	Clearly written Complete sentences Compound/ complex sentences Variety of sentence length	Few or no errors: Capitalization Ending punctuation Commas Paragraphs indented Spelling
3	Most elements of biography developed: who, life span Early years (schooling, family) Contributions/ awards/honors Impressions	General focus on topic Most supporting details included	Most ideas connected Most ideas sequenced and logical	Most sentences clearly written Most sentences complete Simple sentences Some variety of length	Some errors: Capitalization Ending punctuation Commas Paragraphs indented Spelling
2	Few elements of biography developed: who, life span Early years (schooling, family) Contributions/ awards/honors Impressions	Moves away from focus Few supporting details	Some ideas connected Not always sequenced and logical	Some unclear sentences Some run-on, fragmented sentences Little variety	Many errors: Capitalization Ending punctuation Commas Paragraphs indented Spelling
1	Lacks development of elements of biography: who, life span Early years (schooling, family) Contributions/ awards/honors Impressions	Unfocused Lacks detail	Few ideas connected Little sequence and logic	Sentences not clear Frequent fragmented sentences No variety	Serious errors: Capitalization Ending punctuation Commas Paragraphs indented Spelling
0	No attempt	No attempt	No attempt	No attempt	No attempt

Source: Written by Tyler, B., Tyson, R., and Hightower, W. (1998). Tifton, GA: Northside Elementary School, Tift County Schools.

Figure 7.4   A rubric to evaluate biographies.

Evaluating Writing: Persuasive Text

	Elements of Persuasion (5)	Ideas (5)	Organization (5)	Sentence Structure (5)	Mechanics (5)
4	Issue Point of view Defense Conclusion	Fresh, original Focuses on topic Supporting conclusion	Clearly states issue Point of view identified Clear defense of view Brief summary	Clearly written Complete sentences Compound/ complex sentences Variety of sentence length	Few or no errors: Capitalization Ending punctuation Commas Paragraphs indented Spelling
3	Issue Point of view Defense	Most ideas focus on issue Some support of view	States the issue Point of view identified Clear defense of view	Most sentences clearly written Most sentences complete Simple sentences Some variety of length	Some errors: Capitalization Ending punctuation Commas Paragraphs indented Spelling
2	Issue Point of view	Few ideas focus on issue Moves away from issue Lack of support for viewpoint	States the issue Identifies point of view Defense is present	Some unclear sentences Some run-on, fragmented sentences Little variety	Many errors: Capitalization Ending punctuation Commas Paragraphs indented Spelling
1	Issue	Incomplete ideas No support of issue Lacks detail	States the issue	Sentences not clear Frequent fragmented sentences No variety	Serious errors: Capitalization Ending punctuation Commas Paragraphs indented Spelling
0	No attempt	No attempt	No attempt	No attempt	No attempt

Source: Written by Spencer, C., Stewart, M., Edwards, S., and Whitehead, D. (1998). Tifton, GA: Charles Spencer Elementary School, Tiff County Schools.

Figure 7.5 An example of a rubric for evaluating persuasive writing.

about reading, writing, and just thinking. Teachers are encouraged to keep their own Wonder Book to serve as a model for students and to promote lifelong learning as well. Sharing with first through third graders Byrd Baylor's (1995) *I'm in Charge of Celebrations* as a read-aloud then having students generate a class list of ideas as to what events should be celebrated can be a great start. Celebrate birthdays, holidays, the first snowfall, the election of a new president, the 100th day of school, and on and on. Many of these topics can easily be woven into social studies units as part of the curriculum, making the topics more relevant for students.

Wonder Books may include anything that interests students. Often social studies and science mix, but that is acceptable. Spiral notebooks with lined paper make the most practical Wonder Books as they are easily stored away. Harvey (2002, 18) suggests the Wonder Books may include:

- Questions and wonderings
- Passions and interests
- Current thoughts
- Topic lists
- Project ideas
- Observations
- Responses to nonfiction reading
- Notes on reading content (i.e., textbook material)
- Notes on topics of interest
- Notes on field research
- Notes on inquiry projects
- Bibliographic information on books that were read
- Lists of helpful resources: Web sites, readings, conversations, etc.
- Outlines, webs, and other graphic organizers
- Interviews
- Letters
- Poems and rhymes
- Drawings, sketches, cartoons, and doodles
- Maps, charts, graphs, and diagrams
- Photographs, pictures, and postcards
- Assorted artifacts
- Quotes from books, writers, teachers, other students
- Models of beautiful language and well-written nonfiction
- Drafts of nonfiction writing

Wonder Books can be the source of topics for related writing in social studies.

Multigenre Writing for Research

Students may use or include different types of writing genres for a social studies research project. They may include three or four of these in their report. The following are some examples that students may opt to do.

Newspaper/magazine article: feature story
Newspaper article: obituary
Newspaper article: column
Newspaper article: personal or want ad
Newspaper/magazine article: news story
Newspaper (tabloid): cover with headlines
  and subheadlines
Newspaper review of movie, book, concert, etc.
Newspaper letter to editor
List (achievements, events, names, supplies, etc.)
Narrative story
Greeting card
Sheet music
Personal letter or note
E-mail dialogue
Journal/diary entries
Descriptive paragraph
Television/radio ad
Poster (wanted, playbill, concert, movie, etc.)
Recipe

Trivia Facts
Quotes
Play
Game
Book Cover
Map
Memo
Poem
Definition
Receipt
Photo caption (with photo
  or illustration)
Conversation/dialogue
Dual thoughts (inner dialogue)
Stream of consciousness
Eulogy
Wedding invitation
Doctor's report
Birth certificate

Reports may be on individuals (Joan of Arc, Princess Diana, Alexander Graham Bell, Albert Einstein, Al Capone, etc.), a group (Roger's Rangers, The Tuskegee Airmen, etc.), or an event (the attack on the *Maine,* the Holocaust, the first American in space, etc.).

Structuring the Writing Research Project

Modeling research strategies provides guidance for youngsters. Giving them parameters along with a rubric provides structure to make them feel more secure in their initial efforts to uncover the great "unknown" in social studies. As they venture forth reading and gleaning information to put in a research report, they need efficient ways of recording the information and putting it into a useful format. For second through third grade students, folding a sheet of paper in half length ways and then again in the opposite direction (known as the "hot dog" and "hamburger" folds) provides a note sheet with four rectangles. Students can label each rectangle with a heading for which they are to locate information. For instance, if the students are writing biographies, the headings may be: childhood events, education, travels, and interesting facts. All the information may come from a single biography or autobiography with the book reference written on the back of the note sheet.

The teacher should first read aloud a picture book biography such as *A Picture Book of Patrick Henry* (Adler 1991). After reading the book, have a transparency with four squares labeled with the headings mentioned earlier. Have the students supply factual information from the book for each square.

Fourth through eighth grade students should keep a folder of their research as they collect it. Each page should indicate the citation that will be used in the paper's bibliography. The teacher should demonstrate how to cite quotes as well as how to put information in one's own words. Some teachers like for students to use index cards, however, many students will lose some if not all of their research notes if the project is over a week or two in duration due to the small size of the 3 by 5 inch cards. Folders, too, can be misplaced. At the beginning of the project, students need to be given due notice that they are responsible for their research. If necessary, attach the note cards to a key ring using a hole punch. Brightly colored folders are less apt to go missing.

Internet Searches

When having students search for information on the Internet, have them use the following "search" framework as suggested by Laurie Henry (2006), a classroom teacher.

1. **Set a purpose for searching.** Identifying the task at hand initially will prevent students from going down blind alleys. Have the students define their task by asking themselves, "What am I supposed to do?" "What information do I need in order to do this?" The students should then make a list to follow. The list should be shared with other students to come up with other possibilities.

2. **Employ effective search strategies.** Creating a K-W-L chart or concept maps helps students focus and results in an efficient use of their time.

3. **Analyze search engine results.** Searching the Internet for information requires that students read strategically. The tendency is for students to become overwhelmed by the numerous possibilities they encounter. The key is for students to determine which search results provide the most relevant information for the task. Skimming and scanning techniques are essential.

4. **Read critically and synthesize information.** Conventional text found in nonfiction books and journal articles provides accuracy; Internet sources may or may not be accurate. Facts may be distorted as the material has not been reviewed by editors. In short, anyone can put anything on the Web. Have students visit reputable Web sites such as the Library of Congress America's Story pages for students (www.americaslibrary.gov/cgi-bin/page.cgi).

5. **Cite your sources.** Landmarks Citation Machine is a free citation service that provides citations in both Modern Language Association (MLA), which most school districts use, as well as the American Psychological Association (APA). This site is located at http://citationmachine.net and is relatively easy to use.

6. **How successful was your search?** By reflecting on the search process, students can determine what worked and what did not, which will aid future search engine ventures.

A simple search for the Holocaust will turn up over 800,000 hits on the Internet. Even a topic from the same period in time that is more defined, such as "World War II Pacific naval battles and American involvement," will yield around 200,000 results. Helping students to refine their searches will target their task and assist them as researchers.

Another way to assist both elementary and middle school students is to direct them to the American Library Association's Web site (www.ala.org) and have them go to Great Websites for Kids. This site has literally thousands of links of well-developed and accurate Web sites that students can investigate as part of their research. A key indicates the level of difficulty for each site. Topics include biographies, American Revolutionary War, Civil War, Industrial Revolution, World War I, World War II, the civil rights movement, and many, many more.

Another Web site for upper elementary and middle schoolers is A&E's Biography Web site (www.biography.com), which has over 20,000 entries for students to consider. The Gallery of Achievers (www.achievement.org/galleryachieve.hml) is a Web site that features achievements of famous individuals of the twentieth century.

Aesthetic and Efferent Reading and Writing

Aesthetic and efferent reading and writing were first identified by Rosenblatt (1978) back in the 1930s. Readers have different purposes for reading—for instance, reading for enjoyment and reading for information. Reading for pleasure is referred to as **aesthetic reading.** Reading to find out information is referred to as **efferent reading.** According to Rosenblatt, nearly every reading experience requires a balance between aesthetic and efferent reading. As students read, they move back and forth between the aesthetic and efferent stances. Tompkins (2005) believes that literature, however, should be read primarily from the aesthetic stance. Thus, when having students read picture or chapter books, or historical novels, it is important that teachers keep foremost in mind that the experience be a pleasurable one. This is true even though students will be gaining information, the efferent side of reading, as they read such books.

Likewise, writing has its own aesthetic and efferent sides. Poetry and narratives are considered more aesthetic while expository writing (persuasive, descriptive, and explanatory) is from the efferent stance. Autobiographies and biographies contain both aesthetic and efferent elements as personal insights and facts about the individual are revealed.

Social studies requires both aesthetic and efferent reading and writing. Researching informational books relies largely on efferent reading, as does writing a descriptive report. However, there are several different types of activities that allow students to utilize efferent reading with aesthetic and efferent writing. For instance, fourth graders through middle schoolers are hooked on music. They know the latest CDs and the top tunes on the charts. One way to incorporate music into the social studies is to have the student write lyrics and do a karaoke sing-along. A list of karaoke CD titles available from Sound Choice can be purchased for one dollar. This company offers the oldies as well as current hits. The address is:

Sound Choice
14100 South Lakes Drive
Charlotte, NC 28273
Web site: www.soundchoice.com

Below is an example of a song written by a fifth grader after studying the 1600s in a social studies unit.

In the 1600s
(Sing to the tune of "In the Navy" by the Village People)
In the 1600s, you could sail the seven seas,
In the 1600s, men wore wigs if they pleased.
In the 1600s, London burned to smithereens,
In the 1600s, Elizabeth was Queen.
In the 1600s, Louis XIV ruled France,
In the 1600s, he wore fancy coats and pants.
   (Clap, Clap, Clap
   Clap, Clap, Clap
   Clap, Clap, Clap
   Clap, Clap, Clap, Clap, Clap, Clap)
(CHANT) We want witches!
We want witches!
We want witches to burn today! Yeah!
In the 1600s, you could start a war over taxes,
In the 1600s, you could kill your enemies with broad axes.
In the 1600s, women wore long dresses,
In the 1600s, men hunted with blunderbusses.
   (Clap, Clap, Clap
   Clap, Clap, Clap
   Clap, Clap, Clap, Clap, Clap, Clap)
(CHANT) We want witches!
We want witches!
We want witches to burn today! Yeah!

—By Kurtis

This not only is an enjoyable culminating activity for students, but it offers an excellent means of alternative assessment. By having students work with a partner, they can often come up with a wide variety of lyrics based on the content covered in the unit. The teacher can specify the number of facts, and other elements, to be included.

Poetry formats have versatility, flexibility, and diversity. Poetry is a superb way to link content area concepts and motivation to learn. Writing poetry helps students develop their abilities to record vivid, precise descriptions and visualize ideas. As such, it aids in concept development and retention.

Historical Documents: Diaries, Journals, Letters, and Newspapers

Upper elementary and middle school students can learn a great deal about social studies through reading the diaries, journals, letters, and newspaper articles written during the various periods of history, for instance from the journals and and letters of local men and women who were engaged in World War II or the Vietnam War. The local historical society oftentimes has collections of diaries and letters donated by families over periods of time. Also, recall from chapter 1 that students used books and the Internet to access journal entries about the Lewis and Clark expedition's harsh journey during the exploration of the newly purchased Louisiana Territory. Students discovered that Meriwether Lewis, who was well-educated, and William Clark, a former army officer, were able to engage in mostly peaceful encounters with various Native American tribes, something that was lost on later generations of governmental officials.

While students can encounter historical journals via books and the Internet, they also need to become aware of how to use actual, authentic historical documents and artifacts. One way is to share your own family's letters, that is, letters from soldiers to their loved ones, or letters from family members who moved to another state and described the differences in geography, and so on. Many local libraries and historical societies have letters, diaries, and journals dating back a hundred years or more. It is best to introduce such documents that have been laminated with a protective covering. Then move to the actual document that has been handed down and preserved. Students must be taught how to handle such documents without damaging them. They need to learn to open old newspapers and letters slowly and carefully so they won't tear. Their hands need to be both clean and dry, so allow time for a trip to the restroom to thoroughly wash away dirt and grime from playing on the playground or from leftover lunch spills.

One period that offers a rich source of diaries, journals, letters, and newspapers is that of the Civil War. Upper elementary and middle school students can compare the letters of the various soldiers as to their views of the war, which lends itself to the fourth standard of Individual Development and Identity. By comparing letters from brothers, students can discern which brother had received the greater education before going off to war. Local historical societies and libraries are good sources of such writings. Students may also locate such materials on the Web site of the Library of Congress.

During the Civil War, children's magazines were published. *Lessons of War: The Civil War in Children's Magazines* (Marten 1998) is a collection of essays, editorials, articles, poetry, short stories, and letters from children's magazines from the period. By reading from this collection students gain insight into what children of the period experienced from events such as raising funds for soldiers to the loss and sacrifice of family members. A sense of the southern and northern cultures during this period of history can be extracted by students as they read actual articles written during that time.

Letters and journals of soldiers can be difficult for young readers to discern. In *Soldier's Heart,* Gary Paulsen (1998) depicts the life of Charley Goddard of Winona, Minnesota, who at age 15 enlisted in the First Minnesota Volunteers. Paulsen relied heavily on Goddard's letters and journals to write a story about the trauma soldiers encountered in battle, and the mental scars left behind for soldiers to endure. This is a superb book for fifth graders as it presents in a simple, straightforward text the problems of a young man facing war. Teachers must be careful in selecting such books to make certain the historical information presented is accurate.

Prior to going to battle, Civil War soldiers from both sides were asked to write letters to their loved ones—a practice that continues to this day. Here is an excerpt from such a letter written by Major Sullivan Ballou, a Union soldier, to his wife, Sarah, while he was stationed in Washington, DC. Ballou wrote the letter on July 14, 1861, a week prior to Ballou's regiment being engaged in the first battle of Bull Run (or Manassas as it was referred to by the Confederates).

> Sarah, my love for you is deathless. It seems to bind me with mighty cables that nothing but omnipotence can break. And yet my love of country comes over me like a strong wind and bears me irresistibly with all those chains to the battlefield.
>
> If I do not return, my dear Sarah, never forget how much I loved you, nor that when my last breath escapes me on the battlefield, it will whisper your name.
>
> Forgive my many faults and the many pains I have caused you and how thoughtless, how foolish, I have sometimes been. But oh, Sarah, if the dead can come back to the earth and flit unseen around those they love, I shall always be with you, in the brightest day and the darkest night. Always. Always.
>
> And when the soft breeze fans your cheek, it shall be my breath; or the cool air your throbbing temple, it shall be my spirit passing by.
>
> Sarah, do not mourn me dead. Think: I am gone, and wait for me. For we shall meet again.

A week after writing this letter, Ballou died at Bull Run. Someone, or, more likely, several people, took care to preserve this wonderful letter for posterity.

Another soldier in the same battle of Bull Run was Elisha Hunt Rhodes of Cranston, Rhode Island, a descendent of Roger Williams. Rhodes entered the Army of the Potomac as a private in 1861 and participated in every campaign from Bull Run to the surrender proceedings at Appomattox in 1865. Following is Rhodes's letter to his sister after he fought in the first battle of Bull Run (Manassas).

> Camp Clark, Washington, DC
>
> July 28, 1861
>
> My Dear Sister,
>
> I rec'd your letter last night. I will try to give you all the particulars of the Battle. We left our camp on Sunday, July 21st at 2 o'clock in the morning. We started without breakfast and only a little hardbread in our haversacks. We marched until about 10 o'clock AM when our pickets were fired upon. We were on a road with woods on one side. In a few minutes we received a volley and the orders were given for the 2nd R.I. Reg. to charge. We started and charged through the woods into an open field. We had about 700 men. We came out upon about 5,000 of the Rebels who started on the run for the woods on the other side of the valley. We marched to the brow of the hill and fired. Our battery came up and opened fire. The enemy opened fire from several masked forts and cut down our men in great numbers. We loaded and fired as fast as we could. This was the time that Wm. Aborn was shot. He fought bravely when he was shot through the neck. (Rhodes 1991)

Fighting in 20 battles, Rhodes rose from the ranks of private to lieutenant colonel and commander of a regiment by the end of the war. After the Civil War was over, Rhodes returned to work in the cotton and woolen mill business. He was elected Brigadier General of the Rhode Island Militia. Rhodes died at age 75 on January 14, 1917.

Another important Civil War battle was that of Gettysburg, a bitterly fought engagement in which both sides lost several thousand men. Major General George Picket led 15,000 men in the biggest and most deadly cavalry charge of the Civil War. Today it is remembered as "Picket's Charge," the last such unified massive cavalry charge across an open field in history. Following is a portion of a journal from the battle of Gettysburg kept by a 19-year-old lieutenant named John Dooley. Like many Southern officers, Dooley had brought along one of his family's slaves to cook, wash, and run errands. Dooley wrote the following entry into his journal as he marched as a member of the Confederate Army. The route the soldiers took was along narrow, rutted dirt roads as they made their way from Richmond, Virginia, north to Gettysburg, Pennsylvania. They passed farmland that had been the scene of a recent battle.

> Scarce a farmyard that is not stained by human blood. Scarce a field unpolluted by the enemy's touch. The fences are burned, the meadows trampled down, the cattle all gone and the harvests unharvested; proud homesteads in ruins. . . .

By nature a peaceful and gentle person, Dooley became angered at seeing the ravaged countryside. He wrote that it was the work of Northern invaders, that "party of brutal men, uneducated, unrefined, unprincipled, inhuman, and criminal" (Murphy 1992, 10).

The realities of the time and the desperate situations that the soldiers and their loved ones faced are presented to students in a much different light when the accounts come from those actually present at the scene. Through diaries, journals, and letters, students learn to develop empathy for soldiers and their families on both sides. A good activity is to have students pretend they were living during the war and have them write letters to friends and family members or keep a journal of their feelings as the war progressed.

Using Technology to Keep Abreast of Current Events

Having students become aware of current events is a way that they can become active citizen participants. Ben Bradlee, former editor of the *Washington Post*, once said that a newspaper contained "the first rough draft of history" (Ellis 1998). Newspaper articles are an attempt to record accurately the events of the day. Besides current events, death notices offer the opportunity to teach about culture, grocery and car ads reflect economics, events in other parts of the world provide geographic awareness, editorials give insights into political science, and major news stories may go down as historic events. With access to 24-hour news on television and the Internet, increasingly fewer families subscribe to a daily newspaper or weekly news magazine so many students lack access to one for current events assignments. However, access to television and radio is almost universal for most children.

The Internet, with the Associated Press, CNN, and other news media, offers an almost instantaneous source of news events for upper elementary and middle school students complete with videos and frequent updates of pending situations. Many newspapers offer articles on their Internet Web sites, although some charge a subscription fee for access.

In studying current events, one approach is to coincide the event with a thematic unit. For instance, in science the study of plants can be accompanied by having students gather current events on agricultural and weather conditions, whereas the study of space can be accompanied by having students examine news articles on space travel, NASA's research using their Web site, and congressional appropriations for further space launches.

Another intriguing activity is to have students select a date in the near future and then download newspaper articles from throughout the United States, and even the world, on that date. Newspaper Web pages can be found through the Google search engine. For example, a fifth-grade class chose May 1, 2006, the day boycotts of businesses and marches in large cities were held by Hispanic immigrants in support of immigrant rights. Among the newspapers downloaded were the *Arizona Daily Republic,* the *Chicago Tribune,* the *Denver Post*, the *Miami Herald*, the *New York Times*, and the *St. Louis Post Dispatch*. A unique fact was garnered from nearly every article. For instance, the *Chicago Tribune* group read that there were an estimated 10,000 illegal immigrants from Ireland in the United States and an even greater number of Indians, while the students had previously believed the issue was just with Hispanics coming across the border from Mexico. The *New York Times* group reported that busy 14th Street in Manhattan saw only a few shops and one restaurant closed as compared to the findings of the *Los Angeles Times* group, which found that one in three restaurants and businesses closed. Each group also noted other national stories, such as the resignation from NASA of the first woman to command a space shuttle mission, the benefits for preschoolers of a flu-spray vaccine, raids by federal agents on people trafficking humans, and possible reasons for the high cost of gasoline. Students read about a sodium tank explosion in India and the nationalizing of Bolivian natural gas fields.

Besides newspapers and news magazines, electronic news sources can be used for current events. Here are some that students can find via surfing the Internet:

MSNBC	http://www.msnbc.msn.com
CNN Student News	http://www.cnn.com/EDUCATION/
CNN Interactive	http://www.cnn.com
USA Today News	http://www.usatoday.com/news/nfront.htm
World Newspapers	http://www.world-newspapers.com/world-news.html

Other sources of current events include faxed statements or Web sites by politicians indicating their stance on various issues. These may be obtained by contacting state legislators or members of Congress via e-mail if their Web site lacks an opinion on a specific political issue.

Discussion

In teaching social studies, the teacher must give children the opportunity to discuss topics of interest to them. This may be done by allowing groups of students to find a topic of common interest and report back to the class about that topic. More formal types of discussion include panel presentations in which students are assigned to or elect to serve in a group of three or four students. Each group member researches a specific aspect of the topic, and all members make the final presentation to the entire class.

A structured form of discussion for older students is the debate. This very democratic process is a formal discussion of a topic, question, or issue in which opposing sides take turns presenting arguments to the audience. A timed format is established in advance for opening statements from both sides and questions for both sides from the audience. The audience evaluates the debate and votes for the winning team. Debates require the students to research their position and to develop oral language skills.

Through discussion, students develop both listening and speaking skills. They also develop confidence in speaking before their peers, something that is an asset later in life. Literature circles offer students the opportunity to engage in reading the same book, discussing it, and sharing a project based on the book with the class.

Reading, Writing, and Discussing as Learning Strategies

It is important to assist children in developing and applying the appropriate strategy for different types of reading material. For instance, in gathering factual information about the economy of the state of Arizona as compared with that of New Mexico, a student may need to read graphs. However, locating information about the capital of the state of Iowa may require a student to be able to scan through text. To find the main idea of a political speech, the student must be able to skim for information and then create a summary.

Literature Circles

Literature circles are groups of three to eight students who are reading the same story, article, or historical novel selected and introduced in a book talk by the teacher. Since self-selection is part of literature circles, groups change depending on each student's current interest. Thus, students who have selected the same title to read make up a literature circle (Knoeller 1994; Scott 1994). The group usually meets two times a week to talk about the book they are reading. On the other days, the students read the assigned readings from the book and complete tasks related to the book. Here are some examples of tasks for literature circles:

- Discussion Leader: Monitors other group members and gives assistance with tasks when needed. Leads the discussion when the group meets together.
- Historian: Traces the major historical events of the chapter.
- Geographer/Cartographer: Draws a map related to the setting of the book and depicts journeys of the main character.
- Word Warrior: Keeps a list of unusual or unfamiliar words from the book along with writing the sentences in which they were used and their definitions.
- Phrase Keeper: Jots down interesting phrases from each chapter, noting the page numbers for each.
- Character Analyst: Compares and contrasts the main characters of the book.

With literature circles, students are assigned a task for their group. Then the students are assigned to read a set number of chapters, usually one to three chapters, and complete their tasks before meeting as a group. The teacher walks around the classroom and intercedes only if a student appears to need assistance. During the group discussion, students share their reactions to the book along with the final results of their assigned tasks. Students then rotate tasks for the next reading assignment from the book.

Students can also engage in other activities as they read the book. Here are two suggestions.

- As a group, make a character web that depicts the main character's relationship with other characters. Discuss the character web at each group meeting and make changes when appropriate (Kauffman and Yoder 1990).
- Each student keeps a literature response journal and shares reactions to the book as part of the group discussion.

The process of reading, doing the assigned tasks, and meeting and sharing with the group continues until the book is finished. At that point a culminating activity takes place. Some examples of culminating activities are:

- Rewrite an exciting portion of the book as a play and perform it for the class.
- Write and perform a reader's theater from an important exchange of dialogue in the book.
- Write a critique of the book, using samples of book reviews from the local newspaper.
- Make a mural or diorama depicting a scene from the book.
- Stage a mock interview of major characters in the book.

Tips for Initiating Literature Circles

The teacher needs to select books, usually two to four, that will appeal to the students and that relate to the social studies topic to be covered. This guarantees that the material selected is not overly difficult for some of the students. ELLs and struggling readers can be assigned lower reading ability historical fiction or picture books that share the same topic and theme (Farris, Nelson, and L'Allier 2007). Books on tape and graphic novels can also be used to help support lower ability students.

The teacher then does a brief read-aloud from a portion of each of the available books or chooses a picture book on the same theme. The read-aloud may be one or two pages or the prologue of a book. The brief passage may be from the beginning or an interesting point in the middle of the book. The idea is to read enough to whet students' appetites. After reading the passage to the class, the teacher asks the students to react to what has been read and share their thoughts. The class briefly discusses the events shared and makes predictions about what will happen next. Then the teacher goes on to another book and the process is repeated until all the available books have had a portion shared and discussed.

An ideal group size for literature circles is four or five students. For the first couple of attempts, the teacher should assign the students to their groups and tasks to facilitate a smooth and productive outcome. Be sure to place students who are leaders and on task in each group.

Students need to be reminded that literature circles are a collaborative activity. Everyone in the group must read the book and do their assigned task as well as join in the discussion during the group meetings.

SQ3R

A study strategy introduced more than 40 years ago and still in wide use is **SQ3R** (Robinson 1970). Students independently work through five steps:

1. *Surveying* the material by skimming through the chapter.
2. Formulating *questions* by changing the chapter's subheadings into questions.
3. *Reading* to answer the questions that were generated.
4. *Reciting* answers to the questions after reading the chapter.
5. *Reviewing* the answers to the questions.

PQRST

A variation of SQ3R is **PQRST** (preview, question, review, summarize, and test), which was developed by Spache and Berg (1966). This strategy may be used independently or in pairs. It, too, involves five steps:

1. *Previewing* the material to get an idea of the primary emphasis and main points of the chapter or passage.
2. Developing *questions* to be answered while reading the material.
3. *Reviewing* what was read.
4. *Summarizing* either orally or on paper the main points of the passage.
5. *Testing* to find out how familiar the student is with the material.

Literature Response Journals

Literature response journals allow students the freedom to write down their thoughts about a book as they read it. To identify what passage they are reading when they write down their comments and/or reactions, students can jot down the page number in the margin. Students should be instructed to leave four or five lines of space after their entry so that the teacher can question or respond to what they have written.

Students may elect to write as if they were the main character in the book or as if they were the main character's good friend. Students may write to each other in dialogue journals, reflecting on the chapters as they read. Students also may make any comments or illustrations they wish in such journals. The teacher responds by asking short, provocative, nonjudgmental questions. Literature response journals are described in more detail in chapter 10.

QAR

QAR is question, answer, and reflect on what has been read. As students read, they develop questions and seek out answers. After reading the text, they review and try to integrate their newly gained knowledge. This approach is good to use with a social studies journal.

RAFT

RAFT was designed by Santa, Havens, and Harrison (1989) as a strategy for students to use to write for a specific audience. RAFT is an acronym for the *role* of the writer, *audience* to whom the writing is directed, *format* of the writing, and *topic* of the piece itself.

The student identifies a theme about which to write—such as the Revolutionary War—identifies the audience, and selects a format. Possible formats include advice columns, editorials, advertisements, horoscopes, invitations, diaries, journals, songs, obituaries, and poetry. Thus, a RAFT outline about the Revolutionary War might look like this:

R: Members of the Sons of Liberty
A: King George III
F: A rap song
T: Why people living in the New England colonies should support the separation of the colonies from England

At this point, the students create their own rap song to share with the class.

RESPONSE: An Interactive Approach to Study Skills

The old proverb "the worst pencil is better than the best memory" has merit. Students need to be taught how to take notes. **RESPONSE** is a study strategy that involves writing down major points and concepts from the text as well as asking questions about what one has read and determining new vocabulary words and their meaning. Developed by Jacobson (1989), RESPONSE was designed with the purpose of creating written interaction between the student and teacher.

The teacher assigns a passage or chapter to be read by the student. As the student reads the text, he or she uses a RESPONSE form to make notations, write down questions, and jot down unfamiliar concepts or names (see figure 7.6).

Upon receiving the student's RESPONSE sheet, the teacher reviews it, responding to questions or unfamiliar terms that the student has marked with an asterisk. In addition, the teacher clarifies any errant statements or misunderstandings the student may have shown. For instance, in figure 7.6, Kenny had written under "New Words/Concepts/Vocabulary/Names" "Patrick Henry" followed by "The Great Compromiser." However, Henry Clay was known as the "Great Compromiser," so Kenny had confused the two men. His teacher clarified the differences between Clay and Henry so that Kenny could better understand the contributions of each of these leaders.

By combing all the students' questions and unknown terms, the teacher forms a picture of what the students understand and what is unclear to them. Rather than trusting to instinct, the teacher uses RESPONSE sheets as a more precise assessment measure of what direction the class discussion should take.

By writing notes in the margins of the RESPONSE sheet, the teacher can give positive feedback to a student as well as offer guidance in finding information. In doing this, it is important to personalize the comments by using the student's first name. For instance, Carol Fuhler, Kenny's teacher, wrote this as her final comment to Kenny: "Very Complete, Ken—nice job!"

Name: *Kenny Maxwell*   Date: Oct. 27

Chapter: *Nine, Section 2*

IMPORTANT POINTS: As you read, write down important information and the page on which you found the information.

p. 174 Patrick Henry and Samuel Adams thought that making the government more powerful would harm the freedoms won in the Revolutionary War

p. 174 The delegates decided to write a new constitution and give more power to the central government.

p. 174 They were called the Founding Fathers and the meeting was known as the Constitutional Convention. They met in 1787

p. 174 Each state had different concerns.

p. 177 Problems were settled by compromises.

p. 177 Congress would have two house—Senate and House of Representatives—both needed to agree on a law—The Great Compromise

p. 177 Three-Fifths Compromise—of every five slaves only three would be counted for state.

p. 177 National government divided into three parts. Legislative made up of two houses of congress They made the laws. Executive headed by the president. See that the laws of Congress were carried out. Communicated with foreign governments. Judicial the federal courts.

QUESTIONS: As you read, write down any questions that you may have along with the page number. Some questions will be for our class discussion. If you want an answer to a question, place an asterisk (*) by it.

p. 177 How could one part of the government make certain other part followed the law?

NEW WORDS/CONCEPTS/VOCABULARY/NAMES: Write the word or phrase along with the page number on which you found it. Place an asterisk (*) by those you would like to have defined or explained.

p. 174   Patrick Henry, "The Great Compromiser"

p. 174   Three-Fifths Compromise

Figure 7.6   An example of a RESPONSE form.

RESPONSE can be used as a group activity. Each student completes a RESPONSE sheet and shares the information with the other members of the group. The group then discusses each of the important points, questions, and words/concepts and creates a RESPONSE form that summarizes what the group believes is significant. The students hand in their individual forms and the group form to the teacher. Used in this manner, RESPONSE becomes a cooperative learning activity. The teacher, in turn, reviews the groups' RESPONSE sheet as a means of determining what needs to be taught. If a couple of groups have the same question, then that concept needs to be covered in the class discussion.

Cooperative Learning

Although whole class instruction tends to be the predominant method of instruction, cooperative learning has proved to be an effective, noncompetitive instructional approach that allows for student interaction. According to Gunter, Estes, and Schwab (1990, 169), "Working *cooperatively*. . . may be the most critical social skill that students learn, when one considers the importance of cooperation in the workplace, in the family, and in leisure activities." Reading, writing, and discussing are essential elements of cooperative learning because each student must contribute to the group's overall success. The basic premise of **cooperative learning** is that each student must contribute for the goal of the group to be accomplished.

Students need to be allowed to work cooperatively, in particular, to be given ample opportunities to interact and discuss with each other matters of substance. Calkins and Harwayne (1991) point out, "If we were designing schools from start to finish, clearly we'd build in hours and hours of interactive learning. Youngsters need to talk about books, molecules, the Civil War, and current events" (100).

Studies of children who have engaged in cooperative learning activities on a regular basis found that the students gained in self-esteem and were more accepting of cultural and individual differences (Slavin 1983). Augustine, Gruber, and Hanson (1989/1990) are three elementary teachers who have used cooperative learning for several years in their classrooms (grades 3, 4, and 6). They believe that cooperative learning promotes higher achievement, develops social skills, and places the responsibility of learning on the student. "If other educators believe as we do that higher achievement, increased acceptance of differences, improved attitudes towards school, and enhanced self-esteem are valuable goals for all children, then we all need to promote the continued use of cooperative learning" (7). Johnson and Johnson (1993) outlined five elements of cooperative learning. Each element is essential if cooperative learning is to be successfully established as an instructional strategy in a classroom. The elements particularly foster civics education. Here are the five elements:

1. Positive interdependence must be developed. Students must care about each other's learning and understand that "they are responsible for and benefit from one another's learning" (44).

2. Students need lots of opportunities and time to interact with one another to elaborate, bolster, and compromise on issues.

3. Individual accountability must be present in any cooperative learning activity. Students need to realize they are each responsible for their own learning. No free rides are available.

4. Social skills need to be taught for cooperative learning to be successful. Students need to understand how to communicate, serve as an effective group leader, build trust, compromise, and resolve differences.

5. Group processing or group assessment needs to occur on a regular basis so that the group can determine its strengths and weaknesses and can determine how to perform better in the future.

A cooperative learning activity that can be used as part of a social studies unit is roulette writing (Farris 1998). Students in groups of four or five each write about the same topic. After writing for approximately three minutes, each student hands his or her piece of writing to the student on the left. Upon receiving a new writing piece, the student reads what has been written and then continues the piece until the teacher indicates that it is time to pass the paper to the next writer. Each successive writer receives additional time to read what has already been written and to think about how to continue the work. The object of the activity is to continue the same theme and content the first writer in the group used. The last student who writes on the piece writes the conclusion. This is an excellent cooperative learning activity because a student need only contribute one sentence to be a part of a successful activity.

Figure 7.7 (on pp. 269–270) shows an example of roulette writing based on a pioneer unit in a fifth-grade class. This group's topic was "The Day Our School Burned Down." Different handwriting indicates where one student stopped writing and the next began. Notice that the final piece sounds as though it was written by one author, not six.

Group investigation is another cooperative learning strategy that is effective in social studies instruction and relies on the use of reading, writing, and discussion skills. Sharan and Sharan (1989/1990) believe that group investigation focuses on children's individual interests and gives them control over their learning. In group investigation, the teacher initially presents a broad, multifaceted topic to the class for discussion. Groups are formed as subtopics emerge and students indicate their interests. The group members plan how they will investigate their particular subtopic and then carry out their research investigations. Next, the groups reconvene to review and discuss all the information gathered as well as to synthesize, analyze, and summarize the information in their final report. Then all groups present the final reports (Sharan and Sharan 1989/1990).

Field Trips

Social studies lends itself to a wide variety of **field trips**—local community governmental offices, historical museums, visits to senior citizen centers to interview those present about their recollections of a certain period in history, and so on. When deciding on engaging in a field trip with your class, it is important to do some spadework ahead of time. First investigate the location. What are the advantages to having your students visit this site? What are the disadvantages? Is the site age appropriate for your students? Look around during your visit to the location and see if children and adolescents your students' age are enjoying themselves and are benefiting from their experience. Next, find out what the school board policies and procedures are regarding field trips. Some school districts prohibit overnight

The Day Our School Burned Down

The year was 1870. It was hot, and we found it difficult to pay attention to the teacher in the stuffy class room. The building was all made of wood.

Laura Ingalls was our teacher. She tried disparately to make the day a good one but it was no use, it was just too hot. She dismissed us earlier than usual. We all ran across the lane to the creek.

While playing in the creek, we noticed a grey cloud of smoke rising above the trees. We followed the smoke to see where it came from. It was our school! Our school was on fire! Miss Ingalls ran to the saw mill down the road to get Pa Ingalls. He and the other mill workers began bringing water down to put out the fire.

But it was too late. The school was gone and so too was the church. Where would we learn and pray? The children cried.

(continued)

Figure 7.7 An example of roulette writing.

The adults cried. Then Pa
Ingalls prayed for divine guidance.
Right then we decided to rebuild.
The debris would be cleared tomorrow and the next day everyone
would come and help build a new
school. The children could do
the running, the women the
cooking, and the man the building.
Yes we would have a bigger and
better schoolhouse than before. We'd
even have new desks, slates and
books. It'd be hard work, but
together we could do it.

Figure 7.7 *(continued)*

field trips. Others have time stipulations. For instance, a fifth-grade teacher wanted to take her students to visit the state capital, a four-hour drive one way, on a day trip. Her school district's field trip policy included a provision that the time at the location must be equal to or exceed the travel time. Since her students would have had to be at the capital for eight hours plus the eight-hour bus trip, the teacher opted for an overnight visit. The students were then given the additional opportunity to visit a museum as well.

Most school districts insist upon having signed permission forms or slips from the student's parent or guardian. The letter to the parents and guardians should give details as to what to expect from the field trip. This includes the time and day of departure and return, the reason for the field trip, suggestions as to what their children should wear, whether money is needed to cover expenses or make purchases at a gift shop, and any other information you believe is important to include. You may wish to request that parents volunteer as chaperones for the trip as part of your permission form. These letters must be sent out in advance with extra copies made for those students who lose them on the way home from school. A checklist should be kept of the permission slips as they are returned so that those students who still need to return their forms may be reminded to do so. All permission forms should be kept in a secure location.

Field trips require an extra measure of security procedures. Remember that it is the teacher's responsibility to give the bus driver specific directions to the site in advance. Keep in mind that a bus cannot be maneuvered as easily as a car or minivan. Make a phone tree of parents' and the school's phone numbers in case the bus breaks down, delaying the return to school. To be extra safe, take a cellular phone with you on the field trip. Be prepared for bee or wasp stings during early fall field trips. Some students will be allergic to nuts, chocolate, or strawberries. A trip to the local custard shop might require that they be watched for what they can safely eat. If your class will stop at a gift shop, let the students know in advance. It is usually wise to suggest that a modest amount of money be brought or some students will bring a large amount to spend. Gift shops can be tempting to students so be aware that this stop will require additional time.

When planning a field trip with an elementary class, you may want to share poetry from *Mrs. Brown on Exhibit and Other Museum Poems* by Susan Katz (2002). Mrs. Brown, the queen of field trips, heads her class to see everything from mummies to candy to the Merry-Go-Round Museum. The poetry points out what things are available and can be found at museums—brochures, hands-on activities, and don't touch displays. Thus, the book helps to set parameters on the do's and don'ts for students as they venture forth on the field trip. The class can generate a list of appropriate behavior (asking questions of docents, not "hogging" a popular hands-on activity but taking turns, etc.). Featured in the back of the book is an extensive list of museums arranged by state.

On the day before the field trip, go over your classroom rules as well as any other rules of behavior you believe the students need to review (thanking museum guides, docents, and chaperones, standing quietly and listening to presentations, getting into line without pushing and shoving, staying with their assigned group, being prompt, etc.).

Chaperones are usually parents or grandparents of your students. All chaperones should be trained for the field trip. Give them an outline of the day's events. Describe in detail what they are to do with their group. Try to give each chaperone four or five students at the most. Be certain to provide the chaperones this information a week before the field trip along with your home and school numbers and e-mail address—if any questions arise or they cannot attend and need a substitute, they can contact you.

Some schools require students to wear name tags while others think it can cause potential problems as strangers can learn the students' names. Find out what your school district's policy is and follow it. Many schools identify only the student's first name so strangers cannot track them by using the phone book for that area.

The best field trips occur when the students visit a site that they have been studying in social studies. A visit to a Rendezvous after studying about trapping and trading with American Indians can be very enriching. Going to the Rendezvous without having some background can be nothing more than a wasted learning opportunity. Let the students know what to look for during the trip. Giving them small, pocket-size notebooks and pencils they can use to jot down notes along the way can be helpful. Have the class make a K-W-L chart before you depart with the students listing what they already know (K) and what they want to learn (W) on the field trip. The day after the field trip, have the class complete the K-W-L chart with what they learned (L).

NCSS STANDARDS-LINKED LESSON PLAN

Researching Medical Practices

Theme: Medical Advancements
Source: Pamela Farris, Northern Illinois University
Grades: 6–8
Objectives:
• Students will research and summarize actual medical practices.

• Students will understand how to prepare questions for a guest speaker or "ask an expert" using the Internet.

• Students will create and deliver a PowerPoint presentation or use Hyperstudio to compare medical advancements.

• Students will share information with another class using e-mail and the Internet.

NCSS Themes:
   I. Culture
VIII. Science, Technology, and Society

Materials: Heavy weight construction paper or white tag board, book binding material, drawing utensils, glue, medical books, computer with Internet capabilities and PowerPoint or Hyperstudio.
   This activity fits a number of books with social studies themes: *The Midwife's Apprentice*, the novel about the Middle Ages by Karen Cushman; *Johnny Tremain*, the novel about the Revolutionary War by Esther Forbes; *Pink and Say*, the picture book about the Civil War by Patricia Polacco; *With Every Drop of Blood*, the Civil War novel by Christopher Collier, etc.

Process:
• Students will be put into groups and assigned a historical period (the Middle Ages, Revolutionary War and colonial times in America, Civil War, World War I, World War II, the Vietnam War, etc.).

• Students will use library sources and the Internet to research prevailing medical practices of the period.

• Students will summarize the information in a PowerPoint presentation for the class.

• Using the Internet, students contact another class to communicate information and request additional insight.

• Have a local doctor or pharmacist as a visitor to the class.

   Instructional Comments: This is an activity that respectfully acknowledges diversity among students while gaining insight into cultures. For instance, students learn that cats, not rats, were thought to be carriers of the plague during the Middle Ages, with local townspeople killing the felines until it was discovered that a village with lots of cats had no people who had the plague. From early America, such as General George Washington's foresight in having his troops inoculated for small pox, to two significant advancements that overlapped with Word War II—the development of penicillin during the middle of the twentieth century and the creation of plasma— the range of possibilities for student exploration is broad. Strange discoveries often are found by students, such as tomatoes being considered poisonous by many in the 1800s, while now they are considered to help prevent cancer!

Learning Styles Addressed: Verbal/Linguistic, Visual/Spatial, Interpersonal, Intrapersonal, Mathematical/Logical, Emotional

Standards Addressed: Students will seek information from a variety of sources that include experts within their families and medical professionals.

Evaluation: The rubric for this lesson should acknowledge the extent to which the group conducts its research. Also included should be the impact of the PowerPoint or Hyperstudio presentation.

Modifications for Diverse Learners: Students may work in diverse cooperative groups. Adult assistance may be requested.

Variations: Students may hold a "Health Fair" to share their knowledge. The "Health Fair" may introduce health workers in the community.

Chapter Summary

Reading, writing, and discussion skills are important in social studies instruction. Modeling by the teacher is vital if students are to develop these communication skills. Recently published children's literature offers students new perspectives and insights into the social studies. The literature can be used not only to stimulate reading and discussion but also to suggest ideas for writing as well.

The writing process is composed of five stages: prewriting, drafting, revising, editing, and publishing/sharing. Through these stages, the students reflect on what they want to convey to their audience of readers and how their message will be interpreted. Among the different types of writing are narrative, poetic, persuasive, and expository writing.

An approach similar to the writing process should be introduced in reading. Students need to learn a variety of reading strategies for different types of text.

In developing communication skills, it is important to foster group interaction. Cooperative learning is one way to encourage the interdependence of students when conducting small-group activities or projects.

Reading, writing, and discussing are essential in the development and refinement of thinking skills. By encouraging the development of these skills, the classroom teacher can assist students in some very fundamental aspects of being a good citizen. Without these skills, it is questionable whether a democracy can exist.

Children's Literature Recommendations

Adler, D. 1991. *A Picture Book of Patrick Henry.* New York: Holiday House. Patrick Henry was one of the more vocal Founding Fathers. (Gr. 2–4)

Bausum, A. 2004. *With Courage and Cloth: Winning the Fight for a Woman's Right to Vote.* New York: Simon & Schuster and National Geographic. Details the period between 1906 and 1920 and the leaders in the women's suffrage movement. (Gr. 5–8)

Baylor, B. 1995. *I'm in Charge of Celebrations.* Illus. P. Parnall. New York: Aladdin. Rich prose tells of a child's desire to celebrate the important things in nature. (Gr. K–8)

Bodkin, O. 1998. *The Crane Wife.* Illus. G. Spirin. New York: Gulliver. A retelling of a popular love story. (Gr. K–8)

Bridgeman, R. 2002. *1,000 Inventions and Discoveries.* New York: DK Publishing. A history of significant inventions. (Gr. 4–8)

Bunting, E. 1988. *How Many Days to America?* Illus. B. Peck. Boston: Clarion. Boat people from the Caribbean flee to America. (Gr. 2–5)

Collins, M. 2003. *Airborne: A Photobiography of Wilbur and Orville Wright.* Washington, DC: National Geographic. A lively portrayal of the famous brothers of flight. (Gr. 4–8)

Freedman, R. 1997. *Lincoln: A Photobiography.* New York: Clarion. A tapestry of words are woven together in this rich biography of our sixteenth president. (Gr. 4–8)

Golenbock, P. 1992. *Teammates.* Illus. P. Bacon. San Diego: Harcourt Brace. When Jackie Robinson becomes the first African American to play in the major leagues, he is faced with shouts of racial slurs and forced to stay in "colored" hotels away from the team. But when Pee Wee Reese, a born Southerner and captain shortstop of the team, embraces Jackie on the field, the prejudice against Jackie dies down. (Gr. 2–7)

Harness, C. 1998. *Mark Twain and the Queens of the Mississippi.* New York: Simon & Schuster. Dramatic panoramas of the Mississippi River and its steamboats are accompanied by quotes from Samuel Clemens's writings in this picture book for older students. (Gr. 5–8)

Hoyt-Goldsmith, D. 1991. *Pueblo Storyteller.* Photo. L. Migdale. New York: Holiday House. A young Pueblo Indian girl, the tribal storyteller, tells the old tales of her tribe. (Gr. 4–8)

Katz, S. 2002. *Mrs. Brown on Exhibit and Other Museum Poems.* Illus. R. W. Alley. New York: Simon & Schuster. When your teacher is the field trip queen, be prepared to cavort from museum to museum. List of actual museums in every state is included at the back of the book. (Gr. K–5)

MacLachlan, P. 1985. *Sarah, Plain and Tall.* New York: Harper & Row. Sarah is a mail order bride who leaves her home in Maine to travel to the plains of Nebraska. (Gr. 3–5)

Marten, J., ed. 1998. *Lessons of War: The Civil War in Children's Magazines.* Wilmington, DE: Scholarly Resources. This is a collection of actual letters, articles, essays, and poetry from children's magazines from both the northern and southern states during the Civil War period. Good for intermediate through middle school. (Gr. 5–8)

Mochizuki, K. 1995. *Baseball Saved Us.* Illus. D. Lee. New York: Lee and Low. During World War II, young Japanese children living in the U.S. were sometimes separated from their parents who were sent to internment camps. Ken Mochizuki tells how baseball gave him and his friends a purpose in life and a way to pass the time. (Gr. 1–5)

Murphy, J. 1992. *The Long Road to Gettysburg.* New York: Prentice-Hall. This book gives an overview of the battle of Gettysburg as viewed through the eyes of a Confederate officer. Excellent for upper elementary and middle school students. (Gr. 4–8)

Myers, W. D. 1991. *Now Is Your Time! The African American Struggle for Freedom.* New York: HarperCollins. A nonfiction historical account of African Americans in America. (Gr. 5–8)

Nixon, J. L. 1992. *Land of Hope.* New York: Bantam Starfire. A young Jewish girl escapes Russia in the early 1900s and yearns for education. (Gr. 5–8)

———. 1993. *Land of Promise.* New York: Bantam Starfire. Kristyn leaves Sweden for a life on a Minnesota farm in the early 1900s. (Gr. 5–8)

———. 1994. *Land of Dreams.* New York: Bantam Starfire. Rose, an Irish Catholic, comes to America to live with her family in Chicago early in the twentieth century. (Gr. 5–8)

Paterson, K. 1991. *Lyddie.* New York: Dutton/Lodestar. Lyddie works in the cotton mills of Massachusetts during the Industrial Revolution. Child labor and harsh working conditions are explained in this book. (Gr. 4–8)

Paulsen, G. 1998. *Soldier's Heart: Being the Story of the Enlistment and Due Service of the Boy Charley Goddard in the First Minnesota Volunteers.* New York: Delacorte. Charley Goddard enlisted in the Union Army at age fifteen. Charley's first battle is Bull Run and later he fights at Gettysburg. (Gr. 5–8)

Rhodes, R. H., ed. 1991. *All for the Union: The Civil War Diary and Journal of Elisha Hunt Rhodes.* New York: Orion. Elisha Hunt Rhodes served in the Army of the Potomac from the battle of Bull Run through the surrender at Appomattox Courthouse. Superb reference material for middle schoolers. (Gr. 6–9)

Ritter, J. H. 1998. *Choosing Up Sides*. New York: Philomel. Luke tries to please his father but he's a talented southpaw pitcher. And his father, a conservative preacher, believes left-handedness is the devil's work. (Gr. 5–8)

Rylant, C. 1982. *When I Was Young in the Mountains*. Illus. D. Goode. New York: Dutton. This book portrays life in the Appalachian Mountains. (Gr. K–3)

St. George, J. 2002. *So You Want to Be an Inventor?* Illus. D. Small. New York: Philomel. The inventions of 40 inventors are shared. (Gr. 3–7)

Slate, J. 2002. *The Great Big Wagon that Rang: How the Liberty Bell Was Saved*. New York: Cavenish. Story of how farmers saved the Liberty Bell from the British. (Gr. K–3)

Stanley, J. 1992. *Children of the Dust Bowl: The True Story of the School at Weedpatch Camp*. New York: Crown. True stories of Oklahoma families who lived in Weedpatch Camp in California during the Great Depression. (Gr. 4–8)

Thimmesh, C. 2000. *Girls Think of Everything: Stories of Ingenious Inventions by Women*. Illus. M. Sweet. Boston: Houghton Mifflin. Scotchgard, Kevlar, liquid paper, windshield wipers, and other inventions by women are described in this interesting book. (Gr. 4–6)

———. 2002. *The Sky's the Limit: Stories of Discovery by Women and Girls*. Illus. M. Sweet. Boston: Houghton Mifflin. Discoveries of note such as the making of tools by chimpanzees by Jane Goodall and many others are examined in this book. (Gr. 5–8)

Turner, A. 1987. *Nettie's Trip South*. Illus. R. Himler. New York: Macmillan. The author depicts life in the South before the Civil War as her great-great-grandmother wrote about it in a diary. She sees a black person for the first time. Later she witnesses a slave auction. (Gr. 3–8)

Vagin, V. 1998. *The Enormous Carrot*. New York: Scholastic. A well-known Russian folktale about working together to get a deed accomplished. (Gr. K–3)

Weatherford, C., and B. O'Neill. 2005. *A Negro League Scrapbook*. Honesdale, PA: Boyd's Mill Press. An enriching overview of the Negro Baseball League, with several photos depicting the many outstanding players and the social conditions they faced during segregation. (Gr. 4–7)

Weitzman, D. 1982. *Windmills, Bridges, and Old Machines: Discovering Our Industrial Past*. New York: Macmillan. A nonfiction book that relates inventions to industrial efficiency. (Gr. 5–8)

Wisniewski, D. 1991. *Rain Player*. New York: Clarion. A Mayan Indian legend about a young boy who challenges the rain god to a ball game. (Gr. 1–8)

Yep, L. 1991. *Tongues of Jade*. Illus. D. Wiesner. New York: HarperCollins. Seventeen Chinese folktales are shared in this book. (Gr. 5–8)

Related Technology Tools

Web Sites

History Channel

    http://www.historychannel.com

    This Web site is the home of the History Channel. Periodically, activities accompanying movies and documentaries are shared for teachers to use with their students.

Library of Congress

    www.libraryspot.com

    This is a superb Web site for upper elementary and middle school students to use to conduct social studies research. This site is linked to more than 150 major libraries in the United States as well as all 50 state libraries and the Library of Congress.

www.americaslibrary.gov/cgi-bin/page.cgi

    Great site for students doing research

National Council for the Social Studies
www.ncss.org
This is the Web site of the National Council for the Social Studies.
UNICEF
http.www.unicef.org/voy
Voices of Youth is an Internet project of the United Nations Children's Fund (UNICEF). The site offers learning activities and materials. Online discussions include such topics as child labor, armed conflict, HIV/AIDS, and discrimination.
Writing and Reading Across the Curriculum Resources
www. indiana.edu/~ericrec/bks/wac.html
This site includes specific suggestions for implementing approaches to reading and writing in school social studies programs.
CNN Student News
http://www.cnn.com/EDUCATION
An interactive Web site for students. Teachers can access guides to daily programming on CNN.
Online English Grammar
www.edunet.com/english/grammar/index.cfm
Students can ask an "expert" questions regarding English grammar.
Citations
http://citationmachine.net
Provides citations in Modern Language Association (MLA) and American Psychological Association (APA) format.

WebQuests
Role of Women in World War II (Gr. 5–8)
http://www.spa.3.k12.sc.us/WebQuests.html

Software and Videos
Storybook Weaver Deluxe Upgrade. CD-ROM. The Learning Company. Available from www.amazon.com. Students ages 6–12 can write and illustrate their own stories in English or Spanish using over 1,000 story images. The text-to-speech feature lets students hear their story read aloud.
Kid Pix Studio Deluxe. CD-ROM. Broderbund. Available from www.amazon.com. Kid Pix Studio Deluxe is expertly designed, with a collection of 30 lesson plans that were created and used by teachers in classrooms across the country.

References

Abel, F., J. Hauwiller, and N. Vandeventer. 1989. "Using Writing to Teach Social Studies." *Social Studies* 80 (1): 17–20.

Alvermann, D., L. C. Smith, and J. E. Readance. 1985. "Prior Knowledge Activation and the Comprehension of Compatible and Incompatible Text." *Reading Research Quarterly* 20 (4): 420–36.

Augustine, D. K., K. D. Gruber, and L. R. Hanson. 1989/1990. "Cooperation Works!" *Educational Leadership* 47 (4): 4–7.

Banks, J. A. 1991/1992. "Multicultural Education for Freedom's Sake." *Educational Leadership* 49 (4): 32–35.

Barillas, M. 2001. "Literacy at Home: Honoring Parent Voices through Writing." *The Reading Teacher,* 54 (3): 302–8.

Boyer, E. L. 1990. "Civic Education for Responsible Citizens." *Educational Leadership* 48 (3): 4–7.

Burns, K. 1990. *The Civil War.* Videocassette series. Public Broadcasting System.

Buzzeo, T. 2003. "Exploring Social Studies: Shining the Light, Meeting the Standards: Books about Lighthouses." *Book Links* 12 (4): 51–57.

Calkins, L. M., and S. Harwayne. 1991. *Living Between the Lines.* Portsmouth, NH: Heinemann.

Culham, R. 2003. *6 + 1 Traits of Writing: The Complete Guide.* New York: Scholastic.

———. 2005. *6 + 1 Traits of Writing: The Complete Guide for the Primary Grades.* New York: Scholastic.

DeMott, B. 1990. "Why We Read and Write." *Educational Leadership* 47 (6): 6.

Ellis, A. K. 1998. *Teaching and Learning Elementary Social Studies.* 6th ed. Boston: Allyn & Bacon.

Farris, P. J. 1998. "Roulette Writing." *The Reading Teacher* 42 (1): 91.

———. 2005. *Language Arts: Process, Product, and Assessment.* 4th ed. Long Grove, IL: Waveland Press.

Farris, P. J., P. A. Nelson, and S. L'Allier. 2007. "Using Literature Circles with ELLs at the Middle School Level." *Middle School Journal.*

Gammill, D. M. 2006. "Learning the *Write* Way." *The Reading Teacher* 59 (8): 754–62.

Graves, D. H. 1983. *Writing: Teachers and Children at Work.* Portsmouth, NH: Heinemann.

Gunter, M. A., T. H. Estes, and J. H. Schwab. 1990. *Instruction: A Model Approach.* Boston: Allyn & Bacon.

Harvey, S. 2002. "Nonfiction Inquiry: Using Real Reading and Writing to Explore the World." *Language Arts* 80 (1): 12–22.

Harvey, S., and A. Goudvis. 2000. *Strategies That Work: Teaching Comprehension.* York, ME: Stenhouse.

Henderson, A. T., and N. Berla. 1994. *A New Generation of Evidence: The Family is Critical to Student Achievement.* Washington, DC: National Committee for Citizens in Education.

Henry, L. A. 2006. "SEARCHing for an Answer: The Critical Role of New Literacies while Reading on the Internet." *The Reading Teacher* 59 (7): 615–27.

Jacobson, J. M. 1989. "RESPONSE: An Interactive Study Technique." *Reading Horizons* 29 (2): 85–92.

Johnson, D. W., and R. T. Johnson. 1993. "What to Say to Advocates for the Gifted." *Educational Leadership* 50 (2): 44–47.

Kaltsounis, T. 1990. "Interrelationships between Social Studies and Other Curriculum Areas: A Review." *Social Studies* 81 (6): 283–86.

Kauffman, G., and K. Yoder. 1990. "Celebrating Authorship: A Process of Collaborating and Creating Meaning." In *Talking about Books*, ed. K. G. Short and K. M. Pierce, pp. 135–54. Portsmouth, NH: Heinemann.

Knoeller, C. P. 1994. "Negotiating Interpretations of Text: The Role of Student-Led Discussions in Understanding Literature." *Journal of Reading* 37: 572–80.

Kohn, A. 1996. *Beyond Discipline: From Compliance to Community.* Alexandria, VA: Association for Supervision and Curriculum Development.

Kuhrt, B. L. 1989. The Effects of Expressive Writing on the Composing and Learning Processes of Sixth-Grade Students on Social Studies. PhD diss., Northern Illinois University, DeKalb, IL.

Langer, J., and A. Applebee. 1987. *How Writing Shapes Thinking: A Study of Teaching and Learning* (NCTE Research Report No. 22). Urbana, IL: National Council of Teachers of English.

Loftis, S. S. 1996. "Women and the Way West." *Book Links* 5 (3): 29–41.

McGowan, T., and B. Guzzetti. 1991. "Promoting Social Studies Understanding through Literature-Based Instruction." *Social Studies* 33 (4): 16–21.

Marchisan, M. L., and S. R. Alber. 2001. "The Write Way: Tips for Teaching the Writing Process to Resistant Writers." *Intervention in School and Clinic* 36: 154–56.

Miller, F. 2000. "Biography Buddy: Interviewing Each Other." *Social Studies and the Young Child* 12 (3): 13–14.

Rico, G. L. 1983. *Writing the Natural Way.* Los Angeles: Tarcher.

Robinson, F. P. 1970. *Effective Study.* New York: Harper and Row.

Rosenblatt, L. 1978. *The Reader, the Text, and the Poem.* Carbondale: Southern Illinois University Press.

Santa, C., L. Havens, and S. Harrison. 1989. "Teaching Secondary Science through Reading, Writing, Studying, and Problem Solving." In *Content Area Reading and Learning*, ed. D. Lapp, J. Flood, and N. Farnan, pp. 137–51. Englewood Cliffs, NJ: Prentice-Hall.

Scales, P. 1995. "Studying the First Amendment." *Book Links* 5 (1): 20–24.

Schaps, E., and D. Solomon. 1990. "Schools and Classrooms as Caring Communities." *Educational Leadership* 48 (3): 38–42.

Schiller, L. 1996. "Coming to America: Community from Diversity." *Language Arts* 73 (1): 46–51.

Scott, J. E. 1994. "Literature Circles in the Middle School Classroom: Developing Reading, Responding, and Responsibility." *Middle School Journal* 26 (2): 37–41.

Sharan, Y., and S. Sharan. 1989/1990. "Group Investigation Expands Cooperative Learning." *Educational Leadership* 47 (4): 17–21.

Slavin, R. 1983. *Cooperative Learning.* New York: Longman.

Spache, G. D., and P. C. Berg. 1966. *The Art of Efficient Learning.* New York: Macmillan.

Tompkins, G. E. 2004. *Teaching Writing.* 4th ed. Columbus, OH: Merrill.

———. 2005. *Language Arts: Content and Teaching Strategies.* 6th ed. Columbus, OH: Merrill.

Walley, C. 1991. "Diaries, Logs, and Journals in the Elementary Classroom." *Childhood Education* 67 (3): 149–54.

> *A child's world is one that supports questioning minds by offering a variety of "doings" designed to satisfy and extend a child's natural sense of wonder.*
>
> —George W. Maxim,
> Social Studies and the Elementary School Child, *6th ed.*

Chapter Eight

Early Childhood Social Studies

Billie Jo Thomas, Northern Illinois University

CHAPTER OUTLINE

Introduction	Methods and Developmental Limitations
Early Childhood	Techniques of Interdisciplinary Instruction
Curriculum Content and Social Studies	Sample Social Studies Activities
Egocentrism and Eight Circles of Awareness	Chapter Summary

CHAPTER OBJECTIVES

Readers will

- become familiar with early childhood social studies curriculum content;
- understand the eight circles of awareness;
- be able to demonstrate techniques of interdisciplinary instruction in teaching preschool through second grade students; and
- understand the role of interdisciplinary instruction in early childhood social studies.

Introduction

Integrating social studies instruction enables children to be active participants in their learning. At the early childhood level, this translates into many opportunities for firsthand social studies experiences. These experiences should be accompanied by the students' language questioning to discover more information, probing ideas, making connections with previously gained knowledge, and making predictions about what to expect next.

Literacy and language are part of everything the teacher does in the classroom. There is no need to set aside a special time for language or literacy development when instruction is integrated. Regardless of the discipline, students will be using spoken language, listening skills, nonverbal communication, music, pictures, books, writing instruments, and field trips. This approach is successful from early childhood through postdoctoral education. Young children, in their desire to learn about the world around them, practice oral and written language skills, nonverbal communication, and print awareness that create later literacy (Seefeldt 1997).

"Learning to deal with the words in reading and writing is part of developing literacy, but it is not the ultimate goal, which is meaning construction" (Cooper 1997, 167). Hence, for the young child, integrating social studies and reading and writing is a natural combination.

If equal instructional time is devoted to physical, cognitive, social, and emotional development, teachers should spend 25 percent of their instructional time on the social studies knowledge base. They cannot wait until children are in fourth grade to begin teaching social studies for the same reasons they would not wait until then to teach mathematics or literacy. Fourth grade is too late; children's basic attitudes and concepts are formed by then. Lessons in which 25 percent of the curriculum content comes from social studies will help shape the citizens of tomorrow.

Early Childhood

Early childhood is the period of development from birth to eight years of age. It includes infants, toddlers, and children in nursery school, kindergarten, and grades one through three. This chapter focuses on methods, materials, and activities for preschool through grade 2 students. The traditional early childhood curriculum areas are language arts, science, mathematics, physical development, social studies, fine arts, and creativity.

While children differ in gender, personality, learning style, talents, language, cultural backgrounds, and in other ways, all children have the capacity to learn from their experiences. As teachers of social studies, we must combine academic and natural learning by creating environments that interest students while adhering to curriculum standards. Teaching this way leads to the development of genuine understanding as it blends academic knowledge, application, social learning, and higher order thinking while it strikes a cord with students' interests and motivation to learn (Caine and Caine 2006).

Curriculum Content and Social Studies

Each curriculum area contains a body of knowledge that includes vocabulary, facts, and concepts defining the discipline. This body of knowledge is what educators call curriculum content. Information is the content of the lesson being taught about the discipline (Brown and Brown 1985; Smith 1982). This chapter addresses the matter of how to teach the curriculum content for social studies in preschool through second grade through an interdisciplinary approach based on social studies standards.

Social studies content is taken from the knowledge base concerning human groups and how they behave. Emotional studies and social studies are often confused in classrooms. A simple way to differentiate them is to think of emotional as internal and social as external. The subject of emotional studies involves learning about what takes place within the individual. Feelings such as love, hate, fear, anxiety, hope, and so forth are part of the emotional knowledge base. Social studies, on the other hand, always involves at least two people. The social studies knowledge base thus refers to groups, whether large or small in number.

Sometimes there is confusion about the difference between the social studies knowledge base and the social process of being in groups in the classroom. Preschool teachers sometimes say, "I teach social studies during recess and lunch." However, this is incorrect because these teachers are not transmitting information from the social studies knowledge base to the child. The child is in a social situation, but we are often in social situations. This does not mean we are learning anything from a knowledge base. Being in a social group does not mean we are learning social studies; we may even be in a social group learning about another knowledge base, such as science or music (Charlesworth and Lund 1990).

The traditional social studies curriculum at the preschool and lower grade levels focuses on content that teaches about groups of people in terms of the following: current topics, economics, geography, history, and international and global education. A brief description of each area follows with a few samples of content.

The content of *current topics* varies, depending on current topics of interest in the newspaper, on television, in the family, and in the community. Common topic content includes political concepts, environment, peace and war, safety, news, and career education.

The content of *economics* in preschool and kindergarten includes information about *wants and needs* (there is a big difference between the two, as well as between supply and demand), *doing without* (to paraphrase a popular rock song, when you request something, you may not get what you want but you may get something you need), and *money,* such as types of paper and coins, different countries' currency, and what money represents.

The content of *geography* in preschool and kindergarten includes information about the *earth,* such as roundness, movement, earth, sky, and water; *direction,* such as east, west, north, south, up, and down; *location,* such as poles, equator, beside, between, through, and on top of; *regions,* such as awareness of oceans, continents, halves, and so on; and *maps* as print experiences and a beginning awareness of maps representing something else in the real world.

The content of *history* in preschool and kindergarten includes information about developmentally appropriate approaches to *time,* such as yesterday, today and tomorrow; *change,* such as growth, beginnings, and endings; *continuity of human life,* such as child, parents, grandparents, great-grandparents; *the past,* such as the pet Daddy had when he was a little boy, Daddy's baby picture, and so forth; and *holidays,* such as the Fourth of July, Thanksgiving, and birthdays.

The content of *international and global education* taps a wide range of a child's previously gained knowledge. Developmentally appropriate content would include *children* in different nations, *families* around the world, *similarities* in people (for example, all people eat and have or had mothers), *conflict* between nations, and the *interdependence* of people (Why does it matter to us what happens in Somalia or China?).

Egocentrism and Eight Circles of Awareness

In early childhood, in all five of the social studies curriculum areas, the child learns first about himself or herself. The three main areas of interest for young children are *me, myself,* and *I.* **Egocentrism** is the starting point for *all* curriculum areas in early childhood; then learning broadens into wider and wider circles of awareness, each directly linked to the children's *me, myself,* and *I.* The eight circles shown in figure 8.1 represent the levels of awareness about self, family, neighborhood, community, state, nation, world, and universe.

Teachers should be familiar with the eight circles of awareness because children learn the values, beliefs, and stereotypes of the community in which they live (Banks 1992). By being introduced to the contributions of other cultures, children can learn to celebrate the diversity of humankind. When teachers help them to discover diversity, starting with their own classmates, children can learn to respect and appreciate the differences that are part of their daily lives. The examples in figures 8.2, 8.3, and 8.4 help children become aware of that diversity as they expand their circles of awareness.

To understand how a child's awareness of the social studies environment moves from the egocentrism of self through the other seven encompassing circles, one could consider a specific topic, for instance, hair color, food preferences, means of transportation to school, or ways of celebrating certain family events. Let's take the specific topic of hair color as an example. First, the child learns about his or her own hair color, then about the hair color of family members and close friends, then

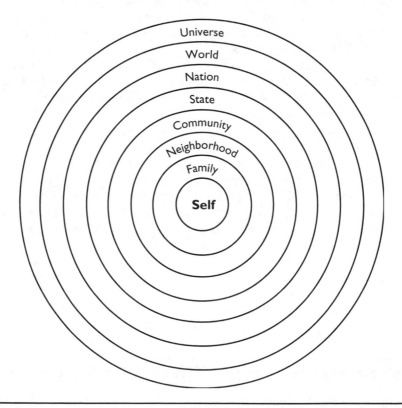

Figure 8.1   The child's widening awareness of the social studies environment.

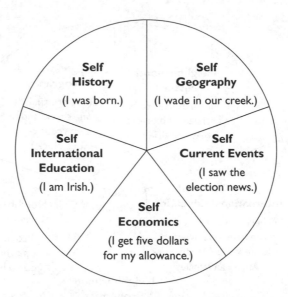

Figure 8.2   Examples of concepts of self in the five social studies curriculum areas.

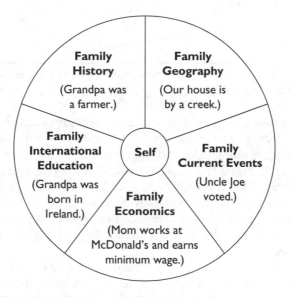

Figure 8.3   Examples of family building on self in the five social studies curriculum areas.

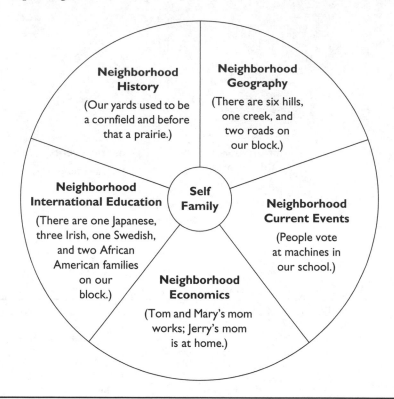

Figure 8.4 Examples of neighborhood building on self and family in the five social studies curriculum areas.

about the hair color of neighbors and community acquaintances. Next, the child begins to form an impressionistic awareness of people (usually somehow related to him or her) in other states and their hair color, say, Grandpa's and Uncle Joe's; then the child begins to gain an awareness that people everywhere have hair and it has color. First, however, the child must learn about his or her hair; then the child relates further knowledge to himself or herself. The child must be exposed through whole language experiences to the vocabulary, facts, and concepts so that she or he can formulate mental ideas about hair color and acquire sufficient vocabulary to learn more.

Figure 8.1 illustrates how the child builds one concept of hair color from the inner, self dimension through the other seven levels to the universe dimension. The five areas of the social studies curriculum all build on these eight levels of awareness. Each level builds on the foundation of the previous narrower one. Figure 8.2 provides examples of activities for the self-dimension for each of the five curriculum areas. A good book to share with kindergarteners and preschoolers is *The Hello, Goodbye Window* by Norton Jester (2005) in which a youngster sees people passing by the house, each engaged in doing different and distinctive activities.

Figure 8.3 gives examples of activities for the family dimension and shows how this dimension builds around self. The recently published picture book *Raisin and Grape* (Amico and Proimos 2006) shares a grandfather's visit plus reasons why grandparents sometimes do the things they do, a perfect book for kindergarteners and first graders as they explore families. Figure 8.4 gives examples of how neighborhood builds around family, which has built around self.

First grade social studies units generally focus on the family unit and expand to communities in second grade. Second graders can reflect on *In November* (Rylant 2000) in which the author shares the sights, smells, noises, and the like of this special month. For instance November food is "an orange smell. A squash and pumpkin smell." After sharing as a read-aloud students can then create a class book later in the school year for January or May to present a distinct contrast to November.

Methods and Developmental Limitations

To be successful in early childhood classrooms, interdisciplinary instruction must operate within certain limitations that apply to all early childhood learning. Activities must be concrete, real, and relevant to the child and his or her world; they must be child directed (this implies choices by the child). Detailed guidelines provided by the National Association for the Education of Young Children (NAEYC) appear in Bredekamp (1987).

Simply put, *concrete* means that the materials can be perceived by the senses of touch, sight, hearing, smell, and taste (Gilbert 1989). *Real* means that the actual object should be there. For example, if you're talking about an orange, use a real one rather than a plastic one or a picture of one or a story of one. Young children engage in optimal learning when they use their senses to explore something real.

☞ **IN THE CLASSROOM**

Thematic Unit: Getting Along with Others, Grades 1–3

Ada, A. F. 2000. *Frog Friend.* Illus. L. Lohstoeter. New York: Scholastic. Great book to talk about becoming a friend with someone who is different. (Gr. K–2)

Carlson, N. 1989. *I Like Me.* New York: Viking Penguin. This is an upbeat book about the importance of liking yourself. (Gr. K–2)

Cosby, B. 1998. *The Meanest Thing to Say.* Illus. V. P. Honeywood. New York: Cartwheel. Part of the Little Bill series, two friends have a disagreement.

Cutler, J. 1993. *Darcy and Grams Don't Like Babies.* Illus. Susannah Ryan. New York: Scholastic. A little girl adjusts to having a new sibling. (Gr. K–2)

Duffey, B. 1990. *The Math Whiz.* Illus. J. Wilson. New York: Viking Penguin. Marty can solve any math problem but he hates P.E. He resolves it with some help from his teacher. (Gr. 2–3)

Golenbock, P. 1990. *Teammates.* Illus. P. Bacon. San Diego, CA: Harcourt Brace. The true story of the friendship between Pee Wee Reese, an all-star shortstop, and Jackie Robinson, the first African American to play major league baseball. They were teammates on the Brooklyn Dodgers. (Gr. 2–3)

Heine, H. 1986. *Friends.* New York: Aladdin. Imagine a rooster, a mouse, and a pig as best friends. As they go through the day they each make a contribution to the various games they play. And in the end they learn to accept each other's uniqueness. (Gr. K–3)

Kellogg, S. 1986. *Best Friends*. New York: Dial. Kathy is jealous of Louise, who gets to go away to summer camp. When Louise returns and gets a new puppy, Kathy feels sorry for herself. In the end, the two girls share the puppy. (Gr. K–3)

Leverich, K. 1991. *Best Enemies, AGAIN*. New York: Morrow. Priscilla and Felicity find it difficult to get along. Felicity always picks on Priscilla until one day Felicity gets her due reward. (Gr. 2–3)

Moore, I. 1991. *Little Dog Lost*. New York: Macmillan. The importance of making new friends and of cooperating with others are the themes of this book. Two lonely children who have recently moved to the country make friends who help them find their lost dog. (Gr. K–3)

Raschka, C. 1993. *Yo? Yes!* New York: Orchard. Two young boys from different cultures strike up a friendship. (Gr. K–4)

Rohmann, E. 2002. *My Friend Rabbit*. Boston: Millbrook. Mouse talks of his friend, Rabbit, who means well but who has a penchant for trouble. (Gr. K–2)

Rylant, C. 1998. *Poppleton and Friends*. Illus. M. Teague. Poppleton the Pig learns the value of having friends. (Gr. Preschool–1)

Steig, W. 1971. *Amos and Boris*. New York: Farrar, Straus, and Giroux. This is the classic picture book that has friendship as a major theme. It also points out that size is not really important. (Gr. K–3)

Zamorano, A. 1997. *Let's Eat!* Illus. J. Vivas. New York: Scholastic. Set in Spain, this is a delightful story of a family preparing for the birth of a new baby. (Gr. K–3)

Primary Focus Book

For this thematic unit, *Amos and Boris* is read aloud with the class. As the teacher reads the book, questions can be posed.

How did Amos become friends with Boris?

Why would Amos want to be Boris's friend? Why would Boris want to be Amos's friend?

How can Amos save Boris?

Why didn't Amos go out during low tide?

Have you ever had a good friend move away? How did it make you feel?

What makes someone a best friend?

The next day, read aloud *My Friend Rabbit*. Have the students describe Mouse's friend. Make a Venn diagram to compare and contrast Mouse and Rabbit.

Suggested Activities

• Have students draw pictures of themselves playing or working with a friend.

• Have students write about a time they had a disagreement with a friend or a brother or sister. How did they resolve it?

• Discuss ways to get along with a bully.

• Have students list three things they like about themselves.

• Bring in an assortment of poetry about friends and read a poem each day to the class. Write the poem on chart paper and read it through with the class three or four times during the day. Give each student a copy to put in a ring binder as part of their own poetry collection.

• Invite the students to help create a bulletin board on friends. What would they like included? Who will be responsible for each part?

• The students may draw pictures of something they like to do with a friend.

• The children can write a poem about a friend with the help of the teacher, a teacher's aide, or an older student.

• The students can make a collage of things that friends do together.

• If a student has moved away, the class can write letters and mail them to the student's new address.

Putting students in small groups allows the teacher to focus on concept development as well as to assess overall growth in social studies surroundings.

While doing this, they acquire vocabulary about the real thing. In the case of an orange, words such as *round, soft, color, orange, peel, sweet,* and *juicy* might constitute acquired vocabulary. *Relevant* means that what the child is learning about should be present in the child's natural environment. Therefore, the child would be expected to use this material or behavior in his or her home or community. For example, we teach young children about cars, buses, and trains (always remember the egocentrism and start with the family's main mode of transportation, be it bicycle, bus, or car) before we teach them about rickshaws. We teach first about what is concrete, real, and relevant. And when we use realia and manipulatives that children can see, touch, smell, and taste, we are also helping our English language learners to develop new vocabulary in English, along with conceptual knowledge.

Rosemary Wells's (2004) *My Kindergarten* presents in context for youngsters the distinct events of a typical school year including introducing democracy, as the students vote to indicate their preference, as well as other events, such as recess, Valentine's Day, and so on. Another relevant activity is the celebration of the first 100 days of school, something most kindergarten and first grade classrooms do. Having students collect special items to total one hundred (Popsicle sticks, polka dots, ribbons, yogurt tops, etc.) and then having a celebration on the 100th day can make for an interesting gathering. Sharing *100th Day Worries* by Margery Cutler (2000) depicting a child who worries about everything, particularly what to collect for the 100th day of school, will touch a chord with more than one student. An accompanying book is *Miss Bindergarten Celebrates the 100th Day of School* (Slate 2002), a rollicking rhyme of animals from A to Z who share their unusual collections can entice children to thinking about how their own collection is like or different from that of their classmates. And yet another book on this topic is Rosemary Wells's (2000) *Emily's First 100 Days of School*, in which Emily's teacher teaches students to find something new every day (five different vegetables in her father's vegetable soup to 51 reasons why Emily's older sister can't go to the city with her friends, to only 89 calories in her tomato soup, and so on).

Returning to the orange example, we teach about oranges, bananas, and other familiar fruits because we can make certain that we have them for a class snack. Later, in the intermediate grades, teachers can help children build on these early concrete, hands-on experiences and, after physical brain development is complete, relate them to kiwis, kumquats, tangelos, and other fruits.

There are limits to the type of abstract language and abstract thinking that children under eight years of age can engage in because of their normal but incomplete physical brain and nerve development. What concerns us here is that children in preschool and kindergarten need to choose from developmentally appropriate hands-on activities that are concrete, real, and relevant to their world (Bredekamp 1987; Hamilton and Flemming 1990; Hunt and Renfro, 1982).

The NAEYC defines what is developmentally appropriate in terms of age and the individual (Bredekamp 1987, 2):

> *Age appropriateness.* Human development research indicates that there are universal, predictable sequences of growth and change that occur in children during the first 9 years of life. These predictable changes occur in all domains of development—physical, emotional, social, and cognitive. Knowledge of typical development of children within the age span served by the program provides a framework from which teachers prepare the learning environment and plan appropriate experiences.

> *Individual appropriateness.* Each child is a unique person with an individual pattern and timing of growth, as well as individual personality, learning style, and family background. Both the curriculum and adults' interactions with children should be responsive to individual differences. Learning in young children is the result of interaction between the child's thoughts and experiences with materials, ideas, and people. These experiences should match the child's developing abilities while also challenging the child's interest and understanding.

Techniques of Interdisciplinary Instruction

With a knowledge of the limitations on how young children learn, teachers can use developmentally appropriate, child-directed, hands-on activities with concrete, real, and relevant materials. They need to use the child's egocentrism and ever-widening social perspective (Piaget 1952), represented by the eight circles of awareness, as the foundation for their social studies curriculum plans. Building on this foundation, teachers are able to use an interdisciplinary approach in teaching the social studies curriculum content. Appropriate techniques include teaching vocabulary, facts, and concepts through speaking and listening vocabulary; dictated and written stories; books, magazines, and other printed materials; the child's drawn pictures and written print; nonverbal communication; field trips and print in the environment; and music.

Speaking and Listening Vocabulary

Speaking and listening vocabulary is built into everything teachers do in the classroom. The one-on-one "good morning" greeting between teacher and child is an example of social development while language and literacy skills are also being expanded. Films, DVDs, and videotapes also aid vocabulary development. Other sample activities follow. The primary curriculum content area for each is given in parentheses.

- Informal small group discussion about the aquarium during free playtime (science).
- Large-group discussion with a classroom visitor from another country, such as France (social studies).
- Experimentation with the five types of magnets in the science corner (science).
- Listening for higher or lower (or louder or softer) sounds on the new instruments on the music table (music).
- Talking about and looking for the mile markers on a field trip (mathematics).
- Playing in the sociodramatic play area while dressing, talking, and listening like a chosen character would (social development).
- Describing facial expressions in pictures held by the teacher, and discussing when they are appropriate and when they are not (emotional development).
- Telephoning ill classmates from the principal's office to say the class misses them and hopes they are well soon (social development).
- Making pancakes: measuring, stirring, baking, and following the rebus-picture recipe (physical development and mathematics).

In all the foregoing activities, the main content knowledge base being taught is language or literacy. However, all the activities will directly develop skills necessary for early literacy, important for mastering learning in social studies.

Morning Message

The morning message is a terrific activity to engage young students in social studies. Typically the teacher establishes the framework of the message so it includes the date, day of the week, and the primary information to be shared that day. Writing on the white board, the teacher can stretch students' social studies knowledge. At the first grade level, the teacher may point out the features of the town in which the students live as the morning message for an entire week. For instance,

Monday, September 18, 2006
Today is Joey's birthday.
Today is sunny.
We live in Omaha, Nebraska,
on the banks of the
Missouri River.

Tuesday, September 19, 2006
Today is a rainy day.
Omaha was where Indian tribes lived.

Wednesday, September 20, 2006
Today is cloudy.
Many pioneers stopped at Omaha
as they moved westward.

Thursday, September 21, 2006
Today is sunny. It is PE day.
Trains brought cattle and hogs to Omaha.

Friday, September 22, 2006
Today is sunny. It is "Hot Dog" day!
Hurrah!
Omaha meatpackers shipped beef and hogs back
to the eastern cities. They made hot dogs, too.

Thus in a week's time span, the first graders have a thumbnail history of their hometown. The teacher can combine phonics instruction with the social studies lesson by having students write the morning message on lined paper on clipboards and then underlining the phonics chunks to be taught that day. For instance the *sun* of sunny or *cat* of cattle. At the end of the week, the teacher may send a weekly newsletter home with the students containing all of the morning messages for the week along with other information and learning activities.

Language Experience Approach

The Language Experience Approach (LEA) supports having young students dictate their thoughts to the teacher or an aide who writes them down exactly as the child presented the information. The teacher then reads aloud what was written and the child then reads along with the teacher. This is a great activity for beginning readers and writers as well as ELLs who may not have sufficient command of English words and spelling to compose a piece in a reasonable amount of time. Whole class LEA stories and informational summaries can be written on chart paper and then taped or posted around the classroom for reference by the students. From time to time the teacher can have the students "read the room" and reshare the written LEA pieces.

Sharing books such as the Arthur series by Marc Brown, Henry and Mudge books by Cynthia Rylant, Judy Moody books by Megan McDonald, and the irascible Ramona books by Beverly Cleary help students deal with the everyday events of life as a young child—loosing a tooth, dealing with a bully, having a pesky sibling. LEA stories can then be enriched as the budding writer gleans vocabulary from the books shared as read-alouds by the teacher and in his or her own reading to create stories. The students move from LEA to their own writing, using temporary or invented spelling (as students are in late kindergarten and early first grade) to jot down their thoughts.

Letters, Songs, and Lists as Social Studies Resources

Along with dictated and written stories, teachers can use letters, songs, and lists across the curriculum. Social studies content activities, such as the French visitor mentioned above, often lend themselves to dictated, written communications such as invitations, time schedules, maps of where to park and how to find the classroom, thank-you notes, an order for a thank-you flower arrangement, and so on. Because of their developmental level, most kindergartners and preschoolers verbally dictate these to the teacher, who then prints them for the children. The teacher should print each communication exactly as dictated, errors included, because it is the children's creation.

Although a child may write an entire message alone, this does not always happen at the kindergarten level. Most five-year-olds should be able to sign their name and, using invented spelling, print a few letters or words. Oftentimes they will draw a picture and label it with a letter or series of letters. It should be noted that it is harmful to force young children to copy words and phrases over and over. By first grade, children are using invented, or temporary, spelling as they move toward conventional spelling.

Teachers should be aware that children from first language backgrounds other than English often have different patterns in their inventive spelling. For example, native Spanish-speaking children will use more vowels in their writing, whereas native English-speaking children will use more consonants (Escamilla 2000). Other languages will likely exhibit patterns that are different than English inventive spelling. This is a natural progression in children's acquisition of a second language.

"Picture storybooks provide many sources for expressive and imaginative writing" (Norton 2003, 259). Norton believes that by having children write letters to friends, family members, teachers, and librarians they will be encouraged to write expressively. She suggests such books as *The Jolly Postman* (Ahlberg and Ahlberg 1986), a book in which a postman delivers letters to fairy-tale characters such as the Three Bears, the Big Bad Wolf, and Cinderella, and *Stringbean's Trip to the Shining Sea* (Williams 1988), in which a boy sends postcards back home during a camping trip across the United States.

Here are some examples of other social studies content activities that involve writing:

- Writing to the local mass transit authority for information about the system
- Writing a history of the child's life or a family history
- Writing a shopping list for purchases at the grocery store
- Writing to a kindergarten class in a foreign country
- Writing to a local politician
- Writing to the president of the United States
- Writing to someone the child has seen on the television news or in the newspaper

Having children write about their own life after hearing a story about another child lets children understand that there are similarities among children and their families. For instance, *My Father's Boat* (Garland 1998) is the story of a Vietnamese boy whose father teaches him how to fish. The story tells of how the grandfather taught the boy's father to fish. The book is based on the Vietnamese proverb, "When you are young, you need your father; when you are old, you need your son." After hearing the story, children can write and illustrate about something they were taught by a parent or grandparent or guardian. Children whose English language resources are still developing can also participate in the activity by making drawings that tell a story or illustrate a process, and adding labels or short phrases according to their ability levels.

Books, Magazines, and Other Printed Materials

As discussed earlier, all printed materials used in the classroom should be concrete, real, and relevant to the lives of young children. This means that they should not be specially published just for education. They should exist outside of classrooms and be found, instead, in such environments as the home, workplace, grocery store, church, gas station, and so forth. Books written for young children's enjoyment, such as fairy tales, nursery rhymes, and popular tales like *The Very Hungry Caterpillar* (Carle 1986), *Lilly's Purple Plastic Purse* (Henkes 1996), *Lilly's Big Day* (Henkes 2006), *Chrysanthemum* (Henkes 1991), and *Koala Lou* (Fox 1989) are also good choices because they were not created just to meet language or literacy goals (such as learning five new vocabulary words per day).

A well-stocked book corner is an asset to any early childhood classroom. It should include a wide variety of books, including mail-order catalogs, a first encyclopedia, phone books, nursery rhymes, fairy tales, big books (both commercially published and those made in class), modern books, traditional fables, poetry, children's magazines (such as *Ladybug, Spider, Appleseed,* and *Our Big Outdoors*—see chapter 7), brochures, music, and maps. A common rule of thumb is to have six books for each child in the class. By displaying the books in a gutter under the white board so that the front of each book is prominently displayed, children will be more apt to pick them up and peruse them. It is important to change the featured books every two to three weeks as well as to allow the children to have daily browsing time. This enables students to choose their books. A rack of colorful plastic bins labeled with blue dots for folktales and fairy tales, yellow for informational books, green for chapter books, and so forth, teaches the students to be responsible for returning the books to their proper category just by looking at the code on the bin and the color of the dot pasted on the front cover of the book.

Books should also reflect the diversity within the classroom and the community so that children see themselves represented in these stories. This might include books whose contents or characters reflect different cultures, ethnicities, religions, genders, physical and mental abilities, social classes, and so forth. Books that reflect the children's own lives engage their personal interest and also invite them to look at different aspects of other people's lives.

The books and other printed materials should include content from all curriculum areas, including social studies. Examples of books that contain information from the social studies knowledge base are listed in the Children's Literature Recommendations section at the end of this chapter. Suggestions for antibias criteria for the selection of books for young children are given in chapter 4. In addition, Huck, Hepler, Hickman, and Kiefer (2004) provide lists of books celebrating culturally diverse families.

Interactive Storybook Read-Alouds

All children benefit from interactive storybook read-alouds, particularly those with limited experiences with books. Such reading builds vocabulary, language development in terms of sentence structure, and literacy understanding as well as encourage oral responses to literature. From time to time, the teacher stops during interactive storybook reading to pose questions that lead the students to understanding the text. Thus, as the storybook is used as a read-aloud, the teacher supports it with ongoing conversation that helps the students use the book's content to reveal its meaning by putting bits and pieces of information together.

The following steps are suggested to present a successful interactive read-aloud:

- Select a high-interest book with rich language and multiple layers of meaning.
- If a picture book or chapter book, the plots should be absorbing plots and the characters lively, appealing.
- If an informational book, the information shared should be appealing and accurate while still being presented in rich language and having multiple layers of meaning.
- Read the book to yourself three times—once silently, followed by an oral reading, then again silently, the last time to plan goals for the listeners.
- Identify and use sticky notes in the portions of the book where children should predict what will happen next, discuss, reflect, or connect (to self, other texts, or the world).
- Anticipate where you may need to do some back filling of student knowledge (i.e., unknown vocabulary such as "curds and whey," describing a procedure such as churning butter, and so on).
- Consider how you might entice students to participate in the read-aloud (join in on repetitive phrases, etc.).
- Be prepared for students who jump in unexpectedly with comments—be flexible but don't let a student get the group off task and on another tangent.
- After sharing the read-aloud, have a means of sharing it a second time within a few days, perhaps having the children consider another tack or dimension of the story.

The list of books below make for good interactive fiction read-alouds in social studies.

Cooney, Barbara. 1982. *Miss Rumphius.* New York: Viking.
Fleming, Candace. 2001. *Who Invited You?.* New York: Atheneum.
Fleming, Candace. 2004. *This is the Baby.* New York: Farrar, Strauss, and Giroux.
Fleming, Denise. 1993. *In the Small, Small Pond.* New York: Holt.
Henkes, Kevin. 1996. *Lilly's Purple Plastic Purse.* New York: Greenwillow.
Henkes, Kevin. 2006. *Lilly's Big Day.* New York: Greenwillow.
Lobel, Arnold. 1970. *Frog and Toad Are Friends.* New York: Harper & Row.
Rathman, Peggy. 1995. *Officer Buckle and Gloria.* New York: Putnam.
Taback, Simms. 1999. *Joseph Had a Little Overcoat.* New York: Viking.
Yolen, Jane. 2000. *Off We Go!.* New York: Little Brown.

The list of informational books below is recommended for social studies.

Adler, David. 2005. *George Washington.* New York: Holiday House.
Chandra, D., and M. Comora. 2003. *George Washington's Teeth.* New York: Farrar.
Cole, Henry. 1997. *Jack's Garden.* New York: Harper Trophy.
Gibbons, Gail. 1986. *The Post Office Book.* New York: Holiday House.

Gibbons, Gail. 1987. *Fire! Fire!*. New York: Holiday House.
Gibbons, Gail. 1990. *Farming*. New York: Holiday House.
Gibbons, Gail. 1998. *Knights in Shining Armor.* New York: Holiday House.
Gibbons, Gail. 2006. *Ice Cream: The Full Scoop.* New York: Holiday House.
Houston, Gloria. 1991. *My Great Aunt Arizona.* New York: Harper.

Informational books can share a wealth of social studies topics during the interactive read-aloud, hitting upon more than one social science. For instance, Gail Gibbons's *Ice Cream: The Full Scoop* (2006) weaves a historical tale with Marco Polo's travels to China where he learned about spices, silks, and ice cream. The book goes on to share that Thomas Jefferson would bring to America the recipe for this delectable dessert. The ingenuity of an ice cream vendor at the World's Fair in St. Louis who rolled waffles into cones to serve as eatable, portable dishes reveals a lesson in economics.

Drawing Pictures and Writing Print

Drawing and writing require eye–hand coordination, visual discrimination, and fine muscle development, all of which are necessary for literacy. It is important that from day one in kindergarten, the teacher demonstrate how to properly grip a pencil for drawing and writing—then make certain the children use the grip. Have the students put a pencil on the table in front of them and point it at their bellybutton. Then using the thumb and index finger, pick up the pencil where the bare wood meets the paint, use the middle finger to flip the pencil up and rest upon.

Regardless of what children are drawing or writing, eye–hand coordination, visual discrimination, and fine muscle control are skills that develop anyway, but for some children sooner than others. Drawing a flower is of as much benefit as printing a capital *P* over and over. If a child chooses to print the *P* over and over again, that is acceptable; otherwise, the skills will develop as the child uses instruments to draw or write whatever she or he wants to draw or write.

Five-year-olds practice using pencils, pens, markers, and crayons. They also need paper that is at least 11 inches by 14 inches. A variety of writing instruments and kinds of paper are desirable so that children can learn about the physical limitations of each kind.

Nonverbal Communication

Gestures, dress, and facial expressions are types of **nonverbal communication.** Young children need to learn to discern meaning when nonverbal communication accompanies verbal communication. For example, someone yelling, "Stop!" with a smile on her face is communicating something very different from someone yelling, "Stop!" with a fist held up. Following are some other examples of activities involving nonverbal communication; again, curriculum content areas are given in parentheses. All these activities contribute to literacy and language development.

- The look on the bus driver's face when all 30 of us board the city bus (social development).

- A class discussion about what we and others do with our mouths when we are angry, happy, sad, and so on (social development).

- Reading a story about a girl who is afraid of flying and how her body expresses fear (emotional development).

Discussing nonverbal communication in a diverse classroom is a perfect opportunity to invite children to share and compare gestures that they, their family, relatives, or neighbors use that might be different from (or the same as) what other people use. Teachers can also investigate some culturally different gestures and ask students to consider them, such as pointing with one's lips (Puerto Rico) or beckoning someone by wiggling one's fingers with the palm facing outward (Philippines).

Field Trips and Print in the Environment

Field trips and print in the environment stimulate so much spoken language and discussion, trigger so much new vocabulary, and provide so many concrete, real, and relevant materials and activities that almost everything about them contributes directly to language and literacy development. Written communication is stimulated through invitations, thank-you notes, maps, and so forth. Print is available everywhere in the environment, and children are motivated to read or pay attention to signs and then later to follow up with books and stories. Some field trips with content in various curriculum areas, but still developing literacy, are trips to the following places:

- Science museum (science)
- Bakery (social studies)
- Grocery store (social studies, mathematics)
- Mathematics academy (mathematics)
- Music store (music)
- Circus (physical education, social studies)
- Garden (science, social studies)

Programs for young children should include as many field trips as time allows. One transported trip per month and another as a walking field trip per week are a minimum.

Field trips are useful in all areas of social studies as indicated in the following:

- History: visit our old park, our old school, our old classroom.
- Economics: visit stores, banks, factories.
- Current events: visit a newspaper office, television station.
- International education: visit homes of people from other nations, ethnic museums.
- Geography: visit hills, lakes, mountains, islands, whatever is in the local environment.

Music

Music involves auditory communication, written communication through notes, visual memory, pattern repetition, visual discrimination, and so on. It is an important component of any integrated approach, and the skills developed through music are directly applicable to literacy and language skills. The following music activities for the social studies content area would be desirable for literacy development:

- Writing to a kindergarten class in Honduras and asking what their favorite songs are.
- Playing tone bells or the xylophone by color coded musical notes. (The C tone bell, xylophone C bar, and the C note on the music sheet are all red; B is blue on all; C is yellow; and so on.)
- Listening to different kinds of recorded music and identifying what country the music is from, such as jig, polka, can-can.
- Listening to musical selections such as a funeral dirge, the "Wedding March," and Sousa marches and deciding when it is appropriate to play each and when it is not.

Sample Social Studies Activities

Examples of general plans for vocabulary, materials, and content are shown in the following outline. The outline includes all five social studies curriculum areas for the self dimension of awareness shown in figure 8.1 and the examples of concepts of self presented in figure 8.2. Child-directed, developmentally appropriate, hands-on, concrete, real, and relevant materials and activities are used.

Circle of Awareness: SELF

III. Social studies area: HISTORY

    A. Possible vocabulary

        Birth, death, generations, grandfather, grandmother, aunt, uncle, cousin, brother, sister, old, new, antique, was, is, will be, past, present, future, growth

    B. Concrete materials

      1. Photographs of the child at birth, of birthdays, of parent at birth, of parents on birthdays, of relatives

      2. Baby clothing worn by the child, by other family members; the child's old and new toys

      3. Child's old and new Valentines, birthday cards, or other greeting cards; family's cards

      4. Graphs charting child's height during the year, showing growth

      5. Puppets available in classroom showing the progression of development from birth through 6 years of age

      6. Books, films, and tapes available in the classroom that depict children in the first 6 years of life; that depict families with older, middle-aged, and young adults and teenagers, young children and infants; that depict pioneer families, Depression-era families, gay nineties families, future families, and so forth

      7. Short-lived animals (gerbils, caterpillars, and so on) in the classroom so that children have the opportunity to experience life and death

      8. A short video showing how a person walks during different stages of life

C. Activities

1. Have class, large-group, and small-group discussions about the foregoing materials and make sure each child has a concrete article to relate to, such as a photograph of himself or herself at birth, at each discussion.

2. Have children paint or draw a picture of the historical family they liked most in the film they just saw.

3. Have each child dictate a short letter to some older person in his or her family.

4. Have children sing songs with you about the special occasions shown on the cards they have brought to school. Make up songs or rhymes.

5. Have several books about families, babies, birth, and death available in the book corner for children to choose from.

6. Take a field trip to a busy place and watch how different people walk differently at different ages.

II. Social studies area: ECONOMICS

A. Possible vocabulary
Money, coins, nickels, dimes, quarters, dollars, allowance, gift, presents, want, need, purchase, buy, receipt, sell, trade, honesty, cheat, greed, sharing, charity

B. Concrete materials

1. Nickels, dimes, quarters, dollars, sample checks

2. Mail order catalogs

3. Wooden puzzles about coins

4. Paper puzzles about different paper money for each child to cut up

5. Classroom dramatic play area set up as a grocery store or a flower store or a clothing store, and so on

6. Examples of good chairs, cheap chairs, good shirts, cheap shirts, sturdy materials and easily broken materials, such as drinking glasses

7. Books about money, honesty, greed, sharing, and charity available in the book corner for children to choose from

C. Activities

1. Have the class choose something in the room or make something that they would be willing to give to another class or group. Then have them dictate a letter about it, and deliver the letter and gift to the other group.

2. Have class members draw a picture of something they would never give away.

3. Make a large wall graph with pictures of items the children feel they must have and another with pictures of items they would like to have but could do without. They can draw them or cut them out of catalogs, or you can draw them.

4. Discuss and show pictures of nonverbal communication. Can you tell whether someone wants to get into the movie theater but has no money? Can you tell whether someone is hungry but cannot eat? Can you tell when someone has money to spend?

5. Sing songs about money, wishes, and hopes.

6. Use flash cards of pictures of children being honest and dishonest. Each time a picture shows honesty, have the children play their rhythm instrument triangles. Every time a picture shows greed, have the children blow on kazoos.

III. Social studies area: GEOGRAPHY

A. Possible vocabulary

Land, water, air, hill, mountain, rock, sand, mud, valley, sky, waterfall, cornfield, island, cliff, on, under, inside, between

B. Concrete materials

1. Sand and water table

2. Dirt and water table

3. Boxes of different kinds of rocks and dirt

4. Puppets and a box to use with prepositions such as *on, in, through,* and *above*

5. Slides, films, and tapes of mountains or other geographical features not present in the immediate locale

6. Musical recordings about the earth—for example, "This Land Is Your Land, This Land Is My Land" and "The Garden Song"

7. Travel posters depicting geographical forms such as lakes and islands

8. Modeling clay to form earth features such as hills and valleys

9. Books indicating maps and directions such as *I'll Follow the Moon* by Stephanie Tara (2005) and *The Red Book* by Barbara Lehman (2004)

C. Activities

1. Take a walking field trip and have a picnic. Discuss the land forms in the immediate environment.

2. Have children dictate letters to people who live in different places asking them for photographs and information about local landforms.

3. Make a collage from travel magazines of lakes, mountains, valleys, and so on.

4. Have children draw pictures with felt-tipped markers showing where they would like to live.

5. Have a picture-sorting activity using magazine pictures of environmentally healthy or unhealthy mountains, islands, lakes, and so forth.

6. Have the children match calendar pictures (or other scenic outdoor pictures) to different musical compositions and explain why they matched each picture to each musical composition.

IV. Social studies area: CURRENT EVENTS

A. Possible vocabulary

Newspaper, television news, tabloid, community, state, nation, catastrophe, human interest story, weather, hurricane, accident, celebration, Hollywood, movies

B. Concrete materials

1. Newspaper articles brought by the children from home

2. Videotapes of television news programs

3. Bulletin board on which to display stories and reports

4. Weather maps

C. Activities

1. Discuss each article or picture the children bring in and put it on the bulletin board.

2. Show videotapes of television news and discuss which stories are about disasters, which are about the weather, which are about celebrations, and so on.

3. At the end of the day, have the children vote on what they would consider the "current event of the day" in the classroom.

4. Take a field trip to a local newspaper.

5. Have a local newspaper or television reporter visit the classroom.

6. Have the children forecast the weather for the next day. Make a picture record of the forecast, and check it the next day.

7. Keep a record of new art and music releases.

V. Social studies area: INTERNATIONAL AND GLOBAL EDUCATION

A. Possible vocabulary

Country, world, sharing, foreign languages, Spain, France, Third World, food, toys, homes, clothing, flag, stamps, military, war

B. Concrete materials

1. Snack foods from different countries

2. Clothing from different countries

3. Pictures of homes in different countries

4. Toys from different cultures and countries

5. Books about other countries in other languages and about war

6. Recordings of music from other countries, such as the cancan, Irish jig, polka, and so on; and recordings of various national anthems

7. Recordings of the same story being read in different languages

8. Films and pictures of modes of transportation in different countries

9. A picture chart showing how children can help one another

C. Activities

1. Discuss similarities in pictures showing where people live or find shelter in different countries.

2. Show films and posters from embassies of different countries.

3. Begin a resource file of children's games from around the world, and teach one game to a small group of children.

4. Have children dictate letters to children or schools in other countries asking about the similarities and differences in their schools and ours.

5. Sort pictures that depict war and those that depict peace, and make a two-part bulletin board display.

6. Have children draw pictures showing the places they would most like to visit.

7. Have the children demonstrate dances from other nations.

8. Have people from other nations visit the classroom and bring samples of baby clothes, food, toys, and music.

9. Take a field trip to homes of people who have lived in other countries.

These activities are some of many that could be developed for the dimension of self. Moreover, many similar lesson plans could also be developed for each of the other seven dimensions of social awareness. (Figures 8.3 and 8.4 present examples of the family and neighborhood dimensions.) The possibilities are limitless.

Science, Technology, and Early Childhood Social Studies

Early childhood social studies instruction largely focuses on the child, family, neighborhood, and community. Science and technology may be referred to as part of a field trip to the local hospital with a nurse or doctor telling the students about medicines and medical equipment that is used in health care. An accompanying Web site for National Nutrition Month is http://kidshealth.org that has activities young children can engage in via the Internet. Or perhaps after a visit to the fire station, as a follow-up activity the teacher can use the computer to go to appropriate Web sites such as the United States Fire Administration http://www.usfa.fema.gov/kids or locate fire prevention activities at http://firesafety.buffnet/activity.htm.

A particularly popular government Web site for young students is The White House (http://www.whitehouse.gov/kids/) that has several different activities hosted by currently residing White House pets, presently two dogs and a Longhorn bull residing at the Crawford, Texas, ranch of President George W. Bush. When studying money, two good sites are the U.S. Treasury Department http://www.kids.gov/k_money.htm and the Sovereign Bank's http://www. kidsbank.com. An accompanying game for second graders and advanced first graders is Lemonade Stand in which youngsters can try their hand in the business world (http://www.lemonadestand.com).

Sites for young students may need to be accessed first by the classroom teacher, an aide, or a social studies buddy from an upper grade level. Oftentimes, once a site has been accessed and "bookmarked," students then can assist each other in regaining access. New Web sites are popping up every day but the wise teacher always checks the site first to determine if it is too difficult, too easy, or has inappropriate content.

NCSS STANDARDS-LINKED LESSON PLAN

Community Helpers

Theme: Become aware of workers who contribute to a successful community

Source: Donna Werderich

Grades: K–2

Objectives:

• Students will be able to define community.

• Students will realize that it takes many, varied jobs for a city or town to work as a community.

• Students will learn about the different roles workers play in the community.

NCSS Themes:

III. People, Places, and Environment

Materials: Chart paper, construction paper, markers, pencils, crayons, newspaper and magazine advertisements, "tools of the trade"

Process:

• Have students explain what they think community means.

• Read, *Communities* and *What is a Community from A to Z? Discuss* with students the main idea of community.

• Using a K-W-L chart paper, make a list together as a class of the many jobs people might have in a community. Ask students to share what jobs their family members have.

• Have students share questions they may have about different community helpers. Add these to the "W" column in the K-W-L chart.

• Explain that community helpers use "tools of the trade" to help them with their job.
  — What tool(s) would a firefighter use?
  — What tool(s) would a mail carrier use?
  — What tool(s) would a carpenter use?
  — What tool(s) would a pizza maker use?

• Begin reading *Community Helpers from A to Z* over the next several days. Write each letter and career on a separate piece of chart paper. Include specific vocabulary and "tools of the trade."

• Have students look through magazines and newspapers for pictures that correspond to the different community helpers to be glued to the chart paper.

• Invite family and community members to be classroom Community Helper speakers. Ask that they try and bring in their "tools of the trade."

• Ask students to share what they have learned about the different community helpers. Comments can be added to the "L" column in the K-W-L chart.

• The students can draw and tell about what they might like to do when they grow up.

• Create a classroom of community helpers. Brainstorm a list of jobs for each student to have. Discuss their role and tool. Rotate jobs so that each student may have the opportunity to experience each role.

Children's Literature:

Caseley, J. 2002. *On the Town: A Community Adventure.* Greenwillow. Grades K–2.

Kalman, B. 1998. *Community Helpers from A to Z.* New York, NY: Crabtree. Grades K–2.

Kalman, B. 2000. *What Is a Community from A to Z.* Crabtree. Grades K–2.

Trumbauer, L. 2000. *Communities.* Pebble. Grades K–2.

Extension Activities:
1. Take field trips to appreciate the jobs performed by the various helpers.
2. Create community helper centers in the classroom. Provide pictures, books, paper, pencils, crayons, dress-up clothes, tools of the trade. Suggested children's literature include: *How a House Is Built, The Post Office Book: Mail and How It Moves, Fire! Fire!*
3. Allow students to role play different community helper roles.
4. Draw a community with houses, streets, and places of business.
5. Read additional children's literature to learn about communities in different cultures.

Learning Styles Addressed: Verbal/linguistic, visual/spatial, body/kinesthetic, interpersonal, intrapersonal.

Evaluation: Reflect on the quality of students' oral responses. See if students can explain the meaning of a community and different roles of community helpers. Does the students' writing and drawing illustrate their understanding of a community helper?

Chapter Summary

While mindful of the limitations on how young children learn, teachers can use child-directed, hands-on activities with concrete, real, and relevant materials for teaching social studies via an integrated approach. These activities should be based on the child's egocentrism and ever-widening social perspective represented by eight circles of awareness as the foundation for social studies curriculum plans. Building on this foundation, teachers can use different whole language activities (speaking and listening vocabulary; dictated and written stories; books, magazines, and printed materials; the child's own drawn pictures and written print; nonverbal communication; field trips; and music) to teach the five social studies curriculum areas (history, economics, geography, international and global education, and current events).

Children's Literature Recommendation

Ada, A. F. 2000. *Frog Friend.* Illus. L. Lohstoeter. New York: Scholastic. Field mouse seeks out a friend and discovers Frog. But Frog is so different from himself. She is bigger and has a loud voice and loves to jump in the water. How can they be friends? Great for talking about accepting differences. (Gr. K–2)

Ahlberg, J., and A. Ahlberg. 1986. *The Jolly Postman.* Boston: Little, Brown. A postman makes his rounds delivering letters to nursery rhyme and fairy-tale characters. (Gr. K–2)

Amico, T., and J. Proimos. 2006. *Raisin and Grape.* New York: Dial. A wise grandfather visits and shares some reasons grandparents do the things they do. Giving advice such as holding your grandfather's hand when crossing the street (because not doing this is how grape juice is made). (Gr. K-2)

Anno, M. 1977. *Anno's Counting Book.* New York: HarperCollins. Each spread of this wordless counting book (which counts from 0–12) shows a panorama of a developing town. Students can count the number represented on each page (i.e., pine trees versus deciduous trees; buildings, people, animals). Very good for language development as children share their interpretations of the pages. (Gr. K–2)

Barger, T. 1980. *Special Friends.* New York: Julian Messner. A girl tells of her rewarding and enjoyable visits with her elderly neighbor. This book reveals the differences that occur as one becomes older. (Gr. 1–2)

Bauer, C. 1985. *My Mom Travels a Lot.* New York: Frederic Warne. A little girl points out the good and bad things about a mother's job that takes her away from home a lot. (Gr. 1–2)

Brown, M. 1998. *D.W.'s Lost Blankie.* Boston: Little, Brown. When Arthur's little sister D.W. loses her blankie, she doesn't think she'll ever be able to sleep again. (Gr. K–1)

Bunting, E. 1997. *A Day's Work.* Illus. R. Himler. Boston: Houghton Mifflin. The touching story of a day's work for a migrant family. (Gr. K–2)

———. 1998. *Going Home.* Illus. D. Diaz. New York: HarperTrophy. When their parents get excited about an upcoming visit to Mexico, the children don't understand what the fuss is all about. Then when they realize their parents came to America for better opportunities and left their family and friends behind, they understand the sacrifice their parents have made for them. (Gr. K–3)

Carle, E. 1986. *The Very Hungry Caterpillar.* New York: Philomel. Colorful illustrations and fluid text explain the many ways the caterpillar satisfies its hunger and grows. (Gr. K–2)

Caseley, J. 1998. *Mickey's Class Play.* New York: Greenwillow. When Mickey's costume is destroyed before the play, the entire family pitches in to make another duck suit. Children will focus on the thrill of being the center of attention. (Gr. 1–3)

Chandra, D., and M. Comora. 2003. *George Washington's Teeth.* Illus. B. Cole. New York: Farrar. With wit, verve and sympathy for poor George, the dental mystery is solved. (Gr. K–3)

Clifton, L. 1983. *Everett Anderson's Goodbye.* New York: Holt, Rinehart and Winston. Everett Anderson comes to terms with his grief after his father dies. (Gr. 2–3)

Cosby, B. 1998. *The Meanest Thing to Say.* Illus. V. P. Honeywood. New York: Cartwheel. Part of the Little Bill series by Bill Cosby, this story tells of two friends and how they interact with each other. (Gr. K–2)

———. 1998. *Shipwreck Saturday.* Illus. V. P. Honeywood. New York Cartwheel. Two friends spend Saturday sailing the boy's new sailboat. Unfortunately the boat accidentally gets broken. (Gr. K–1)

Cutler, M. 2000. *100th Day Worries.* New York: Simon & Schuster. Jessica is a worrier by nature so when her first-grade class is to celebrate the 100th day of school, she worries about what her 100-objects collection should be. (Gr. K–1)

Everitt, B. 1992. *Mean Soup.* San Diego, CA: Harcourt Brace Jovanovich. Horace has a bad day. His mother boils a pot of water and then screams into it. Horace joins her, and together they make "mean soup." The book shares a way to let out emotions without hurting others. (Gr. K–2)

Feiffer, J. 1998. *I Lost My Bear.* New York: Morrow. When a little girl loses her teddy bear, no one will help her find it. She ventures out on her own and discovers more than anyone ever expected. (Gr. K–1)

Fisher, I. 1987. *Katie-Bo.* New York: Adama. At first Jim and his brother, Teddy, are confused and nervous when they learn their family is going to adopt a Korean baby. However, both come to agree that adoption is a very special way to have a sister, and Katie-Bo becomes a very special sister. (Gr. K–3)

Fox, M. 1989. *Koala Lou.* Illus. P. Lofts. San Diego, CA: Harcourt Brace Jovanovich. Koala Lou is the oldest child in a large family. Because her mother is busy with the younger children, Koala Lou believes her mother no longer loves her. But when Koala Lou finishes second in a tree climbing race, her mother gives her a big hug and tells her that she loves her, always has, and always will. (Gr. K–1)

Garland, S. 1998. *My Father's Boat.* Illus. T. Rand. New York: Scholastic. A Vietnamese boy learns to fish on his father's shrimp boat. (Gr. 2–3)

Gibbons, G. 1982. *The Post Office Book: Mail and How It Moves.* New York: HarperTrophy. A great book to share before a field trip to the post office. Follow it up with a letter-writing activity. (Gr. K–2)

———. 1984. *Fire! Fire!* New York: HarperTrophy. The tools of firefighters are shared. How fires are fought in cities and forests as well as on the waterfront is explained. (Gr. K–2)

———. 1985. *Check It Out: The Book about Libraries.* San Diego, CA: Harcourt. This book depicts how libraries are organized and the services they provide. (K–2)

———. 1990. *How a House Is Built.* New York: Holiday. The "measure twice, cut once" philosophy of carpenters is wise advice. The steps for constructing a house, from bare ground to the final roofing nail, are presented in this informational book. (Gr. K–2)

———. 1994. *Emergency!* New York: Holiday. This book depicts emergency workers in a city. (Gr. K–2)

———. 1996. *Recycle! A Handbook for Kids.* New York: Little, Brown. In simple terms, Gibbons describes the need to preserve our natural resources by recycling. Good read-aloud before starting a class recycling program of paper, aluminum cans, and plastic bottles. (Gr. K–3)

Greenspun, A. A. 1992. *Daddies.* New York: Philomel. The author tells how she lost her own father at an early age. She then presents a collection of pictures of fathers and their young children. (Gr. 1–3)

Hazen, B. 1985. *Why Are People Different?* Racine, WI: Western. This story helps children understand the differences in people so that they will not be frightened of others but instead will develop relationships with children who are different. (Gr. 1–3)

Henkes, K. 1991. *Chrysanthemum.* New York: HarperCollins/Greenwillow. After being ridiculed on the first day of school, Chrysanthemum believes her absolutely perfect name is absolutely dreadful. At last, the music teacher, Mrs. Delphinium Twinkle, shows Chrysanthemum's classmates the beauty of a unique name. (Gr. K–3)

———. 1996. *Lilly's Purple Plastic Purse.* New York: HarperCollins/Greenwillow. Lilly loves everything about school—especially her teacher, Mr. Slinger. But when Mr. Slinger punishes her for breaking the rules, Lilly gets revenge by drawing a nasty picture of him. Eventually, Lilly discovers that her actions do not change how Mr. Slinger feels about her, and she decides to treat him with respect. (Gr. K–2)

———. 2006. *Lilly's Big Day.* New York: Greenwillow. Lilly's teacher is getting married and she's going to the wedding. (Gr. K–2)

Howe, J. 1987. *I Wish I Were a Butterfly.* San Diego, CA: Harcourt Brace Jovanovich. The little cricket will not sing because he thinks he is ugly. He wants to be beautiful like a butterfly. However, the cricket finds out that everyone is special in some way, and he starts to sing. The butterfly hears him and wishes he were a cricket. This book lets each child know that he or she is special. The artwork is beautiful. (Gr. K–2)

Jester, N. 2005. *The Hello, Goodbye Window.* Illus. C. Raschka. New York: Michael Di Capua Books. A young child views the world as people pass by the window. (Gr. K)

Johnson, A. 1992. *The Leaving Morning.* Illus. D. Soman. New York: Orchard. This book describes the emotions of leaving one home and learning to love another home. (Gr. K–3)

Krauss, R. 1998. *You're Just What I Need.* Illus. J. Noonan. New York: Trophy. A mother plays hide-and-seek with her young child. (Gr. K–1)

Lehman, B. 2004. *The Red Book.* Boston: Houghton Mifflin. A young child gets lost in a book that contains an island and a map. (Gr. K–1)

Lobel, G. 2002. *Does Anybody Love Me?* Illus. R. Beardshaw. New York: Good Books. After her parents scold her for making "chocolate pudding" from mud, Charlie runs away from home. (Gr. K–1)

McBratney, S. 1997. *Guess How Much I Love You.* Illus. I. Bates. Boston: Candlewick. The sharing of love between parent and child is conveyed in this delightful picture book. (Gr. K–1)

———. 1998. *Just You and Me.* Illus. I. Bates. Boston: Candlewick. When a storm approaches, shy Little Goosey doesn't want to share shelter with anyone but her dad. He understands how Little Goosey feels. (Gr. K–1)

McDermott, G. 1972. *Anansi the Spider.* New York: Holt, Rinehart and Winston. This folktale from the Ashanti in Ghana tells the story of Anansi, an animal with human qualities who gets into trouble. (Gr. 1–3)

Milich, Z. 2001. *The City ABC Book.* San Francisco: Kids Can. Black-and-white photos reveal letters are hidden in a city's structures (example: A-shaped windows). Have children find letters as they walk or ride the bus to school (i.e., an X on a barn door, an H formed with shutters and a window, an O with an oval shaped window). (Gr. K–2)

Morris, W. 1987. *The Magic Leaf.* New York: Atheneum. Long ago in China, Lee Foo, a smart man, seeks and finds the magic leaf. He also finds a lot of trouble. (Gr. K–2)

Norac, C. 1998. *I Love You So Much.* Illus. C. K. Dubois. New York: Doubleday. Lola the hamster wakes up each morning with some important words to say. But she doesn't know who to say them to. Her cheeks puff out with the words but she still doesn't say them. At the end of the day, her magical message bursts forth! (Gr. K–1)

Osborne, M. P. 2002. *New York's Bravest.* Illus. S. Johnson and L. Fancher. New York: Knopf. Based on the true life of the legendary New York firefighter Mose Humphreys who lived in the mid-1800s. (Gr. K–2)

Polacco, P. 1993. *The Bee Tree.* New York: Philomel. Mary Ellen tires of reading so Grampa takes her and eventually the entire neighborhood on a rollicking jaunt as they follow a swarm of bees to their bee tree. Grampa smokes the bees out and gathers the honey for a festive party for all. (Gr. K–3)

———. 1998. *Thank You, Mr. Falker.* New York: Philomel. Little Trisha has problems learning to read. The letters get all jumbled up to her until her fifth-grade teacher helps her learn to read. This is the autobiographical story of Patricia Polacco's struggle with dyslexia and her tribute to the teacher who helped her deal with it. (Gr. 1–3)

Pratt, D. 2000. *Hey Kids! You're Cookin' Now!* Illus. J. Winter. New York: Harvest Hill Press. A terrific cookbook for children and their adult helpers. Winner of several awards. (Gr. K–4)

Reiser, L. 1998. *Cherry Pies and Lullabies.* New York: Greenwillow. Four generations of American mothers sign lullabies, bake a favorite food, make a quilt, and create a crown of flowers. (Gr. K–2)

———. 1998. *Tortillas and Lullabies (Tortillas y Cancionitas).* New York: Greenwillow. Four generations of Costa Rican mothers sign lullabies, bake a favorite food, make a quilt, and create a crown of flowers. (Gr. K–2)

Rodriguez, L. J. 1998. *America is Her Name.* Illus. C. Vazquez. New York: Curbstone Press. America is a Mixteca Indian girl who lives in a barrio in Chicago. She dreams of the state of Oaxaca in Mexico where she was born. America's father loses his job and her uncle drinks too much. When a poet comes to her class and encourages the students to think of themselves as writers, America encourages her mother and sister to write down their thoughts on paper. (Gr. 2–3)

Rylant, C. 1998. *Poppleton and Friends.* Illus. M. Teague. New York: Blue Sky Press. This book focuses on Poppleton the Pig and his friends. Poppleton learns that if you want to live to be 100, eating grapefruit might help, but having friends definitely will. (Gr. 1–2)

———. 2000. *In November.* New York: Harcourt. The senses are piqued by the tantalizing elements offered in November. (Gr. 1–3)

Say, A. 1993. *Grandfather's Journey.* Boston: Houghton Mifflin. The Caldecott Award–winning book about a Japanese man who travels to the United States to live but who returns to his homeland that he loves. (Gr. K–6)

Seuss, Dr. 1984. *Butter Battle Book.* New York: Random House. This story depicts the difficulties of battle and the possible outcomes. (Gr. 2–3)

Shyer, M. 1985. *Here I Am, An Only Child.* New York: Scribner. A little boy explains the advantages and disadvantages of being an only child. (Gr. 1–2)

Simon, N. 1976. *All Kinds of Families.* Chicago: Albert Whitman. Exploring in words and pictures what a family is and how families vary in makeup and lifestyle, this book celebrates happy times but also shows that some relationships are troubled ones. Separations and sadness occur, yet the positive values of lives shared endure to provide foundations for future families. (Gr. P–2)

Slate, J. 2002. *Miss Bindergarten Celebrates the 100th Day of School.* Illus. Ashley Wolff. New York: Puffin. Miss Bindergarten's unusual class of animals each collects a bizarre 100 items for the 100th day celebration. (Gr. K–1)

Steptoe, J. 1997. *In Daddy's Arms, I Am Tall: African American Celebrating Fathers.* New York: Lee & Low. A collection of poems celebrating fatherhood. (Gr. K–2)

Stewart, S. 2002. *The Library.* Illus. D. Small. New York: Farrar, Straus & Giroux. A beautifully illustrated book about a library. Share and then take the students to the local library for storytime. (Gr. 1–4)

Tara, S. 2005. *I'll Follow the Moon.* Illus. L. E. Fodi. New York: Brown. A baby sea turtle uses the moon as a navigational device to reunite with its mother. (Gr. K–1)

Wells, R. 2000. *My Kindergarten.* New York: Hyperion. Describes a year of kindergarten by introducing the significant aspects of a school year, including voting. (Gr. K)

———. 2004. *Emily's First 100 Days of School.* New York: Hyperion. Emily is back and Miss Cribbage teaches the students something new each day from "Tea for Two" to school bus number 3, to day four and the four corners of a square in square dancing and so on. (Gr. K–1).

Williams, V. 1988. *Stringbean's Trip to the Shining Sea.* New York: Greenwillow. A boy sends back postcards from his camping trip across the western United States. (Gr. 2–3)

Yolen, J. 1993. *Weather Report.* Illus. A. Gusman. Honesdale, PA: Boyds Mills Press. A book of poetry about the weather. Includes poems about rain, sun, wind, snow, and fog. (Gr. 1–3)

Zamorano, A. 1997. *Let's Eat!* Illus. J. Vivas. New York: Scholastic. A family awaits the arrival of a new baby. (Gr. K–3)

Related Technology Tools

WebQuests

Abraham Lincoln (Gr. 1–4)
   http://www.spa3.k12.sc.us/WebQuests.html

Clifford Interactive Storybooks (Scholastic) (Gr. K–2)
   http://teacher.scholastic.com/clifford1/
   Clifford the lovable Big Red Dog series demonstrates a variety of useful behaviors—helping others, being kind and considerate, and so on. This site has interactive games and reading and writing activities to accompany the Clifford books.

Harriet Tubman (Gr. 2)
   http://www2.lhric.org/pocantico/tubman/tubman.html

National Association for the Education of Young Children (NAEYC)
   www.naeyc.org
   The nation's largest and most influential organization of early childhood educators and others dedicated to improving the quality of programs for children from birth through third grade.

PBS *Between the Lions* (Gr. K–2)

http://pbskids.org/lions/

This companion Web site to the television series *Between the Lions* offers interactive games, printable coloring sheets, video clips, and a 200-word illustrated speaking glossary. There are over 70 interactive online stories that are printable. Very helpful for striving readers and ELLs.

Carmen Sandiego

www.carmensandiego.com

A virtual detective game that helps build students' skills in geography, history, math, and grammar. The new 2007 geography edition is out.

HyperHistory Online

www.hyperhistory.com

Explore over 3,000 years of world history through interactive time lines that chart people, history, events, and maps.

Software and Videos

Designing Developmentally Appropriate Days. NAEYC. 28 minutes. Available at www.naeyc.org. Teaches about the fundamentals of developmentally appropriate practice for all children.

Carmen Sandiego. The Learning Company. Available at www.carmensandiego.com. A virtual detective game that helps build student's skills in geography, history, math, and grammar. The new 2007 geography edition is out.

My First Amazing History Explorer CD-ROM. DK Multimedia. Available from www.amazon.com. An invaluable introduction to history, the CD-ROM combines insight into the past with a sense of playful adventure, transporting children back through time to past worlds, such as the great Roman Empire and the high mountain home of the Incas.

I Love the USA CD-ROM. Global Software Publishing. Available from www.amazon.com. Designed for ages 6 to 9, kids learn about the states as well as their capitals, culture, and history. Raise the Flag quizzes let kids periodically test their knowledge.

Travel the World with Timmy CD-ROM. IBM. Available from www.amazon.com. Students ages 4–7 can travel to visit friends in Argentina, Kenya, and Japan and learn interesting facts about the people, places, and animals of other countries while painting and decorating cultural artwork.

References

Banks, J. A. 1992. "Multicultural Education for Freedom's Sake." *Educational Leadership* 49 (4): 32–35.

Bredekamp, S. 1987. *Developmentally Appropriate Practice in Early Childhood Programs Serving Children from Birth through Eight.* Washington, DC: National Association for the Education of Young Children.

Brown, C., and G. Brown. 1985. *Play Interactions.* Skillman, NJ: Johnson and Johnson.

Caine, R. N. and G. Caine. 2006. "The Way We Learn." *Educational Leadership* 64 (1): 50–54.

Charlesworth, R., and K. Lund. 1990. *Math and Science for Young Children.* New York: Delmar.

Cooper, J. D. 1997. *Literacy: Helping Children Construct Meaning.* 3rd ed. Boston: Houghton Mifflin.

Escamilla, K. 2000. "Bilingual Means Two: Assessment Issues, Early Literacy and Spanish-Speaking Children." *Research Symposium on High Standards in Reading for Students from Diverse Language Groups: Research, Practice and Policy*, pp. 1–18. Washington, DC: Retrieved online from http://www.ncbe.gwu.edu/ncbepubs/symposia/reading/bilingual5.html.

Gilbert, L. 1989. *Do Touch.* Mt. Rainier, MD: Gryphon House.

Hamilton, D., and H. Flemming. 1990. *Resources for Creative Teaching in Early Childhood Education*. 2nd ed. Orlando, FL: Harcourt Brace Jovanovich.

Huck, C. S., S. Hepler, J. Hickman, and B. Kiefer. 2004. *Children's Literature in the Elementary School*. 7th ed. Dubuque, IA: Brown and Benchmark.

Hunt, T., and N. Renfro. 1982. *Puppetry in Early Childhood Education*. New York: Nancy Renfro Studios.

Maxim, G. W. 1998. *Social Studies and the Elementary School Child*. 6th ed. Columbus, OH: Prentice-Hall.

Norton, D. 2003. *Through the Eyes of a Child*. 6th ed. Columbus, OH: Merrill.

Piaget, J. 1952. *The Origins of Intelligence in Children*. New York: International Universities Press.

Seefeldt, C. 1997. *Social Studies for the Preschool Primary Child*. Columbus, OH: Merrill.

Smith, C. 1982. *Promoting the Social Development of Young Children*. Mountain View, CA: Mayfield.

> The knowledge and habits of mind to be gained from the study of history are indispensable to the education of citizens in a democracy.
>
> —The Bradley Commission on History in Schools

Chapter Nine

History
Connecting Children to the Past

Richard A. Fluck, Northern Illinois University;
Mary Beth Henning, Northern Illinois University

CHAPTER OUTLINE

CHAPTER OBJECTIVES

Readers will

- appreciate the importance of history in teaching social studies;

- understand the role of historians in preserving history;

- learn a variety of methods and materials to stimulate children's interest in history; and

- review a variety of children's literature that introduces historical themes and concepts.

Introduction

Alicia Bierstodt's fourth grade class is having a "history encounter" as Alicia refers to it. The class is reading about the history of baseball—discovering that the sport is more than just Derek Jeter, Albert Pujols, and Barry Zito. Unearthing its historical roots, the class found out that baseball was played by pioneers as they moved westward and its popularity spread by Civil War soldiers. Racial issues were also discussed by the students as they learned about Negro League stars such as Satchel Paige, Josh Gibson, and "Cool Papa" Bell. Jackie Robinson, also a player in the Negro League, became the first African American to break into major league baseball. Racial tensions eased when Pee Wee Reese, the Brooklyn Dodgers star infielder and a native of the southern state of Kentucky, welcomed Jackie as a teammate, putting his arm around Jackie's shoulders during infield practice prior to a game. The class talked about the threats Hank Aaron received when he was attempting to break Babe Ruth's home run record.

Alicia had students locate pictures of catchers' uniforms from different time periods and compare how each piece of equipment improved safety. After viewing a photograph of Yogi Berra sans a catcher's helmet, one student remarked, "So that's why that guy talks so funny. He kept getting hit on the head with foul balls." Economic issues were also touched on as they learned about Curt Flood, who sued major league baseball for the right to play for the team he wanted to play for and not for the team who "owned" his contract, thereby starting free agency. Students learned that baseball was first introduced in Japan in 1870 by an American teacher and that it is now Japan's most popular sport. According to Alicia, history encompasses

> everything and anything. All the social studies relate back to history—geography, economics, civics, sociology, and anthropology—all of them. With baseball, we have had a World Series played during an earthquake. It was a reminder for us after September 11 that we must go on with our lives. Baseball is a part of Americana and our history.

What took place yesterday, the week before, and the century before: that is **history.** Our link to the past surrounds us. History is not only about our own personal history and that of our families, it also traces our communities, the United States, the world, and indeed the entire universe. History is a chronological study of what happened to humanity in the past. It is also the study of controversial issues and changing interpretations of the past. Oral or written records as well as physical remains contribute to our historical knowledge. One seventh grader remarked, "History is a noun because it's people, places, and things." Through the gathering of information and the careful examination of the lives of people (where they lived and traveled, and their possessions), we gain an understanding of the human condition throughout the ages.

According to David W. Blight (2002), an award-winning **historian**:

> *History*—what trained historians do—is a reasoned reconstruction of the past rooted in research; it tends to be critical and skeptical of human motive and action. . . . History can be read by or belong to everyone; it accesses change and progress over time. (3)

In Blight's view, history differs from memory inasmuch as memory is "often treated as a sacred set of potentially absolute meanings and stories, possessed as the heritage or identity of a community. Memory is often owned; history interpreted" (3). In considering the tragic events of September 11, 2001, in which the World Trade Center and Pentagon were attacked by terrorists who had taken over commercial aircraft, Alan Brinkley, a history professor at Columbia University, states:

> We need to make a distinction between history and memory. In the memory of everyone old enough to have experienced September 11, this date will remain one that we will remember the rest of our lives, just as almost all Americans old enough to do so remember the Kennedy assassination every November 22. But that's not the same as becoming a major event in history. For example, JFK's death is a huge event in memory. It may or may not have been a truly major event in history. September 11 is similar. We may not know for years or decades whether it truly changed the course of history. (Meacham 2002, 63)

In teaching history, we must make clear the distinction between what is recalled and what is interpreted.

History must be taught in a way that appeals to students. Far too often students remark that they find history to be dull, boring (Loewen 1995). David McCullough, award-winning biographer of *Truman* (1992) and *John Adams* (2001) and former history professor at Cornell University, notes that he was not satisfied in teaching history unless each student had fallen in love with history. He soon realized, however, that unless the student was on a quest to discover some aspect of history that meant something to her, she wouldn't fall in love with the subject. Thus, as teachers, our mission is to set all of our students on personal quests to uncover history in an invigorating, relevant manner that creates a love affair with the past.

History's Role in Elementary and Middle School Social Studies Curriculum

Although it would be an oversimplification to accept that history is the unquestioned basis of social studies instruction, it would be safe to say that there have always been some who believed that teaching history is at the basis of a democratic education (Nelson 1996; Saxe 1991). Even with the National Council for the Social Studies (1994) adopting more of a citizenship focus to their definition of social studies, social studies educators from Mary Ritter Beard to Diane Ravitch have argued that the core of social studies should continue to be the study of history.

A perennial question in teaching history is what is the best pedagogical approach. Should it be the presentation of facts and information? Or should we concentrate on developing students' thinking skills? This chapter will present a variety of methods and materials useful for teaching history to elementary and middle school students. One of the earliest women social educators, Emma Willard (1787–1870), wrote best-selling history textbooks that promoted the use of graphic representations and charts to teach chronology and historical events in the 1830s. Willard believed that studying history should lead students to develop habits of the mind (or critical thinking skills). In the late 1800s, Mary Sheldon Barnes advocated using **primary source materials** and "object lessons" (taking current events, controversies, or **historical relics**) to make history come alive for students (Monteverde 1999).

Recent concerns over the lack of historical knowledge by high school seniors in the United States have resulted in additional questions as to how we should teach history in kindergarten through twelfth grade. Today's high-stakes, standardized testing emphasizes the acquisition of factual knowledge, usually measured through multiple-choice achievement tests rather than essay tests. Clearly history's people, places, and things are perfect for designers of such multiple-choice exams. That said, echoing from the past are the words of Shirley Engle (1987), who over 40 years ago proclaimed that "in teaching social studies, we should emphasize decision making as against mere remembering" (74). Examining decisions that people made in the past serves as a springboard for students' own inquiries into the future.

Writes C. Frederick Risinger (2002), a former president of the National Council for the Social Studies:

> There is a growing backlash against high-stakes testing, and there may be a time when authentic assessment of student achievement will replace the fact-based, multiple-choice tests that dominate the standards and testing movement today. Until that time, social studies teachers will have to grapple with the dilemma of teaching students the information they need to pass the test while trying to prepare them for their role as informed, participatory citizens in a rapidly changing world. (233)

One needs to have broad knowledge of history and the ability to apply analytical and decision-making skills to make informed decisions. As we teach history as part of social studies instruction we will continue to weigh to what degree we need to teach factual knowledge as opposed to decision making.

Integrating children's literature in the teaching of history is a tried and true method for capturing children's imagination as they begin to examine topics and skills important to historians. The National Council for the Social Studies has produced two excellent books that annotate and link children's literature to the social studies standards. Teachers who would like to build their social studies programs around children's literature will find *Children's Literature in Social Studies: Teaching to the Standards* (Krey 1998) and *Linking Literature with Life: The NCSS Standards and Children's Literature for the Middle Grades* (Sandmann and Ahern 2002) to be excellent resources. Throughout this textbook are references to quality children's literature, both fiction and nonfiction, that lends itself to the teaching of history in grades K–8.

The Role of the Historian

One of the goals of history education has been to help children "think like historians." But historians vary in the way they approach their discipline as much as teachers do. Levstik and Barton (1996) have warned that to oversimplify the work of historians may give children false ideas. Particularly in the last 20 years, historians have become more alert to the multiple interpretations of different perspectives on history and how people's values influence their interpretations of events and people (Hartzler-Miller 2001). But, at some level, historians try to determine the accuracy of historical evidence that is presented. To do so, in many ways the historian needs to think and act like a scientist by practicing the following principles:

• Search carefully for facts.

• Use a variety of sources for evidence.

Having students follow historical events can include using maps to trace battles in a war and conducting word searches to become familiar with the towns and rivers.

- Without exhibiting any personal bias, judge the evidence for accuracy.
- Write about the facts objectively.

This is easier said than done. Think of something you are passionate about studying. Now try to present that information in a nonbiased manner. An arduous assignment indeed. Children need to be taught the investigative strategies that historians use. While the Internet offers a lot of valuable information, many sites are biased. Teaching students to go to several different sources on the Internet to find information about a specific historical event is one way to verify historical information. A site with a bibliography citing the same person repeatedly may not be accurate and is likely to be biased. Sites funded by specific groups are generally biased to the political leanings of that group. In order to help students understand the concept of ideology when they are using the Internet, the teacher can explain how strongly sets of beliefs are reflected in an author's work by using particularly biased Web sites as examples (Lee 2002).

Inquiry is a method of helping children learn how to evaluate different hypotheses about history. Massialas and Cox (1966) historically pressed for inquiry in social studies, while Van Fossen and Shiveley (1997) have more recently taken up inquiry's mantle. In the reflective inquiry tradition originally identified by Barth and Shermis (1970), inquiry is a process-driven approach in which students grapple with "significant problems" by forming hypotheses and gathering data from a variety of sources (749). Students are expected to use data to develop well-reasoned judgments about social and historical problems. An inquiry lesson that is literature based will allow children to read various books espousing different perspectives on a historical event or person; then they can create their own hypothesis and evidence-based conclusion about the question at hand. Ideally, inquiry should help children to learn something about the past that will inform their present lives (Whelan 2001).

One way to create an inquiry lesson would be to pose the question "What kind of person was Christopher Columbus?" Students could then read different books about Christopher Columbus to help answer their meaningful question. Books such as *Encounter* (Yolen 1992), *Christopher Columbus: Voyager to the Unknown* (Levinson 1990), and *Discovering Christopher Columbus: How History is Invented* (Pelta 1991) present different information about Columbus. After evaluating different sources and perspectives on Christopher Columbus, children would draw their own conclusions and present them to an audience. Historical inquiry helps children to recognize that history is more about interpretation than it is about simply condensing the facts (Levstik and Barton 2001; Whelan 2001). Research has shown that children's interest in history is stimulated when they use historical narratives to try to learn "what really happened" or when they feel they are searching for the "truth" (Levstik and Pappas 1992, 378). Students' interest will be aroused by issues of emotion and judgment in history more than from reading a textbook (Downey and Levstik 1991; Levstik and Barton 1996).

Perspectives on History

Stories handed down from one generation to another in the oral tradition are part of history. **Primary witness** accounts are recollections of an event and make valuable contributions to the record of the human condition. The person who was at the stadium when Mark McGuire broke Roger Maris's home run record can give a first person account. However, the fan who listened to the event on the radio as described by announcer Jack Buck is a secondary witness since that person received the information secondhand from the play-by-play announcer. The account of a **secondary witness** is less credible since he or she received information of an event as interpreted by another individual.

People attending the same event at the same time often have different versions of that event. Personal bias can play a role in the retelling of what occurred. A Confederate and a Union soldier who fought each other during Pickett's charge at the battle of Gettysburg would likely have much different versions of the encounter. Another factor influencing the degree of accuracy in recall is that human memory is not perfect. The excitement of the event, a poor vantage point, or previously known or unknown knowledge all can interfere in recalling events. For instance, when President John F. Kennedy was assassinated, his wife Jacqueline reached out her arm and assisted a secret service agent as he climbed into the speeding convertible. Later, she recalled holding her husband's head in her lap and denied pulling the secret service agent into the black presidential limo. However, a home movie clearly showed Mrs. Kennedy stretched out on the trunk of the car with her arm extended to the agent. A good book to share on the event is *Kennedy Assassinated! The World Mourns: A Reporter's Story* (Hampton 1997). Children may compare Hampton's recollections to the accounts of their grandparents, great aunts and uncles, or older neighbors' memories of that day. These examples indicate that history presents primary and secondary witness accounts that must be weighed for credibility.

Helping children to recognize the different perspectives that various witnesses to history represent is one of the goals of teaching history. Books such as *The Boys' War* (Murphy 1990) present excerpts of original letters written by children who fought in the Civil War. *A Separate Battle: Women and the Civil War* (Chang 1991) also presents excellent examples of letters, diaries, and true stories from the perspective of women in the Civil War era.

Students learning about the Holocaust will appreciate the true stories presented by 20 different young people who experienced the Holocaust in Europe between 1933 and 1945 in *Tell Them We Remember: The Story of the Holocaust* (Bachrach 1994). Using materials and ideas from the United States Holocaust Memorial Museum (http://www.ushmm.org/) provides primary source documents and an introduction to the museum. Note that students need guidance on this topic because there are over 600,000 other Web sites on the Holocaust and they can easily get distracted from the task at hand.

☞ IN THE CLASSROOM

An Oral History Project

To help students feel what it is like to be a historian, one of the most powerful experiences is to complete an oral history. Teachers may choose a topic, theme, or subject to explore through oral history, or students may choose their own line of inquiry. What works best is for students to consider a topic that can be illuminated through an interview. A local history event provides wonderful fodder for rich interviews. Social history is also an excellent avenue to explore. For example, learning about dating in generations past or understanding how discrimination affected people in your community are popular topics among older students. Several interviews on the same topic will show students how events can be interpreted differently by various primary sources. Preparation for an oral history project should include some research about the topic in order to create more informed questions. For younger children, an oral history project can be accomplished by inviting guest speakers to the class and interviewing the "witness to history" as an entire class.

Oral history offers elementary and middle school students an opportunity to interview people and gain their perspective about a certain event or time period. Oral history can be done with third through eighth graders. It is critical that the teacher first develop students' questioning strategies so that their interviews will go well. It is best for students to begin with recall questions and then move to higher-level questions. The five Ws—who, when, where, what, and why—of newspaper and television reporting are a good starting point for students. The teacher should model questions that the students might ask and then have students get into pairs to generate additional questions. Remind students to leave ample space between questions to write the response of the person they are interviewing.

Mary Conner (1998, 424), a teacher in Pasadena, California, gives these suggestions to her students for conducting oral history interviews:

• You may wish to tape-record the interview. If you do, ask permission first. Using a tape recorder can intimidate some people.

• Make an appointment with the person. Thirty minutes to an hour of time should be ample for each interview.

- Thank the person in advance for agreeing to help you with your assignment. Follow up with a brief thank-you note after the interview.

- Keep in mind that most adults love to talk about their own life experiences.

- The person may not be able to answer all of your questions. If a question makes a person seem uneasy, move on to another question.

- If the person doesn't give you specific details, ask them to tell you more or elaborate.

- If you are uncertain as to what the person is talking about, ask them to explain.

A particular theme or time period should be chosen for the oral history project. Themes may include such topics as immigration, World War II, the space race between the United States and the former U.S.S.R., the Vietnam War, or the assassinations of President John F. Kennedy or Martin Luther King, Jr. Themes may be localized; for example, students who live in Louisiana may interview residents who lived through Hurricane Katrina or California students may interview people about earthquakes or the Rodney King trial. A time period might be when the individual interviewed was an elementary student of the 1960s or 1970s.

Begin the year by having students interview one another to develop and write a biography of another classmate. Using a computer, color printer, and a digital camera, the students can produce biographies complete with color photos of their subjects.

Students will often find it edifying to interview a grandparent or neighbor who has colorful stories to share. Some teachers will find that an organized visit to a local nursing home or retirement village offers a plethora of opportunities to garner from local sources. Permission should be granted in advance from those who will be interviewed with willing participants being informed of who will hear the interview tape. Help the class brainstorm appropriate questions that may lead to interesting stories from the interviewee. Prior to the interview session, students should be given the opportunity to practice interviewing each other in order to improve their questioning, listening, and optional note-taking skills. Practicing with a cassette recorder and microphone is also essential. Interviews may last anywhere from 20 minutes to over an hour. Much depends on the skill of students in asking questions (and listening) and the personality of the interviewee. Those witnesses to history who are naturally more talkative and energetic often produce better interviews. Families may be enlisted for assistance if students will be completing their interviews independently. Teachers may ask students to transcribe their favorite part of the interview or digitize it so it can be shared with others. Those who contribute to the project should be thanked with a follow-up note. Students will often report that an oral history project was the most meaningful assignment they completed all year.

Primary Source Documents

One of the most important tools of a historian's trade is a **primary source document.** Children will enjoy getting right to the source and examining it rather than just reading a textbook. As children examine primary source documents, they construct their own meanings about history. Letters, diaries, photos, and legal documents are all examples of primary sources. Recent issues of *Social Education* (the professional journal of the National Council for Social Studies) often feature primary source documents that teachers can copy with accompanying lesson plans.

Jackdaw kits, named for the jackdaw bird, a black European member of the crow family known for collecting bits and pieces of materials for its nest, (http://

wwwjackdaws.com) are favorites of teachers because each includes primary source documents for children to examine (Dowd 1990; Martorella and Beal 2002; Rasinski 1983). They also provide an excellent means of individualizing instruction as each student can have his or her own kit, work with a partner, or participate in a small group, thereby meeting the learning needs of all students. Jackdaws organize a variety of primary source documents and other materials, such as artifacts about a single topic from a historical time period placed in a large folder or sturdy box such as a plastic container with a lid. A jackdaw on the civil rights movement might contain an audiotape of Martin Luther King, Jr.'s, "I Have a Dream" speech, pictures of water fountains or restrooms labeled "whites only" or "colored," a copy of the Norman Rockwell painting of Ruby Bridges being escorted to school by federal marshals, photos of civil rights protests, and photos of riots after Martin Luther King, Jr., was assassinated. These containers then become ready-made sources for lesson ideas. Possible jackdaws can be about an individual, an event, a document, an issue, or a place. Here are a few examples:

Primary Grades
  Community jackdaws
    Bank
    Fire department
    Hospital
    Police department
    Post Office
  Native Americans
    Plains Indians
    Woodland Indians
    Coastal Indians
  Famous Americans
    Betsy Ross
    Benjamin Franklin
    George Washington
    Abraham Lincoln
    Martin Luther King, Jr.
    Thomas Edison
    Sarah Breedlove Walker
Intermediate Grades
  The Declaration of Independence
  Famous People
    Simón Bolívar
    George Washington Carver
    Madam Curie
    Dorothea Dix
    Catherine the Great
    Napoleon Bonaparte
    Theodore Roosevelt
    Booker T. Washington

       Great Inventions
          Printing press
          Electricity
          Telegraph
          Telephone
          Airplane

Middle School

       People Who Promoted Peace
          Jimmy Carter
          Mahatma Ghandi
          Martin Luther King, Jr.
          Nelson Mandela
          Eleanor Roosevelt
          Woodrow Wilson
       The Bill of Rights
       The U.S. Constitution
       People Who Changed the Way People Think
          Leonardo da Vinci
          Bill Gates
          Aristotle
          Mother Theresa
          Sacajawea

Authors and their works, for example, Jean Fritz's series on the Revolutionary War and David Adler's biographies of George Washington, Betsy Ross, Benjamin Franklin, and others, can accompany jackdaw kits. Such jackdaws might focus on Tories, Minutemen, Molly Pitcher, King George III, Benedict Arnold, George Washington, Martha Washington, Benjamin Franklin, George Rogers Clark, John Adams, Abigail Adams, Samuel Adams, John Hancock, Dr. Joseph Warren, Paul Revere, Billy Dawes, Crispus Attucks, Marquis de Lafayette, General Gage, Hessians, Thomas Paine, Betsy Ross, James Armistead Lafayette, and so on.

Relics from World War II such as ration coupons, buttons or chevron ranks from uniforms, newspaper clippings, and letters from soldiers fighting at the front can make up a jackdaw. Examining printed materials from the past can help students relate to those individuals who lived in another time and place and develop a personal attachment. Each jackdaw usually contains suggested accompanying activities that the students may be assigned. Giving students a number of possible activities from which to select enables them to make choices by interest and ability level.

Historical Connections with the Local Community

Beginning with your own community, find an interesting period of time synonymous with a period your students will be studying as part of your curriculum. Launch an investigation by poking around the community for information. Peruse your historical museum for letters and legal documents as well as pictures and photos. The local newspaper or public library will have an archive where you can find old articles and sales ads. Your hospital may have historical records to share. If your town is a county seat, the county's courthouse is a great repository of historical documents—land titles, survey plats from over the years, and birth and death records. Other good sources include churches and the Internet. If a college or university is within 30 miles of your school, scrounge around the various documents or library there. You may find some fascinating information that few local residents are aware of. Don't be surprised if your community was once the site of a prisoner of war camp (either from the Civil War or World War II), a famous discovery, or the beginning of a well-known company. Each community has its own unique history.

Here are some examples of information uncovered by teachers from throughout the United States that they and their students pursued through searching documents in their own communities and sometimes beyond.

• The creation and later decline of Route 66 across America and its current presence in Flagstaff, Arizona.

• In the 1920s, the Ku Klux Klan moved into the area of southern Clay County, Indiana, gaining some local support but was thwarted by local citizens during the Great Depression.

• During the latter part of the Civil War an arsonist burned granaries in the town of Hickory Grove, Illinois, only to be hung when vigilantes stormed the jail. Referred to afterward as "Hangtown," the community suffered during the years following the war from lack of growth. One day a group of the town's leaders gathered in the local pharmacy, agreeing that the town should be renamed. Picking a bottle of Rochelle Salts off the shelf, a man declared that Rochelle would be a good name and the deed was done.

Sometimes documents verify that the person who receives the most fame is not necessarily the individual most deserving of the credit. Students in Albany, New York, wanted to combine the study of history with the study of science in their invention unit. Knowing that Robert Fulton had successfully built the first steamboat, the *Clermont,* and navigated it from Albany to New York City, they inquired as to what further advancements to the steamboat were made. Their natural curiosity led them to Henry Miller Shreve, whose brilliantly inventive efforts created the very successful steamboat the *Washington*, a vessel 148 feet in length powered by a lightweight engine, unlike the weighty engine of Fulton. In 1816, the *Washington* successfully sailed down the Ohio River and down the Mississippi to New Orleans in the unheard of time of two weeks. Shreve's work opened the waterways of what became the midsection of the country. The town of Shreveport, Louisiana, was named for Colonel Shreve, leaving a regional legacy in comparison to the more international fame achieved by Fulton.

Science and history can make for an excellent combination as the human condition continues to be improved through scientific advancements. Local businesses and major corporations can be sources of historical information on inventions that might not be widely known. Here are some examples:

• Barbed wire, invented by Joseph Glidden of DeKalb, Illinois, permitted the affordable confinement of cattle in vast ranges of western range land.

- Chocolate chip cookies were an accidental discovery in the 1930s when Ruth Wakefield used an old colonial cookie recipe for guests at her Toll House Inn, so named for having housed passengers overnight on the toll road from Boston to New Bedford. Rushed to prepare a new batch of cookies, Ruth tossed into the batter chunks of dark chocolate rather than melting it. Hence the name, Toll House cookies.

- The creation of the automatic-oiler for train steam engines by Elijah McCoy, a black engineer from Detroit, making oiling the equipment by hand no longer necessary. So successful was his invention it also provided a cliché we still use today. Engineers insisted on Elijah's automatic-oiler by saying they wanted "the real McCoy."

- The famous design of the Coca-Cola bottle was invented not in Atlanta, Georgia, home of Coca-Cola, but hundreds of miles away in Terre Haute, Indiana, in a glass factory owned by Chapman Root.

- In 1905, 11-year-old Frank Epperson of New Jersey left a stick in his soda pop mixture in a cup outside. When the temperature dipped below freezing, voila, the Popsicle was created. But he didn't sell his invention until 18 years later in 1923, calling them Epsicles.

Nearly every town, no matter how small, has contributed a significant piece of history. Local businesses and national corporations may share an untold wealth of historical documentation of inventions or businesses that were initiated from relatively small beginnings. The Smithsonian (http://www.siris.si.edu/) and National Archives (http://www.archives.gov/education/index.html) provide Web sites that are virtual gold mines for primary source documents.

Artifacts

Artifacts, actual items used by people from another time period, pique the interest of students. Being able to hold and touch an artifact helps the student to transcend time and go back to the era from which the artifact originated. Artifacts often inspire children to engage in their own inquiries as questions are sparked. Carol Fuhler, a middle school teacher and collector of antiques and memorabilia, uses artifacts to open a unit of study. Carol initially models the steps in the investigative process by first explaining to the class the meaning of an artifact, reminding students that it is likely to be old and needs to be handled with great care. Next she carefully unwraps tissue and bubble wrap to reveal an artifact that is a clue to what the students will be studying. In this case, a small carbide miner's light offers food for thought. Thinking aloud, the teacher demonstrates how she formulates questions and uses her previously gained knowledge to indicate what the light reminds her of and the reasons why. She then uses the overhead transparency projector to begin to fill in the "Speculations and Ponderings" sheet (see In the Classroom: Forging Connections with Artifacts). Now Carol uncovers the flat newspaper-covered object to reveal *In Coal Country* (Hendershot 1987) (Note: Another possible picture book is *Mama Is a Miner* by Lyon [1994]), which she reads aloud to the class. To motivate the class as she reads, Carol asks the students to identify clues that will reveal the purpose of the artifact and what time period it came from. After she finishes reading, she queries the students to share their reactions: How is the artifact related to the story? What do they surmise as the artifact's identity? Why did they make their decision that it was a miner's light? Can they pinpoint the historical period? Can they justify their answer? With a partner they complete the "Speculations and Ponderings" sheet (Fuhler, Farris, and Nelson 2006). Next she goes to the Web site the Old Country in the New World, which gives students information on the history and hazards of coal mining where they can learn more about the topic (www.amphilsoc.org/library/exhibits/wallace/work.htm).

The teacher then places a carefully wrapped artifact, a picture book wrapped in newspaper, and five copies of a historical fiction novel wrapped in brown grocery bags into a colorful gift bag. She gives a colorful bag to every group of four or five students. Some of the artifacts she uses are framed pictures from the period, articles of clothing such as a belt buckle or a hat, jewelry such as a brooch or watch, documents such as a draft notice or a ration coupon encased in a plastic cover, or military gear such as a lead bullet, belt buckle, or tin cup. Keeping an eye out for newly released historically based picture books, Carol is careful that the accompanying picture book and historical novel are properly matched with the artifact. She also finds a nonfiction, information book that explains some aspect of the period or theme. Fortunately, the major historical periods have numerous picture books as well as historical fiction from which to choose. There are more and more information books being published. The last item in the group's bag is an envelope containing a Web site that relates to the historical period.

When given the special bag, students first examine the artifact and answer questions about it: What is it? When would it have been used? Does it remind you of something you've seen before or an experience you've had? What kind of person would have owned the artifact? Next, the group takes turns reading aloud from the picture book and then discuss the theme of the book. Finally, the group reads the historical novel as a literature circle activity (see chapter 7 for more on literature circles). By assigning students to groups, the teacher can provide for struggling readers as well as gifted readers.

If actual artifacts are not readily available, items can be substituted. For instance, a tin pie pan, a pair of worn Levi's, a quilt, and an old horse bridle could be used for sharing the westward movement. Accompanying historical fiction could be *The Ballad of Lucy Whipple* (Cushman 1997), the story of a family that moves to California during the gold rush, or a biography such as *Riding Freedom* (Ryan 1998) depicting the adventurous life of Charlotte "Charley" Parkhurst, a superb horsewoman and stagecoach driver as well as the first woman to vote in California and most likely the United States.

Artifact collections may be checked out from local libraries and museums for a short period of time. Some large school districts have their own collections. Many such collections have accompanying activities that have been designed by teachers for use with elementary and middle school students. Holding a tin cup used by a soldier during the Civil War or touching a flight jacket worn by a Tuskegee Airman or one of the first female astronauts to fly in the space shuttle spins an entirely different perspective on the social studies lesson. Suddenly it is real and relevant.

☞ IN THE CLASSROOM

Forging Connections with Artifacts

Steps to Discovery

• Very carefully unwrap the artifact from the tissue paper and bubble wrap as it is likely to be very old. Examine the object inside.

• Discuss the item, giving each member of your group a turn to voice observations regarding the age of the artifact, where it might have originated, and what use it might have had. As a group, answer the prompts on the "Speculations and Ponderings" sheet. Individuals can jot brief notes on their own copy.

• Next, unwrap the book that is covered in newspaper. Examine the cover. Is it possible to make a connection between the book and the artifact at this point?

• Take turns reading aloud, listening to see how the book might be used to extend your knowledge of the artifact or the historical period with which it is connected. After discussing the book with your group members, record any additional information on the data collection sheet.

• Review what you've learned so far. What do you still want to know?

• Visit the Web site to gather additional information.

• Stop again and discuss what you have learned so far. Adjust the recorded speculations as needed.

• Wrap up this part of your work by practicing your summarization skills. First, summarize the picture book you read. Then, summarize the information you have gathered about the artifact. As a group, be prepared to present an overview of your work to the entire class.

• In a presentation to the class, show your artifact. Pass it around so that your classmates can study it. Share a few of your initial speculations. Next, give a brief summary of your picture book. Explain how it helped you to learn about your artifact. Finally, summarize your group's thoughts up to this point. Be prepared for questions and input from your classmates.

Speculations and Ponderings Data Collection Sheet

1. Examine your artifact. Brainstorm ideas about what it is and what its use might have been. Who might have used it? What conclusions are you drawing from your own background knowledge as you ponder?

2. What period of history or particular event does this item bring to mind?

3. Do you think your item has a general geographic home? Might it be more likely to be found in one part of the United States than another?

4. Read the accompanying picture book. Based upon the additional clues from the story, adjust your speculations accordingly, if need be.

5. Where might you go for additional information on the artifact and the topic it represents?

6. Investigate a relevant Web site and add several facts to document your speculations or extend your understanding. Use the back of this sheet to record your information and note the Web site. Finally, discuss the role that technology can play as a companion to the books you are reading.

(Adapted from Fuhler, C. J., P. J. Farris, and P. A. Nelson. 2006. "Building Literacy Skills across the Curriculum: Forging Connections with the Past through Artifacts." *The Reading Teacher* 59 (7): 646–59. Used by permission.)

Teachers can create their own boxes, trunks, suitcases, or time capsules made from empty paper towel rolls and fill them with artifacts from their own families. Hickey (1997) has suggested that an excellent way to introduce family history to children is to put together a collection of artifacts from your own life, such as photos, yearbooks, newspaper clippings, stuffed animals, a symbolic piece of clothing, and family bibles. The teacher assembles these items in a trunk to show students how much they can learn from artifacts about a person and time period. Students' examination of someone else's time capsule or treasure chest can inspire them to create their own "trunks" of artifacts to illustrate their lives.

Students can also create history museums by organizing an educational display of their collected artifacts (Levstik and Barton 2001). Many teachers are familiar with the idea of science projects that display students' research questions, hypothesis, and research. A history museum can be similar to a science fair. History museum displays can be presented to other students, parents, intergenerational

---

☞ IN THE CLASSROOM

Inquiries about Ancient Egypt

Egypt is a popular history topic in upper elementary and middle grades. The Egyptian culture lends itself to inquiry that uses the World Wide Web since so much is available online. Children generate many excellent inquiry questions that can be explored through the use of multiple resources. An excellent inquiry, for example, would be to explore the question, "How exactly were the pyramids built?" One of the reasons that this is an excellent inquiry question is because historians continue to debate this issue. One of many hypotheses is that the pyramids were built by slaves while another suggests that farmers were paid during the summer and fall months to build the pyramids. Historians are not certain if the structures were made by carrying blocks one by one, using lift machines, ramps, or some other means.

Web sites that pursue mysteries in history, such as http://unmueseum.org/bldpyram.htm and http://www.users/clhost.com/ata/egypt.htm, do an excellent job of making this debate accessible to students. Another Web site that illuminates this topic (but is difficult to read because there is so much information; hence it is better for middle school students and gifted intermediate students) is http://www.pbs.org/wgbh/nova/pyramid/. An easier Web site for students to use is http://www.ancientegypt.co.uk/pyramids/index.html, produced by the British Museum. This Web site actually presents conflicting theories about why Egyptians used the pyramid shape. The site http://www.touregypt.net/construction/ explores ways the pyramids might have been constructed.

Below are some accompanying books on ancient Egypt.

Colman, P. 1997. *Corpses, Coffins, and Crypts: A History of Burial.* New York: Holt. (Gr. 6–8)
Hawcock, D. 2000. *Amazing Pop-Up Pull-Out Mummy Book.* London: Dorling Kindersley. (Gr. 4–7)
Logan, C. 2002. *The 5,000-Year-Old Puzzle: Solving a Mystery of Ancient Egypt.* Illus. M. Sweet. New York: Farrar/Melanie Kroupa. (Gr. 3–6)
McIntosh, J. 2000. *Archaeology.* London: Dorling Kindersley. (Gr. 2–7)
Pemberton, D. 2001. *Egyptian Mummies: People from the Past.* San Diego, CA: Harcourt. (Gr. 2–6)

Using the Internet as a source for inquiry in history gives teachers a superb opportunity to help children learn to evaluate the quality of sources. This skill is one that historians must use in order to evaluate their subjects.

groups, or be massaged into entries to the National History Day competition. National History Day (http://www.nationalhistoryday.org) gives students in grades 6 through 12 the opportunity to present to judges exhibits, documentaries, papers, or performances.

Place in History

Where people lived gives us clues as to their lives. This includes their domicile as well as if they moved from place to place during their lifetime. Hogans and pueblos, also called cliff dwellings, are housing structures of the southwestern United States, yet each housed a different culture of Native American people. Appreciating the context of place gives children a better understanding of history. Some research on children's historical thinking suggests that children have a limited appreciation of history because they are confused about how history occurs in different places at the same time (Barton and Levstik 1996).

An interesting study for third and fourth graders is to go to the Internet and locate pictures of the homes owned by presidents when they were elected to office. From the prestigious Virginia plantation of Mount Vernon owned by President George Washington, to John Adams's simple farmhouse in Quincy, Massachusetts, to Thomas Jefferson's European-influenced Monticello (which he designed himself), to the clapboard two-story Springfield home of Abraham Lincoln, to Harry Truman's charmingly modest house that he bought from his in-laws, our presidents' homes attest that they came from very different economic backgrounds. Indeed, many came from humble, meager beginnings not unlike the lifestyles of many students themselves.

The climate and environment influence the culture of people. For instance, language, an aspect of culture, is reflective of the needs of people. Inuits have several different words in their language for snow, depending upon the texture and quality of the flakes and severity of the snowstorm. The Hopi tribe has only four color words. As the need for new vocabulary arises, due to the effects of globalism, economy, and technology, new words are created and added to a language. As an example, let's consider that Coca-Cola and Levi's are two words known in nearly every language in the world as a result of trade. The Vietnam War resulted in the development of the rapid medical treatment center called triage. And the development of a thin, portable computer called a laptop has become an essential tool for men and women throughout the world. The Internet makes it easy for elementary students in Nashville, Tennessee, to send messages to their friends and download and burn the latest top 40 hits onto CDs. That same Internet permits Masai tribesmen to sell their cattle as they herd their bovines across the savannahs of Africa.

We are influenced by the places we have lived as well as where we have traveled. Consider Thomas Jefferson: known as the author of the Declaration of Independence, he served as both secretary of state and president of the United States. While carrying out his duties as a diplomat, he was greatly influenced by his travels to France and Great Britain. As a result he brought back some very significant dishes that kids adore: macaroni and cheese, ice cream, and potato chips. George

Abraham Lincoln's home in Springfield, Illinois, was within walking distance to his law office and the state capitol building.

Washington Carver saw the farmland where he grew up depleted of its nutrients after years of producing cotton. Carver used scientific experiments to help farmers use southern land productively by finding another successful agrarian product. The outcome yielded peanuts as a cash crop and several new products, including another great food children love—peanut butter. Had George Washington Carver lived in Minnesota or Pennsylvania, peanut butter might not have been created for decades.

A beautiful picture book that illustrates climate and compares a young girl's memory of New York City to Long Island is the autobiographical sketch of Margaret Wise Brown. Children who love Brown's picture books will enjoy reading *The Days Before Now: An Autobiographical Note by Margaret Wise Brown* (Blos 1994) and might even be inspired to write their own stories of their childhood. *Our House: The Stories of Levittown* (Conrad 1995) recounts the lives of children from each of the decades from the 1940s to the 1990s. What unifies these stories of the second half of the twentieth century is the sense of place that is important to Levittown, Pennsylvania.

Another picture book with a social studies theme is *Paddle-to-the-Sea* (Holling 1941), a classic story that illustrates the journey of a Native American boy's home-made toy. The boy creates a canoe to fulfill his dream and the reader learns about the Paddle Person's journey from the Great Lakes to the ocean. This fabulous book integrates history, geography, and a message about keeping dreams alive.

Stories of human tragedy are often part of history. Consider *Katie's Wish* (Hazen 2002), a picture book that examines the feelings of a young Irish child whose mother feeds her family nutritious potatoes. But having plain old potatoes day after day becomes too much for little Katie who wishes them away. Soon after, a rot spreads across the potato fields, withering the crop and causing people to become ill and die. Sent with her cousin to Boston to join her father, Katie still blames herself. Half the population of Ireland either died or fled the Emerald Isle as a result of the Irish potato famine.

An even greater tragedy occurred during the Middle Ages in Europe. "And no bells tolled, and nobody wept no matter what his loss because almost everybody expected death. . . . And people said and believed, 'This is the end of the world,'" wrote Agnolo di Tura in 1347, conveying the reaction of the community to the bubonic plague, the Black Death that swept across Europe in the fourteenth century. The devastation caused by the plague and resultant spirited interest in science are probed in *When Plague Strikes: The Black Death, Smallpox, and AIDS* by James Cross Giblin (1995), who is an award-winning author of nonfiction books for children. Upper elementary and middle school students will be captivated by this book, which depicts human fear of the unknown and resultant scientific advancements in the field of medicine.

Tragedies of violations of human rights pepper history. Life in Russia during the pogroms (mass killings) is illustrated along with the significance of Ellis Island in *The Memory Coat* (Woodruff 1999). Emphasizing the importance of family and the reasons for emigration, this fictional story helps young children appreciate the challenges of entering America at the turn of the twentieth century. A good accompanying novel for upper elementary and middle schoolers is *Letters from Rifka* (Hesse 1992), which depicts a Russian Jewish girl's life as she leaves her native land for America. The plight of the Chinese during Chairman Mao's Cultural Revolution can be explored by middle schoolers in the autobiographical *Red Scarf Girl: A Memoir of the Cultural Revolution* (Jiang 1997).

Time in History

A continuing question over the years has been when are elementary students mature enough to grasp various historical concepts and understandings. Research has suggested that students' ability to understand the concept of historical time is developmental in nature (Thornton and Vukelich 1988). Levstik and Barton (2001) have completed research that shows that even kindergartners are adept at sequencing and chronology, but that specific dates are more troublesome for young children to learn. Dates have little meaning to children under the age of nine (Thornton and Vukelich 1988), but children as young as seven and eight are able to conceptualize "history" when using narratives (such as historical fiction) (Levstik and Pappas 1992). Even the youngest of school-aged children can accurately talk about "long ago" and times "close to now" (Levstik and Barton 2001). Rather than worrying so much about specific dates with youngest children, what may be more natural for children is to focus on the "what" of history rather than the "when" (Barton and Levstik 1996). By about fifth grade, generally students are developmentally ready to use dates in their discussions of history, although even third and fourth graders are developmentally beginning to understand the concept of dates

(Barton and Levstik 1996). Using a chronological framework that is concrete, such as a brief time line (1400s, 1500s, 1600s, and 1700s) showing the progression of major events from the discovery of America to the founding of the United States, may help older students grasp the relatively abstract concept of time. Pictures seem to be particularly useful to children learning the meaning of dates and time lines (Levstik and Barton 2001). Students at various age levels enjoy creating time lines of their own lives, complete with illustrations or pictures marking significant events. Older students will benefit from creating time lines that compare their own lives to world history, American history, and cultural events.

Literature that helps children understand the concept of time, chronology, and sequencing can build fundamental skills important to the development of historical knowledge. Narratives can help even the youngest children appreciate the passage of time. A picture book that elegantly describes the passage of time is *Who Came Down That Road?* (Lyon 1992). Great-grandparents, Indians, mammoths, and questions are all featured along one road that represents the history of the Earth. The story makes time relevant to a young boy and thus is a good entry point for introducing time lines at the primary level.

A whimsical picture book that appeals to children who wish that they could see real dinosaurs is *Time Train* by Paul Fleischman (1991). The story describes a class field trip on the Rocky Mountain Unlimited, which takes a group of students to the time of the dinosaurs. Although children must learn that people were not alive at the same time as dinosaurs, this book captures an imaginary encounter between children and prehistorical beasts.

Picture books can make a time period come alive for young children. Aliki's (1983) *A Medieval Feast* illuminates the preparations for a feast with a king during the Middle Ages. Young children will focus on the unusual foods prepared for the king, and teachers can emphasize the social structure illustrated in this book.

Nelson (1998) has suggested that teaching the history of the calendar can help children to appreciate how different calendars have emerged in different cultures. A picture book such as *Till Year's Good End: A Calendar of Medieval Labors* by Nikola-Lisa (1997) illustrates how the months might be experienced by working people in the Middle Ages. Understanding the establishment of the international date line and standardized time and distance in 1884 helps to demystify for children the concept of time and space.

Classroom calendars are an important way to indicate what has taken place during the school year and what is yet to occur. Nearly every kindergarten and first grade in the United States celebrates the "100th day of school." Linking calendars to historical study is a way to integrate some early understanding of time with current events for the youngest children. *Miss Bindergarten Celebrates the 100th Day of Kindergarten* (Slate 1998) is a must for all school libraries.

Calendars should be presented from the very beginning of the school year. On the first day of school, invite students to make a giant birthday calendar by chronologically getting in order their birthdays. Place signs with the names of the months around the classroom. Make the task more challenging for fourth through eighth graders by not permitting them to speak—allow them to use hand signals only. These activities can help children learn the important skill of sequencing.

Science, Technology, and History

Science and technology are intertwined with history as new advancements and improvements change the human condition. Medical advancements from herbal home remedies to Leonardo da Vinci's meticulous illustrations of the human circulatory system to Jonas Salk's discovery of a vaccine to prevent polio have changed how people live. Technological advancements in travel from the inventions of the wheel, two-horse chariot of Roman times, stagecoach, railroad, steamship, automobile, and airplane have resulted in the rapid movement of people over long distances. The course of history has been changed by such military advancements as the catapult, gunpowder, machine gun, tank, airplane, mobile radio, aircraft carrier, and nuclear bomb. The fear of chemical warfare and nuclear bombs looms over us today as heads of nations seek to flex their muscles and extend their territory and power base.

History and science blend together for interesting study for elementary and middle school students. Intermediate grade students will find *The Cod's Tale* (Kurlansky 2001), an informational picture book, to be a historical perspective of the cod. Included in this well-written book is humankind's thousand year relationship with this fish, once so plentiful that merely lowering a basket into the ocean resulted in several being hauled in as catch. Along with a scientific description of the life cycle and natural enemies of the cod is a historical perspective including culture, geography, technology, trade, and boundary law. A time line runs along the bottom of the pages. Mark Kurlansky's (2006) *The Story of Salt* is likewise intriguing—wars have been fought over this precious mineral.

Another book that weaves scientific facts and geographic information is the fascinating book *The Man-Eating Tigers of Sundarbans* by Sy Montgomery (2001). Living in a mangrove swamp on the Bay of Bengal, the Sundarbans tigers' forest is approachable only by boat. As men venture there for wood, fishing, and honey some are stalked by the tigers who hide in the water only to leap toward their victims, grabbing them by the back of their necks. A scientific perspective as well as native folklore and religious beliefs are all shared in this book.

The study of endangered species links history and science as does the examination of ecology and ecosystems of the world. An examination of human interference with ecology, such as the introduction of rabbits to Australia, destruction of the rain forests of the world, or takeover of farmland for housing developments, can raise awareness of the need for humans to be more discriminatory in their actions to preserve a balance with nature. The picture book *A River Ran Wild* (Cherry 1992) demonstrates the environmental changes of a river throughout its life, including the pollution by factories in the 1800s and 1900s and resultant efforts by community groups to restore the quality of the water. A complementary book is Kathryn Lasky's (1995) *She's Wearing a Dead Bird on Her Head*, which depicts a fictionalized account of Harriet Hemenway and Minna Hall, the nineteenth-century founders of the Massachusetts Audubon Society. This picture book not only highlights the environmental movement but also the women's rights movement.

Biographies

People make up the various cultures of our world. History is the record of the human condition of homo sapiens. Race, beliefs, and traditions influence families and each subsequent generation. Understanding how cultures are alike and how they differ is a primary social studies benchmark at all grade levels. A classroom rich in biographies might tempt children to learn about significant individuals from the past. Examining biographies can make a time period come alive for children, offer students a perspective on how other people have made decisions, or illustrate important values and character traits. Using an individual's life as a case study is an excellent way to help children learn about the larger lessons of citizenship.

Biographies offer case studies into how people have made decisions in the past. Jean Fritz's series on Revolutionary War heroes is a superb way to introduce primary through intermediate elementary students to famous individuals of the period. Her books include *And Then What Happened, Paul Revere?* (1973) and *Can't You Make Them Behave, King George?* (1977). Judith St. George's (2005) picture book *You're on Your Way, Teddy Roosevelt* describes his struggles as a youngster to become stronger as well as his curiosity about nature and animals. *Lou Gehrig: The Luckiest Man* (Adler 1997), an excellent biography for the primary grades, illustrates how a baseball star showed courage and commitment to his community in the face of a fatal disease. *Only Passing Through: The Story of Sojourner Truth* (Rockwell 2000), with gorgeous illustrations by R. Gregory Christie, teaches children about the example set by Sojourner Truth, who was released from slavery and used the law and her voice to advocate for abolition. Children may be surprised to learn that there was slavery in New York in the 1820s. The picture book *Flight* (Burleigh 1991) portrays the incredible journey of Charles Lindbergh as he became the first person to fly across the Atlantic Ocean. *Eleanor Roosevelt: A Life of Discovery* (Freedman 1993) presents the fascinating story of one of the most important women in American history. Personal and political details provide context to children who want to learn about the Great Depression, presidential politics, World War II, and the United Nations. *Martin's Big Words* (Rappaport 2001), a picture book biography, tells of young Martin Luther King, Jr., and how he became a leading spokesperson for the civil rights movement of the 1950s and 1960s. *Through My Eyes* (Bridges 1999), another picture book, is Ruby Bridges's autobiographical telling of her breaking the color barrier by becoming the first African American to attend an all-white elementary school in New Orleans, Louisiana, in the fall of 1960.

An important leader in women's rights was Amelia Bloomer, who started her own newspaper, fought for the vote for women, and started a fashion trend. Not content wearing uncomfortable corsets and hoop skirts, Amelia invented an early version of billowy slacks for women that earned the name "bloomers." The picture book *You Forgot Your Skirt, Amelia Bloomer!* (Corey 2000) is a delightful biography as well as a depiction of women's suffrage for first through fifth graders.

Upper elementary and middle school students will find *Tecumseh and the Shawnee Confederation* (Stefoff 1998) presents an interesting story of a man who attempted to unite the tribes of the Old North West (now Indiana, Illinois, and Ohio) to confront the invasion of settlers into their native lands. Middle schoolers can gain insight into the Lakota tribe from the time of the Louisiana Purchase to the massacre at Wounded Knee with *Tatan'ka Iyota'ke: Sitting Bull and His World* (Marrin 2001). From being trained to become a brave warrior early in his boyhood to becoming the supreme war chief and leader of the Lakota nation, Sitting Bull's truth, courage, spirituality, and love for his people make him a historical character worth studying. His reign as chief and subsequent life on a reservation are accurately depicted along with his brief sojourn with Buffalo Bill Cody's Wild West Show and death at the massacre at Wounded Knee.

The most influential and famous people of the last millennium are included in a reference book entitled *1000 Years of Famous People* (Gifford 2002). Students can read the thumbnail sketch of an individual and then seek out additional information in a biography. Upper elementary and middle school students find *Never Give Up and Go For It! Letters from American Heroes* (Andrews 2002) to be a fascinating book as several individuals and their brave deeds are depicted. A good activity is to place the heroes and heroines' names in a hat and have each student select one. The student then writes a letter to their hero or heroine commending the person's accomplishments.

To celebrate Women's History Month, visit "4000 Years of Women in Science" at http://crux.astr.ua.edu/4000ws/4000ws.html, which combines science and history education. Another beneficial site (http://www.rochester.edu/SBA/suffragehistory.html) for gathering information is maintained by the Susan B. Anthony Center for Women's Leadership at the University of Rochester. Teachers might select a book for a read-aloud such as *Let it Shine: Stories of Black Women Freedom Fighters* by Andrea Pinkney (2001). This excellent introductory book chronicles black women who have spoken out for economic, political, and social rights. Speaking in many forms and forums, these women labored in the struggle for freedom against overwhelming odds. The author portrays women from the Civil War period through today: Harriet Tubman's aiding slaves in escaping, Sojourner Truth's fight for freedom and equality for blacks and women, Mary McCleod Bethune's fight for better education, Ella Josephine Baker's breaking into the entertainment field, Rosa Parks's refusal to give up her bus seat to a white man, Shirley Chisholm's triumph at becoming the first black woman elected to Congress. Pinkney stresses the theme of service to others to benefit all. Middle school students will gain insight from the efforts of these African American women.

Several publishers have biography series that are appropriate for social studies. *My First Book of Biographies* (Marzollo 1994) offers brief introductions to pique young students' interest. A very easy to read biographical series is produced by Capstone Press and includes such famous individuals as George Washington, Cesar Chavez, and Martin Luther King, Jr. Other easy to read series are "American Legends" by Rosen Publishing, which includes books about Johnny Appleseed, Daniel Boone, and Jim Bowie, and the "LifeTimes" series by Chrysalis Education, which includes more recent historical leaders such as Anne Frank, Mother Theresa, and Nelson Mandela. For upper elementary students, the "People Who Made a Difference" series, published by Rourke Publishing, includes biographies on Jane Addams, Thomas Edison, Henry Ford, John Muir, and Florence Nightingale. A final suggestion is the series on community builders put out by Scholastic. This series features Andrew Carnegie, Bill Gates, and Milton Hershey, among others.

Some biographical Web sites include the following:

Amelia Earhart

http://www.ellensplace.net/cae_intr.html
This site is divided into three sections: The Early Years, The Celebrity, and The Last Flight.

Simón Bolívar

http://www.geocities.com/Athens/Acropolis/7609/eng/toc.html
The life of the great South American general is covered in a biography at this Web site.

Harriet Tubman

http://www.incwell.com/Biographies/Tubman.html
This site is about Harriet Tubman, the former slave who helped slaves escape on the Underground Railroad.

Students seeking information on presidents of the United States can go to the White House Web site and search for a biography of a particular president by using either the first and last initials of the president or by the numerical order of the president. For instance, http://www.whitehouse.gov/history/presidents/tj3.html is the site for Thomas Jefferson, the third president of the United States, and http://www.whitehouse.gov/history/presidents/al16.html is the site for Abraham Lincoln, sixteenth president of the United States.

Night is the autobiographical account by Nobel Prize winner Elie Wiesel (1972/2006) of how his Jewish family was taken from their home in 1944 to the Auschwitz concentration camp and then on to Buchenwald. Appropriate for eighth graders, this book vividly gives details of the harshness and horror inflicted on the Jews by the guards and members of the German SS.

Middle school students may go to more detailed Web sites. However, many biographical Web sites are maintained by universities and may overwhelm students with vast quantities of information. Chapter 10 discusses biographies further and provides additional titles.

Historical Fiction

One of the best ways to "make history come alive" is through storytelling and the use of historical fiction (Brophy 1992). Good historical fiction includes accurate facts of the period as well as descriptions of life during the time portrayed. Fortunately, there is an abundance of quality historical fiction suitable for grades K–8 with additional titles coming out each year.

For second and third graders the short, simple, heartwarming tale *Sarah, Plain and Tall* (MacLachlan 1985) tells of a woman from Maine who responds to a letter from a farmer who is seeking a wife and mother for his two young children. This book is also readily available in Spanish. Third and fourth graders enjoy the exhilarating adventure and unexpected tragedy of a dogsled race in the classic *Stone Fox* (Gardiner 1980).

Suspense always intrigues upper elementary and middle school students. Such is *The Witch of Blackbird Pond* (Speare 1978), a Newbery Award-winning novel set in

Puritan New England. Kit is different from other girls as she knows how to swim in an era when swimming was something only boys and men did. When she teaches a youngster how to read, she is accused of witchcraft. This book offers insights to the Salem witch trials and is suitable for grades five through eight (see chapter 1 for an interdisciplinary unit on the Salem Witch Trials).

A Cinderella story in reverse, *Esperanza Rising* (Ryan 2000) offers a tale of a Mexican girl who was born to wealth and privilege as the daughter of a rich land-owner. Her father's untimely death leads to her and her mother fleeing to the United States and freedom. But the year is 1924 and the only work they can find is in the fields as laborers planting, cultivating, and harvesting vegetables and fruits. Another tale of the Great Depression is shared in the Newbery Award-winning *A Year Down Yonder* (Peck 2001). The setting is rural downstate Illinois in a small town where everyone knows their neighbors and almost everyone is destitute due to the poor economy.

A book that is not to be overlooked is *Neela: Victory Song* (Divakaruni 2003), which shares the story of a 12-year-old girl in 1939 who lives through India's struggle for independence and who resists an arranged marriage by her family. More examples of historical fiction are shared throughout this book and particularly in the next chapter.

Nonfiction, Informational Books

While most textbooks gloss over historical topics or contain more breadth than depth, nonfiction books give students a greater opportunity to construct their own understandings (Tomlinson, Tunnell, and Richgels 1993; Zarnowski 1998). By selecting several nonfiction books on a theme or topic, teachers can help students consider different authors' voices and multiple perspectives on a person, event, or idea. Particularly appropriate are books that integrate primary source material and vivid descriptions with pictures (Zarnowski 1998).

Reading nonfiction text should be modeled by the teacher so that students will better understand how to approach the format and how to incorporate previously gained knowledge. Using the teacher's best media friends, overhead projectors and sticky notes, here are steps to modeling nonfiction reading with students that have been adapted from Stephanie Harvey and Anne Goudvis's (2000) suggestions for improving reading comprehension:

1. Make an overhead transparency of a nonfiction piece, such as an article from the children's social studies magazines *Cobblestone*, *Calliope*, or *Scholastic News*, and place it on an overhead projector. Start with something short, only a page or two.

2. Read the passage aloud, stopping and rereading aloud important points. Explain why you believe each point is significant (caption, defines a new word or concept, shares critical information, etc.).

3. Relate information from the piece to your previously gained knowledge. Tell the students what you already know from other sources (perhaps a television documentary, a newspaper or magazine article, a book, etc.).

4. Continue reading the piece, stopping and questioning or responding when appropriate.

5. Use a second overhead projector to write comments. Divide an overhead transparency into three columns—Facts, Questions, and Responses (FQRs). Write down the information you gathered, questions that came to mind, and responses to the newly gained information.

6. Have students use color-coded sticky notes (Facts—green; Questions—yellow; Responses—blue) to write down their own FQRs and then place them on the chalkboard under the three categories.

7. Have a few students share their sticky notes, beginning with Facts and progressing to Questions and, lastly, Responses. Comment on the thinking of each student: Are they relating previously gained knowledge? Making predictions? Using context clues to make suppositions? Developing thoughtful questions that may, or may not, have answers?

8. Next, have students write in their social studies learning log (a spiral notebook solely for writing about social studies) what they learned from the topic shared in the information, nonfiction piece.

9. After five minutes have passed, have a few students share what they have written about the topic.

If there are ample quantities of a text so that each student can have a copy, such as the *Weekly Reader, Scholastic News, Time for Kids,* or *National Geographic in the Classroom,* students can follow along at their seats or sitting on the floor. Putting the students in work groups of three to produce a FQR sheet for another piece of text is also helpful. Scholastic News provides features such as headings and bold print that are synonymous with informational text.

An interesting twist to informational books is Phillip M. Hoose's (2001) *We Were There, Too: Young People in U S. History,* a book targeted at intermediate and middle schoolers. Beginning with a 12-year-old who sailed with Christopher Columbus as a cabin boy, nearly 70 young people who either intentionally or unintentionally made major contributions to the history of the United States are described. A brief follow-up regarding their adult lives is also included. This makes for a great writing stimulus.

Many informational books are filled with facts but presented in an appealing manner, thereby making them palatable for students. Such is *Black Potatoes: The Story of the Great Irish Famine, 1845–1850* (Bartoletti 2001), a well-researched book that relies upon original sources such as diaries, archives, and newspapers of the period. Heartrending accounts of local Irish who died of starvation while rich landlords exported food to England are shared. Like a number of informational books, this book includes a bibliography, source list, and Web site addresses for teachers and students to use. Companion books might include the informational book *We Came to North America: The Irish* (Nickles 2001) and *Feed the Children First: Irish Memories of the Great Hunger* (Lyons, 2002), a collection of narrative accounts from the children and grandchildren of the survivors of the great famine that brings home for readers the human element behind history.

Topics of study can be enriched through nonfiction books. A study of jazz can combine biographies of such great jazz legends as Louis Armstrong, Cab Calloway, Count Basie, Pearl Bailey, Duke Ellington, Ella Fitzgerald, Billie Holiday, and others. Students can work in pairs to report on one of these major contributors to jazz. Through use of the Internet, they can download a recording from their musician and share it as part of their presentation. *The Sound that Jazz Makes* by Carole Boston Weatherford (2001) is a book that traces the roots of jazz back to African rhythms in song and dance found through songs shared by slaves during fieldwork. Jazz's influence on ragtime and opera written by such noted American composers as Irving Berlin and George Gershwin makes for a challenge to gifted students. Other topics of study could be vocal or dance styles as well as an in-depth study of jazz lyrics. Another could be of famous jazz clubs such as the Cotton Club and Birdland Club.

Children's Books about Jazz

Curtis, C. P. 1999. *Bud, Not Buddy.* New York: Delacorte. (Gr. 5–8)

Diamond, B. 2001. *Louis Armstrong: Jazzing Up the Music.* Illus. L. Harden. New York: McGraw-Hill. (Gr. 1–3)

Gray, L. M. 1996. *Little Lil and the Swing-Singing Sax.* New York: Simon & Schuster. (Gr. 2–4)

Orgill, R. 1997. *If I Only Had a Horn: Young Louis Armstrong.* Boston: Houghton Mifflin. (Gr. 2–6)

Pinkney, A. D. 1998. *Duke Ellington: The Piano Prince and His Orchestra.* Illus. B. Pinkney. New York: Hyperion. (Gr. 2–6)

Raschka, C. 1992. *Charlie Parker Played Be Bop.* New York: Orchard. (Gr. 2–8)

Schroeder, A. 1996. *Satchmo's Blues.* Illus. F. Cooper. New York: Doubleday. (Gr. 2–8)

This topic of study gives students the opportunity to listen to jazz and consider how the music might be reflective of what is happening in American history. Teachers can also refer to the following NCSS Standards-Linked Lesson Plan on jazz as a reflection of the 1920s.

NCSS STANDARDS-LINKED LESSON PLAN

Jazz as a Reflection of the 1920s

Theme: 1920s

Source: Mary Beth Henning, Northern Illinois University

Objectives:

• Students will discuss how jazz music might be reflective of the events occurring in the 1920s.

• Students will discover some of the cultural/musical/historical roots of jazz music. Students will define jazz music.

NCSS Themes:

I. Culture—Social studies program should include experiences that provide for the study of culture and cultural diversity, so that

• The early grade learner can describe ways in which language, stories, folktales, music, and artistic creations serve as expressions of culture and influence the behavior of people living in a particular culture; and

- The middle grade learner can explain and give examples of how language, literature, the arts, architecture, other artifacts, traditions, beliefs, values, and behaviors contribute to the development and transmission of culture.

Materials: Jazz selections such as "Grandpa's Spells," "Blue Horizons," or others that would be reflective of the different moods of the 1920s, samples of music that could be considered jazz roots, such as "Guinea Hunter's Dance" or gospel.

Process:
- Music can tell us a lot about a decade. The 1920s is sometimes called the Jazz Age. I am going to play a couple selections of jazz music for you today. I would like you to listen to the music and see if you can interpret what the musicians might have been feeling when they wrote and played this music.
  Play "Grandpa's Spells"
  —Ask students, "What do you think the musicians were feeling when they made this music?"
  —Can you guess what might have been happening in the 1920s that would make people feel like making this kind of music?
  —Sadness, discrimination

- Some people say that jazz is the first form of truly American music.
  —Who do you think created jazz music?
  —African Americans, Duke Ellington, Louis Armstrong, etc., city music (New Orleans)
  —Where do you think the ideas for jazz came from?
  —Gospel, traditional African music, also blues
  Play samples of gospel and Guinea dance
  —Have a student point out Guinea on a map (West Africa).
  —Ask students to compare how this music sounds like jazz.
  —Can you guess what might have been happening in the 1920s that would make people feel like making this kind of music?
  —Prosperity, happiness, dancing
  Play "Blue Horizons"
  —Ask students, "What do you think the musicians were feeling when they made this music?"

- Ask students to define jazz now that they have heard a couple different selections.
  —Improvised, syncopated, ensemble playing

- Ask students to think about other kinds of music that might be unique to different decades in American history. How might that kind of music reflect the events and feelings of the decades? The previous and current decades?

- Conclusion: Ask students to review what they have learned today about music and the 1920s.

Learning Styles Addressed: Verbal/linguistic, music/rhythm, visual/spatial, interpersonal

Evaluation: Reflect on the quality of students' oral responses to the discussion. See if students can find music to use in their own presentations of other decades in history.

Extension Activities: Read students books such as *The Sound that Jazz Makes* by Carole Boston Weatherford (2000) or *Jazz ABZ* by Wynton Marsalis (2005). In *Jazz ABZ* poetry, wordplay, free verse, and more are teamed with famous jazz musicians in this sophisticated and elegant alphabet book. Have the entire class read *Bud, Not Buddy,* the Newbery Award-winning book by Christopher Paul Curtis (1999) about a young boy who tries to find his trumpet-playing father as he roams across the country with a small-time jazz band during the Great Depression.

Chapter Summary

History is the thread that ties social studies together with people, places, and things. Certainly it serves as a foundation block in social studies instruction. Through a meticulous study of documents, oral histories, and artifacts historians give a perspective of the events and issues that have influenced humankind.

History can be shared through a variety of different teaching approaches. Jackdaws (containing artifacts and real documents) and WebQuests, as well as different forms of literature (picture books, historical fiction, and nonfiction books), all serve as viable means of history instruction.

Children's Literature Recommendations

Adler, D. A. 1997. *Lou Gehrig: The Luckiest Man.* San Diego, CA: Gulliver. Gentle pictures accompany the story of a man honored as the "greatest prototype of good sportsmanship and citizenship." This book illustrates life in the early twentieth century and will appeal to baseball fans. (Gr. 1–6)

Aliki. 1983. *A Medieval Feast.* New York: Thomas Crowell. Children will marvel at the edible extravagance of blackbirds baked in a pie and marzipan sculptures that were created for the king's feast. Life on a medieval estate comes to life in this story. (Gr. 1–6)

Andrews, A. 2002. *Never Give Up and Go For It! Letters from American Heroes.* New York: Dalmation Press. Upper elementary and middle schoolers will find this book to be of interest. Outstanding accomplishments of famous Americans are portrayed. (Gr. 4–8)

Bachrach, S. D. 1994. *Tell Them We Remember: The Story of the Holocaust.* Boston: Little, Brown. Individuals' stories are placed in historical context to make the Holocaust more personal. (Gr. 4–8)

Bartoletti, S. C. 2001. *Black Potatoes: The Story of the Great Irish Famine, 1845–1850.* Boston: Houghton Mifflin. During the latter 1840s, Ireland is hit by a great famine when a potato blight destroys the crops. Thousands become ill and die while thousands of others flee to mainland Europe and the United States. (Gr. 6–8)

Blos, J. W. 1994. *The Days Before Now: An Autobiographical Note by Margaret Wise Brown.* New York: Simon & Schuster. Blos has adapted an autobiographic note written by Margaret Wise Brown for the Junior Book of Authors into a beautiful picture book sure to appeal to young children. (Gr. Pre-K–4)

Bridges, R. 1999. *Through My Eyes.* New York: Scholastic. On November 14, 1960, escorted by federal marshals, six-year-old Ruby Bridges became the first African American ever to attend all-white William Frantz Elementary School in New Orleans, Louisiana. (Gr. 1–8)

Burleigh, R. 1991. *Flight: The Journey of Charles Lindbergh.* New York: Philomel. A retelling of the first famous flight across the Atlantic that will appeal to even young children. (Gr. K–5)

Chang, I. 1991. *A Separate Battle: Women and the Civil War.* New York: Lodestar. The role of women as nurses, soldiers, spies, and abolitionists is explored in this nonfiction book. (Gr. 4–8)

Cherry, L. 1992. *A River Ran Wild.* San Diego, CA: Harcourt Brace. A nonfiction historical account of a river in the eastern United States and how local citizens took action to make it environmentally safe again. (Gr. K–8)

Conrad, P. 1995. *Our House: The Stories of Levittown.* New York: Scholastic. Although the houses might all look the same in Levittown, Pennsylvania, the stories told from children's perspectives in each of the decades from 1940–1990 reveal the unique experience of each family and each time period. This book shares stories from the first planned community. (Gr. 3–8)

Corey, S. 2000. *You Forgot Your Skirt, Amelia Bloomer!* Illus. C. McLaren. New York: Scholastic. Amelia Bloomer starts her own newspaper, tries to change the voting laws, and creates a new fashion for women—freeing them of hoop skirts and tight-fitting corsets. (Gr. 1–5)

Curtis, C. P. 1999. *Bud, Not Buddy.* New York: Delacorte. During the Great Depression, a young boy seeks to find his father who is a member of a traveling band. (Gr. 5–8)

Cushman, K. 1997. *The Ballad of Lucy Whipple.* Boston: Houghton Mifflin. When her family pulls up stakes in Massachusetts to venture with other gold rushers of 1849, Lucy proves to be reluctant. (Gr. 4–7)

Divakaruni, C. B. 2003. *Neela: Victory Song.* Madison, WI: American Girl. Twelve-year-old Neela observes the arranged marriage of her sister and wonders why boys receive a better education. The backdrop is India's struggle for independence from Great Britain. (Gr. 5–8)

Fleischman, P. 1991. *Time Train.* New York: HarperCollins. For teachers who might wish to introduce the idea of time travel, this book provides just the train ticket. (Gr. K–5)

Freedman, R. 1993. *Eleanor Roosevelt: A Life of Discovery.* New York: Clarion Books. This Newbery Honor book combines a frank text with primary source documents and photos of Eleanor Roosevelt's life. (Gr. 4–8)

Fritz, J. 1973. *And Then What Happened, Paul Revere?* New York: Coward, McCann & Geoghegan. One of Fritz's earliest stories of the Revolutionary period. Her delightful prose and the engaging illustrations make this a classic. (Gr. 2–6)

———. 1977. *Can't You Make Them Behave, King George?* New York: Coward, McCann & Geoghegan. Another one of Fritz's popular texts characterized by her engaging storytelling and historical facts interwoven in the text. (Gr. 2–6)

Gardiner, J. 1980. *Stone Fox.* Illus. M. Sewall. New York: Holt. The family farm is at stake when grandpa suffers a stroke, but can a young boy and his beloved dog, Searchlight, win the dogsled race against Stone Fox? (Gr. 3–5)

Giblin, J. C. 1995. *When Plague Strikes: The Black Death, Smallpox, and AIDS.* Woodcuts, D. Frampton. New York: HarperCollins. The plague and its various episodes in history open this book along with how society and leaders reacted. Later events of smallpox and the more recent discovery of AIDS are posed from an historical perspective. (Gr. 5–8)

Gifford, C. 2002. *1000 Years of Famous People.* New York: Kingfisher. Movers and shakers are described in this reference book. (Gr. 3–8)

Hampton, W. 1997. *Kennedy Assassinated! The World Mourns: A Reporter's Story.* Cambridge, MA: Candlewick Press. This is a first-person account of a young reporter's actions in Dallas, Texas, on the famous day, November 22, 1963. A variety of press photographs is included. (Gr. 4–8)

Hazen, B. S. 2002. *Katie's Wish.* Illus. E. A. McCully. New York: Dial. Young Katie grows tired of eating potatoes so she wishes they'd go away. Then the potato famine begins and she blames herself. Great picture book to use as a read-aloud to introduce a unit on the potato famine. (Gr. K–3)

Hesse, K. 1992. *Letters from Rifka.* New York: Holt. A young Russian Jewish girl writes about life and discrimination. (Gr. 6–8)

Hendershot, J. 1987. *In Coal Country.* New York: Knopf. Coal mining in Appalachia is described. (Gr. 2–6).

Holling, H. C. 1941. *Paddle-to-the-Sea.* Boston: Houghton Mifflin. This Caldecott Honor book tells a wonderful story of place and sea journeys from the perspective of a "Paddle Person" created by an American Indian boy. The Paddle Person fulfills the boy's dream of adventures along its way from Lake Nipigon, Canada, to the Gulf of St. Lawrence and France. (Gr. 2–6)

Hoose, P. M. 2001. *We Were There, Too: Young People in U.S. History.* New York: Farrar, Straus & Giroux. Contributions of over 60 young people who made major contributions to the history of the United States are shared in chronological order. A brief follow up on their adult lives is also included. (Gr. 4–8)

Jiang, J. 1997. *Red Scarf Girl: A Memoir of the Cultural Revolution.* New York: HarperCollins. A young girl recalls the chaotic events under Chairman Mao's cultural revolution in Communist China in the 1960s. (Gr. 7–8)

Kurlansky, M. 2001. *The Cod's Tale.* Illus. S. D. Schindler. New York: Putnam. A scientific and historical look at the cod fish. Excellent for linking science and social studies. (Gr. 2–6)

———. 2006. *The Story of Salt.* Illus. S. D. Schindler. New York: Putnam. A scientific and historical look at salt, a mineral needed for humans to survive. Excellent for linking science and social studies. (Gr. 2–6)

Lasky, K. 1995. *She's Wearing a Dead Bird on Her Head.* Illus. D. Catrow. New York: Hyperion. A fictionalized account of Harriet Hemenway and Minna Hall, the nineteenth-century founders of the Massachusetts Audubon Society. The environmental and women's rights movements are portrayed in this book. (Gr. 1–5)

Levinson, N. 1990. *Christopher Columbus: Voyager to the Unknown.* New York: Dutton, Lodestar. A biography of Christopher Columbus that portrays the dangers of the trip. (Gr. 1–5)

Lyon, G. 1992. *Who Came Down That Road?* New York: Richard Jackson. This gorgeously illustrated book lyrically describes how different people and animals have traveled down an "old, old, old, old road." Beginning with a little boy's great-grandma and great-grandpa, the travelers on the road represent the passage of time. (Gr. Pre-K–3)

———. 1994. *Mama Is a Miner.* New York: Orchard. Illus. P. Catalanotto. The life of a mother who is also an underground coal miner is depicted. (Gr. 3–6)

Lyons, M., ed. 2002. *Feed the Children First: Irish Memories of the Great Hunger.* New York: Atheneum. Organized themes including The People, The Houses, The Land, and Searching for Food will help students learn about the famine through the voices of the Irish who encountered it. This book brings home for readers the human element behind the history. (Gr. 4–8)

MacLachlan, P. 1985. *Sarah, Plain and Tall.* New York: Harper & Row. An award-winning novel about a mail order bride who leaves her home on the East Coast to go to the prairie. (Gr. 2–4)

Marrin, A. 2001. *Tatan'ka Iyota'ke: Sitting Bull and His World.* New York: Dutton. From learning to hunt to becoming supreme war chief, Sitting Bull's life is eloquently described. (Gr. 7–8)

Marsalis, W. 2005. *Jazz ABZ: An A to Z Collection of Jazz Portraits.* Cambridge, MA: Candlewick Press. Twenty-six famous jazz musicians are portrayed through poetry in this vibrant picture book. (Gr. 4–8)

Marzollo, J. 1994. *My First Book of Biographies.* New York: Scholastic. Forty-five brief biographies with engaging pictures introduce children to a multitude of men and women from different times and cultures. (Gr. 1–5)

Montgomery, S. 2001. *The Man-Eating Tigers of Sundarbans.* Photo. E. Briggs. Boston: Houghton Mifflin. Nonfiction account of the Sundarbans tigers accompanied by native folklore and religious beliefs. (Gr. 2–3)

Murphy, J. 1990. *The Boys' War: Confederate and Union Soldiers Talk about the Civil War.* New York: Clarion. Primary source documents are woven throughout the text. Although some photos are gruesome, the book makes the point that the Civil War was fought by many children. (Gr. 3–8)

Nickles, G. 2001. *We Came to North America: The Irish.* New York: Crabtree. Actual newspaper articles, personal accounts, and more are shared in this overview of the Irish coming to America in the 1600s and after. (Gr. 3–8)

Nikola-Lisa, W. 1997. *Till Year's Good End: A Calendar of Medieval Labors.* New York: Atheneum. Inspired by the Books of Hours from the Middle Ages, this children's book puts a different twist on learning about the months of the year. (Gr. 1–6)

Peck, R. 2001. *A Year Down Yonder.* New York: Penguin. A young girl from Chicago stays with her grandmother in rural Illinois during the Great Depression. (Gr. 6–8)

Pelta, K. 1991. *Discovering Christopher Columbus: How History Is Invented.* San Antonio, TX: Lerner. A portrayal of how historians work. (Gr. 2–5)

Pinkney, A. D. 2001. *Let it Shine: Stories of Black Women Freedom Fighters.* Illus. S. Alcorn. San Diego, CA: Gulliver. Taking its title from the phrase "letting the light shine," a term used by Ida Wells-Barnett's work through the media to stop the lynching in the middle of the night of black men by Ku Klux Klan members. Ten African American women over a 150-year period in the United States who fought for civil rights and liberties are portrayed. (Gr. 5–8)

Rappaport, D. 2001. *Martin's Big Words.* Illus. B. Collier. New York: Jump at the Sun. A picture book depicting the civil rights movement of the 1950s and 60s and how it influenced Martin Luther King, Jr. (Gr. 1–4)

Rockwell, A. 2000. *Only Passing Through: The Story of Sojourner Truth.* New York: Alfred A. Knopf. Tells the story of Sojourner Truth from age 9 to age 46. Morals of speaking up, valuing family, and using your voice are conveyed. (Gr. 1–8)

Ryan, P. Muñoz. 1998. *Riding Freedom.* Illus. B. Selznick. New York: Scholastic. A biography of Charlotte "Charley" Parkhurst, a famous horsewoman who was the first woman to vote in California. (Gr. 3–6)

———. 2000. *Esperanza Rising.* New York: Scholastic. When a wealthy girl's father dies, she and her mother escape from Mexico to the United States. A reverse Cinderella tale that gives pause for thought to readers. (Gr. 5–8)

St. George, J. 2005. *You're on Your Way, Teddy Roosevelt.* New York: Philomel. Pale and puny, asthmatic young Teddy Roosevelt and his family are the focus of this book. Although wealthy, Teddy's family struggled to help him change from a weakling into the hearty world leader and environmentalist he later became. (Gr. 3-5)

Slate, J. 1998. *Miss Bindergarten Celebrates the 100th Day of Kindergarten.* Illus. A. Wolff. New York: Dutton. The famous dog teacher and her delightful students celebrate the 100th day of kindergarten. Adam the alligator collects 100 Popsicle sticks and Brenda the beaver makes 100 loops for a construction paper chain. Miss Bindergarten does 100 sit-ups and makes 100-day punch from 100 cherries and 100 ice cubes. Delightful time story. (Gr. K–1)

Speare, E. 1978. *The Witch of Blackbird Pond.* New York: Laurel Leaf. Set during the Salem witch trials, teenage Kit arrives from Barbados and befriends Quakers. When she teaches a child to read, she is accused of witchcraft. (Gr. 5–8)

Stefoff, R. 1998. *Tecumseh and the Shawnee Confederation.* New York: Facts on File. Chief Tecumseh led tribes of the Midwest against settlers and the Army during the early days of the United States. (Gr. 6–8)

Weatherford, C. B. 2001. *The Sound that Jazz Makes.* Illus. E. Velasquez. New York: Walker and Company. This marvelously written book traces the history of jazz back to its African roots. It is filled with illustrations that bring history to life and evoke powerful emotions in the reader. This is an excellent classroom resource that belongs in every elementary school library. (Gr. 1–5)

Wiesel, E. 1972/2006. *Night.* New York: Hill and Wang. The true story of how Wiesel's family was taken away in the night and how he never again saw his mother or sisters. (Gr. 8)

Woodruff, E. 1999. *The Memory Coat*. New York: Scholastic. A young Russian immigrant wears a homemade coat sewn by his mother. When the doctor marks him as a reject at Ellis Island, he turns his coat inside out so the chalk won't show. (Gr. 3–8)

Yolen, J. 1992. *Encounter*. San Diego, CA: Harcourt. This book illuminates the perspective of the Taino people who first met Columbus in the New World. (Gr. 1–5)

Related Technology Tools

Web Sites

Individual History of the 50 States

State History

http://www.50states.com

This site contains general information about state capitals, flags, songs, and locations.

Colonial America

Life on a Colonial Farm

http://www.pbs.org/ktcaniberty/perspectives/dailylife.html

Students can view life on a colonial farm. Highlighted are the lives of children, their clothing, games they played, and their chores.

Colonial Williamsburg

http://www.history.org

Learn about life during the colonial times by taking a virtual tour of the National Historic site of Colonial Williamsburg.

America's Homepage

http://www.pilgrims.net/plymouth

The Revolutionary War

The American Revolution for Kids

http://www.kidinfo.com/American_History/American_Revolution.html

Slavery and the Underground Railroad

The Underground Railroad (National Geographic)

www.nationalgeographic.com/features/99/radroad/

"Born in Slavery: Slave Narratives from the Federal Writers' Project, 1936–1938"

http://memory.loc.gov/ammem/snhtml/snhome.html

Civil War

The American Civil War Homepage

http://sunsite.utk.edu/civil-war/

Great American History's Outline of the Civil War

http://members.tripod.com/~greatamericanhistory/

The Civil War Home Page

http://www.civil-war.net

World War II

National World War II Memorial

http://www.wwiimemorial.com/Education/index.htm

Holocaust

The United States Holocaust Memorial Museum

http://www.ushmm.org/education/foreducators/

A Cybrary of the Holocaust

http://remember.org/index.html#Top

Packed with primary source documents and discussions geared toward students and teachers, this Web site focuses on the Holocaust.

The Cold War
CNN
  http://www.cnn.com/SPEC/ALS/cold.war/
Civil Rights
Martin Luther King, Jr., Research and Education Institute
  http://www.stanford.edu/group/King/
The Civil Rights Movement (CNN)
  http://www.cnn.com/EVENTS/1997/mlk/links.html
Photo Tour of the Civil Rights Movement
  http://seattletimes.nwsource.com/mlk/movement/PT

WebQuests
A Bomb is Dropped and Our Lives are Changed (Gr. 7–8)
  http://students.itech.sfsu.edu/itec815_s99/rfishtrom/
American Revolution Project (Gr. 5)
  http://www.esc20.net.etprojects/formats/webquests/fal199/revol/
Avoid It Like the Plague!!! (Gr. 6–8)
  http://www.techtrekers.com/webquests/#Social%20Studies
Donner Online (Story of the Donner Party) (Gr. 5–8)
  http://www.kn.pacbell.com/wired/donner/index.html
Jazz Age (Gr. 7–8)
  http://wapiti.pvs.k12.nm.us/~Computer/jazzage.htm
Jamestown: The First Permanent Settlement in the New World (Gr. 5–6)
  http://www.nevada/edu/~rpeters/peterswebquest.htm
A Journey on the Oregon Trail (Gr. 5–8)
  http://www.plainfield.k12.in.us/hschool.webq/webq58/pagethtm
Presidents Day (Gr. 3–6)
  http://its.guilford.k12.nc.us/webquests/presidents/pres.htm
Titanic—Sink or Swim (Gr. 3–5)
  http://www.esc20.net/etprojects/formats/webquests/spring2000/ulvalde2282k/hsddwq/
  default.htm

Software and Videos
Fun Facts of American History. Teacher's Video Company. Available from www.teachers-video.com. Do your students know that we had a president serve for only one day? Why do we drive on the right-hand side of the road? What is the origin of the tepee?
Little Known Facts of American History. Teacher's Video Company. Available from www.teachersvideo.com. Learn about the origins of the Ferris wheel, tissue paper, and potato chip. Meet the first stagecoach drivers, phone operators, and baseball umpires. Discover how time zones and road maps changed life in America.
World War II Chronicles. 1995. A E Home Video. Seven 70-minute videos. Available at Teacher's Discovery, 800-543-4180. Produced using rare archival footage and expert commentary, this series gives a complete account of World War II.
Carmen Sandiego Junior Detective Edition. 1995. Broderbund, San Rafael, CA. There are a multitude of "Where in _____ is Carmen Sandiego?" titles that teach geography. Students like them and many schools and parents have purchased at least one of the programs from Broderbund.
Sim Town. 1995. Software for Kids, Theatre Square, Orinda, CA. This is the version of the popular Sim series that appeals to the youngest set. Children create their own town as they learn about what makes a neighborhood. *Picture Atlas of the World,* 1995, National

Geographic Society, Washington, DC. A wonderful geography resource that children can use to explore culture, people, and geography of different countries.

Oregon Trail III. 2000. Minnesota Educational Computer Consortium, St. Paul, MN. This "oldie but goodie" is still a wonderfully interactive program that children love. Students have the opportunity to make choices that will affect the outcome of their simulated journey on the Oregon Trail.

Maya Quest. 1995. Minnesota Educational Computer Consortium, St. Paul, MN. Made by the same company that markets Oregon Trail, this is an inquiry into the Mayan culture.

Jean Fritz Videos. Sundance. Available at www.sundancepub.com. Set includes nine videos also sold separately. These videos are based on the popular Jean Fritz books that explore social studies themes.

References

Barth, J. L., and S. S. Shermis. 1970. "Defining the Social Studies: An Exploration of Three Traditions." *Social Education* 34 (7): 743–51.

Barton, K. C., and L. S. Levstik. 1996. "Back When God Was Around and Everything: Elementary Children's Understanding of Historical Time." *American Educational Research Journal* 33 (2): 419–54.

Blight, D. W. 2002. *Beyond the Battlefield: Race, Memory, and the American Civil War.* Cambridge, MA: Harvard Press.

Bradley Commission on History in Schools. 1988. *Building a History Curriculum: Guidelines for Teaching History in Schools.* Washington, DC: Educational Excellence Network.

Brophy, J. 1992. "Fifth-Grade U.S. History: How One Teacher Arranged to Focus on Key Ideas in Depth." *Theory and Research in Social Education* 20 (2): 141–55.

Dowd, F. S. 1990. "What's a Jackdaw Doing in Our Classroom?" *Childhood Education* 66: 228–31.

Downey, M. T., and L. S. Levstik. 1991. "Teaching and Learning History." In *Handbook of Research Studies Teaching and Learning*, ed. J. P. Shaver, pp. 400–10. New York: MacMillan.

Engle, S. 1987. *Voices of Social Education: 1937–1987.* New York: Macmillan.

Fuhler, C. J., P. J. Farris, and P. A. Nelson. 2006. "Building Literacy Skills across the Curriculum: Forging Connections with the Past through Artifacts." *The Reading Teacher* 59 (7): 646–59.

Hartzler-Miller, C. 2001. "Making Sense of 'Best Practice' in Teaching History." *Theory and Research in Social Education* 9 (4): 672–95.

Harvey, S., and A. Goudvis. 2000. *Strategies That Work: Teaching Comprehension to Enhance Understanding.* Portland, ME: Stenhouse.

Hickey, M. G. 1997. "Bloomers, Bell Bottoms, and Hula Hoops." *Social Education* 61 (5): 293–99.

Krey, D. M. 1998. *Children's Literature in Social Studies: Teaching to the Standards.* Washington, DC: National Council for the Social Studies.

Lee, J. K. 2002. "Ideology and the Web." *Social Education* 66 (3): 161–65.

Levstik, L. S., and K. C. Barton. 1996. "'They Still Use Some of Their Past': Historical Salience in Elementary Children's Chronological Thinking." *Journal of Curriculum Studies* 28 (5): 531–76.

———. 2001. *Doing History: Investigating with Children in Elementary and Middle Schools.* 2nd ed. Mahwah, NJ: Lawrence Erlbaum.

Levstik, L. S., and C. C. Pappas. 1992. "New Directions for Studying Historical Understanding." *Theory and Research in Social Education* 20 (4): 369–85.

Loewen, J. 1995. *Lies My Teacher Told Me: Everything Your American History Textbook Got Wrong.* New York: New Press.

McCullough, D. 1992. *Truman*. New York: Simon & Schuster.

———. 2001. *John Adams*. New York: Simon Schuster.

Martorella, P. H., and C. Beal. 2002. *Social Studies for Elementary School Classrooms*. 3rd ed. Upper Saddle River, NJ: Merrill.

Massialas, B. G., and C. B. Cox. 1966. *Inquiry in Social Studies*. New York: McGraw-Hill.

Meacham, J. 2002 (September 9). "A Date with History: A *Newsweek* Conversation with Some Leading American Historians." *Newsweek*, 62–65.

Monteverde, F. E. 1999. "Considering the Source: Mary Downing Sheldon Barnes." In *Bending the Future to Their Will: Civic Women, Social Education, and Democracy*, ed. M. S. Crocco and O. L. Davis, Jr. Lanham, MD: Roman & Littlefield.

National Council for the Social Studies. 1994. *Expectations of Excellence: Curriculum Standards for Social Studies*. Washington, DC: Author.

Nelson, J. L. 1996. "The Historical Imperative for Issues-Centered Education." In *Handbook on Teaching Social Issues*, ed. R. W. Evans and D. W. Saxe, pp. 14–24. Washington, DC: National Council for the Social Studies.

Nelson, M. R. 1998. *Children and Social Studies: Creative Teaching in the Elementary Classroom*. 3rd ed. Ft. Worth, TX: Harcourt Brace.

Rasinski, T. 1983. *Using Jackdaws to Build Background and Interest for Reading* (ERIC Document Reproduction Service. No. ED 234351). Washington, DC: U.S. Department of Education, National Institute of Education.

Risinger, C. F. 2002. "Two Different Worlds: The Dilemma Facing Social Studies Teachers." *Social Education* 66 (4): 231–33.

Sandmann, A. A., and J. F. Ahern. 2002. *Linking Literature with Life: The NCSS Standards and Children's Literature for the Middle Grades*. Washington, DC: National Council for the Social Studies.

Saxe, D. W. 1991. *Social Studies in Schools: A History of the Early Years*. Albany: State University of New York Press.

Thornton, S. J., and R. Vukelich. 1988. "Effects of Children's Understanding of Time Concepts on Historical Understanding." *Theory and Research in Social Education* 16 (1): 69–82.

Tomlinson, C. M., M. O. Tunnell, and D. J. Richgels. 1993. "The Content and Writing of History in Textbooks and Trade Books." In *The Story of Ourselves: Teaching History Through Children's Literature*, ed. R. Ammon and M. O. Tunnell, pp. 51–62. Portsmouth, NH: Heinemann.

Van Fossen, P. J., and J. M. Shiveley. 1997. "Things that Make You Go 'Hmmm . . .': Creating Inquiry 'Problems' in the Elementary Social Studies Classroom." *The Social Studies* 88 (2): 71–77.

Whelan, M. 2001. "Why the Study of History Should Be the Core of Social Studies Education." In *The Social Studies Curriculum: Purposes, Problems, and Possibilities*, ed. E. W. Ross, pp. 43–56. Albany: State University of New York.

Zarnowski, M. 1998. "It's More than Dates and Places: How Nonfiction Contributes to Understanding Social Studies." In *Making Facts Come Alive: Choosing Quality Nonfiction Literature K–8*, ed. R. A. Bamford and J. V. Kristo, pp. 93–108. Norwood, MS: Christopher-Gordon.

> *The thread of people's lives weaves through the past, the present, and into the future . . . through the pages of historical fiction, the past becomes alive.*
>
> —*Donna E. Norton,*
> Through the Eyes of a Child, *6th ed.*

Chapter Ten

Another Time, Another Place
Bringing Social Studies to Life through Literature

Marjorie R. Hancock, Kansas State University

CHAPTER OUTLINE

Introduction

Across the U.S.A. (and Around the World)
with Picture Books

Meeting Famous People Face-to-Face
through Biography

Sharing Personal Responses to
Historical Fiction through Journals

Putting It All Together:
Thematic Social Studies Unit

Science, Technology, and History

Chapter Summary

CHAPTER OBJECTIVES

Readers will

- understand how the literary genres of historical fiction, nonfiction, and biography can build students' historical and geographical knowledge and understanding;

- understand how recently published biographies present history in a realistic and entertaining way;

- understand how response journals can be used with historical fiction to help students better understand historical events; and

- be able to develop thematic units for the teaching of social studies.

Introduction

Just as literature brings life to the philosophy of integrated instruction, so too does literature breathe life into an elementary social studies program. The wealth of literature linked to social studies spans all **literary genre** and provides a complement, indeed a possible alternative, to the factualized textbook that has long been the mainstay of the traditional social studies curriculum. Levstik (1990, 850) quotes a fifth grader who preferred reading historical novels about the Revolutionary War rather than her social studies textbook. According to this student, the textbook "just says that Americans were right, but doesn't tell you exactly why they were right or why the British fought."

The trend toward integrated instruction and its dependence on literature has obviously influenced an explosive increase in quality children's trade books, many of which are linked to teaching social studies (Perry 1998; Trofanenko 2002). This new bounty of literature is embellished with rich, realistic detail and historical characters with whom the reader may easily identify; it also provides an unprecedented way to make social studies interesting and meaningful to the elementary reader. Literature has the power to transport readers to another place and allow them to become part of it. Literature provides the opportunity to transport readers to another time and allow them to become a part of history. Literature possesses the magic to bring social studies to life and, at the same time, to bring deeper understanding and meaning to students of social studies.

What young American could resist the detailed research and captivating documentation of a Russell Freedman biography, *The Voice that Challenged a Nation: Marian Anderson and the Struggle for Equal Rights* (2004), or his award-winning informational book, *Children of the Great Depression* (2005)? What child's sense of patriotism would not be aroused by the vivid illustrations of The American Revolution in Wendell Minor's (2006) vividly illustrated *Yankee Doodle America: The Spirit of 1776 from A to Z*? What reader's empathy for the trails of the westward exploration would not be enhanced through the well-research focus of *York's Adventures with Lewis & Clark: An African American's Part in the Great Expedition* (2004) by Rhoda Blumberg? What amazement might result upon reading a historically based account of *Rosa* (2005) by Nikki Giovanni revealing the moment of defiance of Rosa Parks that changed our views of equal rights? What child will not remember the blend of fear and friendship surrounding the Civil War and the power of "touching the hand of Abraham Lincoln" in Patricia Polacco's *Pink and Say* (1994)? What adolescent would not empathize with the pain and courage of Billie Jo in forgiving herself a family tragedy occurring during the dire economic and natural conditions of the Oklahoma Dust Bowl in the Newbery award-winning *Out of the Dust* (Hesse 1997)?

Advocates of integrated instruction have strongly encouraged teachers to expand the use of literature in their classrooms to enhance reading and writing (Hancock, 2004; Kiefer, Hepler, and Hickman, 2007). Now the literature connection is also being extended to the realm of social studies as a means of personalizing and making the social science more relevant to the lives and needs of students (Ammon and Weigard 1993; Ceprano and English 1990; Sanacore 1990). Quality children's literature linked to the social studies curriculum encompasses both geographic and historical concepts. It also encompasses a variety of literary genre (picture books, folklore, poetry, historical fiction, biography, informational books) that have been found to provide effective links to the curriculum (Johnson and Ebert 1992; Moir 1992).

This chapter provides the classroom teacher with a supply of ideas for incorporating literature into an integrated social studies program. Practical reading and writing applications supported by recent research and built around the literary genre of picture books, historical fiction, and biography are suggested. The integrated ideal of thematic units is addressed through sample concept-based units. These integrated applications of literature to an elementary social studies program provide only a beginning for classroom teachers as they start to bring social studies to life through the use of literature. Teachers' personal perspectives, knowledge of literature, and related activities can provide even further impetus for implementing an integrated perspective of elementary social studies.

Across the U.S.A. (and Around the World) with Picture Books

Picture books have been found to be an excellent means of conveying an understanding of both geography and history to elementary-level students (Dowd 1990; Pritchard 1989; Sisson 1990). Once considered the realm of primary grades, picture books now provide a means of adding a lively dimension to social studies teaching whatever the age or grade of the student. Quality picture books can capture student interest in the places associated with characters. Picture books with geographic features motivate students' interest in maps and geographic information (Levstik 1985). As Louie (1993, 17) writes: "Whereas textbooks present factual information and explanation, literature can make geographic concepts come alive for children. When teachers use literature as a medium to teach location, they also extend children's love of stories to geographic concepts."

A challenging means of combining a geography and history trip across the nation (or around the world) is through an exploration of children's picture books with settings in our country (or around the globe). The integration of social studies, reading, and writing is effectively accomplished through a classroom journey in which picture books transport students to another time and another place while providing information about our country or the world today. Although this section of the chapter focuses on our nation's regions, similar activities can be used with a world map and literature related to settings around the world.

A large outline map of the United States is required for this journey. Throughout the unit (or even throughout the school year), names and symbols of books will be added to this map, until it finally becomes a class **mural.**

A whole-class activity built around *My America: A Poetry Atlas of the United States* by Lee Bennett Hopkins (2000) can serve as an introduction to the entire United States. This poetry anthology is organized by the eight geographical sections of America. Prefacing each section is a map of the section and fascinating facts about each state and its capital. Stephen Alcorn's powerful paintings provide a visual dimension to the poetic journey shared by Langston Hughes, David McCord, Carl Sandburg, and a host of other beloved poets. A choral reading performance of these poems will take the class from the coast of Maine to the Hawaiian Islands, as the poetic journey provides the initial information for the class map/mural.

Students' initial exposure to a journey across America can be enhanced by an oral reading, singing, and discussion of *This Land Is Your Land* (Guthrie 1998). The classic folk song is brought to life through richly illustrated folk art spanning the "redwood forest" to the "Gulf Stream waters" and the "wheat fields waving" to the "diamond desert." An unforgettable portrait of the diversity of our land inspires the handing of our national treasure to each succeeding generation.

A sampling of picture books dealing with the various regions and states of the United States is briefly described in the rest of this section.

The Northeast

Let's journey to Maine where Peter Parnell's *Winter Barn* (1986) provides the tranquil setting for the activities of creatures who inhabit a memorable barn during the long, cold New England winter. Moving to Vermont, the reader appreciates the wonder of intricate snowflakes through the determined lens of the photographer in *Snowflake Bentley* (Martin 1998) through the Caldecott award-winning woodcuts of Mary Azarian. The devastation of the 9/11 twin towers of New York City are nostalgically visited though an exciting event in Mordecai Gerstein's *The Man who Walked between the Towers* (2003). A sensitive and informative view of the Amish is captured with colored photographs in *Amish Home* (Bial 1993), while the spirit of Amish community inspires Jane Yolen's *Raising Yoder's Barn* (1998). Lynn Curlee's *Liberty* (2000) and *Brooklyn Bridge* (2001) capture the history and longevity of these landmarks, which exemplify the stature, freedom, and bravery of the city of New York. On the road to rural Massachusetts the reader encounters D. B. Johnson's *Henry Hikes to Fitchburg* (2000), *Henry Builds a Cabin* (2002), and *Henry Climbs a Mountain* (2003) reflecting the conservative spirit and appreciation of nature of Henry David Thoreau.

The Southeast

The nation's capital, Washington, D.C., provides a perfect location for a journey through the Southeast by introducing David Small's Caldecott award-winning, cartoon-like presidential caricatures in *So You Want to Be President?* (St. George 2000). Little-known facts surround these presidents while providing humor and general facts about these national leaders.

The folk traditions of Appalachia are captured in a fanciful collection of rhymes, riddles, and verse aptly titled *Granny Will Your Dog Bite? And Other Mountain Rhymes* (Milnes 1990). These humorous portrayals can be tempered with Cynthia Rylant's serious recollections of the land were she grew up, in *Appalachia: The Voice of Sleeping Birds* (1991). An uncelebrated Kentucky heroine is shared in *Mary on Horseback* (Wells 1998), a story of an extraordinary nurse who brought health care to skeptical mountain people. Set in a Quaker school in post–Civil War Jonesborough, Tennessee, *Virgie Goes to School with Us Boys* (Howard 2000) captures the challenges of a determined African American girl and her quest to attend school in the Southeast in the 1860s. Based on a true family story, Elizabeth Fitzgerald Howard provides a historical note showcasing the importance of education for former slaves during the Reconstruction period.

Heading farther south, the reader explores the music and culture of the true South through Walter Dean Myers *Blues Journey* (2003) and Barbara T. Russell's *Maggie's Amerikay* (2006), an immigration story of friendship in the 1898 port of New Orleans.

The Midwest and Great Plains

The agricultural belt of the Midwest and Great Plains is the next stop on our literary journey. Carl Sandburg's poetry blends with the artwork of Wendell Minor in portraying *Grassroots* (1998), celebrating the beauty and ruggedness of middle America. Westward migration through the rugged prairie lands of Missouri, Kansas, and Oklahoma are revealed through *Grandma Essie's Covered Wagon* (Williams 1993), a true tale adapted from the authentic oral history of the author's grandmother. *Mississippi Mud: Three Prairie Journals* (Turner 1997) shares journal entries of three children on their Conestoga wagon journey from Kentucky to Oregon across the tallgrass prairie of the Great Plains.

The Oklahoma Land Rush of 1893 and the role of black settlers in westward expansion is told through *I Have Heard of a Land* (Thomas 1998). The author's great-grandparents traveled on a wagon train to stake their claim for land, a symbol of freedom and a new life for many former slaves. Ken Robbins's *Thunder on the Plains* (2001) captures the demise of the buffalo in the Great Plains through authentic photographs.

In a more contemporary setting, *The Bravest of Us All* (Arnold 2000) introduces the Kansas tornado as a test of the courage of a young girl. *The Journey* (Stewart 2001) features an Amish girl who travels from her farm to the city of Chicago showcasing the contrasts between urban and rural life through diary entries. Finally, *Rushmore* (Curlee 1999) brings the history of the beloved South Dakota monument to life, supporting the patriotism and steadfastness of the heartland of America.

The Southwest

Turning southward, the literary road leads to Texas and *The Best Town in the World* (Baylor 1983). Life in this small country town in the Texas hills around the turn of the century seems little different from that of many American towns of that era. However, its residents take special pride in it. While in Texas, share Tomie de Paola's Comanche tale, *The Legend of the Bluebonnet: An Old Tale of Texas* (1983). The beautiful state flower results from the selflessness of an Indian girl who sacrifices her dearest possession to bring rain to save her people. Steven Kellogg's tall tale of *Pecos Bill* (1986) describes how the title character is raised by a pack of coyotes and grows up to become a legendary Texas cowboy.

The changing faces of the desert area of the Southwest are portrayed through *Storm in the Desert* (Lesser 1997), which lyrically describes an approaching storm and its effect on plant and animal life. *Desert Scrapbook* (Wright-Frierson 1997) utilizes sketches, journal notes, and artifacts to share the flora, fauna, and fluctuating moods of the Sonoran Desert. A companion book would be *Cactus Hotel* (Guiberson 1991), which describes the life of the saguaro cactus.

The Far West

The character of the West is often linked to westward expansion. Ann Turner's (1999) *Red Flower Goes West* is a poignant portrayal of the hardships and joys of this defining period in history. Tony Johnston's (2002) *Sunsets of the West* captures the geographic wonders and spirit of the land through Ted Lewin's vivid watercolors.

Western folklore and legends abound. *The Cremation of Sam McGee* (Service 1987) details the adventures of a Yukon prospector during the Alaskan gold rush. Among the legends about the huge expanse of remote western mountains and valleys is *The Legend of the Indian Paintbrush* (de Paola 1988), the story of a beautiful western flower. T. A. Barron creates an admirable legend through a true mountain adventure of a girl who climbs Long's Peak in Colorado in *High as a Hawk* (2004).

Gathering the Sun (Ada 1997) salutes the migrant workers who for decades have brought in the California harvest through their fortitude and hard work. This alphabetical book blends poetry in both Spanish and English with sun-drenched illustrations to celebrate the harvest and the workers in this warm, year-round climate that produces an abundance of fruits and vegetables. Katherine Krull's biography of Cesar Chavez, *Harvesting Hope* (2003), extends the tribute to the role of migrants in America.

Linking Regions Together

As teachers read a wide selection of books to their students and students read even more books independently, the mural map will come alive with literary memories of the regions of the United States. Students might record the author, title, location, and time period of each book on a "sticky note" and attach it in the proper place on the map. They might also draw a picture or symbol of each story on the map to create a permanent memory of each book read. Barbara Younger's *Purple Mountains Majesty* (1998) is a superb book to share as a culminating read-aloud as it tells the intriguing story of Katharine Lee Bates's journey across America as an inspiration for her beloved poem/song "America the Beautiful." Louise Borden's (2002) *America Is . . .* and Lynn Cheney's (2002) *America: A Patriotic Primer* as read-alouds also provide inspiration for understanding the foundation of freedom and honor that crosses all regional and state boundaries in building our national pride and spirit. A plentiful list of book titles for travel across the United States for all grade levels can be obtained through the *Exploring the United States through Literature* series (Latrobe 1994).

Devin Scillian's (2001) *A is for America* is the opening book in a series of state books published by Sleeping Bear Press. The two-tiered form provides both rhymed text for primary students (K–2) and expanded expository text for grades 3–6. The series includes titles like *B is for Beaver* for Oregon, *H is for Hoosier* for Indiana, and *M is for Maple Syrup* for Vermont. The books physically represent the breadth and depth of our national landscape.

Discovering our country's geography and history through picture books can be a unit lasting a few weeks. It can also be expanded to cover the entire school year. What is created on the classroom wall map is a collage of literature experiences ranging in location "from sea to shining sea."

Extending Our Journey to the World

Although this section of the chapter focuses on the geography and history of the United States, teachers can easily adapt strategies and locate literature to move beyond our own borders to discover the world through picture books. A good beginning is Anita Lobel's *Away from Home* (1994), which takes us alphabetically to the far corners of the world. This alliterative pattern book becomes a model for your students' own journey across the globe. *How to Make an Apple Pie and See the World* (Priceman 1994) whisks readers to several countries to gather world-class ingredients for a sumptuous apple pie. These two books provide motivating activities that can easily build into a parallel unit for a worldwide trip through picture books. The classroom becomes a collage of literature-based experiences that definitely transport students across the globe.

The following list will provide a few picture book titles for your journey:

Chin-Lee, *A is for Asia* (1997)
Curlee, *Seven Wonders of the Ancient World* (2002)
Curlee, *Parthenon* (2004)
Dooley, *Everyone Bakes Bread* (1996)
Johnson, *Mapping the World* (1999)
Knight, *Talking Walls: The Stories Continue* (1996)
Lewin, *Market!* (1996)
Norges, *Hana in the Time of the Tulips* (2004)
Sturges, *Bridges Are to Cross* (1998)

 IN THE CLASSROOM

Reflecting on History through Reader's Theater

Reader's theater provides an exciting format for blending oral language, dramatic reading, careful listening, and quality literature into a memorable experience (Young and Vardell 1993). Not only can reader's theater improve reading fluency and attitudes toward reading, but it can also aid in an understanding of historical contexts and attitudes. Whether reading from the text as prepared script or altering the text to afford a reader's theater format, the value of this activity spans the outcomes of language arts and social studies.

Bull Run by Paul Fleischman (1993) suggests a perfect opportunity for dramatic reading by up to 16 students. The text provides two-page reflections by eight Northern and eight Southern characters of different stature and backgrounds before, during, and after the historic Battle of Bull Run. The perspectives of soldiers, common folk, and leaders reflect the changing thoughts and views about war itself. A mixture of male and female roles provide choice for your performers. The words are powerful and reflect the reality of the period at the onset of the Civil War. Have your students practice to improve reading fluency, articulation, and expression. The performance read from the text will blend the powerful voices as they recur intermittently throughout the script. Encourage your students to let their voices exude the changing tones that the onset of war brings. This activity allows choice and places the reader in the role of a historical character.

Katie's Trunk by Anne Turner (1992) contains a blend of both narrative and dialogue by several characters. With some writing alterations, a script reflecting the tone of the text can be prepared. Based on a true incident that happened to one of the author's ancestors, the reader's theater will give an exciting glimpse into the beginnings of the American Revolution. Tories, rebels, and patriotic allegiances fill the life of Katie. Papa, Mama, Walter, Hattie, and Katie are joined by the rebellious likes of John Warren and Ruben Otis. History will be brought to life in a dramatic reading of the words of these common people who witnessed the disagreement that led to the fight for America's freedom.

Historical fiction picture books (Ellen Levine's *Henry Freedom Box*, 2006) provide an essential resource for scriptwriting for reader's theater in the intermediate grades. A chapter from historical fiction (Jim Murphy's *Desperate Journey*, 2006) can provide another opportunity for script writing in the middle school. Literature provides an authentic, integrated language arts activity encompassing reading, writing, listening, and speaking through reader's theater.

Meeting Famous People
Face-to-Face through Biography

Biography has provided a natural literature link to social studies for decades. The serial biographies of the past provided dry, factual information about famous people. Current authors, however, have begun to present authentic, flesh-and-blood individuals to elementary-grade readers by relating interesting historical information in a realistic, entertaining manner. Authors such as David Adler, Jean Fritz, Russell Freedman, James Cross Giblin, Diane Stanley, and Leonard Everett Fisher have introduced students to the multidimensional characteristics of famous people and their public and private lives.

Children in the intermediate grades seem to be almost magnetically drawn to the achievements of those who have overcome obstacles on their journey toward personal success. According to Levstik (1993), older elementary students link themselves closely with biographical characters. Biographies enable readers to experience real life vicariously by tapping the experiences of achievers while providing a historical context for understanding such people's lives. Biographies are written about people who have had a positive impact on society and therefore leave the reader with an optimistic view of his or her potential as an individual in our society (Zarnowski 1990).

Perhaps Jean Fritz's explanation of the appeal of biography over time and generations best explains why biographical accounts should be included in the social studies curriculum:

> We all seek insight into the human condition, and it is helpful to find familiar threads running through the lives of others, however famous. We need to know more people in all circumstances and times so we can pursue our private, never-to-be-fulfilled quest to find out what life is all about. (Quoted in Commire 1982, 80)

Extending biography beyond famous individuals in American history to those renowned throughout the world can increase student awareness of the traits that characterize past and present global leaders. Two activities can be used to bring children face-to-face with historical figures. The first involves exposing students to picture book biographies and then having the students write biographical poems (bio-poems) describing traits of these famous individuals. The second activity, geared more toward intermediate-level students, involves making biographical comparisons to better understand the researching and writing of biographies of famous figures. Author studies and comparative biographical readings focus on the process of biography and can lead students to biographical composition efforts.

From Simple Biographies to Bio-Poems

A plentiful supply of simple biographies that combine a picture book format with historical data on famous persons are available for third- through fifth-grade students. Reading these biographies, learning the historical background surrounding a famous person, and incorporating a related writing activity is an efficient way to use a whole language approach to social studies. Picture book biographies such as David Adler's *A Picture Book of Samuel Adams* (2004) and *A Picture Book of Lewis and Clark* (2003), Robert Burleigh's *The Secret of the Great Houdini* (2002), and James Cross Giblin's *The Amazing Life of Benjamin Franklin* (2000) are brief but accurate accounts of the lives of famous Americans. Diane Stanley's *Michelangelo* (2000) introduces the reader to a genius of the Italian Renaissance, while one of her most recent picture book biographies portrays a lesser-known world hero, *Saladin: Noble Prince of Islam* (2002). This book depicts an Islamic warrior known for his civility who tried to maintain his honor and chivalry in the midst of horrendous fighting.

A related writing activity emerging naturally from a study of historical figures involves composing a nine-line bio-poem (Danielson 1989) about the individuals portrayed in picture book biographies. Here is the format of the nine-line bio-poem:

Line 1: First name of biographical subject
Line 2: Four Adjectives describing the subject
Line 3: Husband/wife/sibling, etc., of . . .
Line 4: Lover of . . . (three people, places, things)
Line 5: Who feels . . . (three things)
Line 6: Who fears . . . (three things)
Line 7: Who would like to see . . . (three things)
Line 8: Resident of . . . (city, state, country)
Line 9: Last name of biographical subject

Following the reading of *Good Queen Bess* (Stanley and Vennema 1990), Sarah, a sixth-grade student, composed a bio-poem highlighting the personality and achievements of Queen Elizabeth I of England (figure 10.1 on the following page).

A collection of such bio-poems may be displayed on a "Who's Who" bulletin board. A class discussion often elicits common traits, goals, and accomplishments of famous people. The bio-poem provides an encapsulated view of these people.

Becoming an Expert on Biographers and Their Subjects

Becoming a "biography buff" (Zarnowski 1990) involves not only learning about famous historical figures but also learning about the literary genre of biography in the process. Students can become biography buffs by reading (1) biographies of different subjects written by the same author and (2) biographies about the same subject written by different authors. Some specific examples and suggestions should help further this use of biography in the social studies curriculum.

Several children's authors are known for their special treatment of historical figures in their well-written, award-winning biographies. Ingri and Edgar d'Aulaire, Jean Fritz, Milton Meltzer, F. N. Monjo, and Diane Stanley have each written a number of high-quality biographies of historical figures.

An interesting interdisciplinary idea is to study not only the historical characters that biographers portray in their works but to become an expert on the biographers themselves. Students can do this by reading several biographies by the same author. For example, Jean Fritz is known for her motivating titles of books about the Revolutionary War heroes, including *And Then What Happened, Paul Revere?* (1973), *Can't You Make Them Behave, King George?* (1982), *Where Was Patrick Henry on the 29th of May?* (1975), *Why Don't You Get a Horse, Sam Adams?* (1974), and *Will You Sign Here, John Hancock?* (1976). Students not only learn from and enjoy the unique portrayals of these historical subjects but may come to understand the significance and style of

Elizabeth I
Well-educated, intelligent, cautious, loyal
Daughter of Henry VIII and Anne Boleyn
Lover of England, Robert Dudley, and her
    loyal subjects
Who feels more powerful than most men,
    capable of ruling her homeland, and
    proud to serve her people
Who fears her imprisonment in the Tower,
    leaving no heir to the throne, and the
    treasonous Mary Queen of Scots
Who would like to see the defeat of the
    Spanish Armada, the flowering of the
    Elizabethan Age, and herself remembered
    as a great monarch
Resident of London
Queen of England 1558-1603.

Figure 10.1 By writing and sharing biographical poetry about famous leaders, students gain greater insights into historical figures (Danielson 1989).

biography itself. An analysis of Fritz's books for writing style, sense of humor, historical accuracy and documentation, characterization, and theme can provide students with some general insights into Fritz's process of writing her biographies.

Ideas gleaned from a similar analysis of several works by the same author may inspire a young writer of biography to research and construct a biographical sketch of a favorite historical personality. Other authors to study include F. N. Monjo, who often tells his stories from an outsider's point of view as in *Poor Richard in France* (1973), told from his grandson's point of view. Milton Meltzer is another biographer famous for his use of authentic voices and words from the past, as in *Voices from the Civil War* (1989), with excerpts from documents, diaries, interviews, and speeches. Russell Freedman's photobiographic essays, including *Indian Chiefs* (1987a) and *Franklin Delano Roosevelt* (1990b), provide another means of sharing biography. Kathryn Lasky's (2000) *Vision of Beauty: The Story of Sarah Breedlove Walker* tells the amazing success story of a girl born to former slaves in the language Walker would have used. The varied techniques of these biographers introduce exemplary styles and models for young biographers in the elementary classroom.

Another way to become a biography buff is to become a expert on one historical figure by reading several biographies of the same person. A compare-and-contrast chart can be used to determine each author's portrayal of the individual's strengths and weaknesses, use of authentic materials for conveying the story (maps, documents, photographs, etc.), style of writing (point of view/tone), documentation, and type of biography (complete or partial). Such comparisons and contrasts may reveal a variety of information, even conflicting information, on the subject. As a culminating activity, students might share their findings by dressing and speaking in the first-person voice of their subject.

For example, through the years, many authors have attempted to capture the life of Abraham Lincoln in their own special styles. The d'Aulaires's (1957) classic illustrated portrayal of the life of Lincoln is a good place to begin. In contrast, Russell Freedman won a Newbery Medal for *Lincoln: A Photobiography* (1987b). Other authors have presented portions of Lincoln's life, including Carl Sandburg in *Abe Lincoln Grows Up* (1985) and Ann Turner's (2001) *Abe Lincoln Remembers*. These titles serve as a beginning for developing expertise on this great statesman. Students' comparisons and contrasts will clarify their own preference for biographical portrayal and lead them toward the development of their own written portrayal of Lincoln or another figure.

Another example might carry the reader back in time and beyond our borders to the Middle Ages in France and the story of Joan of Arc. Two fine picture book biographies, *Joan of Arc* (Poole 1998) and *Joan of Arc* (Stanley 1998) provide well-researched information and a humanistic portrayal of this young heroine. Comparing and contrasting facts, illustrations, and historical notes provide an adventure through the eyes of historian, researcher, and artist.

The possibilities seem unlimited as integrated instruction and the genre of biography work together in a meaningful reading and writing interaction. The emphasis of integrated instruction on process supports the use of authors' studies and comparative studies to assist young writers in developing their own writing style. The integration of reading and writing through the use of biography epitomizes the philosophy of integrated instruction.

Sharing Personal Responses to Historical Fiction through Journals

Historical fiction has long-held literary ties to the social studies curriculum. The benefits of using historical fiction to enhance social studies instruction have been enumerated (Cianciolo 1981; Gallo and Barksdale 1983). Historical fiction can help children "experience the past—to encounter the conflicts, the suffering, and the despair of those who lived before us. . . . Well-written historical fiction offers young people the vicarious experience of participating in the life of the past" (Kiefer, Hepler, and Hickman 2007, 543). The case for historical fiction has been convincing indeed. Teachers have traditionally responded by reading historical fiction aloud to their classes and by assigning book reports on historical fiction.

A response-based view of the role of children's literature in the elementary classroom, however, has been brought to the attention of researchers and teachers

(Galda 1988; Hancock, 2004); that is, children are encouraged to respond to literature by writing as they read. Researchers inform us that written language captures ideas concretely and may even influence the development of reading (Langer and Applebee 1987).

The need for encouraging personal responses to literature has been supported by Louise Rosenblatt (1976, 1978), whose transactional theory of reader response articulates the essential reciprocal relationship between the reader and the literary text. Likewise, children as readers have their own story to tell as they interact with the pages of the book. The **reader response theory** further suggests that readers be active participants in making meaning from the literature they encounter (Probst 1984).

Too often, when teachers assign historical fiction "book reports," students choose a book from a list and summarize the content after they have read the book. But what about the informative thoughts they experienced while reading the book? What about these connections students have made with the historical facts that have become part of their reading schema? How can those connections be captured so that teachers and students alike can experience the link between historical fiction and historical fact?

Responding to historical fiction by writing in a variety of **journal** formats is an effective way of capturing this personal interaction of the reader with a part of history brought alive through quality children's literature. The textbook may be essential for presenting the facts of a historic period, but the catalyst that can bring those facts to life may be books of historical fiction that place "real" characters in "authentic" periods of history allowing the reader to "live through" the life and times portrayed.

The insightful interactions of the reader with historical fiction may be lost if thoughts, emotions, and responses are not permanently captured throughout the reading of the book. The solution, therefore, is to capture the internal connections between historical fact and historical fiction by writing a journal. A historic response journal, a character journal, or both aids students in connecting fact and fiction by allowing them to vicariously experience an unfolding piece of history as they read historical fiction.

Historical Fiction Response Journals

A response journal is a place for students to express their thoughts, insights, feelings, reactions, questions, connections, and opinions while reading a book (Hancock 1993c). According to Hancock (1993b, 467), "Written response to literature is a powerful means of preserving those special transactions with books that make reading a rewarding, personal journey." The teacher might give brief talks on a variety of historical fiction books geared to a particular period of American or world history. After the students have personally chosen one of these books, the teacher should encourage them to record their individual thoughts while they are reading the book. Students must be assured that the journals will not be graded and that spelling and punctuation will not be corrected. Emphasis should be on the free expression of ideas as the students interact with literature.

The resultant journal entries may include a transfer of the reader to another time and place in history. Readers tend to bring life to fictional characters, and the students may talk to, advise, and judge the actions of a character within the context of history in their journal entries. The student may also make mention of historical facts and names that are part of the background for reading and discuss the historical setting. In reading journal entries, the teacher may discover the personal connection with history as a student assumes the guise of a fictional character. Identification with a character can transport the reader to a historical period that is brought alive through reading.

Some teachers find it difficult to turn students loose with an assignment as free as the foregoing. They prefer giving students a list of response prompts that focus their responses more on the historical aspects of the books they are reading. Here are a few sample response prompts:

• What historical facts are mentioned in the book that you already knew from our study of this historical period?

• What new and interesting historical facts were presented?

• How does the life of the main character fit into the historic period (education, dress, expectations of society)?

• How do the actions of the main character fit into the standards of the historical period?

• What impression of life during this historic period is projected?

If teachers prefer prompts to free expression and impressions, it is still essential to capture responses to these prompts *while* the students are reading the book rather than retrospectively after they have completed it. Growth in understanding the historical period can only be indicated through the unfolding reactions of the reader during the reading process.

Suggested historical fiction trade books for the literature response journal include:

Avi, *Crispin: The Cross of Lead* (2002); *Crispin: At the Edge of the World* (2006)
Curtis, *Bud, Not Buddy* (1999)
Cushman, *The Ballad of Lucy Whipple* (1996)
Cushman, *Catherine, Called Birdy* (1994)
Hesse, *Out of the Dust* (1997)
Holm, *Boston Jane: An Adventure* (2001)
Lisle, *The Art of Keeping Cool* (2000)
Pearsall, *Trouble Don't Last* (2002)
Salisbury, *Under the Blood Red Sun* (1994)

Character Journals

Another interesting way of extending response to historical fiction while ensuring the reader's vicarious interaction with history is to have the student write in a character journal (Hancock 1993a). The character journal encourages the reader to "become" the main character. Entries in the journals are written as if the reader/ writer were that character. Entries are usually written down at the end of each chapter in diary form.

An excellent book that models a character journal is *Letters from Rifka* (Hesse 1992). Written in the first-person narrative style, the story is presented as a series of journal entries written by Rifka in the margins of the treasured book of poetry by Russian author Pushkin. In these entries, Rifka reveals her hopes and dreams as well as the obstacles she and her Jewish family had to overcome to reach America in 1919. Strong examples of a character journal are titles in the *Dear America* and *My Name Is America* series (Scholastic). For example, *The Journal of William Thomas Emerson: A Revolutionary War Portrait* (Denenberg 1998) shares first-person journal entries filled with the authentic voice of a 12-year-orphan who joins the cause of the patriots in the prerevolutionary Boston. This well-researched fictional journal format provides a model for character journals for intermediate and middle-level students.

The type of historical fiction that lends itself best to character journals must have a strong main character with whom the reader can identify. The character and plot must be closely linked, and a strong sense of the historical period should be present.

Suggested historical fiction trade books for the character journal include:

Conrad, *Prairie Songs* (1985)
Cushman, *Rodzina* (2002)
DeFelice, *The Apprenticeship of Lucas Whitaker* (1996)
Friedman, *Escaping into the Night* (2006)
Hill, *Dancing at the Odinochka* (2005)
Karr, *Bone Dry* (2002)
Moses, *The Legend of Buddy Bush* (2004)
O'Dell, *My Name Is Not Angelica* (1990)
Paterson, *Lyddie* (1991)
Paterson, *Jip* (1996)

Putting It All Together: Thematic Social Studies Units

Because interdisciplinary instruction advocates the teaching of integrated rather than isolated pieces of information, the thematic unit becomes an essential component of social studies teaching. The selection and elaboration of a social studies theme or concept through literature, reading, and writing symbolize the synthesis of integrated instruction. A similar concept-based interdisciplinary approach to teaching social studies with literature has been introduced by James and Zarrillo (1989). Thematic units built around a central theme can lead students beyond facts and dates to a deeper understanding of a concept (Lipson et al. 1993; Manning, Manning, and Long 1994).

Designing classroom instruction based on related titles and planning an array of response-based literature activities associated with them provide a solid base for effective teaching (Pappas, Kiefer, and Levstik 1996). Hancock (2004) enumerates several benefits to teaching thematic units through a literature base:

• Thematic units expose students to all literary genre.

• Thematic units based on literature contain multiage possibilities.

• Thematic units provide a broader vision and higher-level exploration of a topic.

• Thematic units naturally use fact and fiction for both enjoyment and learning.

Hancock (2004) also suggests the following five steps for planning a thematic unit:

1. Choose a broad-based theme and title.
2. Brainstorm titles of related children's literature.
3. Locate additional children's books through library searches or Internet Web sites.
4. Create a graphic web or organizer reflecting the connectedness of the literature or subthemes.
5. Plan literature-based activities for whole class, small group, and individual participation.

Two thematic social studies units are described below. The first, "Change," is appropriate for students in the primary and early-intermediate grades and is closely tied to the NCSS themes on Time, Continuity, and Change. The second, "In Quest of Freedom," is suited for children in the upper-intermediate and middle school levels and links to the NCSS themes of People, Places, and Environments; Individual Development and Identity; and Power, Authority, and Governance. Although these units focus on social studies concepts, the literature, reading, and writing activities incorporate a true integrated, interdisciplinary instructional perspective.

Thematic Concept: Change

The world is changing constantly. The horror of the 9/11 tragedy weighs heavily on our minds and hearts as the threat of loss of personal freedom looms over a nation. Young and old alike have witnessed change and its impact on our lives. Looking back over the past century, we realize the Soviet Union no longer exists; the two German states have been reunited. In the United States, suburbs creep into farmlands, local roads become interstate highways, and small towns grow into booming cities. For some people, change signals progress. For others, change can be stressful and disappointing. The more-personal aspects of our daily life also change. New jobs, moves to a new location, and the fluid structure of the family unit can be unsettling for ourselves and our students.

Reading about changes that occur in the familiar ways of life can help children put change in a proper perspective. Books can help them understand the loss of something special while coming to understand that places and people are always evolving. Literature about change in towns, communities, and cities can lead to insightful discussions and activities that may help young children cope with the unsettling changes that take place around them. A thematic unit built on quality literature and enhanced by writing and discussion activities can awaken students to this broad concept that will sweepingly affect their future.

City changes, although expected, can seem overwhelming over time. *New Providence: A Changing Cityscape* (Von Tscharner and Fleming 1987) looks at the development of the downtown area in a fictitious city between 1910 and 1987. The town is viewed historically through changing architecture, vehicles, and storefronts. One building, for example, changes from a dry goods store to a pharmacy to a computer outlet during its 77-year history. The book provides a natural extension for gathering photographs, maps, and newspapers from your own city or town to discover how history had been reflected over the years in its development. Eco-

Project boards can be effective means for students to share an overview of their work on a unit of study. This display accompanies a research paper in which the student sought out children's literature including informational books in the library as well as Web sites as sources.

nomic and sociological changes as well as political influence over time might also be examined.

Alice and Martin Provensen's *Shaker Lane* (1987) follows the evolution of a community from farmland to growing rural area to sprawling suburb on the shores of a new reservoir. While the community changes, some people like Old Man Van Sloop stay and adjust to the changes. To complete this book, the class might invite a longtime resident of the community to share an oral history of change. Some students might be encouraged to interview several longtime residents and record their perspectives in a permanent written record of community reflections.

The classic *The Little House* by Virginia Lee Burton (1942) can serve as a transitional book from an urban to a rural perspective of change. The encroachment of the city on the country is portrayed through the house that stood on the hill and watched day by day as the seasons passed. Gradually a road is built, traffic increases, and a city surrounds the little house. A happy ending is ensured because the house is relocated by the great-great-granddaughter of the man who built it.

The rural perspective of change is also represented in children's literature. *Toddlecreek Post Office* (Shulevitz 1990) takes the reader to a small town whose small post office serves as the activity center for townspeople and dogs. Although the kindly postmaster, Vernon Stamps, has spent years listening to people's joy and woes on their daily visits, his mail dispersal becomes inefficient. The building is eventually torn down, and the locals lose their gathering place. This portrait of vanishing small-town America possibly reflects a deeper vanishing American way of life. Related activities might include a debate on changes in one's own community and whether they are beneficial.

A personal connection to change is shared by reading *Letting Swift River Go* by Jane Yolen (1992). In the middle of this century, many towns across America were purchased by the government and drowned in order to form reservoirs. This dramatic event is captured by a west Massachusetts child's perspective as her childhood memories are submerged so urban areas can be supplied with water. Sally Jane recalls playing by the Old Stone Mill, harvesting maple sap, and walking to school down a country road. Although her vivid memories have been transformed by progress, Sally learns that memories become part of life forever. Students can speculate on exploring the history of their own towns, roads, and geographic surroundings. The interaction of facts and speculation provide an exciting outlet for exploring change in the students' own environment.

Although cast in a farm setting, *Time to Go* (Fiday and Fiday 1990) captures a child's emotion about moving and giving up a special place. This story of loss of a family farm describes a child's feelings as he recalls a happy past on the day that it is time to go and accept change. Our nation has become increasingly mobile, and children need to know they are not alone in their feelings of loss. A written, chronological reflection on change in a child's life can provide personal insights to the classroom teacher. Voluntary sharing of such reflections can help children cope when it is "time to go."

A historical perspective on change can be viewed through the eyes of immigrants who left their homes and traveled to a strange, new land during the past century. While they chose to create a new identity, they retained bits of their culture and traditions as they helped blend the country that today is America. *A House of Tailors* (Giff, 2004) shows the loss of family, the hard work, and the disappointment that accompany immigrating in search of new opportunities. This story details a young woman's courageous journey to a new land and her adaptation and preservation within the context of her uncle's home. In a fictional account, *When Jessie Came Across the Sea* (Hest 1997), Jessie must travel alone to America and leave her grandmother behind. Transcending time and culture, this title is a tribute to all who seek a better life and see change as a positive reward.

Another historical perspective on personal change occurs in Rosemary Wells's *Wingwalker* (2002), which showcases the outcome of the Depression and the Dust Bowl. Reuben's family leaves Oklahoma for Minnesota where his father gets as job as a carnival wingwalker. Not only must Reuben adjust to a new home, but he must overcome his fear of flying to show his respect for his father's efforts to support the family in trying times.

A higher-level comparison on change occurs through the reading, examination, and reflection on *Dateline: Troy* (Fleischman 2006). A retelling of the classic story of the Trojan War is juxtaposed with newspaper clippings of modern news events. Guided discussion can lead to the discovery of the tragic parallels between ancient and modern history and the realization that change does not necessarily mean progress, but that history repeats itself.

The foregoing books and suggested extension activities provide a simple beginning for a thematic unit on change. Although limited to personal and historical perspectives on change, these resources provide a model of how interdisciplinary teaching and learning transcend the traditional textbook. The unit could last a few weeks or be expanded to include the additional perspectives over a period of several more weeks. The concept of change will be better understood because the students' own lives and community will have become an integrated part of the study. Reading, writing, researching, reflecting, and discussion activities that augment quality literature will give students a multidimensional perspective on change in the community and their own lives.

An Investigative Thematic Unit: The Quest for Freedom

A journey through history provided a multitude of views on the struggle for the attainment of freedom. A thematic unit based on the general concept of freedom can provide a thought-provoking perspective for studying the effects of people striving to achieve independence, emancipation, civil liberty, or autonomy that ultimately leads to self-respect and self-determination. Throughout history, the quest for freedom has spanned the globe and the ages. Exploring personal stories of difficult struggles to achieve freedom provides an exciting vehicle from which to study this broad historical topic. Although this thematic unit will be limited, it can be covered in three to nine weeks, depending on teacher augmentation and student motivation.

This particular unit is designed to be used with three groups of students within a classroom. Each group of students should investigate one type of freedom from a specific historical perspective: political freedom (based on the Revolutionary Period, 1773–1785), personal freedom (based on the struggle of African Americans for equality), and freedom from persecution (based on the Holocaust of World War II).

Researching

Each group begins the unit by defining its type of freedom, discussing what group members already know about it, and deciding what they would like to learn from their research and reading. Although the initial work involves research from textbooks and encyclopedias, findings should be geared toward answering the following questions from a variety of literature:

- What were the causes of this quest for freedom?
- What effects did lack of freedom impose on the individual involved?
- What steps did those involved directly take to move toward freedom?
- What individuals emerged as catalysts in supporting the quest for freedom?
- What outcome prevailed as a result of this quest?
- Does this quest for freedom still continue today? If so, how? If not, why not?

The three groups come together at the end of their investigation and share the information they have discovered, citing the literature that led them to their discoveries. All groups compare and contrast their answers to the foregoing guideline questions. Commonalities and generalities often emerge as students engage in higher-level reasoning and thinking.

Reading

Along with informational books and encyclopedias, a wealth of literature of all genres can assist students in achieving a fuller understanding of the quest for each type of freedom. The following lists suggest a variety of literary genres that can be used in this investigative unit.

Political Freedom for a Nation

Adler, *B. Franklin: Printer* (2001) (biography)

Ammon, *Valley Forge* (2004) (nonfiction)

Avi, *The Fighting Ground* (1984) (historical fiction)

Clapp, *I'm Deborah Sampson: A Soldier in the War of the Revolution* (1977) (biography)

Collier and Collier, *My Brother Sam is Dead* (1985) (historical fiction)

Fleming, *Everybody's Revolution* (2006) (nonfiction)

Freedman, *Give Me Liberty! The Story of the Declaration of Independence* (2000) (nonfiction)

Longfellow, *The Midnight Ride of Paul Revere* (2001) Illus. C. Bing (poetry/picture book)

Rinaldi, *Cast Two Shadows: The American Revolution in the South* (1998) (historical fiction)

A classroom library with a mixture of fiction and informational books is important if students are encouraged to read independently about social studies.

Schanzer, *George vs. George: The American Revolution Seen from Two Sides.* (nonfiction)

Personal Freedom and Individual Equality

Adler, *Enemies of Freedom* (2004) (biography)

Hamilton, *Anthony Burns: The Defeat and Triumph of a Fugitive Slave* (1988) (biography)

Lester, *To Be a Slave* (1968/1998) (firsthand accounts)

McKissick and McKissick, *Christmas in the Big House, Christmas in the Quarters* (1994) (informational picture book)

Meltzer, *The Black Americans: A History in Their Own Words, 1619–1983* (1984) (letters, speeches, diaries, documents)

Paulsen, *Nightjohn* (1993) (fiction)

Pinkney, *Let it Shine: Stories of Black Women Freedom Fighters* (2000) (biography)

Rappaport, *Free at Last: Stories and Songs of Emancipation* (2004) (nonfiction)

Rockwell, *Only Passing Through: The Story of Sojourner Truth* (2000) (biography)

Weatherford, *Moses: When Harriet Tubman Led her People to Freedom* (historical fiction)

Freedom from Persecution—The Holocaust

Bartoletti, *Hitler Youth: Growing up in Hitler's Shadow* (2005) (nonfiction)

Bitton-Jackson, *I Have Lived a Thousand Years: Growing up in the Holocaust* (1997) (autobiographical memoir)

Meltzer, *Never Forget: The Jews of the Holocaust* (1976) (quotes/journal entries)

Millman, *Hidden Child* (2006) (biography)

Mochizuki, *Passage to Freedom: The Sugihara Story* (1997) (picture book)

Tunnell and Chilcoat, *Children of Topaz* (1996) (informational/diary)

Warren, *Surviving Hitler* (2001) (biography)

Writing

Each group of students incorporates the information compiled from the various types of literature into a newspaper explaining the struggle for freedom. Group members cooperatively choose an appropriate name for their newspaper. Each stu-

---

☞ IN THE CLASSROOM

Literature-Based Time Lines

A collaborative method of recording the wealth of social studies related literature shared during a unit or throughout the entire academic year is by keeping a cumulative literature-based time line. The following steps will help your students achieve a chronological log of trade books recorded through a historical perspective.

1. From the content of a single unit or the coverage of your social studies curriculum, determine the time span that the time line will cover. (Consider the time units of the U.S. History Standards for American History.)

2. Create a time line around the upper walls of your classroom with yarn, colored strips of paper, or a roll of twelve-inch-wide shelf paper.

3. Let students calculate appropriate units and appropriate mathematical spacing of prominent historical events during the chosen time span. Use a social studies textbook as an anthology for dates and events.

4. Use word processing and computer-generated graphics to mark years and selected images of chosen historical events.

5. Each time a student reads a book within the unit or curricular span (biography, historical fiction, informational), add a self-illustrated drawing of the historical message of the text. Under the drawing, copy one quote from the text that best represents the historical context of the book.

6. Prepare a three-by-five-inch index card that includes the author and title of the book.

7. Attach the drawing and the index card to the time line within the appropriate historical time frame.

8. As the time line fills in with literature, students place dates and events in a historical framework. They also remember and connect the related literature experiences that helped bring history to life.

dent then writes a feature or column on information gleaned from a particular book that was read or shared. The newspaper may be a mix of fact and fiction, but it must stay within the historical context of the quest for freedom. Diary entries, personal vignettes, and anecdotes can be written to capture the human spirit of individuals struggling toward freedom.

The use of word processing or software programs in newspaper format is highly desirable. Duplication of each newspaper for each member of the class will provide a means to share and compare information from each group. The cooperative group effort required during this unit not only provides a wealth of information on the topic of freedom and the spirit of those who fought for it but may also increase each student's desire to further explore an aspect of freedom surveyed by other members of the class.

The development of thematic units is limited only by the desire of the teacher to integrate reading, writing, and social studies in the curriculum. An interdisciplinary approach enables the classroom teacher to tear down traditional curricular boundaries while providing meaningful integration through unit teaching.

Science, Technology, and History

When twin texts meet technology, and science is added in, the result can be a strong interdisciplinary unit of instruction. In the world of interdisciplinary instruction, both nonfiction books and related fiction titles can actually enhance comprehension of both facts and story (Camp 2000). In addition, the infusion of a technology Web site can add visual representation to the learning model (Hancock 2002). Fiction (picture and chapter books across genres) plus nonfiction (informational/biographical titles) plus technology (an Internet Web site) provides endless benefits to the reader of each. Extended learning, enhanced comprehension, higher-level connections, aesthetic/efferent response, motivation for reading, and critical evaluation of information are certain benefits when twin texts meet technology in interdisciplinary teaching and learning.

Examples from three social studies and science interdisciplinary areas provide concrete titles and Web sites to better understand this powerful trio of resources.

The California Gold Rush

Nonfiction: Stanley, J. 2000. *Hurry Freedom: African Americans in the Gold Rush.* New York: Crown. (2001 Orbis Pictus Award) (Gr. 4–6)

Fiction: Cushman, K. 1996. *The Ballad of Lucy Whipple.* New York: Crown. (Gr. 4–5)

Web site: http://www.museumca.org/goldrush

Sponsored by the Oakland Museum of California, this Web site includes a tour of authentic artwork depicting the Gold Rush as well as a virtual tour of the museum's Gold Rush exhibit. Multicultural connections are provided.

The Irish Famine

Nonfiction: Lyons, M. 2002. *Feed the Children First: Irish Memories of the Great Hunger.* New York: Atheneum. (Gr. 5–8)

Fiction: Giff, P. R. 2000. *Nory Ryan's Song.* New York: Delacorte. (Gr. 4–8)

Web site: http://www.lyonsdenbooks.com

This author site contains reader response activities related to her books. In this case, students empathize with the plight of children during the Famine by viewing an authentic artwork from the late 1850s in Ireland.

The Blizzard of 1888
Nonfiction: Murphy, J. 2000. *Blizzard!* New York: Scholastic. (Gr. 4–8)
Fiction: Ehrlich, G. 1999. *A Blizzard Year.* New York: Scholastic. (Gr. 4–8)
Web site: http://memory.loc.gov
The American Memory Digital Collection of the Library of Congress. Testimonials from the survivors of the powerful blizzard of 1888 by the staff of the WPA (1936–40) can be accessed. Linked to copies of original recordings. Gateway to rich primary sources related to American history.

The potential scenarios for combining these three perspectives for teaching are endless and vary from grade level to grade level.

Primary Grades

Web site	Teacher Prior Knowledge	Fiction	Teacher Read-Aloud
Fiction	Teacher Read-Aloud	Nonfiction	Teacher Read-Aloud
Nonfiction	Teacher Read-Aloud	Web site	Student Activity

Intermediate Grades

Nonfiction	Teacher Read-Aloud	Nonfiction	Independent Reading
Fiction	Independent Reading	Fiction	Teacher Read-Aloud
Web site	Before/During/After Reading	Web site	After Reading

Middle School

Web site	Pre Reading Activity	Nonfiction	Independent Reading
Fiction	Independent Reading	Fiction	Independent Reading
Nonfiction	Teacher Read-Aloud	Web site	Evaluating Facts

Those who know content, literature, and quality Web sites thrive in creating these powerful trios of nonfiction, fiction, and Web sites to enhance overall comprehension and historical understandings.

Chapter Summary

Integrated instruction has provided classroom teachers with a justification to introduce quality literature across the curriculum. The realm of social studies has always been associated with biography and historical fiction, but integrated instruction has provided inclusion of these genre with related writing and discussion activities. In addition, the world of picture books provides an extension of literature into both geographic and historical concepts.

Literature linked to social studies widens a child's world by providing the opportunity to participate in new experiences, visit new places, and be a genuine part of the past. The rich resources of literature available for use in interdisciplinary instruction brings social studies to life through literary journeys that offer meaningful links to the child's own life and world.

NCSS STANDARDS-LINKED LESSON PLAN

Voice of Everyday People Who Make History

Theme: Using Primary Source Material to Document Community History
Grade Level: Grades 6–8
Source: Marjorie Hancock, Kansas State University
Objectives:

- Students will dramatically read aloud accounts of young people and their roles in U.S. history from Phillip Hoose's *We Were There, Too! Young People in U. History* (Farrar, Straus & Giroux 2001).

- Students will experience and value the use of primary sources including journals, interviews, first-person accounts.

- Students will select a senior community member and create a written and oral presentation of the individual using primary sources of photographs, interview transcripts, and first-person accounts.

NCSS Objectives:
   I. Culture
   II. Time, Continuity, and Change
   IX. Global Connections

Materials:
Hoose, P. 2001. *We Were There, Too! Young People in US. History.* New York: Farrar, Straus & Giroux. (Gr. 4–8)
Audiotaping and/or videotaping equipment, digital cameras, word processing program, scanner

Process:

Dramatic Read-Alouds

- Students will each select one of over 60 accounts of young boys and girls who made contributions throughout U.S. history.

- Each student will prepare a dramatic read-aloud of his/her choice emphasizing authentic voice and spirit.

- During preparation, students will evidence the effect of the use of primary sources as a means of bringing authenticity to their presentation.

- Students will share an oral presentation of each account with a goal of inspiring their audience.

Interviews/Primary Sources

- Students will select a senior community member who has had some influence on the community in which they live.

- Students will brainstorm questions that will bring forth quality information from those to be interviewed.

- Students will make arrangements to interview and audiotape/videotape their subject and to elicit personal voice and memories of his/her community contributions over a lifetime.

- Students will elicit other primary sources to enhance their written and oral presentation (i.e., photographs, letters, diaries, posters).

Presentation/Written and Oral

- Students will prepare a written project modeled after the 2- to 4-page format of the Phillip Hoose book. They will include authentic text from the interview along with photographs, maps, handwritten notes, etc., to enhance and authenticate the presentation.

- Students will use technology to transcribe interviews, scan artifacts, and design their written and visual presentations.

• Students will prepare an oral report to share with peers to bring each subject to life through primary source material.

Community Contribution

• Students will gather all written reports and create a CD to share with the community. In addition, a printed copy of the reports will be laminated and bound for use at the community and school library.

Instructional Comments: Teacher modeling is essential, so it is suggested that the teacher prepare a model of both an oral and a written presentation prior to instruction. While the trade book serves as the student model, the teacher will work through the process as he/she prepares his/her own interview enhanced by primary sources.

Learning Styles Addressed: Verbal/linguistic; visual/spatial; interpersonal

Evaluation: The final products will reflect the following traits:

• The student uses at least three primary sources to project authenticity of information.

• The text reflects quality interview data that have been selectively transcribed and sequenced.

• The oral presentation is dramatic and appears filled with the voice of the interviewed subject.

• The written presentation reflects the use of a layout modeled after that in the Phillip Hoose book titled, *We Were There, Too!*

Modifications for Diverse Learners:

• Students may pair up as interview teams for verbal and artistic support in completing the assignment.

• Students may creatively use technology to create the design and layouts of their presentations.

• Students may use videotapes (with permission) to create iMovies of the memoirs of community leaders.

Extensions:

• Students can access other quality nonfiction historical texts to determine how primary sources are used to enhance transmission of information.

• Students can create a bibliography of nonfiction books that use primary sources as the key to authenticity.

• Students can share their performance and written presentations at a community open house.

Children's Literature Recommendation

Ada, A. F. 1997. *Gathering the Sun: An Alphabet in Spanish and English.* Trans. R. Zubizaretta. Illus. S. Silva. New York: Lothrop. Sun-drenched paintings and twenty-eight poems transport the reader to the fields and orchards of California where migrant workers create the harvest each year. (Gr. K–3)

Adler, D. A. 2001. *B. Franklin: Printer.* New York: Holiday House. Packed with information for young report writers, this book has maps, engravings, paintings, drawings, and letters on almost every page as it brings the Franklin era to life through primary sources. (Gr. 4–6)

———. 2003. *A Picture Book of Lewis and Clark.* New York: Holiday House. The famous travels of Lewis and Clark are shared. (Gr. K–2)

———. 2003. *A Picture Book of Samuel Adams.* Illus. J. Fisher. New York: Holiday House. The story of a lesser known, but prominent statesman of the new American nation. One of the many fine picture books by Adler that make biography accessible to young students. (Gr. K–2)

———. 2004. *Enemies of Slavery*. Illus. D. A. Smith. New York: Holiday House. Fourteen men and women stand as enduring champions of freedom in a time of slavery. They include John Brown, Frederick Douglass, Lucretia Mott, Nat Turner, and others. (Gr. 4–6)

Allen, T. B. 1989. *On Grandaddy's Farm*. New York: Knopf. Events from the 1930s, when the author and his cousin spent summers on their grandparents' farm in the hills of Tennessee. (Gr. 2–4)

Ammon, R. 2004. *Valley Forge*. Illus. B. Farnsworth. New York: Holiday House. During the freezing winter of 1777–78, the Continental army transformed itself from a ragtag outfit to a professional army at Valley Forge under the direction of General George Washington. (Gr. 2–4)

Arnold, M. D. 2001. *The Bravest of Us All*. Illus. B. Sneed. New York: Dial. When a tornado blows through a Kansas farm, Velda Jean must overcome her fear and show courage in time of trouble. Brad Sneed's watercolor art has the characters literally blowing across the pages during the storm. (Gr. 1–5)

Avi. 1984. *The Fighting Ground*. Philadelphia: Lippincott. Thirteen-year-old Jonathan goes off to fight in the Revolutionary War and discovers the real war is being fought within himself. (Gr. 6–8)

———. 2002. *Crispin: The Cross of Lead*. New York: Hyperion. Set in 14th century England, an orphan learns his real name is Crispin and faces a mortal enemy. Clutching his only possession, a lead cross, Crispin escapes to a new world of opportunity and terror. Nail-biting tension and a gripping ending. (Gr. 6–8)

———. 2006. *Crispin: At the Edge of the World*. New York: Hyperion. The second book in the planned trilogy follows Crispin and Bear in their lives as free men. When Bear is badly wounded, Crispin becomes the decision maker even when it means confronting death to maintain their freedom. (Gr. 6–8)

Barron, T. A. 2003. *High as a Hawk: A Brave Girl's Historical Climb*. Illus. T. Lewin. New York: Philomel. The courageous climb of a young girl up Long's Peak in Colorado is documented with some true facts of the journey. (Gr. 2–4)

Bartoletti, S. C. 2005 *Hitler Youth: Growing Up in Hitler's Shadow*. New York: Scholastic. Hitler's rise to power is told through the firsthand experiences of young followers. The Hitler Youth Movement is traced from the early 1930s until the defeat of Hitler. (Gr. 6–8)

Baylor, B. 1983. *The Best Town in the World*. Illus. R. Himler. New York: Scribner. Life in a small country town in the Texas hills around the turn of the century poetically reveals the "best" of everything. (Gr. 2–6)

Bial, R. 1993. *Amish Home*. Boston: Houghton Mifflin. A sensitive, informative view of the spirit and beliefs of the Amish told through photographs. (Gr. K–4)

Bitton-Jackson, L. 1997. *I Have Lived a Thousand Years: Growing Up in the Holocaust*. New York: Simon & Schuster. An unforgettable memoir that details the horrible experiences of Auschwitz and the perseverance and twists of fate that allow Elli Friedmann to survive the death camp. (Gr. 6–8)

Blumberg, R. 2004. *York's Adventures with Lewis & Clark: An African American's Part in the Great Expedition*. New York: HarperCollins. The Orbis Pictus Award for 2005 celebrates a lesser-known perspective on the 100th anniversary of the Great Expedition west. Archived artwork, endnotes, and research source work bring quality to this nonfiction work (Gr. 4–8)

Borden, L. 2002. *America Is . . .* Illus. S. Schuett. New York: McElderry. A textual and visual mural of all the unique qualities that makes America the greatest nation and the source pride in its citizens. (Gr. K–4)

Burleigh, R. 2002. *The Secret of the Great Houdini*. Illus. L. Gore. New York: Atheneum. A little boy finds himself mesmerized by the powers of freedom and human will that Houdini represents. Houdini is portrayed as testing the boundaries of his body, the forces of nature, and his imagination. (Gr. 2–6)

Burton, V. L. 1942. *The Little House.* Boston: Houghton Mifflin. A country house is unhappy when the city, with all its buildings and traffic, grows up around it. (Gr. K–2)

Cheney, L. 2002. *America: A Patriotic Primer.* Illus. R. P. Glasser. New York: Simon & Schuster. An alphabetical tribute to all that is America—from historical facts to historical personalities, from national monuments to national symbols. Filled with countless bits of information about our nation. (Gr. K–4)

Chin-Lee, C. 1997. *A is for Asia.* Illus. Y. Heo. New York: Orchard. A panoramic glimpse into a continent that covers one-third of the earth through an alphabetical format. (Gr. K–3)

Clapp, P. 1977. *I'm Deborah Sampson: A Soldier in the War of the Revolution.* New York: Lothrop. Real-life adventure of a New England woman who, posing as a man, served for more than a year in the Continental Army. (Gr. 4–6)

Collier, J., and C. Collier. 1985. *My Brother Sam Is Dead.* New York: Four Winds. A family is divided by the Revolutionary War as the protagonist is caught between his loyalist father and his rebel brother. (Gr. 6–8)

Conrad, P. 1985. *Prairie Songs.* New York: Harper & Row. Louisa's life in a loving pioneer family on the Nebraska prairie is altered by the arrival of a new doctor and his beautiful, tragically ill wife. (Gr. 3–5)

Curlee, L. 1999. *Rushmore.* New York: Atheneum. A tribute to the genius of the sculptor and the fearless workers who made a dream of this symbol of America a national reality. (Gr. 4–8)

———. 2000. *Liberty.* New York: Atheneum. The story behind the building of the Statue of Liberty is told through well-researched text and outstanding illustrations, including cross-sections and interior views of this symbol of America's freedom. (Gr. 4–8)

———. 2001. *Brooklyn Bridge.* New York: Atheneum. This legacy to New York's skyline and architecture is revealed through its rigorous building as an exceptional engineering project. Outstanding diagrams and varied viewpoints provide additional visual understanding of the role of this bridge in New York's history. (Gr. 4–8)

———. 2002. *Seven Wonders of the Ancient World.* New York: Atheneum. Outstanding artwork shares the spotlight with the facts, figures, dimensions, and architectural efforts behind each of the world's great wonders. (Gr. 4–8)

———. 2004. *Parthenon.* New York: Atheneum. A tribute to the architecture, construction, and symbolism of the temple to honor Athena in Athens. (Gr. 5–8)

Curtis, C. P. 1999. *Bud, Not Buddy.* New York: Delacorte. Set in the Depression era in Detroit, orphaned Bud seeks his roots in Grand Rapids. Finally locating his elderly grandfather, Bud not only finds a sense of family and a future career in music, but also learns answers to many questions about his deceased mother. (Gr. 5–8)

Cushman, K. 1996. *The Ballad of Lucy Whipple.* New York: Clarion. The rough life of a California mining town provides the backdrop for Lucy's initial reluctance to adapt to the gold rush and her growing maturity as she finds her way home. (Gr. 3–5)

———. 2002. *Rodzina.* New York: Clarion. The Orphan Train journey from the east to the west exposes Rodzina to rejection and mistreatment before reaching the love and family of which she dreams. (Gr. 4–6)

d'Aulaire, I., and E. P. d'Aulaire. 1957. *Abraham Lincoln.* Rev. ed. New York: Doubleday. Classic children's biography of Lincoln from his birth through the Civil War by a famed author-illustrator team. (Gr. 2–6)

DeFelice, C. 1996. *The Apprenticeship of Lucas Whitaker.* New York: Farrar, Straus & Giroux. After his family dies of consumption in 1849, Lucas becomes Doc Beecher's apprentice and exposes the macabre practices for fighting tuberculosis. (Gr. 5–8)

Denenberg, B. 1998. *The Journal of William Thomas Emerson: A Revolutionary War Portrait* (*My Name Is America* series). New York: Scholastic. A young tavern boy overhears the activities of the committee while proving himself a true patriot during prerevolutionary days. (Gr. 4–6)

de Paola, T. 1983. *The Legend of the Bluebonnet: An Old Tale of Texas.* New York: Putnam. A retelling of the Comanche lesson of how a little girl's sacrifice brought the bluebonnet to Texas. (Gr. K–4)

———. 1988. *The Legend of the Indian Paintbrush.* New York: Putnam. Little Gopher becomes an artist for his people and brings the colors of the sunset down to earth as his paintbrushes are transformed into brilliantly colored western flowers. (Gr. K–4)

Dooley, N. 1996. *Everyone Bakes Bread.* Illus. P. J. Thornton. Minneapolis, MN: Carolrhoda. A tour of the globe reveals many countries and cultures with commonalities in culinary traditions. (Gr. K–3)

Fiday, B., and D. Fiday. 1990. *Time to Go.* Illus. T. B. Allen. San Diego, CA: Gulliver. As a child and his family prepare to leave, he takes one last look at the family farm. (K–3)

Fleischman, P. 1993. *Bull Run.* Illus. D. Frampton. Woodcuts. New York: HarperCollins. The voices of 16 characters before, during, and following the historic Civil War battle bring life and personal commitment from people from all walks of life—slaves, free people, soldiers. Includes notes from the book to be used as a reader's theatre. (Gr. 5–8)

———. 2006 (updated edition). *Dateline: Troy.* Collages by F. Frankfeldt and G. Morrow. Cambridge, MA: Candlewick Press. A retelling of the story of the Trojan War juxtaposed with newspaper clippings of modern news events revealing the tragic parallels of ancient and modern history. (Gr. 6–8)

Fleming, T. 2006. *Everybody's Revolution: A New Look at the People who Won America's Freedom.* New York: Scholastic. The diversity of America at the time of the Revolutionary War included women, African Americans, Jews, Native Americans, Hispanic Americans, European immigrants, and young adults who played leading roles in the struggle against Britain. (Gr. 4–6)

Freedman, R. 1987a. *Indian Chief.* New York: Clarion. Famous Native American leaders of the old West are depicted. (Gr. 4–8)

———. 1987b. *Lincoln: A Photobiography.* New York: Clarion. An absorbing look into Lincoln's career shown through numerous photographs, prints, and reprints of original documents. The 1988 Newbery Medal winner. (Gr. 4–8)

———. 1990a. *Cowboys of the Wild West.* New York: Clarion. Photos of cowboys in the late 1800s along with narration about their lifestyle, cattle drives, and the hardships they faced. (Gr. 3–6)

———. 1990b. *Franklin Delano Roosevelt.* New York: Clarion. A photobiography of our longest serving president. (Gr. 4–8)

———. 2000. *Give Me Liberty! The Story of the Declaration of Independence.* New York: Holiday House. Opens with a lively account of the Boston Tea Party and moves to tell the story of how the Declaration came to be an affirmation of human rights and representative government. (Gr. 4–8)

———. 2004. *The Voice that Challenged a Nation: Marian Anderson and the Struggle for Equal Rights.* New York: Clarion. Marian Anderson's brilliant voice helped her spread the cause for equal rights among Americans. (Gr. 4–8)

———. 2005. *Children of the Great Depression.* New York: Clarion. The Orbis Pictus Award winner for 2006 showcases photography that captures the emotions and challenges of this stark period in history. (Gr. 4-8)

Friedman, D. D. 2006. *Escaping into the Night.* New York: Simon & Schuster. The underground forest encampment is a place to which Halina escapes in fleeing the Polish ghetto. In an effort to protect herself from the advancing Germans, she must learn to live without the mother who was left behind. (Gr. 5–8)

Fritz, J. 1973. *And Then What Happened, Paul Revere?* Illus. M. Tomes. New York: Coward, McCann. A description of the well-known and lesser-known details of Paul Revere's life and exciting ride. (Gr. 2–4)

————. 1974. *Why Don't You Get a Horse, Sam Adams?* Illus. M. Tomes. New York: Coward, McCann. The blatant defiance of British authority is exemplified by the behavior of this noble statesman. (Gr. 2–4)

————. 1975. *Where Was Patrick Henry on the 29th of May?* Illus. M. Tomes. New York: Coward, McCann. A brief biography of Patrick Henry that traces his progress from planter to statesman. (Gr. 2–4)

————. 1976. *Will You Sign Here, John Hancock?* Illus. T. S. Hyman. New York: Coward, McCann. John Hancock's vanity and penchant for flourishes is captured in this brief biography. (Gr. 2–4)

————. 1982. *Can't You Make Them Behave, King George?* Illus. T. de Paola. New York: Coward, McCann. Unpopular English monarch George III is viewed through a humorous, yet historical perspective. (Gr. 2–4)

Gerstein, M. 2003. *The Man who Walked between the Towers*. New York: Roaring Brook Press. Based on a historical account of a tightrope walker who showed his courage in the air between the New York towers that tumbled on 9/11/01. (Gr. 2–4)

Giblin, J. C. 2000. *The Amazing Life of Benjamin Franklin*. Illus. M. Dooling. New York: Scholastic. Brilliant writing enhanced by watercolor illustrations bring this American icon to life. Both author and illustrator notes indicate the research involved in creating this *Orbis Pictus* Honor Book. (Gr. 2–5)

Giff, P. R. 2004. *A House of Tailors*. New York: Random House. Traveling to America to her uncle's home proves to be an adjustment and a challenge for Dina. Opportunity turns to horror when the family home and business burns. (Gr. 4–6)

Giovanni, N. 2005. *Rosa*. Illus. B. Collier. New York: Henry Holt. This masterfully illustrated account of Rosa Parks's life is linked with other events embedded in the civil rights movement. (Gr. 2–4).

Gregory, K. 1996. *The Winter of the Red Snow: The Revolutionary War Diary of Abigail Jane Stewart* (*Dear America* series). New York: Scholastic. Fictionalized journal entries written in Valley Forge, Pennsylvania, in the winter of 1777–78 enhanced by authentic portraits, drawings, and documents from the period. (Gr. 3–6)

Guiberson, B. Z. 1991. *Cactus Hotel*. Illus. M. Hoyd. New York: Henry Holt. The saguaro cactus serves as a home to birds and other Sonoran Desert creatures. (Gr. 1–4)

Guthrie, W. 1998. *This Land Is Your Land*. Illus. K. Jakobsen. Boston: Little, Brown. This well-known folk song and tribute to Woody Guthrie is accompanied by folk art that guides the reader on a coast-to-coast tour of America. (Gr. K–4)

Hamilton, V. 1988. *Anthony Burns: The Defeat and Triumph of a Fugitive Slave*. New York: Knopf. A biography of the slave who escaped Boston in 1854, was arrested at the instigation of his owner, and whose trial caused a furor between abolitionists and supporters of the Fugitive Slave Act. (Gr. 5–8)

Hesse, K. 1992. *Letters from Rifka*. New York: HarperCollins. Rifka, a Russian Jewish girl in the early twentieth century, writes about her hopes in immigrating to America. (Gr. 5–8)

————. 1997. *Out of the Dust*. New York: Scholastic. Set in the Oklahoma Dust Bowl during the Great Depression, this free verse novel tells of Billie Jo's struggle to forgive herself and heal her heart when a family tragedy overwhelms her spirit. (Gr. 5–8)

Hest, A. 1997. *When Jesse Came across the Sea*. Illus. P. J. Lynch. Cambridge, MA: Candlewick Press. An inspiring tale of a young immigrant girl's life in America and the threads that bind her to her European heritage. (Gr. 2–5)

Hill, K. 2005. *Dancing at the Odinochka*. New York: McElderry. Owned by the Russians, the Odinochka is a trading post where native people in Alaska trade furs, listen to stories and music, and dance. When the U.S. purchases a part of Alaska from Russia, Erinia and her people must adjust to becoming American Alaskans. (Gr. 6–8)

Holm J. L. 2001. *Boston Jane: An Adventure*. New York: HarperCollins. Jane Peck ventures to the Pacific Northwest to wed her childhood idol, William Baldt. The crude life of the wilderness causes Jane to discover a new self as a courageous woman of the frontier and to question her impending marital destiny. (Gr. 5–8)

Hopkins, L. B., ed. 2000. *My America: A Poetry Atlas of the United States*. Illus. S. Alcorn. New York: Simon & Schuster. Fifty poems are grouped by geographic region to paint a portrait of the breadth of our country. Both honored poets and new voices combine in a visual and textual tribute to the wide-ranging, ever-changing landscape of America. (Gr. 4–6)

Howard, E. F. 2000. *Virgie Goes to School with Us Boys*. Illus. E. B. Lewis. New York: Simon & Schuster. A determined Virgie wants to go to school with her brothers, but they keep saying she is too little for the seven-mile walk and that girls don't need school. Based on a true story from the author's family from the Civil War Reconstruction period. (Gr. 2–4)

Johnson, D. B. 2000. *Henry Hikes to Fitchburg*. Boston: Houghton Mifflin. Henry and his friend decide to go to Fitchburg, MA, but each takes a different journey. Henry chooses to walk because it is faster and puts him in touch with nature, while his friend chooses to work to earn enough money to buy a train ticket there. Even though the train is faster, Henry has a pail of blackberries in hand to illustrate the fruits of his journey. (Gr. 2–4)

———. 2002. *Henry Builds a Cabin*. Boston: Houghton Mifflin. People wonder why Henry Bear would build a cabin away from town. While he sketches a floor plan, he interacts with nature's animals. Johnson captures the work ethic, love of nature, and environmental philosophy of Henry David Thoreau through his expressionist illustrations. (Gr. 1–4)

———. 2003. *Henry Climbs a Mountain*. Boston: Houghton Mifflin. The natural experience and vigor of mountain climbing inspire Henry in his writing when he returns home. (Gr. 1–4)

Karr, K. 2002. *Bone Dry*. New York: Hyperion. Matthew Morrisey and Dr. Asa B. Cornwall search for the skull of Alexander the Great. This sequel to *Skullduggery* follows Matthew from Paris to northern Africa in 1840 and shares the bizarre and deadly world of the Sahara Desert. (Gr. 4–6)

Kellogg, S. 1986. *Pecos Bill*. New York: Morrow. Incidents from the life of the legendary cowboy, from his life among the coyotes to his unusual wedding day. (Gr. K–3)

King, C., and L. B. Osborne. 1997. *Oh, Freedom! Kids Talk about the Civil Rights Movement with the People Who Made It Happen*. New York: Knopf. The voices of young and old explore the feelings, experiences, and events during the civil rights movement through interviews conducted by children with family members, friends, and activists. (Gr. 5–8)

Knight, M. B. 1996. *Talking Walls: The Stories Continue*. Illus. A. S. O'Brien. Gardiner, ME: Tilbury House. A sequel to *Talking Walls* (1992) takes the reader around the world to revere the role famous walls have played in past and current history. (Gr. 4–8)

Krull, K. 2003. *Harvesting Hope: The Story of Cesar Chavez*. Illus. Y. Morales. San Diego: Harcourt. Vivid illustrations showcase the struggle and the courage of the leader of migrant workers in California. (Gr. 3–6)

Lasky, K. 2000. *Vision of Beauty: The Story of Sarah Breedlove Walker*. Illus. N. Bennett. Boston: Candlewick. The first child born to a family after slavery was abolished, Sarah was orphaned at age 7. She went on to design hair products, becoming the first black millionairess in America. (Gr. 2–4)

Leitner, K. 1992. *The Big Lie: A True Story.* New York: Scholastic. A stark, autobiographical account of how the author's family was rounded up in Hungary and taken to Auschwitz, where her mother and younger sister died. (Gr. 5–8)

Lesser, C. 1997. *Storm in the Desert.* Illus. T. Rand. San Diego: Harcourt Brace. Poetic narrative and dynamic watercolors describe the effects of a desert storm on the landscape and inhabitants. (Gr. 2–6)

Lester, J. 1968. *To Be a Slave.* New York: Dial. The verbatim testimony of former slaves is combined with the author's own commentary on the conditions and inequality of slavery. (Gr. 4–8)

Levin, E. (2006). *Henry's Freedom Box: A True Story from the Underground Railroad.* Illus. Kadir Nelson. New York: Scholastic. When Henry's family of slaves is sold and separated from him, Henry makes a harrowing journey in a wooden crate to find freedom. Based on a true story, Henry "Box" Brown's life is revealed with courage and grace. (Gr. K–2).

Lewin, T. 1996. *Market!* New York: Lothrop, Lee & Shepard. From the chilly Andes Mountains to the sultry jungles of Africa, from the souks of Morocco to the New York waterfronts . . . people come to market to buy and sell what they grow, catch, or make. (Gr. K–4)

Lisle, J. T. 2000. *The Art of Keeping Cool.* New York: Simon & Schuster. In 1942, Robert and his cousin, Eliot, uncover long-kept family secrets. They become involved with a German artist suspected of being a spy. Robert must detach himself when suspicions and prejudice result in violence. (Gr. 5–8)

Lobel, A. 1994. *Away from Home.* New York: Greenwillow. This around-the-world journey follows the alphabet to the far corners of the world. Alliterative sentences share names, action verbs, and cities of the world. (Gr. K–3)

Locker, T. 1998. *Home: A Journey through America.* San Diego, CA: Harcourt Brace. This tribute to America blends selected writings and poems that vividly describe the landscape where writers call home with Locker's oil paintings for a vision of our varied and special land. (Gr. 2–5)

Longfellow, H. W. 2001. *The Midnight Ride of Paul Revere.* Illus. C. Bing. Handprint. This new edition of a classic poem features maps and digitally scanned artifacts that add detail to the watercolor-tinted scratchboard drawings. (Gr. 5–8)

McKissick, P. C., and F. L. McKissick. 1994. *Christmas in the Big House, Christmas in the Quarters.* Illus. J. Thompson. New York: Scholastic. The documented text compares and contrasts how Christmas was celebrated in the big Virginia plantation house and the slave quarters in the period just before the Civil War. (Gr. 2–5)

Martin, J. B. 1998. *Snowflake Bentley.* Illus. M. Azarian. Boston: Houghton Mifflin. The Caldecott Medal was awarded for the dimensional woodcuts in this picture book biography of this photographer of snowflakes. (Gr. 1–4)

Matas, C. 1993. *Daniel's Story.* New York: Scholastic. Published in conjunction with the opening of the United States Holocaust Memorial Museum, this novel tells the composite story of millions of children who lived through the Holocaust. (Gr. 4–8)

Meltzer, M. 1976. *Never Forget: The Jews of the Holocaust.* New York: Harper & Row. A history of the atrocities committed against the courageous Jews documented by historical sources. (Gr. 3–6)

————. 1984. *The Black Americans: A History in Their Own Words, 1619–1983.* New York: Cromwell. A history of African Americans in the United States told through authentic documents and eyewitness accounts. (Gr. 5–8)

————. 1989. *Voices from the Civil War: A Documentary History of the Great American Conflict.* New York: Cromwell. Authentic source material documents the life and events of the four years of the Civil War. (Gr. 4–8)

Meyers, W. D. 2003. *Blues Journey.* Illus. C. Meyers. New York: Holiday House. The joy of music follows a twosome on a journey to New Orleans. (Gr. 2–4)

Millman, I. 2005. *Hidden Child.* New York: Farrar. Jewish children who survived WWII went into hiding. Isaac Millman was one of those survivors who tells his secret story. (Gr. 4–6)

Milnes, G. 1990. *Granny Will Your Dog Bite? And Other Mountain Rhymes.* Little Rock, AR: August House. A lively collection of traditional rhymes, songs, and riddles about mountain life. (Gr. 3–8)

Minor, W. 2006. *Yankee Doodle America: The Spirit of 1776 from A to Z,* New York: Putnam. An alphabet book revisits the key moments, symbols, and issues of the Revolutionary War. (Gr. K–4)

Mochizuki, K. 1997. *Passage to Freedom: The Sugihara Story.* Illus. D. Lee. New York: Lee & Low. Against the order of the government, a Japanese diplomat issues thousands of visas to Jewish refugees to escape the wrath of the Nazis. (Gr. 4–8)

Monjo, F. N. 1973. *Poor Richard in France.* Illus. B. Turkle. New York: Holt, Rinehart, & Winston. Benjamin Franklin's trip to France is revealed from the view of his seven-year-old grandson. (Gr. 1–3)

Moses, S. 2004. *The Legend of Buddy Bush.* New York: McElderry. Buddy Bush ends up in jail in North Carolina when falsely accused of a crime against a white woman. Pattie Mae adores her Uncle Buddy and sets off on the hard road to expose the truth. (Gr. 5–8)

Murphy, J. 1996. *A Young Patriot: The American Revolution as Experienced by One Boy.* New York: Clarion. Fifteen-year-old Joseph Plumb Martain shares his experience in the army from 1776 to 1783 in his own words, including the leadership of Washington, Lafayette, and Steuben, the battle of Yorktown, and the winter at Valley Forge. (Gr. 6–8)

———. 2006. *Desperate Journey.* New York: Scholastic. When her father and uncle are arrested, twelve-year old Maggie Haggerty must haul the heavy cargo through the Erie Canal in the mid-1800s to recover a monetary bonus for her family. (Gr. 4–8)

Norges, D. 2004. *Hana in the Time of the Tulips.* Illus. B. Ibatoulline. Cambridge, MA: Candlewick. Exquisite art in the style of Rembrandt showcases the story of the monetary value of the tulip in Holland in the 1600s as well as the changing relationship of a loving daughter and her entrepreneur father. (Gr. 4–8)

O'Dell, S. 1990. *My Name Is Not Angelica.* New York: Dell/Yearling Books. Raisha and her betrothed, Konje, an African tribal chief, are captured and sold into slavery in the West Indies. Konje escapes and becomes a leader of a band of runaway slaves, while Raisha, called Angelica by her owner, waits their reunion. (Gr. 6–8)

Parnell, P. 1986. *Winter Barn.* New York: Macmillan. A dilapidated old barn shelters a wide variety of animals during the subzero temperatures of a Maine winter. (Gr. K–3)

Paterson, K. 1991. *Lyddie.* New York: Dutton. A Vermont farm girl goes to work in deplorable conditions of a factory during the Industrial Revolution in Lowell, Massachusetts. (Gr. 5–7)

———. 1996. *Jip.* New York: Dutton. A Vermont orphan finds his roots while befriending a mentally unstable prisoner. (Gr. 3–5)

Paulsen, G. 1993. *Nightjohn.* New York: Delacorte. Nightjohn, an escaped slave, believes that reading is the key to freedom. He returns to the South where beatings and mutilations never deter him from his goal of teaching slaves to read. For mature readers. (Gr. 6–8)

Pearsall, S. 2002. *Trouble Don't Last.* New York: Knopf. Samuel is forced to run away with Harrison, an old slave, from a Kentucky plantation to Ohio and Canada. The hardships and prejudice that runaway slaves encounter on their journey to freedom is harsh and realistic. (Gr. 5–8)

Peck, R. 2003. *The River between Us.* New York: Dial. Two young women depart in a boat from a small southern Illinois town at the start of the Civil War. Racism reigns as they struggle to decide which side to be on and why. (Gr. 6–8)

Polacco, P. 1994. *Pink and Say.* New York: Philomel. This Civil War story of friendship and fear has been passed through Polacco's family. It celebrates shared humanity in a war-torn nation. (Gr. 3–8)

Poole, J. 1998. *Joan of Arc.* Illus. A. Barrett. New York: Knopf. Meticulously researched, this chronology of the events surrounding Joan's remarkable life captures her courage and humanity while sharing the drama, triumph, and tragedy of her crusade. (Gr. 5–8)

Priceman, M. 1994. *How to Make an Apple Pie and See the World.* New York: Knopf. Readers are whisked around the world to gather the necessary ingredients for a sumptuous apple pie. Social studies, math, and taste buds are integrated when the recipe becomes reality. (Gr. K–3)

Provensen, A., and M. Provensen. 1987. *Shaker Lane.* New York: Viking. When the town decides to build a reservoir on its land, the residents of Shaker Lane move away rather than fight to keep their homes. (Gr. 2–4)

Rappaport, D. 2004. *Free at Last! Stories and Songs of Emancipation.* Illus. S. W. Evans. Cambridge, MA: Candlewick. True accounts put readers in the shoes of men and women who fought for their freedom through defiance and resistance. (Gr. 6–8)

Rinaldi, A. 1998. *Cast Two Shadows: The American Revolution in the South.* San Diego: Harcourt Brace. Claiming she wants no part of war, Caroline Whitaker endures much heartache as her family is torn apart and her best friend is hanged during 1780 with a differing view of the war than that fought in the North. (Gr. 5–8)

Robbins, K. 2001. *Thunder on the Plains: The Story of the American Buffalo.* New York: Atheneum. The loss of the buffalo through wasteful killings and abandonment are showcased through color tinted photographs authentic to this historical period. (Gr. 3–6)

Rockwell, A. 2000. *Only Passing Through: The Story of Sojourner Truth.* Illus. R. Gregory Christie. New York: Knopf. Isabella, a mistreated slave girl, transforms herself into Sojourner Truth, one of the most powerful antislave and human rights messengers in history. The physical and mental strength of this extraordinary woman are symbolized by the expressive artwork that accompanies the text. (Gr. 4–8)

Russell, B. T. 2006. *Maggie's Amerikay.* Illus. J. Burke. New York: Farrar. An Irish immigrant and an African American boy discover kinship through music in the port of New Orleans. (Gr. 4–6)

Rylant, C. 1991. *Appalachia: The Voices of Sleeping Birds.* San Diego: Harcourt Brace. Poetic collections of the author growing up in Appalachia are enhanced by evocative, full color portraits of the region. (Gr. 2–4)

St. George, J. 2000. *So You Want to be President?* Illus. D. Small. New York: Philomel. The 2001 Caldecott Medal award book shares lesser-known facts about each of the presidents. The art of David Small captures the humor and uniqueness each brought to the White House. (Gr. 2–4)

Salisbury, C. 1994. *Under the Blood Red Sun.* New York: Delacorte. Friendships and Japanese American family ties are strained following the bombing of Pearl Harbor. (Gr. 5–8)

Sandburg, C. 1985. *Abe Lincoln Grows Up.* Illus. J. Daugherty. San Diego: Harcourt Brace. Reprinted from Sandburg's *Abraham Lincoln: The Prairie Years.* (Gr. 6–8)

———. 1998. *Grassroots.* Illus. W. Minor. San Diego: Harcourt Brace. Beautiful oil paintings blend with the treasured poetic voice of Sandburg to share timeless observations of the Midwest—America's heartland. (Gr. 5–8)

Schanzer, R. 2004. *George vs. George: The American Revolution as Seen from Both Sides.* Washington, DC: National Geographic. George Washington was the man who freed the

American colonies from the British, and George III was the British king who lost them. There are two sides to every story. (Gr. 4–6)

Service, R. 1987. *The Cremation of Sam McGee.* New York: Greenwillow. An illustrated version of a well-known poem that captures the mystery and romance of the Alaska gold rush and tells the tale of an interesting Yukon prospector. (Gr. 5–8)

Scillian, D. 2002. *A is for America.* Illus. P. Carroll. Chelsea, MI: Sleeping Bear Press. Opening book to a series about the 50 states. Each book provides rhymed text for the youngest reader and expanded text for the intermediate-level student. Titles include: *B is for Beaver* (Oregon), *H is for Hoosier* (Indiana), *M is for Maple Syrup* (Vermont), and 47 others. (Gr. 3–5)

Shulevitz, U. 1990. *Toddlecreek Post Office.* New York: Farrar, Straus & Giroux. Vanishing small-town America is portrayed as the local post office, the center of town activity, is closed down and a town faces a lost identity. (Gr. 2–4)

Stanley, D. 1998. *Joan of Arc.* New York: Morrow. At seventeen she rode into battle and was proclaimed the savior of France; at nineteen she was condemned to a terrible death; five hundred years later she becomes a saint. History is brought to life through rich narrative and gilded illustrations. (Gr. 3–6)

———. 2000. *Michelangelo.* New York: HarperCollins. Combined authentic and computer-generated art helps in telling the story of this artistic genius who created *The Pieta,* the statue of *David,* and painted the ceiling of the Sistine Chapel in the Vatican in Rome. (Gr. 4–8)

———. 2002. *Saladin: Noble Prince of Islam.* New York: HarperCollins. A little-known biographical subject, Saladin is an Islamic warrior noted for his civility in times of horrendous fighting. His honor and chivalry are portrayed as are exquisite paintings of Islamic artwork. (Gr. 5–8)

Stanley, D., and P. Vennema. 1990. *Good Queen Bess.* New York: Four Winds. The life of the strong-willed queen of England during the time of Shakespeare and the defeat of the Spanish Armada is presented through beautiful illustrations and text. (Gr. 4–7)

Stewart, S. 2001. *The Journey.* Mankato, MN: Farrar, Straus & Giroux. Readers learn about Chicago from the perspective of a young Amish girl. (Gr. 1–4)

Sturges, P. 1998. *Bridges Are to Cross.* Illus. G. Laroche. New York: Putnam. A journey to famous bridges around the globe reflects the significance of bridges as cultural symbols, celebrations, and solutions in our world. (Gr. 3–6)

Taylor, M. 2001. *The Land.* New York: Putnam. A prequel to Taylor's *Roll of Thunder, Hear My Cry* is told by Paul-Edward, born part Indian, part African slave—an identity that almost destroys him. He pursues his dream of owning the land through backbreaking work. (Gr. 6–8).

Thomas, J. C. 1998. *I Have Heard of a Land.* Illus. F. Cooper. New York: HarperCollins. The Oklahoma Territory invited the strength and determination of men, women, and newly freed African Americans to stake their claim in quest of a new life and courageous dream. (Gr. 2–5)

Toll, N. S. 1993. *Behind the Secret Window: A Memoir of a Hidden Child During World War II.* New York: Dial. When she was eight, the author and her mother were hidden from the Nazis by a Gentile couple in Poland. The 64 authentic watercolors illuminate the experiences of a child in hiding. (Gr. 4–8)

Tunnell, M. O., and G. Chilcoat. 1996. *The Children of the Topaz: The Story of a Japanese American Internment Camp Based on a Classroom Diary.* New York: Holiday House. Based on a teacher's diary as a primary source, the book deals with the impact of forced imprisonment on Japanese Americans during World War II and includes diary reproductions and authentic information on the conditions at Topaz. (Gr. 4–6)

Turner, A. 1992. *Katie's Trunk*. Illus. R. Himler. New York: Macmillan. The two sides of the American Revolution confront each other as Katie finds that true friendship extends beyond the lines drawn by war. (Gr. 3–6)

————. 1997. *Mississippi Mud: Three Prairie Journals*. Illus. R. Blake. New York: HarperCollins. Through poetic journal entries, Amanda, Caleb, and Lonnie reveal different dreams and personalities on their journey from Kentucky to Oregon. (Gr. 3–6)

————. 1999. *Red Flower Goes West*. Illus. D. Nolan. New York: Hyperion. A family of settlers leaves behind family, friends, and way of life as they travel to the gold rush of California. Only one piece of their former life, a red geranium, accompanies them on the hard journey to be planted as a symbol of hope at their destination. (Gr. 2–5)

————. 2001. *Abe Lincoln Remembers*. Illus. W. Minor. New York: HarperCollins. Preparing for a night at Ford's Theater with Mrs. Lincoln, the president reminisces about his life. The first-person fictionalized voice is a poignant retrospective on his accomplishments and trials and his joy that the Civil War is at last over. (Gr. 3–5)

Von Tscharner, R., and R. Fleming. 1987. *New Providence: A Changing Cityscape*. San Diego: Harcourt Brace. A visual treatment of the emerging urban environment as an imaginary town moves through economic, political, and architectural changes from 1910 to 1987. (Gr. 2–6)

Warren, A. 2001. *Surviving Hitler*. Boston: Houghton Mifflin. The author uses her interview style to gather the memories of a boy captured and interred in a Nazi concentration camp. His memoir is a tribute to his courage and the life he has salvaged from his near death experience. (Gr. 4–6)

Weatherford, C. B. (2006). *Moses: When Harriet Tubman Led Her People to Freedom*. Illus. K. Nelson. New York: Jump at the Sun/Hyperion. The spiritual journey of Harriet Tubman follows the voice of God as she travels north to freedom to escape slavery. (Gr. 4–6)

Wells, R. 1998. *Mary on Horseback: Three Mountain Stories*. New York: Dial. Nurse Mary Breckenridge travels on horseback to the isolated mountains of Kentucky and exhibits the goodness and vitality of an undercelebrated heroine. (Gr. 4–6)

————. 2002. *Wingwalker*. Illus. B. Selznick. New York: Hyperion. The drought of the Dust Bowl drives Reuben's family north to Minnesota for work. His father is forced to take a job as an airplane wingwalker, and Reuben is forced to overcome his fear of flying to prove his support and love of his family. (Gr. 3–5)

Williams, D. 1993. *Grandma Essie's Covered Wagon*. Illus. W. Sadowski. New York: Knopf. A vivid account of the joys and challenges of a move from Missouri to Kansas to Oklahoma in the late 1800s. Adapted from the authentic oral history of the author's grandmother. (Gr. 2–5)

Wright-Frierson, V. 1997. *A Desert Scrapbook*. New York: Simon & Schuster. The flora and fauna of the Sonoran Desert is portrayed through sketches, journal entries, painted snapshots, and watercolored artifacts of this ever-changing habitat. (Gr. 3–6)

Yolen, J. 1992. *Letting Swift River Go*. Illus. B. Cooney. Boston: Little, Brown. Sally Jane experiences changing times in rural America as the Swift River town in western Massachusetts is enveloped by a water reservoir. The story eloquently reveals that while change is constant, the memory of a place can stay with you forever. (Gr. 1–4)

————. 1998. *Raising Yoder's Barn*. Illus. B. Fuchs. Boston: Little, Brown. A strong community allegiance prevails when a devastating fire ravishes the barn of an Amish family in Pennsylvania. (Gr. 1–4)

Younger, B. 1998. *Purple Mountains Majesties: The Story of Katharine Lee Bates and "America the Beautiful."* Illus. S. Schuett. New York: Dutton. A summer cross-country train trip inspires scholar/poet/professor Bates to write her famous tribute to the beauty and grandeur of the nation's physical blessings—mountains, plains, and shining seas. (Gr. K–5)

Related Technology Tools

Web Sites

www.win.tue.nl/cs/fm/engels/discovery
  Discovery Web—Exploration from Roman Empire period to twentieth century. (Gr. 5–8)
http://lcweb2.gov/ammem/
  American Memory: Historical Collections for the National Digital Library. (Gr. 4–8)
http://www.execpc.com/~dboals
  History and social studies Web site for K–12 teachers.
http://www.pagesz.net/~stevek/resources.html
  Resources for historians. (Gr. 5–8)
http://www.pages.net/~stevek/history.html
  What is history? A sampler.
http://www.cr.nps.gov/nr/twhp/home.html
  National Register of Historical Places (good for showing local historical places to grades 2–8).
http://library.advanced.org/10966/index.html
  The Revolutionary War: A Journey Towards Freedom. (Gr. 5–8)
http://users.southeast.net/~dixe/amrev/index.htm
  The American Revolution: On-Line
www.isu.edu/~trinmich/Oregontrail.html
  The Oregon Trail—contains Fantastic Facts and Historic Sites sections. (Gr. 3–8; excellent supplement to Oregon Trail CD-ROM)
www.sunsite.utk.edu/civil-war/warweb.html
  American Civil War home page: Comprehensive site. (Gr. 5–8)
http://lincoln.lib.niu.edu
  Lincoln/Net: Official Abraham Lincoln Web site of Illinois. (Gr. 7–8)
www.ellisisland.org
  Ellis Island: Immigration history. (Gr. 4–8)
www.grolier.com/wwii/wwii_mainpage.html
  World War II: Comprehensive Web site. (Gr. 5–8)
www.loc.gov/folklife/vets
  Web site of interviews of U.S. veterans. (Gr. 4–8)
www.stanford.edu/group/King
  Martin Luther King, Jr.: Biography

WebQuests

Abraham Lincoln (Gr. 1–4)
  http://spa3.k12.sc.us/WebQuests.html
Charles Lindbergh (Gr. 6)
  http://www.education.umd.edu/Depts/EDCI?edci385/webquests3/Webquests3/
  Webquest4/webquests4.html
Diary of Anne Frank (Gr. 6–8)
  http://www.spa3.k12.sc.us/WebQuests.html
Westward Ho! (Gr. 4–6)
  http://www.germantown.k12.i1.html/webquest.html

Technology Resources

Notable Social Studies Trade Books
  www.ncss.org/resources/notable
  Selected by a Book Review Committee appointed by National Council for the Social Studies (NCSS) and assembled in cooperation with the Children's Book Council.

Aesop's Fables Online Exhibit
www.AesopFables.com
An online collection of Aesop's Fables that includes a total of 655+ Fables, indexed in table format, with morals listed.

Fairfax County Virginia Libraries
www.cofairfax.va.us/library/homepage.htm
Travel through American History with juvenile fiction picture books geared for intermediate grades.

Software and Videos

Crazy Horse—A & E Biography. Teacher's Video Company. Available from www.teachers-video.com. One of the fiercest Native American warriors, Crazy Horse was the last to give up the fight. He became famous at Little Big Horn.

"Dear America: Friend to Friend CD-ROM." 2000. Knowledge Adventure. Available from www.amazon.com. Based on the scholastic book and television series of the same name, "Dear America: Friend to Friend" introduces role models for young women that teach history, social studies, and creative expression.

"Eyewitness Children's Encyclopedia." Global Software and Videos Publishing. Available at www.gspna.com.

Ancient Rome Video Set. (1998). Teacher's Discovery. 200 minutes total. Available at 800-543-4100. Travel back to an empire that ruled the world and learn about the ancient myths, modern discoveries, and secrets of Rome.

Children's Literature Listservs

Child_Lit<listserv@email.rutgers.edu>
This children's Literature Criticism and Theory group is the most academic of the listservs. This discussion group fosters the sharing of ideas by researchers engaged in scholarship on any topic.

Kidlit_Lit<listserv@bingvmb.cc.binghamton.edu>
Children's literature supporters discuss teaching, innovative ideas, current research and share ideas, questions, and stories with the group.

CCBC-Net<listserv@ccbc.cc.binghamton.edu>
The Cooperative Children's Book Center at the University of Wisconsin focuses on a monthly theme, author, subject, or issue.

Other Literature-Related Web Sites for Teachers

http://www.aaronshep.com/rt/RTE.html
Aaron Shepard's Reader's Theater Editions
Stories including humor, fantasy, and retold tales from different cultures are adapted into reader's theater scripts for third grade and above.

http.//ericir.syr.edu
AskERIC Home Page
Literature-based lesson plans, virtual libraries, full texts of fairy tales and fables, bibliographies, and links to other Web sites are available through this home page.

http://bdd.com/teachers
BDD Books for Young Readers
The Teachers Resource Center shares teaching tools to bring quality books to life for young readers.

References

Ammon, R., and J. Weigard. 1993. "A Look at Other Trade Book Topics and Genres." In *The Story of Ourselves,* ed. M. O. Tunnel and R. Ammon. Portsmouth, NH: Heinemann.

Camp, D. 2000. "It Takes Two: Teaching with Twin Texts of Fact and Fiction." *The Reading Teacher* 53: 400–8.

Ceprano, M., and E. B. English. 1990. "Fact and Fiction: Personalizing Social Studies through the Tradebook-Textbook Connection." *Reading Horizons* 30: 66–77.

Cianciolo, P. 1981. "Yesterday Comes Alive for Readers of Historical Fiction." *Language Arts* 58: 452–61.

Commire, A., ed. 1982. *Something About the Author.* Detroit, MI: Gale Research.

Danielson, K. E. 1989. "Helping History Come Alive with Literature." *Social Studies* 80: 65–68.

Dowd, F. 1990. "Geography Is Children's Literature, Math, Science, Art and a Whole World of Activities." *Journal of Geography* 89: 68–73.

Galda, L. 1988. "Readers, Texts, Contexts: A Response-Based View of Literature in the Classroom." *The New Advocate* 1: 92–102.

Gallo, D. R., and E. Barksdale. 1983. "Using Fiction in American History." *Social Education* 47: 286–89.

Hancock, M. R. 1993a. "Character Journals: Initiating Involvement and Identification through Literature." *Journal of Reading* 37: 42–50.

———. 1993b. "Exploring and Extending Personal Response through Literature Response Journals." *The Reading Teacher* 46 (6): 466–74.

———. 1993c. "Exploring the Meaning-Making Process through the Content of Literature Response Journals." *Research in the Teaching of English* 27: 335–68.

———. 2002. "When Twin Texts Meet Technology: Gateway to Enhanced Inquiry and Comprehension." Paper presented at the International Reading Association 47th Annual Convention, San Francisco, CA, April 30.

———. 2004. *A Celebration of Literature and Response: Readers, Books, and Teachers in K–8 Classrooms.* 2nd ed. Columbus, OH: Prentice-Hall/Merrill.

James, M., and J. Zarrillo. 1989. "Teaching History with Children's Literature: A Concept-Based, Interdisciplinary Approach." *Social Studies* 80: 153–58.

Johnson, N. M., and M. J. Ebert. 1992. "Time Travel Is Possible: Historical Fiction and Biography—Passport to the Past." *Reading Journal* 45: 488–95.

Kiefer, B. Z., S. Hepler, and J. Hickman. 2007. *Charlotte Huck's Children's Literature.* 9th ed. Boston: McGraw-Hill.

Langer, J., and A. Applebee. 1987. *How Writing Shapes Thinking: A Study of Learning and Teaching.* Urbana, IL: National Council of Teachers of English.

Latrobe, K. H., series ed. 1994. *Exploring the United States Through Literature Series.* Phoenix, AZ: Oryx Press (seven volumes: Northeast, Southeast, Great Lakes, Plains, Southwest, Mountain, and Pacific states).

Levstik, L. 1985. "Literary Geographic and Mapping." *Social Education* 77: 38–43.

———. 1990. "Research Directions: Mediating Content through Literary Texts." *Language Arts* 67: 848–53.

———. 1993. "'I Wanted to Be There': The Impact of Narrative on Children's Thinking." In *The Story of Ourselves,* ed. M. O. Tunnel and R. Ammon. Portsmouth, NH: Heinemann.

Lipson, M. Y., S. W. Valencia, K. K. Wixson, and C. Peters. 1993. "Integration and Thematic Teaching: Integration to Improve Teaching and Learning." *Language Arts* 70: 252–63.

Louie, B. Y. 1993. "Using Literature to Teach Location." *Social Studies and the Young Learner* 5: 17–18, 22.

Manning, M., G. Manning, and R. Long. 1994. *Theme Immersion: Inquiry-Based Curriculum in Elementary and Middle Schools.* Portsmouth, NH: Heinemann.

Moir, H., ed. 1992. *Collected Perspectives: Choosing and Using Books for the Classroom.* Boston: Christopher Gordon.

Norton, D. E. 2003. *Through the Eyes of a Child.* 6th ed. Columbus, OH: Merrill.

Pappas, C., B. Kiefer, and L. Levstik. 1996. *An Integrated Language Perspective in the Elementary School: Theory in Action.* 2nd ed. New York: Longman.

Perry, P. J. 1998. *Exploring Our Country's History: Linking Fiction to Nonfiction.* Englewood, CO: Teacher Ideas.

Pritchard, S. F. 1989. "Using Picture Books to Teach Geography in the Primary Grades." *Journal of Geography* 88: 126–27, 137.

Probst, R. E. 1984. *Adolescent Literature: Response and Analysis.* Columbus, OH: Merrill.

Rosenblatt, L. 1976. *Literature as Exploration.* New York: Appleton-Century-Crofts.

———. 1978. *The Reader, The Text, The Poem.* Carbondale: Southern Illinois University Press.

Sanacore, J. 1990. "Creating the Lifetime Reading Habit in Social Studies." *Journal of Reading* 3: 414–18.

Sisson, J. 1990. "Read Your Way across the U.S.A." *Journal of Geography* 89: 175–77.

Trofanenko, B. 2002. "Images of History in Middle-Grade Social Studies Trade Books." *The New Advocate* 15: 129–32.

Young, T., and S. Vardell. 1993. "Weaving Reader's Theater and Nonfiction into the Curriculum." *The Reading Teacher* 46: 396–406.

Zarnowski, M. 1990. *Learning about Biographies: A Reading-and-Writing Approach for Children.* Urbana, IL: National Council of Teachers of English.

> *What is needed is a mutual commitment to the learning of geography and to understanding the learning of geography. It is our common agenda.*
>
> —Anne K. Petry,
> *"Future Teachers of Geography: Whose Opportunity?"*

Chapter Eleven

Geography
Exploring the Whole World through Interdisciplinary Instruction

Maria P. Walther, Gwendolyn Brooks Elementary School, Aurora, IL

CHAPTER OUTLINE

CHAPTER OBJECTIVES

Readers will

- understand the geography for life standards;
- demonstrate competency in applying the six essential elements of geography;
- be able to utilize children's literature in the teaching of geography; and
- be able to incorporate Web sites throughout the world in the teaching of geography.

Introduction

Geography surrounds us. Without thinking about it, we make decisions based on geographical knowledge every day—we dress appropriately for the weather, plan the quickest route for doing errands, and draw maps to places we want others to find. There is an ongoing interaction between humans and the geography that surrounds them. It is this interaction that teachers must share with their students.

Geography should come alive in the classroom, and the 1994 National Geography Standards reflect this idea in the title *Geography for Life*. The Standards state, "Geography is for life in every sense of that expression: lifelong, life sustaining, and life enhancing. Geography is a field of study that enables us to find answers to questions about the world around us—about where things are and how and why they got there. We can ask questions about things that seem very familiar and are often taken for granted" (Geography Education Standards Project 1994, 11).

It is important to note that the whole thrust of the Standards is on questioning why things are the way they are. There is no better way to get students thinking, discussing, and analyzing information than through the use of children's literature. The social students curriculum offers curious students and their teachers rich opportunities to "mine the treasures in literature" (Laminack and Wadsworth 2006, 139). As you read this chapter, you will find a healthy balance between fiction and nonfiction texts. Fiction texts offer learners rich stories about diverse people and other lands. Authentic nonfiction texts provide "the widest range of topics, subjects, people, issues, events, and thoughts to explore. Nonfiction breeds passionate curiosity; passion leads to engagement" (Harvey 2002, 15). By reading fiction and nonfiction texts, children can travel to other lands and be a part of the events that shaped our world. Literature is an ideal way for students to gain the geographical knowledge that they need in order to be productive citizens in a global community. "Geographers believe that their goal of understanding how all of the parts of the world are globally interrelated is very important for today's citizens" (Sunal and Haas 2000, 269). Literature encourages questioning and discussion. It provides a common ground for continued study. As Louie (1993, 18) states, "Whereas textbooks present factual information and explanation, literature can make geographic concepts come alive for children." It is through the use of quality children's literature and literature-based reading, writing, thinking, and listening activities that geography will come to life in the classroom.

According to Madeline Gregg and Diane Carver Sekeres (2006, 103):

> Teachers in the early grades spend a great deal of time helping children see and understand phenomena (things) and processes (actions) in the world around them. Geography lessons are full of activities that help children identify, describe, and categorize objects and processes. Many of these objects are not found in the children's daily lives, for reasons of size, geographic distribution, danger, or cost. Icebergs, wild animals, and the position of the sun at midsummer in the Arctic are examples. Similarly, many of the processes are invisible to the children. The water cycle, the differential heating of the planet by the Sun, the migration of animal populations—these are all examples of processes that children cannot directly see.

Gregg and Sekeres go on to state that the teacher's own passion for geography is important for motivating students. Likewise using realia—actual objects students can see and touch such as a globe or stuffed toy penguins and polar bears—assist children in understanding phenomena. Demonstrations by the teacher are also needed to demonstrate geographical processes so students view changes in systematic ways. Such use of realia and demonstrations "not only engage the students' interest and curiosity, but they also provide a context in which to introduce the vocabulary that is necessary to support discussions and then readings about the unit's topics. Expository texts often contain new and challenging vocabulary words" (2006, 105) and that is true with geography informational texts.

This chapter gives practical ideas on how to incorporate geographic subject matter, skills, and perspectives—as identified by the 1994 National Geography Standards—into a social studies classroom through the use of children's literature activities, research and writing activities, and thematic units. A beginning step for both teachers and students when incorporating geography in their classroom and

---

☞ IN THE CLASSROOM

Six Essential Elements and Eighteen Geography Content Standards

The geographically informed person knows about and understands:

The World in Spatial Terms

1. How to use maps and other geographic representations, tools, and technologies to acquire, process, and report information from a spatial perspective.

2. How to use mental maps to organize information about people, places, and environments in a spatial context.

3. How to analyze the spatial organization of people, places, and environments on Earth's surface.

Places and Regions

4. The physical and human characteristics of places.

5. That people create regions to interpret Earth's complexity.

6. How culture and experience influence people's perceptions of places and regions.

Physical Systems

7. The physical processes that shape the patterns of Earth's surface.

8. The characteristics and spatial distribution of ecosystems on Earth's surface.

Human Systems

9. The characteristics, distribution, and migration of human populations on Earth's surface.

10. The characteristics, distribution, and complexity of Earth's cultural mosaics.

11. The patterns and networks of economic interdependence on Earth's surface.

12. The processes, patterns, and functions of human settlement.

13. How the forces of cooperation and conflict among people influence the division and control of Earth's surface.

Environment and Society

14. How human actions modify the physical environment.

15. How physical systems affect human systems.

16. The changes that occur in the meaning, use, distribution, and importance of resources.

The Uses of Geography

17. How to apply geography to interpret the past.

18. How to apply geography to interpret the present and plan for the future.

in their lives is to adjust their mind-set about what geography is. In this chapter, geography comes to life through the use of the high-quality children's books. Educators must reinforce the ideas that the Standards (1994, 18) espouse: "Geography is not a collection of arcane information. Rather, it is the study of spatial aspects of human existence. Geography has much more to do with asking questions and solving problems than it does with rote memorization of isolated facts." Boehm and Petersen (1994, 211) expand on this idea when they state: "Geography is an eclectic subject that ranges from the physical sciences through the social sciences to the arts and humanities." By integrating geography into all subject areas of the curriculum, students will begin to see that geography truly plays a part in all aspects of their lives.

A Look at the Geography for Life Standards

The Standards (1994) present teachers with an outline of what students should know and be able to do at the end of three benchmark grades: four, eight, and twelve (see In the Classroom box page 403). They were developed through a consensus process by geographers, teachers, parents, and others. The Standards are based on the five fundamental themes that were identified in 1984 in the *Guidelines for Geographic Education: Elementary and Secondary Schools* (Committee on Geographic Education, 1984). "The five themes have become an integral element of social studies education, appearing in all geography textbooks and most social studies programs as a context for geographic education" (Boehm and Petersen 1994, 211). The themes are (1) location, (2) place, (3) relationships within places (human–environmental interaction), (4) relationships between places (movement), and (5) regions. The five themes were meant to convey to the nation's teachers the message that it is no longer acceptable to stop teaching geography after teaching only location and place (Boehm and Petersen 1999). (See In the Classroom: The Five Themes of Geography and Related Teaching Ideas.) The Standards expand on the five themes and assist educators in answering two important questions: What is most worth knowing about geography? and What content, skills, and perspectives are essential for students to know and use? The five themes give meaningful guidance to educators and curriculum developers about best practices in geography education (Bednarz and Bednarz 1994).

The study of geography comprises three interrelated and inseparable parts: subject matter, skills, and perspectives. The subject matter of geography is the essential knowledge that students should acquire. It is on this essential knowledge that the skills are based. The skills include asking geographic questions, acquiring, organizing, and analyzing geographic information, and answering geographic questions. The knowledge and skills are viewed from two perspectives: spatial and ecological. Students must master all three components of geography to become geographically informed citizens (Geography Education Standards Project 1994).

☞ IN THE CLASSROOM

The Five Themes of Geography and Related Teaching Ideas

Location: This theme answers the question, "Where is that?"
• Assist young students as they learn their street address. This helps them understand that their home is a definite spot on Earth.

• Use maps and globes to locate settings of read-aloud stories.

Place: This theme answers the question, "What is it like there?"
• Encourage youngsters to use their five senses to note the physical and cultural features of places they visit on field trips and during other experiences outside the classroom.

Relationships within Places (Human-Environmental Interaction): This theme answers the question: "What do people have to do to live there?"
• Work together with your class to beautify the school grounds by planting flowers, plants, or trees.

• Visit a construction site and watch the progress.

• Students examine photographs of their school, home, or neighborhood to see the changes that have occurred over time.

Relationships between Places (Movement): This theme answers the question: "How do people, goods, and ideas get from one place to another?"
• Read stories, learn words, and sing songs from other lands.

• Invite family members to send postcards from their travels or other places. Discuss how postcards get from one place to another.

• Request that students bring in a favorite stuffed animal with a tag. Locate the place of origin on a map.

Regions: This theme answers the question: "How are places alike?"
• Identify the different regions in your classroom: reading center, writing center, or other areas of the room.

Source: Adapted from: M. Schoenfeldt. 2001. "Geographic Literacy and Young Learners," *The Educational Forum* 66 (1): 26–31.

The Geographic Skills

The geographic skills offer a framework for developing lessons. A brief explanation of each skill and a sample activity follows:

1. **Asking geographic questions.** Students will find the answers to the questions Where? and Why there?

   After fifth-graders read the book *Follow the Drinking Gourd* (Winter 1988), the teacher and students identify the locations of the Underground Railroad stations that are hinted at in the lyrics. A class discussion about why those locations were chosen as part of the Underground Railroad ensues (Louie 1993). When teaching the same concept to younger students, it is important that they understand that the Underground Railroad was not a train, but a series of safe hiding places for escaping slaves. Three engaging picture books that introduce the concept of the Underground Railroad to young learners are *The Underground Railroad* (Bial 1995), *Barefoot: Escape on the Underground Railroad* (Edwards 1997), and *Secret Signs Along the Underground Railroad* (Riggio 1997).

2. **Acquiring geographic information.** Students will gather information from array of sources and in a variety of ways.

   When acquiring geographic information, involve students in fieldwork. Young fieldwork participants conduct research in the community by distributing questionnaires, taking photographs, recording observations, interviewing citizens, and collecting samples (Geography Education Standards Project 1994). Another plentiful source of geographic information is the Internet (see the Web sites section at the end of the chapter).

3. **Organizing geographic information.** Learners will organize and display information in ways that help with analysis and interpretation of data. They must be able to both decode and encode maps.

   Involve middle school students in a "Top 10" project. Begin by sharing the picture book *Hottest, Coldest, Highest, Deepest* (Jenkins 1998) describing the remarkable natural wonders on Earth. Divide your class into small groups to collect, organize, analyze, and display information about their chosen top 10 natural wonders. Other books that are helpful for this project include *America's Top Ten Rivers* (Tesar 1998b), *America's Top Ten Mountains* (Tesar 1998a), and *America's Top Ten Natural Wonders* (Ricciuti 1998).

4. **Analyzing geographic information.** Junior geographers will look for patterns, relationships, and connections.

   After fourth graders study a map of the Oregon Trail and read from the many diaries available, invite them to draw inferences and suggest reasons why people migrated and why they chose particular routes. One such diary is *Rachel's Journal* (Moss 1998), which gives a fictional account of a 10-year-old girl traveling from Illinois to California and provides young readers with a sense of what it would have been like to journey on the Oregon Trail.

5. **Answering geographic questions.** Students will develop generalizations and conclusions based on geographic knowledge.

   Students choose a topic of interest to them (e.g., the best place to go in-line skating, where the town should build a bike trail) and research the topic by doing fieldwork. They compile the research by using charts, maps, and graphs and present their findings to the class or to the agency that might consider implementing their ideas.

The Six Essential Elements

The Standards identify six essential elements that are used to plan and organize themes in the classroom. Of course, as with any integrated theme or unit of study, the subject matter will reach far beyond geography. Following are brief descriptions of each element to help in the selection of related themes.

1. **The World in Spatial Terms**—Studying the relationship between people, places, and environments by mapping information about them in a spatial context.

2. **Places and Regions**—Discovering how the identities and lives of individuals are rooted in particular places and in human constructs called regions.

3. **Physical Systems**—Examining the physical processes that shape Earth's surface and that interact with plant and animal life to create, sustain, and modify ecosystems.

4. **Human Systems**—Looking first at population, and then at the human activities, from culture to economics, to settlement, and to conflict and cooperation.

5. **Environment and Society**—Understanding the intersection of physical and human systems.

6. **The Uses of Geography**—Learning how geography, when taken as a whole, helps us understand the past, interpret the present, and plan for the future (Geography Education Standards Project 1994).

The remainder of this chapter addresses each of these six elements and demonstrates how teachers, through the use of literature based activities, can incorporate each element into their existing themes and units. For each element, a sample theme, unit, or list of activities is offered. It is my hope that these themes and ideas will start you on the road to becoming a geographically informed citizen who will, in turn, provide your students with a wealth of opportunities to experience, question, and make decisions based on their geographical knowledge.

The World in Spatial Terms

Around the World with Exciting Books

Children are fascinated with travel and far away places. Kapp (1991) explains a clever way to introduce the concept of travel to young children. Begin by reading Shel Silverstein's poem "Magic Carpet" found in *A Light in the Attic* (1981). While your class sits on an oriental rug invite them to tell about their choice of a travel spot. Record their travel destinations on a chart and save it for future reference. Kapp discovered that "by the end of the year in which geography was regularly infused into the curriculum, the chart demonstrates that young travelers have expanded their horizons" (1991, 174). Children who, at the beginning of the year, chose either Walt Disney World or Grandma's house were now choosing places from other continents. One way to infuse geography into the classroom is through the use of a read-aloud activity called "Around the World with Exciting Books." As an addition to your regular read-aloud, build in a time to read books from around the world and locate the settings on a world map bulletin board (see figure 11.1). As children journey from continent to continent through fine literature, offer opportunities for students to write descriptions of the continents from the information gathered in the books. Younger students can draw an illustration of each book read. Post either the descriptions or illustrations on the bulletin board. A compelling book that will give students further insight into the diversity of the world's cultures and climates is Yann

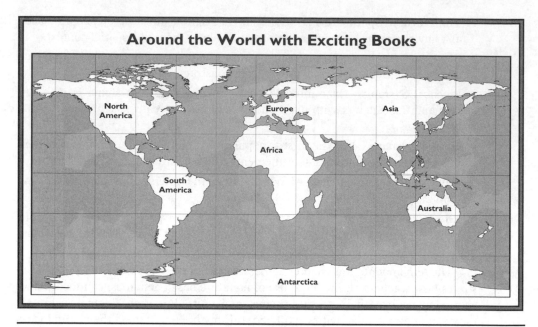

Figure 11.1 Around-the-world bulletin board.

Arthus-Bertrand's (2002) *Earth From Above for Young Readers.* This idea is easily adapted for intermediate students as a way to encourage independent reading in a variety of genres. Older readers can keep track of their own reading using an individual world map where they record the titles and authors of both fiction and nonfiction books they read about each continent. I've included a sampling of books for primary and intermediate grade children that represent each continent in our world.

Africa—Primary
Brett, *Honey, Honey—Lion! A Story of Africa* (2005)
Brown, *Uncommon Traveler* (2000)
Diakité, *I Lost My Tooth in Africa* (2006)
Feelings, *Jambo Means Hello: A Swahili Alphabet Book* (1974)
Hoffman, *Boundless Grace* (1995)
London, *Ali: Child of the Desert* (1997)
Musgrove, *Ashanti to Zulu: African Traditions* (1976)
Africa—Intermediate
Smith, *Thunder Cave* (1995)
Antarctica—Primary
Glimmerveen, *A Tale of Antarctica* (1989)
Spinelli, *Something to Tell the Grandcows* (2004)
Antarctica—Intermediate
McMillan, *Penguins at Home: Gentoos of Antarctica* (1993)
Antarctica—Middle School
Armstrong, *Shipwreck at the Bottom of the World: The Extraordinary True Story of Shackleton and the Endurance* (1998)

Bledsoe, *How to Survive Antarctica* (2006)

McKernan, *Shackleton's Stowaway* (2005)

Asia—Primary

Dolphin, *Our Journey from Tibet* (1997)

Levinson, *Our Home Is the Sea* (1988) (China)

Tejima, *Bear's Autumn* (1986) (Japan)

Young, *Monkey King* (2001)

Asia—Intermediate

Macdonald, *Marco Polo: A Journey through China* (1998)

Neuberger, *The Girl-Son* (1995)

Australia—Primary

Baker, *Where the Forest Meets the Sea* (1987)

Fox, *Possum Magic* (1983)

Ormerod, *Lizzie Nonsense* (2005)

Wheatley and Rawlins, *My Place* (1988)

Australia—Intermediate

Oodgeroo, *Dreamtime: Aboriginal Stories* (1994)

Europe—Primary

Bemelmans, *Madeline* (1939) (France)

Huck, *The Black Bull of Norroway: A Scottish Tale* (2001)

Europe—Intermediate

Brewster, *Anastasia's Album* (1996)

Krasilovsky, *The Cow Who Fell in the Canal* (1957) (Netherlands)

Krasilovsky, *The First Tulips in Holland* (1982) (Netherlands)

Middle East—Intermediate/Middle School

Rumford, *Traveling Man: The Journey of Ibn Battuta, 1325–1354* (2001)

North America—Primary

Ancona, *Piñata Maker/El Piñatero* (1994) (Mexico)

Binch, *Gregory Cool* (1994) (Caribbean)

MacLachlan, *All the Places to Love* (1994)

Winslow, *Dance on a Sealskin* (1995) (Alaska)

North America—Intermediate

Jacobs, *A Passion for Danger: Nansen's Arctic Adventures* (1994)

Parker, *Land Ho! Fifty Glorious Years in the Age of Exploration* (2001)

Ryan, *Becoming Naomi León* (2004)

North America—Middle School

Creech, S. *Walk Two Moons* (1994)

Creech, S. *The Wanderer* (2000)

Curtis, C. P. *The Watsons Go to Birmingham—1963* (1995)

Curtis, C. P. *Bud, Not Buddy* (1999)

South America—Primary

Alexander, *Llama and the Great Flood* (1989)

Cherry, *The Great Kapok Tree: The Tale of the Amazon Rain Forest* (1990)

Dorros, *Tonight Is Carnaval* (1991)

South America—Intermediate

Kurtz, *Miro in the Kingdom of the Sun* (1996)

☞ **IN THE CLASSROOM**

Creative Road Trips

Students need to learn how to read maps. In particular, they need to become familiar with their own state. Most state tourism departments will provide enough state maps for your class. After making certain your students can locate the major cities on the map, have them make up "creative road trips." These can then be written on cards and shuffled. One student reads the cards while the others locate the two cities. Use an atlas to expand the activity to the entire United States or the world. Here are some examples:

Weed Patch, California, to Garden Grove, California
Accident, Maryland, to Rescue, Virginia
Speed, North Carolina, to Trooper, Pennsylvania
Doctor Phillips, Florida, to Medicine Hat, Alberta, Canada
Sleepy Eye, Minnesota, to Coffee, Georgia
Ball Club, Minnesota, to Diamond, Illinois
Talent, Oregon, to Hollywood, California

A variation for middle school students is to use cities named for names of capitals and countries.
Havana, Illinois, to Cuba, New Mexico
Moscow, Idaho, to Russia, Indiana

Historical events can also be used for yet another variation.
Napoleon, Ohio, to Waterloo, Iowa
Custer, Kentucky, to Little Bighorn (National Monument), Montana

☞ **IN THE CLASSROOM**

Latitude and Longitude Activities

To have a firm understanding of the concept of latitude and longitude (the system of east–west lines, called parallels of **latitude,** and north–south lines, called meridians of **longitude),** students must begin by understanding the grid system as a place location device. After they gain this understanding they then can begin to transfer it to latitude and longitude. The **parallels of latitude** measure distances in degrees north and south of the equator (designated as zero degrees latitude). The **meridians of longitude** converge at both poles and measure distances in degrees east and west of the prime meridian (designated as zero degrees longitude). The following activities build on each other and strengthen a child's concept of latitude and longitude:

1. Prepare a simple grid with squares along the top identified by numbers and squares along the side identified by letters. Design a simple shape—heart, pumpkin, house—by coloring in certain squares. Give students blank copies of the grid and by using coordinates (A–1, B–2, C–3, and so on); instruct students to color in all the squares to create the shape.

2. Provide your class with a basic outline map of the world. The map should include the lines of latitude and longitude and a simple compass rose. Play "Find a Continent" by giving coordinates and having students locate the nearest continent.

3. Before reading a book about another country, display the coordinates of longitude and latitude that fall within the boundaries of the country in the book. Ask students to use the coordinates to identify the country; have them color in the country on their own outline map of countries they have read about.

4. Write an itinerary for a journey to various cities in the world. Instead of naming the cities, identify them only by longitude and latitude. Have students plot each city on a world outline map and determine a route for the journey.

5. After enjoying the book *Sarah, Plain and Tall* (MacLachlan 1985), readers compare and contrast Sarah's home in Maine and the Whitting's home on the prairie. Each student chooses a city, determine its latitude and longitude, and describe its prominent features.

MacLachlan, P. 1985. *Sarah, Plain and Tall*. New York: Harper & Row.

Mental Maps

"The Standards redefine place-location literacy as having an accurate **mental map.** A mental map is a picture of the world and its features carried by individuals in the 'mind's eye'" (Bednarz and Bednarz 1994, 194). Mental maps are effective tools for students and teachers. Providing learners with various opportunities to draw mental maps freehand as part of their class work will help them to see maps as instruments for expressing ideas. It gives them a tool for both learning and demonstrating knowledge (Hayes 1993).

An idea for introducing mental maps to seventh graders, called "Write It! Map It! Sail It!" (Hollister 1994, 279), engages them in both describing a route in writing and drawing a map. Students choose a familiar location and write detailed directions for reaching that place. They pass these directions to a classmate who draws a map from the written directions. The maps are displayed for positive comments from the class. Through this activity, students discover that it is difficult to verbally describe how to get somewhere clearly enough for someone else to map.

Mental maps can also be used in the middle school to represent ideas found in books. For example, the book *Anno's U.S.A.* (Anno 1983) gives readers a more in-depth understanding of the United States. Using their prior knowledge of U.S. geography, learners trace the traveler's route and discuss the characteristics of the different locations in terms of landscape, history, and story settings (Louie 1993).

Middle school teachers will find mental maps are a helpful instructional tool to illustrate geographic ideas and work through problems associated with places. Mental maps are useful because they emphasize key information and eliminate irrelevant details often found on wall maps and textbooks (Hayes 1993).

Third and fourth graders will find it a challenge to map the activities of the canoeists in the book *Three Days on a River in a Red Canoe* (Williams 1981). Using the map in the book showing the first day's activities, learners make maps of the activities that the families engage in on the remaining days (Louie 1993). This lively book motivates children to become budding cartographers!

Children in the early primary grades can also use mental maps. Many picture books lend themselves to the use of mental maps. "In the early grades, students should come to see maps, like the written word, as a source of information about their world" (Geography Education Standards Project 1994, 63). First graders can follow the example of Sara Fanelli (1995), a young girl who drew maps of her world in *My Map Book*. Sara includes map symbols such as a direction key for north, south, east, and west and labels of important elements including bridges, school, and the playground. Children can create a map of the route the characters took when they were looking for Simon's missing items in *Adèle & Simon* (McClintock 2006). After reading the book *Around the Pond: Who's Been Here?* (George 1996), youngsters can draw a map of the route Cammy and William took on their walk, then compare it with the map in the book. The multicultural tale of *My Little Island* (Lessac 1984) can be mapped to show the different places the boy visits when he returns home, and the charming story of *The Little Band* (Sage 1991) lends itself to a map showing the places the band passed on its march through the town. Finally, the humorous story *The Scrambled States of America* (Keller 1998) is a lively introduction to mentally mapping the United States.

Using Literature to Teach Mapping Skills

There are many outstanding and informative nonfiction books for teaching students of all grade levels about how maps are made and how to use maps. The following list gives just a few:

Berger and Berger, *The Whole World in Our Hands: Looking at Maps* (1993) (Gr. 2–4)
Carey, *How to Use Maps and Globes* (1983) (Gr. 3–5)
Clouse, *Puzzle Maps, U.S.A.* (1990) (Gr. 2–4)
Crewe, *Maps and Globes* (1996) (Gr. 1–4)
Hartman, *As the Crow Flies: A First Book of Maps* (1991) (Gr. K–1)
Knowlton, *Maps and Globes* (1985) (Gr. K–3)
Leedy, *Mapping Penny's World* (2000) (Gr. K–2)
Lye, *Measuring and Maps* (1991) (Gr. 2–5)
Rabe, T. *There's a Map in My Lap: All about Maps* (2002) (Gr. 1–3)
Sipiera, *Globes* (1991) (Gr. 3–5)
Weiss, *Getting from Here to There* (1991) (Gr. 2–5)

There are also fiction books that lend themselves to teaching various map skills. The difficult skill of recognizing and using symbols is introduced to young children in the book *My Camera: At the Aquarium* (Marshall 1989). Readers follow the photographer's footprints on a map of the aquarium to see the many different sea creatures. They can then make symbols for each sea creature on their own map of the aquarium (Louie 1993). Intermediate students can practice measuring distance on maps using the nonfiction book *Measurement* (Sammis 1998) where, through activities, they learn to make distance measurements on maps using scale bars, color keys, and contour lines. The story *Jeremy's Tail* (Ball 1990) helps young children discover the similarities and differences between people in their community and the people Jeremy meets in the book. Using the clues in the illustrations, work with your class to trace Jeremy's journey on a globe. The class can also map the same journey on a flat map and collect postcards and other travel information from the different locations (Louie 1993). Intermediate students also enjoy tracking a story's progress on a map. The book *Paddle-to-the-Sea* (Holling 1991) is full of maps that guide the reader along the way as the canoe named Paddle journeys from Canada through inland waterways and finally crosses the Atlantic Ocean. Students can use a large reference map to chart the canoe's progress.

Stories of getting lost will resonate with any reader who, too, has once been lost. Jennifer Dewey's (2001) *Finding Your Way: The Art of Natural Navigation* is a collection of stories and experiences of those who have been lost in such places as the Antarctic, the desert, and cities around the world. Consider reading this book aloud to children in grades two through four.

Historical fiction novels present opportunities for older readers to trace travels of the main character via a land map. Thirteen-year-old Sophie travels from Virginia to Connecticut where she joins her cousins and three uncles to make a transatlantic trip by sailboat to England in Sharon Creech's (2000), *The Wanderer.* The journey of a family from Michigan to Alabama during the Civil Rights movement years is portrayed in *The Watsons Go to Birmingham—1963* (Curtis 1995) where the family stumbles into the Birmingham church bombing and race riots. A second book by Christopher Paul Curtis (1999) is *Bud, Not Buddy,* which traces the travels of the orphan boy Bud across Michigan in search of his father based on clues he finds in his dead mother's belongings. *Walk Two Moons* (Creech 1994) tells the story of a young girl who makes a journey from Ohio to Idaho with her grandparents to find her mother. Books such as these can be the focus of a literature circle with a role of a mapmaker being added as one of the tasks of the group (see chapter 7).

Several informational picture books for primary through middle school students highlight geography and the use of maps. Englishwoman Mary Kingsley's travels in the 1890s to West Africa are described in Don Brown's (2000) *Uncommon Traveler.* The story *Traveling Man: The Journey of Ibn Battuta, 1325–1354* (Rumford 2001) tells about Ibn Battuta who traveled from his home in Morocco to the Rock of Gibraltar to Beijing, China. During his travels of over 75,000 miles, this Muslim pilgrim faced rebels, shipwrecks, illness, and freezing weather. As you read this book aloud, track Ibn Battuta's journey on a world map. Pair this with *Marco Polo: A Journey through China* (Macdonald 1998), depicting the earlier travels of Marco Polo from Italy through the Middle East to China. A meaningful activity is to compare Ibn Battuta's 14th century travels with those of Marco Polo in the 13th century on the same map.

Yet another picture book of an explorer is *A Long and Uncertain Journey: The 27,000 Mile Voyage of Vasco da Gama* (Goodman 2001) set 150 years after Ibn Battuta's journey. This book is an account of Vasco da Gama's voyage from Europe around Africa to the Orient and back, enabling Portugal to gain a foothold in the Muslim world and its desirable trade routes. Included in this book is a foldout map of da Gama's route. Twelve European explorers who reached the New World, from Columbus to Cabrillo, during the golden age of exploration are introduced to students in *Land Ho! Fifty Glorious Years in the Age of Exploration* (Parker 2001). Maps and labeled illustrations add to the information shared in this picture book.

For the intermediate grades, Walter Oleksy's (2002) *Mapping the World* provides a history of cartography covering mapmaking from the ancient world to modern times including a time line, glossary of map terms, and a list of additional sources. A companion book is *Small Worlds: Maps and Mapmaking* (Young 2002). If a university is nearby, a field trip to a cartography lab would be appropriate for fourth graders through middle schoolers.

Nonfiction books that are enticing to intermediate and middle school readers include the biography *Shipwreck at the Bottom of the World: The Extraordinary True*

Mapmaking can be a challenging spatial skill requiring students to give thought to location and perspective as well as involving math skills when drawing to scale.

Story of Shackleton and the Endurance (Armstrong 1998), a detailed account of the now famous Shackleton expedition aboard the ship *Endurance* from England to Antarctica in search of the South Pole. When their ship was crushed by ice, Shackleton and his men pulled their small lifeboats across the ice, eating their sled dogs when their food ran out.

Treasure Maps

Another way to entice students to create and use maps is through a unit on buried treasure. Two intermediate fiction books that will get readers thinking about hidden treasure are Will Hobbs's *Ghost Canoe* (1997) and Paul Fleischman's *The Ghost in the Noonday Sun* (1989). Both books contain young protagonists involved in looking for treasure. Two nonfiction books that describe true stories of hidden treasure are *True-Life Treasure Hunts* (Donnelly 1984) and *The Children's Atlas of Lost Treasures* (Reid 1997). Learners use the information gained from the nonfiction books and ideas in the fiction books to write their own treasure hunt stories. These stories should include maps that lead to the treasure their main character is trying to find. Another enjoyable activity for older students is to hide "treasures" for younger students and draw simple treasure maps to help guide the younger hunters to the treasure.

Places and Regions—
A Primary Unit about Native American Tribes

The Native Americans of North America formed tribes that lived in different regions of our country. By studying different Native American tribes and the region in which they lived, children begin to understand the concept that a region is an area of the earth's surface with unifying geographic characteristics and that these characteristics affect the humans that inhabit the region. An example of a primary grade unit on Native Americans is described here. Primary students study and learn about three Native American tribes and the regions in which they live: the Wampanoag Tribe of the Northeast, the Sioux Tribe of the Plains, and the Pueblo Tribe of the Southwest (see figure 11.2). To learn a bit about each tribe's customs and traditions, young learners listen to both fiction and nonfiction books set in that region. After gathering information about each tribe, budding writers use what they have learned to complete the expository writing frame or the chart found in table 11.1. The frame helps young writers organize their information and shows them the basic elements of report writing. It also serves as a way to compare and contrast the different tribes and their regions.

Choose from the growing collection of Native American tales to help students gather information. *The Rough-Face Girl* (Martin 1992) is the Algonquin Cinderella tale giving children a glimpse into how the Algonquin lived in the Northeast Woodlands. The award-winning story *Arrow to the Sun* (McDermott 1974) comes alive with

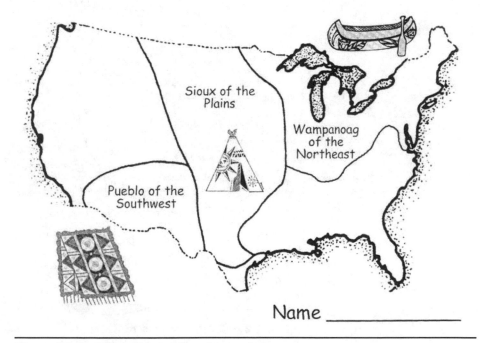

Figure 11.2 Map of Native American regions.

Table 11.1   Expository writing frame

The _____ tribe lived in _____ .

Their homes were _____ made of _____ .

They ate _____ .

They _____ and _____ .

the brilliant colors that the Pueblo Tribe of the Southwest used in their artwork. *The Legend of the Indian Paintbrush* (de Paola 1988) tells the tale of Little Gopher who lived in the Plains region and painted the stories of his tribe. To culminate the unit, read *Children of the Earth and Sky* (Krensky 1991) featuring tales about children from different Native American tribes. To complement the fiction texts consider including these nonfiction selections: *Dancing Rainbows: A Pueblo Boy's Story* (Mott 1996), *Tapenum's Day: A Wampanoag Indian Boy in Pilgrim Times* (Waters 1996), and *Many Nations: An Alphabet of Native America* (Bruchac 1998). The Native Americans who lived, and still live, in these three regions share many similar customs and traditions and also have their own unique traditions. After students have studied and written reports about each tribe, work together to make a class Venn diagram (see figure 11.3) to organize their information and compare and contrast the three Native American Tribes.

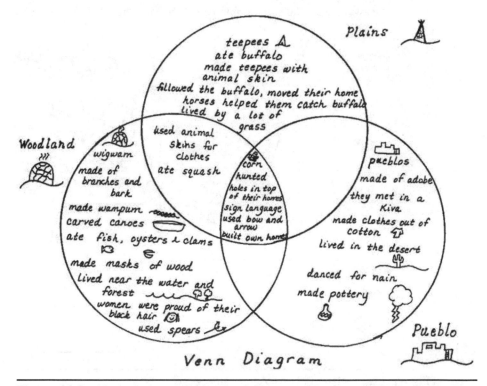

Figure 11.3   Venn diagram of Woodland, Plains, and Southwest Native Americans.

☞ **IN THE CLASSROOM**

Mapping Ideas

1. As a homework assignment during Fire Prevention Week, request that students and parents plan a safe escape route from their home and a meeting place outside the house. The family can work together to draw a map of this route to share with the class.

2. Using a map with five major cities on it, middle schoolers pretend that they are a bus driver and have to pick up and deliver passengers to all five cities. Students begin by determining the most efficient route. Next, they generate a passenger schedule for one bus based on this route. For an extra challenge, they can create a schedule for two buses (Gregg 1997).

3. When a new child joins your class, students can draw a map of the school to help the new classmate find his or her way.

4. Work together with your class to make a three-dimensional map of the classroom. Ask students to save half pint milk containers from their lunches; tell them to cut the top off where it meets the side, so the box is open, then turn it over and cut away parts of the sides with scissors so that it resembles the legs of a desk (see figure 11.4). Children decorate their desks and place them on a large piece of paper on the floor. Request that students bring in various size boxes from home; use them to make the other furniture in the room (Maxim 2002). Once your three-dimensional map is complete, read aloud *Roxaboxen* (McLerran 1991), a tale about Marian and her playmates building an imaginary town on a hill.

5. Younger learners can make "Me Maps." With a partner, students take turns tracing each other's body shape on large pieces of paper. The children then label their body parts using agreed upon symbols for eyes, nose, mouth, ears, waist, and elbows in the correct location on their body maps (Sunal and Haas 2000). Read *My Map Book* (Fanelli 1995) to show young cartographers all the other things they can map.

6. Using the book *Me on the Map* (Sweeny 1996) as a model, students make a diagram showing their global address. Beginning with a world map, they can mark the continent that they live on, then the country within that continent, then the state within that country, and finally, the city within that state.

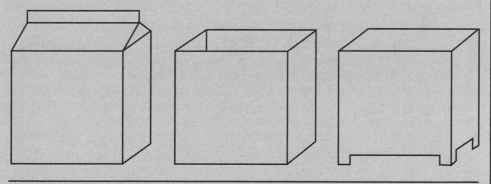

Figure 11.4 Milk carton desk.

Physical Systems—
How Climate and Weather Affect Our Lives

Physical process can be grouped into four categories according to where the process operates: (1) atmosphere (climate and meteorology), (2) lithosphere (plate tectonics, erosion, and soil formation), (3) hydrosphere (the circulation of the oceans and the hydrologic cycle), and (4) biosphere (plant and animal communities and ecosystems). Children must understand the interaction within and between these categories of physical processes (Geography Education Standards Project 1994). The study of atmospheric processes of climate and meteorology provides an excellent basis for an integrated social studies unit on weather and its effect on human beings. As the Standards point out, "Climate and weather affect more than just personal decision-making on a daily basis. They are major factors in understanding world economic conditions over longer periods" (76). Through the study of weather and different weather events, students are given an opportunity to use other data-collecting tools to represent their ideas. In primary classrooms, many teachers graph the daily weather on a weather chart. Teachers must take this graphing activity a step further and begin to ask their class questions about how the weather is affecting their lives. If it has been raining for a week straight, for example, teachers can ask their students, How has the weather affected the place that you choose to play after school? This idea can then be broadened to include climates in other places: How does the climate in the desert affect the plant and animal life there? A book that illustrates the delicate balance between plants and animals in the desert is *Desert Trip* (Steiner 1996). To show how life in a small town is connected to the desert environment, read *Desert Town* (Geisert, 2001). Using a large, shallow cardboard box, the class can make a desert diorama with sand and models of desert plants and animals. The diorama can be used as a springboard for writing activities and discussion about desert climate and its effects. Nonfiction titles at various grade levels are also available. Beginning readers will learn many facts from the *Rookie Read-About Science Series* book *It Could Still Be a Desert* (Fowler 1997) and for older readers Gail Gibbons's (1996) *Deserts* is bursting with information.

In *The Cloud Book* (de Paola 1975) Tomie cleverly presents basic information about the 10 most common cloud types and how they indicate coming weather changes. After reading, take your class outside to observe the clouds each day and record on a chart or graph the types of clouds they see. Young meteorologists can write their daily prediction about the weather in a learning log and check their prediction the following day. Extend the concept of clouds and cloud formation into a creative writing and art activity by reading *It Looked Like Spilt Milk* (Shaw 1947). To make their own book, give students torn pieces of white paper mounted on nine-by-twelve-inch sheets of blue paper; students look at their "cloud" and write what they imagine their "cloud" looks like.

Older learners discover how devastating tornadoes are to both the land and the people when they read *Night of the Twisters* (Ruckman 1988). Intermediate grade students who want to learn more about tornadoes, their behavior, and the way meteorologists track them should reach for *Storm Chasers: Tracking Twisters* (Herman 1997), *Tornadoes* (Murray 1996), and *Tornado Alert* (Branley 1988). Another violent weather event that affects both the environment and the people living in the area is a hurricane. The book *The Day the Hurricane Happened* (Anderson 1974) describes a family's experience when they encounter a hurricane on the Caribbean island of St. John. Two nonfiction books that explain hurricanes, thunderstorms, and other weather events are *Wild, Wet and Windy* (Llewellyn 1997) and *I Didn't Know that People Chase Twisters and Other Amazing Facts about Violent Weather* (Petty 1998). To study both weather events at once, divide your class into two groups: one studying tornadoes and the other, hurricanes. Gather fiction and nonfiction resources about the weather events. Each group presents their findings through the use of maps, charts, graphs, and written or oral reports. Their presentation should include what causes each type of storm, how it affects both the people and the environment, and what safety measures can be taken to help survive violent weather.

Human Systems— Westward Expansion in the United States

In an interdisciplinary unit on westward expansion, students will use maps, diaries, and fiction and nonfiction books to draw inferences about why people migrated and why they chose certain routes. As Rocca (1994, 114) states, "Students will benefit from tracing migration routes and learning why these movements were necessary." The interdisciplinary unit illustrated in figure 11.5 (on the following page) is designed for either primary grades or intermediate grades. Children in the intermediate grades can be divided into small groups to read the various texts. If you are working with learners in the primary grades, read aloud books from the collection to your students.

Environment and Society—Protecting Our Earth

When studying the environment and society, students become aware of how human actions modify the physical environment. They begin to understand the causes and implications of different kinds of pollution, resource depletion, and land degradation. A unit on environment and society can be divided into three parts: endangered species, endangered environment, and pollution. Using children's books and other resources learners explore each topic and decide what steps they can take, either as individuals or as a whole class, to address each environmental issue. To share their suggestions, students create posters to post around the school and the community. The following books paint vivid pictures of the dangers our society will encounter if we do not take steps to protect our earth:

Endangered Species
Seuss, *The Lorax* (1971)
Wallwork, *No Dodos: A Counting Book of Endangered Animals* (1993)
Endangered Environment
Baker, *Where the Forest Meets the Sea* (1987)
Base, *Uno's Garden* (2006)

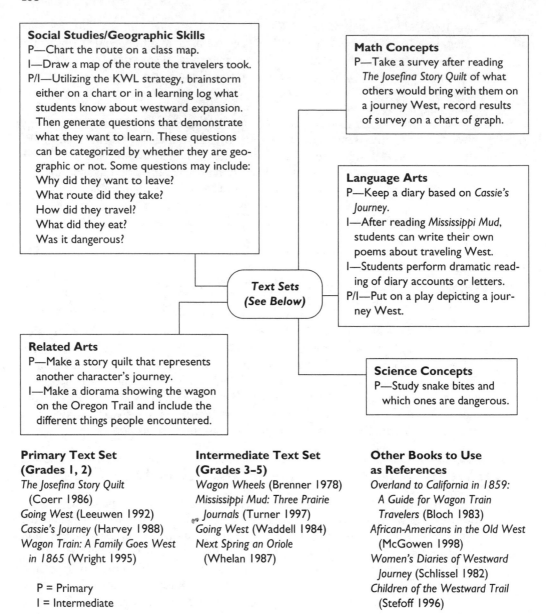

Social Studies/Geographic Skills
P—Chart the route on a class map.
I—Draw a map of the route the travelers took.
P/I—Utilizing the KWL strategy, brainstorm either on a chart or in a learning log what students know about westward expansion. Then generate questions that demonstrate what they want to learn. These questions can be categorized by whether they are geographic or not. Some questions may include:
Why did they want to leave?
What route did they take?
How did they travel?
What did they eat?
Was it dangerous?

Math Concepts
P—Take a survey after reading *The Josefina Story Quilt* of what others would bring with them on a journey West, record results of survey on a chart of graph.

Language Arts
P—Keep a diary based on *Cassie's Journey.*
I—After reading *Mississippi Mud,* students can write their own poems about traveling West.
I—Students perform dramatic reading of diary accounts or letters.
P/I—Put on a play depicting a journey West.

Text Sets (See Below)

Related Arts
P—Make a story quilt that represents another character's journey.
I—Make a diorama showing the wagon on the Oregon Trail and include the different things people encountered.

Science Concepts
P—Study snake bites and which ones are dangerous.

Primary Text Set (Grades 1, 2)
The Josefina Story Quilt (Coerr 1986)
Going West (Leeuwen 1992)
Cassie's Journey (Harvey 1988)
Wagon Train: A Family Goes West in 1865 (Wright 1995)

P = Primary
I = Intermediate

Intermediate Text Set (Grades 3–5)
Wagon Wheels (Brenner 1978)
Mississippi Mud: Three Prairie Journals (Turner 1997)
Going West (Waddell 1984)
Next Spring an Oriole (Whelan 1987)

Other Books to Use as References
Overland to California in 1859: A Guide for Wagon Train Travelers (Bloch 1983)
African-Americans in the Old West (McGowen 1998)
Women's Diaries of Westward Journey (Schlissel 1982)
Children of the Westward Trail (Stefoff 1996)

Figure 11.5   Interdisciplinary literature unit.
NCSS Standard 12: The Processes, Patterns, and Functions of Human Settlement.
Theme: Westward expansion in the United States.

George, *Everglades* (1995)
Hiaasen, *Hoot* (2002) and *Flush* (2005)
McDonald, *Judy Moody Saves the World* (2004)
Pollution
Peet, *The Wump World* (1970)
Van Allsburg, *Just a Dream* (1990)

The Uses of Geography—Reflective Decision Making

National Council for the Social Studies (1993, 213) states: "The primary purpose of the social studies is to help young people develop the ability to make informed and reasoned decisions for the public good as citizens of a culturally diverse, democratic society in an interdependent world." Learners use the knowledge, skills, and perspectives they have gained through the study of geography to make informed decisions. This decision-making process must be practiced regularly in the schools. Reflective decision making requires students to use what they have learned in a new way. They have to solve problems, make predictions, write essays, and hypothesize. Throughout this chapter there have been examples of how learners use children's literature and other resources to gain information and organize this information to demonstrate their knowledge. The next step is for students to use this knowledge in a new way. Through reflective decision making, students apply what they have learned in order to make intelligent and responsible decisions. The challenge of reflective decision making is to perceive a problem in its broadest possible context so that its multifaceted implications are apparent. The problem selected for the classroom must be directly connected to the interests of the students. Reflective decision makers go through the following steps, leading them to social action:

1. Identifying and defining the problem

2. Identifying value assumptions

3. Identifying alternatives

4. Predicting consequences

5. Reaching decisions and justifying decisions

6. Realizing the tentativeness of decision making

7. Acting on the decision

Divide the class into small groups with others who have the same concerns. Freeman and Freeman (1991) state that when youngsters study topics in social studies cooperatively, they begin to view issues critically and plan social action. "But what is crucial is for social studies to result in social action, in really doing social studies" (32). We must model this decision-making process for our students and show them that we value their active participation in reflective decision making. It is important to give students credit for engaging in the process of learning as well as credit for the products they make as individuals or in a group (Freeman and Freeman 1991).

Geography and the Other Social Sciences

Geography's link with the other social sciences is an essential one. We see this as second grade students study their community and the location of the grocery store, bank, and police station, fourth graders track the settling of their state, or eighth graders trace Attila's conquests as he led the Huns from Asia across Europe during the Roman Empire. Geography often provides the critical framework in terms of territories of people so that the other social sciences can be studied. Oceans, rivers, deserts, and mountains restricted the movement of people throughout history. The need for food production resulted in communities being located in fertile areas. State governments were established and moved when the need for a more central location was discovered. We see an example of this in both of the state capitals of Indiana and Illinois when they were moved from areas in the south to centrally located spots (in Indiana, from Corydon to Indianapolis, and in Illinois, from Vandalia to Springfield). Geography clearly plays a vital role in the social sciences.

Science, Technology, and Geography

A volcano erupts in Hawaii and lava flow eventually cools and creates additional rock and land expanding the island. A river changes course over the years causing new bridges to be built. Such are a few of the close links geography has to science and technology. There are numerous Web sites to link geography with science and technology. National Geographic has one of the most interactive, educational Web sites at http://www.nationalgeographic.com/education/, which contains features that change periodically, interactive exhibits, an online world atlas, and other resources to explore the United States and the rest of the world. NASA's interactive education Web site hosts timely topic-specific Web chats. This site allows students to interact with NASA engineers, experts, and even astronauts. The site can be accessed at http://quest.arc.nasa.gov/ with new projects being added from time to time. The U.S. Geological Survey's Learning Web holds a collection of lesson plans, classroom materials, and other science and geography related materials. Interested learners can "Ask the Experts" by directly e-mailing U.S. Geological scientists. Maps may be studied from an historical perspective as well as image galleries. The Web site is http://www.usgs.gov/education/index.html.

The potential of the Internet is used to the fullest extent by some historical map sites that link history and geography. Animation and **Geographic Information System (GIS)** maps are used at the Western Washington University Web site of Professor Emeritus Ed Stephan (www.ac.wwu.edu/~stephan/48states.html). The Web site begins in 1650 and continues to the present showing boundary changes of the contiguous forty-eight states. This site features the development of California's early Catholic missions and its first counties. Ancient Greece is also portrayed with the route of Alexander the Great's conquests. A companion Web site is the Hargrett Collection at the University of Georgia (www.libs.uga.edu/darchive/hargrett) that has a superb collection of historical U.S. maps. This site contains maps for the Colonial Period, the Revolutionary War, Westward Expansion, and the Civil War. Another similar Web site is the Perry-Castañeda Library Map Collection at the

University of Texas (www.lib.utexas.edu/Libs/PCL/Map_collection/histus.html). This Web site is smaller and well indexed. *Periodical Historical Atlas of Europe* (www.euratlas.com/summary.htm) provides a chronological mapping of European history at hundred-year intervals from the beginning of the first millennium to AD 1300. In order to save precious instructional minutes and even hours, it is wise for the teacher to explore each of these Web sites ahead of time and bookmark maps the best accompany each lesson.

NCSS STANDARDS-LINKED LESSON PLAN

Latitude and Longitude

Theme: The World in Spatial Terms
Source: National Geographic Xpeditions (www.nationalgeographic.com)
Grade: 5
Objectives: The learners will:

• Describe what they see on a U.S. and world map;

• Discover lines of latitude and longitude and explain why they are helpful;

• Determine latitude and longitude of their home town and other places;

• Discuss how climate varies with latitude;

• Explain what kinds of clothing they would wear at various latitudes during specified months.

NCSS Themes:

III. People, Places and Environment
    c. use appropriate resources, data sources, and geographic tools such as atlases, databases, grid systems, charts, graphs, and maps to generate, manipulate, and interpret information.

Materials: World outline map with latitude and longitude lines, U.S. outline map with latitude and longitude lines, road atlas (optional), drawing paper.

Process:

1. Divide class into partners.

2. Give each pairing a world outline map and a U.S. outline map.

3. Ask students to look at each map and discuss what they know or notice about the maps.

4. Record their ideas on the chalkboard or a piece of chart paper.

5. Request that students look at the U.S. map and find lines running across and up and down the page. Tell them that the lines across the page are lines of latitude and the lines up and down the page are lines of longitude.

6. Instruct students to find and mark the location of their town and help them to determine its latitude and longitude.

7. Next, choose other places in the United States and find their approximate latitude and longitude.

8. Invite learners to examine the world outline map and discuss the general climate patterns that occur as latitude increases and seasonal temperature variations (focus on the fact that areas further away from the equator tend to be cooler and that, except in places close to the equator, temperatures are cooler in the winter and warmer in the summer).

Instructional Comments: When discussing latitude and longitude make sure that children understand that there are not real lines on the ground, that they were added to the map to help people locate places more easily.

Learning Styles Addressed: Verbal/linguistic, visual/spatial, interpersonal

Standards Addressed: How to use maps and other geographic representations, tools, and technologies to acquire, process, and report information from a spatial perspective.

Evaluation: Have students point out lines of latitude on outline map. Ask students to tell you or write down what they think they would be wearing if they were really in one of these places:

• If you are outside at 60 degrees N latitude, and it is January.

• If you are outside at 10 degrees N latitude, and it is February.

• If you are outside at 35 degrees N latitude, and it is July.

Modifications for Diverse Learners: For visually impaired students lines of latitude and longitude can be enhanced with puffy paint to give them texture.

Extensions: Ask students to draw a picture of themselves at different latitudes in the United States. The picture should include them wearing appropriate clothing and doing activities they think would be appropriate for weather in these places. Post their pictures on a large U.S. map on a bulletin board.

NCSS STANDARDS-LINKED LESSON PLAN

Understanding Scale: Choosing the Right Map

Theme: The World in Spatial Terms
Source: Maria Walther, Gwendolyn Brooks Elementary School
Grade: 3
Objectives: The learners will:

• Compare the scales of three maps;

• Decide which map is appropriate for different situations.

NCSS Themes:

III. People, Places and Environment

d. estimate distance and calculate scale

Materials: The book *The Journey* by Sarah Stewart; three maps from an atlas with different scales ranging from large to small: a map of the state of Illinois—1 inch = 20 miles, a map of the city of Chicago and surrounding suburbs—1 inch = 4 miles, and a map of the city of Chicago—1 inch = 3 miles; rulers; pencils/paper.

Process:

1. Read the book *The Journey* (2001) by Sarah Stewart.

2. Discuss the difference between Hannah's life in her Amish community and her visit to the big city of Chicago.

3. Divide students into small groups and give each group the three maps.

4. Instruct them to examine maps and write down their observations.

5. Point out the different scales on the maps.

6. Pose a variety of questions and have students determine which map would be the most helpful. For example:

   i. Which map would help you find the distance between Sarah's Amish community and Chicago?

   ii. Which map will help you find the distance between the Shedd Aquarium and Macy's?

iii. Which map would help you if you were lost in the city?

iv. Which map contains more detailed information?

v. Which map has a larger scale?

7. Have students work in their small group to create a list of uses for each map.

8. Display the maps and uses on a bulletin board entitled: Choosing the Right Map.

Instructional Comments: This activity can be used with any three maps with varying scales. It is an excellent way to help students choose appropriate maps to answer their geographic questions.

Learning Styles Addressed: Verbal/linguistic, visual/spatial, interpersonal

Standards Addressed: How to use maps and other geographic representations, tools, and technologies to acquire, process, and report information from a spatial perspective

Evaluation: Use the student's responses to the questions asked and their written list of uses of each map to determine their understanding of map scale.

Modifications for Diverse Learners: When creating groups for this lesson, pair supportive students with those who may need extra help. To modify the activity use only the state map and city map to compare and contrast.

Extensions: Have students create three maps with different scales for example: the school grounds, the school building, and the classroom.

Source: S. Stewart. 2001. *The Journey.* Illus. D. Small. New York: Farrar, Straus & Giroux. Hannah, an Amish girl, tells her diary about her first visit to Chicago.

Chapter Summary

The use of stories in social studies is a powerful way to engage students' interest and provide readers with opportunities to develop personal understandings. By developing deeper understanding through reflection on what they have read and felt, social studies students form opinions about what they value in life and choose the actions they will perform (Common 1986). As Oden (1992, 151) points out, "Children love books. Through carefully chosen books, geography can be integrated into the curriculum in a way that will stimulate and excite young students. Geography concepts can be emphasized and strengthened easily and painlessly through the use of literature." The use of quality children's literature to teach geographic knowledge and skills opens for students a world of excitement and information.

Children's Literature Recommendations

Geographic Skills

Bial, R. 1995. *The Underground Railroad.* Boston: Houghton Mifflin. Photos of actual stations are shared. (Gr. 3–5)

Edwards, P. 1997. *Barefoot: Escape on the Underground Railroad.* Illus. H. Cole. New York: HarperCollins. In this dramatic picture book, the forest animals help Barefoot, an escaped slave, elude his pursuers. (Gr. 3–7)

Jenkins, S. 1998. *Hottest, Coldest, Highest, Deepest.* Boston: Houghton Mifflin. Describes some of the most amazing wonders of the world, including the places that hold the records for the hottest, coldest, windiest, and rainiest. (Gr. 1–4)

Moss, M. 1998. *Rachel's Journal.* New York: Harcourt Brace. In her journal, Rachel describes her family's adventures while traveling by covered wagon on the Oregon Trail in 1850. This fictional journal is based on actual experiences of overland emigrants between 1846 and 1868. (Gr. 3–5)

Riggio, A. 1997. *Secret Signs Along the Underground Railroad.* Honesdale, PA: Boyds Mills Press. A young deaf boy must pass along important information about a new hiding place on the Underground Railroad by using his artistic talent to paint a picture of the "safe haven" on a panoramic egg. (Gr. 3–5)

Ricciuti, E. 1998. *America's Top Ten Natural Wonders.* Woodbridge, CT: Blackbirch Press. Introduces ten unique and natural formations in the United States, including the Grand Canyon, Devil's Tower, and Niagara Falls. (Gr. 3–8)

Tesar, J. 1998a. *America's Top Ten Mountains.* Woodbridge, CT: Blackbirch Press. Discusses ten of America's most unique mountains, including the Grand Tetons, Mauna Kea, and Mount Rainier. (Gr. 3–8)

———. 1998b. *America's Top Ten Rivers.* Woodbridge, CT: Blackbirch Press. Explores ten unique rivers in the United States, including the Mississippi, Yukon, and Rio Grande. (Gr. 3–8)

Winter, J. 1988. *Follow the Drinking Gourd.* New York: Alfred A. Knopf. An old sailor named Peg Leg Joe teaches the runaway slaves a song called "Follow the Drinking Gourd," which gives directions to Canada. (Gr. 3–8)

The World in Spatial Terms: Around the World with Exciting Books

Arthus-Bertrand, Y. (Photographer), and R. Burleigh (Text). 2002. Illus. D. Giraudon. *Earth From Above for Young Readers.* New York: Henry N. Abrams. Photos from cameras in space give a different perspective of the earth. (Gr. 4–8)

Berry, J. 2002. *Around the World in Eighty Poems* Illus. K. Lucas. San Francisco: Chronicle. A collection of 80 poems from countries throughout the world. (Gr. 1–8)

Fanelli, S. 1995. *My Map Book.* New York: HarperCollins. A young child's attempt at being a cartographer. (Gr. K–2)

Silverstein, S. 1981. *A Light in the Attic.* New York: Random House. An anthology of humorous poems on a variety of topics. (Gr. 1–6)

Africa

Brett, J. 2005. *Honey, Honey—Lion!: A Story from Africa.* New York: G. P. Putnam's Sons. Brett's detailed illustrations accent this fast-paced version of the legend of the honeyguide, an African bird, and the honey badger. (K–2)

Brown, D. 2000. *Uncommon Traveler.* Boston: Millbrook. The story of the remarkable journey during the 1890s of Mary Kingsley who traveled from England to West Africa. (Gr. 4–6)

Diakité, P. 2006. *I Lost My Tooth in Africa.* Illus. B. W. Diakité. New York: Scholastic. Based on the true story of when the author's little sister lost her tooth in Mali. (Gr. K–4)

Feelings, M. 1974. *Jambo Means Hello: A Swahili Alphabet Book.* Illus. T. Feelings. New York: Dial Books. An alphabet book containing Swahili phonetic spellings, a map of the countries where Swahili is spoken, and descriptive information about Africa. (Gr. K–3)

Hoffman, M. 1995. *Boundless Grace.* Illus. C. Binch. New York: Dial. In this sequel to the book *Amazing Grace,* Grace is invited to visit her father and his new family in Africa. (Gr. K–3)

London, J. 1997. *Ali: Child of the Desert.* Illus. T. Lewin. New York: Lothrop. While Ali and his father are crossing the Saharan Desert on camels a fierce sandstorm separates them. Ali has to decide what would be the best way to find his father. (Gr. K–4)

Musgrove, M. 1976. *Ashanti to Zulu: African Traditions.* Illus. L. Dillon and D. Dillon. New York: Dial. Following letters from A to Z, this source explains traditions and customs of 26 African tribes and includes a map of Africa. (Gr. 1–3)

Smith, R. 1995. *Thunder Cave.* New York: Hyperion. When 14-year-old Jacob travels alone to remote Kenya to find his father, he is drawn into an exciting adventure that revolves around the effects of drought and poaching on the African elephant. (Gr. 6–8)

Antarctica

Armstrong, J. 1998. *Shipwreck at the Bottom of the World: The Extraordinary True Story of Shackleton and the Endurance.* New York: Crown. A superb account of the expedition to the South Pole and how Shackleton braved the ocean waters to rescue his stranded men. (Gr. 6–8)

Bledsoe, L. J. 2006. *How to Survive Antarctica.* New York: Holiday House. Bledsoe's informal narrative is based on her three trips to Antarctica. She shares with interested readers the amazing facts about the science and geography of this mysterious place. (Gr. 5–8)

Glimmerveen, U. 1989. *A Tale of Antarctica.* New York: Scholastic. A story from the penguins' point of view about what happens to their world when humans arrive. (Gr. 1–2)

McKernan, V. 2005. *Shackleton's Stowaway.* New York: Knopf. A historical fiction novel about the 1914 expedition told from the point of view of its youngest crew member, Perce Blackborow. (Gr. 5–9)

McMillan, B. 1993. *Penguins at Home: Gentoos of Antarctica.* Boston: Houghton Mifflin. Children will learn the ways in which gentoo penguins are perfectly adapted to the harsh environment of the Antarctic Peninsula. (Gr. 1–4)

Spinelli, E. 2004. *Something to Tell the Grandcows.* Illus. B. Slavin. Grand Rapids, MI: Eerdmans Books for Young Readers. Spinelli tells the story of Admiral Byrd's expedition from a cow's point of view. (Gr. K–4)

Asia

Dolphin, L. 1997. *Our Journey from Tibet.* Illus. N. J. Johnson. New York: Dutton. This moving book, illustrated with photographs, tells the story of a nine-year-old girl who escapes Tibet through the mountains of the Himalayas so that she can go to school. (Gr. 3–5)

Levinson, R. 1988. *Our Home Is the Sea.* New York: Dutton. A young Chinese boy hurries through a crowded market to his family's houseboat in the Hong Kong harbor to join his father and grandfather in their family profession of fishing. (Gr. 1–3)

Macdonald, F. 1998. *Marco Polo: A Journey through China.* New York: Watts. Marco Polo's travels from Venice to China and back during the thirteenth century are shared with intriguing details. (Gr. 3–6)

Neuberger, A. E. 1995. *The Girl-Son.* New York: Carolrhoda. A true story of a courageous mother in turn-of-the-century Korea who fights prejudice and tradition to educate her daughter. (Gr. 4–6)

Tejima, K. 1986. *Bear's Autumn.* La Jolla, CA: Green Tiger Press. In Hokkaido, the northern island of Japan, a bear cub makes his first dive to catch and eat tasty salmon. (Gr. K–3)

Young, E. 2001. *Monkey King.* New York: HarperCollins. This beautifully illustrated book tells the adventures of the Monkey King, a beloved character from the T'ang Dynasty. (Gr. 2–3)

Australia

Baker, J. 1987. *Where the Forest Meets the Sea.* New York: Greenwillow. On a camping trip in an Australian rain forest, a young boy wonders about the future ecology of the region. (Gr. K–3)

Fox, M. 1983. *Possum Magic.* Illus. J. Vivas. San Diego, CA: Harcourt Brace. When Grandma Poss turns little Hush invisible, she forgets the secret food needed to make Hush visible again. So the two of them set off on a journey to the major cities of Australia to find the remedy. (Gr. K–2)

Ormerod, J. 2005. *Lizzie Nonsense*. New York: Clarion. Lizzie, who lives with her family in the Australian bush, passes the weeks when her father is away using her imagination. (Gr. K–2)

Oodgeroo. 1994. *Dreamtime: Aboriginal Stories*. Illus. B. Bancroft. New York: Lothrop. This book is divided into two parts. In the first half, the author shares stories of her childhood; the second half consists of Aboriginal folktales. (Gr. 4–8)

Wheatley, N., and D. Rawlins. 1998. *My Place*. Australia: Collins Dover. This story takes place on a street in Australia and through narrative text and illustrations, it chronicles the neighborhood's changes from 1988 back to 1788. (Gr. 5–8)

Europe

Bemelmans, L. 1939. *Madeline*. New York: Viking. The classic story of Madeline, who lives in a boarding school in France near the Eiffel Tower and Seine River. (Gr. K–2)

Brewster, H. 1996. *Anastasia's Album*. New York: Hyperion. Through the use of real photographs and letters, readers get a glimpse into the private world of the last Romanovs. (Gr. 4–7)

Huck, C. 2001. *The Black Bull of Norroway: A Scottish Tale*. Illus. A. Lobel. New York: Greenwillow. A retelling of a traditional Scottish tale set in Norway where a courageous girl sets out to seek her fortune and ultimately finds true love. (Gr. 2–5)

Krasilovsky, P. 1957. *The Cow Who Fell in the Canal*. Illus. P. Spier. London: World's Work. A picture book that features the landscape, canals, windmills, and quaint village scenes of the Netherlands. (Gr. K–2)

———. 1982. *The First Tulips in Holland*. New York: Doubleday. Beautiful drawings about spring in Holland. (Gr. K–3)

Middle East

Rumford, J. 2001. *Traveling Man: The Journey of Ibn Battuta, 1325–1354*. Boston: Houghton Mifflin. The 75,000-mile and 29-year journey of Ibn Battuta from his native Morocco on his pilgrimage to Mecca and on to China is described in this fascinating picture book (Gr. 4–8)

North America

Ancona, G. 1994. *Piñata Maker/El Piñatero*. New York: Harcourt Brace. This Spanish/English photo-essay describes how Don Ricardo, a craftsman from Southern Mexico, makes piñatas for the special fiestas held in his village. (Gr. K–3)

Binch, C. 1994. *Gregory Cool*. New York: Dial Books for Young Readers. Young Gregory learns to relax and enjoy the differences in cultures when he travels from his home in America to Tobago, a Caribbean island, to visit his grandparents. (Gr. 3–6)

Creech, S. 1994. *Walk Two Moons*. New York: HarperCollins. Sal makes her way from Ohio to Idaho with her grandparents, hoping to locate her mother who won't be coming back. (Gr. 5–8)

———. 2000. *The Wanderer*. New York: HarperCollins. Thirteen-year-old Sophie travels from Virginia to Connecticut and boards a sailboat with her three uncles and two cousins to make a transatlantic voyage to England. (Gr. 3–7)

Curtis, C. P. 1995. *The Watsons Go to Birmingham—1963*. New York: Delacorte. Young Kenny describes the family's journey during the civil rights period to take his "delinquent" older brother to stay with their grandmother in Birmingham. The family encounters shock and horror when they arrive. (Gr. 6–8)

———. 1999. *Bud, Not Buddy*. New York: Delacorte. During the Great Depression, Bud's mother dies and he sets out across Michigan to locate his father, having only vague clues from his mother's meager possessions. (Gr. 4–8)

Jacobs, F. 1994. *A Passion for Danger: Nansen's Arctic Adventures*. New York: Putnam. This story takes readers on a journey with Fridtjof Nansen, a Norwegian, who traveled to unexplored regions of the world in the 1800s. (Gr. 5–8)

Joseph, L. 1992. *Coconut Kind of Day,* Illus. S. Speidel. New York: Puffin. Poems of the Caribbean Islands including "Steel Drum" and "Morning Songs." (Gr. K–2)

MacLachlan, P. 1994. *All the Places to Love.* Illus. M. Wimmer. New York: HarperCollins. This beautifully illustrated book pays tribute to the American farm. (Gr. 2–4)

Parker, N. W. 2001. *Land Ho! Fifty Glorious Years in the Age of Exploration.* New York: HarperCollins. Twelve European explorers from Columbus through Cabrillo are introduced in this picture book. (Gr. 3–5)

Ryan, P. M. 2004. *Becoming Naomi León.* New York: Scholastic. When her mother appears after seven years of abandonment, Naomi's grandmother helps her find herself. (Gr. 4–6)

Winslow, B. 1995. *Dance on a Sealskin.* Illus. T. Sloat. Alaska: Alaska Northwest. This book takes readers back in time to the ancient culture of the Alaskan Yupik Eskimo and introduces them to the ritual of "the first dance." (Gr. 2–4)

South America

Alexander, E. 1989. *Llama and the Great Flood.* New York: T.Y. Crowell. A Peruvian folktale similar to the Noah's Ark story. The illustrations include mountainous Peruvian landscape and the colorful Peruvian Indian dress. (Gr. K–4)

Cherry, L. 1990. *The Great Kapok Tree: The Tale of the Amazon Rain Forest.* New York: Harcourt Brace. A man threatens the natural habitat of the tropical rain forest animals when he comes along to chop down the great kapok tree. (Gr. K–4)

Dorros, A. 1991. *Tonight Is Carnaval.* New York: Dutton. Illustrated with arpilleras sewn by the members of the Club de Madres Virgen del Carmen of Lima, Peru, this book tells the story of a family in South America that is eagerly preparing for the excitement of Carnaval. (Gr. 2–4)

Kurtz, J. 1996. *Miro in the Kingdom of the Sun.* Illus. D. Frampton. Boston: Houghton Mifflin. An Inca folktale, illustrated with woodcuts, tells the tale of a young Inca girl who succeeds where her brothers and others have failed, when her bird friends help her find the special water that will cure the king's son. (Gr. 1–4)

The World

Goodman, J. E. 2001. *A Long and Uncertain Journey: The 27,000 Mile Voyage of Vasco da Gama.* New York: Mikaya. Vasco da Gama sailed from Europe around Africa to the Orient and returned to Portugal, securing valuable trade routes for his country. Includes a fold-out map of his journey. (Gr. 3–5)

Mental Maps

Anno, M. 1983. *Anna's U.S.A.* New York: Philomel. This wordless book, illustrated by the author, records a traveler's journey from the West Coast of the United States to the East. Anno places his character in both historical and fictional scenes as he stops in villages, towns, and cities. Great for diverse students (LD and English language learners). (Gr. K–3)

George, L. B. 1996. *Around the Pond: Who's Been Here?* New York: Greenwillow. While picking blueberries on a summer afternoon, two children see signs of unseen animals including footprints, a dam, and a floating feather. Other books in this series include: *In the Snow: Who's Been Here?* and *In the Woods: Who's Been Here?* (Gr. K–3)

Keller, L. 1998. *The Scrambled States of America.* New York: Holt. A humorous tale of the time that Kansas got bored and invited all the states to the biggest party ever. When all the states then decided to switch spots, they discovered there is no place like home. (Gr. 1–3)

Lessac, F. 1984. *My Little Island.* New York: Harper & Row. A young boy goes with his best friend to visit the little Caribbean island where he was born. (Gr. 1–3)

McClintock, B. 2006. *Adèle & Simon.* New York: Farrar, Straus and Giroux. Adèle and her younger brother meander through the streets of Paris on their way home from school. Endpaper traces their route on a map of Paris from 1907. (Gr. K–2)

Sage, J. 1991. *The Little Band.* Illus. K. Narahashi. New York: Margaret K. McElderry. A little band of children from various cultures marches through a town and brings joy and music to the people. (Gr. 2–3)

Williams, V. B. 1981. *Three Days on a River in a Red Canoe.* New York: William Morrow. Two children and their mothers spend three days on a river, experiencing and observing nature around them. (Gr. 2–4)

Using Literature to Teach Mapping Skills

Armstrong, J. 1998. *Shipwreck at the Bottom of the World.* (See the Antarctica section.)

Ball, D. 1990. *Jeremy's Tail.* Illus. D. Rawlins. New York: Orchard Books. Jeremy is blindfolded while playing "Pin the Tail on the Donkey" but on his way to the donkey he travels halfway around the world. (Gr. 2–4)

Berger, M., and G. Berger. 1993. *The Whole World in Our Hands: Looking at Maps.* Illus. R. Quackenbush. Nashville, TN: Ideal Children's Books. Explains what maps are and how to use them, discusses map symbols and their meanings, and includes maps of a house, community, city, state, country, and the world. (Gr. 1–4)

Brown, D. 2000. *Uncommon Traveler.* (See the Africa section.)

Carey, H. H. 1983. *How to Use Maps and Globes.* New York: Watts. Explains how maps and globes are designed and how to get the most out of them, including special-purpose maps. Discusses how maps can be used to make written and oral reports more interesting. (Gr. 3–5)

Clouse, N. L. 1990. *Puzzle Maps U.S.A.* New York: H. Holt. Introduces the 50 states and their shapes, showing the states in various configurations aside from their normal arrangement. (Gr. 2–5)

Creech, S. 1994. *Walk Two Moons.* (See the North America section.)

———. 2000. *The Wanderer.* (See the North America section.)

Crewe, S. 1996. *Maps and Globes.* Illus. R. Turvey and S. Tourret. New York: Children's Press. A thorough introduction to maps, globes, and how to use them. (Gr. 2–4)

Curtis, C. P. 1995. *The Watsons Go to Birmingham—1963.* (See the North America section.)

———. 1999. *Bud, Not Buddy.* (See the North America section.)

Dewey, J. O. 2001. *Finding Your Way: The Art of Natural Navigation.* Photo. S. Trimble. Boston: Millbrook. Stories of how real people use natural navigation to find their way back are shared in this picture book. (Gr. 2–4)

Fanelli, S. 1995. *My Map Book.* New York: HarperCollins. A collection of maps provides a childlike view of the owner's bedroom, school, playground, and other places farther away. (Gr. K–2)

Hartman, G. 1991. *As the Crow Flies: A First Book of Maps.* Illus. H. Stevenson. New York: Bradbury Press. A look at different geographical areas from the perspectives of an eagle, rabbit, crow, horse, and gull. (Gr. K–2)

Holling, H. C. 1991. *Paddle-to-the-Sea.* Boston: Houghton Mifflin. This book maps the journey of a toy canoe named Paddle, beginning in Canada north of Lake Superior through the inland waterways across the continent to the Gulf of St. Lawrence and finally across the Atlantic Ocean. (Gr. 2–4)

Knowlton, J. 1985. *Maps and Globes.* Illus. H. Barton. New York: Harper & Row. A brief history of mapmaking, a simple explanation of how to read maps and globes, and an introduction to the many different kinds of maps that exist. (Gr. 2–4)

Leedy, L. 2000. *Mapping Penny's World.* New York: Holt. Lisa and her pet boxer, Penny, discover maps and their parts—the key and symbols, labels, scale, and more. (Gr. K–2)

Lye, K. 1991. *Measuring and Maps.* New York: Gloucester Press. Discusses the science of geography as measured by globes, maps, latitude, longitude, and map symbols and presents related projects. (Gr. 4–6)

Macdonald, F. 1998. *Marco Polo: A Journey through China.* (See the Asia section.)

McLerran, A. 1991. *Roxaboxen.* Illus. B. Cooney. New York: Lothrop, Lee, & Shepard Books. Marian and her playmates build an imaginary town on the hill, complete with houses, stores, and playfields. This book is based on true events in the childhood of the author's mother. (Gr. 3–5)

Marshall, J. P. 1989. *My Camera: At the Aquarium.* Boston: Little, Brown. Young readers visit different sea creatures in this book by using a map of the aquarium marked with the photographer's footprints. (Gr. 2–4)

Oleksy, W. 2002. *Mapping the World.* New York: Watts. This book covers the history of cartography from the ancient world to the use of modern-day computers. It includes a time line. (Gr. 4–6)

Parker, N. W. 2001. *Land Ho! Fifty Glorious Years in the Age of Exploration.* (See the North America section.)

Rabe, T. 2002. *There's a Map in My Lap: All about Maps.* Illus. A. Ruiz. New York: Random House. The Cat in the Hat introduces readers to different kinds of maps (city, state, world, topographic, temperature, and terrain); their formats (flat, globe, atlas, puzzle); the tools needed to read them (key, symbols, scales, grids, and compasses); and funny facts about places ("Michigan looks like a scarf and a mitten! Louisiana looks like a chair you can sit in!"). (Gr. K–2)

Rumford, J. 2001. *The Traveling Man: The Journey of Ibn Battuta.* (See the Middle East section.)

Sammis, F. 1998. *Measurement.* New York: Benchmark. From a series of books entitled *Discovering Geography,* this book explains and gives suggested activities for measuring distance on maps through the use of scale bars, color keys, and contour lines. (Gr. 2–5)

Sipiera, P. P. 1991. *Globes.* Chicago: Children's Press. Describes the usefulness of globes to show the roundness of Earth and the various consequences of that shape. (Gr. 1–3)

Sweeny, J. 1996. *Me on the Map.* New York: Crown. This book describes a child's global address beginning with her room and ending with her universe. (Gr. 1–3)

Weiss, H. 1991. *Getting from Here to There.* Boston: Houghton Mifflin. Discusses various aspects of maps, including direction, distance, symbols, latitude and longitude, how maps are made, and special-purpose maps and charts. (Gr. 2–5)

Young, K. R. 2002. *Small Worlds: Maps and Mapmaking.* New York: Scholastic. This book describes the process of mapmaking. (Gr. 1–3)

Treasure Maps

Donnelly, J. 1984. *True-Life Treasure Hunts.* Illus. C. Robinson. New York: Random House. Compelling stories of pirates, sunken treasure, the Sacred Well at Chicén Itzá in the Yucatán, and King Tut's tomb in Egypt get children interested in hunting for treasure. Includes U.S. lost treasure maps showing where sunken ships and other loot are reportedly located. (Gr. 5–7)

Fleischman, S. 1989. *The Ghost in the Noonday Sun.* Illus. P. Sis. New York: Greenwillow. Twelve-year-old Oliver tries to escape from pirates, who take him to an island to find the ghost and treasure of Gentleman Jack. (Gr. 5–8)

Hobbs, W. 1997. *Ghost Canoe.* New York: Morrow Junior Books. Fourteen-year-old Nathan, fishing with the Makah in the Pacific Northwest, finds himself holding a vital clue when a mysterious stranger comes to town looking for Spanish treasure. (Gr. 5–8)

Reid, S. 1997. *The Children's Atlas of Lost Treasures.* Brookfield, CT: Millbrook Press. This book surveys lost treasures around the world, including pirate loot and treasures lost in wars and natural disasters. (Gr. 4–6)

Places and Regions—A Primary Unit about Native American Regions

Bruchac, J. 1998. *Many Nations: An Alphabet of Native America.* Illus. R. Goetzl. UK: Bridgewater Books. Illustrations and brief text present aspects of the lives of many varied native peoples across North America. (Gr. 1–4) de Paola, T. 1988. *The Legend of the Indian Paintbrush.* New York: Putnam. Little Gopher is not like the rest of the boys in his tribe. He will never be a great warrior or hunter, instead, he records events in brilliant colors on animal hides. (Gr. K–3)

Krensky, S. 1991. *Children of the Earth and Sky.* Illus. J. Watling. New York: Scholastic. Depicts traditions and lifestyles in five different tribes of northern Native Americans through vignettes set almost 200 years ago, when they still had much of the continent to themselves. (Gr. 4–8)

McDermott, G. 1974. *Arrow to the Sun.* New York: Puffin Books. An adaptation of the Pueblo myth that explains how the spirit of the Lord of the Sun was brought to the world of men. (Gr. K–2)

Martin, R. 1992. *The Rough-Face Girl.* Illus. D. Shannon. New York: G.P. Putnam's Sons. In this Algonquin version of the Cinderella story, the Rough-Face Girl and her two beautiful but heartless sisters compete for the affections of the Invisible Being. (Gr. K–3)

Mott, E. C. 1996. *Dancing Rainbows: A Pueblo Boy's Story.* New York: Dutton. A young Tewa Indian boy and his grandfather prepare to take part in the tribe's feast, which will include the special Tewa dance. (Gr. 1–3)

Waters, K. 1996. *Tapenum's Day: A Wampanoag Indian Boy in Pilgrim Times.* Illus. and Photo. R. Kendall. New York: Scholastic. An authentic informative glimpse into a day in the life of a Wampanoag boy. (Gr. 1–3)

Physical Systems—How Climate and Weather Affect Our Lives

Anderson, L. 1974. *The Day the Hurricane Happened.* Illus. A. Grifalconi. New York: Scribner's. On the Caribbean island of St. John, a family experiences the drama, danger, and destruction of a hurricane. (Gr. 4–6)

Branley, F. 1988. *Tornado Alert.* Illus. G. Maestro. New York: Crowell. The often-asked questions of what causes tornadoes, how they move, and what to do if you are near one are all handled in a clear and unsensationalized fashion. (Gr. 2–4)

de Paola, T. 1975. *The Cloud Book.* New York: Holiday House. Introduces the 10 most common types of clouds, the myths that have been inspired by their shapes, and what they tell about coming weather changes. (Gr. K–3)

Fowler, A. 1997. *It Could Still Be a Desert.* New York: Children's Press. Describes the characteristics of deserts, the animals and plants that live in them, and their constantly changing nature. (Gr. 2–4)

Geisert, B. 2001. *Desert Town.* Illus. A. Geisert. Boston: Houghton Mifflin. This story shows a small town in a desert area over a one-year span and how it is connected to the changing seasons and physical environment. (Gr. 1–4)

Gibbons, G. 1996. *Deserts.* New York: Holiday House. An introduction to the characteristics of deserts and the plants and animals that inhabit them. (Gr. K–3)

Herman, G. 1997. *Storm Chasers: Tracking Twisters.* Illus. L. Schwinger. New York: Grosset & Dunlap. A short chapter book that describes the behavior of tornadoes and how meteorologists track these powerful storms. (Gr. 2–3)

Llewellyn, C. 1997. *Wild, Wet and Windy.* Cambridge, MA: Candlewick Press. Gives information about all types of storms and weather, includes a true/false question on every page. (Gr. 2–3)

Murray, P. 1996. *Tornadoes.* New York: Child's World. Full-color photographs and clear text help to explain the fascinating phenomenon of tornadoes to children. (Gr. 2–4)

Petty, K. 1998. *I Didn't Know that People Chase Twisters and Other Amazing Facts about Violent Weather.* Illus. P. Roberts and J. Moore. Brookfield, CT: Copper Beech Books. Provides interesting information about violent weather phenomena such as thunderstorms, lightning, blizzards, monsoons, and sandstorms. Includes glossary and index. (Gr. 2–5)

Ruckman, I. 1988. *Night of the Twisters.* New York: Harper & Row. A fictional account of the night that freakish and devastating tornadoes hit Grand Island, Nebraska, as experienced by a 12-year-old, his family, and his friends. (Gr. 5–8)

Shaw, C. 1947. *It Looked Like Spilt Milk.* New York: Harper & Row. An imaginary look at clouds and the shapes that they form. (Gr. K–4)

Steiner, B. 1996. *Desert Trip.* Illus. R. Himler. San Francisco: Sierra Club Books for Children. As a young girl and her mother hike through the desert they discover the rich variety of life that thrives in the dry desert heat. (Gr. 1–5)

Human Systems—Westward Expansion in the United States

Bloch, L. M. 1983. *Overland to California in 1859: A Guide for Wagon Train Travelers.* New York: Bloch. This book includes quotes from sources actually used by pioneers, which tell about routes, tracking and pursuing Native Americans, deer hunting, rattlesnake bites, and much more. An excellent background book for students who are writing their own short stories or diaries about traveling to the West. (Gr. 4–8)

Brenner, B. 1978. *Wagon Wheels.* Illus. D. Bolognese. New York: HarperCollins. Three young black brothers follow a map to their father's homestead on the western plains to take advantage of the free land offered by the Homestead Act. (Gr. 3–5)

Coerr, E. 1986. *The Josefina Story Quilt.* Illus. B. Degen. New York: Harper & Row. An easy-reader book about Faith, who leaves in May 1850 on a covered wagon from Missouri to California. Faith brings her pet chicken, Josefina, even though it does not lay eggs and is too tough to eat. Faith keeps a record of her trip by sewing a quilt. (Gr. 2–4)

Harvey, B. 1988. *Cassie's Journey: Going West in the 1860s.* Illus. D. K. Ray. New York: Holiday House. A picture book that contains a first-person account of a girl who travels by covered wagon from Illinois to California and encounters buffalo, terrible weather, illness, snakebites, and death. (Gr. 2–4)

Leeuwen, J. V. 1992. *Going West.* Illus. T. B. Allen. New York: Dial. Follows a family's emigration by prairie schooner from the East across the Plains to the West. (Gr. 2–5)

McGowen, T. 1998. *African Americans in the Old West.* New York: Children's Press. Describes the important role of freed slaves and other African Americans in the settlement of the West. (Gr. 4–8)

Schlissel, L. 1982. *Women's Diaries of Westward Journey.* New York: Schocken. Contains diaries of three women. Also includes a table that lists the characteristics of women who traveled West between 1851 and 1859. (Gr. 5–8)

Scott, L. H. 1987. *The Covered Wagon and Other Adventures.* Lincoln: University of Nebraska. The author tells of her family's trip by wagons from St. Paul, Minnesota, to Thermopolis, Wyoming, in 1906 and a later trip to Oregon. (Gr. 5–7)

Stefoff, R. 1996. *Children of the Westward Trail.* Brookfield, CT: Millbrook Press. Describes what life was like for those children who were uprooted from their Midwestern homes and transported by their families across the frontier in wagons and on horseback. (Gr. 3–6)

Turner, A. 1997. *Mississippi Mud: Three Prairie Journals.* New York: HarperCollins. Amanda and her two brothers share their hopes and fears in their journals as they travel west. Each entry is written in the form of a poem. (Gr. 4–8)

Waddell, M. 1984. *Going West.* Illus. P. Dupasquier. New York: Harper & Row. This book contains nine-year-old Kate's diary of a trip across the United States in a covered wagon. (Gr. 3–4)

Whelan, G. 1987. *Next Spring an Oriole.* Illus. P. Johnson. New York: Random House. Ten-year-old Libby travels west by covered wagon with her family for two months and one thousand miles from Virginia to Michigan in 1837. When the family befriends a Potowatomi child with measles, the Native Americans repay the family's kindness by helping them survive the winter with gifts of corn and smoked meat.

right, C. C. 1995. *Wagon Train: A Family Goes West in 1865.* Illus. G. Griffith. New York: Holiday House. This book tells the story of Ginny and her African American family as they travel from Virginia to California using the Oregon Trail. (Gr. 1–3)

Environment and Society—Protecting Our Earth

Baker, J. 1987. *Where the Forest Meets the Sea.* New York: Greenwillow. A boy remembers the past inhabitants of the fantastic forest on a beautiful island but wonders if it will all be lost to land development. (Gr. 3–4)

Base, G. 2006. *Uno's Garden.* New York: Abrams. Uno's forest slowly disappears as a city takes over. (Gr. K–2)

George, J. C. 1995. *Everglades.* Illus. W. Minor. New York: HarperCollins. A Seminole story-teller narrates this story of the river and its vanishing inhabitants. A pictorial symbol chart of vanishing species in the Everglades is included. (Gr. 1–5)

Hiaasen, C. 2002. *Hoot.* New York: Knopf. A young teenager fights a large developer to pre-vent the takeover of a wildlife area that is home to tiny burrowing owls. (Gr. 6–8)

———. 2005. *Flush.* New York: Knopf. Noah and Abbey gather evidence to prove that a casino boat was illegally dumping raw sewage into the ocean. (Gr. 5–8)

McDonald, M. 2004. *Judy Moody Saves the World.* Cambridge, MA: Candlewick. In Judy's third adventure she tries to convince her family and her classmates to be more environ-mentally conscientious. (Grades 1–3)

Peet, B. 1970. *The Wump World.* Boston: Houghton Mifflin. The spunky, pudgy wumps live happily on a lush green planet until the Pollutians come from outer space to take over. (Gr. 1–3)

Seuss, Dr. 1971. *The Lorax.* New York: Random House. A sadder but wiser Onceler tells how he exploited and ruined the local environment in spite of the warnings of the Lorax. (Gr. 1–6)

Van Allsburg, C. 1990. *Just a Dream.* Boston: Houghton Mifflin. A nightmarish trip into a polluted future motivates a boy to be concerned for the environment. (Gr. 1–6)

Wallwork, A. 1993. *No Dodos: A Counting Book of Endangered Animals.* New York: Scholastic. A simple picture book illustrating endangered animals. The endnotes provide detailed information about the threats to the featured animals. (Gr. K–3)

Teaching Resources

Books

Fromboluti, C. S. 1990. *Helping Your Child Learn Geography.* Washington, DC: Office of Edu-cational Research and Improvement. This publication is filled with good ideas for par-ents and educators of young children.

National Organizations

National Council for the Social Studies
3501 Newark Street NW
Washington, DC 20016

NCSS has a Geographic Education Special Interest Group composed of K–12 teachers, curriculum developers, and researchers interested in developing and integrating geography.

National Council for Geographic Education
Department of Geography and Regional Planning
Indiana University of Pennsylvania
Indiana, PA 15705

NCGE is the only organization for teachers that is exclusively devoted to improving geography education. NCGE produces the *Journal of Geography* and distributes geography education materials published by the Geographic Education National Implementation Project (GENIP), a coalition of geographical organizations. GENIP publishes geography education materials and a newsletter that is free of charge for teachers who request it from: Association of American Geographers, 1710 16th St. NW, Washington, DC 20009.

National Geographic Society
P.O. Box 2895
Washington, DC 20077-9960

In an effort to improve geography awareness and education, National Geographic has instituted the Geography Education Program, which offers teacher training and assistance through workshops and model classroom experimentation. Curriculum guidelines and suggestions and a quarterly newsletter inform teachers of classroom ideas and techniques. For a copy of the National Geography Standards, write to: National Geographic Society, P.O. Box 1640, Washington, DC 20013-1640 or call 1-800-368-2728.

Related Technology Tools

Web Sites

(The) CityLink Project
> http://www.neosoft.com/citylink/default.html
> This site is a comprehensive listing, featuring states and cities. Its easy-to-use format provides students with information about various cities including what to see, what to do, and how to find out more information about the city. It would be helpful in creating travel brochures.

Virtual Tourist
> http://www.virtualtourist.com/vt/
> This site offers general information, tourist guides, and pictures for thousands of places.

Earth Day
> http://www.erinoaa.gov/EarthDay/
> This eye-pleasing site offers links to environmental information and projects for the classroom.

Global Learning and Observations to Benefit the Environment
> http://www.globe.gov/fsl/welcome.html
> Students from more than sixty countries help scientists record climate changes.

GORP—National Historic Trails
> http://www.gorp.com/index.htm
> Students can access this site to find maps and detailed descriptions of the old pioneer routes such as the Oregon Trail.

MapQuest
> http://www.mapquest.com
> Get customized maps for places all over the world using this interactive atlas.

National Geographic
> http://www.nationalgeographic.com
> The National Geographic site includes several world-class projects on the environment, wildlife, and preservation.

National Geographic Society Map Machine
> http://www.nationalgeographic.com/ngs/maps/cartographic.html
> A shortcut to National Geographic Society Map Machine is
> http://www.nationalgeographic.com/mapmachine.
> When students need a quick map, facts about a country, state, or province, or a picture of its flag, choose this site with its Map Machine Atlas.

Online Photo Archive

http://ap.accuweather.com

An exciting archive of more than 400,000 photos of news, as well as thousands of historical photos of people, places, and events.

WebQuests

Map Adventure (Gr. 2–4)

http://its.guifford.k12.nc.us/webquests/mapadventure/map.htm

Explore Australia (Gr. 2)

http://www.lfelem.lfc.edu/tech/DuBose/webquest/MRWB/Aus.htm13

Native Americans in the Natural World (Gr. 1–3)

http://its.guilford.k12.nc.us/webquests/native/native.html

Civil War BattleQuest: The War of 10,000 Places (Gr. 5–8)

http://www.techtrekers.com/webquests/#Social%20Studies

Blazing Trails with the Buffalo Soldiers (Gr. 4–6)

http://www.memphis-schools.k12.tn.us/admin/tlapages.buffalo.html

South American Countries (Gr. 5–8)

http://its.guifford.k12.nc.us/webquests/samer/samer.htm

Voyage to Japan (Gr. 5–6)

http://www.spa3.k12.sc.us/WebQuests.html

Where In the World Are We? A WebQuest About Countries (Gr. 6–8)

http://www.memphis-schools.k12.tn.us/admin/tlapages/countries.htm

Technology Resources

Five Activities for Teaching Geography's Five Themes

www.education-world.com/a_lessonnesson071.shtml

This site contains ideas for teaching the geography themes of location, place, human/environment interaction, movement, and region.

Discovery School's A–Z Geography

http://school.discovery.com/homeworkhelp/worldbook/atozgeography/

Find information about regions, countries, and cities around the world. This is a good source if you have a lesser-known topic you want to explore.

Geographic Learning Site

http://geography.state.gov/htmls/statehome.html

The Unites States Department of State developed this site to help teachers not only explore geography, but also learn about U.S. policy and interaction with countries around the world.

Software and Videos

Where in the World Is Carmen Sandiego? (Broderbund) (Mac/Windows) Expands students' knowledge of world geography and cultures as they travel to 50 countries, gather clues, and take guided tours through scrolling landscapes. Designed for grades 4–8. Also available Junior Detective Edition for grades Pre-K–3. (www.broderbund.com)

Where in Time Is Carmen Sandiego? (Broderbund) (Mac/Windows) This program, designed for grades 4–8, includes 18 historical puzzles which allow students to track Carmen from ancient Egypt to the 1960s space race. Along the way they will meet historical figures and be able to explore in greater depth each historical event they are witnessing. (www.broderbund.com)

Learning to Read Maps. Teacher's Video Company. Available from www.teachersvideo.com. Equipped with maps, students can obtain a wealth of information. Investigate the meaning of coordinates, scales, legends, directions, colors, and symbols.

Great American State Quiz. Teacher's Video Company. Available from www.teachersvideo.com. This fun video offers stimulating, interactive quizzes to help students learn state facts, sites, monuments, and geography.

GeoCycle USA. EdVenture Software and Videos. Available from www.edven.com. Learn geography as you experience our country's famous cities and landmarks firsthand.

United States Geography. Fogware Publishing. Available from www.amazon.com. Trace the paths of pioneers and patriots, and witness a country as vast and varied in climate, topography, and natural resources as any place on earth. Ten CDs feature various regions, such as the Northeast, Southwest, and West.

References

Bednarz, S., and R. Bednarz. 1994. "The Standards Are Coming!" *Journal of Geography* 93 (4): 194–96.

Boehm, R. G., and J. F. Petersen. 1994. "An Elaboration of the Fundamental Themes in Geography." *Social Education* 58 (4): 211–13.

Committee on Geographic Education. 1984. *Guidelines for Geographic Education: Elementary and Secondary Schools*. Washington, DC: Association of American Geographers and National Council for Geographic Education.

Common, D. L. 1986. "Students, Stories and Social Studies." *The Social Studies* 77 (5): 246–48.

Freeman, D. E., and Y. S. Freeman. 1991. "'Doing' Social Studies: Whole Language Lessons to Promote Social Action." *Social Education* 55 (1): 29–32, 66.

Geography Education Standards Project. 1994. *Geography for Life: National Geography Standards*. Washington, DC: National Geographic Research and Exploration.

Gregg, M. 1997. "Seven Journeys to Map Symbols: Multiple Intelligences Applied to Map Learning." *Journal of Geography* 96 (3): 146–52.

Gregg, M., and D. C. Sekeres. 2006. "Supporting Children's Reading of Expository Text in the Geography Classroom." *The Reading Teacher* 60 (2): 102–10.

Harvey, S. 2002. "Nonfiction Inquiry: Using Real Reading and Writing to Explore the World." *Language Arts* 80 (1): 12–22.

Hayes, D. A. 1993. "Freehand Maps Are for Teachers and Students Alike." *Journal of Geography* 92 (1): 13–15.

Hollister, V. G. 1994. "Arriving Where We Started: Using Old Maps in a Middle School Social Studies Classroom." *Social Education* 58 (5): 279–80.

Kapp, B. M. 1991. "A Magic Carpet Trip to Learning Geography." *Journal of Geography* 90 (4): 174–78.

Laminack, L. L., and R. M. Wadsworth. 2006. *Reading Aloud across the Curriculum*. Portsmouth, NH: Heinemann.

Louie, B. Y. 1993. "Using Literature to Teach Location." *Social Studies and the Young Learner* 5 (3): 17–18, 22.

Maxim, G. W. 2002. *Social Studies and the Elementary School Child*. 8th ed. Columbus, OH: Merrill.

National Council for the Social Studies. 1993. NCSS Position Statement. "A Vision of Powerful Teaching and Learning in the Social Studies: Building Social Understanding and Civic Efficacy." *Social Education* 57 (5): 213–23.

Oden, P. 1992. "Geography Is Everywhere in Children's Literature." *Journal of Geography* 91 (4): 151–58.

Petry, A. K. 1995. "Future Teachers of Geography: Whose Opportunity?" *Journal of Geography* 51: 487–94.

Rocca, A. M. 1994. "Integrating History and Geography." *Social Education* 58 (2): 114–16.

Schoenfeldt, M. 2001. "Geographic Literacy and Young Learners." *The Educational Forum* 66 (1): 26–31.

Sunal, C. S., and M. E. Haas. 2000. *Social Studies and the Elementary/Middle School Student*. Orlando, FL: Harcourt Brace Jovanovich.

> Democracy is not simply a system whereby people elect
> those who govern them, but a system in which every member
> of the community participates in self-governance.
>
> —Walter C. Parker,
> "Participatory Citizenship: Civics in the Strong Sense"

Chapter Twelve

Civic Education in a Democratic Society

Richard A. Fluck, Northern Illinois University

CHAPTER OBJECTIVES

Readers will

• understand how to create a democratic classroom;

• appreciate and understand the role of the citizen in a democratic society;

• comprehend the role of civic life, politics, and government;

• be able to apply critical thinking skills in teaching civic education;

• understand the importance of teaching character education;

• understand brain research as it relates to character education; and

• appreciate the need to teach about human rights for all citizens.

Introduction

"The essential purpose of social studies is to develop competent and caring individuals who can make decent decisions for the common good," according to Tedd Levy (quoted in Rasmussen 1999, 1), former president of the National Council for the Social Studies and middle school social studies teacher. This means that students should become responsible citizen actors who take responsibility for making decisions. "Civic competence is the study of the ideals, principles, and practices of citizenship that lead to a commitment to action" (Neal and Moore 2003, 1). In our changing global society, the importance of America and its role as the leading democratic society was put forth by Becker (1992, 83–4):

> As citizens living in a large, influential, multicultural, democratic society, our actions have an impact on others as well as on the physical and social environment. . . . Citizen power seems to be on the rise [in the world]. Are we preparing our citizens for a new world order?

Thus, for teachers in the twenty-first century, civic education becomes a challenge they must address. In 1994, the Center for Civic Education (CCE) published *National Standards for Civics and Government* (1994). These standards were grouped into five different categories: civic life, politics, and government; the foundations of the U.S. political system; the values and principles of U.S. constitutional democracy; the relationship of U.S. politics to world affairs; and the role of the citizen (see the Standards later in this chapter).

Social Justice

Social justice is equal rights for all. It involves **human rights** with respect to everyone having the right to freedom of speech and beliefs and the right to basic human needs of nourishment as well as respect. Social justice means that the rules and laws are applied the same way regardless of wealth or political influence. Fairness to all citizens is the underlying theme.

Students in elementary school have an innate sense of fairness and a strong desire to be treated fairly. If the bully in the class is singled out and unduly punished, the other students, despite their dislike of that student, will cry foul. Teachers who weed out certain students and then make fun of them or put them in awkward situations are loathed by the class. The classroom rules apply to all students and any discipline must be measured out accordingly. Likewise, students who treat their peers with less than proper respect provide their classmates with reasons not to become their closest friends as these classmates may be the next target of ridicule or jokes.

Not only must students read about social realities and discuss them but they also need to become knowledgeable of ways to respond to social injustice when they, themselves, encounter it. "Using literature written for children and young adults can help facilitate appreciation of multiple perspectives, respect for cultural differences, understanding that people must not be discriminated against" (Tyson and Park, 2006, 25). Books that relate to social justice in the classroom are becoming more readily available. *The Bully Blockers Club* (Bateman 2004) is one of a series of books by Albert Whitman and Company about bullying and how to resolve it. Lotty Raccoon is bullied by Grant Grizzly, but when she seeks help from adults she is brushed off because Grant is always well behaved in their presence. However, Lotty forms a coalition of friends calling themselves the "Bully Blockers Club," which garners the attention of adults who then resolve the bullying problem. Another book that children will find revealing is *The Recess Queen* (O'Neill 2002), which depicts a child who acts as a dictator on the playground, bossing the other children and not letting them play on the swings or slide without her permission, until a new girl in school challenges her authority. A book that crosses most grade levels and is great for provoking class discussion is *Say Something* (Moss 2004), a picture book about a girl who sees a variety of bullying tactics in school and on the bus but watches in silence. She falls victim when her friends are absent and she eats alone in the cafeteria.

Creating a Democratic Classroom

"Despite the importance of social studies, experts worry that we are failing to prepare students to participate in their neighborhoods, cities, states, nation, and the world" (Rasmussen 1999, 1). It is up to the classroom teacher to plan experiences in which students can engage in active citizenship.

A democratic classroom has several goals. First, the teacher should be a role model. According to Fernlund (1997, 220–21):

> A teacher's actions have a profound influence on the behavior and attitudes of students. If the teacher models democratic practices, the children will absorb powerful lessons. The teacher who shows respect for students when they are expressing their ideas is communicating the importance of each individual's contribution. The teacher who regularly includes alternative points of view in the curriculum is preparing students to live with diversity and to question the truth of just one source of information.

A second goal of a democratic classroom is to foster an open and supportive climate where all ideas and views are given consideration. A third goal is to encourage multiple perspectives and sources. Students learn that knowledge gained through one source alone may not be accurate. They also learn the value of diversity with this goal. A fourth goal is respect and cooperation as both are essential for a productive learning climate. A fifth goal is the idea of shared goals and rules. The last goal of a democratic classroom is that of group decision making (Fernlund 1997).

From the first day of school the teacher can involve students in establishing classroom rules of conduct (Metzger 2000). Kindergartners may decide that they should respect others and their property. As one five-year-old said, "Don't touch somebody else or their things and don't use mean words that hurt." Classroom rules work best if the teacher and the class discuss potential problems at the beginning of the year. Together they come up with a short, clear, and concise list of rules, maybe only three or four. In this way, the students not only feel they have engaged in setting the limits and have ownership, but since the rules are few, they can better keep them in mind.

Beginning at the third-grade level, classes can develop their own classroom constitution. A good way of initiating the school year is to read aloud *Shh! We're Writing the Constitution* (Fritz 1987), which gives insights into the 1787 Constitutional Convention in Philadelphia. When students learn that a **constitution** is "a set of important rules people have discussed and agreed to live by," they are ready to discuss and decide on rules for their own classroom. This is also a good time to introduce the concept of majority rule with a simple majority being more than 50 percent. Stricter requirements of two-thirds majority can also be explained to students. A constitution should have a preamble, or the reason for the constitution. An example would be "We, the students and teacher in 4–K, in order to learn and work together, have agreed to follow the rules listed below." Students and the teacher should all sign the constitution. It is best to hold the discussions and vote on rules when the entire class is present if the constitution is to work effectively. Any new student can have the constitution explained to him or her and they may sign it as well.

Throughout the year there are several opportunities to embrace democracy in the classroom. Students may vote on the kind of projects they want to do that will be displayed for Parent's Night or on which historical novel the entire class reads for the Civil War period. Although these are not major issues to adults, they provide the opportunity for students to participate in an election process and learn the importance of a single vote (see In the Classroom—How Much Is One Vote Worth?).

☞ IN THE CLASSROOM

How Much Is One Vote Worth?

In 1645, one vote gave Oliver Cromwell control of England.
In 1649, one vote caused Charles I of England to be executed.
In 1845, one vote brought Texas into the Union.
In 1868, one vote saved President Andrew Johnson from impeachment.
In 1876, one vote changed France from a monarchy to a republic.
In 1876, one vote gave Rutherford B. Hayes the presidency of the United States.
In 1933, one vote gave Adolph Hitler leadership of the Nazi Party.
In 1960, one vote changed in each precinct in Illinois would have denied John F. Kennedy the presidency.

Source: March Fong Eu, California Secretary of State, 1984. Quoted in Janet Riggs. 1995, March. *Good News.* RUMC, Rochelle, IL.

Role of the Citizen

Students must learn that freedom is accompanied by the *responsibilities of citizenship*. As such, students need to develop personal skills (Engle and Ochoa 1988). Students must learn to express their own personal convictions. This includes being able to communicate their own beliefs, feelings, and convictions. Being able to adjust their own behavior in group situations is yet another skill. Group interaction skills need to be honed so that they can contribute to a supportive climate in working in small or large groups. Another group interaction skill is the ability to participate in making rules and guidelines as well as to be a good group leader or follower. Being able to delegate tasks and duties in addition to organizing, planning, making decisions, and taking an action are other group interaction skills, all of which lend themselves to strong workplace skills when the students enter the workforce.

Interpreting events is one aspect of being a good citizen. In recent years, critical literacy has been advocated in classrooms to involve students in reading not only the social studies textbook but supplementary texts and historical novels. Sharing news clippings, having access to CNN.com and other Internet news Web sites, bringing in news magazines, and the like is needed to expand the students' knowledge of the world by sharing community, state, national, and international events with elementary and middle school students. The idea is for students to develop an understanding that text yields meaning as opposed to containing meaning. Thus students recognize that reading and writing are necessarily interpretive events. By having students engage in student-choice research projects and take social action they understand that reading and writing are part of the habits, customs, and behaviors that shape social relations (Behrman 2006).

A good citizen keeps informed on issues that affect society. Hence the classroom teacher should make certain that students are abreast of the news—local, state, national, and international. Events should be shared on a developmental basis. For instance, in early 1999, the impeachment trial of President Bill Clinton involved several aspects that parents and teachers had difficulty addressing. However, the impeachment issue depended on two very simple issues that elementary and middle school students could readily understand: (1) Did the president lie under oath? and (2) Did he try to cover up his lies? In a national poll of fourth graders taken during the impeachment trial, the children surveyed overwhelmingly voted that President Clinton should be removed from office because he lied.

Social Action Projects

Another social and participation skill that students need to develop is the ability to identify situations in which they themselves should take social action. This may be a service learning project that the class undertakes such as cleaning up a neighborhood park and planting flowers or collecting money through a recycling program (Wade 2000). A class of fifth graders decided to show their support for a fellow student who had cancer by cutting their own hair. The boys got "buzz cuts" while the girls had their hair trimmed. The result was the boy felt he was a part of the group rather than the only one with no hair. Obviously, such a drastic move required that the teacher take part in the hair cutting himself as well as get parental input and support for the students' decision.

Another service learning project example is the Saving Black Mountain Project. Upon learning that the highest peak in Kentucky was slated to be strip mined, students first interviewed miners and mining company officials as well as environmentalists in order to take an informed position on the issue. They visited the mountain on a field trip and took water samples from local wells, which they had tested as part of a science lesson. They then undertook a more assertive role by raising thousands of dollars in donations. Local media (newspapers, radio and television stations) were contacted for press conferences. A ten-page proposal was sent to the appropriate state agency suggesting alternative recommendations. A group of students and their teacher appeared before a subcommittee of the state legislature. Due in part to the efforts of these young students, a compromise solution was adopted by the state of Kentucky and Black Mountain was saved (Powell, Cantrell, and Adams 2001).

If elementary and middle school students are given proper guidance and supervision, they can research social action projects to be able to take an informed position on the issue. Through their social action activities, they can influence changes in their community.

Studying Great Leaders

Studying great leaders such as Indira Gandhi, Martin Luther King, Jr., Nelson Mandela, Golda Maier, and Franklin Delano Roosevelt helps middle schoolers understand and experience the power of language as each of these leaders' rhetoric influenced thinking of citizens and mobilized them into action (Sisk 2002). Biographies should be used to supplement the social studies textbook in order for students to gain in-depth understanding. Songs by contemporary pop artists can provide students with "politically contextualized understandings of issues related to the environment, history, economics, politics, and racism" (Behrman 2006, 492).

When students are encouraged to work individually or with others to decide on a course of action, they are taking responsibility for improving society. By assisting or guiding them, the teacher can point out ways in which they can influence those individuals who are in positions of power to strive for extensions of freedom, social justice, and human rights (Engle and Ochoa 1988).

Civic Life, Politics, and Government

Students need to have the opportunity to "learn and practice essential citizenship skills, respect for human dignity, and the value of the democratic process" (National Council for the Social Studies 1996, 307). Elementary students need to grasp the elements of democratic rules. By middle school, students need to understand other forms of governance such as monarchy, autocracy (as in a dictatorship), military rule, oligarchy (rule by a small group of people), and parliamentary rule.

A thought-provoking book for upper elementary and middle schoolers is *To Establish Justice: Citizenship and the Constitution* (McKissick and Zarembka 2004). Citizens rights as well as the rights of immigrants, women, and minorities are explored. Varying arguments and consequences are examined. This is a particularly timely book in light of the discussions on immigration. As the first ten amendments to the Constitution, the Bill of Rights is a fundamental part of American life and citizenship. To help middle school students understand the basic principles of the Bill of Rights, a good book to share as a read-aloud is Russell Freedman's (2003) *In Defense of Liberty: The Story of America's Bill of Rights*. Freedman explains the need for the Bill of Rights and how each amendment was developed and adopted.

To introduce the three branches of government—**executive, legislative, and judicial branch**—it may be best to create an equilateral triangle for students to visualize that each branch is responsible for certain duties and tasks: the legislative branch passes laws and approves budgets; the executive branch requests funding and carries out and enforce the laws; and the judicial branch enforces the laws. A good book for first and second graders that introduces some of the various tasks a president engages in is *So You Want to be President?* (St. George 2004). The legislative branch can be examined through a picture book that is targeted toward third and fourth graders entitled *My Senator and Me: A Dog's View of Washington, D.C.* by Senator Edward Kennedy (2006). The book describes how a bill, in this case one supporting education and schools, makes its way through Congress. While it simplifies legislative matters, youngsters are taught that a bill first starts as an idea, then goes through the legislative process and is voted upon and signed by the president before it is enacted.

Students can put government into practice by developing their own panel or council. As a longstanding activity to promote and encourage citizenship, a student council can have many different duties, such as conflict res-

President Harry S. Truman campaigns from a train in Fargo, ND. A study of changes in presidential campaigning as part of technological developments is a good project for middle schoolers.

olution. It can also demonstrate democratic processes by having members elected to the council by their peers. J. R. Bolen (1999) went a step further and developed a student **government** based on the model of the three-branch U.S. government at La Mesa Middle School in La Mesa, California. The legislative branch consisted of a Senate and a House of Representatives. Since the middle school was divided into seven teams of learners separated by grade levels, the students decided it would be logical to treat each team as being the equivalent of a state. Each team elected two senators who represented them in the Team Senate. Each team was divided into four to six smaller advisories, each of which elected a representative to the House of Representatives. Three committees were created for the Senate and another three for the House of Representatives. The Senate and House of Representatives met together in joint session to vote on the approval of any bills that came through the committee structure.

The judicial branch was comprised of a panel of four student members and three members of the school staff, including the principal or vice principal of the school. The Judiciary Panel had to abide by the student conduct rules of the school and school district. A case heard by the Judiciary Panel included a situation where the president pro tem of the Team Senate was suspended from school for fighting.

☞ **IN THE CLASSROOM**

The Three Branches of Government

A children's book that describes in detail the executive, legislative, and judicial branches of government is Betsy and Giulio Maestro's (1996) *Voice of the People: American Democracy in Action*. This nonfiction book is appropriate for fifth through eighth graders as it describes the functions of each of the three branches of government. It also goes into great detail in explaining how the president of the United States is elected, including how political conventions and the electoral college work.

Students can be assigned to report on various aspects of the democratic process. For instance, small groups or pairs of students could be assigned to the following topics: House of Representatives, the Senate, how bills are passed, the president's duties and powers, the Supreme Court, the chief justice of the Supreme Court, the appellate court system, and so forth.

Source: Maestro, B., and G. Maestro. 1996. *Voice of the People: American Democracy in Action*. New York: Morrow.

Under the school code, a student suspended from school cannot take part in any extracurricular activities such as student government. The Judiciary Panel ruled that the student could not participate in student government since the Student Body Constitution stated that a member could be removed from office for not fulfilling his or her duties.

The third branch of student government was the executive branch. The students decided to divide the executive branch into two parts: an Executive Board consisting of the president and other officers elected annually by popular vote and the Student Council, which was made up of the Executive Board, cabinet members (who were appointed by the Executive Board), and elected team leaders (governors). The executive branch had limited power under this structure and served to support legislative acts and oversee student activities. The executive branch was responsible for holding bimonthly school spirit assemblies and informing the student body of current events.

As an active and functioning legislative body, a variety of bills were passed by the legislative branch, including the School Safety Act, which directed that students were not allowed to mentally or physically harass other students on their birthdays. Just the airing of this as a problem proved to be a major step for the student body and student behavior changed as a result. Not only was the effective enactment of legislation confirmed, but also the inherent nature of politics in governance. One student asked Mr. Bolen if he supported another person's bill, whether he or she could have the other person vote for his or her bill. Mr. Bolen told the student that this was appropriate and was known as lobbying. Obviously learning about government through active participation helps students to gain insights about governmental processes.

☞ IN THE CLASSROOM

Civic Commitments

Civic dispositions are those attitudes and habits of mind that enhance the individual's ability to participate competently and responsibly in the political system.

I. Civility
Treating others with respect.
Addressing the issue rather than launching personal attacks in public debates.
Respecting the rights of others to be heard.

II. Individual responsibility
Citizens should take responsibility for themselves and their actions.

III. Self-discipline
Citizens freely follow the fundamental rules of the American system without requiring the imposition of external authority.

IV. Civic-mindedness
There are times when citizens should place the common good above their personal interests.

V. Open-mindedness
Citizens should be open to considering opposing positions or modifying their own positions. This does not mean that all views are of equal value.

VI. Compromise
Conflict of principles may require compromise with others to attain an acceptable solution. Some matters are unfit for compromise because they threaten the continued existence of constitutional democracy.

VII. Toleration of diversity
Respect for the rights of others who differ in ideas, ways of life, customs, and beliefs is based on an understanding of the benefits of such diversity within the community.

VIII. Patience and persistence
Forming or changing public policy usually requires a great deal of time and persistent effort.

IX. Compassion
Empathy with others and concern for their welfare are attributes of citizens in a society devoted to the common good.

X. Generosity
Spending time, effort, and resources in a civic context benefits others and the community at large.

Reprinted with permission from Center for Civic Education. *Civitas: A Framework for Civic Education.* 1991. Pp. 14–35. Calabasas, CA,

Developing Critical Thinking Skills

While the development of thinking skills has been addressed in an earlier chapter (see chapter 6), civics education necessitates that students develop the higher-level thinking skills to make judgments and evaluations. The inquiry process of constructivism, sometimes referred to as the scientific method or problem solving, is one approach teachers can use to have students develop new generalizations and correct faulty ones. Students engage in observing, questioning, and even challenging what they already know as they develop a new generalization that is accurate. The teacher sets the stage by providing sets of data surrounding a problem for the students to consider. Students then create their own hypotheses about the likely cause of an event, what is generally true in some area of society, or what might solve a problem. Then the teacher designs a series of activities such as simulations, review of newspaper articles, and so on in which the students gather data to confirm or dispute their hypotheses. As the students collect the information, some pieces will be discarded if they are not relevant (Parker and Jarolimek 2003).

Perhaps the easiest and most relevant way to introduce students in third grade through eighth grade to critical thinking is by having a unit on political advertising during elections. Share Web sites and videotapes of television ads with your class. Have the students try to determine which statements are facts and which are opinions; through their efforts they will begin to understand the need to have valid data. At this point, the various types of propaganda approaches can be introduced. They are:

- Appeal to the elite—the advertiser uses flattery to persuade the listener to buy something.
- Bandwagon—the ad appeals to people's desire to belong to a group.
- Card stacking—the ad presents only one side of an issue.
- Glittering generality—the ads make broad and dazzling claims but they are not backed up with facts.
- Name-calling—the ad, usually political, calls something or someone else by a negative term.
- Plain folks—the ad is designed to appeal to the common person.
- Rewards—"free" prizes or reduced costs are advertised.
- Testimonial—a well-known person serves as a product spokesperson.
- Transference—the ad features a famous person using the product.

Observing and studying propaganda techniques can help students develop a sensitivity to what is factual and what is opinion or fiction. Second graders can identify basic propaganda techniques such as name-calling (which occurs on the playground) or rewards. By fourth grade, students should be able to identify the use of the bandwagon, card stacking, and testimonials. The remaining propaganda techniques can be addressed in fifth grade. For middle schoolers, films, recordings, and posters of political ads from World War II from the U.S. Army, Nazi Germany, and Tokyo Rose can serve to distinguish how propaganda was used during the war both at home and abroad.

The Right to Vote

Citizens' freedom in a democracy carry with it certain rights and responsibilities, including the right to vote. Americans are used to knowing the winner of a presidential election by the following day, thus the delay of the 2000 presidential election results by several weeks was a bit unsettling. However, the American people waited out the counting and recounting process patiently. There were no uprisings or rebellions. Indeed, such was not the first time that a presidential election was not settled in a quick fashion. In the election of 1800, the decision was delayed as the Electoral College voted and voted and voted again. The Federalists, predominantly from New England and the middle-Atlantic states, supported John Adams for a second term. Alexander Hamilton, a New York statesman and creator of the Bank of the United States, led a powerful group of Electoral College members who did not want a Virginian such as Vice President Jefferson to garner the presidency. However, on the sixth day, Hamilton broke the stalemate by releasing his members to vote for Thomas Jefferson as the third president of the United States.

Many elementary and middle schools serve as precinct polling locations for local, state, and national elections. The week prior to the election is often a time when teachers present civic lessons on the right to vote. Topics may include suffrage, voting rights of African Americans, and the lowering of the voting age from 21 to 18. Typically, a mock election is held with the students all participating as "citizens." Students can be selected to serve as prominent candidates (such as presidential, senatorial, or gubernatorial candidates) and present their views on political issues. Teams of students can serve as assistants to the candidate, making posters, helping locate information and data, as well as drafting the final speech to the "citizens." Other students can serve as election judges and news media.

Civics and the Other Social Sciences

Civics education deals with people and their governance, but governance is not something that happens in a vacuum, and decisions that have wide-ranging effects can vary depending on the ideology of the decision makers. Thus, who gets elected affects all the social sciences, including history, economics, and geography. Certainly history has been changed by elections; a liberal politician will take a nation in one direction while his or her conservative counterpart will take it in quite another. Negotiations between leaders may result in redefined boundaries for fishing, thereby affecting the economies of the nations involved. Government policies have resulted in numerous groups leaving their homelands to seek better lives in other countries. A great Web site for history and civics is the History Channel's http://www. historychannel.com/classroom/index.html. Another good Web site is MCI Worldcom's Marco Polo site at http://marcopolo.mci.com/home.aspx, which contains lesson plans across subject matter.

Science, Technology, and Civic Education

Citizenship education has been affected by advancements in media. Long gone are the handwritten accounts of events that were the basis for newspaper articles. Now, even when a local candidate gives a speech, it is recorded on audio and videotape. When the president presents the annual state of the union address it is broadcast live into our living rooms. On the campaign trail, candidates are under

438

☞ IN THE CLASSROOM

**Grades K–4 Content Standards—
National Standards for Civics and Government**

I. WHAT IS GOVERNMENT AND WHAT SHOULD IT DO?
   A. What is government?
   B. Where do people in government get the authority to make, apply, and enforce rules and laws and manage disputes about them?
   C. Why is government necessary?
   D. What are some of the most important things governments do?
   E. What are the purposes of rules and laws?
   F. How can you evaluate rules and laws?
   G. What are the differences between limited and unlimited governments?
   H. Why is it important to limit the power of government?

II. WHAT ARE THE BASIC VALUES AND PRINCIPLES OF AMERICAN DEMOCRACY?
   A. What are the most important values and principles of American democracy?
   B. What are some important beliefs Americans have about themselves and their government?
   C. Why is it important for Americans to share certain values, principles, and beliefs?
   D. What are the benefits of diversity in the United States?
   E. How should conflicts about diversity be prevented or managed?
   F. How can people work together to promote the values and principles of American democracy?

III. HOW DOES THE GOVERNMENT ESTABLISHED BY THE CONSTITUTION EMBODY THE PURPOSES, VALUES, AND PRINCIPLES OF AMERICAN DEMOCRACY?
   A. What is the United States Constitution and why is it important?
   B. What does the national government do and how does it protect individual rights and promote the common good?
   C. What are the major responsibilities of state governments?
   D. What are the major responsibilities of local governments?
   E. Who represents you in the legislative and executive branches of your local, state, and national governments?

IV. WHAT IS THE RELATIONSHIP OF THE UNITED STATES TO OTHER NATIONS AND TO WORLD AFFAIRS?
   A. How is the world divided into nations?
   B. How do nations interact with one another?

V. WHAT ARE THE ROLES OF THE CITIZEN IN AMERICAN DEMOCRACY?
   A. What does it mean to be a citizen of the United States?
   B. How does a person become a citizen?
   C. What are important rights in the United States?
   D. What are important responsibilities of Americans?
   E. What dispositions or traits of character are important to the preservation and improvement of American democracy?
   F. How can Americans participate in their government?
   G. What is the importance of political leadership and public service?
   H. How should Americans select leaders?

Reprinted with permission from Center for Civic Education. National Standards for Civics and Government. © 1994. Pp. 15–83. Calabasas, CA.

☞ **IN THE CLASSROOM**

Grades 5–8 Content Standards—
National Standards for Civics and Government

I. WHAT ARE CIVIC LIFE, POLITICS, AND GOVERNMENT?
   A. What is civic life? What is politics? What is government? Why are government and poli-
   tics necessary? What purposes should government serve?
   B. What are the essential characteristics of limited and unlimited government?
   C. What are the nature and purposes of constitutions?
   D. What are alternative ways of organizing constitutional governments?

II. WHAT ARE THE FOUNDATIONS OF THE AMERICAN POLITICAL SYSTEM?
   A. What is the American idea of constitutional government?
   B. What are the distinctive characteristics of American society?
   C. What is American political culture?
   D. What values and principles are basic to American constitutional democracy?

III. HOW DOES THE GOVERNMENT ESTABLISHED BY THE CONSTITUTION EMBODY
    THE PURPOSES, VALUES, AND PRINCIPLES OF AMERICAN DEMOCRACY?
    A. How are power and responsibility distributed, shared, and limited in the government
    established by the United States Constitution?
    B. What does the national government do?
    C. How are state and local governments organized and what do they do?
    D. Who represents you in local, state, and national governments?
    E. What is the place of law in the American constitutional system?
    F. How does the American political system provide for choice and opportunities for partic-
    ipation?

IV. WHAT IS THE RELATIONSHIP OF THE UNITED STATES TO OTHER NATIONS AND
   TO WORLD AFFAIRS?
   A. How is the world organized politically?
   B. How has the United States influenced other nations and how have other nations influ-
   enced American politics and society?

V. WHAT ARE THE ROLES OF THE CITIZEN IN AMERICAN DEMOCRACY?
   A. What is citizenship?
   B. What are the rights of citizens?
   C. What are the responsibilities of citizens?
   D. What dispositions or traits of character are important to the preservation and improve-
   ment of American constitutional democracy?
   E. How can citizens take part in civic life?

Reprinted with permission from Center for Civic Education. National Standards for Civics and Government.
© 1994. Pp. 15–83. Calabasas, CA.

the microscope regarding their positions on major issues and their own personal behavior. When a candidate announces in Des Moines that he or she is in favor of funding more agriculture programs or says in Los Angeles a tax break would be healthy for the economy it is heard throughout the country.

Due to the fast dissemination of information, election results predictions can be precarious. Should the states' results for the presidency be reserved until all states, including Alaska and Hawaii, have closed their polls? Exit polls were so inaccurate during the 2000 presidential election between George W. Bush and Al Gore that some news networks flip-flopped their predictions throughout the evening, leaving NBC news anchor Tom Brokaw to say, "We don't have egg on our faces, it's an omelet."

While elections have met with changes due to technological advancements, there are political and citizenship issues that involve economics and technology. Consider urban sprawl that has usurped thousands of acres of farms and wetlands. *Hoot,* a novel by Carl Hiaasen (2002), is the tale of a 13-year-old "eco-guerilla" who pits himself against developers who plan to destroy a part of the Florida wilderness home to tiny burrowing owls, transforming the land into part of suburbia. The author's gift for twisted humor coupled with the book's seriousness serve to make this a book students enjoy discussing. A good accompanying book is *Rainforest Explorer* (Nicholson 2002), written in the form of a journal kept by children on an imaginary trip to the Amazon River basin. The field-based science makes for an excellent interdisciplinary study.

Character Education

Character education has been around for centuries. Historically, many leaders such as Aristotle, Quintilian, Muhammad, Martin Luther, Johann Herbart, Horace Mann, and John Dewey advocated character education in schools. Numerous labels have been used for character education including values clarification, moral education, transmission of cultural values, and socialization. Terms commonly used in character education include the following:

Character—refers to a person's moral constitution or a cluster of virtues.

Ethical—refers to universal standards and codes of moral principles.

Moral—the rightness or wrongness of something based on what a community believes to be good or right in conduct or character.

Values—refers to what we desire, a sense of feeling about things.

Virtue—refers to moral qualities, such as courage or generosity.

According to Ella Burnett (2000), "We have a set of learned, internal norms that tell us what is appropriate behavior in a given setting and what is not. We are not usually aware of these norms, which are formed early in our upbringing. We use norms to make sense out of social experiences" (20). Character education helps children to acquire the norms of society.

Brain research by Daniel Goleman (1995) has found that children with what he refers to as **emotional intelligence,** or the ability to understand other people and manage their own emotions, are better able to get along with others. Goleman believes that all children can develop emotional intelligence. His research findings indicate that children with high emotional intelligence are better learners, have fewer behavior problems, feel better about themselves, and are better able to resist peer pressure. Goleman's research also indicated that such children were better at resolving conflicts and were happier, healthier, and more successful. They tended to possess empathy toward others and, as a group, were less violent than their peers.

Goleman has five basic skills of emotional intelligence. Children need to develop self-awareness of what they are feeling and why. A second skill is the ability to manage their own mood, like anger or stress. A third skill is self-motivation, or directing emotions and energy toward goals. The fourth skill is developing empathy toward others. And the last skill is handling relationships, understanding them, resolving conflicts, and being a friend. Some suggestions of activities to help students build their emotional intelligence include the following:

• Have the class visit a nursing home. Keep the visit short and cheerful.

• Have the class collect cartoons and jokes they like for a bulletin board.

• When a child uses a negative label, help the student think of the opposite word (i.e., lose/win, stupid/smart, crybaby/courageous).

• When a child makes a mistake, help the child figure out how to fix it.

• Have jobs in the classroom so students learn responsibility.

• When a child is frustrated and ready to give up, have the student think of two other ways to accomplish the task at hand.

• Have students play charades using body language to depict emotions.

• Have each student give a positive aspect about a topic (school, recycling, etc.).

Critics of character education argue from two viewpoints. Some argue that schools are not teaching **moral principles** and **values.** Other critics state that the values taught in schools are different from their own. **Human rights** is rarely discussed in the elementary curriculum.

R. Freeman Butts (1988) believes that students should be taught the rights and obligations of citizenship. According to Butts, obligations of citizenship include justice, equality, authority, participation, truth, and patriotism. Rights of citizenship in a democratic society include freedom, diversity, privacy, due process, property, and human rights. A primary mission of public school education has long been and continues to be **citizenship education** (Allen and Stevens 1998). The Center for Civic Education (1994, 12) describes effective citizenship as being values for the public good and those of freedom, diversity, and individual rights: "We believe that civic virtue embraces thinking and acting in such a way that individual rights are viewed in light of the public good and that the public good includes the basic protection of individual rights."

Activities for character education begin with kindergartners as we teach them the Pledge of Allegiance. This pledge is the sharing of values, principles, and beliefs that Americans share. Symbols of the shared values, principles, and beliefs of Americans include the flag, the Statue of Liberty, Uncle Sam, the bald eagle, and the national anthem. In addition, certain holidays such as Labor Day, Thanksgiving, Veterans Day, Martin Luther King, Jr.'s, Birthday, and Presidents' Day should be celebrated and discussed with students. As mentioned earlier, character education at the kindergarten level also includes respect for others and their property. This gets into the rights as well as the obligations of individuals.

How we treat others is an important aspect of character education. A book that primary children enjoy is *Snail Started It* by Katja Reider (1998). This circular story includes a lesson about the use of harmful words that hurt others' feelings. Virtue is explored in *The Paper Dragon* (Davol 1998), a book for primary and intermediate levels. This book includes the Chinese characters for courage, loyalty, love, and sincerity that underscore the book's theme of love.

As students progress through the grades, they learn about other values, symbols, and principles of basic documents such as the Declaration of Independence, U.S. Constitution, and Bill of Rights. Students study national and state symbols. Students may nominate and vote on a classroom animal, flag, song, flower, tree, bird, and so on. These can be displayed in the classroom throughout the year.

Older students can delve into the obligations and rights of citizenship. For instance, to open February and Black History Month, a fourth- or fifth-grade teacher may want to share *From Slave Ship to Freedom Road,* a picture book by Julius Lester (1998). The book presents several scenarios about the lives of slaves, from their capture in west Africa to their escape along the Underground Railroad. The author points out that millions of Africans were captured and chained in very confined quarters on the slave ships, placed side by side on wooden shelves like stacks of books. Those who died during the three-month voyage across the Atlantic Ocean to the New World were tossed overboard. So many dead bodies were thrown overboard that sharks swam alongside slave ships. In the book, Lester provides imagination exercises for African Americans and white people. Engaging students in the simulations presented in the book will help students examine their own feelings and values. For black students, Lester challenges them for being resentful that they are descendants of slaves. For white students, Lester dares them to consider how they would feel if a space ship landed and took them away from their parents and later sold them to people to be their slaves and do their work without pay. As slaves Africans weren't even allowed to keep their own names as their owners would give them new ones. How would students react to this kind of exploitation? At the end of the book, Lester defines freedom as having several meanings. Freedom is "to be responsible for oneself and one's time; to own oneself; to be one's own master; and, as a promise we are still learning how to keep" (38). This leads well into a class discussion of freedom as a right. The following two picture books tie in well: *A Place Called Freedom* (Sanders 1998) is a story of a family of freed slaves who settle in Indiana. Each winter the father helps slaves escape and settle near them. The community takes the name of Freedom. *The Strength of These Arms: Life in the Slave Quarters* (Bial 1998) shows haunting photographs of the stark contrast between the homes of the plantations owners and the slave quarters.

The civil rights movement of the 1950s and 1960s is another major topic of study for social studies. In the lower grades, sharing such books as *Martin's Big Words* (Rappaport 2001), the story of Martin Luther King, Jr., and *The Story of Ruby Bridges* (Coles 1995), the story of how Ruby Bridges became the first African American child to attend an all-white New Orleans school, can help students better understand the hardships and prejudice that African Americans encountered. Intermediate-level students can reflect upon Pam Muñoz Ryan's (2003) *When Marian Sang: The True Recital of Marian Anderson* and Russell Freedman's (2004) *The Voice that Challenged a Nation: Marian Anderson and the Struggle for Equal Rights.* Both picture books portray the world renowned opera singer's return to America when she was denied permission to perform in Constitution Hall because she was not white. With the aid of Eleanor Roosevelt, wife of then President Franklin D.

Roosevelt, Anderson performed an outdoor concert at the Lincoln Memorial. This incident is cited as being one of many pivotal events in African American civil rights.

Seventh- and eighth-grade students may read Chris Crowe's (2003) informational book, *Getting Away with Murder*, about Emmett Till, a 14-year-old African American boy from Chicago who was visiting his relatives in Mississippi. On a dare, he whistled at an attractive young woman, the wife of a grocery store owner. A few nights later, Emmett Till was taken from his bed by a group of white men and murdered. His body was later found floating in a river. An excellent pictorial overview of the period is *A Dream of Freedom: The Civil Rights Movement from 1954–1968* (McWhorter 2003). *Promises to Keep: How Jackie Robinson Changed America* (Robinson 2004), a book for middle schoolers, illustrates the burden the young baseball player had when he became the first African American major league baseball player. Racial slurs were hurled at him and he had to perform beyond the normal expectations of a new player. Another book for the middle school level is *Face Relations: Eleven Stories About Seeing Beyond Color* (Singer 2004). *Face Relations* presents both happy and sad stories, but all are thought provoking about contemporary teenagers and the commonplace situations and friendships they encounter.

Marian Anderson

Character Education and Children's Literature

Character education can help create a safe, positive school and community environment. It also increases students' social competence and reduces students' aggressive behaviors as they develop values and ethics (Curtis-Seinik et al. 2006). A number of selections of children's and young adult literature are useful tools in teaching character education. Students can explore the dilemmas protagonists face and relate such situations to real-life experiences they themselves have encountered or predicaments that may arise in the future. A simple book that all kindergarten and first graders can identify with is *Courage* (Waber 2002). A young boy finds bravery in going to bed without a night-light, riding his bicycle the first time without training wheels, and believing in his dreams. Waber defines courage as what we give each other—a good lesson to help build classroom community.

Character development takes a twist in Walter Dean Myers's (2002) *Handbook for Boys: A Novel* that middle schoolers will relish. The proprietor of a Harlem barbershop is appointed by the court to supervise two troubled teenagers. The elder man conveys a strong message that a good future is built on hard work and dependability as well as sustaining one's dreams.

An informational book on civic activism is *Generation Fix: Young Ideas for a Better World* (Rusch 2002), which presents solutions children and teenagers have created on their own, including organizing after-school programs for inner-city schools to planting vegetable gardens to help feed the homeless.

Having students consider different perspectives is one aspect of character education.

Books with Character Education Themes

Through literature, children can gain vicarious experiences and learn about character and virtue. *When I Grow Up* (Harper 2001) is great for grades 1–3 as children share positive character traits such as being brave, understanding, adventurous, thoughtful, generous, and confident. *Gettin' through Thursday,* a picture book by Melrose Cooper (1998), tells the story of Andre, who dreads Thursdays. His mother gets paid on Fridays and by Thursday the family has little or no money left. If Andre makes the honor roll, his mother promises to give him a party. Andre is pleased until he realizes that report card day falls on a Thursday. But his family plans an imaginary celebration with an imaginary cake and candles for Andre to blow out. They even give him make-believe presents. The next day is payday and the family has a real party. Children can relate to this warm story as they themselves have had to wait until payday so their family can afford to buy something they dearly want. Another good book about character is *The Ballad of Lucy Whipple* (Cushman 1996). Lucy's parents dream of living in California. When Lucy's father and little sister die, her mother takes the remaining children to California during the gold rush. Lucy hates the idea of living in California and works to save money to return east. After encountering a former slave and numerous people from different walks of life who had come in search of their own dreams, Lucy decides she is needed in California. She stays and opens a library.

Following is a brief list of children's books that focus on character together with their descriptions:

Gilson, J. 2002. *Stink Alley.* New York: HarperCollins. Set in Leiden, Holland, in the year of 1614, orphan Lizzy Tinker, age 12, belongs to a group of religious refugees (the Pilgrims) led by William Brewster. Encouraged to lead a plain life, she meets up with a little boy, young Rembrandt, who is irreverent and naughty but who possesses great artistic talents and loyalty. When the two of them uncover a spy plot, Lizzy has to question her basic beliefs about lying. (Gr. 4–7, honesty)

Halpin, M. 2004. *It's Your World—If You Don't Like It, Change It: Activism for Teenagers.* New York: Simon and Schuster. An informational book that offers suggestions and guidelines to teenagers in becoming active citizens in order to improve their community. (Gr. 6–8)

Lafaye, A. 2002. *The Strength of Saints.* New York: Simon & Schuster. In 1936, deep in the depths of the Great Depression, young Nissa and her family struggle in Harper, Louisiana, a racially divided town. A cannery is built by a group of northern businessmen. When the cannery offers to hire both blacks and whites, racial tensions are stirred and the ire of Ku Klux Klan members is aroused. Nissa herself must decide whether to permit blacks to use her library. (Gr. 6–8, respect for others)

Silverman, E. 1994. *Don't Fidget a Feather.* Illus. S. D. Schindler. New York: Macmillan. Gander and Duck are so full of self-adulation that they hold contests to see who is the best swimmer and who can fly the highest. Then they decide the real winner will be the one who can freeze in place and not "fidget a feather." But this contest results in Fox taking Gander and Duck back to his stew pot determined to cook Gander. Duck must decide if winning a contest is worth losing a friend. (Gr. K–8, friendship, loyalty)

Spinelli, J. 2002. *Loser.* New York: Joanna Colter Books. A boy fails at everything and is given the moniker of "Loser." Throughout his elementary school years he is mocked. When a child mysteriously disappears, "Loser" sets out to find the youngster, becoming the town hero. (Gr. 4–7, respect for others, courage)

Every year numerous children's books are published that have themes based on character and/or citizenship. Keeping in close contact with the school librarian or the children's literature buyer at a local bookstore can be helpful to teachers looking for additional reading materials in this social studies strand. Following is a list of children's books that focus on character and citizenship:

Armstrong, W. H. 1989. *Sounder.* New York: Harper & Row. (Gr. 7–8, respect, caring, citizenship)

Bauer, M. D. 1986. *On My Honor.* New York: Clarion. (Gr. 6–8, trustworthiness)

Brewster, P. 1988. *Bear and Mrs. Duck.* New York: Holiday House. (Gr. K–3, diversity)

Bunting, E. 1983. *The Wednesday Surprise.* Boston: Houghton Mifflin. (Gr. K–4, understanding, respect)

Clements, A. 2002. *The Jacket.* Illus. M. Henderson. New York: Simon & Schuster. (Gr. 4–7, justice, understanding, respect)

Cohen, B. 1983. *Molly's Pilgrim.* New York: Lothrop, Lee & Shepard. (Gr. K–3, citizenship)

Cowen-Fletcher, J. 1994. *It Takes a Village.* New York: Scholastic. (Gr. K–5, citizenship)

Flournoy, V. 1985. *The Patchwork Quilt.* New York: Dial. (Gr. K–3, respect)

Fox, P. 1984. *One-Eyed Cat.* New York: Bradbury. (Gr. 6–8, responsibility, trustworthiness)

Garland, S. 1998. *My Father's Boat.* New York: Scholastic. (Gr. K–3, citizenship, responsibility, family)

Giff, P. R. 1998. *Lilly's Crossing.* New York: Delacorte. (Gr. 5–7, citizenship, responsibility)

———. 2002. *Pictures of Hollis Woods.* New York: Random House. (Gr. 7–9, responsibility)

Hale, S. 2005. *Princess Academy.* New York: Bloomsbury. (Gr. 5–7, courage, strength)

Hemphill, P. M. 1991. *Sally Thomas: Servant Girl.* New York: Winston-Derek. (Gr. 4–6, citizenship, responsibility)

Hiaasen, C. 2002. *Hoot.* New York: Knopf. (Gr. 5–8, responsibility, citizenship, courage)

Kingsolver, B. 1993. *Pigs in Heaven.* New York: HarperCollins. (Gr. 8, justice, fairness)

Lester, H. 1999. *Hooway for Wodney Wat.* Boston: Houghton/Walter Lorraine. (Gr. K–2, acceptance of others)

Lionni, L. 1973. *Swimmy.* New York: Knopf. (Gr. K–1, friendship)

Lovell, P. 2001. *Stand Tall, Molly Lou Melon.* New York: Putnam. (Gr. K–3, self-confidence)

Lowry, L. 1994. *The Giver.* Boston: Houghton Mifflin. (Gr. 6–8, citizenship, justice, responsibility)

Martin, A. M. 2002. *A Corner of the Universe.* New York: Scholastic. (Gr. 5–8, responsibility)

Murphy, J. 1990. *The Boys' War.* New York: Scholastic. (Gr. 4–8, courage, citizenship)

Park, B. 1995. *Mick Harke Was Here.* New York: Scholastic. (Gr. 4–6, courage, responsibility, family)

Park, L. 2001. *A Single Shard.* Boston: Clarion. (Gr. 5–8, hard work, perseverance)

Paterson, K. 1991. *Lyddie.* New York: Lodestar. (Gr. 6–8, courage, responsibility)

Rathmann, P. 1995. *Officer Buckle and Gloria.* New York: Putnam. (Gr. K–2, responsibility, citizenship)

Rohrmann, E. 2002. *My Friend Rabbit.* New York: Millbrook. (Gr. K–2, friendship, loyalty)

Sachar, L. 1998. *Holes.* New York: Farrar, Straus & Giroux. (Gr. 7–8, justice, responsibility, courage)

Shannon, D. 1998. *No, David.* New York: Scholastic. (Gr. K–2, responsibility, caring, family)

Silverstein, S. 1964. *The Giving Tree.* New York: HarperCollins. (Gr. K–5, caring)

Seuss, Dr. 1940. *Horton Hatches the Egg.* New York: Random House. (Gr. K–1, trustworthiness)

Taylor, M. 1976. *Roll of Thunder, Hear My Cry.* New York: Dial. (Gr. 5–8, fairness, justice)

Taylor, T. 1969. *The Cay.* New York: Doubleday. (Gr. 5–8, respect, caring, trustworthiness)

Wagner, K. 1998. *A Friend Like Ed.* Boston: Walker. (Gr. K–2 friendship)

Walsh, J., and S. Williams. 1992. *When Grandma Came.* New York: Puffin Books. (Gr. K–3, family, caring, responsibility)

White, E. B. 1952. *Charlotte's Web.* New York: HarperCollins. (Gr. 3–5, fairness, responsibility, caring, friendship)

Woodson, J. 2005. *Show Way.* New York: G. P. Putnam. (Gr. 5-8, strength, determination)

Character Building

Developing character means that certain character traits are valued. For kindergartners and first graders, honesty and goodness are traits readily embraced. Second graders may stress the importance of respect for others, while third and fourth graders may emphasize the need to contribute one's best effort on a group project. Certainly character traits have been debated for centuries.

Sharing literature with strong character traits often involves discussing how the book relates to oneself (text to self), another book (text to text), or to the world (text to world). The classic *Charlotte's Web* (White 1952) presents several admirable character traits: friendship, love, honesty, unselfishness. And some not so honorable: greed, self-centeredness, unfeeling, inconsiderate. This is a superb read-aloud for second and third graders as they contemplate their own character development. After each chapter the teacher should pull out significant statements regarding character and share them on an overhead projector. After the class discusses each statement, the sentence could be written on a sentence strip and stapled to the bulletin board. Here are some sample character statements from *Charlotte's Web:*

"Do you want a friend, Wilbur?" it said. "I'll be a friend to you" (31).

"Wilbur was merely suffering the doubts and fears that often go with finding a new friend" (41).

"Underneath her rather bold and cruel exterior, she had a kind heart, and she was to prove loyal and true to the very end" (41).

"The rat had no morals, no conscience, no scruples, no consideration, no decency, no milk of rodent kindness, no compunctions, no higher feeling, no friendliness, no anything" (47).

"He would kill a gosling if he could get away with it—the goose knew that. Everybody knew it" (47).

"But I'm not sure Templeton will be willing to help. You know how he is— always looking out for himself, never thinking of the other fellow" (89).

"The crickets felt it was their duty to warn everybody that summertime cannot last forever" (113).

"He has a most unattractive personality. He is too familiar, too noisy, and he cracks weak jokes" (135).

"It is not often that someone comes along who is a true friend and a good writer. Charlotte was both" (184).

One study of character traits can easily be coupled with the study of World War II. The heroism of soldiers, fighter pilots, and field nurses has been well-documented as well as citizens who found themselves in the way of the Nazi and Japanese war machines. Anne Frank's (1952) diary included several poignant statements regarding character. Consider the following entries in her diary.

> "Whoever is happy will make others happy too. He who has courage and faith will never perish in misery!" (March 7, 1944).

> "[Daddy] said, 'All children must look after their own upbringing.' Parents can only give good advice or put them on the right paths, but the final forming of a person's character lies in their own hands" (July 15, 1944).

> "In spite of everything I still believe people are really good at heart" (July 15, 1944).

Have students select one of Anne Frank's statements and write a justification for it based on their own encounters with others.

Several Web sites focus on character building. Plato's Matching Game (http://www.pbskids.org/adventures/treasurebox/concentration/index.html) for third- and fourth-grade levels familiarizes students with the language of character traits by having them match words. Identifying Respectful Behavior (http://www.charactercounts.org/ideas/ACW/ACW-Ideas-9-11/) has fourth through sixth graders work together in groups to identify what constitutes respectful behavior toward other individuals. Using poetry to express feelings and emotions is the emphasis of Strategies for Empowering Students—I Am Me and Nobody Else (http://www.urbanext.uiuc.edu/ce/strat119.html). This Web site is targeted at fourth through eight graders. Two middle school Web sites that concentrate on character building are The Identity Game's Spin Me a Student (http://www.educplace.com/activity/spin/html), in which students examine their responsibilities, skills, and talents and use them to create a fun visual model, and A Letter to Myself (http://www.educplace.com/activity/spin/html), which requires students to set new personal goals at the beginning of each semester by writing themselves a letter stating how they will meet those goals.

Other Character and Civic Education Sources

Fortunately civic education has several Web sites that can be bookmarked for future reference. The Center for Civic Education (http://www.civiced.org) is perhaps the best known and most recognized organization within social studies circles in the United States. It provides free lesson plans and lists the National Standards for Civics and Government. This Web site also has numerous links to other Web sites that emphasize civic education. The Constitutional Rights Foundations (http.//www.crf-usa.org) is a nonprofit, nonpartisan organization that designs programs and curriculum materials for K–12 teachers and students. It has a mock trial program and a program entitled Sports and the Law, which illustrates issues related to law and society. Another good Web site is CongressLink (http.//www.congresslink.org), which was designed by the Dirksen Congressional Center in Pekin, Illinois, and includes lesson plans, online historical materials, and a list of Web sites especially selected for teachers. C-SPAN in the Classroom (http://www.c-spanclassroom.org) has some outstanding lesson plans, including some with significant speeches appropriate for upper elementary and middle school levels. There are teacher's guides and suggested student projects. This site has "An American Presidents Scavenger Hunt" that includes information on all 43 presidents.

Human Rights

The Convention on the Rights of the Child (CRC), an international treaty, was adopted by the United Nations in 1989. The three main categories that are included are (1) the right to provision of basic needs such as food, shelter, and health care; (2) the right to protection from exploitation, armed conflict, and other threats to health and safety; and (3) the right to participation through expression of opinion, access to information, or in practice of one's culture, religion, and language. Human rights education encourages students to become responsible citizens. For instance, "Children learn to respect the rights of others in a classroom where guidelines are established cooperatively, expression of opinion is encouraged and taken seriously, problems are discussed openly, and responsibilities are shared by all" (Schmidt and Manson 1999, 3).

Both theory and research support the idea that children will express different forms of empathy as they grow older. Teachers can encourage a child to think and act in empathic ways by "acknowledging prosocial statements and behaviors, providing instruction about sharing and being considerate of others, and modeling nurturing behavior and kindness toward others in their classrooms" (Glover and O'Donnel 2003, 17).

Many children's books share the importance of human rights. The picture book *Uncle Willie and the Soup Kitchen* (DiSalvo-Ryan 1991) gives students an introduction to a community soup kitchen where volunteers work to feed those less fortunate. After sharing this book, students may collect canned goods to be used in a soup kitchen or food pantry for disadvantaged members of the community. *Rosa* (Giovanni 2005) is a beautifully depicted picture book that accurately portrays Rosa Parks as a civil rights activist and how she refused to give up her seat on a bus to a white man. This event resulted in the boycott of buses by African Americans in Montgomery, Alabama, and has been noted as the beginning of the civil rights movement.

What it is like to be an orphan in a foreign country and adopted by an American family is shared in the warm story *I Love You Like Crazy Cakes* (Lewis 2000). The author describes how she and her husband adopted an infant Chinese girl who had been given up by her family under the Chinese government's "one family, one child" rule.

Students need to see that famous individuals can be generous to those who are less fortunate than they. Children interested in sports will enjoy *Lives of the Athletes: Thrills, Spills (And What the Neighbors Thought)* (Krull 1997), which tells what makes these individuals great sports figures and interesting human beings. Older children might enjoy learning about Gandhi and his campaign for self-rule using nonviolent means in *Gandhi, Great Soul* (Severance 1997). These books and others can help students understand the need for standing up for human rights for all people.

NCSS STANDARDS-LINKED LESSON PLAN

Walk in Their Shoes

Theme: Taking someone else's perspective

Source: Martha Brady, Northern Arizona University

Objectives:

• Students will reflect upon the lives of other individuals by examining the types of footwear presented.

• Students will make a connection by writing a story about the person and events that took place while the individual was wearing the shoes.

NCSS Themes:

   I. Culture

Materials: Eight pairs of different kinds of shoes (leather hiking boots, sandals, high heels, sneakers, wingtips, leather work shoes, moccasins, loafers, etc.), pencil and paper

Process: This activity should accompany a discussion about cultures.

• Display the eight pairs of shoes by placing them on a table where they can be seen at the front of the classroom. Ask the students the following questions:
Where do you think these shoes may have traveled?
What kind of person wore these shoes?
What did they look like?

• Ask a student to select the pair of shoes of a person who is courageous. Have the student give a reason why. Call on another student to do likewise. Then select another pair of shoes and ask the students what the wearer is like.

• Next, model for the students a short oral story about a pair of shoes and have the students guess which pair of shoes you were thinking about as you made up the story. Then have them give the cues that tipped them off.

• Then have a student select a pair of shoes (but not tell the other students which shoes) and share a quick oral story about what happened to the shoes before they got to your classroom. Again, have the students guess which pair of shoes.

• Finally, have the students go to their desks and write a story about one pair of shoes and the events that pair of shoes took part in.

Instructional Comments: Similar styles of shoes can be used. You may want to visit a resell clothing shop or ask friends and relatives to send any worn shoes your way. The important point is to get students to use point of view and see things from someone else's perspective.

Learning Styles Addressed: Verbal/linguistic, visual/spatial; interpersonal

Standards Addressed: Students express their thoughts through narrative and descriptive writing.

Extensions:

• Show pictures of people from a specific period in time (e.g., the westward movement, Great Depression, the gold rush in Alaska, the fleeing of Poles during World War II).

• Bring in samples of eyeglasses from different periods in history.

• Share pictures of different workers in the same profession throughout history (e.g., construction workers, farmers, actors)

Variations: For first and second graders, use different kinds of hats. Construction hard hat, baseball cap, nurse's hat, fast-food hat, etc.

Chapter Summary

The teacher plays an important role in assisting students in learning to become responsible citizen actors. By teaching about democracy and the rights and obligations of citizenship as well as serving as a role model, the teacher can help children learn the basic rudiments of a democratic government in early elementary school. By the intermediate and middle school grades, civic education and character education can be further refined. Harriet Lipman Sepinwall (1999, 5) writes about young children:

> They need to acquire and practice skills for resolving conflicts peacefully and for living together in a spirit of mutual cooperation and appreciation for the contributions of others. Teachers of young children have an opportunity to lay a foundation . . . which . . . can help to make this a better world.

Children's Literature Recommendations

Bateman, T. 2004. *The Bully Blockers Club*. Morton Grove, IL: Albert Whitman. Lotty is besieged by a bully, discovering that the bully changes tactics when adults are around. So Lotty forms a coalition of friends and names the group the "Bully Blockers Club." The club gets the attention of adults and the bullying stops. (Gr. K–3)

Bial, R. 1998. *The Strength of These Arms: Life in the Slave Quarters*. Boston: Houghton Mifflin. Photographs of plantation homes and slave quarters. (Gr. 3–8)

Coles, R. 1995. *The Story of Ruby Bridges*. New York: Scholastic. A picture book depicting the true story of how six-year-old Ruby Bridges became the first African American to attend an all-white school in New Orleans. (Gr. 1–6)

Cooper, M. 1998. *Gettin' through Thursday*. Illus. N. Bennett. New York: Lee & Low. Andre dreads Thursdays—the day each week when the family has no money. (Gr. 3–4)

Crowe, C. 2003. *Getting Away with Murder*. New York: Dial. An informational account of the incident that led up to the murder of Emmett Till and the resultant legal wrangling that acquitted the men who had murdered him. (Gr. 7–8)

Cushman, K. 1996. *The Ballad of Lucy Whipple*. New York: Clarion. Lucy balks at having to live in a California mining town during the gold rush. (Gr. 4–6)

Davol, M. W. 1998. *The Paper Dragon*. Illus. R. Sabuda. New York: Atheneum. Love, courage, loyalty, and sincerity are examined in this book. (Gr. 1–3)

DiSalvo-Ryan, S. 1991. *Uncle Willie and the Soup Kitchen*. New York: Morrow. Uncle Willie and his friends work as volunteers to help those less fortunate. (Gr. 1–5)

Frank, Anne. 1952. *Anne Frank: The Diary of a Young Girl*. New York: Doubleday. A young Jewish girl keeps a poignant diary as she hides from the Nazis. A classic to be read by all. (Gr. 6–8)

Freedman, R. 2003. *In Defense of Liberty: The Story of America's Bill of Rights*. New York: Clarion. An explanation of the Bill of Rights is presented in palatable terms that middle school students can understand. (Gr. 6–8)

———. 2004. *The Voice that Challenged a Nation: Marian Anderson and the Struggle for Equal Rights*. New York: Clarion. A portrayal of how opera singer Marian Anderson was denied the right to sing at Constitution Hall because she was an African American. (Gr. 2–5).

Fritz, J. 1987. *Shh! We're Writing the Constitution*. Illus. T. de Paola. New York: Putnam. The Constitutional Convention in Philadelphia is recreated in this historically accurate book. (Gr. 2–4)

Giovanni, N. 2005. *Rosa*. Illus. B. Collier. New York: Henry Holt. A picture book outlining the true story of how the bus boycott in Montgomery, Alabama, began when Rosa Parks refused to give up her seat to a white man. (Gr. 2–5)

Harper, C. M. 2001. *When I Grow Up*. San Francisco: Chronicle. Positive character traits (being dependable, optimistic, imaginative, fair) are shared by children. (Gr. 1–3)

Hiaasen, C. 2002. *Hoot*. New York: Knopf. A young teenager fights a developer to prevent the takeover of a wildlife area that is home to owls. (Gr. 6–8)

Kennedy, E. 2006. *My Senator and Me: A Dog's View of Washington, D.C.* New York: Philomel. A picture book of how an idea becomes a bill and passes through Congress. (Gr. 2–5)

Krull, K. 1997. *Lives of the Athletes: Thrills, Spills (And What the Neighbors Thought)*. San Diego, CA: Harcourt Brace. A Notable Children's Book in Social Studies selection tells about the human side and generosity of famous athletes. (Gr. 2–5)

Lester, J. 1998. *From Slave Ship to Freedom Road*. Illus. R. Brown. New York: Dial. Through simulations and vivid paintings, what it was like to be a slave is portrayed in this moving book. (Gr. 4–8)

Lewis, R. 2000. *I Love You Like Crazy Cakes*. New York: Little, Brown. An infant Chinese girl is adopted by American parents. (Gr. K–2)

McKissick, P., and A. Zarembka. 2004. *To Establish Justice: Citizenship and the Constitution*. New York: Knoft. This book is a guide to demonstrate what the U.S. Constitution has meant. It answers basic questions such as who is a citizen and what are the rights of citizens. (Gr. 5–8)

McWhorter, D. 2003. *A Dream of Freedom: The Civil Rights Movement from 1954 to 1968*. New York: Scholastic. A historical overview of the civil rights movement. (Gr. 5–8)

Moss, P. 2004. *Say Something*. New York: Tilbury House. After silently observing a number of different types of bullying a young girl finds herself as a victim. (Gr. 2–5)

Myers, W. D. 2002. *Handbook for Boys: A Novel*. New York: HarperCollins. An older barber is given custody of two troubled teenagers and teaches them the value of hard work and keeping their dreams alive. (Gr. 6–8)

Nicholson, S. 2002. *Rainforest Explorer*. New York: Tangerine/Scholastic. A fictitious journey down the Amazon River is described through journal entries. (Gr. 4–7)

O'Neill, A. 2002. *The Recess Queen*. New York: Scholastic. When a girl dictates that no one gets permission to swing on the swings or slide on the slides, the other kids are intimidated. Then a new girl comes to school and challenges the "Recess Queen." (Gr. K–2)

Rappaport, D. 2001. *Martin's Big Words*. New York: Jump the Sun Publishers. Depicts the life of Martin Luther King, Jr. (Gr. 1–3)

Reider, K. 1998. *Snail Started It*. Illus. Angela von Roehl. New York: North-South Books. Six characters learn a lesson on the use of harmful words. (Gr. K–2)

Robinson, S. 2004. *Promises to Keep: How Jackie Robinson Changed America*. New York: Scholastic. This biography provides insights into the personal side of Jackie Robinson as he broke into the big leagues as the first African American professional sports star during the early years of the civil rights movement. (Gr. 6–8)

Rusch, E. 2002. *Generation Fix: Young Ideas for a Better World*. New York: Beyond Words. The efforts of 15 young people to better the world are shared. (Gr. 5–8)

Ryan, P. M. 2003. *When Marian Sang: The True Recital of Marian Anderson*. New York: Scholastic. Beautifully illustrated picture book that describes Marian Anderson's concert at the Lincoln Memorial in 1939.

St. George, J. (2004). *So You Want to be President?* Illus. D. Small. New York: Philomel. Background facts and humorous incidents along with the actual presidential oath of office are shared in this picture book for primary students. (Gr. 1–3)

Sanders, S. R. 1998. *A Place Called Freedom*. Illus. T. B. Allen. New York: Atheneum. Families of freed and runaway slaves settle in Freedom, Indiana. (Gr. 4–7)

Severance, J. B. 1997. *Gandhi, Great Soul.* New York: Clarion. The life of Mahatma (which means "great soul") Gandhi is documented accompanied by numerous photographs. (Gr. 6–8)

Singer, M. 2004. *Face Relations: Eleven Stories About Seeing Beyond Color.* New York: Simon and Schuster. Stories by noted authors depict contemporary issues that confront today's teenagers. (Gr. 7–8)

Waber, Bernard. 2002. *Courage.* Boston: Houghton Mifflin. With each decision, a youngster moves toward bravery as he sleeps for the first time without a night-light and rides his two-wheeler without training wheels. (Gr. K–1)

White, E. B. 1952. *Charlotte's Web.* Illus. G. Williams. New York: Harper & Row. A moving story of the friendship between a spider and a pig. Should be shared with all children. (Gr. 2–4)

Related Technology Tools

Web Sites
Kids Voting

http://www.kidsvotingusa.org

Kids Voting USA is a nonprofit, nonpartisan, grassroots organization dedicated to securing democracy for the future by involving youth in the election process today.

Center for Civic Education

http://www.civiced.org

Add this Web site for the Center for Civic Education to your computer's favorites. Contains activities pertaining to the U.S. Constitution including Constitution Day. E-books about the Constitution and other topics may be accessed by elementary and middle school students.

Civic Mind

http://www.civicmind.com

This law-related site teaches civics lessons using core documents of American government. Check out the teachers' center and the library of Supreme Court cases and historical documents.

Presidential Libraries and Museums

http://www.nara.gov

Begin by accessing the National Archives and Records Administration (NARA) Web site, which provides links to all the technology resources in the system.

National Archives

http://www.archives.gov/index.html

Home of the nation's important documents, by clicking onto this site students may view such documents as the original Declaration of Independence and the U.S. Constitution as signed by our forefathers.

WebQuests
Ben's Guide to Government for Kids (Contains different materials for various grade levels: Gr. K–2, 3–5, and 6–8)

http://bensguide.gpo.gov/

How a Bill Becomes a Law (Gr. 4)

http://www.ccsd.edu.mis/jim/weblessons/fourthgrade/law/index.htm

Software and Videos
Three Branches of American Government. Teacher's Video Company. Available from www.teachersvideo.com.

Citizenship and State Government. 2001. Teacher's Discovery. Available at 800-543-4180. A 137-page ring binder complete with activities, progress charts, sample letters, a calendar planner, state government resources and much, much more.

The Bill of Rights Video Series. 2000. Teacher's Discovery. Available at 800-543-4180. Individual videos also available. Titles include: *To Keep and Bear Arms, Students' Right to Privacy, One Nation Under God, For Which it Stands,* and *Sentenced to Die.*

References

Allen, M. G., and R. L. Stevens. 1998. *Middle Grades Social Studies.* 2nd ed. Boston: Allyn & Bacon.

Becker, J. 1992. "A New World Order." *Educational Leadership* 49 (5): 83–84.

Behrman, E. H. 2006. "Teaching about Language Power, and Text: A Review of Classroom Practices that Support Critical Literacy." *Journal of Adolescent and Adult Literacy* 49 (6): 490–98.

Bolen, J. R. 1999. "Taking Student Government Seriously." *Middle Level Learning* January/February (4): 6–8.

Burnett, E. M. G. 2000. "Conflict Resolution: Four Steps Worth Taking." *Social Studies and the Young Child* 12 (3): 20–23.

Butts, R. F. 1988. *The Morality of Democratic Citizenship: Goals for Civic Education in the Republic's Third Century.* Calabasas, CA: Center for Civic Education.

Center for Civic Education. 1994. *National Standards for Civics and Government.* Calabasas, CA: Author.

Curtis-Seinik, C., M. McCarthy, K. Nadal, D. Pfeiffer, A. Tella, and N. Wagner. 2006. "Character Education, K–12, in Uniondale." *Social Studies and the Young Learner* 19 (1): 27–29.

Engle, S., and A. Ochoa. 1988. *Education for a Democratic Citizenship.* New York: Teachers College Press.

Fernlund, P. M. 1997. "Civic Education: Building Participation Skills in a Democratic Society." In *Elementary and Middle School Social Studies: A Whole Language Approach,* 2nd ed., ed. P. Farris and S. Cooper, pp. 207–28. Boston: McGraw-Hill.

Glover, R. J., and B. K. O'Donnel. 2003. "Understanding Human Rights! The Development of Perspective-Taking and Empathy." *Social Studies and the Young Child* 15 (3): 15–18

Goleman, D. 1995. *Emotional Intelligence: Why It Can Matter More than IQ.* New York: Bantam.

Metzger, D. 2000. "Young Citizens: Partners in Classroom Management." *Social Studies and the Young Learner* 12 (4): 21–23.

National Council for the Social Studies. 1996. "NCSS Guidelines and Principles for Student Government: NCSS Position Statement." *Social Education* 60 (5): 307.

Neal, L. I., and A. L. Moore. 2003. "When Bad Things Happen to Good People: Human Rights at the Core." *Social Studies and the Young Child* 15 (3): 1–4.

Parker, W. C. 1989. "Participatory Citizenship: Civics in the Strong Sense." *Social Education* 53 (6): 353–54.

Parker, W. C., and J. Jarolimek. 2003. *Social Studies in Elementary Education.* 12th ed. Upper Saddle River, NJ: Prentice-Hall.

Powell, R., S. C. Cantrell, and S. Adams. 2001. "Saving Black Mountain: The Promise of Critical Literacy in a Multicultural Democracy." *The Reading Teacher* 54 (7): 772–81.

Rasmussen, K. 1999 (Winter). "Social Studies: A Laboratory for Democracy." *ASCD Curriculum Update* 1–3, 8.

Schmidt, J., and P. Manson. 1999. "Human Rights Education: A Framework for Social Study from the Interpersonal to the Global." *Social Studies and the Young Child* 11 (3): 1–4.

Sepinwall, H. L. 1999. "Incorporating Holocaust Education into the K–4 Curriculum and Teaching in the United States." *Social Studies and the Young Learner* 11 (3): 5–8.

Sisk, D. 2002. "Critical Literacy Can Help in These Troubled Times." *Understanding Our Gifted* 14 (2): 24–25.

Tyson, C. A., and S. C. Park. 2006. "From Theory to Practice: Teaching for Social Justice." *Social Studies and the Young Learner* 19 (2): 23–25.

Wade, R. C. 2000. "Beyond Charity: Service Learning for Social Justice." *Social Studies and the Young Learner* 12 (4): 6–9.

Educational efforts to improve fundamental mathematic and problem-solving skills can foster knowledgeable consumers who can take full advantage of the sophisticated financial services offered in an ever-changing marketplace.
> —Alan Greenspan, "The Importance of Financial and Economic Education and Literacy"

Chapter Thirteen

Economics Education
Ways and Means

Jill E. Cole, Wesley College;
Richard A. Fluck, Northern Illinois University;
Steven L. Layne, Judson College

■ CHAPTER OUTLINE

CHAPTER OBJECTIVES

Readers will

- understand that economics is based on the concept of scarcity;
- understand that students need to develop decision making in order to become good consumers; and
- be able to incorporate literature in the teaching of economics.

Introduction

A stay-at-home mom in a small town in Indiana opened the mail to find a credit card had been granted in her name. She hadn't requested the card nor the $10,000 credit line offered to her. She called the credit card company to ask a question: How can your company offer a $10,000 line of credit to a woman who has no job? The answer: This is America.

This story should not be surprising. The average American family is more indebted now than at any previous time in history. In the United States, money is easy to spend and everyone is encouraged to do so. Given the current status of economics in our country and the "spend now—pay later" mentality of a large portion of society, it is imperative that our children be educated to understand economics. The children of today are our only hope for change. If change is what we seek, then a working knowledge of economic systems, both past and present, is the best tool educators can provide.

Imagine for a moment that you have just arrived at an elementary school faculty meeting. The principal announces that everyone will spend time working on writing new curricular units during staff in-service days this year and provides a list of topics that need attention. Teachers are to volunteer for the topics they are most interested in researching. Chances are that if "economics" is one of the choices, there will not be an overabundance of volunteers. Economics is a subject area viewed by many adults as dull and highly technical. Many elementary teachers might feel that they "don't have the working knowledge to teach economics," yet they are actually seasoned professionals in using many of the economic principles that children in elementary school are ready to learn.

> Any time children choose from among two or more alternatives, they are making decisions that can be examined using what economists call an economic way of thinking . . . the discipline of economics is often described as the science of analyzing decisions and decision making. (Van Fossen 2003, 90)

This chapter shares information on the most significant tools available to assist teachers in communicating and expanding economic knowledge to their young charges. Through the use of good literature, you can help your students discover how much a million really is, what it was like to be a "street kid" and be sent west on the Orphan Train during the late 1800s and early 1900s because your family lacked food and shelter, what it would be like to live during the Great Depression, or how one grain of rice could turn a peasant into the richest man in all of Japan (Pittman 1986).

What Is Economics?

Economics is two things: a body of knowledge and a way of thinking (Banaszak 1987). It involves the questions of what, how, how much, and for whom. The analysis of what goods and services should be produced, how they are produced, how much is produced, and for whom the goods and services are produced is the study of economics (Allen and Stevens 1998; Warmke and Muessig 1980). In teaching economics to students, we are instructing them on the terms and concepts of the field, but also on a mind-set that will help them become successful consumers in our society. The study of **production, distribution, exchange,** and **consumption** is very important to help students understand the basics of economics, but these concepts need to be tied to the decision-making skills students will use as they grow to adulthood. We must keep in mind that the purpose for having our students study economics is to enable them to use the concepts in their real lives and become informed, competent citizens (Wentworth and Schug 1993).

Economics is based on a concern about **scarcity.** People often want more than the available resources can provide, and then decision-making skills become necessary (Dillingham, Skaggs, and Carlson 1992). It is important that students under-

☞ IN THE CLASSROOM

Economic Terms

Economics education can be divided into three facets: personal economics, consumer economics, and social economics.

Personal Economics

Personal economics deals with individual households, companies, and markets. Students should become aware of terms and concepts they need in the economics of their individual, day-to-day lives. Here are some examples of this category.

* Money—Students need to be aware that money can be used for good or poor choices. Decision-making skills involving money are crucial.

* Budgeting—Even young children can develop a budget for allowance money or class money. A budget answers the question: How am I going to spend this money?

* Banking—The basics of banking can easily be brought into the classroom via a field trip or a guest speaker. Other terms than can be taught while discussing banks are interest, credit, loans, checking accounts, and savings accounts.

* Careers—As students discuss personal economics, the topic of careers is sure to be broached. It's valuable to get students thinking about how they would like to earn a living when they are adults. Related terms are wages and benefits.

The next three terms give students some strategies for determining their personal choices and for using good decision-making skills. The terms themselves might not be used with younger children, but the concepts are very valuable.

* Scarcity—This refers to the situation where there are limited resources to meet unlimited wants. Decisions and choices must be made.

* Opportunity cost—This term describes a student's second choice for a scarce resource.

* Cost-benefit analysis—This is a decision-making process in which the student would weigh the benefits and costs of certain personal choices.

Consumer Economics

Older students who have had experience with personal economics are ready for an introduction to the second facet of economics, *consumer economics*. Consumer economics encompasses our nation as a whole and demonstrates how individuals and groups fit into our economy. Some valuable terms follow.

* Supply and demand—A teacher may use a balance scale to demonstrate supply and demand. As the demand for goods goes up, supply goes down. Then as the supply goes down (scarcity), prices go up, which in turn causes the demand to go down again. This reestablishes the balance.

* GNP—The gross national product is the sum total of goods available in the country. It can be a yardstick of the economy's performance.

* Consumption—the use of goods that have been purchased (e.g., the consumption of snack foods)

* Inflation—Students may be able to understand inflation through this scenario: If you buried $100 in the ground and dug it up ten years later, would you be able to buy more or less with that same $100? If you can buy fewer goods, inflation has occurred. Deflation has occurred if you can buy more goods.

* Stock market—Stocks are ownership of a company. Stocks go up and down based on the perceived value of the company. The stock market is where shares of stock are bought and sold.

- Goods and services—The following activity may help students understand the difference between goods and services. Ask each student what jobs his or her parents hold. On the chalkboard, categorize each job as providing a good or a service.

- Import/export—Our country imports goods from other countries, and we export goods to other countries. A demonstration may be held between two classrooms. One class has apples, the other has bananas. It would get boring eating only one kind of fruit, so one class imports bananas from the other class and exports their own apples. That way, both classes can enjoy both kinds of fruits.

Social Economics

A third facet of economics is *social economics.* Social economics refers to ways the economy affects or is affected by the conditions of our society. Some terms related to social economics include:

- War—Historically affects all societies by increasing the need for supplies and decreasing the available laborers. Rationing may occur so that needed goods are available for those involved in combat.

- Welfare—Society's system for providing necessities to those who are unemployed and lacking a source of income.

- Lottery—Instituted in some parts of the country as a way for local or state governments to fund various projects while promising an economic windfall to the correct ticket holder.

- Homeless—A condition of being without residence, which is becoming an increasing problem for which no viable solutions have been found.

- Wealth—Descriptor indicating a high level of economic and social status.

- Poverty—Descriptor indicating a low level of economic and social status.

- Inflation—A rise in price level related to an increased volume of spending and/or credit with a loss in the value of the currency.

- Depression—Economic condition in which employment, business, and stock market values severely decline.

stand that in making a decision, they are either acting on or reacting to the economy. Students need to be shown how good economic decisions can bring satisfaction and poor economic decisions can bring disappointment.

The determination of specific economic concepts most important to learn will vary by which economist or educator is being consulted (Laney 1993). This chapter provides lists of economic terms (see the boxes) that may be helpful in structuring an economic curriculum that focuses on the nurturing of decision-making strategies and the ability to make good choices.

Classroom Economics

The crux of economics is about choices and decision making. According to Dillingham, Skaggs, and Carlson (1992, 2), "It is not possible for all people to satisfy all their wants in a world of scarce resources; it is impossible to avoid making choices." Perhaps the teacher can take a moment and reflect on classroom routines already in place that would lend themselves to economic study and decision making. It may be surprising how many everyday classroom procedures can be related to economics with just a change in emphasis or a rearrangement of activities.

Sometimes all it takes is an aware teacher ready to teach economics through regular classwork, with just a word to the students to make them aware as well.

For example, as our classrooms make the journey from teacher directed to child centered, giving choices to students is essential. We are not leaving the classroom totally up to the students, but we are providing options so students can determine their preferences and priorities and make appropriate decisions. Every day, students are faced with choices. The advantages and disadvantages of each should be presented, discussed, and weighed. The students should then make the ultimate decision, and the consequences, whether good or bad, should be noted and discussed. Only through consistent practice can students gain the competence in decision making that will make the process easier and more successful for them as adults.

The classroom provides unlimited opportunities for decision making. Students can make choices of food and games to have at a class party, of poems or plays to learn and share with another class, of which friend to read with, or what topic to use for writing workshop. As students become competent at decisions such as these, they can be given even more responsibility in the classroom. Teachers may allow students a choice among books to be studied during reading workshop, various response activities to a book, the amount of time to be spent daily in sustained silent reading, and topics that the class will study together. The teacher may also want to provide math, social studies, and science manipulatives and activities for students to choose between to supplement their learning in those areas as well.

Class meetings are another vehicle that many teachers are using to include decision making and problem solving in the classroom. A short amount of time

Learning how to read and construct charts is part of economics instruction. These girls are tallying items by consumer demand within their class.

can be set aside daily, weekly, or on an as-needed basis for the teacher and students to gather and discuss the happenings of the classroom. Topics may include academic issues but are more likely to focus on social aspects of the classroom—fairness to all students, respect for diversity, kindness on the playground, rules of the classroom, and so forth. This is an excellent time for the teacher to model problem-solving language, decision-making techniques, and openness to diverse views. It's during a time like this, short as it may be, that students learn about their classroom as part of the bigger picture—that it is part of our American society and how they, as citizens, can live in this society successfully.

Economic education has been largely considered a discipline better suited for secondary students, not elementary and middle school students. In 1997, the National Council on Economic Education issued the *Voluntary National Content Standards in Economics.* Sixteen of these standards are appropriate for introduction at the elementary or middle school level. These standards "encompass the most important and enduring ideas, concepts, and issues in the field. Each is a principle of economics that economists, economic educators, and teachers consider essential for students to know" (Meszaros and Engstrom 1998, 7). The following list includes the sixteen content standards that apply to elementary and middle school curriculum along with a suggested children's book for each (Kehler 1998, 26–29; National Council on Economic Education 1997).

Content Standard 1: Productive resources are limited. Therefore, people cannot have all the goods and services they want; as a result, they must choose some things and give up others.
Hutchins (1986), *The Doorbell Rang*

Content Standard 2: Effective decision making requires comparing the additional costs of alternatives with the additional benefits. Most choices involve doing a little more or a little less of something; few choices are all-or-nothing decisions.
Williams (1983), *Something Special for Me*

Content Standard 3: Different methods can be used to allocate goods and services. People, acting individually or collectively or through government, must choose which methods to use to allocate different kinds of goods and services.
Cosgrove (1978), *The Muffin Muncher*

Content Standard 4: People respond predictably to positive and negative incentives.
Kroeger (1996), *Paperboy*

Content Standard 5: Voluntary exchange occurs only when all participating parties expect to gain. This is true for trade among individuals or organizations within a nation, and among individuals or organizations in different nations.
Viorst (1978), *Alexander, Who Used to be Rich Last Sunday*

Content Standard 6: When individuals, regions, and nations specialize in what they can produce at the lowest cost and then trade with others, both production and consumption increase.
Hall (1979), *Ox-Cart Man*

Content Standard 7: Markets exist when buyers and sellers interact. This interaction determines market prices and thereby allocates scarce goods and resources.
Jaffrey (1995), *Market Days: From Market to Market Around the World*

Content Standard 8: Prices send signals and provide incentives to buyers and sellers. When supply or demand changes, market prices adjust, affecting incentives.
Merrill (1972), *The Toothpaste Millionaire*

Content Standard 9: Competition among sellers lowers costs and prices and encourages producers to produce more of what consumers are willing and able to buy.
Hall (1997), *The Milkman's Boy*

Content Standard 10: Institutions evolve in market economies to help individuals and groups accomplish their goals. Banks, labor unions, corporations, legal systems, and not-for-profit organizations are examples of important institutions. A different kind of institution, clearly defined and well-enforced property rights, is essential to a market economy.
Giff (1994), *Count Your Money with the Polk Street School*

Content Standard 11: Money makes it easier to trade, borrow, invest, and compare the value of goods and services.
Wells (1997), *Bunny Money*

Content Standard 13: Income for most people is determined by the market value of the productive resources they sell. What workers earn depends, primarily, on the market value of what they produce and how productive they are.
Stevens (1995), *Tops and Bottoms*

Content Standard 14: Entrepreneurs are people who take the risks of organizing productive resources to make goods and services. Profit is an important incentive that leads entrepreneurs to accept the risks of business failure.
Seuss (1961), *The Sneetches*

Content Standard 15: Investment in factories, machinery, new technology, and the health, education, and training of people can raise future standards of living.
Mitchell (1993), *Uncle Jed's Barbershop*

Content Standard 16: There is an economic role for government to play in a market economy whenever the benefits of a government policy outweigh its costs. Governments often provide for national defense, address environmental concerns, defend and protect property rights, and attempt to make markets more competitive. Most government policies also redistribute income.
Hager and Pianin (1998), *Balancing Act*

Decision making should permeate the curriculum and become a natural process for students. The purpose of economics education is to help prepare students to make choices that will improve their lives, and one way to do that is to include the everyday aspects of economics and decision making in the students' classroom life.

Primary Thematic Unit: Money

A good place to begin teaching economic concepts to our primary students is with money. "Money is linked to changes in economic variables that affect all of us and are important to the health of the economy" (Mishkin 1995, 3). Even the youngest students have come in contact with money and its power. It is part of their own personal economics because it affects them in their everyday life. Since that is the case, it is never too soon to begin teaching not only how much each coin is worth, how to buy items, and how to figure change, but the economic significance of money as well.

The topic of money is taught from the preschool years on up. Most of the time the focus of the lessons is mathematically based, and students are encouraged to manipulate coins and bills in order to count, add, subtract, and exchange money correctly. We should be adding to this list activities that encourage thinking, defining choices, and making decisions. Although it is very important for students to be able to use money accurately, in our society today it is also crucial to use money wisely.

☞ **IN THE CLASSROOM**

Activities for Economics Lessons

Listed here are some additional ideas for bringing decision making and economics into the classroom.

1. Students can help decide on a money-making project for their class. They should be involved in every step of the project, including the decision of what to spend the money on when the project is complete.

2. Near Christmastime, let students write their Christmas wishes to Santa, and then have them prioritize the list and give reasons.

3. Set up a class store that has commonly needed items for sale: pencils, pens, erasers, crayons, and so forth. Students can use real money or class money they have earned through class activities to buy items they need. Keep the store running throughout the school year, stopping often to evaluate and discuss successes, failures, and changes that need to be made.

4. Have a class garage sale. Ask students to bring small items from home that they don't want anymore. They can make posters to advertise their booth, determine prices for their merchandise, and invite other classrooms to their sale. Throughout the activity, discuss supply and demand, goods and services, competition, propaganda, and the use of money.

5. Discuss the difference between using money and bartering. Let students experience both of these systems using the class store and discuss advantages and disadvantages of each.

6. Take a field trip to a local business and ask someone to explain the economic concerns of the business and perhaps how the students can participate or help.

7. Play board games that use money or economic concepts and discuss strategies and choices as the children play.

8. Give each student in the room a job and discuss how the jobs provide goods and services and how they interact with and support each other.

9. Bring in several travel brochures and travel sections from the Sunday newspaper, complete with hotel fees and airfares. Divide the class into groups of three students each, and give each group an imaginary $5,000 to spend on an imaginary vacation. Have each group plan a vacation and give reasons why they selected what they did. You may even arrange for a travel agent to visit the classroom at the beginning of the project.

10. Pair up students and give them each an imaginary $1,000. Give the students a conversion table for foreign currencies. Let the students choose a country and convert their $1,000 into the new currency.

The following examples of thematic units on money stress the importance of thinking about the use of money and the choices and decisions that go along with that process. It is our belief that the medium that can promote such thinking best is children's literature. However, although literature is presented as the base from which this unit grows, it can be used in addition to and entwined with the traditional mathematics unit on money that is often included in the primary curriculum.

Immersion in the Concept of Money

One effective way to introduce students to a concept is to immerse them in physical representations of the topic to be covered. In a classroom where the students are about to study money, you might display posters of coins and bills, money manipulatives set out for children to explore, books about money exhibited attractively, and poems about money on chart paper. There should be a mix of informational and fiction books, letting children know that the characters they read about offer interesting facts that also can be applied to their own lives.

As mentioned earlier, if the teacher takes the approach that the everyday routines of the classroom can be used to teach the topic at hand, money can become a part of the classroom. Story time can include books and poems relating to money, sharing time can encourage "money stories" from the children, and writing workshop can promote pieces where children describe some of their money-spending decisions. These pieces may then be dramatized to practice the use of concrete coins and dollars and to instill the notions of choices and decision making.

An especially powerful example of decision making and finance is a token economy. John Hail (2000) suggests setting up a token economy in the classroom to help students learn various economic principles such as making choices, scarcity, time and money, costs and benefits, and accepting responsibility. He tells students that they will earn one token a day for the rest of the year. They need to take care of their tokens, save, and spend wisely. Getting a drink, going to the restroom, and sharpening a pencil are examples of things that can cost the students tokens. Weighing costs and making decisions immediately come into play. As in a real economy, Hail recommends instituting new expenses, creating opportunities for employment, and enacting price increases as the school year progresses. Problems such as scarcity and disasters also can be built into the program. Time for reflection about the token economy needs to be set aside, perhaps in a class meeting. Discussion about the economic events and decision-making procedures taking place in the classroom are crucial to the students' understanding and to the teacher's insight into whether all students are learning and benefiting from the activity.

An intriguing way to entice upper elementary students is to introduce candy consumption. In 2000, the U.S. population consumed 7.1 billion pounds of candy with 3.3 billion pounds being chocolate candy. That same year sales of chocolate candy reached $13 billion with chewing gum sales of $2 billion. The top candy holiday is of course Halloween with nearly $2 billion in sales. During a two week period, students can track the class's consumption of candy bars, chips, soda pop, and gum. In addition, for each category they can identify the top products in sales (e.g., Snickers, Twix, M&Ms) as selected by classmates. Additional activities can be found at www.candyusa.org and www.hersheys.com to engage students.

Teaching the Concept of Money through Literature

One book that introduces money as well as the existence of choices and the necessity of decision making is *Alexander, Who Used to be Rich Last Sunday* (1978) by Judith Viorst. In this book, Alexander receives a dollar from his grandparents and then makes some choices about spending the money. At the end of the story, Alexander has no money left and is disappointed in the decisions he made. This is a wonderfully humorous book, but it also can encourage discussions of the choices Alexander made. Which were good choices and which were not? Which choices would the students have made themselves? What advice would they give Alexander? How would the students spend the money if they had received the same amount from their grandparents? How do they think Alexander will spend his money next time? Not only does this book provide rich exchanges concerning decision making, but it also includes money math as well. Each time Alexander spends money, the students can subtract the amount from the original dollar he received from his grandparents. A chart may be made to keep track of Alexander's expenditures with one column reserved for the class's opinion of the choice (see figure 13.1).

This book also lends itself to dramatization. One student could act out the part of Alexander while other children could play Alexander's brothers, parents, friends, grandparents, and the storekeepers he visits. Act One may show Alexander making the choices described in the book; Act Two may show the students making their own choices of how to spend the money and how Alexander's satisfaction with his choices could change.

Decision	Amt. spent	class opinion	Better choice
Bubblegum	15¢	OK	just buy one piece
Bets	15¢	poor	Don't bet!
Rented snake	12¢	good	—
Bad words	10¢	Very bad	Don't say bad words.

Figure 13.1 Young students can make a class economic chart to determine the best financial choices.

A book that combines mathematical facts about money and thinking strategies as well is David M. Schwartz's *If You Made a Million* (1989). Each page shows an amount of money from one penny to a million dollars and humorous ways to earn it. The book also introduces such concepts as interest, denominations of bills, checks, banking, loans, down payments, and income tax. It entices students to count money, compare it, and think about its use in our world today. The last page states that money involves choices, and the question posed to the children is, "What would you do with a million dollars?"

This certainly leads directly into a writing project. The students can make their own personal lists of what they would do with one million dollars and prioritize the list, thinking about what they value most and what they feel would constitute wise choices. Then they can move into small groups where they are instructed that they no longer personally have a million dollars, but that their group has a million dollars. Since they can't have all the items on their separate lists, some decision making is required. Which items will stay on the group's list and which will be abandoned? Then the class can reconvene and the students are advised once more that their groups do not have a million dollars, but their class as a whole does. Again, decision making comes into play, and choices have to be made. As the class discusses the situation, the students need to come up with those items that are going to stay on the list and those that can be left off. These choices can be prioritized on the board and a discussion can ensue about what the children find as the most important and valuable ways to spend a million dollars.

After this role-playing activity, it may be appropriate to present the class with some real money and an authentic decision-making situation. If the students have participated in a moneymaking project or have run a class store for a while, perhaps this is a good time to discuss some options for the profits. Encourage them to apply the knowledge they learned from the previous activity to the real-life choices they can make with the money their class actually has.

These are just a few of the books rich in ideas to teach the basics of money, weighing choices, and decision making. Other books that correlate with these subjects are included in table 13.1 (on the following page) and in the annotated bibliography at the end of this chapter.

Using Poetry to Teach the Concept of Money

Poetry can play a large role in helping children understand a variety of topics, money being no exception. Sharing poetry in the classroom can give students a new perspective on the topic as well as foster an ongoing enjoyment of poetry. The whimsical poem below can be an introduction to money that will capture children's imagination and prepare them to discuss money and what it means to them.

I Asked My Mother
I asked my mother for fifty cents
To see the elephant jump the fence.
He jumped so high that he touched the sky
And never came back 'til the Fourth of July.
—Anonymous

Table 13.1 Selected examples of children's literature for teaching economic concepts

Title (Author/Publisher)	Synopsis	Economic Concepts
Charlie Needs a Cloak (Tomie de Paolo, Prentice-Hall, 1973)	Charlie shears the sheep, cards the wool, dies the wool, and weaves to make a new cloak. (Gr. K–2)	factors of production, efficiency
The Confe$$ion$ and $ecret$ of Howard J. Fingerhut (Ester Hershenhorn, Holiday House, 2002)	Howard sets out to win the prize for being the top entrepreneur in his school. (Gr. 3–5)	barter, supply and demand, entrepreneurship
If You Give a Mouse a Cookie (Laura Joffe Numeroff, HarperCollins, 1985)	A little mouse shows up at a young boy's house. A cookie starts a chain of cause-effect events. (Gr. K–3)	unlimited wants, goods/services, sequencing
The Lorax (Dr. Seuss, Random House, 1971)	Despite the warning of the wise Lorax, the "Once-ler" uses up all the Truffula trees to make "thneeds." (Gr. 1–5)	scarcity, natural resources, factors of production, long-run versus short-run
Market! (Ted Lewin, Lothrop, Lee & Shepard, 1996)	Illustrations of marketplaces around the world. (Gr. 2–5)	market, barter, supply and demand
Pancakes, Pancakes (Eric Carle, Aladdin, 1998)	Before Jack can eat his pancake breakfast, he must cut the wheat to grind for flour, gather the eggs, milk the cow, churn the butter, and build a fire. (Gr. K–2)	productive resources, scarcity, opportunity cost, exchange
Uncle Jed's Barbershop (Margaret King Mitchell, Simon & Schuster, 1993)	An African American barber in the south saves enough money to open his own barbershop. (Gr. 2–5)	saving, factors of production, opportunity cost, entrepreneurship
Something from Nothing (Phoebe Gillman, Scholastic, 1992)	An adaptation of a Yiddish folktale. Joseph's grandfather makes something new out of Joseph's blanket, but Joseph must give up something first. (Gr. 1–2)	opportunity cost

Source: Adapted from P. J. Van Fossen. 2003. "Best Practice Economic Education for Young Children? It's Elementary." *Social Education* 67 (2): 90–94.

This next poem was cowritten by a first-grade class and their teacher. After reading many poems about money, they decided they wanted to write one of their own. As they did, they had some wonderful discussions about the significance of money and how the children proposed to use money in their everyday lives.

Money
Money, money, money, money,
Coins, a dollar bill.
Put some money in the bank
Save it if you will.
Money, money, money, money,
Penny, nickel, dime.
A quarter is twenty-five
And all of them are mine!

Another poem written by a nine-year-old comments on an everyday experience common to all schoolchildren—keeping track of lunch money. Students will certainly be able to commiserate with the poet and may be inspired to write their own lunch money "blues."

Lunch Money
I'm in the lunch line.
I have ten dollars. Ten is fine.
A bully takes two. That makes eight.
Eight's still great.
I trip and hit my knee, out falls three.
That makes five. Will I survive?
My friend begs me, so I give her three.
Now I have two. What will I do?
I give it to the lunch lady.
It is just enough.
Boy, getting lunch is really tough.
    —Nina, age 9

Additional poems related to money may be found in various poetry anthologies. Listed here are poems that students might enjoy.

"The Animal Store" by Rachel Field
"Barter" by Sara Teasdale
"The Coin" by Sara Teasdale
"The Falling Star" by Sara Teasdale
"The Fairies Never Have a Penny to Spend" by Rose Fyleman
"For Sale" by Shel Silverstein
"Market Square" by A. A. Milne
"Smart" by Shel Silverstein

Culminating the Unit on Money

As the students close their unit on money, it may be timely to expand their knowledge beyond their own classroom and into other countries around the world. Armstrong and Burlbaw (1991, 143) state that "money fascinates" and this may be even more true as students have the opportunity to look at currency from other countries. Although the primary student would not study foreign banknotes in detail, the understanding that money is used around the world (but may take different forms) helps the children develop an appreciation of various cultures, perhaps even some represented in the classroom.

Samples of foreign currency may be obtained from several sources. Students may have some coins or bills at home they could bring to school, or teachers, friends, and acquaintances may have some that could be borrowed. Put the word out around school and the community that you are looking for examples of foreign money, and you may receive plenty to culminate the class's study of money. Following is the address of a supplier where you may purchase selections of world banknotes or catalogs of world paper money. Catalogs may be available for as little as $1 and banknote selections for approximately $17 (Armstrong and Burlbaw

1991). An especially helpful guide available from Morris Lawing is *Collector's Guide and Catalogue of World Paper Money* by John Aeillo.

Morris Lawing
P.O. Box 9494
Charlotte, NC 28299

Suggested activities with world currency include finding locations on the map that match the foreign money the class is observing, using the pictures on paper money to determine things of value to that country, noting heroes of particular countries from their pictures on the money, listing differences and similarities between foreign and U.S. currency, and being aware of the fact that money can reflect a country's economic values and history. Through participating in these activities, students come to understand their own money system better, as well as learning about the world around them.

Although the thematic unit on money may be concluding in the classroom, the study of money and its relationship to economics can continue throughout the school year. Money, its power, and its problems come into students' lives daily. The choices and decisions facing students are unlimited and deserve the attention of the teacher sensitive to economic issues. As the teacher incorporates decision making into the fabric of the classroom routines, students study economics all year long.

Here are some additional titles relating to money:

Berenstain and Berenstain (1983), *The Berenstain Bears and the Trouble with Money*
Berger and Berger (2001), *Round and Round the Money Goes*
Briers (1987), *Money*
Elkin (1983), *Money*
Facklam and Thomas (1992), *The Kids' World Almanac of Amazing Facts About Numbers, Math, and Money*
Frank (1990), *Tom's Lucky Quarter*
Giff (1994), *Count Your Money with the Polk Street School*
Hoban (1987), *Twenty-Six Letters and Ninety-Nine Cents*
Leedy (2002), *Follow the Money!*
McMillan (1996), *Jelly Beans for Sale*
McNamara (1972), *Henry's Pennies*
Maestro (1993), *The Story of Money*
Maestro and Maestro (1988), *Dollars and Cents for Harriet*
Medearis (1990), *Picking Peas for a Penny*
Mitgutch (1985), *From Gold to Money*
Williams (1982), *A Chair for My Mother*
Zimelman (1992), *How the Second Grade Got $8,205.50 to Visit the Statue of Liberty*

Web Sites for Information on Money
www.treas.gov/topics/currency
www.making-sense.com
www.kidsbank.com
www.aplusmath.com/cgi-bin/flashcards/money

Intermediate Thematic Unit: The Mall of Life (Money)

Using the terminology introduced in the primary grades and expanding upon it in a spiral curriculum approach, fourth, fifth, and sixth graders can learn about money and balancing budgets by engaging in a week-long unit of study called the "Mall of Life." At the beginning of the week the students draw cards for jobs, a salary, and whether they are married, have children, or are single. Then they move around the room to various stations to purchase items (gas and oil change for their car, groceries, clothing, a trip to the doctor's office, a car dealership, a real estate agency to rent apartments or purchase homes, etc.). Much like a classroom version of a modern day Monopoly game, students learn how families have to budget their resources. Each station is manned by a parent volunteer.

In order to create a "Mall of Life," select possible jobs and salaries that might be existing in your local community for the job and salary cards. The salary cards list the take-home salary for the month. Have enough family cards (single without children, single parent with children, married, and married with children) to reflect an equal number for each possibility. Have a set of cards for health insurance, with half of the cards indicating it is being paid by the employer and the rest of the cards containing an amount to be paid by the participant. Print for each student 20 checks and staple them into a checkbook including a deposit form and a register for the checks to be recorded with the balance maintained. Next, set up the various sta-

E-commerce can be utilized in teaching economics by giving students a list of items such as iPods, sneakers, and sports equipment to "purchase" from sources on the Internet. They can then compile the best prices for the objects.

tions. Photos of cars and trucks along with prices and monthly payments should be provided at the "car dealership" station. Likewise, houses with 30-year mortgages at the current mortgage rate and rental apartments are portrayed at the "realtor" station. Grocery ads are taped to a wall. One station has all the utilities: cable, Internet, electricity, gas, water, and cell phone. Since cell phone rates vary, put different rates on cards and have students draw from the cards to determine how much their cell phone bill is. To make it even more motivating, there are some stations for entertainment—movies, pizza parlor, ice-cream sundaes, ball games, bowling, various priced vacations to Florida, Colorado, New York, Yellowstone, Europe, etc. A babysitter station has rates for the evening, the weekend, and a week. Students have to engage in all the stations. That is, they must buy a car, groceries, pay for their cell phone, and so on.

Sixth-grade teacher Pachia Tenpas-Rice found her students better understood their parents' monthly financial dilemmas by having participated in the "Mall of Life." She said she had students say, "I've only got $500 left and I still have to get a car." Tenpas-Rice was fortunate as one of her parents was a car salesman who volunteered to come in for the afternoon to negotiate monthly payments for the vehicles for the students. He found most of the kids were budget conscious and didn't go for the flashy vehicles but saved their money for entertainment and fun stuff (Klopf 2006).

Intermediate Thematic Unit: The Orphan Train

There have been five major U.S. migrations of homeless children, the most recent being the result of the devastation of Hurricane Katrina that hit Alabama, Mississippi, and Louisiana, causing the evacuation of the port city of New Orleans. The first was the Trail of Tears (1838–1839), which forced the relocation of thousands of Cherokee children and their families. The second migration was the Underground Railroad and occurred as a result of slavery, peaking in the years just prior to and during the Civil War. The third was the Orphan Train, which took place from 1853 through the early 1900s due to a lack of jobs. The fourth was the one thousand children who were relocated during the Holocaust from Europe to the United States from 1938 through 1945.

During the late 1800s and early 1900s, many children roamed the streets of large eastern cities. Homeless, abandoned, or orphaned children found themselves as penniless street urchins. Some had been separated in the confusion of the immigration process at Ellis Island. Older children of rural families who had drifted to cities to locate work but were often unable to find jobs found they had to fend for themselves. Others had lost their parents to illness. Still others had been abandoned when their fathers sought a new life in the West, leaving behind their families without financial resources. Mothers with limited or no work simply gave up their children. Often abused or neglected, these children of the streets struggled to survive by selling newspapers or shining shoes. Many resorted to theft or prostitution as a means of providing food and shelter for themselves and often younger siblings. There were no antibiotics, health insurance, sick leave, or labor unions. Many jobs were hazardous with serious accidents resulting in injury or even death. The situation was not unlike what is found today in third world countries.

With limited orphanages and foundling homes in New York City, Charles Loring Brace established the Children's Aid Society in 1853. He believed that the orphan problem could be resolved by "placing out" children by collecting them and sending them to the American West, which was in need of laborers for farms and ranches and for industry. Many families were eager to provide a foster home for a child who was willing to work. A hit or miss affair, many children bounced from one foster home to another with those deemed as "undesirable" being returned to New York City. Thousands of children were adopted by the families with whom they had been placed. Some families were wonderful and caring. Harsh conditions faced other foster children as they were expected to work hard and given little, if any, emotional support.

Between the years 1853 and 1929, over 250,000 children were "emigrated" out of eastern urban areas to the West. Orphan Train children faced the challenge of a new life in an unfamiliar environment and surroundings without the comfort of families and friends. While attempts were made to keep siblings together, it was not unusual for one to be placed in one location and another placed in a foster home in a neighboring, but far away, town or even state. Welfare and child protection laws were nonexistent (Betts 2006).

Upon their arrival at a rural town's rail depot, the Orphan Train children were viewed with a critical eye by prospective foster parents. Selection was not unlike that of the slave auctions of the 1600 and 1700s. Appearance and physical strength weighed heavily in who was and was not selected. Strong boys were needed for farm work. And, in some cases, attractive young girls were selected and sexually abused by foster fathers. Some orphans silently slipped away from the trains when they stopped for water and wood to replenish the steam locomotives and simply vanished. Others ran away from their foster homes.

The need to provide economic resources for children makes a study of the Orphan Trains one pertinent to elementary students. Orphans were sent to Illinois, Missouri, Wisconsin, Minnesota, North Dakota, South Dakota, Kansas, Iowa, Nebraska, and Texas. Estimates indicate that over two million descendents of the Orphan Train riders are alive today (Betts 2006). Below are books that share the problems of the orphans as they made new lives in the West.

Children's Books about the Orphan Trains

Bunting, E. 2000. *Train to Somewhere.* Illus. R. Himler. Boston: Houghton Mifflin. A wonderfully illustrated picture book telling of the apprehension of the orphans as they rode westward to new homes and lives. Terrific read-aloud to open a unit of study on the Orphan Trains. (Gr. 2–5)

Cushman, K. 2003. *Rodzina.* Boston: Clarion. Rodzina is a 12-year-old mean orphan, desperate for a home as she travels West in 1881 from Chicago to California. (Gr. 4–6)

Kerr, R. 1994. *The Texas Orphans: A Story of the Orphan Train Children.* Houston: Eakin Publications. Hundreds of children were taken to Texas by the Orphan Trains. This historical novel is based upon the events and challenges faced by some of them. (Gr. 3–5)

Nixon, J. L. 1996. *A Family Apart*. New York: Laurel Leaf. This historical novel depicts the struggle and heartache encountered when siblings are separated as part of the Orphan Train. (Gr. 4–8)

———. 1999. *A Dangerous Promise*. New York: Laurel Leaf. Another historical fiction novel in the Orphan Train series by Nixon, this one features an adventure. (Gr. 4–8)

———. 2000. *David's Search*. New York: Laurel Leaf. Young David leaves New York City on an Orphan Train to a new home with a compatible family in Missouri in 1866. The family is supportive of the woman's suffrage movement and has a former slave as its hired hand. But Missouri also has the Ku Klux Klan, which David encounters in a frightening experience. (Gr. 4–8)

Warren, A. 2000. *Orphan Train Rider*. Boston: Houghton Mifflin. A nonfiction account of one boy's experience as being an orphan and placed out West as part of the Orphan Train. (Gr. 3–6)

———. 2001. *We Rode the Orphan Trains*. Boston: Houghton Mifflin. A former Orphan Train rider disfigured from battle wounds suffered in World War I roams the community selling produce. (Gr. 2–8)

After reading aloud *Train to Somewhere* (Bunting 2000), give book talks about historical fiction novels focusing on the Orphan Trains, such as books in the Orphan Train series by Joan Lowery Nixon. Have the students select the book that interests them most and put them into literature circle groups (see chapter 7). Have the students each select two roles (word warrior, character captain, passage master, illustrator, summarizer, etc.) and perform one role for each half of the novel. A role may not be duplicated by another group member for the same half of the book. The students make the reading assignments in order to complete the novel and the roles over a two-week period. In addition, the group creates a presentation (reenactment of a scene, a television show such as *The View*, *Oprah*, or *This is Your Life*, or a game show) for the class. They rehearse and then share their presentation with the class (see chapter 14 for Orphan Train lesson plan on drama).

Intermediate Thematic Unit: The Great Depression

Vocabulary related to content area study can often be technical and intimidating. Students may feel that economic terms such as *inflation* or *depression* hold little relevance to their daily lives. Creating an interest and motivation in students to learn about economic concepts can best be achieved by incorporating literature into the curriculum.

The power of literature to put students in touch with another time and place is the vehicle by which even the most technical concepts may be introduced and explored. Students are more willing and able to learn the meanings of economic terms if they are able to associate them with their own lives, the lives of someone they know, or the experiences of a character they meet in a book. Careful integration of children's literature into a study of economics can ensure that every student will be able to relate to the concepts being studied.

One way of addressing some higher-level economic concepts is through a study of the Great Depression that began in the United States in 1929. The historical importance of the Great Depression is primarily due to the economic turmoil with which it is associated. Many students will find learning about economic principles easier if they can make comparisons between what they know about our economy today and what they understand it to have been like many years ago. Students can develop an understanding of the nation's economy during the Great Depression by looking at how it affected the lives of people who lived during those years. Good literature is one way to provide that understanding.

Introducing the Concept with Literature

A strength in the introduction of any concept is to begin with what the children already know. Often students will reveal their knowledge readily when they are relating to a story. A good read-aloud on the Great Depression is *Uncle Jed's Barbershop* (Mitchell 1993), which depicts the true story of an African American barber who loses his savings when his local bank collapses during the economic crisis. A perfect novel for a unit on the Great Depression is Mildred Taylor's *Song of the Trees* (1975). This book, Taylor's first, tells the story of the Logan family suffering through the Depression in rural Mississippi. The father has gone to Louisiana because there is no work in Mississippi, and a white man is pressuring the Logan children's grandmother to sell some of her land. This white man intends to chop down all the beautiful trees and, because of the Depression, is offering very little money for the land.

Quite early in the story, it is discovered that seven-year-old Christopher-John has been up at night eating cornbread. His mother gently chastises him and explains that the family must eat only when they are truly hungry. She gives her young son a simple explanation of the family's limited finances, including the reason why his father had left the family in Mississippi to go to work laying railroad tracks in Louisiana. This simple explanation of the family's economic situation and the concept surrounding it provides an easy introduction to the term *depression*. Students can then focus on other events from the story that they feel might be associated with the Depression.

Taylor's book is very short, making it an ideal springboard into the topic of the Great Depression. Teachers can introduce graphic organizers or other aids to assist students in charting information as they receive it. Economic terms appropriate for discussion following *Song of the Trees* include: unemployment, inflation, and depression. A good follow-up to *Song of the Trees* is Zilpha Snyder's *Cat Running* (1994), which describes the fate of rural children during the Great Depression. Homelessness and wanderers such as the Okies are depicted.

Advancing the Concept with Literature

It may be difficult for students today to directly relate to the desperation that comes with an economic depression. James Lincoln Collier's *Give Dad My Best* (1976) offers them the opportunity to vicariously experience the lengths to which poverty can drive an individual. Jack Lundquist is 14 years old and watching helplessly as his unemployed father allows poverty to overtake the family. Jack's father, a trombone player, made quite a living during the Roaring Twenties. Now the twenties are over and the widowed Mr. Lundquist spends his days waiting for things to get better.

Jack faces considerable inner turmoil as he watches his father lie to his sister, Sal, about buying her a dress for the school play. Later, Jack tries to quell his own fears that his father is spending the precious rent money on jazz albums and beer, until he learns that the family is about to be evicted. To keep the family together, Jack acts on an idea he has considered throughout the entire novel: theft.

Students will see in Jack how truly desperate life can become during an economic depression. When the hero of the novel is driven to thievery by forces beyond his control, the reader is forced to consider the causal factor. Collier's book prepares students to intelligently discuss an economic depression. This book offers teachers a tremendous opportunity for promoting critical thinking about economics by leading students into a discussion of how Mr. Lundquist might have planned his finances and spending more carefully prior to the Great Depression. Likewise, students may discuss the alternatives that they see for the family to remain together. Students may find, as they read and study further, that the alternatives they suggest may or may not have been possible during this time in history.

Phyllis Reynolds Naylor's *Walking Through the Dark* (1976) is a true testimony to the courage of people living in America during the 1930s. This novel provides a disturbing yet poignant look at the effects of the Great Depression on the Wheeler family. Ruth Wheeler, a young teenager, is sick of hearing about "hard times" as the novel opens. In a sense, Ruth is like many of our students; she is uninvolved and uninterested in economic events that have not directly affected her family.

As the story unfolds, Ruth and her family are forced to endure conditions they never could have dreamed possible. Each family member is forced into a form of humility that erases all distinction of economic status. The story is told in such a manner that readers cannot help but feel a sense of guilt for any abundance they enjoy.

Walking Through the Dark will give students a taste of just how devastating the effects of the Great Depression were. Phyllis Reynolds Naylor uses Ruth Wheeler's diary as an introduction to many chapters, and it is through this diary that we begin to see the growth and maturity that hard times often bring. Asking students to keep a character journal would be an ideal way of bringing students into a more affective relationship with the Wheeler family. In addition, this particular novel lends itself to the creation of a time line (see figure 13.2). Students creating a time line of the changes forced on the Wheelers by the economy are interacting with the text in a critical manner.

Extending the Concept with Literature

A name well-known in the field of children's literature is Milton Meltzer. His ability to represent America's past in simple language with attention to historical accuracy has garnered him praise from critics and numerous literary awards. Meltzer's (1969) *Brother Can You Spare a Dime?* is a nonfiction book based on eyewitness accounts of the Great Depression. Included in this book are detailed descriptions of life during the Depression from people who really lived through it, as well as photographs, songs, and political propaganda from the period. Although this type of information might not appeal to students initially, after experiencing the Depression through the characters in some fine pieces of literature students' interest levels are sure to be heightened.

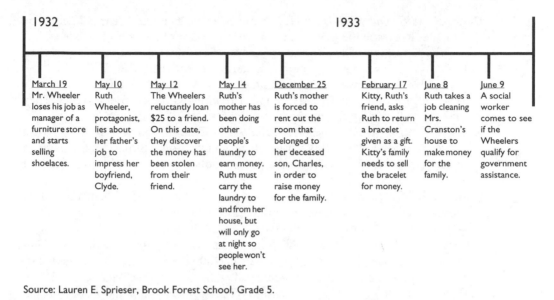

1932					1933		
March 19 Mr. Wheeler loses his job as manager of a furniture store and starts selling shoelaces.	**May 10** Ruth Wheeler, protagonist, lies about her father's job to impress her boyfriend, Clyde.	**May 12** The Wheelers reluctantly loan $25 to a friend. On this date, they discover the money has been stolen from their friend.	**May 14** Ruth's mother has been doing other people's laundry to earn money. Ruth must carry the laundry to and from her house, but will only go at night so people won't see her.	**December 25** Ruth's mother is forced to rent out the room that belonged to her deceased son, Charles, in order to raise money for the family.	**February 17** Kitty, Ruth's friend, asks Ruth to return a bracelet given as a gift. Kitty's family needs to sell the bracelet for money.	**June 8** Ruth takes a job cleaning Mrs. Cranston's house to make money for the family.	**June 9** A social worker comes to see if the Wheelers qualify for government assistance.

Source: Lauren E. Sprieser, Brook Forest School, Grade 5.

Figure 13.2 Chronological time line of the effects of the Great Depression on the Wheeler family. Lauren Sprieser, a fifth grader, created this time line as she read *Walking Through the Dark* (Naylor 1976).

If fictional characters—such as those previously mentioned—can become real to a reader, a natural motivation for learning is created because the reader cares about the people who are experiencing hardship. In Collier's book, students may find music to a song played by Jack's father in *Give Dad My Best* or see a photograph showing a room for rent like the one put out by the Wheelers in *Walking Through the Dark*. The literature used to introduce and advance students' knowledge now provides fuel for them to make connections with more complicated nonfiction material. Other novels based on the Great Depression are listed below:

Antle, N. 1993. *Hard Times: A Story of the Great Depression.* Illus. J. Watling. New York: Viking. This historical novel is about an Oklahoma family during the Great Depression. (Gr. 5–8)

Blumenthal, K. 2002. *Six Days in October: The Stock Market Crash of 1929.* New York: Atheneum. Terrific overview of the collapse of the stock market in 1929. (Gr. 5–8)

Curtis, C. P. 1999. *Bud, Not Buddy.* New York: Delacorte. A young boy searches for his grandfather, a musician, during the Great Depression. (Gr. 5–8)

Evans, W., and C. Rylant. 1994. *Something Permanent.* San Diego, CA: Harcourt Brace. The stories of ordinary people living during the Great Depression are told through poetry and photographs. (Gr. 5–8)

Friedrich, E. 1996. *Leah's Pony.* Illus. M. Garland. Honesdale, PA: Boyds Mills Press. Leah sells her beloved pony in an attempt to save her family's farm. Moved by her personal sacrifice, the neighbors refuse to bid against her as she buys back the tractor her father needs to farm. (Gr. 4–8)

Hesse, K. 1997. *Out of the Dust.* New York: Scholastic. Fifteen-year-old Billie Joe struggles to escape the guilt she feels over the death of her mother while enduring the hardships of life in the Oklahoma dust bowl during the Depression. Billie Joe's free verse adds a unique dimension to the story. (Gr. 5–8)

Hunt, I. 1993. *No Promises in the Wind.* Oakland, CA: Berkley. Josh and his brother Joey, faced with too little food at home, run away with their friend Henry. They find life on their own during the Great Depression to be difficult. (Gr. 5–8)

Karp, N. J. 1974. *Nothing Rhymes with April.* Illus. P. Johnson. New York: Harcourt Brace. Set in the 1930s, this story tells of young Mollie Stone. Mollie enters a poetry contest in hopes of winning a secondhand bicycle her family cannot afford. (Gr. 3–5)

Koller, J. F. 1991. *Nothing to Fear.* San Diego, CA: Harcourt Brace. When his father moves away to find work and his mother becomes ill, Danny struggles to find a way to help the family during the Depression. (Gr. 4–6)

Meyers, A. 1992. *Red-Dirt Jessie.* New York: Walker. Growing up in the dust bowl during the Depression, Jessie struggles to help her father recover from a nervous breakdown while trying to tame an abandoned dog that has become wild. (Gr. 4–6)

Peck, R. 1999. *A Long Way from Chicago.* New York: Dial. Mary Alice and her brother spend hilarious summers with their Grandma Dowdel, despite little money and few material possessions. (Gr. 6–8)

———. 2000. *A Year Down Yonder.* New York: Dial. The Great Depression is raging, and Mary Alice is sent to spend a year with eccentric, but loving Grandma Dowdel. (Gr. 6–8)

Raven, M. T. 1999. *Angels in the Dust.* Illus. R. Essley. New York: Troll. Story of a farm family during the Great Depression enhanced by the rich illustrations. (Gr. 2–8)

Ryan, P. M. 2000. *Esperanza Rising.* New York: Scholastic. Esperanza moves from Mexico to California during the Great Depression and experiences poverty and discrimination, but also determination and hope. (Gr. 5–8)

Stanley, J. 1993. *Children of the Dust Bowl: The True Story of the School at Weedpatch Camp.* New York: Crown. An information book sharing the experiences of a number of children. (Gr. 3–6)

Thesman, J. 1997. *The Storyteller's Daughter.* Boston: Houghton Mifflin. Quinn, the middle child in a working-class family, copes with life during the Great Depression. She learns secrets about her father's strength and optimism. (Gr. 4–6)

Although Meltzer's book is a tremendous nonfiction resource, students should be encouraged to continue their exploration with other readings of expository material. Source ideas include chapters or sections from social studies textbooks at different grade levels, newspaper and magazine articles discussing the Great Depression, or adult books that have some sections appropriate for intermediate students. In addition, the plethora of picture books flooding the publishing market is sure to include some that address the Great Depression.

Books, articles, and poetry inspired by the Great Depression can be challenging for students to read, especially struggling readers. In order for them to be able to comprehend the text and understand the underlying emotions and ideas, strategic reading is necessary. Harvey and Goudvis (2000) describe strategic reading as deep thinking about a text to construct meaning and increase comprehension. They recommend six reading strategies that include making connections, questioning, visualizing, inferring, determining importance, and synthesizing. First, students can be taught to activate prior knowledge by noticing text-to-self, text-to-text, and text-to-world connections in what they read. They can also be instructed how to ask good questions before, during, and after reading and how to visualize by utilizing mental pictures of what they read. Reading between the lines, or inferring, is another strategy that helps students draw conclusions, make predictions, and ascertain themes. Especially significant when reading nonfiction is determining importance; students need to learn to differentiate between "important" and "interesting," and how to remember important information. Finally, synthesizing allows students to generalize, sum-

☞ IN THE CLASSROOM

Economic Activities for Intermediate and Middle School Students

The following ideas may be used to integrate or extend a study of economics in the intermediate or middle school classroom.

1. Create checkbooks for students with registers and a "deposit" system. Allow them to write checks to purchase any number of things, such as time for free reading or the privilege to sit in a special chair. Work with them to balance and maintain accurate records.

2. Research the economic conditions of a country in need. As a class, choose to sponsor the care of a child from that country through an organization. Students should budget expenses to cover the summer months and work to organize moneymaking projects to support the child.

3. Engage students in a study of propaganda techniques. Have them decide which methods they find most persuasive. Ask them to create advertisements for books in the school library using the propaganda techniques they have studied. Keep track of the number of times these titles are checked out and find out which methods were most successful.

4. Have students interview their parents or grandparents on the topic of the economy. The class can formulate general questions that they wish everyone to respond to, and students can write individual questions seeking personal testimony from the persons they are interviewing.

5. Invite a guest speaker in to discuss the stock market with the class. Have this person assist the class in selecting a stock to invest in as a simulation and instruct them on the buying and selling of their stock. Teach students to "read" the stock market report and discuss any decisions they may wish to make regarding their stock.

6. Have students select an item, such as gasoline, that is critical to the daily life of people in our country and chart the price increases and decreases of that item over several weeks. Ask them to hypothesize reasons for these price changes. Consider as a class what would happen if the price increased or decreased drastically. What conditions would cause this to happen? How would people most likely respond? How would society's response help or hurt the situation further?

7. Go to a card shop that sells custom cards called something like "on the day you were born." Select the date that you plan to introduce the unit and request copies from different decades (January 15, 1900; January 15, 1910; January 15, 1920; and so on). Have students discuss the differences in prices for bread, milk, gasoline, and cars. During which two decades did the prices increase the most? What could be the reason for the large increase?

marize, evaluate, and personalize the text. When this arsenal of reading strategies is taught consistently throughout the school year, literature about the Great Depression, both fiction and nonfiction, can be clearer and more enjoyable for students to read.

Literature as a Basis for Economic Comparison

A thematic study is guided by the teacher, who has clearly defined purposes and emphases for the unit. As students look in-depth at the theme of the unit, the teacher will focus on terminology and concepts that suit the needs of the curriculum. For the Orphan Train unit, intermediate-level students will target social issues as well as economic. This is also done in the unit for the Great Depression where middle school teachers might focus heavily on the stock market crash that led to the Depression. Upper-grade elementary teachers might choose only to mention the crash and emphasize instead the crucial elements of decision making in a depressed economy.

Whatever the emphasis, the opportunities for comparison between the economy "then" and "now" are ripe. Picture books or novels that reflect our society as it currently exists offer multiple opportunities for drawing comparisons to a more depressed economy. Students can be asked to focus on a character's appearance in a picture book set in the 1990s and compare it with photographs from Meltzer's (1969) book. Similarly, students may be asked to compare descriptions of the community and characters described in Neal Shusterman's contemporary novel *The Shadow Club* (1988) with those of the Lundquist family in *Give Dad My Best* (Collier 1976). An additional source of comparison for middle school students is to use the futuristic seeing of Lois Lowry's *The Giver* (1993) as a basis for comparison with that of the Wheeler family in *Walking Through the Dark* (Naylor 1976). Each of these stories has endless possibilities for economic comparison if students are guided to focus on what the text and photographs communicate about the economy.

Using Literature to Teach Economics

The amount of children's literature available that can be related to economic concerns is almost unlimited. The teacher who is interested in augmenting the economic curriculum with literature will find that almost any quality children's book can be used toward this purpose. Economics is an everyday concern—thus, the everyday actions described in a good plot would most likely relate to some aspect of economics. Good children's literature gives us insights into the lives of characters and into our own lives as well. Economics is an important part of life and can be illuminated through the characters and plot of a good book.

The following questions can be used to focus students' attention on economic concerns while children's literature is being studied in the classroom. These questions are open ended. More specific questions may be designed according to the piece of literature being used and to meet the needs of a particular group of students.

How is scarcity represented in this book?

How do the characters deal with scarcity?

What resources are involved in the plot?

What are the economic systems described in the story?

What goals do the characters have?

What decisions do the characters make to try to reach their goals?

What choices are made?

How do the characters in the story depend on each other in various ways?

How does money play a role in the book?

What economic lessons do the main characters learn?

What economic terms are used?

What feelings do the characters display in connection with economic successes or failures?

Literature can be used to introduce different aspects of economics. The world of work, for instance, can be explored through picture books such as *Pop's Bridge* (Bunting 2006), the story of a welder and his painter friend who work in 1937 to build the Golden Gate Bridge, and *Sky Boys: How They Built the Empire State Building* (Hopkinson 2006), the story of how the world's tallest building was built during the Great Depression. Another career, teaching in rural America, is explored in *My Great-Aunt Arizona* (Houston 1992/1997), a picture book for first through third graders set in the Blue Ridge Mountains, and *The Teacher's Funeral: A Comedy in Three Parts* (Peck 2004), a historical novel set in rural Indiana at the turn of the twentieth century. The importance and use of natural resources can be explored in books such as Christin Ditchfield's series for primary students: *Coal* (2003), *Oil* (2003), and *Wood* (2003). Taking coal as a theme, the primary-grade teacher might share *In Coal Country* (Hendershot 1992), a picture book focusing on one family who lives in a mining town in Pennsylvania while a middle-grade teacher might also share *Growing Up in Coal Country* (Baroletti 1999), an informational book with anecdotal stories told by people who worked in the coal mines as children before child labor laws forbid them to enter the mines.

Economics and the Other Social Sciences

The economic success of a culture from long ago can be determined by anthropologists as they sift through the artifacts and relics left behind. Archeological diggings uncover both personal belongings and that of businesses of the period. Upon examining the remains of the ancient city of Pompeii, long buried under the volcanic ash of Mount Vesuvius in AD 79, the seaport city was discovered to have been a resort area for Romans. Excavations indicate that wealthy Pompeii residents had plumbing in their homes, something that poor members of society lacked. Artifacts and relics left behind are indicative of the wealth of the culture as well as the economic classes present during the period. During the Middle Ages the emergence of tradespeople with their specialty skills initiated the emergence of a middle class with what appeared to be relatively simple tools—a leather punch, a knife, needles, scissors, candle forms, and so forth. Have students ask their grandparents about the kinds of tools they remember their parents using in their work each day—wrenches, drills, presses, hammers, saws, and so on. Generate a class list on a chart. Compare it with how similar tasks are done today. For instance, most houses used to be built board by board, nail by nail on the building site. Today, many houses are built from structural components that are prefabricated at a factory, shipped on a flatbed semitrailer to the building site, and lifted by a crane into position where the carpenters use nail guns to assemble the structure.

Examination of the economic policies of successful societies such as the Greek and Roman empires and the Chang dynasty can reveal how trade influenced the political thinking of their leaders. Roads were built and rivers navigated to facilitate the buying and selling of raw and finished products. Oftentimes one society will borrow an idea from another society to enhance its own economic system. For instance, the autobahn of Germany in the 1930s and 1940s made for quick transport of supplies and troops for the Nazi war effort. The commander of the Allied Forces, General Dwight D. Eisenhower, took note. Upon becoming president of the United States, Eisenhower mapped out a grand plan of 41,000 miles of multilane divided roads with limited access, engineered for maximum speed and safety. First initiated in 1956, a coast-to-coast, Canada to Mexico highway system was designed to enhance the transportation of goods and people. Today we take the Eisenhower Interstate Memorial Highway system for granted. Create math problems for students to determine the amount of time it would take to truck goods on interstates versus traveling two-lane roads, assuming a 65-miles-per-hour speed limit for the interstate and 55-miles-per-hour for two-lane highways. Using maps from your state, students will gain locational skills. For instance, if you live in Florida, have the students consider a trip from Gainesville to Miami or Jacksonville to Tampa. In Colorado, Denver to Colorado Springs. In Texas, Abilene to Houston or San Antonio to El Paso. This activity can be adjusted for diverse learners by giving them two cities of relatively close proximity, such as San Antonio to Austin or San Antonio to Houston.

Geography also plays other economic roles as it frequently teams with geology. In the 1600s and 1700s, fishing villages near the Grand Banks of the Atlantic Ocean thrived just as today we find natural seaports such as Brisbane, Goa, Hong Kong, Long Beach, New York City, Rotterdam, Singapore, Tangiers, and Veracruz serve as important seaports for their respective countries. Throughout history, locations with ample supplies of natural resources were among those first settled and where towns sprouted. Detroit became a noted automobile and truck manufacturing location due to its proximity to the steel mills of northern Indiana and Ohio. The steel mills, in turn, were located near Lake Michigan and Lake Erie, large bodies of water that easily provide navigation for the barges filled to the brim with iron ore. Have students examine major cities in your state, the United States, or another country to determine how location plays a role in the products the cities produce.

The types of skills of a workforce influence where businesses may decide to locate. A manufacturer may desire a town where there is inexpensive labor. Today, this has been reflected in the number of companies moving their manufacturing divisions to Mexico or southeast Asia. Gateway Computers started in a dairy barn in South Dakota but moved its corporate headquarters to the sunny climate of California to help recruit and retain engineers and corporate leaders for the company. Depending on its economic base some towns are referred to as "white collar" or "blue collar." White collar represents the skills and higher salaries of a corporate executive or office worker while blue-collar workers generally earn a lower salary and perform hands-on or manual labor. Sociologists point out the need to spend government resources for better schools so that people can gain better paying jobs. Upper elementary students can be paired to investigate two cities similar in size but with different demographic and economic situations. Have each set of students access the Web site of the U.S. Census Bureau to gain information from the 2000 census to compare and contrast the economic and social conditions of the two towns. Before assigning the cities to the students, model how to compare and contrast this information by using two nearby towns. Go on the Internet and compare education levels, median incomes, home values, and other information that you and your students believe are part of a city's economic well-being. Make a chart comparing the data for the two cities. Have your students discuss what they think are possible reasons the two cities differ economically. Middle schoolers can survey their parents and neighbors as well as newspaper archives and share their efforts with the class to create an economic picture of their community. For instance, during the past decade, what new businesses have started in the community? Have any businesses moved into the area? Which businesses have left or downsized? What types of businesses have expanded? Declined?

History can affect economics. As new inventions come about, companies may proliferate or decline as those with the most efficient and best products survive, often buying up smaller companies. Consider that there were over 100 different car and truck manufacturers in the early 1900s. Today only two major automakers have corporate headquarters in the United States, Ford and General Motors, both with declining sales and an increasing number of foreign competitors. When personal computers (PCs) were first invented, a similar situation existed. Today the major PC makers in the United States are Dell, Gateway, and Hewlett Packard, with most of them having the components built in other countries.

Certainly wars have changed the course of history as well as the economics of nations. During the American Revolution, the colonies had vast amounts of raw goods such as cotton, grain, tobacco, and wood for shipbuilding and construction but lacked manufactured goods such as needles, cloth, medicines, and finished fine furniture, which England produced. During the American Civil War, the South had raw supplies such as cotton and tobacco, while the North had factories that manufactured clothing, arms, steel, and finished goods. The North also had a more extensive rail system. The sun was said "never to set on the British Empire," yet the end of World War II saw the beginning of the breakup of one of history's most successful and far-reaching empires. The 1991 Persian Gulf War was an attempt by Iraq to take over the oil fields of Kuwait and enhance its economic position. In 2003, Operation Iraqi Freedom was an attempt to rid Iraq of its oppressive regime and turn the country's wealth over to its people. Upper elementary and middle school students can examine the outcomes of wars to determine the economic before and after.

Economics and the other social sciences should be studied together as they are closely related. This helps students gain a better perspective of how the social studies are woven together in a fabric of interrelationships.

Science, Technology, and Economics

Scientific and technological advancements affect economic developments. Consider Eli Whitney's idea of interchangeable parts for guns. Quickly the idea spread to machinery, thereby reducing costs for production and reducing downtime for repairs as the replacement part was more readily available since its size was no longer unique. Likewise, Henry Ford's development of the assembly line for rapid production lowered costs of automobiles and was subsequently used for appliances, furniture, clothing, and the production of food. It was largely the efficiency of assembly lines in the United States that resulted in the mass production of airplanes, jeeps, tanks, guns, and uniforms for the Allies that led to victory in World War II.

Today automated factories produce products quickly. Robotics have replaced humans in many cases. Automobile manufacturers have only a few days of parts on hand as they build new vehicles to customer specifications, thereby saving money for both the seller and the buyer. However, it is the efficiency of the shipping and handling of the parts, made possible by computerized tracking of inventories and fleet transportation cross-country over railways and interstate highways, that yields reduced inventories and fewer warehouses.

Divide students into groups of four. Have them design a product they can make from simple materials (i.e., Popsicle sticks, construction paper, balsa wood, pipe cleaners, empty paper towel rolls, empty clear plastic salad containers, and other inexpensive or free items). Have the students gather the items so they can make at least six final products. Then set aside time to transform the classroom into a factory with the students setting up their assembly lines and making their products. The final products can be sold as part of a token economy program.

Another activity is to have students make quilt squares and piece them together. Small groups of students can set up their own assembly lines for the designing of the squares, cutting, and sewing.

NCSS STANDARDS-LINKED LESSON PLAN

Being an Entrepreneur

Theme: Starting a Business
Source: Pamela J. Farris, Northern Illinois University
Grades: 3–5
Objectives:
• Children will create their own business.

• Children will describe their business in an expository piece of writing.

• Children will advertise their business using persuasive writing in the format of a newspaper, radio, or television (video) ad.

NCSS Themes:
  IV. Individual Development and Identity
   V. Individuals, Groups, and Institutions
  VI. Power, Authority, and Governance
 VII. Production, Distribution, and Consumption
VIII. Science, Technology, and Society
  IX. Global Connections

Materials: White tag board or a computer with PowerPoint, colored markers, blank cassette and/or video tapes, cassette recorder, video camera, a copy of the chapter book for every student.

Children's Book: Hershenhorn, E. 2002. *The Confe$$ion$ and $ecret$ of Howard J. Fingerhut.* Illus. E. Long. New York: Holiday House.

Process: Talk about what it takes to be an entrepreneur and start one's own business. Have the students brainstorm what would be needed (funding, a product, location, labor, etc.). Next introduce the book, *The Confe$$ion$ and $ecret$ of Howard J. Fingerhut.* This activity will take two weeks to complete.

Divide the class into groups of four to five students. Have the students read the book and engage in a literature circle with group members taking turns at the different roles as described in the chapter.

The class will discuss the book using the following questions:

• Why was the H. Marion Muckley Junior Business Person of the Year Award so important?

• Is it important for businesses to win awards?

• What kind of awards can businesses win? (bring in a copy of *Fortune* magazine's annual survey of best corporations to work for)

• Do we have any awards for local businessmen and businesswomen? (students can investigate as a homework assignment)

• What businesses of Howie's classmates were successful?

• What things could Howie have done to make his "A Boy for All Seasons" business a successful enterprise?

• What influence did ads have on the various businesses?

• What makes a business successful?

Next, the students will each create an imaginary business. Using white tag board and colored markers or a computer with PowerPoint, the students will design an ad for their product.

Each student will write out a script for a radio or television ad. Share examples of different newspaper, magazine, radio, and television ads with the students to see what works. Share propaganda techniques and have students identify the technique with the ad:

• Appeal to the elite—Use of flattery to persuade

• Bandwagon—Appeal to desire to "belong" (need for peer approval)

• Card stacking—Presentation of only one side of an issue or product

• Glittering generality—Broad and dazzling but unsubstantiated claims about a product

• Name-calling—Calling another product (or political candidate) a derogatory name

• Plain folks—Used to gain confidence of ordinary people, often used by politicians to convey they are just like any typical citizen

• Rewards—Free prizes, reduced price, rebates, lower interest rates, etc.

• Testimonial—Well-known personality endorses the product

• Transference—Upon seeing or hearing the ad, the person believes that by obtaining the product they will be viewed as being more attractive or appealing like the one giving the sales pitch

The students will be encouraged to use persuasive writing to sell their product. The student will edit their script with a partner before actually recording it.

Using the chapter book as a model, the students will then write a descriptive two-page paper describing their business plan in detail. They will outline how much money they need to start their business, the type of business (product or service) it is, why it is needed, and a plan for its success.

On day 10 of the unit, students will take part in a Business Exposition Fair. They will display their white tag board ads and a model of their product (may be real or an illustration). Each student will give a two-minute speech on their business for the class. Encourage the students to dress up for their presentations. Provide refreshments (cheese, crackers, pretzels, popcorn, and punch or juice boxes). If held during the lunch hour, invite parents to drop in and visit.

During the two-week unit, have two or three local businesspeople share their experiences in operating a successful business. Then have the students tour their businesses. Try to vary the types of businesses (service industry, restaurant, discount store, manufacturer). Some businesses prohibit field trips due to safety concerns.

Instructional Comments: Students are somewhat familiar with the role of the consumer as they have had experience purchasing fast food, toys, and so forth. This activity reverses that role to that of being a businessman or businesswoman.

Learning Styles Addressed: Verbal/linguistic, visual/spatial, mathematical/logical, interpersonal

Standards Addressed: Students will use creative and critical thinking, math, and oral and writing skills to develop and describe a business from an economic perspective.

Evaluation:
• Assess each of the roles of the student as part of the literature circle activity.
• Assess the contributions of the student in the class discussion.
• Evaluate the business in terms of: Does it fill a need? Is it creative? Is it feasible?
• Evaluate the ad in terms of: Does it describe the product? Does it follow one of the propaganda techniques outlined? Is it colorful? Does it have a catchy slogan? Is it persuasive?
• Evaluate the expository descriptive writing on a scale of 1 to 5 (low to high) based on the following:
   —Organization
   —Word choice
   —Details
   —Conventions
• Evaluate the two-minute speech on a scale of 1 to 5 (low to high):
   —Does the opening have a hook that appeals to audience?
   —Is the presentation organized?
   —Is the description clear?
   —Did the student articulate well, using pitch, stress, and juncture?

Modifications for Diverse Learners: Record the book on cassette tape for learning disabled or struggling readers. Have students who have difficulty writing dictate their descriptive writing piece into a cassette recorder to be typed by a teacher's aide or a classroom volunteer later in the day. The teacher should conference with the student and assist him or her with the drafting and development of the final product.

Extensions:
   If it is the winter or rainy season, have students engage in a Monopoly or Life board game contest.
   Have the students play the Stock Market Game during the two-week unit. The game shows how to invest money, create a stock portfolio, manage a budget, and follow a company. The game can be found at: http.//www.smg2000.org.
   If your school doesn't have a school store, have the students set up a small store and sell pencils, pens, notebooks, and other school supplies. Have the students keep accounts, order supplies, and so forth.

Variations: For first and second graders, read the book *Alexander, Who Used to Be Rich Last Sunday* by Judith Viorst (1978). Using real money, model how Alexander spent his allowance during the week. Then hand out an allowance to each student (use paper money you have printed on green paper and cut). Allow them to purchase items during the week (pencils, extra time at the computer, small inexpensive trinkets you've picked up). Good behavior may be rewarded by the classroom paper dollars.

Chapter Summary

Economics education is an important ingredient in developing students who have the kind of decision-making skills necessary to live happy and productive lives. Although economic concepts may intimidate some teachers, careful examination of economic tasks associated with daily living will demonstrate that all educators have the necessary experience to instruct students in some economic principles.

Quality children's books can be effective tools in helping students explore economic concepts and understand the economies of past decades. Using literature allows students to consider the choices made by the characters they have read about and to critically evaluate whether more productive alternatives were possible. Students must carry with them knowledge of economies past and present if they are to lead us into a new age.

Children's Literature Recommendations

Antle, N. 1993. *Hard Times: A Story of the Great Depression.* Illus. J. Watling. New York: Viking. This historical novel is about an Oklahoma family during the Great Depression. (Gr. 5–8)

Baroletti, S. 1999. *Growing Up in Coal Country.* Boston: Houghton Mifflin. Informational book with dramatic descriptions and photos of children working in the dangerous underground coal mines of Appalachia before child labor laws were passed. (Gr. 4–8)

Berenstain, S., and J. Berenstain. 1983. *The Berenstain Bears and the Trouble with Money.* New York: Random House. Brother and Sister Bear learn how to save and spend money. (Gr. K–1)

Berger, M., and G. Berger. 2001. *Round and Round the Money Goes.* Illus. J. McCreary. Nashville, TN: Hambleton-Hill. This book describes how people have used money, from the times of trading to the invention of coins to the use of paper bills. It ends with a discussion of how money is used in society today. (Gr. K–6)

Blumenthal, K. 2002. *Six Days in October: The Stock Market Crash of 1929.* New York: Atheneum. Terrific overview of the collapse of the stock market in 1929. (Gr. 5–8)

Briers, A. 1987. *Money.* New York: Bookwright Press. Chapters in this nonfiction book include "Coins and Paper Money," "Money Around the World," and "Using Money in the Future." (Gr. 5–8)

Bunting, E. 2000. *Train to Somewhere.* Illus. R. Himler. Boston: Houghton Mifflin. A wonderfully illustrated picture book telling of the apprehension of the orphans as they rode westward to new homes and lives. Terrific read-aloud to open a unit of study on the Orphan Trains. (Gr. 2–5)

———. 2006. *Pop's Bridge.* Illus. C. F. Payne. San Diego, CA: Harcourt. In 1937, construction workers build the Golden Gate Bridge. (Gr. 1–4)

Collier, J. L. 1976. *Give Dad My Best.* New York: Four Winds. During the Great Depression (1929–1934), young Jack Lundquist tries to hold his family together despite the seeming indifference of his unemployed father. (Gr. 5–8)

Cosgrove, S. 1978. *The Muffin Muncher.* Los Angeles: Price Stern Sloan. A dragon threatens to burn down the drawbridge if the villagers don't leave him a pile of muffins each day. When the villagers run out of resources, the dragon comes up with a new production plan that results in muffins for everyone. (Gr. K–2)

Curtis, C. P. 1999. *Bud, Not Buddy.* New York: Delacorte. A young boy searches for his grandfather, a musician, during the Great Depression. (Gr. 5–8)

Ditchfield, C. 2003. *Coal.* Hartford, CT: Children's Press. Vivid photographs depict current coal mining techniques in the United States. One of a series of books on natural resources and conservation. (Gr. 2–4)

———. 2003. *Oil.* Hartford, CT: Children's Press. Color photographs depict oil fields and rigging in the United States. (Gr. 2–4)

———. 2003. *Wood.* Hartford, CT: Children's Press. Harvesting and replanting of forests are shown with current photos. Conservation is encouraged. (Gr. 2–4)

Elkin, B. 1983. *Money.* Chicago: Children's Press. The focus of this book is the history of money, but it also includes kinds of money, why we use money, and what we do with it. (Gr. 2–4)

Evans, W., and C. Rylant. 1994. *Something Permanent.* San Diego, CA: Harcourt Brace. The stories of ordinary people living during the Great Depression are told through poetry and photographs. (Gr. 5–8)

Facklam, M., and M. Thomas. 1992. *The Kids' World Almanac of Amazing Facts About Numbers, Math, and Money.* New York: Pharos Books. This fun-filled book is packed with tips, tricks, and shortcuts to help students understand the use of numbers in our world. One chapter is devoted to money. (Gr. 3–6)

Frank, H. 1990. *Tom's Lucky Quarter.* Illus. P. Mangold. Ada, OK: Garrett Educational Corporation. Tom receives a quarter from his father for washing the car. This story follows Tom's quarter from the bookstore where Tom spends his money to buy a book, to the bakery, to the chimney sweep, to the music man, to the bank, to a restaurant, to Tom's father, and then back to Tom! (Gr. K–3)

Friedrich, E. 1996. *Leah's Pony.* Illus. M. Garland. Honesdale, PA: Boyds Mills Press. Leah sells her beloved pony in an attempt to save her family's farm. Moved by her personal sacrifice, the neighbors refuse to bid against her as she buys back the tractor her father needs to farm. (Gr. 4–8)

Giff, P. R. 1994. *Count Your Money with the Polk Street School.* New York: Dell. Ms. Rooney's class is learning all about money and saving. If they learn their lessons well, they'll take a trip together. This easy-to-read chapter book also includes a money board game. (Gr. K–2)

Hager, G., and E. Pianin. 1998. *Balancing Act.* New York: Vintage. Describes how the president works with Congress to pass a balanced budget. For middle school and up. (Gr. 6–8)

Hall, D. 1979. *Ox-Cart Man.* New York: Puffin. Each member of a colonial period family works to produce something the father can trade at the Portsmouth market once a year. (Gr. K–2)

———. 1997. *The Milkman's Boy.* New York: Walker. The Graves family has a small dairy and deliver milk house-to-house. The family faces competition from other dairies. (Gr. 1–3)

Hendershot, J. 1992. *In Coal Country.* New York: Dragonfly. Considered a classic, this picture book shares the life of a family whose father works in the underground mines. (Gr. 2–4)

Hershenhorn, E. 2002. *The Confe$$ion$ and $ecret$ of Howard J. Fingerhut.* Illus. E. Long. New York: Holiday House. Howard sets out to win a prize for being the best entrepreneur despite obstacles that keep surfacing. A humorous book that teaches great economic lessons. (Gr. 3–5)

Hesse, K. 1997. *Out of the Dust.* New York: Scholastic. Fifteen-year-old Billie Joe struggles to escape the guilt she feels over the death of her mother while enduring the hardships of life in the Oklahoma dust bowl during the Depression. Billie Joe's free verse adds a unique dimension to the story. (Gr. 5–8)

Hoban, T. 1987. *Twenty-Six Letters and Ninety-Nine Cents.* New York: Greenwillow. Photographs are used to show numerals and their corresponding coin values. (Gr. K–1)

Hopkinson, D. 2006. *Sky Boys: How They Built the Empire State Building.* Illus. J. Ransome. New York: Schwartz & Wade. During the depths of the Great Depression the Empire State Building is built in record time, creating the world's tallest building. (Gr. 1–4)

Houston, G. 1992/1997. *My Great-Aunt Arizona.* Illus. S. Lamb. New York: Harper Trophy. Named after the state of Arizona where her brother is stationed in an Army cavalry unit, Arizona grows up in the Blue Ridge Mountains where she becomes a teacher in a one-room school. (Gr. 2–5)

Hunt, I. 1993. *No Promises in the Wind.* Oakland, CA: Berkley. Josh and his brother Joey, faced with too little food at home, run away with their friend Henry. They find life on their own during the Great Depression to be difficult. (Gr. 5–8)

Hutchins, P. 1986. *The Doorbell Rang.* New York: Mulberry. Cookies represent an economic concept—scarcity and choice. (Gr. 1–3)

Jaffrey, M. 1995. *Market Days: From Market to Market Around the World.* Boston: Bridgewater. This is a colorful book that gives students a glimpse of the wares sold at marketplaces around the world. (Gr. 1–3)

Karp, N. J. 1974. *Nothing Rhymes with April.* Illus. P. Johnson. New York: Harcourt Brace. Set in the 1930s, this story tells of young Mollie Stone. Mollie enters a poetry contest in hopes of winning a secondhand bicycle her family cannot afford. (Gr. 3–5)

Koller, J. F. 1991. *Nothing to Fear.* San Diego, CA: Harcourt Brace. When his father moves away to find work and his mother becomes ill, Danny struggles to find a way to help the family during the Depression. (Gr. 4–6)

Kroeger, M. K. 1996. *Paperboy.* New York: Clarion. Willie Brinkman sells newspapers to help his family. But how do you sell papers carrying news that no one wants to read? (Gr. 2–4)

Leedy, L. 2002. *Follow the Money!* New York: Holiday House. George the Quarter narrates this book as a day in the life of a coin. Coupons, garage sales, charitable donations, and weekly wages are all included. The back of the book gives the history of money, U.S. currency, and common money words. (Gr. 1–3)

Lowry, L. 1993. *The Giver.* Boston: Houghton Mifflin. Young Jonas, a member of a futuristic community, is assigned the task of holding all memories of emotion and sensation for the members of a seemingly perfect society. (Gr. 6–8)

McMillan, B. 1996. *Jelly Beans for Sale.* New York: Scholastic. This picture book includes realistic, colorful photographs of real children, jelly beans, and the coins it would take to buy the jelly beans. The history of jelly beans, how to make flavored jelly beans, a note from the author, and information on free jelly bean kits for the classroom are also included. (Gr. 1–3)

McNamara, L. 1972. *Henry's Pennies.* Illus. E. McCully. New York: Crown. Henry decides how to spend his pennies. He wants to buy a real elephant at a white elephant sale, but he ends up purchasing a white rabbit instead. (Gr. 1–2)

Maestro, B. 1993. *The Story of Money.* Illus. G. Maestro. New York: Clarion. This book tells the history of our money system and includes many interesting and useful facts. (Gr. 1–3)

Maestro, B., and G. Maestro. 1988. *Dollars and Cents for Harriet.* New York: Crown. Five stories describe how Harriet the elephant earns five dollars to buy something special. (Gr. K–2)

Medearis, A. S. 1990. *Picking Peas for a Penny.* New York: Scholastic. Angeline and John are picking peas for a penny during the Great Depression. This is a rhythmic biographical story that shows just how much a penny can mean. (Gr. 3–6)

Meltzer, M. 1969. *Brother Can You Spare a Dime? The Great Depression 1929–1933.* New York: Alfred A. Knopf. Meltzer's historically accurate chronology of events during the Great Depression are told through eyewitness accounts. (Gr. 4–8)

Merrill, J. 1972. *The Toothpaste Millionaire.* Boston: Houghton Mifflin. Twelve-year-old Rufus Mayflower protests the high price of toothpaste by producing his own. (Gr. 3–5)

Meyers, A. 1992. *Red-Dirt Jessie.* New York: Walker. Growing up in the dust bowl during the Depression, Jessie struggles to help her father recover from a nervous breakdown while trying to tame an abandoned dog that has become wild. (Gr. 4–6)

Mitchell, M. K. 1993. *Uncle Jed's Barbershop.* Illus. J. Ranome. New York: Simon and Schuster. This touching story tells of Uncle Jed traveling throughout southern counties cutting hair and saving money for his dream: his own barbershop. Based on a true story about an African American barber in the south. (Gr. 1–8)

Mitgutch, A. 1985. *From Gold to Money.* Minneapolis: Carolrhoda. This book tells the history of money from bartering to paper money. (Gr. 3–8)

Naylor, P. R. 1976. *Walking Through the Dark.* New York: Atheneum. Diary entries provide the vehicle for this poignant account of the effects of the Great Depression on a family, particularly the eldest daughter. (Gr. 5–8)

Peck, R. 1999. *A Long Way from Chicago.* New York: Dial. Mary Alice and her brother spend hilarious summers with their Grandma Dowdel, despite little money and few material possessions. (Gr. 6–8)

———. 2000. *A Year Down Yonder.* New York: Dial. The Great Depression is raging, and Mary Alice is sent to spend a year with eccentric, but loving Grandma Dowdel. (Gr. 6–8)

———. 2004. *The Teacher's Funeral: A Comedy in Three Parts.* New York: Dial. "If your teacher has to die, August isn't a bad time of year for it" goes the first line of this historical novel. Set in rural Parke County, Indiana, at the turn of the twentieth century, the author shares a tale of a small community and a rural one-room schoolhouse. (Gr. 4–6)

Pittman, H. C. 1986. *A Grain of Rice.* New York: Hastings House. Clever peasant Pong Lo saves the life of the emperor's daughter but is denied the right to marry her because he is poor. Thus, he asks for one grain of rice to be doubled every day for one hundred days, which makes him a rich man. (Gr. 2–4)

Raven, M. T. 1999. *Angels in the Dust.* Illus. R. Essley. New York: Troll. Story of a farm family during the Great Depression enhanced by the rich illustrations. (Gr. 2–8)

Ryan, P. M. 2000. *Esperanza Rising.* New York: Scholastic. Esperanza moves from Mexico to California during the Great Depression and experiences poverty and discrimination, but also determination and hope. (Gr. 5–8)

Schwartz, D. 1989. *If You Made a Million.* Illus. S. Kellogg. New York: Lothrop, Lee & Shepard. This humorous book considers choices children have for spending. (Gr. 2–5)

Seuss, Dr. 1961. *The Sneetches.* New York: Random House. Sylvester McMonkey McBean is an entrepreneur who sells stars as well as removes them for higher and higher prices. This is a good tale for social structure as well. (Gr. 2–4)

———. 1971. *The Lorax.* New York: Random House. A community comes together to set rules to protect the environment. (Gr. 2–6)

Shusterman, N. 1988. *The Shadow Club.* Boston: Little, Brown. In this novel, "second best" high school students play anonymous pranks on their rivals and allow vengeance to get out of control. (Gr. 5–8)

Snyder, Z. K. 1994. *Cat Running.* New York: Delacorte. Cat is a girl growing up in a rural setting during the Great Depression. The big race is coming up and she wants to beat the fastest boy in school, an Okie who lives in a cardboard hut. (Gr. 5–8)

Stanley, J. 1992. *Children of the Dust Bowl.* New York: Crown. Photobiographical account of poor migrant workers from Texas and Oklahoma who traveled to California during the 1930s and opened a school for their children. (Gr. 4–8)

Stevens, J. 1995. *Tops and Bottoms.* San Diego, CA: Harcourt Brace. Lazy Bear agrees to let Hare farm his land in exchange for splitting the harvest. Hare has Bear choose tops or bottoms. Depending on what Bear chooses, Hare plants crops that produce opposite of Bear's choice. (Gr. K–3)

Taylor, M. D. 1975. *Song of the Trees.* Illus. J. Pinkney. New York: Dial. Based on a true story, white lumbermen try to force the Logan family to sell the beautiful trees on their land. (Gr. 5–7)

Thesman, J. 1997. *The Storyteller's Daughter.* Boston: Houghton Mifflin. Quinn, the middle child in a working-class family, copes with life during the Great Depression. She learns secrets about her father's strength and optimism. (Gr. 4–6)

Viorst, J. 1978. *Alexander, Who Used to be Rich Last Sunday.* Illus. R. Cruz. New York: Macmillan. Alexander's grandparents come to visit and bring Alexander a dollar. Will he spend it wisely? (Gr. K–3)

Wells, R. 1997. *Bunny Money.* New York: Dial. Max and Ruby go shopping with their savings. So many choices! (Gr. K–2)

Williams, V. 1982. *A Chair for My Mother.* New York: Greenwillow. A child and her waitress mother save their money to buy a comfortable armchair. (Gr. 1–3)

———. 1983. *Something Special for Me.* New York: Greenwillow. Rosa has saved money to buy a birthday present for herself. Instead, she chooses something everyone can enjoy. (Gr. 1–3)

Zimelman, N. 1992. *How the Second Grade got $8,205.50 to Visit the Statue of Liberty.* Morton Grove, IL: Albert Whitman. The second grade experiences many hilarious setbacks and triumphs as they try to raise money for their trip. In the end, victory is sweet! (Gr. 1–2)

Related Technology Tools

Web Sites

Consumer Education for Teens
http://www.was.gov/ago/youth
This resource, developed by teens, helps teenagers become educated consumers. Teens can learn how to spot fake product and telemarketing scams, how to use credit cards, and more.

EconEdLink
http://www.econedlink.org
More than forty Web-based lessons for K–6 that include topics such as scarcity, opportunity cost, productivity, exchange, money, and specialization. Part of the Marco Polo Network.

Economics and Geography Lessons for Children's Books
http://www.mcps.k12.md.us/curriculum/sociaistd/Econ_Geog.html
Montgomery County, Maryland, public schools share this site with activities created by teachers to accompany over thirty children's literature and young adult books.

Econopolis
http://www.tqjunior.advanced.org/3901
An interactive tutorial on a wide variety of basic economic concepts (scarcity, supply and demand, etc.).

Escape from Knab!
http://www.escapefromknab.com
Students venture to Planet Knab (bank, spelled backward) and must make a series of successful decisions to survive.

FirstGov for Kids
http://www.kids.gov
This is a U.S. government interagency site for children, developed and maintained by the Federal Citizen Information Center. It has links to worthy kids' sites from other organizations, all grouped by subject.

Global Grocery List Project
http://landmark-project.com/ggl
Students collect prices on everyday items in a grocery store. Afterward, students can place those prices on this Web site and compare them to prices around the world.

H.I.P. Pocket Change: The U.S. Mint Site for Kids

http://www.usmint.gov/kids

The History In Your Pocket (H.I.P.) Pocket Change site showcases the connection between this country's coins and its people. Through games, stories, and other engaging activities, the site brings to life both the extraordinary individuals who appear on U.S. coinage and the generations of citizens who've used this pocket change.

Investing for Kids

http://www.tqd.advanced.org/3096

This Web site is designed by kids for kids. It examines stocks, bonds, mutual funds, and the like. It teaches the principles of saving and investing. It also includes a stock game.

InvestSmart

http://library.advanced.org/10326/main.html

A Yahoo Cool Site, this page gives suggestions on how to invest in stocks. Included in the site is a stock market game and investing lessons with realistic examples.

Jump Start Coalition

http://www.jumpstartcoalition.org/http://finance.yahoo.com/?u

The Jump Start Coalition is funded by numerous government and industry trade groups and is appropriate for young learners. The site has a lengthy list of free materials for teachers and students.

Making Change

http://www.funbrain.com/cashreg/index.html

This site requires students to make change. It is short and interesting. It also challenges students to exchange U.S. dollars for Canadian, Mexican, Australian, and British currency.

National Council on Economic Education

http://www.economicsamerica.org/standards.html

This site includes the standards and benchmarks of the twenty suggested economic standards.

A Pedestrian's Guide to the Economy

http://www.amosweb.com

This site is a good resource for teaching basic economic concepts. Especially useful are "GLOSSarama," a database of economic terms and concepts, and "Mister ECONOMY," which provides simple explanations of economic principles. Also provides 35 complete lesson plans for teachers.

ThinkQuest Library: Business and Industry, Money, Economics, and Finance

http://www.thinkquest.org/library/subj_library.shtml

This is a good Web site to model for students. Top quality student work is shared on this Web site. Great place for students to start an economic research project.

UBUYACAR

http://www.mcli.dist.Maricopa.edu/pbl/ubuystudent/index.html

Maintained by Maricopa (Arizona) Community College, this Web site was designed to help consumers make good economic decisions when purchasing a car. Middle school students enjoy engaging in the problem-solving process as they seek to buy a vehicle that meets the budget parameters that constrain them.

U.S. Treasury's Page for Kids

http://www.treas.gov/kids/index.html

This site links to treasury Web sites designed especially for children that discuss coins, currency, savings bonds, etc.

WisePockets

http://www.umsl.edu/~wpockets

Designed to provide educators with strategies for teaching personal finance education in the classroom, including thirteen lesson plans to accompany children's literature. Provides insight for parents helping children learn about personal finance.

Young Biz
  http://www.youngbiz.com
  Published by *Young Biz* magazine, this site has information from young people who have started their own businesses, information on setting up a business, investing, and interesting links to other Web pages dealing with entrepreneurship.

WebQuests

Can You Make "Cents" of Economics (Gr. 2–4)
  http://its.guilfbrd.k12.nc.us/webquests/economics/economics.htm
For Love of the Game: WebQuest On How Professional Athletes Influence Our Values Concerning Money (Gr. 6–8)
  http://www.spa3.k12.sc.us/WebQuests.html
Out of the Dust (Great Depression) (Gr. 6–8)
  http://wwwfiu.edu/~Candl/ENGLISH/fsuwebquest3/dustweb.htm
Show Me the Money (Gr. 6–8)
  http://www.biopoint.com/WebQuests/DGN2/Welcome.html

Software

Classroom Storeworks. Tom Snyder Productions. Students plan their own store from the ground up in this exciting simulation. Tasks include stocking shelves, accepting coupons on goods, keeping track of inventory, monitoring costs, making change, and reviewing sales reports. (Gr. 2–6)

Coin Changer. Heartsoft. Students practice identifying coins and learn money values in this beginning money software. (Gr. 1–4)

Coin Critters. Nordic. Students work through various lessons and skill levels of coin identification, purchasing, and counting change. Tokens can be earned for completing lessons, and the reward is a coin-munching maze game. (Gr. K–6)

Dollars and Cents Series. Attainment. Three levels of this talking software program engage students in essential money skills. Level I is for beginners needing to practice coin identification and counting money, Level II focuses on spending money and shopping, and Level III involves students in purchasing situations and counting change. (Gr. K–8)

Hot Dog Stand: The Works. Sunburst. Students use different tools to run their own business in a real-world challenge they're sure to enjoy. Students are required to accurately compute, interpret graphs, work backward, analyze data, and estimate as they gather information, make purchasing decisions, keep records, and handle unexpected events. (Gr. 5 and up)

Monopoly. Hasbro Interactive. The classic game of money is now available in computer software. (Gr. 4 and up)

Oregon Trail III. MECC. Students engage in various decision-making processes traveling west on the Oregon, California, or Mormon Trail. The level of expertise is student selected so the adventure always varies. (Gr. 4 and up)

Prime Time Math. Tom Snyder Productions. This exciting program engages students in math as it relates to real-life situations, including wilderness search-and-rescue operations, crimes, medical emergencies, and fires. (Gr. 4–9)

SimCity 2000. Maxis. All new scenarios in the latest version of the classic SimCity program make it especially compelling for young learners as they take over running and planning the ultimate city! (Gr. 7 and up)

SimFarm by Maxis
  Students experience the joys and tribulations of running a farm. Lots of good decisions must be made in order to run a farm successfully—this program gives students every opportunity! (Gr. 5 and up)

Videos

The Grapes of Wrath. 1940. 128 minutes. Teacher's Video Company. Available from www.teachersvideo.com.

Brother, Can You Spare a Dime? 1998. The History Channel. Four volumes, 50 minutes each. Available at Teacher's Discovery, 800-543-4180. Great Depression Activity Packet sold separately. Students can see hobos, soup kitchens, mass media, radical politics, and influential people from the stock market crash of 1929 to World War II.

References

Allen, M. G., and R. L. Stevens. 1998. *Middle Grades Social Studies: Teaching and Learning for Active and Responsible Citizenship.* 2nd ed. Boston: Allyn & Bacon.

Armstrong, D., and L. Burlbaw. 1991. "Cashing In on Students' Interest in Money." *The Social Studies* 82:143–47.

Banaszak, R. 1987. *The Nature of Economic Literacy* (ERIC Digest No. 41). Bloomington, IN: Clearinghouse for Social Studies/Social Science Education.

Betts, B. 2006. "Displaced Children in U.S. History: Stories of Courage and Survival." *Social Studies and the Young Learner* 19 (1): 9–12.

Dillingham, A. E., N. T. Skaggs, and J. L. Carlson. 1992. *Macroeconomics.* Needham Heights, MA: Allyn & Bacon.

Greenspan, A. 2003. "The Importance of Financial and Economic Education and Literacy." *Social Education* 67 (2): 70–71.

Hail, J. M. 2000. "Take a Break: A Token Economy in the Fifth Grade." *Middle Level Learning* 8: M5–M7.

Harvey, S., and A. Goudvis. 2000. *Strategies That Work: Teaching Comprehension to Enhance Understanding.* Portland, ME: Stenhouse.

Kehler, A. 1998. "Capturing the 'Economic Imagination': A Treasury of Children's Books to Meet Content Standards." *Social Studies and the Young Learner* 11: 26–29.

Klopf, R. 2006. "Freeport Students Get Head Start with Life Lesson." http://www.wrex.com/News/index.php?ID=2906 (downloaded April 10, 2006).

Laney, J. 1993. "Economics for Elementary School Students." *The Social Studies* 84: 99–103.

Meszaros, B., and L. Engstrom. 1998. "Voluntary National Standards in Economics: 20 Enduring Concepts and Benchmarks for Beleaguered Teachers." *Social Studies and the Young Learner* 11: 7–12.

Mishkin, F. S. 1995. *The Economics of Money, Banking, and Financial Markets.* New York: HarperCollins.

National Council on Economic Education. 1997. *Voluntary National Content Standards in Economics.* New York: Author.

Van Fossen, P. J. 2003. "Best Practice Economic Education for Young Children? It's Elementary!" *Social Education* 67 (2): 90–94.

Warmke, R., and R. Muessig. 1980. *The Study and Teaching of Economics.* Columbus, OH: Merrill.

Wentworth, D., and M. Schug. 1993. "Fate vs. Choices: What Economic Reasoning Can Contribute to Social Studies." *The Social Studies* 84: 27–31.

In order to preserve the genius and developmental potential of childhood, one must quite simply give the universe back to the child in as rich and dramatic form as possible.

—*Jean Houston,* The Possible Human: A Course in Extending Your Physical, Mental, and Creative Abilities

Chapter Fourteen

Social Studies and the Arts
From Inner Journeys to Faraway Lands

Pamela A. Nelson, Northern Illinois University;
Martha Brady, Northern Arizona University

CHAPTER OUTLINE

CHAPTER OBJECTIVES

Readers will

- appreciate the need to integrate the arts and social studies instruction;
- understand that the love of the arts is best established in elementary school; and
- be able to apply art activities in the teaching of social studies.

Introduction

The fifth-grade class sat huddled around two large posters, Andrew Wyeth's *Christina's World* and Diego Rivera's *The Tortilla Maker,* both of which lay in the middle of the classroom floor. Surrounding the prints were dozens of small bits of paper, each containing a handwritten sentence, phrase, or word. Some students were in the midst of writing more sentences and phrases, tossing two or three tiny strips of paper near one or both of the posters. Many of the children merely looked at the paintings in silence, absorbing their beauty. A few students conversed with one another about what they were observing. After some time had passed, the teacher gathered the boys and girls back to their desks and continued the lesson. "Now," she said, "let's talk about the thoughts you wrote down on the slips of paper. By looking at the clues

497

the paintings gave us, what are the cultures of the people we see in the paintings? How are the cultures similar? How are they different? And, this is a hard one, what might these people be thinking about themselves and their lives at this moment?"

Thus began a lesson that touched the perimeters of language arts and math while encompassing art and social studies. The lesson offered, for both teacher and pupils, an example of the value of the arts as a vehicle for making many aspects of certain lessons understandable.

The discussions that followed the introductory activity were rich and connected. Using the paintings as focal points, with the bits of information on the slips of papers as resources and guides for dialogue, the students were able to make connections to clothing and culture, terrain and culture, faces and culture, occupations and culture, and, finally, actions and culture. The teacher then went a step further by having the students engage in reflection. She asked the students to consider what the people in the paintings were thinking about themselves and their lives at that moment. This allowed students opportunities to sympathize, empathize, and relive personal moments. The students were able to make connections to their own places, their own families, their own environments.

Moving along, the teacher then focused on the artistic elements of the paintings and the artists themselves. Sharing maps of Mexico and Maine (the locations of the two settings of the paintings), the teacher brought in geography. Next biographies of Rivera and Wyeth were presented and discussed as well as some of their other paintings. Children used rulers on blank paper to draw the dimensions of the paintings in an attempt for them to grasp the sense of size. Examples of the **media** used by the artists, tempera and oil paints, were shown. Last, the class focused on a geography bulletin board that featured a map of major art museums throughout the world. Using pushpins and labels, students identified the locations of the Museum of Modern Art in New York City, where Wyeth's *Christina's World* is displayed, and the University of California School Museum in San Francisco, where Rivera's *The Tortilla Maker* is exhibited. This powerful and intriguing lesson was an excellent example of the integration of the arts and social studies. The arts can make lessons authentic, touchable, and engaging for all students in the classroom.

Integrating Social Studies and the Arts

Respected researcher Shirley Brice Heath (2004) is most associated with her ethnographic research on language/literacy development and the ways that educators foster communication among people of different cultures and subcultures. In her most recent work, she investigated ways that the arts especially contribute to language/literacy development and to the development of self-efficacy in children. Pointing to the benefits of the arts in cognitive development and involvement in all of the language arts, Heath says:

> As they [students] work on individual pieces . . . they review what they have seen earlier by consulting a book or video/film or by returning to a gallery or museum. They also reflect . . . on past observations and project ahead to their planned performance or production. (339)

Heath also insists that in an era of high stakes testing, we cannot rely only on the student's ability to complete pencil and paper tasks. She notes that observation over time must be included.

Some teachers believe that they must eliminate time spent in the arts in order to adequately prepare students for standardized tests. Kornfeld and Leyden (2005) addressed that in their work in using arts in their classroom. They discovered through their work with drama that their students were still able to demonstrate growth in both language arts standards and history standards. On a more advanced level, Terster, Hammond, and Bull (2005) engaged students with all of the arts as well as content and technology when they had students create short movies that contained images, text, or video accompanied by student narration. The resulting montages allowed students to demonstrate achievement in written and oral discourse as well as content knowledge.

As children begin to create their own views of their strengths and liabilities, we as educators spend very little time watching this phenomenon occur. We are usually too busy attempting to fill their heads with information. What would we see if we stopped to watch these incredible young boys and girls as they move in between tasks that we ask them to do in school? Would we notice that they skip to recess in rhythmic steps, or play an original melody on a tabletop with their fingers? Would we catch them shaping a form out of a crumpled piece of paper before it dive-bombs into the trash can? Or see them follow the path of a raindrop all the way down a windowpane until it slowly disappears into their imagination? Would we notice that they can name, sing their songs, and give a biographic sketch of a popular rock group? Would we ask them to wash away the chalk drawing of the Alamo on the sidewalk before they head home from school? Would we constantly require them to stop doodling, humming, or tapping their pencil? If we did, we might find a way of channeling those idiosyncratic moments that tend to drive some of us crazy. Integrating the social studies curriculum with the arts may help us discover who our children are, what potential hides within them, and whose voices may well create the "choir of the millennium."

Social studies is the perfect curriculum for integration of the arts as it can be vast, deep, mysterious, linear, global, minute, explosive, sweeping, methodical, intricate, intimate, and celebratory. Whatever social studies is, it too is life. The arts can be pulsating, swelling, complicated, intriguing, beguiling, fluid, fast, delicious, consuming, breathless, bountiful, and mirroring. Like social studies, whatever the arts are, they too are life. Hence social studies and the arts can make a wonderful and exciting combination for children. With our diverse student bodies, this combination can be a potent means of social studies instruction.

This chapter describes a variety of methods and strategies for bringing together specific social studies disciplines and the arts (music, drama, and the visual and media arts). In addition, this chapter offers suggestions and examples for applying Howard Gardner's (2006) Multiple Intelligences (MI) to these integrated lessons with attention being given to the elements of fact finding, research, creative writing, personal exploration and connections, and creative expression (see chapter 3 for more on the Multiple Intelligences).

As with any teaching method, there are caveats the teacher needs to adhere to in preparing lesson plans. Cruz and Murthy (2006) list six that are applicable for all the arts:

Maximizing Lesson Plans Integrating the Social Studies and the Arts

- **Careful planning:** Resources, time allocation, special needs of students, and integration of content and skills must be considered. Collaborating with other teachers, the school media specialist, and public librarian can enhance the project.

- **Student choice:** Giving students some freedom, flexibility, and autonomy will result in greater student interest and motivation.

- **Expectations for learning:** Engaging in the arts can be so enjoyable that some students may not realize that they are learning, and not "just having fun," so expectations should be duly noted, both academically and socially. Placing a chart of the goals and expectations on the wall for the unit of study and reviewing it before, during, and just prior to the end of the project will help keep students on task.

- **Student reluctance:** For students who believe they "can't draw," sing, dance, or engage in public speaking needed for drama, you need to reduce their fears or reluctance by assuring them by your example that their contributions are valued. For drama, lots of practice builds confidence. Praise should be sincere. If we, as teachers, point out some of our own limitations in the arts, students can feel more comfortable in dealing with theirs.

- **Classroom management:** The teacher is the facilitator and must be flexible, but having a structured, well-prepared lesson plan is critical. If students need to refresh their memory regarding expectations, then take that group over to the chart with the goals and have them read and explain each. Engaging in the arts doesn't mean that rowdy behavior is acceptable.

- **Assessment:** Combine alternative assessment activities that are evaluated through checklists or rubrics with reports, research papers, and posters. Have students give input as to what is to be evaluated and how.

This chapter presents schemata that can be used to assist teachers to infuse social studies lessons with strong and varied arts components. These are outlined in the Multiple Intelligences (MI) Grids found throughout the chapter and a Theme Outline Tree (Brady 1998), which is a visual organizational formula for presenting specific social studies topics. These MI Grids and the Theme Outline Tree offer mapping strategies for the integration of the arts into all aspects of social studies, whether it be the social sciences or the ten National Council for the Social Studies (NCSS) adopted themes of study. In addition, drama activities tied to the NCSS Standards are outlined.

Picasso defined art as "that which washes from the soul the dust of everyday life" (quoted in Brady 1998, 1). A student in a fourth-grade classroom in Arizona defined social studies as "finding your way." Combining these two definitions may, at last, give us a glimpse of what the content of social studies can be for children.

The Golden Years for the Arts

Ages nine through eleven are considered the golden years for the arts, for it is during this age span that the left and right hemispheres of the brain are completely linked and auditory pathways undergo growth spurts. It is a time when the arts make the most sense to children and when they are most apt to take risks with the arts. After age eleven or twelve, children rarely advance much further in art, music, athletics, grace of movement, or creative writing flair (Coulter 1989).

Younger children, ages five through eight, gather information using all of the senses. At this age it is easier for many of them to show others what they have learned rather than telling others what they know (Coulter 1989). Clearly, this serves as one more reason to include arts activities into our daily lesson planning to ensure that our classrooms are filled with meaningful opportunities for children to make connections with the arts and content. Embellishing our curricular areas, especially social studies, with arts experiences is a natural way for this to occur.

Music Is the Universal Language of Mankind

One of the first arts that children come to love and enjoy is music. Music played during the prenatal period can have a soothing impact on the yet unborn infant. When the same music is played again after the baby is born, that soothing feeling still resides within the infant. Music exists in all cultures throughout the world.

Henry Wadsworth Longfellow, the famous American poet, referred to music as the universal language of mankind. If his words ring true, then teaching social studies through music has limitless possibilities. Music gives us not only the capacity to make connections to information, but to place events, both personal and historical, into emotional arenas. Music massages our unconscious more than any other intelligence (Gardner 2006). It places us "here" and "there." It sets us down into the moment. Music may give us a more complete understanding of the rhythms of a specific time and place as it defines both. An example of that is the picture book *Bring on that Beat* (Isadora 2002), an illustrated poem of the jazz culture and its influence on people in the jazz community.

For children in the primary grades, music creates connections to holidays as well as special ceremonies and traditions that cannot be duplicated in other ways (Mayesky 1995). Additionally, integrating music into the social studies also brings different points of view to students. Boys and girls can use music as a means of understanding the panorama of all the elements that make up the human existence. A clear example of a first-person point of view is Ntozake Shange's (1994) powerful poem, "I Live in Music." Music is used by Shange as a metaphor for her life. In this piece, Shange introduces children not only to the "aura" of music through sensory application, but to her African American cultural background as well. This poem, like other arts-based poetry, lends itself to social studies lessons whereby students research global music and create cultural snapshots from these musical pieces.

To go a bit further, the following line in Shange's poem can be an interesting beginning point in which to direct children to reflect upon their own lives and how they see themselves: " . . . sound falls round me like rain on other folks." This line can be used to encourage intermediate-age boys and girls to create personal music metaphors and then compare those metaphors with the music metaphor pieces they have written about people from other cultures.

Jazz is another musical entry into the people, places, and environments of our world. The only music form that is inherently American, jazz music is a rich and fertile ground for learning about the sociology of the musicians who play jazz and about the communities like New Orleans, Memphis, and St. Louis that are considered birthplaces for this kind of music. In the Newbery Award winner *Bud, Not Buddy* (Curtis 1999), students learn about life as the grandson of a jazz musician during the Great Depression (see chapter 9 for a lesson plan on jazz).

By studying about the jazz artists themselves in *Jazz ABZ* by Wynton Marsalis (2005) pupils gain a better understanding of the history of certain decades, the evolution of the music industry itself, and the culture that is jazz. In the liner notes of her CD, jazz singer Ann Callaway (1996) writes, "In every century there are great musical artists who help us to know ourselves, forgive ourselves, and celebrate ourselves." Perhaps her words, too, are a definition of social studies.

Perfect Harmony: A Musical Journey with the Boys Choir of Harlem (Smith 2002) presents dynamic photographs of the choir accompanying free-form verses. The linkage of poetry and music is a strong one to which many intermediate and middle school students can relate ("rhythm is the/clock/that keeps/vocal cords/on their feet").

The Multiple Intelligence Grid in figure 14.1 is designed to give ideas for integrating music to broaden the social studies curriculum, enliven specific information, and generate renewed interest in the social sciences.

Key to Grids

V/L	Verbal/Linguistic
L/M	Logical/Mathematical
V/S	Visual/Spatial
M/R	Musical/Rhythmic
B/K	Bodily/Kinesthetic
Inter	Interpersonal
Intra	Intrapersonal
Nat	Naturalistic

Visual Arts —The Illustrated Dictionary of Our Time

The arts, in general, are about connections to ourselves and others. The **visual arts,** in particular, give shape and form to those connections. In so doing, they help us better understand our world and the cultures that make up that world. Michael Day, former president of the Art Education Association, points out that art teaches students to make judgments, to think metaphorically, and to provide multiple solutions to problems (Rasmussen 1998). Art does even more. It teaches students how to respond critically. It also transfers the art of articulation from verbal to visual (Rasmussen 1998). Art elicits comparisons and teaches students about quality and personal selections. In the area of social studies, visual arts are the illustrated dictionary of our time. The visual arts are the observable chronology of the world's five Ws—who, what, when, where, and why.

If children use the visual arts as a tool for understanding the world around them, they become eyewitnesses to the genius of humans and to all the accomplishments, risks, dreams, conflicts, goals, and ethics that have emerged from all those who have

Music and Social Studies Early Grades				
V/L	Keep an ongoing list of how music affects your own culture and other cultures.	Read about particular musical instruments and their relation to specific cultures.	Write a community song about unity.	Discuss lyrics to songs that relate to historical folk figures: D. Boone, Abe Lincoln, etc.	With your family, write a song about your family. Use the tune "Old McDonald."
L/M	Make a chart of well-known songs of cultures in your classroom.	Use specific social studies vocabulary words to create a chant.	Create different categories for cowboy songs.	Create fact/fiction cards about cowboys from information obtained in songs.	Make comparisons between your family song and the original "Old McDonald."
V/S	Design and draw an ABC Cowboy Book to accompany the songs.	Draw geographic pictures that represent what the music describes.	Create a mural that defines "America the Beautiful."	Use background music for imagery purposes.	Create your own illustrations for them.
M/R	Listen to musical excerpts.	Sing songs with your family. Teach the class your favorite.	Collect and learn songs that deal with "work," e.g., "John Henry," "I've Been Working on the Railroad."	Write your own song about working in class and/or home.	Listen to common television music jingles.
B/K	Use "junk" or paper rolls to make an invention that creates music.	Find on a map the regions to which the songs relate.	Learn songs from around the world. Create motions to accompany them.	Act out the songs.	Act out scenes from patriotic songs.
Inter	Teach the class a song your grandparents taught you.	With a partner, explore musical customs from another country.	Listen to music of other countries. Debate your likes/dislikes.	Teach the class a "holiday" song in another language.	Research the origin of the song.
Infra	How/when does music make you feel better?	"What kind of music could stop all conflict? Why?"	"When you think of the state you live in, what kind of music comes to mind? Why?"	Create an individual project from this information.	Write an individual report of the relationship between certain musical instruments and the "feeling" of certain music, e.g., Native American.
Nat	Collect environmental sound effects. Categorize them.	Research musical instruments of the rain forests. Collect rain forest music.	Write your own environmental song. Make percussion instruments.	Explore why some of these songs were "survivor" songs.	Show how nature plays a role.

Figure 14.1   Multiple Intelligence Grid: Music and social studies—early grades.

come before. Thus, these visual observations can be guidance systems to our students' own perceptions of what embodies good citizenship, values, and contributions.

All aspects of the visual arts—drawing, illustration, painting, sculpture, printmaking, photography, architecture, graphic design, and landscape design—play easily into a social studies curriculum. How might children make connections between sculpture and people in leadership roles in history? What elements of printmaking define how written communication has advanced through the ages? What imprints do the designs of buildings, tunnels, and bridges have on students and their grasp of a certain historical era? How can we use photographs to document our own personal history and compare that documentation with how the American cowboy was chronicled? How do cars, ships, machines, furniture, city parks, sports complexes, and other designs created by people impact how students view and understand economics and technology, and what are the implications of these worldly necessities to their own lives?

There are as many ideas for using visual arts to create a climate of learning in social studies as there are children who love color, form, shape, and design. Build a scale model of an American colonial village, a 1900 city, or futuristic space colony. Create a visual display of Brazil's exports (Haslinger, Kelly, and O'Lare 1996). Create a relief map of Hannibal's journey from Carthage across the Alps to fight the Romans. Create masks or a piece of art unique to one culture such as an Egyptian sarcophagus to learn more about rituals, traditions, and ceremonies (Greenwald 2000). Draw a mural representing global currency systems or bartering systems of ancient civilizations. Simulate cave drawings in a darkened classroom with brown butcher paper, flashlights covered with colored cellophane, plant dyes, and twigs (Brady 1994). Compare Greek and Roman history by comparing their architecture (Sporre 1987). Sometimes artists document history such as Bernice Sims's painting *The Selma Bridge Crossing*, which depicts state troopers attacking civil rights demonstrators in Selma, Alabama, on March 7, 1965, a day later referred to as Bloody Sunday.

Bringing works of art into the classroom, as suggested in figures 14.2 and 14.3, not only helps students continue to make connections to other times and other lives, but also reinforces some of the skills and attitudes that nurture self-identity and growth. These skills include making choices, thinking critically, and understanding the art of compromising with others. In addition, there are other skills, attitudes, and knowledge to cover.

Comparing Van Gogh's *The Starry Night* with the lyrics to Don McLean's "Vincent" offers children opportunities to see different points of view as demonstrated through different creative arts forms. Discussing Georges Seurat's *Sunday Afternoon on the Island of La Grande Jatte* can lead to conversations about the sociology of recreation. Studying kinetic art (i.e., art that moves) and comparing moving works (such as Rodin's *Flying Figure C* to the *Imunu* figures from the tribes of New Guinea) give students alternative ways in which to learn the importance of and make connections to art, dance, and movement in all cultures, past and present. George Ancona (2003) shares examples of murals from early cave drawings to the present that visually communicate the experiences and values of those who created them in *Murals: Walls That Sing*.

	Art and Social Studies Early Grades				
V/L	Look at design of several food packagings. Discuss "draw" to consumers. Relate to economics.	Look at pictures of people of different cultures. Write about stereotypes.	Look at well-known works of art. Discuss occupations.	Listen to a story about an artist's life. Discuss similarities to yours.	Show environmental pictures. Discuss industries appropriate to the areas.
L/M	Make predictions regarding pollution, weather, population, etc.	Create a pro/con chart for each package.	Create a pro/con chart for selected television advertisements.	Look at art work that represents "long ago" and "now." Make comparisons.	Use city and state maps to assist students in drawing and labeling personal maps from home to school.
V/S	Use sand trays to create and design different landforms.	Use pictorial magazines to create culture montages.	Assemble a portfolio of famous art in relation to one aspect of social studies.	Draw your family. Find well-known works of art that represent your family.	Create a strip cartoon of your physical growth from birth to now.
M/R	Look at and discuss the "art" and design of musical instruments.	Look at cultural art work. Play music appropriate to that culture. Make connections.	Use pictures as a stimulus for creating a sound poem that defines "working."	Create a vocabulary list from geography slides. Create a rhythmic chant using the words.	Find appropriate music to accompany the montages.
B/K	Take a walking field trip around your community. Look for artwork. Talk civic pride.	Use clay to re-create parts of the community you saw on your field trip.	Build your community out of boxes.	Construct an interactive bulletin board with original art work entitled *Tools*.	Using paper rolls, groups can build a sculpture entitled *Conflict*.
Inter	With a partner look for pictures that represent wants and needs.	Turn to a partner and draw what they will look like when they are old.	Use the computer to draw a machine of the future. Teach the class about it.	Interview family members about their favorite foods.	Brainstorm a design for a class logo to be put on T-shirts.
Intra	Think about and illustrate a book on "good deeds."	Reflect on one good deed. Draw a cartoon to depict it.	Use pipe cleaners to show the definition of "Hands Across America."	Draw what you value the most.	Find a painting that represents you the most. Write about the similarities.
Nat	Bring photos of your animals to class. Talk about pet care and responsibility.	Create a filmstrip of objects in your house that make you safe.	Pick one kind of food and create a sequential drawing from "field to table."	Look at pictures of global dwellings. Compare them to the house you live in.	Draw the perfect house for your family.

Figure 14.2 Multiple Intelligence Grid: Art and social studies—early grades.

		Art and Social Studies Middle Grades			
V/L	Research an artist's life from three different historical periods.	Write and illustrate your autobiography.	Use selected works of art in *The Art Book* (1994) to discuss global geographic locations.	Use other works of art to discuss cultural differences as seen by different artists.	Write a story about family traditions. Ask family members to illustrate.
L/M	Create a pictorial time line of a decade in the twentieth century.	Laminate and cut into puzzle pieces.	Compare components of the original ad campaign to an existing one.	Use pictures to categorize architectural styles from different historical periods.	Collect postcards from around the world. Categorize appropriately.
V/S	Use Matthew Brady's photographs to study the Civil War.	Create a visual ad campaign for an original consumer product.	On paper, design a futuristic colony.	Look for abstract art examples that may be similar to structures.	Construct a mobile of presidential facts.
M/R	Create a rap song that describes each structure.	Create ostanatos (repetitive rhythm patterns) with art history facts.	Write a song from a patriotic poster of the 1940s.	Use dust bowl photos and Woody Guthrie songs to write impressions of the period.	Add appropriate music to each year in the decade.
B/K	Use stacked chairs to construct structures defining: war, hunger, skyscrapers, etc.	Use boxes to construct the colony.	Select a visual artist. Create a board game about his work and life.	Take a trip to an art museum.	Go on an "art scavenger hunt" while there, looking for specific social studies facts.
Inter	Bring photos of yourself, birth to now. Teach a lesson about YOU.	In groups, present a report on a "group" in history such as cowboys. Use pictures.	In groups, select a public issue. Represent it through geometric designs on the overhead.	With a partner create a portfolio of print ads that define cultural stereotypes.	Lead a discussion on technology using ads as your resources.
Intra	Keep a reflective sketch journal for social studies.	Using a painting, write a first-person account of "being there."	Create an independent project using art work to study important battles in our nation's history.	Create a diorama of a historical event. Put yourself in the event. Reflect.	Write a report on one Norman Rockwell painting. Compare the painting to your life.
Nat	Through art, show different architectural styles through the ages.	Discuss the design of Frank L. Wright's *Falling Water* residence in relation to environment.	Use other works of art/buildings to learn about geographic regions/environments.	Build global human habitats to describe survival and environment.	Draw a topographical map of your yard, block, street, etc.

Figure 14.3 Multiple Intelligence Grid: Art and social studies—middle grades.

The Pot That Juan Built (Andrews-Goebel 2002) relies on the rhyme "The House That Jack Built" as a framework. This combination poetry-nonfiction picture book introduces children to the fascinating story of the renowned Juan Quezada and the people of Mata Ortiz, Mexico, who create pots inspired by the ancient designs of Casas Grandes potters. Students will be motivated to design and create their own ceramic pots. If the school lacks a kiln, a call to a local hobby shop will usually result in someone willing to donate some "firing time." *Action Jackson* (Greenberg and Jordan 2002) provides a straightforward account of the life of expressionist painter Jackson Pollock. The illustrations by Robert Andrew Parker give intermediate-level students an accurate portrayal of this famous artist. Students will enjoy learning about this artist, who was influenced by Picasso and who developed "action painting."

☞ IN THE CLASSROOM

Using Visual Art to Represent Feelings

Visual art can be a powerful and perfect way of allowing intermediate and middle school students to make meaning of the Holocaust. The following lesson plan integrating the visual art medium of tissue paper art with an extraordinary collection of children's poetry from the Holocaust, *I Never Saw Another Butterfly* (Volavkova 1993), may well be the truest way for children of today to absorb the event that was the Holocaust in a way that has meaning to them. By re-creating the information in art form, they are able to become part of the meaning.

Lesson Plan: Tissue Art

Theme: The Holocaust

Objectives:

• Children will create a tissue paper collage expressing their personal reaction to a literature or textbook reading selection.

• Children will make a connection using a short creative writing exercise.

Materials: Colored tissue paper, heavy-weight construction or white tag board, lots of newspaper, liquid starch, 30 1-inch paint brushes, 30 small paper or plastic cups, 5 × 7 index cards, and one of the following books:

Primary-intermediate elementary:

Bunting, E. 1996. *Terrible Things: An Allegory of the Holocaust.* Illus. S. Gammel. New York: Jewish Publication Society.

Middle school:

Volavkova, H., ed. 1993. *I Never Saw Another Butterfly: Children's Drawings and Poems from Terezin.* New York: Pantheon.

Process: This project is done after the teacher shares a read-aloud with the class. It is recommended that theme music from the following movies be played as various poems are read: *Schindler's List, Somewhere in Time, Beauty and the Beast, Forest Gump.*

• Review or highlight the main points of the historical or societal event being explored. In this case, the Holocaust.

• Softly in the background, play appropriate music.

• Provide students with several colors of tissue paper, white tag board or white heavy construction paper, paintbrush, a cup containing liquid starch, and newspapers to cover the table surface.

• Instruct students to choose one feeling, thought, or word evoked by the text or event being studied.

- Have students use the art materials provided to create a visual expression (collage) of their reflective thoughts.

- To create the collage, have students use their paint brushes to spread a thin layer of liquid starch on the white tag board or construction paper, tear pieces of tissue paper and place in an overlapping manner on the tag board, paint over the tissue paper again with liquid starch. Note: This step will require modeling by the teacher. Notice the students who grasp this technique and have them aid their neighbors.

- Ask students to choose one or two words from a newspaper headline that communicates the theme of their tissue collage and incorporate or bury it into the collage.

- After students have completed the collage, ask them to write a reflective piece to an individual using the historical time frame being explored through the text.

- Let the collages dry completely, displaying them along with the reflective writing pieces on a bulletin board.

Instructional Comments: This is a powerful activity that requires modeling of making a collage. Time should be allocated for reflective thinking, both as individuals and then in small sharing/discussion groups of three to four students.

Multiple Intelligences: Verbal/Linguistic: Students will listen to poetry and reflect upon personal meanings. Visual/Spatial: Students will use shape, form, and color to create a collage. Intrapersonal: Students will reflect upon their own understanding of the Holocaust event. Musical/Rhythmic: Some students may use appropriate music as a stimulus for placing them into an appropriate frame of mind of this activity.

Standards: Students will use a variety of means to express their connections, thoughts, and reactions to literature and historical events.

Evaluation: The collage and writing should address the following questions:
    Does it create a feeling?
    Does the piece have a theme?
    Does it relate to the topic shared?
    For writing, did the student's word choice add to the piece?
    For writing, was it organized?
    For poetry, did it follow the proper format (i.e., cinquain, diamente)?

Modifications for Diverse Learners: Preselect words from headlines that would be appropriate to use. Have an aide or another student assist the student by sharing the word's definition if the diverse learner is unfamiliar with it. Physically challenged students will need to have the materials set up for them.

Extensions: Numerous activities can evolve from this one.

- Have students read *Number the Stars* by Lois Lowry (1989) (intermediate) or *Stones in Water,* by Donna Jo Napoli (1998) (middle school), and keep a journal of their thoughts.

- Have middle school students reenact the events and thoughts of the children in a concentration camp through the presentation of the play based on the play *I Never Saw Another Butterfly* (Raspanti 1980).

- Have students interview neighbors and relatives who served in World War II.

- Take students to a local historical museum to see artifacts and photos of concentration camps.

- Have students complete a WebQuest, either one you create or one already developed.

Variations: Other possibilities would be to use the same activity with appropriate children's literature for such topics as homelessness, slavery, the Great Depression, terrorism, and so on.

Arts consultant Charles Fowler (1994) suggests that a strong school arts program impacts education in the following ways: (1) the arts make education more comprehensive; (2) the arts bring about a more engaging way to learn; (3) the arts make the curriculum more cohesive; (4) the arts create bridges to a broader culture; (5) the inclusion of the arts creates a more humanistic curriculum; and (6) the arts are our best definition of humanity.

How, then, do we plan opportunities for the arts to create meaning in social studies? Perhaps we become less verbal and more visual. When we study about World War II and neutrality in middle school, we show the film *Casablanca*. When we teach about global waterways, we bring in artwork that puts particular rivers, canals, lakes, and oceans into some visual, geographical, and historical perspective. When we research our nation's founding fathers, we bring in portraits to show how different artists "saw" them. When we teach about dignity, we look at black-and-white photographs that capture history's indignities—from Matthew Brady's photographs of Civil War casualties to Depression-era pictures of soup lines to Holocaust victims to current-day photos of starving children in third world countries. When we study native tribes, both in North America and abroad, we include works of art and icons as well as illustrations in children's literature. Such resources give us a clearer understanding of indigenous peoples.

Integrating art into any curriculum requires three basic things: materials, time to explore them, and validation (Clemens 1991). If children are to benefit from connections that come with the integration of the visual arts with social studies, students must be exposed to different art disciplines on a regular basis. They must be given time to make the necessary connections between content and art. Last, they must get from their teacher a sense of encouragement for what they are doing, which helps validate art itself.

Sydney Clemens (1991, 4) wrote that "art has the role in education of helping children become more themselves instead of more like everyone else." That, perhaps, is our true mission as teachers.

Children Are Drama

Tim was small for his age and his face still bore more resemblance to a child than other 13-year-olds in his class. Adorned each day in T-shirts emblazoned with the insignias of a heavy metal rock group, Tim carried an enormous black three-ring binder to class. This was puzzling to the teachers because the thick binder was always empty. Tim did not complete assignments and only rarely arrived at the classroom with the necessary supplies and books. Generally, Tim's performance on examinations was poor and his participation in class discussion was minimal.

Although Tim consistently lost points for not completing daily assignments, his involvement in a program associated with the study of the period prior to the Civil War was complete and positive. For that program the students traveled from their classroom to a local museum village. There the class met with museum staff members to work with primary source materials that indicated the views of local families on such issues as the Fugitive Slave Act, the Missouri Compromise, and the Union. The students then proceeded to homes or businesses staffed by volunteers who portrayed three homemakers of the 1850s. They met the wife of a new attorney and supporter of the Compromise of 1850; the wife of a blacksmith, who was an ardent abolitionist; and the wife of the editor of the newspaper, who strove to remain neutral on political and religious issues of the day.

During their visits with each of the women, the students assumed the role of children in 1856 and engaged in tasks that were common to children of that period. They helped prepare for the visit of a famous Illinois senator, Stephen A. Douglas. They mended clothing for fugitives who were being hidden by "conductors" on the Underground Railroad. They sorted type as apprentices at the newspaper. When they gathered at the schoolhouse to rehearse the choral reading for Douglas's visit, they encountered a fugitive slave and heard the story of his escape and journey to freedom in Canada. In the closing portions of the program, the students were faced with their duty in regard to the Fugitive Slave Law. That law stated it was illegal to aid fugitives from labor in their flight, and that those who knew of such fugitives were legally bound to make their presence known to appropriate law enforcement agents. Should they report the man whom they had seen and tell the official who in the community was hiding him, or should they maintain their silence?

A woman who enacted the role of one of the wives was also involved as a volunteer at Tim's school. Upon her return to the classroom, she was greeted by a number of students with comments on the program. None was more surprising than Tim's. He approached the volunteer and said, "I didn't know. I didn't know. I didn't know all that was going on. All that just livin' and deciding. It was really hard."

Unfortunately, Tim's initial response to history as a part of the social studies, as evidenced by his empty three-ring binder, is not that uncommon. Resources must be devoted to encouraging and supporting classroom teachers and students as agents of change by identifying vital content and selecting, creating, and evaluating resources and methodologies in the teaching of social studies (Kelin 2005; Levstik 1986). Drama plays an important role in conveying social studies concepts.

The late Dorothy Heathcote is generally credited with the new focus on drama as improvisation rather than performance. The drama she encouraged was closely akin to "first person interpretation" that visitors experience at many historical sites—Williamsburg and Plimoth Plantation are some of the best known. This sort of drama is especially appropriate in the classroom. It emphasizes the pursuit of knowledge from multiple sources (Bradley Commission and Gagnon 1989; Gerwin and Zevin 2003; Kobrin 1996; NCSS 1994), understanding of key concepts and events from a variety of perspectives (Egan 1986; Kohlberg 1976; Selman 1971; Shand, May, and Linnell 1990), and the ability to work as part of a group (O'Neill 1985; Putnam 1991; Ritchie 1991).

Drama requires students to create contexts for their characters (Leigh and Reynolds 1997; Wineburg 1999). As a result, they have to find out more about the period, event, or topic and the characters if they want to "play." Cruz and Murthy (2006) suggest having each student read a novel set in the time period and then jot down notes in a notebook. Edinger (2000) suggests that students do the research first and then read the novel. They may find information at period-related Web sites (examples are listed at the end of this chapter), as well as through primary/second-

Drama affords students the opportunity to develop empathy for others. In this case, students are in a one-room schoolhouse on the prairie. Through involvement, children transform factual information into meaningful schemata.

ary resources and oral histories. The students can also view short videos such as those from Scholastic's *Dear America* series (www.scholastic.com/dearamerica). Students will then be better prepared to write scripts for their dramas. Students should submit drafts to the teacher and other students so they can provide suggestions. The final versions are compiled into a script book for students to use in rehearsals for their drama.

Drama cannot be said to enable students to know the attitudes and feelings of people of former times (Shand, May, and Linnell 1990) because student fantasy and imagination play a significant role (Brophy 1992; Elswit 2000; Wineburg 2001). Drama may, however, make it possible for students to generate feelings and understandings that will broaden their perspective (Elswit 2000).

What does drama bring to children? It is suggested that drama offers a creative and psychological balance to more academic instruction. Drama presents magical experiences that embrace play as a means of looking at reality (Nelson 1992). Drama showcases childhood through pretending and wonder. In addition, drama encourages better thinking in children (Cecil and Lauretzen 1994). Drama also brings a child's sense of being, empathy, and the ability to see life from another's perspective, to feel with that person (Heinig 1987). Drama brings to children creative arenas in which boys and girls can place themselves and stay a while, as they generate their own feelings and attitudes about the feelings and attitudes of others.

Drama and historical role-playing support academic learning and cognitive development and help to "develop a wide range of skills including research, reading, writing, and speaking. Students have opportunities to grow socially as they work collaboratively with each member of a group assuming a different role in the production. A deeper and enhanced understanding of historical events and time periods can be achieved" (Cruz and Murthy 2006, 6). Social studies lends itself all facets of drama including formal scripted plays, informal skits/scenes, pantomime, puppet shows, shadow plays, tableaux, circle stories, improvisation, musical theater and opera, reader's theater, or choral reading.

In a scripted play format, students of all ages can select one aspect of social studies, for instance, right or wrong, and then choose a children's book as a focus for interpretation, such as *Riding Freedom* (Ryan 1998) based on the true adventures of Charlotte "Charley" Parkhurst. Disguised as a boy, Charlotte escaped from an orphanage and made her way west. Blind in one eye from an accident, she later became a legendary stagecoach driver and was the first woman to vote in California, and probably in the United States. By writing an original script, youngsters can deliver their own formal performance of Parkhurst's example of courage and good citizenship.

In an informal activity, students use the art of improvisation to bring clarity to a social studies issue, a historic fact, or even a point of view. Pantomime works extremely well in a classroom setting as this dramatic discipline is less threatening to some. Pantomime also works successfully as an alternative review technique. Tableaux bring together students who create a "still life" of an event with dramatic interactions among players of a scene. For example, students may freeze-frame a scene from the Holocaust and then interact verbally with each member who is in the freeze-frame.

Puppet shows, reader's theater, and choral reading are all dramatic events that offer students opportunities to interact with each other for the "common good" while learning the life skills of patience, effort, tolerance, compromise, confidence, and responsibility. In the early grades, puppet shows can be used to learn more about family, neighborhood, and community structure. In the upper grades, puppet shows can be a stage for understanding and comparing global conflicts. Reader's theater, a form of oral presentation with an emphasis on reading aloud rather than on memorization (Bauer 1987), can lead students to improved reading skills while at the same time bringing cultural folktales to life. Choral reading, another form of oral presentation that uses vocal tones as a method of verbally orchestrating a text, can bring a fullness to the meaning and reading of the Gettysburg Address or a deeper understanding of the lyrics to "America the Beautiful."

If one could teach a social studies lesson that includes imaginative thinking, creative problem solving, movement, spatial awareness, sensory awareness and recall, verbalization, structure, characterization, aesthetic development, and intrapersonal and interpersonal development (Cottrell 1987), then one would also be a drama teacher. The Multiple Intelligence Grids for drama that follow give lesson plan ideas for incorporating the preceding elements in the social studies curriculum.

Drama can provide opportunities for students to explore the attitudes, values, and perspectives that others hold and also to consider their own. Drama allows students to interpret and respond to historical content intuitively through movement, construction, and words. It also provides the opportunity for students to use language and problem-solving skills for real and authentic purposes as they work with peers in their classrooms.

Initiating Drama in the Classroom

In preparing to use drama in the social studies classroom it is helpful to work through three planning phases and then plunge in, returning to the same three phases again and again. First, teachers need to engage in a preparation period of reflection on the strengths and needs of their students and on their own personal weaknesses. Second, teachers need to investigate social studies concepts and topics. Third, teachers need to become familiar with new planning formats that will guide them in working with students in the classroom.

Preparatory Reflection

Journaling helps many teachers during the initial phase of adding drama to the social studies program. Reflection is often aided by asking and writing about very basic questions.

Teachers must first consider the students who will be the choreographers of the drama:

- What concepts, topics, or events might be accessible to or developmentally appropriate for these students in terms of their social and emotional characteristics, knowledge base, or academic skills in working with data?
- Which issues within the concept, topic, or event will be of greatest concern to the students?
- What facet of the concept, topic, or event will be the most interesting to the students?

Teachers must then consider the unique perspectives, talents, and abilities that they themselves bring to the classroom:

- What life experiences, course work, and networks throughout the community, nation, and world can they offer on the concept, topic, or event?
- What former travels or occupations might yield new insight and understanding about people as well as the regions and cultures in which those people live?
- To what concepts, topics, or events might they bring unique perspectives?

Teachers must consider the required curriculum and local sources:

- Which topics are most associated with high interest and ready resource—human, media, artifacts, or time?
- Which topics from the curriculum have been especially appealing to the students?
- How much time would it take to add drama to one unit?
- Which goals and objectives of the current curriculum are essential and which may be considered lower priority?
- Which goals and objectives might be better met through work in drama?
- What readily available objects or artifacts from homes, the community, or the school might be springboards to drama?

514

		Drama and Social Studies Early Grades		
V/L	Select a culture-based children's story. As the teacher reads, students perform narrative pantomime.	Research similar global folktales. Create finger puppets to act them out.	Create improvised actions about an experience with your grandparents.	Vocabulary Drama. Call out a vocabulary word. Students act out definition.	Write and act out a folktale from another country.
L/M	Use math skills to "block" the play.	Create a time line of events along the Oregon Trail. Act out the events.	Create a state historical events calendar. Enact events through improvisation.	Gather and categorize hats to be used in drama situations.	Use inductive/deductive reasoning to create "before/after" scenes.
V/S	Use pictures and photos to stimulate drama experiences.	Create global culture masks to distinguish different characters.	Make paper hats to define different characters.	Create "props" (e.g., light bulb). Students act out what happened before and after invention of lightbulb.	Design and draw the program for the holiday play.
M/R	Create "circles of sound" that define different community workers.	With an older class create a social studies music video.	Present a melo-drama of facts about the Old West.	Sing holiday songs with sounds and activities.	Write and perform a holiday play with music and dancing.
B/K	Present a concept about "home." Students create add-on pantomimes to the original idea.	Play the game Spectator. Students act out "watching something."	Take a field trip to a holiday play.	Create past, present, and future scenes about your family.	Students write and present choral reading using the same book.
Inter	In groups, students create simple debates about historical facts or events.	Create pair debate scenarios such as parent/child, policeman/speeder, etc.	Select a culture poem. Organize class in choral reading of the poem.	Partners conduct telephone conversations with two different people in history.	Create point-of-view scenes in groups.
Intra	Create a first-person character monologue of a community helper. Use tape player.	Create a first-person monologue for one of these animals.	Think about how it feels to get up in front of the class and act.	In a circle, students pantomime "Who Am I?"	Create a book-on-tape voice characterization of your family members.
Nat	Role-play two ways to survive in outer space.	Act out "day-in-the-life" of certain animals.	Create frozen sculptures of landforms such as mountains. Create sound/actions.	Act out the water cycle.	Students play "Human Machines" (Brady 1994).

Figure 14.4 Multiple Intelligence Grid: Drama and social studies—early grades.

Drama and Social Studies **Middle Grades**				
V/L	Research the history of the American theater and how it mirrored events taking place in history.	Write a three-part choral reading piece about one event in history, such as the Hindenburg disaster.	Poll community members about how they support their local theater.	Discuss cultural stereotypes as depicted in movies.	Write a puppet show script about transportation. Be factual.
L/M	Chart the economic differences in Broadway theater and movies.	Use math skills to create sets for the documentary.	Compare theater during Greek, Roman, Medieval, and turn of the century times.	Critique it for actual or nonfactual interpretation.	Create a shooting schedule for the documentary.
V/S	Use boxes to design background sets for informal drama scenes.	Watch a movie that has significance to some aspect of social studies (e.g., *Grapes of Wrath*).	Use colored cellophane to create overhead puppetry skits about social studies.	Document a first-person event in history using a video camera.	Create puppets as modes of transportation.
M/R	Rewrite a chapter book with a historical premise into a children's musical.	Act out lyrics from World War II songs.	Explain how certain music sets the mood for dramatic experiences.	Find music or sound effects to accompany commercials dealing with goods and services.	Find sound effects to accompany the puppet show.
B/K	Create verbal scenarios representing American presidents and their moments of greatness.	Select one social studies issue. Act out yesterday, today, and tomorrow skits.	Dramatize points of view from famous women in history.	Act out original commercials appropriate to different historical periods.	Pantomime the Bill of Rights.
Inter	Use the Internet to research "drama success stories" of people of different cultures.	Report the information to the class.	In groups, create a monologue for one significant historical "turning point."	Brainstorm products that are appropriate to certain historical periods.	With a partner act out one significant event in your state's history.
Intra	Independently, research an actor who is a political spokesperson.	Think of the most dramatic moment in American history. Create a video. Play all parts.	Think of one global problem. Create and videotape a request for aid to help solve the problem.	How do movies influence you? Be specific.	Research current events in which tragedies occurred because of a movie's influence.
Nat	Be an environmentalist who will "guide" someone across your state.	Act out nature's cycles.	Create a two-voice poem about some aspect of global weather.	Assume inanimate roles as the guide tours your state.	Create a monologue as a "survivor" of a historical indignity.

Figure 14.5 Multiple Intelligence Grid: Drama and social studies—middle grades.

☞ **IN THE CLASSROOM**

Helping Students Through the Doorway to the Past

1. Select a theme or event.
2. Share related literature, films, and artifacts with the class.
3. Create a dialogue or improvisation based on the theme or event with a colleague as a model.
4. Show or tell about the resources that helped you develop your role.
5. Make resources available to the students in the classroom.
6. Present the basic idea of the plot or problem.
7. Work with students to develop the setting in which the drama will take place.
8. Have each student work to develop his or her character.
9. Divide students into partners. Have students assume their roles and do dialogues with their partners.
10. Give the starting point of the drama and begin.

Finally, teachers must find others who have expertise in using drama with children or who are interested novices:

• Are there other individuals in the building, district, local college, or community who have expertise or interest?

• When and where could meetings for sharing take place?

Teachers who have used drama with their classes stress the need for support from and collaboration with other teachers. Such support groups offer ideas and encouragement as well as sounding boards to teachers who are interested in trying something new. At the end of this planning phase, classroom teachers should have additional insights about their students and themselves, have identified a topic or theme to investigate, and have made contact with others who are engaged in the same process.

Investigating Resources

Some of the resources for drama will be traditional. Teachers and students need background information. This is most often provided by secondary sources—textbooks, informational books, Web sites—that give overviews of concepts, topics, and events.

In working with drama, however, teachers must also locate resources that will both limit and give a sense of the dramatic to the concept, topic, or event being studied. Quite often such resources come from historical fiction, biography, primary source material, and artifacts. Young adult or children's literature is plentiful and of high quality. Listings and reviews of the outstanding children's books for the social studies are published annually in *Social Education,* the journal of the National Council for the Social Studies (NCSS) and listed on its Web site. Examples of primary sources would be letters, diaries, court transcripts, oral histories, and so on. If primary sources are carefully chosen and organized, many are readable and accessible to upper elementary level students. Edinger (2000) insists that with guidance elementary students can be successful in using primary source materials. Resources may be found at the Library of Congress Web site (www.loc.gov) and the National Archives (www.archives.gov). Both agencies have "teacher pages" on their Web sites that provide teacher- and student-friendly materials and plans.

Artifacts or objects may be found in thrift shops or borrowed from museums or libraries. The children themselves may be able to bring in or make objects that are like those used by people of earlier times. Most communities also contain a considerable number of resource persons or groups who are often forgotten in terms of resource location and development (see the Teaching Resources section at the end of the chapter). Teachers find that resources from the community come serendipitously, so they need to be prepared and prepare others in the school to seize opportunities when they surface.

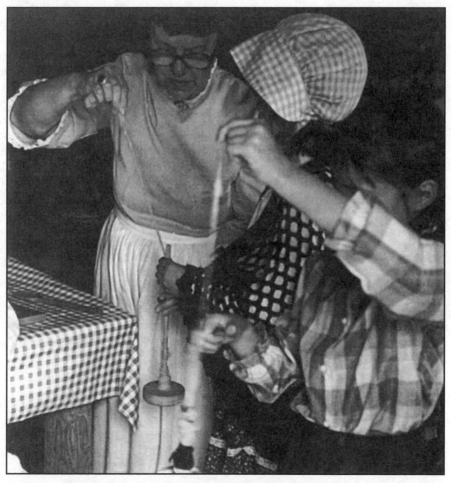

A drama such as the spinning of wool may evolve from a portion of a children's literature book.

Fines and Verrior (1974) and Levstik and Barton (2005) insist that it is important for teachers to become familiar with the most current and valid information and resources on selected topics. As a result, they will be able to guide students toward sources that represent and accurately portray a variety of perspectives (Bartoletti 2000). Edinger (2000), Levstik (1986), and Wineburg (2001) also caution that the emotional loading of narratives used in studying particular issues may lead students to identify with the main characters of the narratives to the exclusion of other views. These authors believe that it is the teacher's responsibility to present students with alternative views and rationales for those views that will help students move beyond a myopic approach to issues and topics. Print, media, and artifacts that support insights into many facets of issues need to be available to students who are using drama as a learning tool.

Developing and Utilizing Specialized Planning Approaches

The most common lesson-planning formats may not be the most effective when planning to teach through drama. The "story form model" of Egan (1986, 1997) offers a more appropriate approach. In using Egan's model, the teacher's first task is to identify the big ideas or issues in the topic and the associated knowledge, skill, and disposition objectives within the required curriculum. The teacher's second task is to identify literature or accounts associated with the events in which story elements (characters, settings, conflicts) are strong. This makes it possible to limit the topic (Brophy 1992) and to identify or locate applicable photographs, artifacts, or props. Based on these resources, the teacher must plan for students to assume the roles of participants and to join the event at some point in time. Finally, the teacher must plan for a period of student reflection and sharing following the drama so students will identify what they learned from the experience (Van Sledright and Brophy 1992).

The following questions provide guidelines for the teacher in the process of character and story development:
Who were the people who took part in this event?
Who were the people affected by the event?
What were their ordinary lives like?
How old were they?
Who were their friends and relatives?
What role or roles should the teacher assume?
What will be the exact words and stimuli used to introduce the drama to the students?
What objects or artifacts might be used to draw the students in?
What will compel this particular group of students to participate?
What areas of the classroom, buildings, or grounds will be used?
Where will the teacher and students look to find supplies, resources, pictures, and
    objects to help develop understanding of the characters or the situation?
How best may students be helped through the initial phases of the drama?
How may the drama be moved if it gets stuck?
How may the teacher help students bring the drama to a conclusion?

The following questions will help the teacher prepare students for the task of reflection on their experiences:

Where will the reflection period take place?

What options will be offered for students to respond to the drama?

Will students talk, write, or draw about their experiences?

How much time will be allotted to individual response and to group response?

Will students share their impressions with those who participated in the drama or with other significant individuals in the school or the community who were not present?

How will students be led from the drama to demonstrate competencies related to national, state, local, and personal thematic strands and goals?

The importance of reflection on both the content and process of dramatizing the event cannot be underestimated. Reflection enables students to consider what they have learned more fully and more critically. The reflective period helps students balance the interpretive and factual aspects of the events. It also helps them as they attempt to apply what they have learned to their lives (Levstik and Barton 2005; Van Sledright and Brophy 1992; Wineburg 1999, 2001).

Resources and Ideas for Drama

The suggestions offered in this section use a variety of dramatic techniques to involve students with historical and contemporary concepts and topics common to most social studies curricula. In each case, the topic is introduced or developed through young adult and children's literature. The suggestion may be developed more fully to form entire units. Each highlights "big ideas" or key concepts and generalizations in the social studies (Banks, Banks, and Clegg 2004). These big ideas should not be identified for the students prior to engaging in the drama itself. The topics also relate to the thematic strands that have been identified as organizers for the social studies curriculum by the most recent curriculum task force of the National Council for the Social Studies (1994).

Drama and Thematic Strands of the Social Studies Curriculum

I. Culture

Social studies programs should develop ideas concerning the unique systems that human beings have created, learned, or adapted to meet their needs so that they will be better able to relate to people in our nation and the world (NCSS 1994, 21).

KEY CONCEPT: Traditions

GENERALIZATION: All societies have a set of traditions that help maintain group solidarity and identity.

Literature Stimulus

Crews (1991), *Big Mama's*

Dooley (1991), *Everybody Cooks Rice*

Garza (1990), *Family Pictures / Cuadros de Familia*

Garza (1996), *In My Family / En Mi Familia*

Rylant (1985), *The Relatives Came*

Dramatic Roles

After reading these books, have students pretend that many years have passed. A scrapbook of the events has been found. Have one student assume the role of an elderly relative who participated as a child. Have another student assume the role of a child who will hear the stories associated with the family gatherings. As an option, students may gather stories about their own family members or individuals whom they are studying, make a scrapbook, and then retell the incidents that are illustrated.

KEY CONCEPT: Rite of passage
GENERALIZATION: All societies have traditional ceremonies and rituals to signal and mark important status changes in a person's life.

Literature Stimulus

Cha (1996), *Dia's Story Cloth: The Hmong People's Journey to Freedom*
Fournot (1985), *The Patchwork Quilt*
Freedman (1994), *A Cloak for the Dreamer*
Guback (1994), *Luka's Quilt*
Shea (1995), *The Whispering Cloth: A Refugee's Story*

Dramatic Roles

In each of the preceding stories, the children of the family are given or assume the task of creating a needlework masterpiece. After reading the stories, arrange students in groups of five and then have them assume roles of other family members—siblings, parents, uncles, aunts, cousins. At that point the "family members" should discuss the changes that they have seen in the main character since the completion of the project. After the role-plays, have the group share the changes that they have talked about.

II. Time, Continuity, and Change

Social studies programs should help students understand their historical roots and locate themselves in time. Students should be given opportunities to learn the processes that historians use as well as to gather information about what has happened in the past and its effects on the present and future (NCSS 1994, 22).

KEY CONCEPT: Historical bias
GENERALIZATION: Historians attempt to reconstruct past events based on sources and artifacts that have been left behind. They must judge the accuracy and authenticity of the data. Their work is influenced by personal biases as well as those of the time in which they live and the audience for whom they are working.

Literature Stimulus

Ballard (1988), *Exploring the Titanic*
Burgess (1997), *Indians of the Northwest: Traditions, History, Legends, and Life*
Goor and Goor (1986), *Pompeii: Exploring a Roman Ghost Town*
Reinhard (1998), *Discovering the Inca Ice Maiden*
Teele (1998), *Step into the Chinese Empire*

Dramatic Roles

Use an artifact very much like those items that are described in the books. After reading one of the books, have two students assume the roles of workers who

A dramatic recreation of a social studies event such as a meeting of the Sons of Liberty can leave a lifetime impression upon students.

have made a great discovery during the exploration. Have another assume the role of the leader of this particular expedition who wants to take the artifacts back to the museum that is underwriting the cost of the work. Have a fourth student assume the role of a famous local archaeologist who does not want artifacts moved from the site. Have the remaining class members assume roles of residents of the nearby community who have come to the site after hearing of the discovery.

KEY CONCEPT: Continuity and change

GENERALIZATION: Although there are constants that run through time, human society is also characterized by change. Conflicts, which have some negative effects, are often the impetus for effective change.

Literature Stimulus

Coles (1995), *The Story of Ruby Bridges*
Erickson (1998), *Daily Life on a Southern Plantation: 1853*
Golenbock (1990), *Teammates*
Lester (1968), *To Be a Slave*
Lyons (1992), *Letters from a Slave Girl: The Story of Harriet Jacobs*
McKissick and McKissick (1994), *Black Diamond: The Story of the Negro Baseball Leagues*
Turner (1997), *Follow in Their Footsteps*

Dramatic Roles

The books suggested for this section represent stories of African Americans in both the nineteenth and twentieth centuries in the United States. Following the sharing of the book, ask one child to assume a role like that played by Works Project Administration workers who gathered the narratives of African Americans. Have another student assume the role of one of the main characters. Have several others assume the roles of individuals who witnessed the events. In each case, it is now 50 years later. Have the writers interview the main characters or witnesses regarding their memories of the actual events and of the impact of those events on the present.

III. People, Places, and Environments

Social studies programs should help students locate geographic regions, towns, cities, and natural and man-made features. Students should also learn of relationships that exists between human beings and the environment (NCSS 1994, 23).

KEY CONCEPT: Human-environment interactions
GENERALIZATION: People work to meet their needs and create places that reflect cultural values and ideas within geographic regions that have certain features.

Literature Stimulus
Begay (1995), *Navajo: Vision and Voices Across the Mesa*
Bruchac (2006), *Navaho Long Walk: The Tragic Story of a Proud People's Forced March from Their Homeland*
Bruchac (2005), *Code Talkers*
O'Dell (1970), *Sing Down the Moon*
Sneve (1993), *The Navajo: A First Americans Book*

Dramatic Roles

Read aloud Bruchac's *Code Talkers*, a book about the Navaho men who served as communications soldiers during World War II because their language was so rare the Japanese could not translate intercepted messages on the battlefields. After locating their reservation area on a map and discussing the physical features of the area, have the students read O'Dell's *Sing Down the Moon* as an entire class. Have the students pantomime their packing and saying farewell to their homes and their land as they begin the march to Fort Sumner. After their pantomimes, have students share their feelings as well as the list of items they'd try to take with them.

IV. Individual Development and Identity

Social studies programs should help students understand the ways in which they learn and make choices. They also need opportunities to come to know how personal identity and decision-making processes are shaped by culture, groups, and institutions (NCSS 1994, 24).

KEY CONCEPT: Immigration.
GENERALIZATION: When people believe that their basic needs and wants may be better or more safely met in another region, they may choose to move there. That decision is influenced by personal, cultural, and institutional values and mores.

Literature Stimulus
Bierman (1998), *Journey to Ellis Island: How My Father Came to America*
Bunting (1994), *A Day's Work*
Caseley (1987), *Apple Pie and Onions*
Fraser (1993), *Ten Mile Day and the Building of the Transcontinental Railroad*
Hoobler and Hoobler (2003), *We Are Americans: Voices of the Immigrant Experience*
Jacobs (1990), *Ellis Island: New Hope in a New Land*
Jimenez (1997), *The Circuit: Stories from the Life of a Migrant Child*
Levinson (1985), *Watch the Stars Come Out*
Strom (1996), *Quilted Landscape: Conversations with Young Immigrants*
Yep (1984), *The Serpent's Children*

Dramatic Roles
After reading the books, have half of the students assume the roles of relatives, children, and friends of people who have decided to leave their homelands. Have the other half assume the roles of individuals who will be leaving their homes for the United States. Have those students tell their friends and relatives why they have decided to risk leaving, how they will deal with hardships, and what they have as goals or hopes.

V. Individuals, Groups, and Institutions

Social studies programs need to help students understand how institutions are formed, what controls and influences them, how they control and influence individuals, and how they can be maintained or changed (NCSS 1994, 25).

KEY CONCEPT: Social organization
GENERALIZATION: Every society consists of smaller units such as classes, families, clubs, communities, and so on. Each of these social units participates in different ways in the total culture to help people meet their needs or to provide for the basic needs and wants of those in the society.

Literature Stimulus
Cooper (2004), *Dust to Eat: Drought and Depression in the 1930s*
Gates (1972), *Blue Willow*
Hesse (1998), *Out of the Dust*
Hunt (1970), *No Promises in the Wind*
Stanley (1992), *Children of the Dust Bowl: The True Story of the School at Weedpatch Camp*

Dramatic Roles
Have three or four students be photographers and journalists who have come to do stories so the plight of these individuals can be addressed. Divide the remaining students into groups so that each photographer and journalist has a group of students to photograph and to talk with as the characters go about their daily business. Have the students role-play common activities mentioned in the books.

VI. Power, Authority, and Governance

Social studies programs should help students understand the historical development of structures of power, authority, and governance in this country as well as in other parts of the world. This would include the study of the role of individuals in a democratic society (NCSS 1994, 26).

KEY CONCEPT: Authority

GENERALIZATION: When authorities feel that the ideology or general well-being of their political system is threatened they may take extreme action against individuals or groups, denying them the basic rights guaranteed under the laws of the state.

Literature Stimulus

Hamanaka (1990), *The Journey: Japanese Americans, Racism and Renewal*

Mochizuki (1993), *Baseball Saved Us*

Oppenheim (2006), *Dear Miss Breed: True Stories of the Japanese American Incarceration During World War II and a Librarian Who Made a Difference*

Spier (1987), *We the People: The Constitution of the United States of America*

Tunnell and Chilcoat (1996), *Children of Topaz: The Story of a Japanese-American Internment Camp Based on a Classroom Diary*

Uchida (1971), *Journey to Topaz*

Welch (2002), *Children of the Relocation Camps*

Dramatic Roles

Most of the books deal with the treatment of Japanese Americans in the United States during World War II. One book offers a pictorial interpretation of the Constitution and of the rights and responsibilities that individuals have in our country. Conduct a congressional hearing on the internment. Have a group of five to ten students assume the role of government officials who will conduct the hearings. Have at least ten other students assume roles of spectators and reporters. Have the remaining students assume roles of Japanese American people who were interned at one of the camps during World War II and who have been asked to tell of their experiences.

VII. Production, Distribution, and Consumption

Social studies programs should help students examine questions of what is to be produced, how production is to be organized, how goods and services are to be distributed, and how unlimited wants and needs will be met with limited resources (NCSS 1994, 27).

KEY CONCEPT: Resources, wants, and needs

GENERALIZATION: Producers of goods and services exchange with others to get resources. Since resources are limited, and wants and needs are relatively unlimited, the situation creates a need for decision making. Choices are based on the individual's value system and the relative scarcity and need for goods, services, or resources.

Literature Stimulus

Atkin (1993), *Voices from the Fields: Children of Migrant Farmworkers Tell Their Stories*

Franklin and McGirr (2000), *Out of the Dump*

Freedman (1994), *Kids at Work*

Parker (1998), *Stolen Dreams: Portraits of Working Children*

Spedden (1994), *Polar: The Titanic Bear*

Dramatic Roles

The preceding books deal with children who lived in the nineteenth and twentieth centuries. The lives of children who worked for a living differed greatly from those of children of the wealthy. Help students create a "general store" from the time period by drawing murals based on Rachel Field's poem and the description of stores in Spedden's book. After reading the books, have one-half of the students assume roles of children who worked. Have the other half assume the roles of the wealthy. Give each 10 cents. Have them pantomime their selection process in the store you have created. After their experience, have students share what they discovered about their choices.

VIII. Science, Technology, and Society

Social studies programs should provide students with opportunities to consider the implications of technology in our lives and of the ethical issues surrounding its use (NCSS 1994, 28).

KEY CONCEPT: Technological change

GENERALIZATION: Technological change alters established relationships among cities, towns, people, and the environment.

Literature Stimulus

Cherry (1992), *A River Ran Wild*

Hiscock (1998), *The Big Rivers: The Missouri, the Mississippi, and the Ohio*

Jackson (1998), *Turn of the Century*

Millard (1999), *A Street through Time: A 12,000 Year Walk through History*

Von Tscharner, Fleming, and The Townscape Institute(1987), *New Providence: A Changing Cityscape*

Dramatic Roles

Have each student assume the role of a person who grew up in one of the towns, moved away, and has returned for a high school reunion. Have the students design picture postcards that might have been available at the time of the visit. While they are still in role, have them write messages to friends who weren't able to come to the reunion. In those messages they should tell about the changes they've noticed in the community because of new technologies.

IX. Global Connections

Social studies programs should offer students opportunities to understand the increasingly important and diverse global connections among world societies. They should be able to identify national interest and global priorities and how they may contribute to or offer solutions to problems throughout the world (NCSS 1994, 29).

KEY CONCEPT: Exploration

GENERALIZATION: Explorations that people made into what were, to them, strange territories resulted in tremendous cultural exchange as well as conflict between different cultural and ethnic groups. In general, more technologically advanced cultures have assimilated or destroyed cultures that were less technologically developed.

Literature Stimulus
Johnson (1998), *Tomatoes, Potatoes, Corn, and Beans: How the Foods of the Americas Changed Eating around the World*
Sis (1991), *Follow the Dream: The Story of Christopher Columbus*
Yolen (1992), *Encounter*

Dramatic Roles
    After reading the books, which tell of Columbus's journey across the ocean, have the students assume the roles of the Taino people who were present for the initial meeting with the Spanish and for the exchange of gifts. The teacher may assume the role of the elder. The improvisation should be conducted in the hope of determining a course of action toward the outsiders. The question might be whether to continue to work to develop relationships with these newcomers or to imprison or kill them.

X. Civic Ideals and Practices

    Social studies programs should offer students an understanding of the civic ideals and practices of citizenship in our democratic republic and of other forms of political organization in other parts of the world (NCSS 1994, 30).

KEY CONCEPT: Political participation
GENERALIZATION: Private citizens act by voting, lobbying, campaigning, attending political meetings, preparing petitions, and running for office.

Literature Stimulus
Bang (2000), *Nobody Particular: One Woman's Fight to Save the Bays*
Blos (1987), *Old Henry*
Bunting (1994), *Smoky Night*
Martin (1998), *The Green Truck Garden Giveaway: A Neighborhood Story and Almanac*
Provensen and Provensen (1987), *Shaker Lane*

Dramatic Roles
    These stories tell of the lives of citizens in this country and the events they experienced in their communities. In each of these cases, the neighbors have prejudices regarding each other, and they ultimately come together. Select one of the stories and have each student assume the role of a member of one of the communities. Arrange for each student to have a partner who is from the "other" community. Move the students beyond the ending of the story to subsequent days. What will happen?

KEY CONCEPT: Pressure groups
GENERALIZATION: Individuals and groups resort to extreme methods to change public policy when they believe that authorities are unresponsive to their needs or that legitimate channels for the alleviation of grievances are ineffective.

Literature Stimulus
Bachrach (1994), *Tell Them We Remember: The Story of the Holocaust*
Cox (1998), *Fiery Vision: The Life and Death of John Brown*
Haskins and Benson (1998), *Bound for America: The Forced Migration of Africans to the New World*
Innocenti (1985), *Rose Blanche*
Oppenheim (1992), *The Lily Cupboard*

Dramatic Roles

Ask one of the students to assume the role of a child who sees his or her best friend being arrested or taken away. Have a second student assume the role of the soldier or slaver, and a third student assume the role of the friend. Have four or five other children involved as friends and observers who happen to be nearby.

Putting It All Together in Interdisciplinary Instruction

Teaching social studies in a loose, eclectic manner is not effective with children, particularly younger students. Teachers who use "a little bit of this and a little bit of that" often have lessons and units that constitute chaos of mind and body in the classroom. Rather, interdisciplinary lessons should have foundational components and experiences. Whether you use the expanding environment approach, the spiral curriculum approach, or even the NCSS Standards (Welton and Mallan 1996), connections must be made from one element of social studies to another. For example, for primary grade students who are learning about Native Americans, an umbrella of lessons that include all of the social sciences along with the 10 themes of study should be presented. Too often we spend the majority of our lessons on the names and locations of tribes, headbands, dances, and houses, instead of creating an entire picture of the Native American. For all students, we must bring a menu of experiences that lead to a complete understanding of the topic. Visual organizational tools assist teachers in creating units and lessons that are not watered down or unbalanced. They can also be used as guides for where to place arts experiences in the curriculum. Grids, outlines, or webs work wonders in this regard. Creating a social studies visual formula, such as the social studies unit tree (figures 14.6 and 14.7), reminds teachers of the areas where they devote too much time and the areas they lightly touch or omit altogether.

Chapter Summary

Teaching social studies with a rich smattering of drama, music, visual art, or other arts disciplines gives students front-row center access to experiences that can develop new knowledge, strategies, and attitudes. It forces students to take internal journeys as they navigate among the highways of facts, figures, and hard information. The arts make the trip a much more meaningful and authentic experience. Integrating arts and social studies in this way touches base with every kind of learner, with every multiple intelligence, with group dynamics of every configuration. It shifts the focus from vertical to horizontal, from linear to arches, from black and white to the entire spectrum of colors. It emphasizes the nuances of life instead of the products of life. It specializes in emotion. But more than anything, teaching social studies in an arts-integrated fashion is about valuing what makes us human, makes us continue to go forward, and gives the world some sense of believability and hope. Perhaps Perry Glasser (1997, 4) summed it up best: "When the classroom door is closed and it's just you and them, give your students who you are and what you know. All of it. Not half. Not some. Everything. The rest is bunk." In social studies, the arts touch everything. For many students, they are everything.

528

Unit Tree

Cowboys

Cowboys Past and Present—K–3

Focus

Anthropology	Economics
Create an archeological midden with cowboy artifacts. Ask another class to "dig" and assess.	Make a list of goods used in your daily life that rely somewhat on cowboys. Draw those goods.

History	Geography	Political Science
Use old photos and music to understand the history of cowboys.	Use the Internet to find information about where cowboys are located in your state.	If a cowboy were president how might the country look different? Journal entry.

Sociology
Discuss facts about a cowboy's life, past and present. Create a picture book depicting both.

Culture	Time/Cont/Change	People/Pls/Environs	Self
Dress as a cowboy. Discuss YOUR cowboy culture. See a cowboy movie. Discuss authenticity.	Chart and compare cowboys through dress, effects, jobs.	Create a cowboy habitat peep box. Add fact cards to the peep box.	Take a photo of yourself in cowboy garb. Write your cowboy autobiography.

Indvs/Grps/Instits	Pwr/Auth/Gov	Prod/Dist/Consump	Science/Tech/Society
Research rodeos. Create rodeo scene using sandboxes.	Create five laws cowboys should live by. Research old jails. Role-play Old West conflicts.	Bring a hamburger wrapper to class. Draw a mural showing the path the burger took from cowboy to dinner table.	Show video clips of herding cattle with helicopters. Explore other technological advances.

Global Connections	Civic Ideals
Create an illustrated booklet of how cows/sheep are herded in Africa, Hawaii, Japan, and the United States.	Journal about ways cowboys are/were good/ornery citizens.

Assessment	Reflection	Literature	Music
Create a class mural of a cowboy's life. Label. Make a cowboy fact book. Learn a cowboy song.	"What's the hardest part of a cowboy's life?" "Tell me about a cowboy you know." "Draw the perfect cowboy."	Pecos Bill Texas Alphabet Cowboy Pictorials	Trail songs Cowboy movie sound tracks

Figure 14.6 Unit tree: Cowboys (K–3).

Unit Tree

Cowboys

Cowboys 'Round the World —Gr. 4–6

Focus

Anthropology

Create an archeological midden with cowboy artifacts. Ask another class to "dig" and assess.

Economics

Use the Internet to collect data on the beef industry. Categorize using visual montages, webs, spirals, graphs, charts.

History

Write a report on differences/ similarities of North and South American cowboys.

Geography

Use map skills to locate global areas that depend on cowboys for herding, ranching, etc.

Political Science

"Why would you trust/not trust a cowboy who runs for office?" Journal.

Sociology

Use creative writing skills and illustrations to describe: rodeo culture, cowboy culture, gaucho culture, etc.

Culture

Create facts/fiction cards. Research five basic global cowboy cultures for: food, clothing, recreation, job, dances, music.

Time/Cont/Change

Use any area of visual arts to create a then/ now report on cowboys.

People/Pls/Environs

Interview real cowboys. Connect local environment to cowboys. Dramatize information.

Self

What about YOU, could you do the job of a cowboy? What couldn't you do? Reflect.

Indvs/Grps/Instits

Create a graph comparing the social classes cowboys are placed in around the globe.

Pwr/Auth/Gov

Research Old West laws vs. modern day laws. Create a cowboy code.

Prod/Dist/Consump

Bring a hamburger wrapper to class. Draw a mural showing the path the burger took from cowboy to dinner table.

Science/Tech/Society

Using magazine pictures, create a montage of technological advances that have influenced cowboy life.

Global Connections

Write a song about the day in the life of a cowboy from another country. From this country.

Civic Ideals

"Why do you think cowboys are viewed as honest, hardworking individuals?" Write a report.

Assessment

Class mural
Cowboy diary
Test of facts
Map test
Biography
Interview

Reflection

Why are cowboys almost obsolete? Cowboys in other countries seem _____. Cowboys get to _____.

Literature

Biographies
Pictorials

Music

Gene Autry songs
Trail songs
Movie sound tracks

Figure 14.7 Unit tree: Cowboys (gr. 4–6).

NCSS Standards-Linked Lesson Plan

Drama

Theme: Orphan Train Riders
Source: Pamela A. Nelson, Northern Illinois University
Grade: 5
Objective:
• Students will use a variety of resources to become an Orphan Train rider. (The Orphan Trains ran from 1850 to 1929. You would need to limit the time period based on your curriculum and resources, as well as the students' interests and needs.)

NCSS Themes:
   II. Time, Continuity, & Change
   IV. Individual Development & Identity

Materials:
Children's Literature
Primary
   Nixon, J. L. The Orphan Train Children
   ———— . 1999. *Lucy's Wish.* New York: Yearling.
   ———— . 1999. *Will's Choice.* New York: Yearling.
   ———— . 2000. *Aggie's Home.* New York: Yearling.
   ———— . 2000. *David's Search.* New York: Laurel Leaf.
Middle Level Elementary/Middle School
   Bial, R. 2002. *Tenement: Immigrant Life on the Lower East Side.* Boston: Houghton Mifflin.
   Bunting, E. 2000. *A Train to Somewhere.* Illus. R. Himler. Boston: Houghton Mifflin.
   Cushman, K. 2003. *Rodzina.* Boston: Clarion.
   Littlefield, H. 2001. *Children of the Orphan Trains.* Minneapolis: Carolrhoda.
   Nixon, J. L. The Orphan Train Adventures
   ———— . 1996. *Caught in the Act.* New York: Laurel Leaf.
   ———— . 1996. *A Family Apart.* New York: Laurel Leaf.
   ———— . 1996. *In the Face of Danger.* New York: Laurel Leaf.
   ———— . 1996. *Keeping Secrets.* New York: Laurel Leaf.
   ———— . 1996. *A Place to Belong.* New York: Laurel Leaf.
   ———— . 1999. *A Dangerous Promise.* New York: Laurel Leaf.
   Reef, C. 2005. *Alone in the World: Orphans and Orphanages in America.* New York: Clarion.
   Tamar, E. 2000. *The Midnight Train Home.* New York: Alfred A. Knopf.
   Warren, A. 2000. *Orphan Train Rider: One Boy's True Story.* Boston: Houghton Mifflin.
   ———— . 2001. *We Rode the Orphan Trains.* Boston: Houghton Mifflin.

Additional Resources
Public Libraries
   Caney, S. 1978. *Steven Caney's Kids' America.* New York: Workman.
   Dooley, D. 1975. *Better Homes and Gardens Heritage Cook Book.* Des Moines, IA: Meridith.
   Fry, A. 1974. "The Children's Migration." *American Heritage* 83: 4–10ff.
   Levy, T. 1982. "Crusader with a Camera." *Cobblestone* 3: 16–21.
Video Libraries
   Public Broadcasting System. 1997. *American Experience: The Orphan Trains.* New York: PBS.
University Libraries
   Brace, C. L. 1890. *The Dangerous Classes of New York, and Twenty Years' Work Among Them.* New York: Wynkoop & Hallenbeck.

Riis, J. 1901. *How the Other Half Lives: Studies Among the Tenements of New York.* New York: Charles Scribner's Sons.

Rothman, D., ed. 1971. *Annual Reports of the Children's Aid Society.* New York: Arno Press and *The New York Times.*

Internet

Orphan Train Heritage Society of America (OTHSA), 4912 Trout Farm Road, Springdale, AR 72762 (http://www.pbs.org/wgbh/amex/orphan/).

Artifacts

Recipes and cookbooks

Songs, music, dances

Maps from the period

Photographs (photocopied or actual)

Reprints of artwork

Newspaper articles and advertisements (photocopied or reproduction)

Broadsides (posters or handbills)

Diary accounts or letters

Time lines of related events

Household objects

(stencil patterns, stencil brushes, wooden spoons and bowls, dishpans, tin plates and cups, kettles or buckets, lye soap and cloth towels, scrub boards and washtubs, boilers, candles and holders, cookie cutters or molds, lanterns, quilts and blankets, carders and wool, flax and cotton samples, spices, slates and slate pencils, the McGuffey *Readers* and Webster's *Blue Backed Spellers*, pens, copybooks, 100% cotton paper, tools, horseshoes, etc.)

Toys

(hoops and sticks, cornhusk and corncob dolls, peach pits, rag balls, marbles, jacks, string, feathers, reproduction paper dolls, etc.)

Items of clothing

(skirts, slacks, blouses, old hats, ribbons, belts, suspenders, bandannas, drawstring bags, hoop skirts, aprons, waist cinchers, paper collars, etc.)

Process:

• Share one of the books or selections from a book listed above. Then help students highlight the important points and snake connections with the current unit of study. Locate the time of the event on a class time line and the locations involved on a period map.

• Assume the role of an agent of the Children's Aid Society who works with parents who decide to place their children on Orphan Trains. Identify the time period. Tell your students about yourself, your family, daily life, and your decision to work with the Children's Aid Society in the "out-placing" of orphans.

• Distribute a Bio-Form to the students. Tell them that they are going to prepare to become a child who was selected for "out-placing." Use the overhead projector to show the Bio-Form for your character to your students. Be sure to share the resources you used and the ways in which you used them to fill in the blanks.

NCSS STANDARDS-LINKED LESSON PLAN

Bio-Form

I.   Who is your character?
   A. Name:
   B. Age and Birthday:
   C. Height and Size:
   D. Hair and Eye Color:
   E. What do you do all day?
   F. What do you do throughout the year? (holidays, jobs, etc.)
   G. What are your "favorites"? (books, games, foods, possessions, celebrations, places, etc.)

II. Who are the important people in your life? What are they like?
   A. Parents:
   B. Extended Family—Older Relatives:
   C. Siblings:
   D. Cousins:
   E. Neighbors:
   F. Officials:

III. What is your home (school, church, factory, etc.) like?
   A. What does it look like? What is it made of?
   B. List important furnishings:
   C. Draw a floor plan of your house:
   D. Where is your favorite place in your house:
   E. What kinds of things are on your family's shopping list? What is on your wish list?

IV. What is your community like?
   A. Where are you located? What is that area like?
   B. Draw a map of your community. Locate your house and the houses of friends. Where do you like to go in your community?
   C. What kinds of things go on in your community?
   D. What kinds of things are going on in the country? Who is president?
   E. Where do you get things that you need in your community?
   F. What do your clothes look like? Where do you get them?

V. What are the current concerns you face?
   A. How will you explain them?
   B. How will you address them?
   C. How will you act toward other people?
   D. What special object or memory will you carry with you throughout the event?

- Have students use the resources to provide information for the first section, then the second, until all five have been completed. Be sure to have students share their choices with a partner as they gather information for each section. This will help students have consistency and accuracy in regard to their characters.

- When all Bio-Forms are completed, gather all students together. Seat them as partners in alphabetical order by their character's name. Tell them that they are all residents of different Children's Aid Society Orphanages in New York City, and that they will be boarding a train for the west tomorrow. Ask them to introduce themselves to the orphan who is seated beside them.

- Have the orphans write to or draw a picture for their parents or relatives. Use appropriate papers and writing instruments for this task.

- Have the orphans share these in small groups.

- Have the students leave their roles and reflect on the activity. What different perspectives did the students exhibit when they were in role? What "holes" surfaced in their characters? How will they go about filling those gaps? How did the Orphan Trains help solve a problem? How did the Orphan Trains create problems? Why did children, agents, and parents react differently to the solution of the Orphan Trains? How does this fit with other things that were going on at this time? What similar problems do we face in the present? How are current situations similar or different from the past?

Instructional Comments: This activity would take place over a period of days. It is very important that all students have access to resources. As a result, multiple copies of resources at a variety of levels must be obtained. Teachers must also plan for students to gather information from media and artifacts. The activity allows for students to engage in drama in partners before moving to small groups.

Learning Styles Addressed: Verbal/linguistic, visual/spatial, interpersonal, intrapersonal

Standards Addressed:

English Language Arts

a. Listen effectively in formal and informal situations.

b. Speak effectively using language appropriate to the situation and audience.

Social Science

c. Understand economic systems, and that scarcity necessitates choices by all individuals.

d. Apply the skills of historical analysis and interpretation.

e. Understand relationships between geographic factors and society.

f. Understand the historical significance of geography.

g. Explain how social institutions contribute to the development and transmission of culture.

Evaluation:

- Is information on the Bio-Form appropriate to the selected time period?

- Did students help their partners clarify, analyze, or support their choices?

- Did students make use of a variety of resources (print, media, artifact)?

- To what degree were students able to assume the role of a child who lived in the selected period?

Modifications for Diverse Learners: Offer information through print, media (videotapes of former dramatizations or commercial films), and artifacts. Offer information that is below grade level, at grade level, and above grade level. Provide one-on-one or small-group assistance from adults or students who have demonstrated expertise in creating characters for drama. Use sticky notes to mark specific passages or portions of resources.

Extensions:

- Invite older students, aides, or parents to participate in the drama and dramatize other aspects of the orphan's experience. For example, reenact the adoption (selection) process, the arrival at the home of adoptive parents, or a reunion with siblings or parents.

- Make connections with community members who may have ridden Orphan Trains or use technology to connect with the Orphan Train Heritage Society of America.

- Explore more recent situations in the United States. Read Warner's (1995) *The Boxcar Children,* Sachs's (1996) *The Bears' House,* Byars's (1997) *The Pinballs,* and/or Creech's (2002) *Ruby Holler.* Compare them to books in Nixon's The Orphan Train Adventures.

Variations: A variety of topics associated with elementary and middle school curriculum could be considered using this same format. The following suggestions offer appropriate children's literature and activities for drama in all of the social studies disciplines.

Children's Literature Recommendations

Ancona, G. 2003. *Murals: Walls That Sing.* Tarrytown, NY: Cavandish.

Andrews-Goebel, N. 2002. *The Pot That Juan Built.* Illus. D. Diaz. New York: Lee & Low.

Atkin, S. 1993. *Voices from the Fields: Children of Migrant Farmworkers Tell Their Stories.* New York: Little Brown.

Bachrach, S. 1994. *Tell Them We Remember: The Story of the Holocaust.* Boston: Little, Brown.

Ballard, R. 1988. *Exploring the Titanic.* New York: Scholastic.

Bang, M. 2000. *Nobody Particular: One Woman's Fight to Save the Bays.* New York: Henry Holt.

Begay, S. 1995. *Navajo: Visions and Voices Across the Mesa.* New York: Scholastic.

Bierman, C. 1998. *Journey to Ellis Island: How My Father Came to America.* New York: Hyperion.

Blos, J. 1987. *Old Henry.* New York: William Morrow.

Bruchac, J. 2005. *Code Talkers.* New York: Dial

———. 2006. *Navaho Long Walk: The Tragic Story of a Proud People's Forced March from Their Homeland.* Washington, DC: National Geographic.

Bunting, E. 1994. *A Day's Work.* New York: Clarion Books.

———. 1994. *Smoky Night.* New York: Harcourt Brace.

Burgess, T. ed. 1997. *Indians of the Northwest: Traditions, History, Legends, and Life.* Philadelphia: Petre Press.

Byars, B. 1977. *The Pinballs.* New York: Harper & Row.

Caseley, J. 1987. *Apple Pie and Onions.* New York: Greenwillow.

Cha, D. 1996. *Dia's Story Cloth: The Hmong People's Journey of Freedom.* New York: Lee & Low.

Cherry, L. 1992. *A River Ran Wild.* New York: Harcourt Brace.

Coles, R. 1995. *The Story of Ruby Bridges.* New York: Scholastic.

Cooper, M. 2001. *Dust to Eat: Drought and Depression in the 1930s.* New York: Clarion.

Cox, C. 1998. *Fiery Vision: The Life and Death of John Brown.* New York: Scholastic.

Creech, S. 2002. *Ruby Holler.* New York: HarperCollins.

Crews, D. 1991. *Big Mama's.* New York: Greenwillow.

Curtis, C. P. 1999. *Bud, Not Buddy.* New York: Delacorte.

Deedy, C. 1995. *The Last Dance.* Illus. D. Santini. Atlanta: Peachtree Publishers.

The Dine of the Eastern Region of the Navajo Reservation. 1990. *Oral History Stories of The Long Walk: Hweeldi Baa Hane.* Washington, DC: U.S. Department of Education.

Dooley, N. 1991. *Everybody Cooks Rice.* Minneapolis, MN: Carolrhoda.

Erickson, J. 1998. *Daily Life on a Southern Plantation, 1853.* New York: Lodestar.

Fournot, V. 1985. *The Patchwork Quilt.* New York: Dial.

Franklin, K. L., and N. McGirr. 2000. *Out of the Dump.* New York: Lothrop, Lee, & Shepard.

Fraser, M. 1993. *Ten Mile Day and the Building of the Transcontinental Railroad.* New York: Henry Holt.

Freedman, A. 1994. *A Cloak for the Dreamer.* New York: Scholastic.

Freedman, R. 1994. *Kids at Work.* New York: Clarion.

Garza, C. L. 1990. *Family Pictures / Cuadros de Familia.* Emeryville, CA: Children's Book Press.

———. 1996. *In My Family / En Mi Familia.* Chicago: Children's Book Press.

Gates, D. 1972. *Blue Willow.* New York: Viking.

Golenbock, P. 1990. *Teammates.* New York: Harcourt Brace.

Goor, R., and N. Goor. 1986. *Pompeii: Exploring a Roman Ghost Town.* New York: Thomas Y. Crowell.

Greenberg, J., and S. Jordan. 2002. *Action Jackson.* Illus. R. A. Parker. New York: Roaring Brook.

Guback, G. 1994. *Luka's Quilt.* New York: Greenwillow.

Hamanaka, S. 1990. *The Journey: Japanese Americans, Racism and Renewal.* New York: Orchard.

Haskins, J., and K. Benson. 1998. *Bound for America: The Forced Migration of Africans to the New World.* New York: Lothrop, Lee, & Shepard.

Hesse, K. 1998. *Out of the Dust.* New York: Scholastic.

Hiscock, B. 1998. *The Big Rivers: The Missouri, the Mississippi, and the Ohio.* New York: Atheneum.

Hoobler, D., and T. Hoobler. 2003. *We Are Americans: Voices of the Immigrant Experience.* New York: Scholastic.

Hunt, I. 1970. *No Promises in the Wind.* New York: Tempo.

Innocenti, R. 1985. *Rose Blanche.* Mankato, MN: Creative Education.

Isadora, R. 2002. *Bring on that Beat.* New York: Putnam.

Jackson, E. 1998. *Turn of the Century.* Watertown, MA: Charlesburg.

Jacobs, W. 1990. *Ellis Island: New Hope in a New Land.* New York: Charles Scribner's Sons.

Jimenez, F. 1997. *The Circuit: Stories from the Life of a Migrant Child.* Boston: Houghton Mifflin.

Johnson, S. 1998. *Tomatoes, Potatoes, Corn, and Beans: How the Foods of the Americas Changed Eating around the World.* New York: Atheneum.

Lester, J. 1968. *To Be a Slave.* New York: Dial.

———. 2005. *Day of Tears: A Novel in Dialogue.* New York: Hyperion.

Levinson, R. 1985. *Watch the Stars Come Out.* New York: E. P. Dutton.

Lyons, M. 1992. *Letters from a Slave Girl: The Story of Harriet Jacobs.* New York: Charles Scribner's Sons.

McKissick, P., and F. McKissick. 1994. *Black Diamond: The Story of the Negro Baseball Leagues.* New York: Scholastic.

Marsalis, W. 2005. *Jazz ABZ: An A to Z Collection of Jazz Portraits.* Cambridge, MA: Candlewick Press.

Martin, J. 1998. *The Green Truck Garden Giveaway: A Neighborhood Story and Almanac.* New York: Simon & Schuster.

Millard, A. 1999. *A Street through Time: A 12,000 Year Walk through History.* New York: DK Publishing.

Mochizuki, K. 1993. *Baseball Saved Us.* New York: Lee & Low.

Morrison, T. 2004. *Remember: The Journey to School Integration.* Boston: Houghton Mifflin.

O'Dell, S. 1970. *Sing Down the Moon.* New York: Dell.

Oppenheim, J. 2006. *Dear Miss Breed: True Stories of the Japanese American Incarceration During World War II and a Librarian Who Made a Difference.* New York: Scholastic.

Oppenheim, S. 1992. *The Lily Cupboard.* New York: HarperCollins.

Parker, D. 1998. *Stolen Dreams: Portraits of Working Children.* New York: Lerner.

Provensen, A., and M. Provensen. 1987. *Shaker Lane.* New York: Viking Kestrel.

Raspanti, C. 1980. *I Never Saw Another Butterfly: A Play.* New York: Dramatic Club.

Reinhard, J. 1998. *Discovering the Inca Ice Maiden.* New York: National Geographic Society.

Ryan, P. Muñoz. 1998. *Riding Freedom.* Illus. R. Selznick. New York: Scholastic.

Rylant, C. 1985. *The Relatives Came.* New York: Collier Macmillan.

Sachs, M. 1996. *The Bears' House.* New York: Puffin.

Shange, N. 1994. *I Live in Music.* Illus. R. Bearden. New York: Stewart, Tabori, Chang.

Shea, P. 1995. *The Whispering Cloth: A Refugee's Story.* Honesdale, PA: Boyds Mills Press.

Sis, P. 1991. *Follow the Dream: The Story of Christopher Columbus.* New York: Random House.

Smith, C. R., Jr. 2002. *Perfect Harmony: A Musical Journey with the Boys Choir of Harlem.* New York: Hyperion.

Sneve, V. 1993. *The Navajo: A First Americans Book.* New York: Holiday House.

Spedden, D. 1994. *Polar: The Titanic Bear.* New York: Madison Press.

Spier, P. 1987. *We the People: The Constitution of the United States of America.* New York: Doubleday.

Stanley, J. 1992. *Children of the Dust Bowl: The True Story of the School at Weedpatch Camp.* New York: Crown.

Strom, Y. 1996. *Quilted Landscape: Conversations with Young Immigrants.* New York: Simon & Schuster.

Teele, P. 1998. *Step into the Chinese Empire.* New York: Loprenz.

Tunnell, M., and G. Chilcoat. 1996. *The Children of Topaz: The Story of a Japanese-American Internment Camp Based on a Classroom Diary.* New York: Holiday House.

Turner, G. 1997. *Follow in Their Footsteps.* New York: Dutton.

Uchida, Y. 1971. *Journey to Topaz: A Story of the Japanese-American Evacuation.* Berkeley, CA: Creative Arts Book Company.

Volavkova, H., ed. 1993. *I Never Saw Another Butterfly.* New York: Pantheon.

Von Tscharner, R., R. Fleming, and The Townscape Institute. 1987. *New Providence: A Changing Cityscape.* New York: Harcourt Brace.

Walker, S. 2005. *Secrets of a Civil War Submarine: Solving the Mysteries of the* H.L. Hunley. Minneapolis, MN: Carolrhoda Books.

Warner, G. 1995. *The Boxcar Children.* Morton Grove, IL: Albert Whitman.

Weeks, S. 2005. *So Be It.* New York: Harper Trophy.

Welch, C. A. 2002. *Children of the Relocation Camps.* Minneapolis, MN: Carolrhoda.

Yep, L. 1984. *The Serpent's Children.* New York: Harper Trophy.

Yolen, J. 1992. *Encounter.* New York: Harcourt Brace.

Related Technology Tools

Web Sites

http://www.mysticseaort.org/alhfarm
   Association for Living Historical Farms and Agricultural Museums

http://www.house.gov
   U.S. House of Representatives

http://www.yahoo.com/Economy
   Yahoo! Business and Economy

http://sunsite.unc.edu/govdocs.html
   Government documents (SunSITE)

http://www.whitehouse.gov/WH/Cabinet/html/cabinet_links.html
   The President's Cabinet

http://www.whitehouse.gov
   The White House

http://www.si.edu
   Smithsonian Institution home page

http://www.law.cornell.edu/supct/supct.table.html
   Decisions of the U.S. Supreme Court

http://www.usgs.gov/lien/doi_edu.html
   Department of Interior Education and Outreach

http://www.undp.org/un/index.html
   United Nations information

http://www.ncss.org/
   National Council for Social Studies

http://www.historychannel.com
   History Channel

http://www.execpc.com/~dboals
   History and social studies Web sites for K–12 teachers

http://coombs.anu.edu.au/WWWVL-SocSci.html
   Social studies virtual library

http://www.nara.gov/
   National Archives

http://www.cr.nps.gov/nr/twhp/home.html
  National Register of Historic Places
http://www.nativeweb.org/
  Native Web
http://www.lib.berkeley.edu/TeachingLib/Guides/Internet
  University of California Library Web
http://www.mit.edu:8001/people/sorokin/women/index.html
  Women's Studies

WebQuests

A Cowboy Adventure: A Trip to the Ranch (Gr. 1–2)
  http://www.claredon.isd.tenet.edu/ElementarySchool/webquests.htm
Colonial American Art (Gr. 5)
  http://www.teachtheteachers.org/projects/Jsmall/public-htm/amerarilindex.htm

Technology Resources

Arts Education: Basic to Learning
  http://www.nwrel.org/nwedu/summer_99
  Learn about the benefits of arts education by reading various national studies that support the arts as a necessary component of education.
The Kennedy Center's ArtsEdge
  http://artsedge.kennedy-center.org
  Offers teachers materials, programs, strategies, and other information based on the national art education standards.
American Music Conference
  http://www.amc-music.com
  This site offers materials, research, media, and various resources to promote music education.
PBS Teacher Source
  http://www.pbs.org/wgbh/ameilteachers_or.html
  Teachers can use the American Experience films and Web sites to teach about the Orphan Trains. Included is a teacher's guide and resources for active learning.
Scholastic
  www.scholastic.com/dearamerica
  Teachers and students may explore this Web site which contains an interactive time line, discussion guides, and downloadable handouts. There are video clips for students as well as links to related web sites and ideas for crafts from the historical periods being studied.

Software and Videos

Leonardo da Vinci Biography. 1997. A&E Home Video. 50 minutes. Available at 800-543-4180. Reproducible activity packet sold separately. An excellent documentary on the "Renaissance Man."
Discover America Collection. CD-ROM. Scholastic. Available from www.scholastic.com.
Carmen Sandiego's Great Chase Through Time. Broderbund. Available from www.broderbund.com.
A Love of Art. CD-ROM. Topics Entertainment. Available from www.amazon.com. Learn important events in the history of Western art and explore the works of Claude Monet.
Native Land. Teacher's Video Company. Available from www.teachersvideo.com. Learn about the nomads who discovered the Americas thousands of years ago and founded the Aztec and Inca empires. Renowned author Jamake Highwater teaches your students about the early civilizations that created art, tools, pottery, and mythology.
The Crusades. 1995. Teacher's Discovery. Four 50 minute videos. Available at 800-543-4180. Video activity packet sold separately. A great way to teach about the Crusades.

Teaching Resources

The following list of resources is offered as a starting point from which to develop a network:

Community Resources

Libraries (census reports, microfilms of daily and special interest newspapers, published diaries, cookbooks, art books, maps, files of community organizations and resource people)

Historical societies (photographs, maps, diaries and letters, artifact kits, reproduction items from the gift shop, resources materials on using artifacts and primary sources with children)

Courthouses (transcripts of trails, records of political figures, health records of disease control, dates of major epidemics in the area)

Churches (parish list of births and deaths, sacramental records, descriptions of services, statements of positions on local and national issues, cookbooks with household tips produced at different time periods in that community, artifacts associated with various time periods)

Professional organizations (Association of Newspaper Publishers, local chamber of commerce, service organizations, American Bar Association, American Medical Association)

University Libraries

Audiotapes

Microfilm and microfiche (area and national newspapers, special collections of documents and publications associated with local and national movements, bound periodicals)

Government documents and publications (congressional records, presidential papers, contemporary biographies and photographs of political figures, National Park Service travel brochures, current national and international maps prepared by the CIA, transcripts, posters, diaries, indexes for material available from various departments of the federal government)

Special collections (rare books, displays, oversized books, recordings, private papers of individuals associated with an institution)

Videos and DVDs (films, documentaries)

Artifacts

Printed materials (price lists of commonly purchased goods, recipes, time lines of related events, actual or fictional diary accounts or letters, broadsides [posters or handbills], photocopies or reproduction newspaper accounts or documents, patterns for clothing, photographs [photocopied or actual], reprints or artwork, amps, songs, music, dances from the period)

Real or reproduction household objects (stencil patterns, stencil brushes, wooden spoons and bowls, dishpans, tin plates and cups, kettles or buckets, lye soap, cloth towels, scrub boards and washtubs, boilers, candles and holders, cookie cutters or molds, lanterns, quilts and blankets, carders and wool, flax and cotton samples, spices, slates, and slate pencils, the McGuffey *Readers* and Webster's *Blue Backed Spellers,* pens, copybooks, 100 percent cotton paper, tools, horseshoes, hoops, type)

Reproduction toys (whimmy diddles, hoops and sticks, cornhusk and corncob dolls, peach pits, rag balls, marbles, jacks, string, feathers, reproduction paper dolls)

Clothing (skirt, blouses, old hats, ribbons, belts, suspenders, bandanna, drawstring bags, hoop skirts, aprons, waist cinchers, paper collars)

National Resources

National Archives
Education Branch Office of Public Programs
Washington, DC 20408

Earth Sciences Information Centers
U.S. Geological Survey
507 National Center
Reston, VA 22092

National Public Radio Audience Services
2025 M Street NW
Washington, DC 20036

United States Patent and Trademark Office
Commissioner of Patents and Trademarks
Washington, DC 20231

References

Banks, J., C. Banks, and A. Clegg. 2004. *Multicultural Education: Issues and Perspectives.* 5th ed. New York: Wiley.

Bartoletti, S. 2000. "Exploring the Gaps in History." *Book Links* 9: 16–20.

Bauer, C. 1987. *Presenting Reader's Theater.* New York: H. W. Wilson.

Bradley Commission on History in Schools and P. Gagnon. 1989. *Historical Literacy: The Case for History in American Education.* New York: Macmillan.

Brady, M. 1994. *Artstarts.* Englewood, CO: Teacher Ideas Press.

———. 1998. *Social Studies and the Multiple Intelligences: Bringing the World Home to Children.* Sedona, AZ: Pandy Music.

Brophy, J. 1992. "Fifth-Grade U.S. History: How One Teacher Arranged to Focus on Key Ideas in Depth." *Theory and Research in Social Education* 20: 141–55.

Callaway, A. 1996. *To Ella, With Love.* CD. New York: After 9 Records.

Cecil, N., and P. Lauretzen. 1994. *Literacy and the Arts for the Integrated Classroom.* New York: Longman.

Clemens, S. 1991. "Art in the Classroom: Making Every Day Special." *Young Children* 52 (2): 4–11.

Cottrell, J. 1987. *Creative Drama in the Classroom 4–6.* Lincolnwood, IL: National Textbook Company.

Coulter, D. 1989. "The Brain's Timetable for Developing Musical Skill." *General Music Journal* 13 (1): 3–10.

Cruz, B. C., and S. A. Murthy. 2006. "Breathing Life into History: Using Role-Playing to Engage Students." *Social Studies and the Young Learner* 18 (3): 4–8.

Edinger, M. 2000. *Seeking History: Teaching with Primary Sources in Grades 4–6.* Portsmouth, NH: Heinemann.

Egan, K. 1986. *Teaching as Story Telling—An Alternative Approach to Teaching and Curriculum in the Elementary School.* Chicago: University of Chicago Press.

———. 1997. "The Arts as the Basics for Education." *Childhood Education* 73: 341–45.

Elswit, S. 2000. "Playing before You Read: Activities to Enrich the Literature Experience." *Book Links* 9: 41–43.

Fines, J., and R. Verrior. 1974. *The Drama of History—An Experiment in Cooperative Teaching.* Aberdeen, AK: Central Press.

Fowler, C. 1994. "Strong Arts, Strong Schools." *Educational Leadership* 52 (30): 4–9.

Gardner, H. 2006. *Multiple Intelligences.* New York: HarperCollins.

Gerwin, D., and J. Zevin. 2003. *Teaching U.S. History as Mystery.* Portsmouth, NH: Heinemann.

Glasser, P. 1997. "Not Half; Not Some." *Educational Leadership* 78 (7): 504–5.

Greenwald, A. W. 2000. "Team Egypt! Integrating the Disciplines." *Middle Level Learning* 7: M2–M4.

Haslinger, J., P. Kelly, and L. O'Lare. 1996. "Countering Absenteeism, Anonymity, and Apathy." *Educational Leadership* 54 (1): 47–49.

Heath, S. B. 2004. "Learning Language and Strategic Thinking through the Arts." *Reading Research Quarterly* 39: 338–42.

Heinig, R. 1987. *Creative Drama Resource Book (K–3).* Englewood Cliffs, NJ: Prentice-Hall.

Houston, J. 1997. *The Possible Human: A Course in Extending Your Physical, Mental, and Creative Abilities.* New York: Tarcher.

Kelin, D. 2005. *To Be as Our Ancestors Did: Collecting and Performing Oral Histories.* Portsmouth, NH: Heinemann.

Kobrin, D. 1996. *Beyond the Textbook: Teaching History Using Documents and Primary Sources.* Portsmouth, NH: Heinemann.

Kohlberg, L. 1976. "Moral Stages and Moralization." In *Moral Development and Behavior,* ed. T. Lickona. New York: Holt, Rinehart.

Kornfeld, J., and G. Leyden. 2005. "Acting Out: Literature, Drama, and Connecting with History." *The Reading Teacher* 59: 230–38.

Leigh, A., and T. Reynolds. 1997. "Little Windows to the Past." *Social Education* 61: 45–47.

Levstik, L. S. 1986. "The Relationship between Historical Responses and Narrative in a Sixth-Grade Classroom." *Theory and Research in Social Education* 14: 1–19.

Levstik, L. S., and K. Barton. 2005. *Doing History and Investigating with Children in Elementary and Middle School.* 3rd ed. Mahwah, NJ: Lawrence Erlbaum Associates.

Mayesky, M. 1995. *Creative Activities for Young Children.* New York: Delmar.

National Council for the Social Studies (NCSS). 1994. *Expectations of Excellence: Curriculum Standards for Social Studies.* Washington, DC: Author.

Nelson, P. A. 1992. Stories, Memorials, and Games: Fourth Graders Respond to History in Classroom and Museum Settings. Unpublished Doctoral Dissertation, Northern Illinois University, DeKalb, IL.

O'Neill, C. 1985. "Imagined Worlds in Theater and Drama." *Theory into Practice* 24: 158–65.

Putnam, L. 1991. "Dramatizing Non-Fiction with Emerging Readers." *Language Arts* 68: 463–69.

Rasmussen, K. 1998 (June). "Visual Arts for All Students." *Education Update*: 1–6.

Ritchie, G. 1991. "How to Use Drama for Cross Cultural Understanding." *Guidance Counselor* 7: 33–35.

Selman, R. 1971. "The Relation of Role Taking to the Development of Moral Judgment in Children." *Child Development* 45: 803–6.

Shand, G., D. May, and R. Linnell. 1990. "History as Ethnography: A Psychological Evaluation of a Theater in Education Project." *Teaching History* 65: 27–32.

Sporre, D. 1987. *The Creative Impulse: An Introduction to the Arts.* Englewood Cliffs, NJ: Prentice-Hall.

Terster, B., T. Hammond, and G. Bull. 2005. "Primary Access: Creating Digital Documentaries in the Social Studies Classroom." *Social Education* 70: 147–50.

Van Sledright, B., and J. Brophy. 1992. "Storytelling, Imagination, and Fanciful Elaboration in Children's Historical Reconstructions." *American Educational Research Journal* 29: 837–59.

Welton, D., and J. Mallan. 1996. *Children and Their World: Strategies for Teaching Social Studies.* Boston: Houghton Mifflin.

Wineburg, S. 1999. "Historical Thinking and Other Unnatural Acts." *Phi Delta Kappan* 80: 488–99.

———. 2001. *Historical Thinking and Other Unnatural Acts: Charting the Future of Teaching the Past.* Philadelphia: Temple University Press.

Glossary

activating prior knowledge. Part of schema theory, stimulating knowing that comes from a previous experience.

aesthetic reading. The reading for enjoyment such as reading a historical novel because one likes to read about history.

alternative assessment. The use of means of assessment other than standardized tests or teacher-made tests to achieve "direct," "authentic" assessment of student performance on important learning tasks.

anthropology. Field of study or discipline concerned with the discovery of what people were like from earliest existence.

artifact. Simple object such as a tool or ornament from a culture or a historical period.

assessment. The act or process of gathering data (i.e., through testing, portfolios, interviews, observation, evaluation of projects or performance-based criteria) in order to better understand the strengths and weaknesses of student learning.

assistive technology. Devices either purchased or handmade by the teacher that aid special needs students in their learning.

at risk. Referring to a person or group whose prospects for success are marginal or worse.

attention deficit disorder (ADD). A developmental disorder involving one or more of the basic cognitive processes relating to orienting, focusing, or maintaining attention.

attention deficit hyperactivity disorder (ADHD). A student with ADD plus hyperactivity. The child demonstrates inattention, impulsivity, and deficits in rule-governed behavior. Not to be confused with the natural squirming that occurs in childhood.

authentic assessment. A type of assessment that seeks to address widespread concerns about standardized, norm-referenced testing by reflecting the actual learning and instructional activities of the classroom and out-of-school worlds.

autistic. A child or adult with a marked severe developmental disorder in which the individual is so self-centered as to be largely or wholly unable to judge reality.

behaviorist. A person who describes behavior by the actions of the individual under the given circumstances.

bilingual. The ability to speak or understand with some degree of proficiency a language besides one's native language.

biography. A book about a person's life, either the entire life or a portion of it.

Bloom's taxonomy. Six cognitive behaviors from lowest to highest thinking levels (knowledge, comprehension, application, analysis, synthesis, and evaluation).

body and kinesthetic. Relating to the ability to use movement to convey meaning as in dance.

character education. Teaching about values that lead to citizens possessing good moral character.

character journals. Personal reaction to events in historical fiction written as though the reader was the main character.

citizen actors. Person who has learned how citizens in a society make personal and public decisions on issues that affect their destiny.

citizenship education. Instruction to develop students' ability to make good decisions and become involved in the governing process.

civics. The field of study or discipline of how people govern themselves; also referred to as political science.

color. Different hues (i.e., red, yellow, green, black).

communicate. To share information or ideas.

concept muraling. Presenting a series of 4–8 pictures pertaining to a topic of study on an overhead transparency and sharing accompanying concepts/facts about each prior to having the students read about the topic.

concrete activities. The inclusion of hands-on materials as part of a lesson or unit of study.

constitution. The basic principles and laws of a nation, state, or social group that determine the powers and duties of and guarantee certain rights to the people in it.

constructivist. Person who believes an individual's prior experiences, mental structures, and beliefs bear upon how experiences are interpreted; focuses on how knowledge is built rather than the final product produced by the student.

consumption. The needs and wants of the buyer; influenced by the ability of the buyer to purchase goods.

convergent question. Inquiry based upon yielding one common answer (described as spokes on a wheel coming together at the hub).

cooperative learning. Any pattern of classroom organization that allows students to work together to achieve their individual goals.

cultural anthropology. The study of different types of human behavior, past, and present, found throughout the world.

culture. Significant ideas, events, values, and beliefs of a society.

curriculum compacting. The addition of new concepts, ideas, and materials to the school district's curriculum.

curriculum standards for social studies. The topics of study and levels of proficiency of social studies instruction; these may be national or state standards.

decision-making process. The direct study of social problems to find a resolution(s); involves five steps: (1) deriving an issue; (2) expressing tentative choices based on tentative values; (3) gathering information to test choices; (4) evaluating data and identifying tested choices; and (5) acting on choices in society.

democratic classroom. A classroom where the teacher respects the students and they respect him/her. Many decisions are based on discussions and voting by the participants.

design. To conceive, create, and plan out in the mind as well as the final project's overall appearance.

differentiated assignments. Tasks that vary in how they are accomplished but relate to the teaching objective.

differentiated instruction. The provision of varied learning situations (whole-class, small-group, or individual instruction) or tasks to meet the needs of students at different levels of learning.

direct instruction. The explicit teaching of a skill.

distribution. To dispense goods or services.

divergent question. Inquiry based upon having multiple possible solutions (described as spokes going outward on a wheel).

diversity. People with different cultures, abilities, and needs represented in a society.

drafting. Putting down thoughts and content on paper without concern about writing conventions of spelling, grammar, and punctuation.

early childhood. Education from birth through grade 3.

economics. The field of study or discipline concerned with the production, distribution, exchange, and consumption of products.

economist. Person who analyses the production, distribution, exchange, and consumption of products and suggests ways to improve the distribution or production or the economy in general.

editing. Going back over one's draft to correct writing conventions (spelling, grammar, and punctuation).

educationally challenged learner. Student who has special needs in order to gain knowledge.

efferent reading. Reading to gain information.

egocentrism. In Piagetian theory, a child's inability to take or see another's point of view.

emotional intelligence. the ability to understand other people and manage their own emotions, which aids in getting along with others

engaged learners. Students who are interested and motivated to learn, often having their interest piqued by the method the teacher uses to introduce a topic of study; active learners.

English as a second language learner (ESL). See below.

English language learner (ELL). Child or adult who is acquiring English in addition to his/her native language. Also known as English as a second language learner (ESL).

environment. The aggregate of social, cultural, and physical conditions that influence the life of an individual or community. Example: classroom environment.

evaluation. Judgment of performance as process or product of change due to instruction; the process of testing, appraising, and judging achievement, group, product, process, or changes in these, frequently through the use of formal and informal tests.

environment. One's surroundings, conditions, and circumstances considered as a whole.

exchange. To take one thing for another as in trade; may be goods or services for money or other goods or services.

executive branch. One of three branches of government as headed by the president of the United States or, in the case of a state, the governor. The head of the government (the president or governor) gives the final approval for new bills or laws by signing them. If he or she does not approve, then the bill or law is said to be vetoed.

explicit instruction. Teacher or textbook information presented by showing or telling students.

expository. Pertaining to either reading or writing informational text.

field trips. Taking students to a specific site such as a museum for additional study. Often firsthand experiences are stressed, such as making candles, etc.

flexible grouping. Allowing students to work in differently mixed groups depending on the goal of the learning task at hand.

form. Outline and shape of something. According to Frank Lloyd Wright, "form follows function" such as in furniture and lighting fixtures.

formal assessment. The collection of data using standardized tests or procedures under controlled conditions.

formative evaluation. The continuing study of the process of change in an instructional program as it moves toward its goals and objectives by monitoring the learning progress of its participants.

FQR (Facts, Questions, Responses). A strategy developed by Stephanie Harvey and Anne Goudvis to help students organize the information as they read and seek out answers to their questions. Students write down facts, questions, and responses on different colored sticky notes and place them either on the text itself or in a notebook as they read. They go back and review as a closing activity.

Geographic Information System (GIS). An electronic system that uses computers and satellites to locate places on earth.

geography. The field of study or discipline of earth's features and distribution of its human inhabitants.

gifted. Student who possesses special talents or skills such as having a high intelligence.

Global Positioning System (GPS). Use of satellites to pinpoint locations on the earth, now found as an option on cars and trucks.

good citizens. Children and adults who have acquired knowledge of political processes, institutions, and heritage and who use a wide range of information, skills, and values to work within the political system.

government. The exercising of power based upon a set of rules to perform functions for a citizenry.

graphic organizer. A diagram which presents information in an organized structure; often used to introduce a social studies topic and/or as a closing activity to a lesson (i.e., a Venn diagram comparing and contrasting Presidents George Washington and Abraham Lincoln).

guided learning experiences. Instruction in which the teacher provides the structure and purpose for learning social studies and for responding to the discussion/artifacts/ text shared.

guided reading. The teacher's supervision of a reading of a passage by students.

handhelds. Electronic, personal communication devices used to store information such as notes, phone numbers, and other information.

hands-on instruction. The use of concrete items such as artifacts to teach a concept.

hearing impairment. A reduction in hearing acuity.

higher-order thinking. Use of higher order thinking which involves complex thinking especially of a logical or abstract-type.

historian. Person who, using reasoned reconstruction, interprets how people lived in the past.

historical fiction. Chapter books or novels set in a specific period of time with imaginary characters, but the details and major historical events are presented accurately.

historical relics. Materials from another generation or period in time.

history. The field of study or discipline of how people lived in the past; it is a reasoned reconstruction of the past rooted in research.

human rights. The basic rights of people to have food, clothing, and shelter as well as to be respected and treated fairly by others.

human systems. The study of where people migrated and settled and why.

inclusion. The placement of students of all abilities in a classroom with the aim of educating all handicapped children, no matter how severe their disabilities, in ordinary classrooms.

Individualized Education Plan (IEP). A specific instructional plan to meet the specific needs of individual students.

informal assessment. Appraisal by casual observation noted in anecdotal recordkeeping.

inquiry. A process driven approach in which students grapple with significant problems by forming hypotheses and gathering data from a variety of sources.

inquiry-based. Learning based on questioning, searching out additional information, and coming to a resolution of the problem; referred to as problem solving.

integrated instruction. The combining of two or more subject area disciplines in a lesson.

interact. To become involved with others usually through discussion or shared work.

interdisciplinary instruction. A curricular organization intended to bring into close relationship the concepts, skills, and values of two or more separately taught subjects (i.e., art, language arts, math, music, science, and social studies) to make them mutually reinforcing.

interdisciplinary teaching (*see* **interdisciplinary instruction**)

interpersonal. Related to the ability to judge *others'* abilities and feeling.

intrapersonal. Related to the ability to judge *one's own* abilities and feelings.

jackdaw. Named for a bird that collects things, a container with primary source documents and artifacts, usually accompanied by activities for students.

journals. Personal written responses (i.e., reaction to historical fiction, a vacation trip).

judicial branch. One of three branches of government in which the court system interpret the laws of the nation or state. The Supreme Court of the United States hears cases concerning the U.S. Constitution.

K-W-L. Strategy developed by Donna Ogle that is especially useful in identifying purposes for reading expository text such as social studies material (originally: What I **K**now; What I **W**ant to Know; What I have **L**earned); W now is referred to as "Wonder" as What I **W**onder if.

latitude. In geography, the location system of east-west lines called parallels.

learning disability. A generic term that refers to a heterogeneous group of disorders manifested by significant difficulties in the acquisition and use of listening, speaking, reading, writing, or mathematical abilities.

learning strategies. Approaches to efficiently acquire and retain new concepts.

learning strategy. A systematic plan, consciously adapted and monitored, to improve one's performance in mastering a task.

legislative branch. One of three branches of government. Representatives are elected by the people to the legislative branch such as members of the House of Representatives and the Senate. Bills and laws are started and passed here before being sent to the executive branch for final approval (signing) or rejection (vetoing).

linguistic. Pertaining to language use, oral or written.

literary genre. Different types of children's books such as picture books, historical fiction, informational books, fantasy, and biography; for social studies, the primary genres are historical fiction, nonfiction, and biography.

literature circles. A group of students (usually 4–6) meet to discuss the same book (usually historical fiction or biography) they are reading independently. Each group member engages in a specific role (character captain, illustrator, summarizer, word warrior, etc.) for part of the book, trading off at a specified point such as halfway through the book. When the book is finished the group presents it to the class in a creative manner (i.e., dramatic portrayal of an important scene, reader's theatre, variation of a television interview show). Typically a class will cover 5–8 different books per topic.

literature response journals. The written reaction to a piece of literature in which a specific incident from the book is elaborated upon; dialogue journals are responses about the same piece of literature that two students (or the student and teacher) write to each other.

location. Describes where specific places or points are on a map or the earth's surface.

logical-mathematical. Able to think in a "scientific manner" to problem solve.

longitude. In geography, the location system of north-south lines called meridans.

manipulatives. Hands-on objects that students can use to demonstrate knowledge of a particular task or skill.

media. Different ways to present art or information.

mental map. The mental image a person has of a place or area, such as a city, state, or country, including knowledge of its features, the places that surround it, and his/her attitude and perceptions regarding the place.

mental retardation. A markedly lower mental age than chronological age; a significant lack of general intellectual ability and functioning.

meridians of longitude. The system of north-south lines that converge at the north and south poles that measure distances east and west of the prime meridian.

moral principles. The character traits that are desired by a society.

movement. Characterizes how people travel from place to place, how they communicate with each other, and how they depend on products and information from other areas.

multicultural education. Programs and materials designed to illustrate the likenesses and differences among ethnic groups or among cultural subgroups of the same ethnic origin.

multigenre writing. Writing in different genre (i.e., narrative, informational, poetic).

Multiple Intelligences (MI). A theory by Howard Gardner that there are at least nine distinct intelligences in how humans learn (verbal/linguistic; logical-mathematical; visual/spatial; body and kinesthetic; musical; interpersonal; intrapersonal; spiritualistic; and naturalistic).

mural. A work of art, such as a painting on a wall or large piece of paper.

musical. Pertaining to ability to use rhythm and tones.

narrative. A story, actual or fictional.

naturalistic. Classification of items such as those found in nature.

nonverbal communication. Use of body movements, eye contact, etc. to communicate.

oral history. The handing down of information orally through either eyewitness accounts or secondary witness retellings.

parallels of latitude. The system of east-west lines that measure distances north and south of the equator.

perspective. One's point of view; especially important in considering other cultures and societies.

persuasive. A piece of writing or text written to convince someone to change their mind about something.

physical systems. In geography, the study of how climate and weather affect our lives.

picture books. A kind of literary genre for children (Pre-K–8) in which the story or information is shared by relying heavily on illustrations.

place. Describes the unique or distinct characteristics (both physical and human) of a location.

poetic. Referring to prose or poetry.

political science. The field of study or discipline of how people govern themselves; also referred to as civics.

portfolio assessment. A selected, usually chronological collection of a student's work that is evaluated to determine learning progress.

PQRST. A variation of the study technique of SQ3R. (preview, question, review, summarize, and test).

prejudice. Preconceived judgment or opinion usually adverse to a particular social group.

prewriting. Beginning the process of writing about a topic (i.e., forming questions, writing down what you know as with KWL, locating information and taking notes); often called rehearsal.

primary source document. The actual, original document (i.e., diaries, letter, newspaper article, photos, legal documents).

primary witness. An individual who was present at an event and provides recollections (either orally or in writing).

prime meridian. The location plotted as zero degrees longitude.

problem solving. The breaking down of an issue and creating possible solutions.

production. The making of goods and products.

project method. Form of learning in which students work together on an activity.

propaganda. The sending of messages to persuade someone to join the same viewpoint.

publishing/sharing. Presenting the final version of a piece of writing such as an expository report on the westward movement.

QAR. An instructional strategy proposed by Taffy Raphael to help learners know what information sources are available for seeking answers to different types of text questions.

RAFT. An aid for students in writing for a specific audience.

read aloud. To share a book or portion of a book with the entire class; especially good for setting the tone for a social studies topic at the beginning of a unit of study.

reader response. A theory by Louise Rosenblatt that when the reader meets the literary text, a creative act takes place. Thus, an intermingling occurs implying that the reader brings knowledge and motivation to the reading task and gains information and/or enjoyment from engaging in the actual reading.

reader response theory. (see **reader response**)

reader's theater. A performance of literature as a story, play, poetry, etc., read aloud expressively by one or more students rather than acted.

region. Categorizing an area according to its features (climate, landform, land use, natural vegetation, culture, and so forth).

relationships within places. Describes how people react to their environment and the changes they make.

relics. From World War II such as ration coupons, buttons or chevron ranks from uniforms, newspaper clippings, and letters from soldiers fighting in the front can make up a jackdaw

relief map. Use of false-color 3-D shading to show changes of altitude.

RESPONSE. A study guide that a student produces that includes important facts, questions about the text, and new concepts/terms/names.

revising. Making changes to the content or organization of a piece of writing.

rubric. A set evaluation criteria for an assignment or task.

scarcity. The lack of availability of a product or service.

schema (pl. schemata). A view that comprehension depends on integrating new knowledge with a network of prior knowledge.

scope and sequence. The skills and knowledge presented in a curriculum.

secondary witness. Individual who was not present at an event but who interprets what a person who was present shares.

self-assessment. Self-monitoring of one's progress in an area of study.

sequencing of strategies. The structuring of successive learning plans.

social context. Relating to a particular group situation.

social interaction. Getting involved with other members of a social group such as creating a relationship with another person or persons.

social justice. Treating everyone with respect and fairness.

social sciences. Six disciplines of study (anthropology, civics [political science], economics, geography, history, and sociology).

social studies. An integrated study of the social sciences focusing on the teaching of higher-level thinking skills with the purpose of developing good citizens.

social studies learners. Students who are acquiring good citizenship skills through an integrated study of the social sciences.

sociology. The field of study or discipline of humans and their interactions in groups.

spatial. Relating to the ability to judge and use area/space effectively and efficiently.

spiral curriculum. Invented by Hilda Taba, the introduction of social studies concepts in lower elementary grades, which are then reintroduced and further developed in intermediate elementary and middle school.

spiritualistic. Relating to the ability to determine right from wrong; sense of ethics.

SQ3R. A study strategy introduced by Helen Robinson for expository text such as social studies (survey the material; question; read to answer questions; recite answers to questions; and review answers to questions).

standards for teaching the social studies. Required areas and levels of study; sometimes referred to as performance expectations.

strategic reader. Reading using specific skills for specific needs such as previewing a social studies chapter by reading headings and photo captions before reading the entire chapter or writing down facts, questions, and responses while reading.

summative evaluation. Assessment measure to determine the success of a program, such as a standardized achievement test or state social studies test.

ten themes for social studies. The National Council for the Social Studies K–12 themes for instructional study. The themes are interrelated and draw from all the social sciences as well as related fields of study. (I. Culture; II. Time, Continuity, and Change; III. People, Places, and Environments; IV. Individual Development and Identity; V. Individuals, Groups, and Institutions; VI. Power, Authority, and Governance; VII. Production, Distribution, and Consumption; VIII. Science, Technology, and Society; IX. Global Connections; and X. Civic Ideals and Practices.

thematic unit. A study of a topic (i.e., communities, Middle Ages, World War II) for a period of time (usually a few weeks) in which most if not all the 10 themes for social studies as well as other subjects are included.

topographical map. Map in which lines are stretched or straightened for the sake of clarity, but without losing their essential geometric relationships.

topography. The relief and configuration of a landscape including its natural and man-made features.

values. Behaviors that are accepted and fostered by a society.

visual arts. Aspects of the visual arts are drawing, illustration, painting, sculpture, printmaking, photography, architecture, graphic design and landscape design.

visual impairment. The loss of acuity of the visual field because of a physical or physiological defect.

visual literacy. The ability to interpret and communicate with respect to visual symbols in media other than print, as visual literacy in viewing television, art, nature, etc.

WebQuest. Developed by Bernie Dodge, an inquiry-based project that requires students to go to a central Web site to get initial information and directions about a task before gathering information from links to other sites.

zone of proximal development. The distance between a child's actual developmental level as determined through independent problem solving and his potential development level as determined through problem solving under adult guidance or a collaboration with more capable peers.

Name Index

Subject Index

Aesthetic reading, 256
Allies, becoming, 116
Alternative assessment, 87–97
  manipulatives, 97
  portfolio assessment, 92–93
  projects, 93–95
  rubrics, 88–92, 95
  self-assessment, 95–97
Anthropology, 14–15, 22
Artifacts, 15, 324–328, 517–518,
  521, 531, 533, 538–539
Arts, 497–527
  dramatic, 509–527
  integrated instruction with,
    498–501
  music, 501–503
  visual, 502, 507–509
Asian communities, diversity in,
  120–121
Assessment, 73–99
  alternative, 87–97
  in the classroom, 74–76
  definition of, 76
  of English language learners, 97
  evaluation vs., 76–79
  formal and informal, 76
  guidelines for, 74
  methods of, 76, 84–85
  quality, key factors for, 77
  technology and, 87
  tools of, 85–87
Assistive technology, 160–162
Associations, classification of,
  205–207, 209, 214
Attention Deficit Disorder/Atten-
  tion Deficit Hyperactivity
  Disorder ADD/ ADHD,
  156, 160

Basic Interpersonal Conversation
  Skills (BICS), 126

Behaviorism, 45, 190–192
Benchmarks, 84
Bilingual education, 9, 103, 105,
  125–139
Bio-Cube, 250
Bio-forms, 532–533
Biographies, 251, 333–335, 356–359
Bio-poems, 357–358
Bloom's taxonomy of educational
  objectives, 77–79
Brain research, 55, 188–190, 440

Change, thematic concept of, 16,
  363–366. *See also* Time, continuity, and change theme
Character
  character building, 447–448
  character education, 44,
    440–447
  children's literature on, 445
  creating, 114–116
  perspective, 216
  reading and, 109–110
  traits of, 447
Character journals, 361–362
Children's literature
  for all learners, 175–181
  biographical, 356–359
  character-education oriented,
    443–447
  citizenship-related, 445, 447
  civics education-related,
    451–453
  drama/dramatic arts, 519–526,
    530, 534–536
  early childhood, 295–296,
    304–308
  economics-related, 466, 468,
    470, 480–481, 487–491
  environment-related, 407, 409,
    422

geography-related, 396–397,
  400, 413–422
historical fiction, 335–336,
  359–362
history-related, 34–38, 162,
  166, 338, 340–344
Holocaust-related, 37
importance of, in social studies, 234–241, 350
for integrating curriculum,
  68–69
literature-based integrated
  instruction, 372–382
on the Middle Ages, 62–63
multicultural/multiethnic,
  106–107, 140–145
nonfiction/informational
  books, 236–241
picture books, 351–355
for reading, writing, and discussing, 273–275
Revolutionary War, 68–69
for special-needs students, 162,
  166
for strategic instruction, 226
teaching through fiction,
  234–235
World War II, 37–38
Choral reading, 351, 510, 512
Circles of awareness, 283–287, 298
Citizen actors, 23–24, 52–55
Citizenship education, 7–10, 441
Civic ideals and practices theme,
  xii, 13, 137, 526–527. *See also*
  Political science
Civics education
  character education, 44,
    440–447
  citizenship responsibilities,
    430–432
  civic dispositions, 435